Teach Yourself

C for Linux® Programming

in 21 Days

SAMS

A Division of Macmillan USA
201 West 103rd St., Indianapolis, Indiana, 46290 USA

Sams Teach Yourself C for Linux® Programming in 21 Days

Copyright © 2000 by Sams Publishing

International Standard Book Number: 0-672-31597-1

Library of Congress Catalog Card Number: 98-89896

Printed in the United States of America

First Printing: December 1999

01   00   99   4   3   2   1

Trademarks

All terms mentioned in this book that are known to be trademarks or service marks have been appropriately capitalized. Sams Publishing cannot attest to the accuracy of this information. Use of a term in this book should not be regarded as affecting the validity of any trademark or service mark.

Linux is a registered trademark of Linus Torvalds.

Warning and Disclaimer

ASSOCIATE PUBLISHER
Bradley L. Jones

ACQUISITIONS EDITOR
Sharon Cox

DEVELOPMENT EDITOR
Tony Amico

MANAGING EDITOR
Lisa Wilson

PROJECT EDITORS
Elizabeth Roberts
Heather Talbot

COPY EDITOR
Mike Henry

INDEXERS
Kevin Kent
Eric Schroeder

PROOFREADER
Katherin Bidwell

TECHNICAL EDITORS
John Friesen
Bill Ball

TEAM COORDINATOR
Meggo Barthlow

MEDIA DEVELOPER
Dan Scherf

INTERIOR DESIGN
Gary Adair

COVER DESIGN
Aren Howell

COPY WRITER
Eric Borgert

PRODUCTION
Lisa England
Dan Harris

Contents at a Glance

Introduction

WEEK 1 At a Glance

Day 1   Introduction to Linux and the C Programming Language

2   The Components of a C Program: Code and Data

3   Statements, Expressions, and Operators

4   Functions: The Basics

5   Basic Program Control

6   Fundamentals of Input and Output

7   Using Numeric Arrays

WEEK 1 In Review

WEEK 2 At a Glance

Day 8   Understanding Pointers

9   Characters and Strings

10   Structures

11   Understanding Variable Scope

12   Advanced Program Control

13   Working with the Screen and Keyboard

14   Pointers: Beyond the Basics

WEEK 2 In Review

WEEK 3 At a Glance

Day 15   Using Disk Files

16   Manipulating Strings

17   Exploring the C Function Library

18   Working with Memory

19   Processes and Signals

20   Advanced Compiler Use

21   An Introduction to GUI Programming with GTK+

WEEK 3 In Review

Appendix A   ASCII Character Chart

B   C/C++ Reserved Words

C   Answers

Type & Run 1   Printing Your Listings

Type & Run 2   Find the Number

Type & Run 3   Secret Messages

Type & Run 4   Counting Characters

Type & Run 5   Calculating Mortgage Payments

Index

Contents

Introduction

Getting Started with C for Linux Programming..1

This Book's Special Features 1

    Example 1 2

    Example 2 2

Making a Better Book..3

Conventions Used in This Book 4

WEEK 1 At a Glance   **5**

Where You're Going 5

DAY 1 Introduction to Linux and the C Programming Language   **7**

Why Use C? 8

    A Brief History of the C Language...9

Preparing to Program 9

The Program Development Cycle 10

    The C Development Cycle 10

    The Development Tools..12

    Creating the Source Code 12

    Compiling the Source Code 13

    Completing the Development Cycle 15

Getting Started with Linux 16

    Your First C Program 17

    Using the ddd Debugger 21

Summary..22

Q&A 23

Workshop 24

    Quiz 24

    Exercises 24

DAY 2 The Components of a C Program: Code and Data   **27**

A Short C Program 27

The Program's Components 29

    The `main()` Function (Lines 8 Through 23) 29

    The `#include` Directive (Line 2)...29

    The Variable Definition (Line 4) 29

    The Function Prototype (Line 6)...30

    Program Statements (Lines 11, 12, 15, 16, 19, 20, 22, and 28) 30

    The Function Definition (Lines 26 Through 29)...31

Program Comments (Lines 1, 10, 14, 18, and 25) 31
Using Braces (Lines 9, 23, 27, and 29)...33
Running the Program...33
A Note on Accuracy 33
A Review of the Parts of a Program...33
Storing Data: Variables and Constants 36
Variables 37
Variable Names 37
Numeric Variable Types 39
Variable Declarations...42
The typedef Keyword..43
Initializing Variables 43
Constants...44
Literal Constants 45
Symbolic Constants..46
Defining Symbolic Constants 47
Summary..49
Q&A 50
Workshop 51
Quiz 52
Exercises 52

DAY 3 Statements, Expressions, and Operators   55

Statements..55
The Impact of Whitespace on Statements...56
Creating a Null Statement 57
Working with Compound Statements 57
Understanding Expressions..58
Simple Expressions 58
Complex Expressions 58
Operators..59
The Assignment Operator 60
The Mathematical Operators 60
Operator Precedence and Parentheses..64
Order of Subexpression Evaluation..66
The Relational Operators..67
The if Statement 68
The else Clause 71
Evaluating Relational Expressions 73
The Precedence of Relational Operators..75
The Logical Operators 76
More on True/False Values 77
The Precedence of Operators 78
Compound Assignment Operators..80
The Conditional Operator 81
The Comma Operator 81

Operator Precedence Revisited 82
Summary 83
Q&A 84
Workshop 85
   Quiz 85
   Exercises 85

DAY 4 Functions: The Basics   **87**

What Is a Function? 87
   A Function Defined 88
   A Function Illustrated 88
How a Function Works 90
   Functions 91
Functions and Structured Programming 92
   The Advantages of Structured Programming 92
   Planning a Structured Program 93
   The Top-Down Approach 94
Writing a Function 95
   The Function Header 95
   The Function Body 98
   The Function Prototype 103
Passing Arguments to a Function 104
Calling Functions 105
   Recursion 106
Where the Functions Belong 109
Summary 110
Q&A 110
Workshop 111
   Quiz 111
   Exercises 111

DAY 5 Basic Program Control   **113**

Arrays: The Basics 114
Controlling Program Execution 115
   The for Statement 115
   Nesting for Statements 120
   The while Statement 122
   Nesting while Statements 126
   The do...while Loop 128
Nested Loops 132
Summary 133
Q&A 134
Workshop 134
   Quiz 134
   Exercises 135

DAY 6 Fundamentals of Input and Output   **137**

Displaying Information Onscreen...138
    The `printf()` Function 138
    The `printf(` Format Strings 138
    Displaying Messages with `puts()` 146
Inputting Numeric Data with scanf() 147
Summary 152
Q&A 152
Workshop 153
    Quiz 153
    Exercises 154

DAY 7 Using Numeric Arrays   **157**

What Is an Array?...157
    Single-Dimensional Arrays 158
    Multidimensional Arrays 162
Naming and Declaring Arrays 163
    Initializing Arrays 166
    Initializing Multidimensional Arrays 167
    Maximum Array Size 170
Summary 172
Q&A 173
Workshop 174
    Quiz 174
    Exercises 174

WEEK 1 In Review   **177**

WEEK 2 At a Glance   **183**

Where You're Going 183

DAY 8 Understanding Pointers   **185**

What Is a Pointer?..186
    Your Computer's Memory...186
    Creating a Pointer 186
Pointers and Simple Variables 187
    Declaring Pointers 187
    Initializing Pointers 188
    Using Pointers 188
Pointers and Variable Types 191
Pointers and Arrays...192
    The Array Name as a Pointer 192
    Array Element Storage 193
    Pointer Arithmetic 196

Pointer Cautions 200
Array Subscript Notation and Pointers...201
Passing Arrays to Functions 201
Passing Pointers to Functions 206
Type void Pointers 210
Summary 213
Q&A 214
Workshop 215
   Quiz 215
   Exercises 216

DAY 9 Characters and Strings   **217**

The char Data Type 217
Using Character Variables...218
Using Strings...220
   Arrays of Characters 220
   Initializing Character Arrays 220
Strings and Pointers 221
Strings Without Arrays 221
   Allocating String Space at Compilation 222
   The malloc() Function 222
   Using the malloc() Function 224
Displaying Strings and Characters 227
   The puts() Function 227
   The printf() Function 228
Reading Strings from the Keyboard 229
   Inputting Strings Using the gets() and fgets() Functions 229
   Inputting Strings Using the scanf() Function 231
Summary 233
Q&A 234
Workshop 235
   Quiz 235
   Exercises 236

DAY 10 Structures   **239**

Simple Structures 240
   Defining and Declaring Structures 240
   Accessing Structure Members...241
More Complex Structures..243
   Structures That Contain Structures 243
   Structures That Contain Arrays 246
Arrays of Structures 248
Initializing Structures 252

Structures and Pointers 255
    Pointers as Structure Members 255
    Pointers to Structures...257
    Pointers and Arrays of Structures 259
    Passing Structures as Arguments to Functions 262
Unions...264
    Defining, Declaring, and Initializing Unions 264
    Accessing Union Members 265
Creating Synonyms for Structures with `typedef` 269
Summary...270
Q&A 270
Workshop 271
    Quiz 271
    Exercises 272

DAY 11 Understanding Variable Scope   **273**

What Is Scope? 274
    A Demonstration of Scope 274
    Why Is Scope Important? 276
External Variables 276
    External Variable Scope...276
    When to Use External Variables 277
    The `extern` Keyword...277
Local Variables 278
    Static Versus Automatic Variables 279
    The Scope of Function Parameters 282
    External Static Variables 282
    Register Variables 282
Local Variables and the `main()` Function 284
Which Storage Class Should You Use? 284
Local Variables and Blocks..285
Summary...286
Q&A 287
Workshop 288
    Quiz 288
    Exercises 288

DAY 12 Advanced Program Control   **291**

Ending Loops Early 292
    The `break` Statement 292
    The `continue` Statement 294
The `goto` Statement..296
Infinite Loops 298
The `switch` Statement...302

Exiting the Program 310

    The `exit()` Function 310

Executing Commands from Within a Program 311

Summary 313

Q&A 313

Workshop 314

    Quiz 314

    Exercises 314

DAY 13 Working with the Screen and Keyboard   **317**

Streams and C..317

    What Exactly Is Program Input/Output?...318

    What Is a Stream? 319

    Predefined Streams 319

C's Stream Functions 320

    An Example 320

Accepting Keyboard Input 321

    Character Input 321

    Formatted Input 326

Screen Output 334

    Character Output with `putchar()`, `putc()`, and `fputc()` 335

    Using `puts()` and `fputs()` for String Output 336

    Using `printf()` and `fprintf()` for Formatted Output 337

Redirecting Input and Output 344

    Redirecting Input..345

    Piping Between Programs 346

When to Use `fprintf()` 347

    Using `stderr` 347

Summary 348

Q&A 348

Workshop 349

    Quiz 349

    Exercises 350

DAY 14 Pointers: Beyond the Basics   **351**

Pointers to Pointers..352

Pointers and Multidimensional Arrays 353

Arrays of Pointers..361

    Strings and Pointers: A Review...361

    Array of Pointers to Type `char` 362

    An Example 364

Pointers to Functions 370

    Declaring a Pointer to a Function 371

    Initializing and Using a Pointer to a Function 371

Functions That Return a Pointer 380
Linked Lists 382
    Basics of Linked Lists 383
    Working with Linked Lists 384
    A Simple Linked List Demonstration 389
    Implementing a Linked List 392
Summary 400
Q&A 401
Workshop 401
    Quiz 402
    Exercises 403

WEEK 2 In Review   **405**

WEEK 3 At a Glance   **413**

    Where You're Going 413

DAY 15 Using Disk Files   **415**

Streams and Disk Files 415
Types of Disk Files 416
Filenames 416
Opening a File 416
Writing and Reading File Data 420
    Formatted File Input and Output 420
    Character Input and Output 424
    Direct File Input and Output 426
File Buffering: Closing and Flushing Files 430
Sequential Versus Random File Access 431
    The `ftell()` and `rewind()` Functions 432
    The `fseek()` Function 434
Detecting the End of a File 437
File Management Functions 440
    Deleting a File 440
    Renaming a File 441
    Copying a File 442
Using Temporary Files 445
Summary 446
Q&A 447
Workshop 448
    Quiz 448
    Exercises 448

DAY 16 Manipulating Strings **451**

String Length and Storage 451

Copying Strings 453

The strcpy() Function 453

The strncpy() Function 455

The strdup() Function 456

Concatenating Strings 457

The strcat() Function 457

The strncat() Function 458

Comparing Strings 460

Comparing Two Entire Strings 460

Comparing Partial Strings 462

Comparing Two Strings While Ignoring Case 463

Searching Strings 463

The strchr() Function 464

The strrchr() Function 465

The strcspn() Function 465

The strspn() Function 466

The strpbrk() Function 467

The strstr() Function 468

String-to-Number Conversions 469

The atoi() Function 469

The atol() Function 470

The atof() Function 470

Character Test Functions 471

tolower() and toupper() 475

Summary 476

Q&A 477

Workshop 477

Quiz 477

Exercises 478

DAY 17 Exploring the C Function Library **481**

Mathematical Functions 481

Trigonometric Functions 482

Exponential and Logarithmic Functions 482

Hyperbolic Functions 483

Other Mathematical Functions 483

A Demonstration of the Math Functions...484

Dealing with Time 485

Representing Time...485

The Time Functions..486

Using the Time Functions 489

Error-Handling Functions 491
    The assert() Function..491
    The errno.h Header File 493
    The perror() Function 494
Functions That Have Variable Numbers of Arguments 496
Searching and Sorting..499
    Searching with bsearch()..499
    Sorting with qsort() 500
    Searching and Sorting: Two Demonstrations 501
Summary 507
Q&A 507
Workshop 507
    Quiz 508
    Exercises 508

DAY 18 Working with Memory   **511**

Type Conversions 511
    Automatic Type Conversions 512
    Explicit Conversions Using Typecasts 513
Allocating Memory Storage Space..515
    The malloc() Function 516
    The calloc() Function 516
    The realloc() Function 518
    The free() Function 519
Manipulating Memory Blocks 522
    The memset() Function 522
    The memcpy() Function 522
    The memmove() Function 522
Working with Bits..524
    The Shift Operators 525
    The Bitwise Logical Operators 526
    The Complement Operator 528
    Bit Fields in Structures 528
Summary 530
Q&A 530
Workshop 532
    Quiz 532
    Exercises 533

DAY 19 Processes and Signals   **535**

Processes..535
    Starting Another Process Using fork() 539
    Zombie Processes 542
    Replacing One Process with Another 547

Signals..549
    Handling SIGCHLD to Prevent Zombie Child Processes 554
Summary...558
Q&A 558
Workshop 558
    Quiz 559
    Exercises 559

DAY 20 Advanced Compiler Use 561

The C Preprocessor..561
    The #define Preprocessor Directive 562
    The #include Directive 567
    Using #if, #elif, #else, and #endif 568
    Using #if...#endif to Help Debug 569
    Avoiding Multiple Inclusions of Header Files 570
    The #undef Directive..571
Predefined Macros 571
Using Command-Line Arguments 572
Command-Line Arguments Using getopt() 574
Programming with Multiple Source Files 576
    Advantages of Modular Programming 577
    Modular Programming Techniques 577
    Using .o Files...579
    Module Components 579
    External Variables and Modular Programming 580
    Using the make Utility 581
Using Shared Libraries 585
Summary...587
Q&A 587
Workshop 588
    Quiz 588
    Exercises 588

DAY 21 An Introduction to GUI Programming with GTK+ 591

History..591
X Concepts 592
    GTK+—The Gimp Toolkit 592
    Finding GTK+ 593
GUIs and Events 594
    A First GTK+ Program 595
    Buttons..599
Creating a Dialog Box 602
A Simple Text Editor 608
Summary...619

Q&A 619
Workshop 620
    Quiz 620
    Exercises 620

WEEK 3 In Review   **621**

APPENDIX A ASCII Character Chart   **629**

APPENDIX B C/C++ Reserved Words   **633**

APPENDIX C Answers   **637**
Day 1: Introduction to Linux and the C Programming Language 637
    Quiz Answers..637
    Answers to Exercises...638
Day 2: The Components of a C Program: Code and Data................639
    Quiz Answers..639
    Answers to Exercises...639
Day 3: Statements, Expressions, and Operators...........................641
    Quiz Answers..641
    Answers to Exercises...641
Day 4: Functions: The Basics...643
    Quiz Answers..643
    Answers to Exercises...644
Day 5: Basic Program Control 647
    Quiz Answers..647
    Answers to Exercises...648
Day 6: Fundamentals of Input and Output 649
    Quiz Answers..649
    Answers to Exercises...649
Day 7: Using Numeric Arrays 653
    Quiz Answers..653
    Answers to Exercises...654
Day 8: Understanding Pointers...657
    Quiz Answers..657
    Answers to Exercises...658
Day 9: Characters and Strings 660
    Quiz Answers..660
    Answers to Exercises...661
Day 10: Structures 664
    Quiz Answers..664
    Answers to Exercises...664

Day 11: Understanding Variable Scope 666
   Quiz Answers...666
   Answers to Exercises..667
Day 12: Advanced Program Control 670
   Quiz Answers...670
   Answers to Exercises..671
Day 13: Working with the Screen and Keyboard...........................672
   Quiz Answers...672
   Answers to Exercises..673
Day 14: Pointers: Beyond the Basics 673
   Quiz Answers...673
   Answers to Exercises..674
Day 15: Using Disk Files 675
   Quiz Answers...675
   Answers to Exercises..676
Day 16: Manipulating Strings...676
   Quiz Answers...676
   Answers to Exercises..677
Day 17: Exploring the C Function Library 678
   Quiz Answers...678
   Answers to Exercises..678
Day 18: Working with Memory 679
   Quiz Answers...679
   Answers to Exercises..680
Day 19: Processes and Signals 681
   Quiz Answers...681
   Answers to Exercises..681
Day 20: Advanced Compiler Use 682
   Quiz Answers...682
   Answers to Exercises..683
Day 21: An Introduction to GUI Programming with GTK+ 683
   Quiz Answers...683
   Answers to Exercises..683

TYPE & RUN 1 Printing Your Listings   **685**
   The First Type & Run..686

TYPE & RUN 2 Find the Number   **689**

TYPE & RUN 3 Secret Messages   **693**

TYPE & RUN 4 Counting Characters   **697**

TYPE & RUN 5 Calculating Mortgage Payments   **701**

Index   **705**

About the Authors

ERIK DE CASTRO LOPO is a professional research and development engineer who lives and works in Sydney, Australia. He used UNIX extensively while in college and discovered Linux in 1995. He is a regular visitor to the Linux Usenet newsgroups, has contributed bug fixes to many open source projects, and has also released some of his own code under the GNU General Public License. Erik's Web page can be found at http://www.zip.com.au/~erikd/.

PETER AITKEN is an associate professor at Duke University Medical Center, where he uses PCs extensively in his research on the nervous system. He is an experienced author on microcomputer subjects, with some 70 magazine articles and 25 books to his credit. Aitken's writing covers both applications and programming topics. His books include *Sams Teach Yourself Internet Programming with Visual Basic 6 in 21 Days* (Sams Publishing) and *Sams Teach Yourself Microsoft Word 2000 in 10 Minutes* (Sams Publishing). He is a contributing editor at *Visual Developer* magazine, where he writes the popular "Basically Visual" column. Visit Aitken's Web page at http://www.pgacon.com/.

BRADLEY L. JONES is an independent consultant providing not only programming, but also direction and guidance for the development of systems, both small-scale and distributed. He has developed systems using such tools as C, C++, SQL Server, Windows NT, PowerBuilder, Visual Basic, Active Server Pages (ASP), Satellite Forms, and more. Jones' other authoring credits include *Sams Teach Yourself Advanced C in 21 Days* (Sams Publishing) and *Programming PowerBuilder* (Que E&T). Brad also contributes articles to publications such as the *Visual C++ Developer*.

Dedication

To Janet.

Acknowledgments

I would like to thank my coauthors, Peter Aitken and Brad Jones, for providing such a solid foundation for me to build on. I would also like to thank Carol Ackerman, who was my first contact at Macmillan; Sharon Cox, who convinced me this project was achievable given the time constraints; Tony Amico, the development editor, and Jon Friesen, the technical editor, who asked some great questions. A thank you also goes out to Richard Stallman, Linus Torvalds, and the rest of the free software community for making GNU/Linux the best operating system I know of. Finally, but most importantly, I would also like to thank Janet, who, by the time this book hits the shelves, will be my wife.

—Erik de Castro Lopo

First and foremost, my thanks go to my coauthor, Brad Jones, for his hard work and dedication. I am also greatly indebted to all the people at Sams Publishing, unfortunately too many to mention by name, who helped bring this book from concept to completion. The text and programs in this book have been thoroughly edited and tested, and we believe this book to be largely, if not completely, error-free. Should you encounter an error, we would like to know about it. You can contact me via email at `peter@pgacon.com`.

—Peter Aitken

A good book is the result of the symbiosis achieved by a number of people working together. I would like to acknowledge all the people—readers, editors, and others—who have taken the time to provide comments and feedback on this book. By incorporating much of their feedback, I believe that Peter and I have made this the best book for easily learning C.

Finally, I'd like to thank my wife for her continued understanding and patience as I take on such projects as the writing of books.

—Bradley L. Jones
`jones@iquest.net`

Tell Us What You Think!

As the reader of this book, *you* are our most important critic and commentator. We value your opinion and want to know what we're doing right, what we could do better, what areas you'd like to see us publish in, and any other words of wisdom you're willing to pass our way.

As an associate publisher for Sams, I welcome your comments. You can fax, email, or write me directly to let me know what you did or didn't like about this book—as well as what we can do to make our books stronger.

Please note that I cannot help you with technical problems related to the topic of this book, and that due to the high volume of mail I receive, I might not be able to reply to every message.

When you write, please be sure to include this book's title and author as well as your name and phone or fax number. I will carefully review your comments and share them with the author and editors who worked on the book.

Fax: 317-581-4770

Email: adv_prog@mcp.com

Mail: Associate Publisher
          Sams
          201 West 103rd Street
          Indianapolis, IN 46290 USA

Introduction

Getting Started with C for Linux Programming

As you can probably tell from the title, this book is designed to allow you to teach yourself C programming for the Linux operating system. Since its origin in the early 1990s, Linux has grown to become the second most popular desktop and server operating system after the Windows variants produced by Microsoft. In the small server market, Linux is competing directly against and beating Microsoft's flagship product, Windows NT. Linux has gained a reputation for being highly stable, configurable, reliable, and secure.

The Linux operating system kernel is written in the C programming language, as is an overwhelming proportion of the programs that make up a Linux distribution. Despite stiff competition from newer languages such as C++ and Java, C remains the language of choice for people who want to program under Linux and other operating systems. For reasons I will detail on Day 1, "Introduction to Linux and the C Programming Language," you can't go wrong in selecting C as your programming language.

You have made a wise decision selecting this book as your means of learning C. Although there are many books on C, I believe this book presents C in the most logical and easy-to-learn sequence. This book is designed for you to work through the lessons in order on a daily basis. I don't assume any previous programming experience on your part, although experience with any other programming language might help you to learn faster.

This Book's Special Features

This book contains some special features to aid you on your path to C enlightenment. Syntax boxes show you how to use specific C concepts. Each box provides concrete examples and a full explanation of the C command or concept. To get a feel for the style of the syntax boxes, look at the following example. (Don't try to understand the material; you haven't even reached Day 1!)

▼ SYNTAX

```
#include <stdio.h>
printf (format-string[,arguments], ...]);
```

printf() is a function that accepts a series of arguments, each applying to a conversion specifier in the given format string. It prints the formatted information to the standard output device, usually the display screen. When using printf(), you must include the standard input/output header file, stdio.h.

▼ The format-string is required, but arguments are optional. For each argument, there must be a conversion specifier. The format string can also contain escape sequences. The following are examples of calls to printf() and their output.

Example 1

```
#include <stdio.h>
int main(void)
{
    printf ("This is an example of something printed!\n");
    return 0;
}
```

Example 1 Output

```
This is an example of something printed!
```

Example 2

```
#include <stdio.h>
int main(void)
{
    printf ("This prints a character, %c\na number, %d\na floating point, %f\n",
        'z', 123, 456.789);
    return 0;
}
```

Example 2 Output

```
This prints a character, z
a number, 123
a floating point, 456.789
```

▲

Another feature of this book is Do/Don't boxes, which give you pointers on what to do and what not to do.

Do	Don't
DO read the rest of this section. It explains the Workshop section that appears at the end of each day.	**DON'T** skip any of the quiz questions or exercises. If you can finish the day's Workshop, you're ready to move on to the new material.

You'll encounter Tip, Note, and Warning boxes as well. Tips provide useful shortcuts and techniques for working with C. Notes provide special details that enhance the explanations of C concepts. Warnings help you avoid potential problems.

Numerous sample programs illustrate C's features and concepts so that you can apply them in your own programs. Each program's discussion is divided into three components: the program itself, the input required and the output generated by it, and a line-by-line analysis of how the program works. These components are indicated by special icons.

In code listings, the line numbers and colons are for referencing purposes only. When you type in the code, you don't need to type the line numbers or colons.

Each day ends with a Q&A section containing answers to common questions relating to that day's material. There is also a Workshop at the end of each day. It contains quiz questions and exercises. The quiz tests your knowledge of the concepts presented on that day. If you want to check your answers, or if you're stumped, the answers are provided in Appendix C, "Answers."

You won't learn C just by reading this book, however. If you want to be a programmer, you must write programs. Following each set of quiz questions is a set of exercises. I recommend that you attempt each exercise. Writing C code is the best way to learn C.

I consider the BUG BUSTER exercises most beneficial. A *bug* is a program error. BUG BUSTER exercises are code listings that contain common problems. It's your job to locate and fix these errors. If you have trouble busting the bugs, these answers are also in Appendix C.

As you progress through this book, some of the exercise answers tend to be long. Other exercises have a multitude of correct answers. As a result, later days don't always provide answers for all the exercises.

The final feature of this book is the Type & Run sections. You'll find five of these in the book. Each Type & Run contains a short C program that does something fun or useful while it illustrates C programming techniques. You can type these listings in and run them. After you've entered them, you can modify the code to see what else you can make it do. The Type & Run sections are for you to experiment with. We hope you have fun doing so.

Making a Better Book

Nothing is perfect, but I do believe in striving for perfection. This is the first edition of *Sams Teach Yourself C for Linux Programming in 21 Days*. In preparing this book, I have spent a great deal of time and effort to ensure that the information and code examples are correct and accurate. Because this is the first edition, I am interested in hearing from you, the reader, about any inconsistencies or errors you find. These will then be fixed in any future editions of this book.

Conventions Used in This Book

This book uses different typefaces to help you differentiate between code and regular English, and also to help you identify important concepts. Code appears in a special monospace font. In the examples of a program's input and output, what the user types appears in **bold monospace**. Placeholders—terms that represent what you actually type within the code—appear in *`italic monospace`*. New or important terms appear in *italic*.

WEEK 1

At a Glance

As you prepare for your first week of learning how to program the Linux operating system using the C language, you will need a few things: this book, a computer with the Linux operating system installed, a C compiler, and a text editor. The C compiler and the text editor have probably been installed on your computer with the Linux operating system.

This book is set up so that each day ends with a Workshop containing a quiz and some exercises. At the end of each day, you should be able to answer all the quiz questions and complete the exercises. Answers to all the quiz questions and exercises for preceding days are provided in Appendix C, "Answers." On later days, answers are not provided for all exercises because there are many possible solutions. I strongly suggest you take advantage of the exercises and check your answers.

The best way to learn a computer language involves more than just reading a book; it involves entering and running a number of C programs. The many C programs included in this book offer hands-on training for the new programmer. As you learn the C language, you are encouraged to modify and experiment with the programs.

Where You're Going

The first week covers basic material that you need to know to understand C fully. On Day 1, "Introduction to Linux and the C Programming Language," and Day 2, "The Components of a C Program: Code and Data," you'll learn how to create a C program and recognize the basic elements of a simple program. The second part of Day 2 deals with variable types and how to define them. Day 3, "Statements, Expressions, and Operators," takes the variables and adds simple expressions so that new values can be created. This lesson also provides information on how to make decisions and change program flow using `if` statements. Day 4, "Functions: The Basics," covers C functions and structured programming. Day 5, "Basic Program Control," introduces more commands that let you control the flow of your programs. Day 6, "Fundamentals of Input and Output," discusses how to make your program interact with the screen and keyboard. The week ends on Day 7, "Using Numeric Arrays," which deals with how to operate with sets of numbers kept in storage elements called arrays.

In addition to all this material, you will also find a couple of Type & Runs. These are located between Day 1 and Day 2 and between Day 4 and Day 5. The program in the first Type & Run will print your program listings with line numbers. The second Type & Run contains a listing that will let you play a number guessing game.

This is a lot of material to cover in just one week, but if you take the information one day a time, you should have no problems.

DAY **1**

Introduction to Linux and the C Programming Language

Welcome to *Sams Teach Yourself C for Linux Programming in 21 Days*. Today's lesson starts you toward becoming proficient in programming Linux using the C language. Today you will learn

- Why C is the best choice for programming Linux
- About the software tools used to develop C programs under Linux
- Finding the software tools
- The steps in the program development cycle
- How to write, compile, and run your first C program
- About error messages generated by the compiler and linker

If you want to read about the history of Linux or the relationship between Linux and other operating systems, you will find a brief discussion of these matters in Appendix A, "ASCII Character Chart."

Why Use C?

In today's world of computer programming, there are many high-level languages from which to choose, such as C, C++, Perl, Python, Tcl/Tk, BASIC, and Java. These are all excellent languages that are well suited to most programming tasks. Even so, there are several reasons why many computer professionals feel that C is at the top of the list:

- C is a powerful and flexible language. What you can accomplish with C is limited only by your imagination. The language itself places no constraints on you. C is used for projects as diverse as operating systems, word processors, graphics, spreadsheets, and even compilers for other languages. In fact, most C compilers, including GCC, are written in C.

- C is a popular language preferred by professional programmers. As a result, a wide variety of C compilers and helpful accessories are available.

- C is a portable language. *Portable* means that a C program written for one computer system (an IBM PC running Linux, for example) can be compiled and run on another system (a DEC VAX system, perhaps) with little or no modification. This is especially true when moving between any of the members of the UNIX OS family.

  Additionally, a program written to run on the Microsoft Windows operating system console (also known as the *MS-DOS box*) can be moved to a machine running Linux with little or no modification. Portability is enhanced by the ANSI standard for C—the set of rules for C compilers.

- C is a language of few words, containing only a handful of terms, called *keywords* , which serve as the base on which the language's functionality is built. You might think that a language with more keywords (sometimes called *reserved words*) would be more powerful. This isn't true. As you program with C, you will find that it can be used to tackle any programming task.

- C is modular. C code can (and should) be written in routines called *functions*. These functions can be reused in other applications or programs. By passing pieces of information to the functions, you can create useful, reusable code.

- The Linux kernel is written in C, so if you ever need to write (or even debug) a device driver or some other code for the Linux kernel, you will need to understand C.

As these features show, C is an excellent choice for your first programming language. What about C++? You might have heard about C++ and the programming technique called *object-oriented programming*. Perhaps you're wondering what the differences are between C and C++ and whether you should be teaching yourself C++ instead of C.

Fortunately there's nothing to worry about. C++ is a superset of C, which means that C++ contains everything C does, plus new additions for object-oriented programming. For a person learning to program, there are probably advantages to learning a small, reasonably simple language like C rather than a large complex language like C++. If you do go on to learn C++, almost everything you learn about C will still apply to the C++ superset. In learning C, you are not only learning one of today's most powerful and popular programming languages, but you are also preparing yourself for object-oriented programming.

Another language that has received lots of attention is Java. Java is based on C++, which in turn is based on C. If later you decide to learn Java, you will find that almost everything you learned about C can be applied to Java.

A Brief History of the C Language

The C language was created by Dennis Ritchie at the Bell Telephone Laboratories in 1972. The language was created to make programming the UNIX operating system easier than programming in assembly language. It also made it far easier to move programs between computers with different hardware.

Due to C's power and flexibility, its use quickly spread beyond Bell Labs. Programmers everywhere began using it to write all sorts of programs. Soon, however, different organizations began utilizing their own versions of C, and subtle differences between implementations started to cause programmers headaches. In response to this problem, the American National Standards Institute (ANSI) formed a committee in 1983 to establish a standard definition of C, which became known as *ANSI Standard C*. Later, in the early 1990s, the International Standards Organization (ISO) released another standard, this time recognized internationally. With few exceptions, every modern C compiler has the ability to adhere to these standards.

The C language was named *C* because its predecessor was named B. The B language was developed by Ken Thompson of Bell Labs. You should be able to guess why it was called B.

Preparing to Program

Programs solve problems. They can't solve all problems, but they can solve computer-related problems. If you want to browse the World Wide Web, there is a program called a *Web browser* that can solve that problem for you. This is an existing problem with an existing solution—a Web browser. Other computer-related problems may not have solutions or may have sub-optimal solutions. Carrying on our discussion of Web browsers, you may have come up with an idea for a new Web browser feature that you would like to implement. You therefore have a programming problem to solve.

To solve this programming problem, you should take certain steps. First, you must define the problem. If you don't know what the problem is, you can't find a solution! Once you know what the problem is, you can devise a plan to fix it. Once you have a plan, you can usually implement it. After the plan is implemented, you must test the results to see whether the problem is solved. This same logic can be applied to many other areas, including programming.

When creating a program in C (or in any language, for that matter), you should follow a similar sequence of steps:

1. Determine the objective(s) of the program.
2. Determine the methods you want to use in writing the program.
3. Create the program to solve the problem.
4. Run the program to see the results.

An example of an objective (see step 1) might be to write a word processor or database program. A much simpler objective is to display your name onscreen. If you didn't have an objective, you wouldn't be writing a program, so you already have the first step done.

The second step is to determine the methods you want to use to write the program. Do you need a computer program to solve the problem? What information needs to be tracked? What formulas will be used? During this step, you should try to determine what you need to know and in what order the solution should be implemented.

As an example, assume that someone asks you to write a program to determine the area inside a circle. Step 1 is complete, because you know your objective: determine the area inside a circle. Step 2 is to determine what you need to know to ascertain the area. In this example, assume that the user of the program will provide the radius of the circle. Knowing this, you can apply the formula $pi*r^2$ to obtain the answer. Now you have the pieces you need, so you can continue to steps 3 and 4, which are called the *Program Development Cycle*.

The Program Development Cycle

The Program Development Cycle has its own steps. In the first step, you use an editor to create a disk file containing your source code. In the second step, you compile the source code to create an executable file. The third step is to run the program to see whether it works as originally planned.

The C Development Cycle

▼ SYNTAX

Step 1 Use an editor to write your source code. By tradition, C source code files have the extension .c (for example, myprog.c, database.c, and so on).

Step 2 Compile the program using a compiler. If the compiler doesn't find any

▼ errors, it will perform a link phase and produce an executable, so go on to step 3. If it does find errors, you need to return to step 1 and correct them.

Step 3 Execute the program. You should test to determine whether it functions properly. If not, start again with step 1 and make modifications and additions to
▲ your source code.

Figure 1.1 shows the program development steps. For all but the simplest programs, you might go through this sequence many times before finishing your program. Even the most experienced programmers can't sit down and write a complete, error-free program in just one step. Because you'll be running through the edit-compile-link-test cycle many times, it's important to become familiar with your tools—the editor and the compiler gcc.

FIGURE 1.1.

The steps involved in C program development.

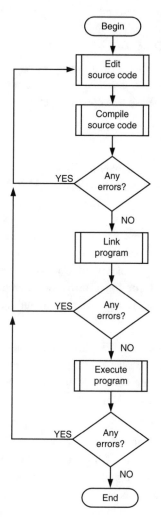

The Development Tools

To write programs in C under Linux, you will need some other programs that are probably already on your machine. You will need a text editor, a C compiler, and tools such as
a make utility and a debugger. We will look at what is available as we require them.

> **Note**   Many other systems, such as Apple Macintosh and Microsoft Windows, have
> Integrated Development Environments (IDEs), which combine a text editor, a
> compiler, and other tools into one integrated package. During 1999, IDEs
> like this have started to become available for Linux, but the vast majority of
> Linux developers still use separate tools.

Creating the Source Code

NEW TERM   *Source code* is a series of statements or commands that are used to instruct the
computer to perform your desired tasks. As mentioned, the first step in the
Program Development Cycle is to enter source code into an editor. For example, the following is a line of C source code:

```
printf("Hello, Mom!");
```

This statement instructs the computer to display the message "Hello, Mom!" onscreen.
(For now, don't worry about how this statement works.)

Using an Editor

When you create source code files, you use a text editor rather than something like a
word processor. Most word processors use special codes embedded within the document
to specify formatting. These extra codes make word processors unsuitable for editing
source code. The American Standard Code for Information Interchange (ASCII) has
specified a standard text format that nearly any program, including the C compiler, can
use.

When you save a source file, you must give it a name. The name should describe what
the program does. In addition, when you save C program source files, give the file a .c
extension. Although you could give your source file any name and extension, .c is recognized as the appropriate extension to use.

There are many text editors available for Linux, such as vi, emacs, joe, ed, vim, crisp, and
jed. Some of these editors can be run at the console (the black and white screen you see
when Linux starts and before the GUI starts), while others require the X Window System
GUI. A couple of GUI-only editors that are highly recommended are nedit, gnp, and kedit.
Using any of these text editors should be second nature to anybody who has ever used a
word processor. The three editors are shown together on one screen in Figure 1.2.

Note

To find out if you have any of these editors available on your machine, you can type their names on the command line followed by the ampersand character (&, produced by holding down the Shift key and pressing the 7 key simultaneously). This runs the editor as a background task and allows further commands to be typed at the terminal window.

FIGURE 1.2.

Three Linux text editors: nedit (top), gnp (middle), and kedit (bottom).

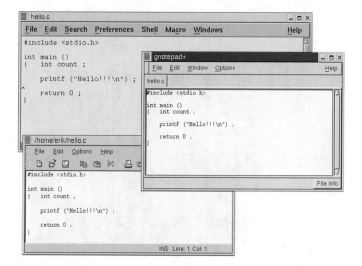

Note

To find alternative text editors for Linux, you could find one of the many Web Sites on the Internet with listings of programs available for Linux or use an Internet search engine. However, the best place to look is the Web site of the Linux distribution you are using.

Compiling the Source Code

NEW TERM Although you might be able to understand C source code (at least you will be able to after reading this book), your computer can't. A computer requires digital, or binary, instructions in what is called *machine language*. Before your C program can run on a computer, it must be translated from source code to machine language. This translation, the second step in program development, is performed by a program called a *compiler*. The compiler takes your source code file as input and produces a disk file containing the machine language instructions that correspond to your source code statements.

The most common C compiler used on Linux is the GNU C Compiler named gcc.

Note

To see if you have the C compiler installed, type the command **gcc -v** at the command line. If it is installed, you will see a message something like the one in the terminal window of Figure 1.3. Don't worry if you don't get the exact same message, because you might have a slightly different version of the C compiler. If, on the other hand, you get a message saying that the command was not found, you will need to consult the manual that came with your Linux distribution for instructions on how to install the C compiler. When you install the C compiler, you should also install all the other development tools.

FIGURE 1.3.

A typical Red Hat 6.0 user setup with a terminal window showing the results of the gcc -v *and* make -v *commands.*

The gcc compiler runs from the command line. Assuming that the source file radius.c exists in the current directory, the command required to compile it and create an executable is

```
gcc radius.c
```

This produces an output file in the current directory that, for historical reasons, is named a.out. To specify an output filename, gcc can be invoked as

```
gcc radius.c -o radius
```

This command tells gcc to compile a C source code file named radius.c and create an output file called radius. This output file (which can be named something other than radius) is an executable file, which means that the program can be run, or executed, by your computer. To run the program, you can type **./radius** at the command prompt. The dot and the forward slash tell the command interpreter in the terminal window to look for the program named radius in the current directory. Without the ./, the command interpreter would look in what is called the *current path* (execute the echo $PATH command to find out the current path).

Other than compiling your C source code into an executable, one of the main tasks of a C compiler is to give you information about where it encountered compilation errors. It would not be very helpful if all the compiler told you was that there was an error in the source code but not where the error occurred and why. C compilers are also able to generate warning messages about code that it understands but may cause it to generate a program with a bug. Obviously, you, as a programmer, would like to know as much as possible about what may be wrong with your program. It is therefore useful to ask the compiler to generate as many warning messages as possible. In addition, if you want to look at the program with the ddd debugger, you have to tell the compiler to add information to the executable file that is required by the debugger. Turning on all warnings and adding debugging information is done by invoking gcc as shown in the following:

```
gcc -Wall -ggdb radius.c -o radius
```

The -Wall directive tells gcc to print out all the warning messages it can, while -ggdb tells gcc to add debugging information for the gdb debugger, which is used inside ddd. This is the way you will be compiling most of the programs in this book. On Day 20, "Advanced Compiler Use," we will deal with the subject of writing and compiling programs written using multiple C source code files. Until then, however, all the programs will be contained in one single source code file.

Completing the Development Cycle

After your program is compiled and an executable file has been created, you can run it by entering its name in the terminal window, remembering to pre-pend ./ to the name. If you run the program and receive results different from what you expected, you need to go back to the first step. You must identify what caused the problem and correct it in the source code. When you make a change to the source code, you need to recompile the program to create a corrected version of the executable file. You keep following this cycle until you get the program to execute exactly as you intended.

When you begin to write programs, you will find that they rarely do exactly as you planned when you first run them. A common programmer's tool for finding and fixing bugs in programs is a debugger. A *debugger* is a program that allows a programmer to step through a program line by line to find errors in the program. As you can see from Figure 1.4, ddd is a debugger with a graphical user interface. You are encouraged to make use of this program throughout this book. Use it as a learning tool as well as a debugging tool. Use it to step through your programs to see how a program operates. Later, in "Using the ddd Debugger", you will find a very brief introduction on how to use ddd to step through a simple program line by line.

FIGURE 1.4.

The ddd *debugger. It uses two windows: a main window for displaying the code and a second smaller window containing its control buttons (right).*

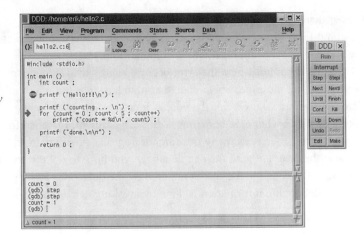

Other Programming Tools

There is one other important programming tool you should test for: the make utility. Typing make -v at the command line should print out a message something like the one shown in Figure 1.3, although it may not be exactly the same. The make utility will not be used until Day 20 when we deal with multi-file compilation.

The final program you will need is something with which to view the programmer's documentation that came with your Linux system. We have already used the manual reader man, but there is also a lot of useful information available in GNU information format that is display using a program named info. Type **info** in the terminal window and you should be presented with an introductory screen to the information system (press **q** to quit). Unfortunately, the info program is not exactly user friendly, but many Linux systems come with alternative information readers such as kdehelp and gnome-help-browser. Check to see if either of these programs are installed on your system by typing their names on the command line of your terminal window. If they are, try to locate the information pages called *System GNU Info Contents* under kdehelp and *Info Pages* under the gnome-help-browser. Also note that both these systems can be used to view the manual pages.

Getting Started with Linux

For the purposes of this book, we will assume that you already have Linux running on your system and have run some of the tests for the presence of the tools. We will also assume that you already have the X Window System Graphical User Interface (GUI) running. If this is not the case, you should install it by following the instructions that came with your Linux distribution.

Once you are able to log in to your system, you will need to start a terminal window (like the one shown in Figure 1.3). This is the standard user setup for a Red Hat Linux 6.0 installation. On other Linux distributions, the terminal may be called an xterm, kconsole, or console window.

Caution

If you are currently running as the root user on your Linux system, you should create an unprivileged user account and use that while you learn to program. The root user account has unrestricted access to the machine and can therefore cause unlimited damage if a program misbehaves. As an unprivileged user on a correctly set up Linux machine, the worst that can happen is that you damage files that you, the unprivileged user, own. It is extremely unlikely that you will damage files owned or required by the operating system.

When you have a terminal window, you should try a couple of the commonly used commands like ls (list directory), pwd (print working directory), ps (list processes), mkdir (make directory), and cd (change directory). All command names in Linux are case sensitive. The command LS (if it exists) is not the same as ls. You can get more information about these programs by reading the manual pages using the man command. For instance, man ls will show information about the ls command. When you have finished viewing the manual page, pressing the **q** key will return you to the command line. Most Linux distributions contain manual pages for almost every program or feature.

Note

The terminal window really consists of two programs, one controlling the window itself and another called the *command interpreter*, which, as its name suggests, interprets and executes the commands given by the user. The most commonly used command interpreter used with Linux is GNU bash (Bourne Again SHell), although many others are available.

For most of this book, the programs you will write as you learn to program in C will be run from a command line in a terminal window.

Your First C Program

You're probably eager to try your first program in C. To help you become familiar with your compiler, Listing 1.1 contains a quick program for you to work through. You might not understand everything at this point, but you should get a feel for the process of writing, compiling, and running a real C program.

This demonstration uses a program named `hello.c`, which does nothing more than display the words "Hello, World!" onscreen. This program, a traditional introduction to C programming, is a good one for you to learn. The source code for `hello.c` is in Listing 1.1. When you type in this listing, you won't include the line numbers on the left or the colons.

LISTING 1.1. `hello.c`.

```
1:  #include <stdio.h>
2:
3:  int main(void)
4:  {
5:      printf("Hello, World!\n\n");
6:      return 0;
7:  }
```

Make sure that you have `gcc` installed and working, as described earlier, and that you have a suitable editor. Once your compiler and editor are ready, follow these steps to enter, compile, and execute `hello.c`.

Entering and Compiling `hello.c`

To enter and compile the `hello.c` program, follow these steps:

1. In the terminal window, change to the directory you want your C program to be in using the `cd` command and start your text editor. If, for instance, you are using `nedit` as your editor, you should type the command **nedit &** at the command prompt.

2. Use the keyboard to type the `hello.c` source code exactly as shown in Listing 1.1. Press Enter at the end of each line.

> **Note** Don't enter the line numbers or colons. These are for reference only.

3. Save the source code. You should name the file hello.c.

4. Verify that `hello.c` is on disk by listing the files in the directory using the `ls` command in the terminal window. You should see `hello.c` within this listing.

5. Compile `hello.c` into a program using the following command in the terminal window.

   `gcc -Wall -ggdb hello.c -o hello`

6. Check the compiler messages. If you receive no errors or warnings, everything should be okay.

If you made an error typing the program, the compiler will catch it and display an error message. For example, if you misspelled the word `printf` as `prntf`, you would see a message similar to the following:

```
hello.c: In function `main':
hello.c:5: warning: implicit declaration of function `prntf'
/tmp/cco48R7q.o: In function `main':
/home/erikd/hello/hello.c:5: undefined reference to `prntf'
collect2: ld returned 1 exit status
```

7. Go back to step 2 if this or any other error message is displayed. Open the `hello.c` file in your editor. Compare your file's contents carefully with Listing 1.1, make any necessary corrections, and continue to step 3.

8. Your first C program should now be compiled and ready to run. If you display a directory listing of all files named hello (with any extension), you should see the following:

> `hello.c` The source code file you created with your editor
>
> `hello.` The executable program created when you compiled and linked hello.c

9. To execute, or run, `hello`, simply enter `./hello`. The message "Hello, World!" is displayed onscreen.

Congratulations! You have just entered, compiled, and run your first C program. Admittedly, `hello.c` is a simple program that doesn't do anything useful, but it's a start. In fact, most of today's expert C programmers started learning C in this same way—by compiling `hello.c`—so you're in good company.

Compilation Errors

A compilation error occurs when the compiler finds something in the source code that it can't compile. A misspelling, typographical error, or any of a dozen other things can cause the compiler to fail. Fortunately, modern compilers don't just fail; they tell you why they're failing and where the problem is. This makes it easier to find and correct errors in your source code.

This point can be illustrated by introducing a deliberate error into the `hello.c` program you entered earlier. If you worked through that example (and you should have), you now have a copy of `hello.c` on your disk. Using your editor, move the cursor to the end of the line containing the call to `printf()`, and erase the terminating semicolon. `hello.c` should now look like Listing 1.2.

LISTING 1.2. hello.c with an error.

```
1:  #include <stdio.h>
2:
3:  int main(void)
4:  {
5:      printf("Hello, World!\n\n")
6:      return 0;
7:  }
```

Next, save the file. You're now ready to compile it. Do so by entering the command for your compiler. Because of the error you introduced, the compilation is not completed. Rather, the compiler displays a message similar to the following:

```
hello.c: In function `main':
hello.c:6: parse error before `return'
hello.c:7: warning: control reaches end of non-void function
```

The small error you introduced caused three compiler messages. Each message gives the name of the C source code file at the start of the line and the second two messages follow the filename with the line number of the source code where the error was found. Notice that the third message is a warning message.

These messages are quite informative, telling you that something is wrong in function `main' and that there was an error in line 6 before `return'. So why is the compiler complaining about something being wrong on line 6 when we removed a semicolon from the end of line 5? The answer is that C doesn't care about things like line breaks between lines. The semicolon that belongs after the printf() statement could have been placed on the next line (although doing so would not have been usual programming practice). Only after encountering the next command (return) in line 6 is the compiler sure that the semicolon is missing. Therefore, the compiler reports that the error is in line 6.

You should also note that sometimes an error in one part of the program (line 6) can cause an error in a later part of the program (line 7). The lesson to learn from all this is as follows: If the compiler reports multiple errors, and you can find only one, go ahead and fix that error and recompile. You might find that your single correction is all that's needed, and the program will compile without errors.

This points out an undeniable fact about C compilers and error messages. Although the compiler is very clever about detecting and localizing errors, it's no Einstein. Using your knowledge of the C language, you must interpret the compiler's messages and determine the actual location of any errors that are reported. They are often found on the line reported by the compiler, but if not, they are almost always on the preceding line. You might have a bit of trouble finding errors at first, but you should soon get better at it.

Using the ddd Debugger

In the section dealing with the C development cycle, the fourth step was to execute the program to figure out if it works correctly. It is perfectly possible to write a C program that compiles without errors but does not meet its objectives. This is what is known as a *logic error* as opposed to the compile errors you looked at earlier. Tracking down logic errors in large programs is much trickier than finding compile errors. However, using a debugger is one very good way to find logic errors because it allows you to step through a program line by line. In this way, you can examine the operation of the program at each line to ensure that it is working the way you hoped it would work when you wrote the program. In this book, we will be using the ddd debugger as a teaching aide rather than as debugging tool.

The ddd debugger requires one simple setup step before it can be used. Assuming you have already obtained ddd, start it from the terminal window by typing **ddd**. If you are running ddd for the first time, you will need to click through one or two startup screens to get to the main window. Then, click the Edit item of the menu bar and choose GDB Settings from that menu. You will then be presented with a dialog box with a scroll bar at the right. Using the scroll bar, scroll down (about half way) until you see the item Autoloading of Shared Library Symbols. You should then click the button to the left of this item until it pops into the "out" position, as shown in Figure 1.5. For this action to be completed, you must then click the OK button and then, using the Edit menu item, click Save Options.

FIGURE 1.5.

Setting up the ddd
debugger.

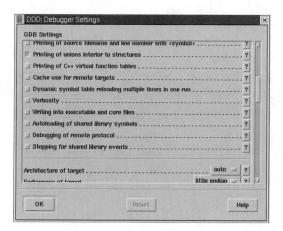

You are now ready to try using ddd on a program. Type in the following program (Listing 1.3) and compile it, remembering to tell gcc to add the debugging information required by the debugger. The executable program should be named hello2.

LISTING 1.3. hello2.c, a program for experimenting with the debugger.

```
1 : #include <stdio.h>
2 :
3 : int main(void)
4 : {    int count ;
5 :
6 :      printf ("Hello!!!\n") ;
7 :
8 :      printf ("counting ... \n") ;
9 :      for (count = 0 ; count < 5 ; count++)
10:          printf ("count = %d\n", count) ;
11:
12:  .  printf ("done.\n\n") ;
13:
14:      return 0 ;
15: }
```

After this program compiles and runs correctly, you are ready to use the debugger. To invoke the debugger on this program type **ddd hello2** at the terminal window command prompt. This should bring up the two ddd normal windows as well as a dialog box with tips on using ddd (which you should close). The main window should contain the source code for hello2.c.

The first step to running ddd is to set an initial breakpoint that gives the debugger a place to stop after initialization. In the main window, click at the far-left side of the first line containing "printf" (line 6) and then click the "break" item (with the stop sign above it) on the toolbar. This should place a stop sign on the line with the printf. You can now click the Run button on the floating button bar, which will make a green arrow appear at the stop sign. Clicking the Step button from the floating button bar will allow you to execute a line of code at a time. The output produced by each line of code will appear in the bottom part of the main window. Obviously, the debugger cannot proceed beyond the end of the program, but, at any time, you can restart the debugger at the top of the program by clicking the Run button.

You are encouraged to experiment with the debugger on the example programs in this book. Using the debugger will give you a much clearer insight into how the C programming language and your computer actually operate.

Summary

After reading this lesson, you should feel confident that selecting C as your programming language for Linux is a wise choice. C offers an unparalleled combination of power, popularity, and portability. These factors, together with C's close relationship to the C++ object-oriented language, as well as to Java, make C unbeatable.

This lesson explained the various steps involved in writing a C program—the process known as *program development*. You should have a clear grasp of the edit-compile-test cycle, as well as the tools to use for each step.

Errors are an unavoidable part of program development. Your C compiler detects errors in your source code and displays an error message, giving both the nature and the location of the error. Using this information, you can edit your source code to correct the error. Remember, however, that the compiler can't always accurately report the nature and location of an error. Sometimes you need to use your knowledge of C to track down exactly what is causing a given error message.

Q&A

Q If I start using one text editor and find I don't like it, can I change to another one without re-typing all the code? Are text editors compatible with one another?

A Yes, all text editors are compatible. If you are using a text editor rather than a word processor, all the files you generate will contain nothing but ASCII characters. Changing text editors should make no difference although some text editors may display the <tab> character slightly differently, making it equivalent to four spaces rather than the normal value of eight.

Q If I want to give someone a program I wrote, which files do I need to give them?

A One of the nice things about C is that it is a compiled language. This means that after the source code is compiled, you have an executable program. This executable program is a standalone program. If you wanted to give `hello` to all your friends who also have computers running Linux, you could. All you need to give them is the executable program, `hello`.

If, however, you want to allow that person to modify the program for his or her own use or use it on a different kind of computer, you need to give him or her the C source code. He or she will then need to compile it so it can run on his or her machine. You may also need to provide him or her with instructions for compiling your program.

Q After I create an executable file, do I need to keep the source file (`.c`)?

A If you get rid of the source file, you have no way to make changes to the program in the future, so you should keep this file. As long as you keep the source file (`.c`), you can always re-create the other files.

Q Can I ignore warning messages?

A Some warning messages don't affect how the program runs, and some do. If the compiler gives you a warning message, it's a signal that something isn't right. You should look at each warning and make a determination. It's always best to try to write all your programs with absolutely no warnings or errors. (With an error, your compiler won't create the executable file.)

Workshop

The Workshop provides quiz questions to help you solidify your understanding of the material covered and exercises to provide you with experience using what you've learned. Try to understand the quiz and exercises before continuing to the next lesson. Answers are provided in Appendix C, "Answers."

Quiz

1. Give three reasons why C is the best choice for a programming language.
2. What does the compiler do?
3. What are the steps in the Program Development Cycle?
4. What command do you need to enter to compile a program called myprog from a C source file called program1.c with gcc?
5. What extension should you use for your C source files?
6. Is filename.txt a valid name for a C source file?
7. If you execute a program that you have compiled and it doesn't work as you expected, what should you do?
8. What is machine language?
9. What does the debugger do?
10. What information is required by the debugger and provided by the compiler?

Exercises

1. Use your text editor to look at the executable file created by Listing 1.1. Does the executable look like the source file? (Don't save this file when you exit the editor.)
2. Enter the following program and compile it. What does this program do? (Don't include the line numbers or colons at the beginning of the lines.)

```
1:  #include <stdio.h>
2:
3:  int radius, area;
4:
```

```
5:  int main(void)
6:  {
7:     printf( "Enter radius (i.e. 10): " );
8:     scanf( "%d", &radius );
9:     area = (int) (3.14159 * radius * radius);
10:    printf( "\n\nArea = %d\n", area );
11:    return 0;
12: }
```

3. Enter and compile the following program. What does this program do?

```
1:  #include <stdio.h>
2:
3:  int x,y;
4:
5:  int main(void)
6:  {
7:     for ( x = 0; x < 10; x++, printf( "\n" ) )
8:         for ( y = 0; y < 10; y++ )
9:             printf( "X" );
10:
11:    return 0;
12: }
```

4. **BUG BUSTER:** The following program has a problem. Enter it in your editor and compile it. Which lines generate error messages?

```
1:  #include <stdio.h>
2:
3:  int main(void);
4:  {
5:     printf( "Keep looking!" );
6:     printf( "You\'ll find it!\n" );
7:     return 0;
8:  }
```

5. **BUG BUSTER:** The following program has a problem. Enter it in your editor and compile it. Which lines generate problems?

```
1:  #include <stdio.h>
2:
3:  int main(void)
4:  {
5:     printf( "This is a program with a " );
6:     do_it( "problem!");
7:     return 0;
8:  }
```

6. Make the following change to the program in exercise 3. Recompile and rerun this program. What does the program do now?

```
9:  printf( "%c", 1 );
```

DAY 2

The Components of a C Program: Code and Data

Every C program consists of several components combined in a certain way. Most of this book is devoted to explaining these various program components and how you use them. To help illustrate the overall picture, you should begin by reviewing a complete (though small) C program with all its components identified. Today you will learn

- The purpose of each program component
- How to compile and run a sample program
- How a program stores data
- The difference between a variable and a constant

A Short C Program

Listing 2.1 presents the source code for multiply.c. This is a very simple program. All it does is accept two numbers that are entered from the keyboard and calculate their product. At this stage, don't worry about understanding the details of the program's workings. The point is to gain some familiarity with the parts of a C program so that you can better understand the listings presented later in this book.

NEW TERM Before looking at the sample program, you need to know what a function is, because functions are central to C programming. A *function* is an independent section of program code that performs a certain task and has been assigned a name. By referencing a function's name, your program can execute the code in the function. The program also can send information, called *arguments,* to the function, and the function can return information to the main part of the program. The two types of C functions are *library functions,* which on Linux are really part of the operating system, and *user-defined functions,* which you, the programmer, create. You will learn about both types of functions in this book.

Note that, as with all the listings in this book, the line numbers in Listing 2.1 are not part of the program. They are included only for identification purposes, so don't type them.

LISTING **2.1**. multiply.c—A program that multiplies two numbers.

```
1:  /* Program to calculate the product of two numbers. */
2:  #include <stdio.h>
3:
4:  int a,b,c;
5:
6:  int product(int x, int y);
7:
8:  int main(void)
9:  {
10:      /* Get the first number */
11:      printf("Enter a number between 1 and 100: ");
12:      scanf("%d", &a);
13:
14:      /* Get the second number */
15:      printf("Enter another number between 1 and 100: ");
16:      scanf("%d", &b);
17:
18:      /* Calculate and display the product */
19:      c = product(a, b);
20:      printf ("%d times %d = %d\n", a, b, c);
21:
22:      return 0;
23: }
24:
25: /* Function returns the product of the two values provided */
26: int product(int x, int y)
27: {
28:      return (x * y);
29: }
```

OUTPUT
```
Enter a number between 1 and 100: 35
Enter another number between 1 and 100: 23
35 times 23 = 805
```

The Program's Components

The following sections describe the various components of Listing 2.1. Line numbers are included so that you can easily identify the program parts being discussed.

The `main()` Function (Lines 8 Through 23)

The only component that must appear once and only once in every executable C program is the `main()` function. In its simplest form, the `main()` function consists of the name `main` followed by a pair of parentheses (`()`) containing the C keyword `void` and a pair of braces (`{}`). Within the braces are statements that make up the main body of the program. Under normal circumstances, program execution starts at the first statement in `main()` and terminates at the last statement in `main()`.

The `#include` Directive (Line 2)

 The `#include` directive instructs the C compiler to add the contents of an include file into your program during compilation. An *include file* is a separate disk file that contains information needed by your program or the compiler. Several of these files (sometimes called *header files*) are supplied as part of your Linux distribution. You never have to modify the information in these files; that's why they're kept separate from your source code. Include files should always have an .h extension (for example, stdio.h).

You use the `#include` directive to instruct the compiler to add a specific include file to your program during compilation. In Listing 2.1, the `#include` directive is interpreted to mean "Add the contents of the file stdio.h." Most C programs require one or more include files. More information about include files is presented on Day 20, "Advanced Compiler Use."

The Variable Definition (Line 4)

NEW TERM A *variable* is a name assigned to a data storage location. Your program uses variables to store various kinds of data during program execution. In C, a variable must be *defined* before it can be used. A *variable definition* informs the compiler of the variable's name and the type of data it is to hold. In Listing 2.1, the definition on line 4, `int a,b,c;`, defines three variables—named a, b, and c—that will each hold an integer value. More information about variables and variable definitions is presented in the section "Storing Data: Variables and Constants" later in the day.

The Function Prototype (Line 6)

NEW TERM A *function prototype* provides the C compiler with the name and arguments of the functions contained in the program. It must appear before the function is used. A function prototype is distinct from a *function definition*, which contains the actual statements that make up the function. (Function definitions are discussed in more detail later today.)

Program Statements (Lines 11, 12, 15, 16, 19, 20, 22, and 28)

The real work of a C program is done by its statements. C statements display information onscreen, read keyboard input, perform mathematical operations, call functions, read disk files, and perform all the other operations that a program has to perform. Most of this book is devoted to teaching you the various C statements. For now, remember that in your source code, C statements are generally written one per line and always end with a semicolon. The statements in multiply.c are explained briefly in the following sections.

The printf() Statement

The printf() statement (lines 11, 15, and 20) is a library function that displays information onscreen. The printf() statement can display a simple text message (as in lines 11 and 15) or a message and the value of one or more program variables (as in line 20).

The scanf() Statement

The scanf() statement (lines 12 and 16) is another library function. It reads data from the keyboard and assigns that data to one or more program variables.

The program statement on line 19 calls the function named product(). In other words, it executes the program statements contained in the function product(). It also sends the arguments a and b to the function. After the statements in product() are completed, product() returns a value to the program. This value is stored in the variable named c.

The return Statement

Lines 22 and 28 contain return statements. The return statement on line 28 is part of the function product(). It calculates the product of the variables x and y and returns the result to the program that called product(). The return statement on line 22 returns a value of 0 to the operating system just before the program ends.

The Function Definition (Lines 26 Through 29)

NEW TERM   A *function* is an independent, self-contained section of code that is written to perform a certain task. Every function has a name, and the code in each function is executed by including that function's name in a program statement. This execution is known as *calling* the function.

The function named `product()`, in lines 26 through 29, is a user-defined function. As the name implies, *user-defined* functions are written by the programmer during program development. This function, which is included in lines 26 to 29, is simple. All it does is multiply two values and return the answer to the program that called it. On Day 4, "Functions: The Basics," you will learn that the proper use of functions is an important part of good C programming practice.

Note that in a real C program, you probably wouldn't use a function for a task as simple as multiplying two numbers. It has been done here for demonstration purposes only.

C also includes library functions that are a part of the operating system or the C compiler package. Library functions perform most of the common tasks (such as screen, keyboard, and disk input/output) your program needs. In the sample program, `printf()` and `scanf()` are library functions.

Program Comments (Lines 1, 10, 14, 18, and 25)

NEW TERM   Any part of your program that starts with /* and ends with */ is called a *comment*. The compiler ignores all comments, so they have absolutely no effect on how a program works. You can put anything you want into a comment, and it won't modify the way your program operates. A comment can span part of a line, an entire line, or multiple lines. Here are three examples:

```
/* A single-line comment */

int a,b,c; /* A partial-line comment */

/* a comment
spanning
multiple lines */
```

You should not use nested comments. A *nested* comment is a comment that has been put into another comment. The GNU C compiler will not accept the following:

```
/*
/* Nested comment */
*/
```

Some compilers do allow nested comments. Although this feature might be tempting to use, you should avoid doing so. One of the benefits of C is portability, and using a feature such as nested comments can limit the portability of your code. Nested comments also can lead to hard-to-find problems.

Many beginning programmers view program comments as unnecessary and a waste of time. This is a mistake! The operation of your program might be quite clear when you're writing the code. However, as your programs become larger and more complex, or when you have to modify a program you wrote six months ago, you will find comments invaluable. Now is the time to develop the habit of using comments liberally to document all your programming structures and operations.

Note

> Many people have started using a newer style of comments in their C programs. Within C++ and Java, you can use double forward slashes to signal a comment. Here are two examples:
>
> ```
> // This entire line is a comment
>
> int x;  // Comment starts with slashes.
> ```
>
> The two forward slashes signal that the rest of the line is a comment. Although many C compilers support this form of comment, you should avoid it if you're interested in writing C programs that are portable.

Do	Don't
DO add abundant comments to your program's source code, especially near statements or functions that could be unclear to you or to someone who might have to modify it later.	**DON'T** add unnecessary comments to statements that are already clear. For example, entering
DO learn to develop a style that will be helpful. A style that's too lean or cryptic doesn't help. A style that is verbose can cause you to spend more time commenting than programming!	``` /* The following prints Hello World! on the screen */ printf("Hello World!\n"); ``` might be going a little too far, at least after you're completely comfortable with the printf() function and how it works.

Using Braces (Lines 9, 23, 27, and 29)

NEW TERM   You use braces ({}) to enclose the program lines that make up every C function—including the main() function. A group of one or more statements enclosed within braces is called a *block*. As you will see in later days, C has many uses for blocks.

Running the Program

Take the time to enter, compile, and run multiply.c. It provides additional practice in using your editor and compiler. Recall these steps from Day 1, "Introduction to Linux and the C Programming Language":

1. Change to the directory where you want to write your program.

2. Start your editor.

3. Enter the source code for multiply.c exactly as shown in Listing 2.1, but be sure to omit the line numbers and colons.

4. Save the program file.

5. Compile the program by entering the appropriate command(s). Remember to tell gcc to turn on all warnings and to include debugging information. If no error messages are displayed, you can run the program by entering ./multiply at the command prompt.

6. If any error messages are displayed, return to step 2 and correct the errors.

A Note on Accuracy

A computer is fast and accurate, but it also is completely literal. It doesn't know enough to correct your simplest mistake; it takes everything you enter exactly as you entered it, not as you meant it!

This goes for your C source code as well. A simple typographical error in your program can cause the C compiler to choke, gag, and collapse. Fortunately, although the compiler isn't smart enough to correct your errors (and you will make errors—everyone does!), it *is* smart enough to recognize them as errors and report them to you. (You saw in yesterday's material how the compiler reports error messages and how you interpret them.)

A Review of the Parts of a Program

Now that all the parts of a program have been described, you should be able to look at any program and find some similarities. Look at Listing 2.2 and see whether you can identify the different parts.

LISTING 2.2. list_it.c—A program to list a code listing.

```
1 : /* list_it.c__This program displays a listing with line numbers! */
2 : #include <stdio.h>
3 : #include <stdlib.h>
4 :
5 : void display_usage(void);
6 : int line;
7 :
8 : int main( int argc, char *argv[] )
9 : {
10:     char buffer[256];
11:     FILE *fp;
12:
13:     if( argc < 2 )
14:     {
15:        display_usage();
16:        return 1;
17:     }
18:
19:     if (( fp = fopen( argv[1], "r" )) == NULL )
20:     {
21:         fprintf( stderr, "Error opening file, %s!\n", argv[1] );
22:         return 1;
23:     }
24:
25:     line = 1;
26:
27:     while( fgets( buffer, 256, fp ) != NULL )
28:        fprintf( stdout, "%4d:\t%s", line++, buffer );
29:
30:     fclose(fp);
31:     return 0;
32: }
33:
34: void display_usage(void)
35: {
36:         fprintf(stderr, "\nProper Usage is: " );
37:         fprintf(stderr, "\n\nLIST_IT filename.ext\n" );
38: }
```

OUTPUT

```
./list_it list_it.c
    1:  /* list_it.c__This program displays a listing with line numbers!
*/
    2:  #include <stdio.h>
    3:  #include <stdlib.h>
    4:
    5:  void display_usage(void);
    6:  int line;
    7:
    8:  int main( int argc, char *argv[] )
```

```
 9:  {
10:      char buffer[256];
11:      FILE *fp;
12:
13:      if( argc < 2 )
14:      {
15:          display_usage();
16:          return 1;
17:      }
18:
19:      if (( fp = fopen( argv[1], "r" )) == NULL )
20:      {
21:          fprintf( stderr, "Error opening file, %s!", argv[1] );
22:          return 1;
23:      }
24:
25:      line = 1;
26:
27:      while( fgets( buffer, 256, fp ) != NULL )
28:          fprintf( stdout, "%4d:\t%s", line++, buffer );
29:
30:      fclose(fp);
31:      return 0;
32:  }
33:
34:  void display_usage(void)
35:  {
36:          fprintf(stderr, "\nProper Usage is: " );
37:          fprintf(stderr, "\n\nlist_it filename.ext\n" );
38:  }
```

ANALYSIS   The list_it.c program in Listing 2.2 displays C program listings that you have
saved. These listings are displayed on the screen with line numbers added.

Looking at this listing, you can summarize where the different parts are. The required
main() function is in lines 8 through 32. Lines 2 and 3 have #include directives. Lines
6, 10, and 11 have variable definitions. A function prototype, void
display_usage(void), is in line 5. This program has many statements (lines 13, 15, 16,
19, 21, 22, 25, 27, 28, 30, 31, 36, and 37). A function definition for display_usage()
fills lines 34 through 38. Braces enclose blocks throughout the program. Finally, only
line 1 has a comment. In most programs, you should probably include more than one
comment line.

List_it.c calls many functions. It calls only one user-defined function, display_usage().
The library functions that it uses are fopen() in line 19; fprintf() in lines 21, 28, 36,
and 37; fgets() in line 27; and fclose() in line 30. These library functions are covered
in more detail throughout this book.

Storing Data: Variables and Constants

In Listing 2.1, you saw that three variables are defined in line 4. Computer programs usually work with different types of data and need a way to store the values being used. These values can be numbers or characters. C has two ways of storing number values—variables and constants—with many options for each. A variable is a data storage location that has a value that can change during program execution. In contrast, a constant has a fixed value that can't change. Before you get to variables, however, you need to know a little about the operation of your computer's memory.

If you already know how a computer's memory operates, you can skip this section. If you're not sure, read on. This information will help you better understand certain aspects of C programming.

A computer uses random access memory (RAM) to store information while it is operating. RAM is located in integrated circuits, or *chips*, inside your computer. RAM is *volatile*, which means that it is erased and replaced with new information as often as needed. Being volatile also means that RAM "remembers" only while the computer is turned on and loses its information when you turn off the computer.

Each computer has a certain amount of RAM installed. The amount of RAM in a system is usually specified in megabytes (MB), such as 1MB, 8MB, 32MB, 64MB, or more. One megabyte of memory is 1,024 kilobytes (KB). One kilobyte of memory consists of 1,024 bytes. Thus, a system with 4MB of memory actually has 4×1,024KB, or 4,096KB of RAM. This would be 4,096KB×1,024 bytes for a total of 4,194,304 bytes of RAM.

A *byte* is the fundamental unit of computer data storage. Day 18, "Working with Memory," has more information about bytes. For now, Table 2.1 provides you with an idea of how many bytes it takes to store certain kinds of data.

TABLE 2.1. Memory space required to store data.

Data	Bytes Required
The letter x	1
The number 500	2
The number 241.105	4
The phrase *Teach Yourself C*	17
One type-written page	Approximately 3,000

The RAM in your computer is organized sequentially, one byte following another. Each byte of memory has a unique address by which it is identified—an address that also distinguishes it from all other bytes in memory. Addresses are assigned to memory locations in order, starting at zero and increasing to the system limit. For now, you don't have to worry about addresses; they are handled automatically by the C compiler.

For what is your computer's RAM used? It has several uses, but only data storage need concern you as a programmer. *Data* is the information with which your C program works. Whether your program is maintaining an address list, monitoring the stock market, keeping a household budget, or tracking the price of hog bellies, the information (names, stock prices, expense amounts, or hog futures) is kept in your computer's RAM while the program is running.

Now that you understand a little about the nuts and bolts of memory storage, you can get back to C programming and how C uses memory to store information.

Variables

NEW TERM
A *variable* is a named data storage location in your computer's memory. By using a variable's name in your program, you are, in effect, referring to the data stored there.

Variable Names

To use variables in your C programs, you must know how to create variable names. In C, variable names must adhere to the following rules:

- The name can contain letters, digits, and the underscore character (_).
- The first character of the name must be a letter. The underscore is also a legal first character, but its use is not recommended at the beginning of a name.
- Case matters (that is, uppercase and lowercase letters). C is case sensitive. Thus, the names `count` and `Count` refer to two different variables.
- C keywords can't be used as variable names. A keyword is a word that is part of the C language. (A complete list of the C keywords can be found in Appendix B, "C/C++ Reserved Words.")

The following list contains some examples of legal and illegal C variable names:

Variable Name	Legality
`Percent`	Legal.
`y2x5__fg7h`	Legal.
`annual_profit`	Legal.
`_1990_tax`	Legal but not advised.

Variable Name	Legality
savings#account	Illegal: Contains the illegal character #.
double	Illegal: This is a C keyword.
9winter	Illegal: The first character is a digit.

The C language is case sensitive, so the names percent, PERCENT, and Percent would be considered three different variables. C programmers commonly use only lowercase letters in variable names, although this isn't required. Using all uppercase letters is usually reserved for the names of constants (which are covered later today).

For many compilers, a C variable name can be up to 31 characters long. (It can actually be longer than that, but the compiler looks at only the first 31 characters of the name.) With this flexibility, you can create variable names that reflect the data being stored. For example, a program that calculates loan payments could store the value of the prime interest rate in a variable named interest_rate. The variable name helps make its usage clear. You could also have created a variable named x or even johnny_carson; it doesn't matter to the C compiler. The use of the variable, however, wouldn't be nearly as clear to someone else looking at the source code. Although it might take a little more time to type descriptive variable names, the improvements in program clarity make it worthwhile.

Many naming conventions are used for variable names created from multiple words. You've seen one style: interest_rate. Using an underscore to separate words in a variable name makes it easy to interpret. The second style is called *camel notation*. Rather than use spaces, you capitalize the first letter of each word. Instead of interest_rate, the variable would be named InterestRate. Camel notation is gaining popularity because it's easier to type a capital letter than an underscore. The underscore is used in this book because it's easier for most people to read. You should decide which style you want to adopt.

Do	**Don't**
DO use variable names that are descriptive.	**DON'T** start your variable names with an underscore unnecessarily.
DO adopt and stick with a style for naming your variables.	**DON'T** name your variables with all capital letters unnecessarily.

Numeric Variable Types

C provides several types of numeric variables. You need different types of variables because different numeric values have varying memory storage requirements and differ in the ease with which certain mathematical operations can be performed on them. Small integers (for example, 1, 199, and –8) require less memory to store, and your computer can perform mathematical operations (addition, multiplication, and so on) with such numbers very quickly. In contrast, large integers and floating-point values (123,000,000, 3.14, or 0.000000871256, for example) require more storage space and more time for mathematical operations. By using the appropriate variable types, you ensure that your program runs as efficiently as possible.

C's numeric variables fall into the following two main categories:

- Integer variables hold values that have no fractional part (that is, whole numbers only). Integer variables come in two flavors: Signed integer variables can hold positive or negative values, whereas unsigned integer variables can hold only positive values (and 0).

- Floating-point variables hold values that have a fractional part (that is, real numbers).

Within each of these categories are two or more variable types.

Listing 2.3 contains a program that will tell you the size of the different kinds of variables on your computer. Why run a program to generate this information? Well, as explained briefly in Day 1, Linux runs on many kinds of computer hardware. The size of some of these variable types on a Linux machine utilizing an Intel Pentium (part of Intel's IA32 family) processor will differ from the size on a Linux machine running a DEC/Compaq Alpha processor.

LISTING 2.3. sizeof.c—A program for displaying the size in bytes of various variable types on your computer. It also displays the maximum and minimum values of integer variable types.

```
 1 : /* A program to print the size of the different    */
 2 : /* kinds of C variables on your machine.            */
 3 : #include <stdio.h>
 4 : #include <limits.h>
 5 :
 6 : int main(void)
 7 : {
 8 :     printf ("Signed   : Size %20s %22s\n", "Min", "Max") ;
 9 :     printf ("char     : %d %22d %22d\n",
10:             (int) sizeof (char), CHAR_MIN,CHAR_MAX);
```

continues

LISTING 2.3. continued

```
11:     printf ("short    :  %d %22d %22d\n",
12:             (int) sizeof (short), SHRT_MIN,SHRT_MAX);
13:     printf ("int      :  %d %22d %22d\n",
14:             (int) sizeof (int), INT_MIN,INT_MAX);
15:     printf ("long     :  %d %22ld %22ld\n",
16:             (int) sizeof (long), LONG_MIN,LONG_MAX);
17:     printf ("\n") ;
18:
19:     printf ("Unsigned : Size %20s %22s\n", "Min", "Max") ;
20:     printf ("char     :  %d %22d %22u\n",
21:             (int) sizeof (unsigned char),0,UCHAR_MAX);
22:     printf ("short    :  %d %22d %22u\n",
23:             (int) sizeof (unsigned short),0,USHRT_MAX);
24:     printf ("int      :  %d %22d %22u\n",
25:             (int) sizeof (unsigned int),0,UINT_MAX);
26:     printf ("long     :  %d %22d %22lu\n",
27:             (int) sizeof (unsigned long),0,ULONG_MAX);
28:     printf ("\n") ;
29:
30:     printf ("single prec. float : %d\n", (int) sizeof (float));
31:     printf ("double prec. float : %d\n", (int) sizeof (double));
32:
33:     return 0 ;
34: }
```

Don't worry if you don't understand how the program works. Although some items are new, such as `sizeof`, others should look familiar. Lines 1 and 2 are comments about the name of the program and a brief description. Lines 3 and 4 include two header files that are standard will all ANSI/ISO C compilers. This is a simple program in that it contains only a single function, `main()` (lines 6 through 34). Lines 9 through 31 are the bulk of the program. Each of these lines prints a textual description with the size of each of the variable types, which is done using the `sizeof` operator. Day 17, "Exploring the C Function Library," covers the `sizeof` operator in detail. As well as printing out the size of each variable type, it prints the maximum and minimum values contained in the `limits.h` header file. (You should note that this file does not contain maximum and minimum values for the floating-point data types.) Line 33 of the program returns the value 0 to the operating system before ending the program.

Here is the output of the program sizeof.c compiled and run on an Intel x86–based Linux machine.

```
./sizeof
Signed   : Size              Min                 Max
char     : 1               -128                 127
short    : 2             -32768               32767
int      : 4        -2147483648          2147483647
long     : 4        -2147483648          2147483647
Unsigned : Size              Min                 Max
char     : 1                  0                 255
short    : 2                  0               65535
int      : 4                  0          4294967295
long     : 4                  0          4294967295
single prec. float : 4
double prec. float : 8
```

Here is the output of the program sizeof.c compiled and run on an DEC/Compaq Alpha microprocessor–based Linux machine.

OUTPUT
```
./sizeof
Signed   : Size              Min                 Max
char     : 1               -128                 127
short    : 2             -32768               32767
int      : 4        -2147483648          2147483647
long     : 8     -9223372036854775808   9223372036854775807
Unsigned : Size              Min                 Max
char     : 1                  0                 255
short    : 2                  0               65535
int      : 4                  0          4294967295
long     : 8                  0    18446744073709551615
single prec. float : 4
double prec. float : 8
```

Notice that no special keyword is necessary to make an integer variable signed (integer variables are signed by default). Also, note how the results on the two processors are the same for char, short, and int but very different for long values. This is because the Alpha processor is a 64-bit processor capable of representing integers up to $2^{64}-1$, whereas the Intel Pentium family of processors is 32-bit and capable of representing numbers up to only $2^{32}-1$. Programmers who want to write C code that is portable between Pentium-based and Alpha-based processors must keep these differences in mind.

Although the size of the data types can vary, depending on your computer's processor, C does make some guarantees, thanks to the ANSI/ISO Standard. There are five things you can count on:

- The size of a char is one byte.
- The size of a short is less than or equal to the size of an int.

- The size of an int is less than or equal to the size of a long.
- The size of an unsigned is equal to the size of an int.
- The size of a float is less than or equal to the size of a double.

Floating-point variables hold values in a way that is similar to the scientific notation you probably learned in high school. Floating-point numbers are represented in three parts: a sign (+ or - to represent positive or negative numbers), a mantissa (a value between 0 and 1), and an exponent. Using this method, a number such as 238.5 would be represented as +0.2385E2: a positive number equal to 0.2385 times 10 squared (that is, 100). The exponent (in this case, 2) can be both positive and negative, allowing the floating-point representation to hold both very large and very small numbers.

However, this floating-point representation cannot represent all numbers with complete accuracy. Many numbers such as 1/3 can only be approximated using floating-point numbers. 1/3 is correctly represented as 0.333333..., with an infinitely repeating string of 3s. Floating-point numbers can retain only a certain number of these repeating 3s. The single precision representation of 1/3 retains about 7 of these repeating 3s, and the double precision representation retains about 19 digits.

The single and double precision floating-point representations also differ in the range of numbers they can store. Double precision variables can store much larger and much smaller numbers than single precision variables. This is because the exponent of the double precision representation can hold a larger range of numbers than the single precision representation. A comparison of the range and precision of single and double precision floating-point numbers appears in Table 2.2.

TABLE 2.2. Range and precision of floating-point numbers.

	Range	Precision
Single precision	1.2E–38 to 3.4E38	7 digits
Double precision	2.2E–308 to 1.8E308	19 digits

Variable Declarations

Before you can use a variable in a C program, it must be *declared*. A variable declaration tells the compiler the name and type of a variable. The declaration may also initialize the variable to a specific value. If your program attempts to use a variable that hasn't been declared, the compiler generates an error message. A variable declaration has the following form:

```
typename varname;
```

2

typename specifies the variable type and must be one of the keywords listed in Table 2.2. varname is the variable name, which must follow the rules mentioned earlier. You can declare multiple variables of the same type on one line by separating the variable names with commas:

```
int count, number, start;    /* three integer variables */
float percent, total;        /* two float variables */
```

On Day 11, "Understanding Variable Scope," you will learn that the location of variable declarations in the source code is important because it affects the ways in which your program can use the variables. For now, you can place all the variable declarations together just before the start of the main() function.

The typedef Keyword

The typedef keyword is used to create a new name for an existing data type. In effect, typedef creates a synonym. For example, the statement

```
typedef int integer;
```

creates integer as a synonym for int. You then can use integer to define variables of type int, as in this example:

```
integer count;
```

Note that typedef doesn't create a new data type; it only lets you use a different name for a predefined data type. The most common use of typedef concerns aggregate data types, as explained on Day 10, "Structures." An aggregate data type consists of a combination of data types presented today.

Initializing Variables

When you declare a variable, you instruct the compiler to set aside storage space for the variable. However, the value stored in that space—the value of the variable—isn't defined. It might be zero, or it might be some random "garbage" value. Before using a variable, you should always initialize it to a known value. You can do this independently of the variable declaration by using an assignment statement, as in this example:

```
int count;   /* Set aside storage space for count */
count = 0;   /* Store 0 in count */
```

Note that this statement uses the equal sign (=), which is C's assignment operator and is discussed further on Day 3, "Statements, Expressions, and Operators." For now, you need to be aware that the equal sign in programming is not the same as the equal sign in algebra. If you write

```
x = 12
```

in an algebraic statement, you are stating a fact: "x equals 12." In C, however, it means something quite different: "Assign the value 12 to the variable named *x*."

You can also initialize a variable when it's declared. To do so, follow the variable name in the declaration statement with an equal sign and the desired initial value:

```
int count = 0;
double percent = 0.01, taxrate = 28.5;
```

Be careful not to initialize a variable with a value outside the allowed range. Here are two examples of out-of-range initializations:

```
int weight = 10000000000000;

unsigned int value = -2500;
```

Fortunately, the GNU C compiler gives a warning when asked to compile such code. It is, however, only a warning. Your program will still be compiled, but it is unlikely to behave as you expected.

Do	Don't
DO understand the number of bytes that variable types take for your computer.	**DON'T** use a variable that hasn't been initialized. The results can be unpredictable.
DO use `typedef` to make your programs more readable.	**DON'T** use a `float` or `double` variable if you're only storing integers. Although they will work, using them is inefficient.
DO initialize variables when you declare them, whenever possible.	**DON'T** try to put numbers into variable types that are too small to hold them.
	DON'T put negative numbers into variables with an unsigned type.

Constants

Like a variable, a *constant* is a data storage location used by your program. Unlike a variable, the value stored in a constant can't be changed during program execution. C has two types of constants, each with its own specific uses:

- Literal constants
- Symbolic constants

Literal Constants

NEW TERM — *A literal constant* is a value that is typed directly into the source code wherever it is needed. Here are two examples:

```
int count = 20;
```

```
float tax_rate = 0.28;
```

The 20 and the 0.28 are literal constants. The preceding statements store these values in the variables `count` and `tax_rate`. Note that one of these constants contains a decimal point, whereas the other does not. The presence or absence of the decimal point distinguishes floating-point constants from integer constants.

A literal constant written with a decimal point is a floating-point constant and is represented by the C compiler as a double precision number. Floating-point constants can be written in standard decimal notation, as shown in these examples:

```
123.456
```

```
0.019
```

```
100.
```

Note that the third constant, `100.`, is written with a decimal point even though it's an integer (that is, it has no fractional part). The decimal point causes the C compiler to treat the constant as a double precision value. Without the decimal point, it is treated as an integer constant.

Floating-point constants also can be written in scientific notation. You might recall from high school math that scientific notation represents a number as a decimal part multiplied by 10 to a positive or negative power. Scientific notation is particularly useful for representing extremely large and extremely small values. In C, scientific notation is written as a decimal number followed immediately by an E or e and the exponent:

1.23E2	1.23 times 10 to the 2nd power, or 123
4.08e6	4.08 times 10 to the 6th power, or 4,080,000
0.85e–4	0.85 times 10 to the –4th power, or 0.000085

A constant written without a decimal point is represented by the compiler as an integer number. Integer constants can be written in three notations:

- A constant starting with any digit other than 0 is interpreted as a decimal integer (that is, the standard base-10 number system). Decimal constants can contain the digits 0 through 9 and a leading minus or plus sign. (Without a leading minus or plus, a constant is assumed to be positive.)

- A constant starting with the digit 0 is interpreted as an octal integer (the base-8 number system). Octal constants can contain the digits 0 through 7 and a leading minus or plus sign.

- A constant starting with 0x or 0X is interpreted as a hexadecimal constant (the base-16 number system). Hexadecimal constants can contain the digits 0 through 9, the letters *A* through *F*, and a leading minus or plus sign.

Symbolic Constants

NEW TERM   A *symbolic constant* is a constant that is represented by a name (symbol) in your program. Like a literal constant, a symbolic constant can't change. Whenever you need the constant's value in your program, you use its name as you would use a variable name. The actual value of the symbolic constant must be entered only once, when it is first defined.

Symbolic constants have two significant advantages over literal constants, as the following example shows. Suppose that you're writing a program that performs a variety of geometrical calculations. The program frequently needs the value π (3.14) for its calculations. (You might recall from geometry class that π is the ratio of a circle's circumference to its diameter.) For example, to calculate the circumference and area of a circle with a known radius, you could write

```
circumference = 3.14 * (2 * radius);
area = 3.14 * (radius)*(radius);
```

The asterisk (*) is C's multiplication operator and is covered on Day 3. Thus, the first of these statements means "Multiply 2 times the value stored in the variable radius, and then multiply the result by 3.14159. Finally, assign the result to the variable named circumference".

If, however, you define a symbolic constant with the name PI and the value 3.14, you could write

```
circumference = PI * (2 * radius);
area = PI * (radius)*(radius);
```

The resulting code is clearer. Rather than puzzle over what the value 3.14 is for, you can see immediately that the constant PI is being used.

The second advantage of symbolic constants becomes apparent when you have to change a constant. Continuing with the preceding example, you might decide that for greater accuracy your program needs to use a value of PI with more decimal places: 3.14159 instead of 3.14. If you had used literal constants for PI, you would have to go through your source code and change each occurrence of the value from 3.14 to 3.14159. With a symbolic constant, you have to make a change only in the place where the constant is defined.

Defining Symbolic Constants

C has two methods for defining a symbolic constant: the #define directive and the const keyword. The #define directive is used as follows:

```
#define CONSTNAME literal
```

This creates a constant named CONSTNAME with the value of literal. literal represents a literal constant, as described earlier. CONSTNAME follows the same rules described earlier for variable names. By convention, the names of symbolic constants are uppercase. This makes them easy to distinguish from variable names, which by convention are lowercase. For the previous example, the required #define directive for a constant named PI would be

```
#define PI 3.14159
```

Note that #define lines don't end with a semicolon (;). #defines can be placed anywhere in your source code, but they are in effect only for the portions of the source code that follow the #define directive. Most commonly, programmers group all #defines together, near the beginning of the file and before the start of main().

How a #define Works

The precise action of the #define directive is to instruct the compiler as follows: "In the source code, replace CONSTNAME with literal." The effect is exactly the same as if you had used your editor to go through the source code and make the changes manually. Note that #define doesn't replace instances of its target that occur as parts of longer names, within double quotes, or as part of a program comment. For example, in the following code, the instances of PI in the second and third lines would not be changed:

```
#define PI 3.14159
/* You have defined a constant for PI. */
#define PIPETTE 100
```

Note

The #define directive is one of C's preprocessor directives, and it is discussed fully on Day 20, "Advanced Compiler Use."

Defining Constants with the const Keyword

The second way to define a symbolic constant is with the const keyword. const is a modifier that can be applied to any variable declaration. A variable declared to be const can't be modified during program execution—only initialized at the time of declaration. Here are some examples:

```
const int count = 100;
const float pi = 3.14159;
const long debt = 12000000, float tax_rate = 0.21;
```

const affects all variables on the declaration line. In the last line, debt and tax_rate are symbolic constants. If your program tries to modify a const variable, the compiler generates an error message. The following code would generate an error:

```
const int count = 100;
count = 200;        /* Does not compile! Cannot reassign or alter */
                    /* the value of a constant. */
```

What are the practical differences between symbolic constants created with the #define directive and those created with the const keyword? The differences have to do with pointers and variable scope. Pointers and variable scope are two very important aspects of C programming, and they are covered on Day 8, "Understanding Pointers," and Day 11.

Now take a look at a program that demonstrates variable declarations and the use of literal and symbolic constants. Listing 2.4 prompts the user to input his or her weight and year of birth. It then calculates and displays the user's weight in grams and his or her age in the year 2010. You can enter, compile, and run this program using the procedures explained on Day 1.

LISTING 2.4. A program that demonstrates the use of variables and constants.

```
 1 : /* Demonstrates variables and constants */
 2 : #include <stdio.h>
 3 :
 4 : /* Define a constant to convert from pounds to grams */
 5 : #define GRAMS_PER_POUND 454
 6 :
 7 : /* Define a constant for the start of the next century */
 8 : const int TARGET_YEAR= 2010;
 9 :
10: /* Declare the needed variables */
11: int weight_in_grams, weight_in_pounds;
12: int year_of_birth, age_in_2010;
13:
14: int main(void)
15: {
16:     /* Input data from user */
17:
18:     printf("Enter your weight in pounds: ");
19:     scanf("%d", &weight_in_pounds);
20:     printf("Enter your year of birth: ");
```

```
21:      scanf("%d", &year_of_birth);
22:
23:      /* Perform conversions */
24:
25:      weight_in_grams = weight_in_pounds * GRAMS_PER_POUND;
26:      age_in_2010 = TARGET_YEAR - year_of_birth;
27:
28:      /* Display results on the screen */
29:
30:      printf("\nYour weight in grams = %d.", weight_in_grams);
31:      printf("\nIn 2010 you will be %d years old.\n", age_in_2010);
32:
33:      return 0;
34: }
```

OUTPUT

```
Enter your weight in pounds: 175
Enter your year of birth: 1960
Your weight in grams = 79450
In 2010 you will be 50 years old
```

ANALYSIS   This program declares the two types of symbolic constants in lines 5 and 8. In line 5, a constant is used to make the value 454 more understandable. Because it uses GRAMS_PER_POUND, line 25 is easy to understand. Lines 11 and 12 declare the variables used in the program. Notice the use of descriptive names such as weight_in_grams. You can tell what this variable is used for. Lines 18 and 20 print prompts onscreen. The printf() function is covered in greater detail later. To allow the user to respond to the prompts, lines 19 and 21 use another library function, scanf(), which is covered later. scanf() gets information from the screen. For now, accept that this works as shown in the listing. Later, you will learn exactly how it works. Lines 25 and 26 calculate the user's weight in grams and his or her age in the year 2010. These statements and others are covered in detail in tomorrow's lesson. To finish the program, lines 30 and 31 display the results for the user.

Do	Don't
DO use constants to make your programs easier to read.	DON'T try to assign a value to a constant after it has already been initialized.

Summary

Today's lesson introduces you to the major components of a C program and explores numeric variables, which are used by a C program to store data during program execution. You learned that the single required part of every C program is the main() function. You also learned that a program's real work is done by program statements that instruct the computer to perform your desired actions. You were also introduced to variables and variable definitions, and you learned how to use comments in your source code.

In addition to the `main()` function, a C program can use two types of subsidiary functions: library functions, supplied as part of the compiler package, and user-defined functions, created by the programmer.

You've seen that there are two broad classes of numeric variables: integer and floating point. Within each class are specific variable types. Which variable type—`int`, `long`, `float`, or `double`—you use for a specific application depends on the nature of the data to be stored in the variable. You've also seen that in a C program, you must declare a variable before it can be used. A variable declaration informs the compiler of the name and type of a variable.

You also learned about C's two constant types: literal and symbolic. Unlike variables, the value of a constant can't change during program execution. You type literal constants into your source code whenever the value is needed. Symbolic constants are assigned a name that is used wherever the constant value is needed. Symbolic constants can be created with the `#define` directive or with the `const` keyword.

Q&A

Q What effect do comments have on a program?

A Comments are for programmers. When the compiler converts the source code to object code, it throws the comments and the whitespace away. This means that they have no effect on the executable program. A program with many comments will execute just as fast as a program with very few comments. Comments do make your source file bigger, but this is usually of little concern. To summarize, you should use comments and whitespace to make your source code as easy to understand and maintain as possible.

Q What is the difference between a statement and a block?

A A block is a group of statements enclosed in braces (`{}`). A block can be used in most places that a statement can be used.

Q How can I find out which library functions are available?

A Linux comes standard with hundreds of libraries. You can see some of them by listing the directories /lib and /usr/lib. The most important library is the standard C library, which will be named something like /lib/libc-2.1.1.so. This library contains a huge number of predefined functions for handling things like keyboard and screen input/output, file input/output, string handling, mathematics, memory allocation, and error handling. These various predefined functions are all fully documented in the

libc section of the GNU info pages and categorized according to their function. The documentation can be viewed using one of the info viewers listed in Day 1. To go direct to the libc section, you can use one of the following commands:

```
gnome-help-browser info:libc
```

```
info libc
```

kdehelp does not have a way to go directly to the libc documentation, but it is relatively easy to find the System GNU info pages and then the libc section within it.

2

Q What happens if I assign a number with a decimal to an integer?

A You can assign a number with a decimal to an `int` variable. If you're using a constant variable, your compiler probably will give you a warning. The value assigned will have the decimal portion truncated. For example, if you assign 3.14 to an integer variable called `PI`, `PI` will contain only 3. The .14 will be chopped off and thrown away.

Q What happens if I put a number into a type that isn't big enough to hold it?

A Many compilers will allow this without signaling any errors. The number is wrapped to fit and therefore won't be correct. For example, if you assign 32768 to a 2-byte signed integer, the integer really contains the value -32768. If you assign the value 65535 to this integer, it really contains the value -1. Subtracting the maximum value that the field will hold generally gives you the value that will be stored.

Q What happens if I put a negative number into an unsigned variable?

A As the preceding answer indicated, your compiler might not signal any errors if you do this. The compiler does the same wrapping as if you assigned a number that was too big. For instance, if you assign -1 to an unsigned integer variable that is 2 bytes long, the compiler will put the highest number possible in the variable (65535).

Q What are the practical differences between symbolic constants created with the `#define` directive and those created with the `const` keyword?

A The differences have to do with pointers and variable scope. Pointers and variable scope are two very important aspects of C programming and are covered on Days 8 and 11. For now, know that by using #define to create constants, you can make your programs much easier to read.

Workshop

The Workshop provides quiz questions to help you solidify your understanding of the material covered and exercises to provide you with experience in using what you've learned. The answers to the quiz and exercises are provided in Appendix C, "Answers."

Quiz

1. What is the term for a group of one or more C statements enclosed in braces?

2. What is the one component that must be present in every C program?

3. How do you add program comments, and why are they used?

4. What is a function?

5. C offers two types of functions. What are they, and how are they different?

6. For what is the #include directive used?

7. Can comments be nested?

8. Can comments be longer than one line?

9. What is another name for an include file?

10. What is an include file?

Exercises

1. Write the smallest program possible.

2. Consider the following program:

```
1 : /* ex2-2.c */
2 : #include <stdio.h>
3 :
4 : void display_line(void);
5 :
6 : int main(void)
7 : {
8 :     display_line();
9 :     printf("\n Sams Teach Yourself C In 21 Days!\n");
10:     display_line();
11:     printf("\n\n");
12:      return 0;
13: }
14:
15: /* print asterisk line */
16: void display_line(void)
17: {
18:     int counter;
19:
20:     for( counter = 0; counter < 34; counter++ )
21:         printf("*" );
22: }
23: /* end of program */
```

2

      a. Which line(s) contain statements?

      b. Which line(s) contain variable definitions?

      c. Which line(s) contain function prototypes?

      d. Which line(s) contain function definitions?

      e. Which line(s) contain comments?

3. Write an example of a comment.

4. What does the following program do? (Enter, compile, and run it.)

```
 1 : /* ex2-4.c */
 2 : #include <stdio.h>
 3 :
 4 : int main(void)
 5 : {
 6 :     int ctr;
 7 :
 8 :     for( ctr = 65; ctr < 91; ctr++ )
 9 :         printf("%c", ctr );
10:
11:   printf ("\n\n");
12:     return 0;
13: }
14: /* end of program */
```

5. What does the following program do? (Enter, compile, and run it.)

```
 1 : /* ex2-5.c */
 2 : #include <stdio.h>
 3 : #include <string.h>
 4 : int main(void)
 5 : {
 6 :     char buffer[256];
 7 :
 8 :     printf( "Enter your name and press <Enter>:\n");
 9 :     fgets( buffer,256,stdin );
10:
11:     printf( "\nYour name has %d characters and spaces!\n",
12:                     strlen( buffer )-1);
13:
14:     return 0;
15: }
```

DAY **3**

Statements, Expressions, and Operators

C programs consist of statements, and most statements are composed of expressions and operators. You must understand statements, expressions, and operators to be able to write C programs. Today you will learn

- What a statement is
- What an expression is
- C's mathematical, relational, and logical operators
- What operator precedence is
- The `if` statement

Statements

NEW TERM   A *statement* is a complete direction instructing the computer to carry out some task. In C, statements are usually written one per line, although some statements span multiple lines. C statements always end with a semicolon (except for preprocessor directives such as `#define` and `#include`, which are discussed on Day 20, "Advanced Compiler Use"). You've already been introduced to some of C's statement types. For example

```
x = 2 + 3;
```

is an assignment statement. It instructs the computer to add 3 to 2 and assign the result to the variable x. Other types of statements will be introduced as needed throughout this book.

The Impact of Whitespace on Statements

NEW TERM   The term *whitespace* refers to spaces, tabs, and blank lines in your source code. The C compiler isn't sensitive to whitespace. When the compiler reads a statement in your source code, it looks for the characters in the statement and for the terminating semicolon, but it ignores whitespace. Thus, the statement

```
x=2+3;
```

is equivalent to this statement:

```
x = 2 + 3;
```

It is also equivalent to this:

```
x          =
2
      +
3  ;
```

This gives you a great deal of flexibility in formatting your source code. However, you shouldn't use formatting like the previous example. Statements should be entered one per line with a standardized scheme for spacing around variables and operators. If you follow the formatting conventions used in this book, you should be in good shape. As you become more experienced, you might discover that you prefer slight variations. The point is to keep your source code readable.

The rule that C doesn't care about whitespace has one exception. Within literal string constants, tabs and spaces aren't ignored; they are considered part of the string. A *string* is a series of characters. Literal string constants are strings that are enclosed within quotes and interpreted literally by the compiler, space for space. An example of a literal string is

```
"How now brown cow"
```

This literal string is different from the following:

```
"How    now    brown    cow"
```

The difference is a result of the additional spaces. With a literal string, C keeps track of the whitespace.

Although it's extremely bad form, the following is legal code in C:

```
printf(
"Hello, world!"
);
```

This, however, is allowed by the GNU C compiler but is not legal C. This means that even though gcc allows this expression, you should not use it if you ever want to compile the code with another C compiler.

```
printf("Hello,
world!");
```

To break a literal string constant line, you must use the backslash character (\) just before the break. Thus, the following is legal and will work with all ANSI C compilers:

```
printf("Hello,\
world!");
```

Creating a Null Statement

NEW TERM If you place a semicolon by itself on a line, you create a *null statement*— a statement that doesn't perform any action. This is perfectly legal in C. Later in this book, you will learn how a null statement can be useful.

Working with Compound Statements

NEW TERM A *compound statement*, also called a *block*, is a group of two or more C statements enclosed in braces. Here's an example of a block:

```
{
    printf("Hello, ");
    printf("world!");
}
```

In C, a block can be used anywhere that a single statement can be used. Many examples of this appear throughout this book. Note that the enclosing braces can be positioned in different ways. The following is equivalent to the preceding example:

```
{printf("Hello, ");
printf("world!");}
```

It's a good idea to place braces on their own lines, making the beginning and end of blocks clearly visible. Placing braces on their own lines also makes it easier to see whether you've left one out.

Do	Don't
DO stay consistent with how you use whitespace in statements. **DO** put block braces on their own lines. This makes the code easier to read. **DO** line up block braces so that it's easy to find the beginning and end of a block.	**DON'T** spread a single statement across multiple lines if there's no need to do so. Limit statements to one line if possible.

Understanding Expressions

NEW TERM In C, an *expression* is anything that evaluates to a numeric value. C expressions come in all levels of complexity.

Simple Expressions

The simplest C expression consists of a single item: a simple variable, literal constant, or symbolic constant. Here are four expressions:

Expression	Description
PI	A symbolic constant (defined in the program)
20	A literal constant
rate	A variable
-1.25	Another literal constant

NEW TERM A *literal constant* evaluates to its own value. A *symbolic constant* evaluates to the value it was given when you created it using the #define directive. A variable evaluates to the current value assigned to it by the program.

Complex Expressions

NEW TERM *Complex expressions* consist of simpler expressions connected by operators. For example

```
2 + 8
```

is an expression consisting of the subexpressions 2 and 8 and the addition operator +. The expression 2 + 8 evaluates, as you know, to 10. You can write C expressions of great complexity:

```
1.25 / 8 + 5 * rate + rate * rate / cost
```

When an expression contains multiple operators, the evaluation of the expression depends on operator precedence. This concept is covered later today, as are details about all of C's operators.

C expressions get even more interesting. Look at the following assignment statement:

```
x = a + 10;
```

This statement evaluates the expression a + 10 and assigns the result to x. In addition, the entire statement x = a + 10 is itself an expression that evaluates to the value of the variable on the left side of the equal sign. This is illustrated in Figure 3.1.

FIGURE 3.1.

An assignment statement is itself an expression.

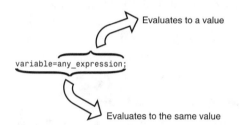

Evaluates to a value

`variable=any_expression;`

Evaluates to the same value

3

Thus, you can write statements such as the following, which assigns the value of the expression a + 10 to both variables, x and y:

```
y = x = a + 10;
```

You can also write statements such as this:

```
x = 6 + (y = 4 + 5);
```

The result of this statement is that y has the value 9 and x has the value 15. Note the parentheses, which are required in order for the statement to compile. The use of parentheses is covered later today.

Operators

NEW TERM   An *operator* is a symbol that instructs C to perform some operation, or action, on one or more operands. An *operand* is something that an operator acts on. In C, all operands are expressions. C operators fall into several categories:

- The assignment operator
- Mathematical operators
- Relational operators
- Logical operators

The Assignment Operator

The *assignment operator* is the equal sign (=). Its use in programming is somewhat different from its use in regular math. If you write

```
x = y;
```

in a C program, it doesn't mean "x is equal to y." Instead, it means "assign the value of y to x." In a C assignment statement, the right side can be any expression, and the left side must be a variable name. Thus, the form is as follows:

```
variable = expression;
```

When executed, `expression` is evaluated, and the resulting value is assigned to `variable`.

The Mathematical Operators

C's mathematical operators perform mathematical operations such as addition and subtraction. C has two unary mathematical operators and five binary mathematical operators.

The Unary Mathematical Operators

The *unary* mathematical operators are so named because they take a single operand. C has two unary mathematical operators, which are listed in Table 3.1.

TABLE 3.1. C's unary mathematical operators.

Operator	Symbol	Action	Examples
Increment	++	Increments the operand by one	++x, x++
Decrement	--	Decrements the operand by one	--x, x--

The increment and decrement operators can be used only with variables, not with constants. The operation performed is to add one to or subtract one from the operand. In other words, the statements

```
++x;
--y;
```

are the equivalent of these statements:

```
x = x + 1;
y = y - 1;
```

You should note from Table 3.1 that either unary operator can be placed before its operand (*prefix* mode) or after its operand (*postfix* mode). These two modes are not equivalent. They differ in terms of when the increment or decrement is performed:

- When used in prefix mode, the increment and decrement operators modify their operand before it's used.

- When used in postfix mode, the increment and decrement operators modify their operand after it's used.

An example should make this clearer. Look at these two statements:

```
x = 10;
y = x++;
```

After these statements are executed, x has the value 11, and y has the value 10. The value of x was assigned to y, and then x was incremented. In contrast, the following statements result in both y and x having the value 11. x is incremented and its value is assigned to y.

```
x = 10;
y = ++x;
```

Remember that = is the assignment operator, not a statement of equality. As an analogy, think of = as the "photocopy" operator. The statement y = x means to copy x into y. Subsequent changes to x, after the copy has been made, have no effect on y.

The program in Listing 3.1 illustrates the difference between prefix mode and postfix mode.

LISTING 3.1. unary.c—Demonstrates prefix and postfix modes.

```
1:   /* Demonstrates unary operator prefix and postfix modes */
2:
3:   #include <stdio.h>
4:
5:   int a, b;
6:
7:   int main(void)
8:   {
9:       /* Set a and b both equal to 5 */
10:
11:      a = b = 5;
12:
13:      /* Print them, decrementing each time. */
14:      /* Use prefix mode for b, postfix mode for a */
15:
16:      printf("\nPost  Pre");
17:      printf("\n%d      %d", a--, --b);
18:      printf("\n%d      %d", a--, --b);
19:      printf("\n%d      %d", a--, --b);
20:      printf("\n%d      %d", a--, --b);
21:      printf("\n%d      %d\n", a--, --b);
22:
23:      return 0;
24:   }
```

OUTPUT

```
Post  Pre
5     4
4     3
3     2
2     1
1     0
```

ANALYSIS This program declares two variables, a and b, in line 5. In line 11, the variables are set to the value of 5. With the execution of each `printf()` statement (lines 17 through 21), both a and b are decremented by one. After a is printed, it is decremented, whereas b is decremented before it is printed.

The Binary Mathematical Operators

C's binary operators take two operands. The binary operators, which include the common mathematical operations found on a calculator, are listed in Table 3.2.

TABLE 3.2. C's binary mathematical operators.

Operator	Symbol	Action	Example
Addition	+	Adds two operands	x + y
Subtraction	-	Subtracts the second operand from the first operand	x - y
Multiplication	*	Multiplies two operands	x * y
Division	/	Divides the first operand by the second operand	x / y
Modulus	%	Gives the remainder when the first operand is divided by the second operand	x % y

The first four operators listed in Table 3.2 should be familiar to you, and you should have little trouble using them. The fifth operator, modulus, might be new. Modulus returns the remainder when the first operand is divided by the second operand. For example, 11 modulus 4 equals 3 (that is, 4 goes into 11 two times with 3 left over). Here are some more examples:

```
100 modulus 9 equals 1
10 modulus 5 equals 0
40 modulus 6 equals 4
```

Listing 3.2 illustrates how you can use the modulus operator to convert a large number of seconds into hours, minutes, and seconds.

LISTING 3.2. seconds.c—Demonstrates the modulus operator.

```
1:   /* Illustrates the modulus operator. */
2:   /* Inputs a number of seconds, and converts to hours, */
3:   /* minutes, and seconds. */
```

```
 4:
 5:    #include <stdio.h>
 6:
 7:    /* Define constants */
 8:
 9:    #define SECS_PER_MIN 60
10:    #define SECS_PER_HOUR 3600
11:
12:    unsigned seconds, minutes, hours, secs_left, mins_left;
13:
14:    int main(void)
15:    {
16:        /* Input the number of seconds */
17:
18:        printf("Enter number of seconds : ");
19:        scanf("%d", &seconds);
20:
21:        hours = seconds / SECS_PER_HOUR;
22:        minutes = seconds / SECS_PER_MIN;
23:        mins_left = minutes % SECS_PER_MIN;
24:        secs_left = seconds % SECS_PER_MIN;
25:
26:        printf("%u seconds is equal to ", seconds);
27:        printf("%u h, %u m, and %u s\n", hours, mins_left, secs_left);
28:
29:        return 0;
30:    }
```

INPUT/ OUTPUT
Enter number of seconds : **60**
60 seconds is equal to 0 h, 1 m, and 0 s

INPUT/ OUTPUT
Enter number of seconds : **10000**
10000 seconds is equal to 2 h, 46 m, and 40 s

 ANALYSIS The program in Listing 3.2 follows the same format that all the previous programs have followed. Lines 1 through 3 provide some comments to state what the program does. Line 4 is whitespace to make the program more readable. Just like the whitespace in statements and expressions, blank lines are ignored by the compiler. Line 5 includes the necessary header file for this program. Lines 9 and 10 define two constants, SECS_PER_MIN and SECS_PER_HOUR, that are used to make the statements in the program easier to read. Line 12 declares all the variables that will be used. Some people choose to declare each variable on a separate line rather than all on a single line. As with many elements of C, this is a matter of style. Either method is correct.

Line 14 is the main() function, which contains the bulk of the program. To convert seconds to hours and minutes, the program must first get the values it needs to work with. To do this, line 18 uses the printf() function to display a statement onscreen, followed by line 19, which uses the scanf() function to get the number that the user entered. The scanf() statement then stores the number of seconds to be converted into the variable seconds. The printf() and scanf() functions are covered in more detail on Day 6, "Fundamentals of Input and Output." Line 21 contains an expression to determine the number of hours by dividing the number of seconds by the constant SECS_PER_HOUR. Because hours is an integer variable, the remainder value is ignored. Line 22 uses the same logic to determine the total number of minutes for the seconds entered. Because the total number of minutes figured in line 22 also contains minutes for the hours, line 23 uses the modulus operator to divide the hours and keep the remaining minutes. Line 24 carries out a similar calculation for determining the number of seconds that are left. Lines 26 and 27 are similar to what you have seen before. They take the values that have been calculated in the expressions and display them. Line 29 finishes the program by returning 0 to the operating system before exiting.

Operator Precedence and Parentheses

In an expression that contains more than one operator, what is the order in which operations are performed? The importance of this question is illustrated by the following assignment statement:

x = 4 + 5 * 3;

Performing the addition first results in the following, and x is assigned the value 27:

x = 9 * 3;

In contrast, if the multiplication is performed first, you have the following, and x is assigned the value 19:

x = 4 + 15;

Clearly, some rules are needed about the order in which operations are performed. This order, called *operator precedence,* is strictly spelled out in C. Each operator has a specific precedence. When an expression is evaluated, operators with higher precedence are performed first. Table 3.3 lists the precedence of C's mathematical operators. Number 1 is the highest precedence and, thus, is evaluated first.

TABLE 3.3. The precedence of C's mathematical operators.

Operators	Relative Precedence
++ --	1
* / %	2
+ -	3

Looking at Table 3.3, you can see that in any C expression, operations are performed in the following order:

- Unary increment and decrement
- Multiplication, division, and modulus
- Addition and subtraction

If an expression contains more than one operator with the same precedence level, the operators are generally performed in left-to-right order as they appear in the expression. For example, in the following expression, the % and * have the same precedence level, but the % is the leftmost operator, so it is performed first:

```
12 % 5 * 2
```

The expression evaluates to 4 (12 % 5 evaluates to 2; 2 times 2 is 4).

Returning to the previous example, you see that the statement x = 4 + 5 * 3; assigns the value 19 to x because the multiplication is performed before the addition.

What if the order of precedence doesn't evaluate your expression as needed? Using the previous example, what if you wanted to add 4 to 5 and then multiply the sum by 3? C uses parentheses to modify the evaluation order. A subexpression enclosed in parentheses is evaluated first, without regard to operator precedence. Thus, you could write

```
x = (4 + 5) * 3;
```

The expression 4 + 5 inside parentheses is evaluated first, so the value assigned to x is 27.

You can use multiple and nested parentheses in an expression. When parentheses are nested, evaluation proceeds from the innermost expression outward. Look at the following complex expression:

```
x = 25 - (2 * (10 + (8 / 2)));
```

The evaluation of this expression proceeds as follows:

1. The innermost expression, 8 / 2, is evaluated first, yielding the value 4:
   ```
   25 - (2 * (10 + 4))
   ```
2. Moving outward, the next expression, 10 + 4, is evaluated, yielding the value 14:
   ```
   25 - (2 * 14)
   ```
3. The last, or outermost, expression, 2 * 14, is evaluated, yielding the value 28:
   ```
   25 - 28
   ```
4. The final expression, 25 - 28, is evaluated, assigning the value -3 to the variable x:
   ```
   x = -3
   ```

You might want to use parentheses in some expressions for the sake of clarity, even when they aren't needed for modifying operator precedence. Parentheses must always be in pairs, or the compiler generates an error message.

Order of Subexpression Evaluation

As was mentioned in the previous section, if C expressions contain more than one operator with the same precedence level, they are evaluated left to right. For example, in the expression

```
w * x / y * z
```

w is first multiplied by x, the result of the multiplication is then divided by y, and the result of the division is then multiplied by z.

Across precedence levels, however, there is no guarantee of left-to-right order. Look at this expression:

```
w * x / y + z / y
```

Because of precedence, the multiplication and division are performed before the addition. However, C doesn't specify whether the subexpression w * x / y is to be evaluated before or after z / y. It might not be clear to you why this matters. Look at another example:

```
w * x / ++y + z / y
```

If the left subexpression is evaluated first, y is incremented when the second expression is evaluated. If the right expression is evaluated first, y isn't incremented, and the result is different. Therefore, you should avoid this sort of indeterminate expression in your programming.

Near the end of today's lesson, the section "Operator Precedence Revisited" lists the precedence of all of C's operators.

Do	Don't
DO use parentheses to make the order of expression evaluation clear.	DON'T overload an expression. It is often more clear to break an expression into two or more statements. This is especially true when you're using the unary operators (- -) or (++).

The Relational Operators

C's relational operators are used to compare expressions, asking questions such as, "Is x greater than 100?" or "Is y equal to 0?" An expression containing a relational operator evaluates to an integer value of 1 or 0. The value 1 may be viewed as true and the value 0 may be viewed as false. C's six relational operators are listed in Table 3.4.

Table 3.5 shows some examples of how relational operators might be used. These examples use literal constants, but the same principles hold with variables.

 Note | Every relational statement always evaluates to 0 or 1. Any integer variable containing a number other than zero will be considered as containing a true value. Only an integer value of zero is false.

3

TABLE 3.4. C's relational operators.

Operator	Symbol	Question Asked	Example
Equal	==	Is operand 1 equal to operand 2?	x == y
Greater than	>	Is operand 1 greater than operand 2?	x > y
Less than	<	Is operand 1 less than operand 2?	x < y
Greater than or equal to	>=	Is operand 1 greater than or equal to operand 2?	x >= y
Less than or equal to	<=	Is operand 1 less than or equal to operand 2?	x <= y
Not equal	!=	Is operand 1 not equal to operand 2?	x != y

TABLE 3.5. Relational operators in use.

Expression	How It Reads	What It Evaluates To
5 == 1	Is 5 equal to 1?	0 (false)
5 > 1	Is 5 greater than 1?	1 (true)
5 != 1	Is 5 not equal to 1?	1 (true)
(5 + 10) == (3 * 5)	Is (5 + 10) equal to (3 * 5)?	1 (true)

Do	**Don't**
DO learn how C interprets true and false. When working with relational operators, false is equal to 0 and any value other than 0 is true.	**DON'T** confuse ==, the relational operator, with =, the assignment operator. This is one of the most common errors that C programmers make.

The `if` Statement

Relational operators are used mainly to construct the relational expressions used in `if` and `while` statements, covered in detail on Day 5, "Basic Program Control." For now, you will learn the basics of the `if` statement to show how relational operators are used to make program control statement*s*.

NEW TERM You might be wondering what a program control statement is. Statements in a C program normally execute from top to bottom, in the same order as they appear in your source code file. A *program control statement* modifies the order of statement execution. Program control statements can cause other program statements to execute multiple times or to not execute at all, depending on the circumstances. The `if` statement is one of C's program control statements. Others, such as `do` and `while`, are covered on Day 5.

In its basic form, the `if` statement evaluates an expression and directs program execution depending on the result of that evaluation. The form of an `if` statement is as follows:

```
if (expression)
    statement;
```

If *expression* evaluates to true, *statement* is executed. If *expression* evaluates to false, *statement* is not executed. In either case, execution then passes to whatever code follows the `if` statement. You can say that execution of *statement* depends on the result of *expression*. Note that both the line `if (expression)` and the line *statement*; are considered to make up the complete `if` statement; they are not separate statements.

An `if` statement can control the execution of multiple statements through the use of a compound statement, or block. As defined earlier today, a block is a group of two or more statements enclosed in braces. A block can be used anywhere a single statement can be used. Therefore, you could write an `if` statement as follows:

```
if (expression)
{
    statement1;
    statement2;
    /* additional code goes here */
    statementn;
}
```

Do	**Don't**
DO indent statements within a block to make them easier to read. This includes the statements within a block in an `if` statement.	**DON'T** forget that if you program too much in one day, you'll get C sick.

Caution

Don't make the mistake of putting a semicolon at the end of an `if` statement. An `if` statement should end with the conditional statement that follows it. In the following, *statement1* executes whether or not x equals 2 because each line is evaluated as a separate statement, not together as intended:

```
if( x == 2 );          /* semicolon does not belong!  */
statement1;
```

In your programming, you will find that `if` statements are used most often with relational expressions; in other words, "Execute the following statement(s) only if such-and-such a condition is true." Here's an example:

```
if (x > y)
    y = x;
```

This code assigns the value of x to y only if x is greater than y. If x is not greater than y, no assignment takes place. Listing 3.3 illustrates the use of `if` statements.

LISTING 3.3. list0403.c:—Demonstrates `if` statements.

```
 1:   /* Demonstrates the use of if statements */
 2:
 3:   #include <stdio.h>
 4:
 5:   int x, y;
 6:
 7:   int main(void)
 8:   {
 9:       /* Input the two values to be tested */
10:
11:       printf("\nInput an integer value for x: ");
12:       scanf("%d", &x);
13:       printf("\nInput an integer value for y: ");
14:       scanf("%d", &y);
15:
16:       /* Test values and print result */
```

continues

LISTING 3.3. continued

```
17:
18:        if (x == y)
19:            printf("x is equal to y\n");
20:
21:        if (x > y)
22:            printf("x is greater than y\n");
23:
24:        if (x < y)
25:            printf("x is smaller than y\n");
26:
27:        return 0;
28:    }
```

INPUT/ OUTPUT   Input an integer value for x: **100**

Input an integer value for y: **10**
x is greater than y

INPUT/ OUTPUT   Input an integer value for x: **10**

Input an integer value for y: **100**
x is smaller than y

INPUT/ OUTPUT   Input an integer value for x: **10**

Input an integer value for y: **10**
x is equal to y

ANALYSIS   list0403.c shows three if statements in action (lines 18 through 25). Many lines in this program should be familiar. Line 5 declares two variables, x and y, and lines 11 through 14 prompt the user for values to be placed into these variables. Lines 18 through 25 use if statements to determine whether x is greater than, less than, or equal to y. Note that line 18 uses an if statement to see whether x is equal to y. Remember ==, the equal operator, means "is equal to" and should not be confused with =, the assignment operator. After the program checks to see whether the variables are equal, in line 21 it checks to see whether x is greater than y, followed by a check in line 24 to see whether x is less than y. If you think this is inefficient, you're right. In the next program, you will see how to avoid this inefficiency. For now, run the program with different values for x and y to see the results.

Note   You will notice that the statements within an if clause are indented. This is a common practice to aid readability.

The else Clause

An if statement can optionally include an else clause. The else clause is included as follows:

```
if (expression)
    statement1;
else
    statement2;
```

If *expression* evaluates to true, *statement1* is executed. If *expression* evaluates to false, control goes to the else statement, *statement2*, which is then executed. Both *statement1* and *statement2* can be compound statements or blocks.

Listing 3.4 shows the program in Listing 3.3 rewritten to use an if statement with an else clause.

3

LISTING 3.4. An if statement with an else clause.

```
1:    /* Demonstrates the use of if statement with else clause */
2:
3:    #include <stdio.h>
4:
5:    int x, y;
6:
7:    int main(void)
8:    {
9:        /* Input the two values to be tested */
10:
11:       printf("\nInput an integer value for x: ");
12:       scanf("%d", &x);
13:       printf("\nInput an integer value for y: ");
14:       scanf("%d", &y);
15:
16:       /* Test values and print result */
17:
18:       if (x == y)
19:           printf("x is equal to y\n");
20:       else
21:           if (x > y)
22:               printf("x is greater than y\n");
23:           else
24:               printf("x is smaller than y\n");
25:
26:       return 0;
27:   }
```

INPUT/
OUTPUT
```
Input an integer value for x: 99

Input an integer value for y: 8
x is greater than y
```

INPUT/
OUTPUT
```
Input an integer value for x: 8

Input an integer value for y: 99

x is smaller than y
```

INPUT/
OUTPUT
```
Input an integer value for x: 99
Input an integer value for y: 99
x is equal to y
```

ANALYSIS   Lines 18 through 24 are slightly different from the previous listing. Line 18 still checks to see whether x equals y. If x does equal y, x is equal to y appears onscreen, just as in Listing 3.3 (list0403.C). However, the program then ends, and lines 20 through 24 aren't executed. Line 21 is executed only if x is not equal to y, or, to be more accurate, if the expression "x equals y" is false. If x does not equal y, line 21 checks to see whether x is greater than y. If so, line 22 prints x is greater than y; otherwise (else), line 24 is executed.

Listing 3.4 uses a nested if statement. Nesting means to place (nest) one or more C statements inside another C statement. In the case of Listing 3.4, an if statement is part of the first if statement's else clause.

The if Statement

▼ **SYNTAX**

Form 1

```
if( expression )
    statement1;
next_statement;
```

▼ This is the if statement in its simplest form. If *expression* is true, *statement1* is executed. If *expression* is not true, *statement1* is ignored.

Form 2

```
if( expression )
    statement1;
else
    statement2;
next_statement;
```

This is the most common form of the if statement. If *expression* is true, *statement1* is
▼ executed; otherwise, *statement2* is executed.

▼ **Form 3**

```
if( expression1 )
    statement1;
else if( expression2 )
    statement2;
else
    statement3;
next_statement;
```

This is a nested `if`. If the first expression, `expression1`, is true, `statement1` is executed before the program continues with the `next_statement`. If the first expression is not true, the second expression, `expression2`, is checked. If the first expression is not true, and the second is true, `statement2` is executed. If both expressions are false, `statement3` is executed. Only one of the three statements is executed.

Example 1

```
if( salary > 45,0000 )
    tax = .30;
else
    tax = .25;
```

Example 2

```
if( age < 18 )
    printf("Minor");
else if( age < 65 )
    printf("Adult");
else
    printf( "Senior Citizen");
```

Evaluating Relational Expressions

Remember that expressions using relational operators are true C expressions that evaluate, by definition, to an integer value. Relational expressions evaluate to a value of either false (0) or true (1). Although the most common use of relational expressions is within `if` statements and other conditional constructions, they can be used as purely numeric values. This is illustrated in Listing 3.5.

LISTING 3.5. Evaluating relational expressions.

```
1:    /* Demonstrates the evaluation of relational expressions */
2:
3:    #include <stdio.h>
4:
5:    int a;
```

continues

LISTING 3.5. continued

```
6:
7:    int main(void)
8:    {
9:        a = (5 == 5);              /* Evaluates to 1 */
10:        printf("\na = (5 == 5)\na = %d", a);
11:
12:        a = (5 != 5);              /* Evaluates to 0 */
13:        printf("\na = (5 != 5)\na = %d", a);
14:
15:        a = (12 == 12) + (5 != 1); /* Evaluates to 1 + 1 */
16:        printf("\na = (12 == 12) + (5 != 1)\na = %d\n", a);
17:        return 0;
18:    }
```

OUTPUT
```
a = (5 == 5)
a = 1
a = (5 != 5)
a = 0
a = (12 == 12) + (5 != 1)
a = 2
```

ANALYSIS The output from this listing might seem a little confusing at first. Remember, the most common mistake people make when using the relational operators is to use a single equal sign—the assignment operator—instead of a double equal sign. The following expression evaluates to 5 (and also assigns the value 5 to x):

```
x = 5
```

In contrast, the following expression evaluates to either 0 or 1 (depending on whether x is equal to 5) and doesn't change the value of x:

```
x == 5
```

If, by mistake, you write

```
if (x = 5)
    printf("x is equal to 5");
```

the message always prints because the expression being tested by the `if` statement always evaluates to true, no matter what the original value of x happens to be. Fortunately, if you compile this statement with all warnings turned on (using gcc -Wall as described in Day 1) gcc will give you a warning message: "suggest parentheses around assignment used as truth value".

Looking at Listing 3.5, you can begin to understand why a takes on the values that it does. In line 9, the value 5 does equal 5, so true (1) is assigned to a. In line 12, the statement "5 does not equal 5" is false, so 0 is assigned to a.

To reiterate, the relational operators are used to create relational expressions that ask questions about relationships between expressions. The answer returned by a relational expression is a numeric value of either 1 (representing true) or 0 (representing false).

The Precedence of Relational Operators

Like the mathematical operators discussed earlier in today's lesson, the relational operators each have a precedence that determines the order in which they are performed in a multiple-operator expression. Similarly, you can use parentheses to modify precedence in expressions that use relational operators. The section "Operator Precedence Revisited" near the end of today's lesson lists the precedence of all of C's operators.

First, all the relational operators have a lower precedence than the mathematical operators. Thus, if you write the following, 2 is added to x, and the result is compared to y:

```
if (x + 2 > y)
```

This is the equivalent of the following line, which is a good example of using parentheses for the sake of clarity:

```
if ((x + 2) > y)
```

Although they aren't required by the C compiler, the parentheses surrounding (x + 2) make it clear that it is the sum of x and 2 that is to be compared with y.

There is also a two-level precedence within the relational operators, as shown in Table 3.6.

TABLE 3.6. The order of precedence of C's relational operators.

Operators	Relative Precedence
< <= > >=	1
!= ==	2

Thus, if you write

```
x == y > z
```

it is the same as

```
x == (y > z)
```

because C first evaluates the expression y > z, resulting in a value of 0 or 1. Next, C determines whether x is equal to the 1 or 0 obtained in the first step. You will rarely, if ever, use this sort of construction, but you should know about it.

Do	Don't
	DON'T put assignment statements in the expression block of an if statement. This can be confusing to other people who look at your code. They might think it's a mistake and change your assignment to the logical equal statement.

DON'T use the "not equal to" operator (!=) in an if statement containing an else. It's almost always clearer to use the "equal to" operator (==) with an else. For instance, the following code

```
if ( x != 5 )
    statement1;
else
    statement2;
```

would be better written as this

```
if (x == 5 )
    statement2;
else
    statement1;
```

The Logical Operators

Sometimes you might need to ask more than one relational question at once. For example, "If it's 7:00 a.m. and a weekday and not my vacation, ring the alarm." C's logical operators let you combine two or more relational expressions into a single expression that evaluates to either true or false. Table 3.7 lists C's three logical operators.

TABLE 3.7. C's logical operators.

Operator	Symbol	Example
AND	&&	exp1 && exp2
OR	¦¦	exp1 ¦¦ exp2
NOT	!	!exp1

The way these logical operators work is explained in Table 3.8.

TABLE 3.8. C's logical operators in use.

Expression	What It Evaluates To
(exp1 && exp2)	True (1) only if both exp1 and exp2 are true; false (0) otherwise.
(exp1 ¦¦ exp2)	True (1) if either exp1 or exp2 is true; false (0) only if both are false.
(!exp1)	False (0) if exp1 is true; true (1) if exp1 is false.

You can see that expressions that use the logical operators evaluate to either true or false depending on the true/false value of their operand(s). Table 3.9 shows some actual code examples.

TABLE 3.9. Code examples of C's logical operators.

Expression	What It Evaluates To
(5 == 5) && (6 != 2)	True (1), because both operands are true
(5 > 1) ¦¦ (6 < 1)	True (1), because one operand is true
(2 == 1) && (5 == 5)	False (0), because one operand is false
!(5 == 4)	True (1), because the operand is false

You can create expressions that use multiple logical operators. For example, to ask the question "Is x equal to 2, 3, or 4?" you could write

```
(x == 2) ¦¦ (x == 3) ¦¦ (x == 4)
```

The logical operators often provide more than one way to ask a question. If x is an integer variable, the preceding question also could be written in either of the following ways:

```
(x > 1) && (x < 5)
```

```
(x >= 2) && (x <= 4)
```

More on True/False Values

You've seen that C's relational expressions evaluate to 0 to represent false and to 1 to represent true. It's important to be aware, however, that any numeric value is interpreted as either true or false when it is used in a C expression or statement that is expecting a logical value (that is, a true or false value). The rules for this are as follows:

- A value of zero represents false.
- Any nonzero value represents true.

This is illustrated by the following example, in which the value of x is printed:

```
x = 125;
if (x)
    printf("%d", x);
```

Because x has a nonzero value, the if statement interprets the expression (x) as true. You can further generalize this because, for any C expression, writing

(*expression*)

is equivalent to writing

(*expression* != 0)

Both evaluate to true if *expression* is nonzero and to false if *expression* is 0. Using the not (!) operator, you can also write

(!*expression*)

which is equivalent to

(*expression* == 0)

The Precedence of Operators

As you might have guessed, C's logical operators also have a precedence order, both among themselves and in relation to other operators. The ! operator has a precedence equal to the unary mathematical operators ++ and --. Thus, ! has a higher precedence than all the relational operators and all the binary mathematical operators.

In contrast, the && and ¦¦ operators have much lower precedence, lower than all the mathematical and relational operators, although && has a higher precedence than ¦¦. As with all of C's operators, parentheses can be used to modify the evaluation order when using the logical operators. Consider the following example:

You want to write a logical expression that makes three individual comparisons:

1. Is a less than b?
2. Is a less than c?
3. Is c less than d?

You want the entire logical expression to evaluate to true if condition 3 is true and if either condition 1 or condition 2 is true. You might write

```
a < b ¦¦ a < c && c < d
```

However, this won't do what you intended. Because the && operator has higher precedence than ¦¦, the expression is equivalent to

a < b ¦¦ (a < c && c < d)

and evaluates to true if (a < b) is true, whether or not the relationships (a < c) and (c < d) are true. You need to write

(a < b ¦¦ a < c) && c < d

which forces the ¦¦ to be evaluated before the &&. This is shown in Listing 3.6, which evaluates the expression written both ways. The variables are set so that, if written correctly, the expression should evaluate to false (0).

LISTING 3.6. Logical operator precedence.

```
1:    #include <stdio.h>
2:
3:    /* Initialize variables. Note that c is not less than d, */
4:    /* which is one of the conditions to test for. */
5:    /* Therefore, the entire expression should evaluate as false.*/
6:
7:    int a = 5, b = 6, c = 5, d = 1;
8:    int x;
9:
10:   int main(void)
11:   {
12:       /* Evaluate the expression without parentheses */
13:
14:       x = a < b ¦¦ a < c && c < d;
15:       printf("\nWithout parentheses the expression evaluates as %d", x);
16:
17:       /* Evaluate the expression with parentheses */
18:
19:       x = (a < b ¦¦ a < c) && c < d;
20:       printf("\nWith parentheses the expression evaluates as %d\n", x);
21:       return 0;
22:   }
```

OUTPUT
```
Without parentheses the expression evaluates as 1
With parentheses the expression evaluates as 0
```

ANALYSIS Enter and run this listing. Note that gcc will give you a warning message stating:

```
list0306.c:14: warning: suggest parentheses around && within ¦¦
```

This is okay in this instance because we are actually trying to demonstrate the problem the compiler is complaining about. More importantly, note that the two values printed for the expression are different even though the only difference between them is that the statement on line 19 has parentheses.

This program initializes four variables, in line 7, with values to be used in the comparisons. Line 8 declares x to be used to store and print the results. Lines 14 and 19 use the logical operators. Line 14 doesn't use parentheses, so the results are determined by operator precedence. In this case, the results aren't what you wanted. Line 19 uses parentheses to change the order in which the expressions are evaluated.

Compound Assignment Operators

C's compound assignment operators provide a shorthand method for combining a binary mathematical operation with an assignment operation. For example, say you want to increase the value of x by 5, or, in other words, add 5 to x and assign the result to x. You could write

```
x = x + 5;
```

Using a compound assignment operator, which you can think of as a shorthand method of assignment, you would write

```
x += 5;
```

In more general notation, the compound assignment operators have the following syntax (where op represents a binary operator):

exp1 op= exp2

This is equivalent to writing

exp1 = exp1 op exp2;

You can create compound assignment operators using the five binary mathematical operators discussed earlier today. Table 3.10 lists some examples.

TABLE 3.10. Examples of compound assignment operators.

When You Write This...	It Is Equivalent to This
x *= y	x = x * y
y -= z + 1	y = y - z + 1
a /= b	a = a / b
x += y / 8	x = x + y / 8
y %= 3	y = y % 3

The compound operators provide a convenient shorthand. The advantages are particularly evident when the variable on the left side of the assignment operator has a long name. As with all other assignment statements, a compound assignment statement is an expression and evaluates to the value assigned to the left side. Thus, executing the following statements results in both x and z having the value 14:

```
x = 12;
z = x += 2;
```

The Conditional Operator

The conditional operator is C's only *ternary* operator, meaning that it takes three operands. Its syntax is

```
exp1 ? exp2 : exp3;
```

If *exp1* evaluates to true (that is, nonzero), the entire expression evaluates to the value of *exp2*. If *exp1* evaluates to false (that is, zero), the entire expression evaluates as the value of *exp3*. For example, the following statement assigns the value 1 to x if y is true and assigns 100 to x if y is false:

```
x = y ? 1 : 100;
```

Likewise, to make z equal to the larger of x and y, you could write

```
z = (x > y) ? x : y;
```

Perhaps you've noticed that the conditional operator functions somewhat like an if statement. The preceding statement could also be written like this:

```
if (x > y)
z = x;
else
z = y;
```

The conditional operator can't be used in all situations in place of an if...else construction, but the conditional operator is more concise. The conditional operator can also be used in places you can't use an if statement, such as inside a call to another function such as a single printf() statement:

```
printf( "The larger value is %d", ((x > y) ? x : y) );
```

The Comma Operator

The comma is frequently used in C as a simple punctuation mark, serving to separate variable declarations, function arguments, and so on. In certain situations, the comma acts as an operator rather than just as a separator. You can form an expression by separating two subexpressions with a comma. The result is as follows:

- Both expressions are evaluated, with the left expression being evaluated first.
- The entire expression evaluates to the value of the right expression.

For example, the following statement assigns the value of b to x, increments a, and then increments b:

```
x = (a++ , b++);
```

Because the ++ operator is used in postfix mode, the value of b—before it is incremented—is assigned to x. Using parentheses is necessary because the comma operator has low precedence, even lower than the assignment operator.

As you'll learn tomorrow, the most common use of the comma operator is in for statements.

Do	Don't
DO use (expression == 0) instead of (!expression). When compiled, these two expressions evaluate the same; however, the first is more readable.	**DON'T** confuse the assignment operator (=) with the equal to (==) operator.
DO use the logical operators && and ¦¦ instead of nesting if statements.	

Operator Precedence Revisited

Table 3.11 lists the C operators in order of decreasing precedence. Operators on the same line have the same precedence.

TABLE 3.11. C operator precedence.

Level	Operators
1	() [] -> .
2	! ~ ++ — * *(indirection)* & *(address of)* (type)
	sizeof + *(unary)* - *(unary)*
3	* *(multiplication)* / %
4	+ -
5	<< >>

Level	Operators
6	< <= > >=
7	== !=
8	& (*bitwise* AND)
9	^
10	¦
11	&&
12	¦¦
13	? :
14	= += -= *= /= %= &= ^= ¦= <<= >>=
15	,

() is the function operator; [] is the array operator.

3

 Tip | This is a good table to keep referring to until you become familiar with the order of precedence. You might find that you need it later.

Summary

Today's lessons covered a lot of material. You learned what a C statement is, that whitespace doesn't matter to a C compiler, and that statements always end with a semicolon. You also learned that a compound statement (or block), which consists of two or more statements enclosed in braces, can be used anywhere a single statement can be used.

Many statements are made up of some combination of expressions and operators. Remember that an expression is anything that evaluates to a numeric value. Complex expressions can contain many simpler expressions, which are called subexpressions.

Operators are C symbols that instruct the computer to perform an operation on one or more expressions. Some operators are unary, which means that they operate on a single operand. Most of C's operators are binary, however, operating on two operands. One operator, the conditional operator, is ternary. C's operators have a defined hierarchy of precedence that determines the order in which operations are performed in an expression that contains multiple operators.

The C operators covered today fall into three categories:

- Mathematical operators perform arithmetic operations on their operands (for example, addition).

- Relational operators perform comparisons between their operands (for example, greater than).
- Logical operators operate on true/false expressions. Remember that C uses 0 and 1 to represent false and true, respectively, and that any nonzero value is interpreted as being true.

You've also been introduced to C's if statement, which lets you control program execution based on the evaluation of relational expressions.

Q&A

Q What effect do spaces and blank lines have on how a program runs?

A Whitespace (lines, spaces, tabs) makes the code listing more readable. When the program is compiled, whitespace is stripped and thus has no effect on the executable program. For this reason, you should use whitespace to make your program easier to read.

Q Is it better to code a compound if statement or to nest multiple if statements?

A You should make your code easy to understand. If you nest if statements, they are evaluated as shown today. If you use a single compound statement, the expressions are evaluated only until the entire statement evaluates to false.

Q What is the difference between unary and binary operators?

A As the names imply, unary operators work with one variable, and binary operators work with two variables.

Q Is the subtraction operator (-) binary or unary?

A It's both! The compiler is smart enough to know which one you're using. It knows which form to use based on the number of variables in the expression that is used. In the following statement, it is unary:

```
x = -y;
```

versus the following binary use:

```
x = a - b;
```

Q Are negative numbers considered true or false?

A Remember that 0 is false, and any other value is true. This includes negative numbers.

Workshop

The Workshop provides quiz questions to help you solidify your understanding of the material covered and exercises to provide you with experience in using what you've learned. The answers to the quiz and exercises are provided in Appendix C, "Answers."

Quiz

1. What is the following C statement called, and what is its meaning?

```
x = 5 + 8;
```

2. What is an expression?

3. In an expression that contains multiple operators, what determines the order in which operations are performed?

4. If the variable x has the value 10, what are the values of x and a after each of the following statements is executed separately?

```
a = x++;
a = ++x;
```

5. To what value does the expression `10 % 3` evaluate?

6. To what value does the expression `5 + 3 * 8 / 2 + 2` evaluate?

7. Rewrite the expression in question 6, adding parentheses so that it evaluates to 16.

8. If an expression evaluates to false, what value does the expression have?

9. In the following list, which has higher precedence?

    a. `==` or `<`

    b. `*` or `+`

    c. `!=` or `==`

    d. `>=` or `>`

10. What are the compound assignment operators, and how are they useful?

Exercises

1. The following code is not well-written. Enter and compile the code to see whether it works.

```
#include <stdio.h>
int x,y;int main(void){ printf(
"\nEnter two numbers");scanf(
"%d %d",&x,&y);printf(
"\n\n%d is bigger",(x>y)?x:y);return 0;}
```

2. Rewrite the code in exercise 1 to be more readable.

3. Change Listing 3.1 to count upward instead of downward.

4. Write an `if` statement that assigns the value of x to the variable y only if x is between 1 and 20. Leave y unchanged if x is not in that range.

5. Use the conditional operator to perform the same task as in exercise 4.

6. Rewrite the following nested `if` statements using a single `if` statement and logical operators.

```
if (x < 1)
   if ( x > 10 )
      statement;
```

7. To what value does each of the following expressions evaluate?

    a. `(1 + 2 * 3)`

    b. `10 % 3 * 3 - (1 + 2)`

    c. `((1 + 2) * 3)`

    d. `(5 == 5)`

    e. `(x = 5)`

8. If x = 4, y = 6, and z = 2, determine whether each of the following evaluates to true or false.

    a. `if( x == 4)`

    b. `if(x != y - z)`

    c. `if(z = 1)`

    d. `if(y)`

9. Write an `if` statement that determines whether someone is legally an adult (age 21), but not a senior citizen (age 65).

10. **BUG BUSTER:** Fix the following program so that it runs correctly.

```
/* a program with problems... */
#include <stdio.h>
int x= 1:
int main(void)
{
   if( x = 1);
      printf(" x equals 1" );
   otherwise
      printf(" x does not equal 1");
   return 0;
}
```

DAY 4

Functions: The Basics

Functions are central to C programming and to the philosophy of C program design. You've already been introduced to some of C's library functions, which are complete functions supplied as part of your compiler. This chapter covers user-defined functions, which, as the name implies, are functions defined by you, the programmer. Today you will learn

- What a function is and what its parts are
- The advantages of structured programming with functions
- How to create a function
- How to declare local variables in a function
- How to return a value from a function to the program
- How to pass arguments to a function

What Is a Function?

Today you will learn the answer to the question "What is a function?" in two ways. First, you will learn what functions are, and then you will learn how they are used.

A Function Defined

NEW TERM   First, the definition: A *function* is a named, independent section of C code that
           performs a specific task and optionally returns a value to the calling program.
Now, take a look at the parts of this definition:

- *A function is named.* Each function has a unique name. By using that name in
  another part of the program, you can execute the statements contained in the function. This is known as *calling* the function. A function can be called from within
  another function.

- *A function is independent.* A function can perform its task without interference
  from or interfering with other parts of the program.

- *A function performs a specific task.* This is the easy part of the definition. A task is
  a discrete job that your program must perform as part of its overall operation, such
  as sending a line of text to a printer, sorting an array into numerical order, or calculating a cube root.

- *A function can return a value to the calling program.* When your program calls a
  function, the statements it contains are executed. If you want them to, these statements can pass information back to the calling program.

That's all there is to the "telling" part. Keep the previous definition in mind as you look
at the next section.

A Function Illustrated

Listing 4.1 contains a user-defined function.

LISTING 4.1. A program that uses a function to calculate the cube of a number.

```
1:   /* Demonstrates a simple function */
2:   #include <stdio.h>
3:
4:   long cube(long x);
5:
6:   long input, answer;
7:
8:   int main(void)
9:   {
10:      printf("Enter an integer value: ");
11:      scanf("%ld", &input);
12:      answer = cube(input);
13:      /* Note: %ld is the conversion specifier for */
14:      /* a long integer */
15:      printf("\nThe cube of %ld is %ld.\n", input, answer);
```

```
16:
17:      return 0;
18:   }
19:
20:   /* Function: cube() - Calculates the cubed value of a variable */
21:   long cube(long x)
22:   {
23:       long x_cubed;
24:
25:       x_cubed = x * x * x;
26:       return x_cubed;
27:   }
```

OUTPUT

Enter an integer value: **100**

The cube of 100 is 1000000.

OUTPUT

Enter an integer value: **9**

The cube of 9 is 729.

OUTPUT

Enter an integer value: **3**

The cube of 3 is 27.

4

 Note   Rather than explain the entire program, the following analysis focuses on the components of the program that relate directly to the function.

ANALYSIS

NEW TERM

Line 4 contains the *function prototype,* a model for a function that will appear later in the program. A function's prototype contains the name of the function, a list of variables that must be passed to it, and the type of variable it returns, if any. Looking at line 4, you can tell that the function is named cube, that it requires a variable of the type long, and that it will return a value of type long. The variables to be passed to the function are called *arguments,* and they are enclosed in parentheses following the function's name. In this example, the function's argument is long x. The keywordbefore the name of the function indicates the type of variable the function returns. In this case, a type long variable is returned.

Line 12 calls the function cube and passes the variable input to it as the function's argument. The function's return value is assigned to the variable answer. Notice that both input and answer are declared on line 6 as long variables, in keeping with the function prototype on line 4.

NEW TERM   The function itself is called the *function definition.* In this case, it's called cube and is contained in lines 21 through 27. Like the prototype, the function definition has several parts. The function starts out with a function header on line 21. The *function header* is at the start of a function, and it gives the function's name (in this case, cube). The header also gives the function's return type and describes its arguments. Note that the function header is identical to the function prototype (minus the semicolon).

The body of the function, lines 22 through 27, is enclosed in braces. The body contains statements, such as in line 25, that are executed whenever the function is called. Line 23 is a variable declaration that looks like the declarations you have seen before, with one difference: It's local. *Local* variables are declared within a function body. (Local declarations are discussed further on Day 11, "Understanding Variable Scope.") Finally, the function concludes with a return statement on line 26, which signals the end of the function. A return statement also passes a value back to the calling program. In this case, the value of the variable x_cubed is returned.

If you compare the structure of the cube() function with that of the main() function, you will see that they are the same. main() is also a function. Other functions that you already have used are printf() and scanf(). Although printf() and scanf() are library functions (as opposed to user-defined functions), they are functions that can take arguments and return values just like the functions you create.

How a Function Works

NEW TERM   A C program doesn't execute the statements in a function until the function is called by another part of the program. When a function is called, the program can send the function information in the form of one or more arguments. An *argument* is program data needed by the function to perform its task. The statements in the function then execute, performing whatever task each was designed to do. When the function's statements have finished, execution passes back to the same location in the program that called the function. Functions can send information back to the program in the form of a return value.

Figure 4.1 shows a program with three functions, each of which is called once. Each time a function is called, execution passes to that function. When the function is finished, execution passes back to the place from which the function was called. A function can be called as many times as needed, and functions can be called in any order.

You now know what a function is and how important a function is. Lessons on how to create and use your own functions follow.

Figure 4.1.

When a program calls a function, execution passes to the function and then back to the calling program.

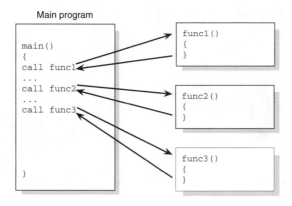

Functions

▼ SYNTAX

Function Prototype

```
return_type function_name( arg-type name-1,...,arg-type name-n);
```

Function Definition

```
return_type function_name( arg-type name-1,...,arg-type name-n)
{
    /* statements; */
}
```

A *function prototype* provides the compiler with a description of a function that will be defined at a later point in the program. The prototype includes a return type indicating the type of variable that the function will return. It also includes the function name, which should describe what the function does. The prototype also contains the variable types of the arguments (`arg type`) that will be passed to the function. Optionally, it can contain the names of the variables that will be passed. A prototype should always end with a semicolon.

A *function definition* is the actual function. The definition contains the code that will be executed. If the prototype contains the names of the variables, the first line of a function definition, called the *function header,* should be identical to the function prototype, with the exception of the semicolon. A function header shouldn't end with a semicolon. In addition, although the argument variable names are optional in the prototype, they must be included in the function header. Following the header is the function body, containing the statements that the function will perform. The function body should start with a opening bracket and end with a closing bracket. If the function return type is anything other than `void`, a `return` statement should be included, returning a value matching the

▼   return type.

▼ **Function Prototype Examples**

```
double squared( double number );
void print_report( int report_number );
int get_menu_choice( void );
```

Function Definition Examples

```
double squared( double number )          /* function header */
{                                        /* opening bracket */
    return(  number * number );          /* function body   */
}                                        /* closing bracket */
void print_report( int report_number )
{
    if( report_number == 1 )
        puts( "Printing Report 1" );
    else
        puts( "Not printing Report 1" );
▲   }
```

Functions and Structured Programming

NEW TERM   By using functions in your C programs, you can practice *structured programming,* in which individual program tasks are performed by independent sections of program code. "Independent sections of program code" sounds just like part of the definition of functions given earlier, doesn't it? Functions and structured programming are closely related.

The Advantages of Structured Programming

Why is structured programming so great? There are two important reasons:

- It's easier to write a structured program because complex programming problems are broken into a number of smaller, simpler tasks. Each task is performed by a function in which code and variables are isolated from the rest of the program. You can progress more quickly by dealing with these relatively simple tasks one at a time.

- It's easier to debug a structured program. If your program has a *bug* (something that causes it to work improperly), a structured design makes it easy to isolate the problem to a specific section of code (such as a specific function).

A related advantage of structured programming is the time you can save. If you write a function to perform a certain task in one program, you can quickly and easily use it in another program that has to execute the same task. Even if the new program needs to accomplish a slightly different task, you will often find that modifying a function you created earlier is easier than writing a new one from scratch. Consider how much you've used the two functions `printf()` and `scanf()` even though you probably haven't seen the code they contain. If your functions have been created to perform a single task, using them in other programs is much easier.

Planning a Structured Program

If you're going to writea structured program, you have to do some planning first. This planning should take place before you write a single line of code, and it usually can be done with nothing more than pencil and paper. Your plan should be a list of the specific tasks your program performs. Begin with a global idea of the program's function. If you were planning a program to manage your name and address list, what would you want the program to do? Here are some obvious things:

- Enter new names and addresses
- Modify existing entries
- Sort entries by last name
- Print mailing labels

With this list, you've divided the program into four main tasks, each of which can be assigned to a function. Now you can go a step further, dividing these tasks into subtasks. For example, the "Enter new names and addresses" task can be subdivided into these subtasks:

- Read the existing address list from disk.
- Prompt the user for one or more new entries.
- Add the new data to the list.
- Save the updated list to disk.

Likewise, the "Modify existing entries" task can be subdivided as follows:

- Read the existing address list from disk.
- Modify one or more entries.
- Save the updated list to disk.

You might have noticed that these two lists have two subtasks in common—the ones dealing with reading from and saving to disk. You can write one function to "Read the existing address list from disk," and that function can be called by both the "Enter new names and addresses" function and the "Modify existing entries" function. The same is true for "Save the updated list to disk."

Already you should see at least one advantage of structured programming. By carefully dividing the program into tasks, you can identify parts of the program that share common tasks. You can write "double-duty" disk access functions, saving yourself time and making your program smaller and more efficient.

This method of programming results in a *hierarchical,* or layered, program structure. Figure 4.2 illustrates hierarchical programming for the address list program.

FIGURE 4.2.

A structured program is organized hierarchically.

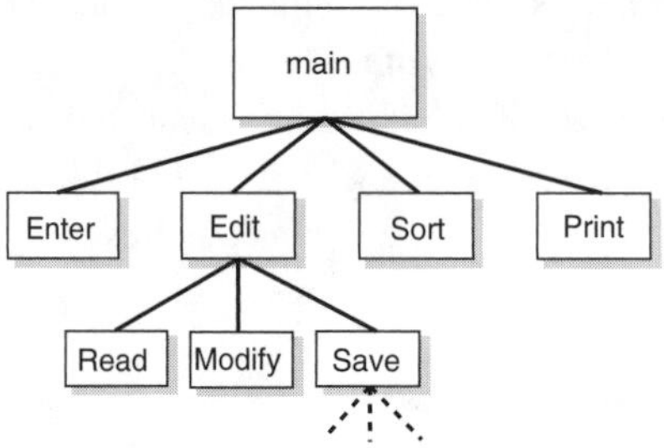

When you follow this planned approach, you quickly make a list of discrete tasks that your program has to perform. Then you can tackle the tasks one at a time, giving all your attention to one relatively simple task. When that function is written and working properly, you can move on to the next task. Before you know it, your program starts to take shape.

The Top-Down Approach

By using structured programming, C programmers take the *top-down approach.* You saw this illustrated in Figure 4.2, where the program's structure resembles an inverted tree. Many times, most of the real work of the program is performed by the functions at the tips of the "branches." The functions closer to the "trunk" primarily direct program execution among these functions.

As a result, many C programs have a small amount of code in the main body of the program—that is, in main(). The bulk of the program's code is found in functions. In main(), all you might find are a few dozen lines of code that direct program execution among the functions. Often, a menu is presented to the person using the program. Program execution is branched according to the user's choices. Each branch of the menu uses a different function.

Note   Using menus is a good approach to program design. Day 12, "Advanced Program Control," shows how you can use the switch statement to create a versatile menu-driven system.

Now that you know what functions are and why they're so important, the time has come for you to learn how to write your own.

Do	Don't
DO plan before starting to code. By determining your program's structure ahead of time, you can save time writing the code and debugging it.	**DON'T** try to do everything in one function. A single function should perform a single task, such as reading information from a file.

Writing a Function

The first step in writing a function is to know what you want the function to do. When you know that, the actual mechanics of writing the function aren't particularly difficult.

The Function Header

The first line of every function is the function header that has three components, each serving a specific function. They are shown in Figure 4.3 and explained in the following sections.

FIGURE 4.3.

The three components of a function header.

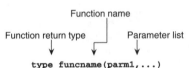

The Function Return Type

The return type of a function specifies the data type that the function returns to the calling program. The function return type can be any of C's data types: `char`, `int`, `long`, `float`, or `double`. You can also define a function that doesn't return a value by using a return type of `void`. Here are some examples:

```
int func1(...)          /* Returns a type int.   */
float func2(...)        /* Returns a type float. */
void func3(...)         /* Returns nothing.      */
```

In these examples, you can see that *func1* returns an integer, *func2* returns a floating-point number, and *func3* doesn't return anything.

The Function Name

You can name a function anything you like, as long as you follow the rules for C variable names given in Day 2, "The Components of a C Program: Code and Data." In C programs, a function name must be unique (not assigned to any other function or variable). It's a good idea to assign a name that reflects what the function does.

The Parameter List

Many functions use *arguments*, which are values passed to the function when it's called. A function must know what kinds of arguments to expect—the data type of each argument. You can pass a function any of C's data types. Argument type information is provided in the function header by the parameter list.

For each argument passed to the function, the parameter list must contain one entry. This entry specifies the data type and the name of the parameter. For example, here's the header from the function in Listing 4.1:

```
long cube(long x)
```

The parameter list consists of `long x`, specifying that this function takes one type `long` argument, represented by the parameter x. If there is more than one parameter, each must be separated by a comma. The function header

```
void func1(int x, float y, char z)
```

specifies a function with three arguments: a type `int` named x, a type `float` named y, and a type `char` named z. Some functions take no arguments, in which case the parameter list should consist of `void`, like this:

```
int func2(void)
```

just like the `main(void)` function.

Note   You do not place a semicolon at the end of a function header. If you mistakenly include one, the compiler will generate an error message.

Sometimes confusion arises about the distinction between a parameter and an argument. A *parameter* is an entry in a function header; it serves as a "placeholder" for an argument. A function's parameters are fixed; they do not change during program execution.

An *argument* is an actual value passed to the function by the calling program. Each time a function is called, it can be passed different arguments. In C, a function must be passed the same number and type of arguments each time it's called, but the argument values can be different. In the function, the argument is accessed by using the corresponding parameter name.

An example will make this more clear. Listing 4.2 presents a very simple program with one function that is called twice.

LISTING 4.2. The difference between arguments and parameters.

```
 1:   /* Illustrates the difference between arguments and parameters. */
 2:
 3:   #include <stdio.h>
 4:
 5:   float x = 3.5, y = 65.11, z;
 6:
 7:   float half_of(float k);
 8:
 9:   int main(void)
10:   {
11:       /* In this call, x is the argument to half_of(). */
12:       z = half_of(x);
13:       printf("The value of z = %f\n", z);
14:
15:       /* In this call, y is the argument to half_of(). */
16:       z = half_of(y);
17:       printf("The value of z = %f\n", z);
18:
19:       return 0;
20:   }
21:
22:   float half_of(float k)
23:   {
24:       /* k is the parameter. Each time half_of() is called, */
25:       /* k has the value that was passed as an argument. */
26:
27:       return (k/2);
28:   }
```

OUTPUT
```
The value of z = 1.750000
The value of z = 32.555000
```

Figure 4.4 shows the relationship between arguments and parameters.

FIGURE 4.4.

Each time a function is called, the arguments are passed to the function's parameters.

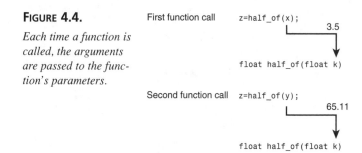

First function call   z=half_of(x);
                                      3.5

                       float half_of(float k)

Second function call   z=half_of(y);
                                      65.11

                       float half_of(float k)

ANALYSIS Looking at Listing 4.2, you can see that the `half_of()` function prototype is declared on line 7. Lines 12 and 16 call `half_of()`, and lines 22 through 28 contain the actual function. Lines 12 and 16 each send a different argument to `half_of()`. Line 12 sends x, which contains a value of 3.5, and line 16 sends y, which contains a value of 65.11. When the program runs, it prints the correct number for each. The values in x and y are passed into the argument k of `half_of()`. This is like copying the values from x to k, and then from y to k. `half_of()` then returns this value after dividing it by 2 (line 27).

Do	Don't
DO use a function name that describes the purpose of the function.	DON'T pass values to a function that it doesn't need.
	DON'T try to pass fewer (or more) arguments to a function than there are parameters. In C programs, the number of arguments passed must match the number of parameters.

The Function Body

The *function body* is enclosed in braces, and it immediately follows the function header. It's in the function body that the real work is done. When a function is called, execution begins at the start of the body and *terminates* (returns to the calling program) when a `return` statement is encountered or when execution reaches the closing brace.

Local Variables

NEW TERM You can declare variables within the body of a function. Variables declared in a function are called *local variables*. The term *local* means that the variables are private to that particular function and are distinct from other variables of the same name declared elsewhere in the program. This will be explained shortly; for now, you should learn how to declare local variables.

A local variable is declared like any other variable, using the same variable types and rules for names that you learned on Day 2. Local variables can also be initialized when they are declared. You can declare any of C's variable types in a function. Here is an example of four local variables being declared within a function:

```
int func1(int y)
{
    int a, b = 10;
    float rate;
    double cost = 12.55;
    /* function code goes here... */
}
```

The preceding declarations create the local variables a, b, rate, and cost, which can be used by the code in the function. Note that the function parameters are considered to be variable declarations, so the variables, if any, in the function's parameter list also are available.

When you declare and use a variable in a function, it is totally separate and distinct from any other variables declared elsewhere in the program. This is true even if the variables have the same name. Listing 4.3 demonstrates this independence.

LISTING 4.3. A demonstration of local variables.

```
 1:   /* Demonstrates local variables. */
 2:
 3:   #include <stdio.h>
 4:
 5:   int x = 1, y = 2;
 6:
 7:   void demo(void);
 8:
 9:   int main(void)
10:   {
11:     printf("\nBefore calling demo(), x = %d and y = %d.", x, y);
12:     demo();
13:     printf("\nAfter calling demo(), x = %d and y = %d\n.", x, y);
14:
15:     return 0;
16:   }
17:
18:   void demo(void)
19:   {
20:       /* Declare and initialize two local variables. */
21:
22:       int x = 88, y = 99;
23:
24:       /* Display their values. */
25:
26:       printf("\nWithin demo(), x = %d and y = %d.", x, y);
27:   }
```

OUTPUT
```
Before calling demo(), x = 1 and y = 2.
Within demo(), x = 88 and y = 99.
After calling demo(), x = 1 and y = 2.
```

ANALYSIS
Listing 4.3 is similar to the previous programs you have seen today. Line 5 declares variables x and y. These are declared outside any functions and therefore are considered global. Line 7 contains the prototype for the demonstration function, named demo(). It doesn't take any parameters, so it has void in the prototype. It also

doesn't return any values, giving it a return type of void. Line 9 starts the main() function, which is very simple. First, printf() is called on line 11 to display the values of x and y, and then the demo() function is called. Notice that demo() declares its own local versions of x and y on line 22. Line 26 shows that the local variables take precedence over any others. After the demo function is called, line 13 again prints the values of x and y. Because you are no longer in demo(), the original global values are printed.

As you can see, local variables x and y in the function are totally independent from the global variables x and y declared outside the function. Three rules govern the use of variables in functions:

- To use a variable in a function, you must declare it in the function header or the function body (except for global variables, which are covered on Day 11).

- For a function to obtain a value from the calling program, the value must be passed as an argument.

- For a calling program to obtain a value from a function, the value must be explicitly returned from the function.

To be honest, these rules are not strictly applied; you will learn how to get around them later in this book. However, follow these rules for now, and you should stay out of trouble.

Keeping the function's variables separate from other program variables is one way in which functions are independent. A function can perform any sort of data manipulation you want, using its own set of local variables. There's no worry that these manipulations will have an unintended effect on another part of the program.

Function Statements

There is essentially no limitation on the statements that can be included within a function. The only thing you shouldn't do inside a function is to define another function (the GNU C compiler does allow this, but it is not portable to other compilers). You can, however, use all other C statements, including loops (these are covered on Day 5, "Basic Program Control"), if statements, and assignment statements. You can call library functions and other user-defined functions.

What about function length? C places no length restriction on functions, but as a matter of practicality, you should keep your functions relatively short. Remember that in structured programming, each function is supposed to perform a relatively simple task. If you find that a function is getting long, perhaps you're trying to perform a task too complex for one function alone. It probably can be broken into two or more smaller functions.

How long is too long? There's no definitive answer to that question, but in practical experience it's rare to find a function longer than 25 or 30 lines of actual code. You have to use your own judgment. Some programming tasks require longer functions, whereas many functions are only a few lines long. As you gain programming experience, you will become more adept at determining what should and shouldn't be broken into smaller functions.

Returning a Value

To return a value from a function, you use the `return` keyword, followed by a C expression. When execution reaches a `return` statement, the expression is evaluated, and execution passes the value back to the calling program. The return value of the function is the value of the expression. Consider this function:

```
int func1(int var)
{
    int x;
    /* Function code goes here... */
    return x;
}
```

When this function is called, the statements in the function body execute up to the `return` statement. The `return` terminates the function and returns the value of x to the calling program. The expression that follows the `return` keyword can be any valid C expression.

A function can contain multiple `return` statements. The first `return` executed is the only one that has any effect. Multiple `return` statements can be an efficient way to return different values from a function, as demonstrated in Listing 4.4.

LISTING 4.4. Using multiple `return` statements in a function.

```
 1:   /* Demonstrates using multiple return statements in a function. */
 2:
 3:   #include <stdio.h>
 4:
 5:   int x, y, z;
 6:
 7:   int larger_of( int a, int b);
 8:
 9:   int main(void)
10:   {
11:       puts("Enter two different integer values: ");
12:       scanf("%d%d", &x, &y);
13:
14:       z = larger_of(x,y);
15:
16:       printf("\nThe larger value is %d.\n", z);
17:
18:       return 0;
19:   }
```

continues

LISTING 4.4. continued

```
20:
21:   int larger_of( int a, int b)
22:   {
23:       if (a > b)
24:           return a;
25:       else
26:           return b;
27:   }
```

OUTPUT
```
Enter two different integer values:
200 300

The larger value is 300.
```

OUTPUT
```
Enter two different integer values:
300
200

The larger value is 300.
```

ANALYSIS As in other examples, Listing 4.4 starts with a comment to describe what the program does (line 1). The stdio.h header file is included for the standard input/output functions that allow the program to display information to the screen and get user input. Line 7 is the function prototype for larger_of(). Notice that it takes two int variables for parameters and returns an int. Line 14 calls larger_of() with x and y. The function larger_of() contains the multiple return statements. Using an if statement, the function checks whether a is bigger than b on line 23. If it is, line 24 executes a return statement, and the function immediately ends. Lines 25 and 26 are ignored in this case. If a isn't bigger than b, line 24 is skipped, the else clause is instigated, and the return on line 26 executes. You should be able to see that—depending on the arguments passed to the function larger_of()—either the first or the second return statement is executed and that the appropriate value is passed back to the calling function.

One final note on this program. Line 11 is a function we used but you might not have noticed. puts() (meaning *put string*) is a simple function that displays a string to the standard output, usually the computer screen. Strings are covered on Day 9, "Characters and Strings." For now, know that they are just quoted text.

Remember that a function's return value has a type that is specified in the function header and function prototype. The value returned by the function must be of the same type, or the compiler generates an error message.

Note

Structured programming suggests that you have only one entry and one exit in a function. This means that you should try to have only one `return` statement within your function. At times, however, a program might be much easier to read and maintain with more than one `return` statement. In such cases, maintainability should take precedence.

The Function Prototype

A program should include a prototype for each function it uses. You saw an example of a function prototype on line 4 of Listing 4.1, and there have been function prototypes in the other listings as well. What is a function prototype, and why is it necessary?

You can see from the earlier examples that the prototype for a function is identical to the function header, with a semicolon added at the end. Like the function header, the function prototype includes information about the function's return type, name, and parameters. The prototype's job is to tell the compiler about the function's return type, name, and parameters. With this information, the compiler can check every time your source code calls the function and verify that you're passing the correct number and type of arguments to the function and using the return value correctly. If there's a mismatch, the compiler generates an error message.

Strictly speaking, a function prototype doesn't have to exactly match the function header. The parameter names can be different, as long as they are the same type and number and in the same order. There's no reason for the header and prototype not to match; having them identical makes source code easier to understand. Matching the two also makes writing a program easier. When you complete a function definition, use your editor's cut-and-paste feature to copy the function header and create the prototype. Be sure to add a semicolon at the end.

Where should function prototypes be placed in your source code? They should be placed before the start of `main()` or before the first function is defined. For readability, it's best to group all prototypes in one location.

4

Do	DON'T
DO use local variables whenever possible. **DO** limit each function to a single task.	**DON'T** try to return a value that has a type different from the function's type. **DON'T** let functions get too long. If a function becomes long, try to break it into separate, smaller tasks. **DON'T** have multiple return statements if they aren't necessary. You should try to have one return when possible; however, sometimes having multiple return statements is easier and clearer.

Passing Arguments to a Function

To pass arguments to a function, you list them in parenthesesfollowing the function name. The number of arguments and the type of each argument must match the parameters in the function header and prototype. For example, if a function is defined to take two type int arguments, you must pass it exactly two int arguments—no more, no less, and no other type. If you try to pass a function an incorrect number and/or type of argument, the compiler will detect it, based on the information in the function prototype.

If the function takes multiple arguments, the arguments listed in the function call are assigned to the function parameters in order: The first argument to the first parameter, the second argument to the second parameter, and so on, as shown in Figure 4.5.

FIGURE 4.5.

Multiple arguments are assigned to function parameters in order.

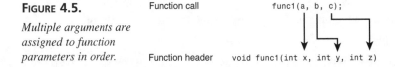

Each argument can be any valid C expression: a constant, a variable, a mathematical or logical expression, or even another function (one with a return value). For example, if half(), square(), and third() are all functions with return values, you could write

```
x = half(third(square(half(y))));
```

The program first calls half(), passing it y as an argument. When execution returns from half(), the program calls square(), passing half()'s return value as an argument. Next, third() is called with square()'s return value as the argument. Then, half() is called again, this time with `third()`'s return value as an argument. Finally, `half()`'s return value is assigned to the variable x. The following is an equivalent piece of code:

```
a = half(y);
b = square(a);
c = third(b);
x = half(c);
```

Calling Functions

There are two ways to call a function. Any function can be called by simply using its name and argument list alone in a statement, as in the following example. If the function has a return value, it is discarded.

```
wait(12);
```

The second method can be used only with functions that have a return value. Because these functions evaluate to a value (that is, their return value), they are valid C expressions and can be used anywhere a C expression can be used. You've already seen an expression with a return value used as the right side of an assignment statement. Here are some more examples.

In the following example, `half_of()` is a parameter of a function:

```
printf("Half of %d is %d.", x, half_of(x));
```

First, the function `half_of()` is called with the value of x, and then `printf()` is called using the values "Half of %d is %d.", x, and `half_of(x)`.

In this second example, multiple functions are being used in an expression:

```
y = half_of(x) + half_of(z);
```

Although `half_of()` is used twice, the second call could have been any other function. The following code shows the same statement, but not all on one line:

```
a = half_of(x);
b = half_of(z);
y = a + b;
```

The following final two examples show effective ways to use the return values of functions. Here, a function is being used with the `if` statement:

```
if ( half_of(x) > 10 )
{
    /* statements; */        /* these could be any statements! */
}
```

4

If the return value of the function meets the criteria (in this case, if `half_of()` returns a value greater than 10), the `if` statement is true, and its statements are executed. If the returned value doesn't meet the criteria, the statements in the `if` are not executed.

The following example is even better:

```
if ( do_a_process() != OKAY )
{
    /* statements; */          /* do error routine */
}
```

Again, actual statements are not provided, nor is `do_a_process()` a real function; however, this is an important example. The return value of a process is checked to see whether it ran correctly. If it didn't, the statements take care of any error handling or cleanup. This is commonly used with accessing information in files, comparing values, and allocating memory.

> **Caution**   If you try to use a function with a `void` return type as an expression, the compiler generates an error message.

Do	**Don't**
DO pass parameters to functions in order to make the function generic and thus reusable.	**DON'T** make an individual statement confusing by putting a bunch of functions in it. You should put functions into your statements only if they don't make the code more confusing.
DO take advantage of the ability to put functions into expressions.	

Recursion

NEW TERM   The term *recursion* refers to a situation in which a function calls itself either directly or indirectly. *Indirect recursion* occurs when one function calls another function that then calls the first function. C allows recursive functions, and they can be useful in some situations.

For example, recursion can be used to calculate the factorial of a number. The factorial of a number x is written x! and is calculated as follows:

```
x! = x * (x-1) * (x-2) * (x-3) * ... * (2) * 1
```

However, you can also calculate x! like this:

```
x! = x * (x-1)!
```

Going one step further, you can calculate $(x-1)!$ using the same procedure:

$(x-1)! = (x-1) * (x-2)!$

You continue calculating recursively until you're down to a value of 1, in which case you're finished. The program in Listing 4.5 uses a recursive function to calculate factorials. Because the program uses `unsigned` integers, it's limited to an input value of 14; the factorial of 15 and larger values are outside the allowed range for unsigned integers.

LISTING 4.5. Using a recursive function to calculate factorials.

```
 1:   /* Demonstrates function recursion. Calculates the */
 2:   /* factorial of a number. */
 3:
 4:   #include <stdio.h>
 5:
 6:   unsigned int f, x;
 7:   unsigned int factorial(unsigned int a);
 8:
 9:   int main(void)
10:   {
11:       puts("Enter an integer value between 1 and 14: ");
12:       scanf("%d", &x);
13:
14:       if( x > 14 || x < 1)
15:       {
16:           printf("Only values from 1 to 14 are acceptable!\n");
17:       }
18:       else
19:       {
20:           f = factorial(x);
21:           printf("%u factorial equals %u\n", x, f);
22:       }
23:
24:       return 0;
25:   }
26:
27:   unsigned int factorial(unsigned int a)
28:   {
29:       if (a == 1)
30:           return 1;
31:       else
32:       {
33:           a *= factorial(a-1);
34:           return a;
35:       }
36:   }
```

OUTPUT
```
Enter an integer value between 1 and 14:
6
6 factorial equals 720
```

ANALYSIS   The first half of this program is like many of the other programs you have
worked with so far. It starts with comments on lines 1 and 2. On line 4, the
appropriate header file is included for the input/output routines. Line 6 declares a couple
of `unsigned` integer values. Line 7 is a function prototype for the factorial function.
Notice that it takes an `unsigned int` as its parameter and returns an `unsigned int`.
Lines 9 through 25 are the `main()` function. Lines 11 and 12 print a message asking for a
value from 1 to 14 and then accept an entered value.

Lines 14 through 22 show an interesting `if` statement. Because a value greater than 14
causes a problem, this `if` statement checks the value. If it's greater than 14, an error message is printed; otherwise, the program figures the factorial on line 20 and prints the
result on line 21. When you know that such a problem might exist, such as a limit on the
size of a number, add code to detect the problem and prevent it.

The recursive function, `factorial()`, is located on lines 27 through 36. The value passed
is assigned to a. On line 29, the value of a is checked. If it's 1, the program returns the
value of 1. If the value isn't 1, a is set equal to itself times the value of `factorial(a-1)`.
The program calls the factorial function again, but this time the value of a is (a-1). If
(a-1) isn't equal to 1, `factorial()` is called again with ((a-1)-1), which is the same as
(a-2). This process continues until the `if` statement on line 29 is true. If the value of the
factorial is 3, the factorial is evaluated to the following:

```
3 * (3-1) * ((3-1)-1)
```

To better understand recursion, you might want to load the program in Listing 4.5 into
the ddd debugger. As described on Day 1, set a breakpoint at the first statement of line
11 by first clicking at the far left side of the line and then clicking the Stop button on the
toolbar. This will place a stop right at the start of the line. If you then click the Run button from the smaller floating window, a green arrow will appear beside the stop sign. You
may then step through your program using the Step button from the floating window.

You will notice that the output of your program appears at the bottom part of the main
window. When you arrive at the line with the `scanf()` and click the Step button, the program will stop and wait for you to input a number. Click in the bottom part of the main
ddd window, which is displaying the output from your program, and enter a number
between 1 and 14. Press the Enter key. The green arrow should now be next to the first
`if` statement of the `main()` function.

It is now possible to step through the rest of the program. Notice that when the debugger
jumps into the function `factorial()`, the lower part of the main window displays the
function name and the value of the argument passed to the function. While inside the

`factorial()` function, holding the cursor over the a (the name of the variable) displays the value of the variable at the bottom of the ddd window. As you step through the `factorial()` function, you will see the value of a decrease every time it is called until a is equal to 1. Then it will return the calculated value of a however many times the function was called. Step through this program a number of times to get an understanding of how recursion works.

Do	**Don't**
DO understand and work with recursion before you use it in a program you are going to distribute.	**DON'T** use recursion if there will be extensive iterations. (An *iteration* is the repetition of a program statement.) Recursion uses many resources because the function has to remember where it is.

Where the Functions Belong

You might be wondering where in your source code you should place your function definitions. For now, they should go in the same source code file as `main()` and after the end of `main()`. Figure 4.6 shows the basic structure of a program that uses functions.

FIGURE 4.6.

Place your function prototypes before `main()` *and your function definitions after* `main()`.

```
/* Start of source code *
    …
    prototypes here
    …
    main()
    {
        …
        …
    }
    func1()
    {
        …
    }
    func2()
    {
        …
    }
/* end of source code*
```

4

You can keep your user-defined functions in a separate source-code file, apart from `main()`. This technique is useful with large programs and when you want to use the same set of functions in more than one program. It is discussed on Day 20, "Advanced Compiler Use."

Summary

This chapter introduces you to functions, an important part of C programming. Functions are independent sections of code that perform specific tasks. When your program needs a task performed, it calls the function that performs that task. The use of functions is essential for structured programming—a method of program design that emphasizes a modular, top-down approach. Structured programming creates more efficient programs and also is much easier for you, the programmer, to use.

You also learned that a function consists of a header and a body. The header includes information about the function's return type, name, and parameters. The body contains local variable declarations and the C statements that are executed when the function is called. Finally, you saw that local variables—those declared within a function—are totally independent of any other program variables declared elsewhere.

Q&A

Q What if I must return more than one value from a function?

A Many times you will have to return more than one value from a function, or, more commonly, you will want to change a value you send to the function and keep the change after the function ends.

Q How do I know what a good function name is?

A A good function name describes as specifically as possible what the function does.

Q When variables are declared at the top of the listing, before `main()`, they can be used anywhere, but local variables can be used only in the specific function. Why not just declare everything before `main()`?

A Variable scope is discussed in more detail on Day 11. You will learn at that time why it is better to declare variables locally within functions instead of globally before `main()`.

Q What other ways are there to use recursion?

A The factorial function is a prime example of using recursion. The factorial number is necessary in many statistical calculations. Recursion is just a loop; however, it differs from other loops in one way. With recursion, each time a recursive function is called, a new set of variables is created. This is not true of the other loops that you will learn about in the next chapter.

Q Does `main()` have to be the first function in a program?

A No. It is a standard in C that the `main()` function is the first function to execute; however, it can be placed anywhere in your source file. Most people place it either first or last so that it's easy to locate.

Workshop

The Workshop provides quiz questions to help you solidify your understanding of the material covered and exercises to provide you with experience in using what you've learned. The answers to the quiz and exercises are provided in Appendix C, "Answers."

Quiz

1. Will you use structured programming when writing your C programs?
2. How does structured programming work?
3. How do C functions fit into structured programming?
4. What must be the first line of a function definition, and what information does it contain?
5. How many values can a function return?
6. If a function doesn't return a value, what type should it be declared?
7. What's the difference between a function definition and a function prototype?
8. What is a local variable?
9. How are local variables special?
10. Where should the `main()` function be placed?

Exercises

1. Write a header for a function named `do_it()` that takes three type `char` arguments and returns a type `float` to the calling program.
2. Write a header for a function named `print_a_number()` that takes a single type `int` argument and doesn't return anything to the calling program.
3. What type values do the following functions return?

    a. `int print_error( float err_nbr);`

    b. `long read_record( int rec_nbr, int size );`

4. **BUG BUSTER:** What's wrong with the following listing?
```
#include <stdio.h>
void print_msg( void );
int main(void)
{
    print_msg( "This is a message to print" );
    return 0;
}
void print_msg( void )
{
    puts( "This is a message to print" );
    return 0;
}
```

5. **BUG BUSTER:** What's wrong with the following function definition?

```
int twice(int y);
{
    return (2 * y);
}
```

6. Rewrite Listing 4.4 so that it needs only one `return` statement in the `larger_of()` function.

7. Write a function that receives two numbers as arguments and returns the value of their product.

8. Write a function that receives two numbers as arguments. The function should divide the first number by the second. Don't divide by the second number if it's zero. (Hint: Use an `if` statement.)

9. Write a function that calls the functions in exercises 7 and 8.

10. Write a program that uses a function to find the average of five type `float` values entered by the user.

11. Write a recursive function to take the value 3 to the power of another number. For example, if 4 is passed, the function will return 81.

DAY 5

Basic Program Control

Day 3, "Statements, Expressions, and Operators," covered the `if` statement, which gives you some control over the flow of your programs. Many times, though, you need more than just the ability to make true and false decisions. Today's lesson introduces three new ways to control the flow of the program. Today you will learn

- How to use simple arrays

- How to use `for`, `while`, and `do...while` loops to execute statements multiple times

- How you can nest program control statements

This is not intended to be a complete treatment of these topics, but rather, today's lesson provides enough information for you to be able to start writing real programs. These topics are covered in greater detail on Day 12, "Advanced Program Control."

Arrays: The Basics

Before we cover the `for` statement, you should take a short detour to learn about the basics of arrays. (See Day 7, "Using Numeric Arrays," for a complete treatment of arrays.) The `for` statement and arrays are closely linked in C, so it's difficult to define one without explaining the other. To help you understand the arrays used in the `for` statement examples to come, a quick treatment of arrays follows.

NEW TERM An *array* is an indexed group of data storage locations that have the same name and are distinguished from each other by a *subscript,* or *index*—a number following the variable name, enclosed in brackets. (This will become clearer as you continue.) Like other C variables, arrays must be declared. An array declaration includes both the data type and the size of the array (the number of elements in the array). For example, the following statement declares an array named `data` that is type `int` and has 1,000 elements:

```
int data[1000];
```

The individual elements are referred to by subscript as `data[0]` through `data[999]`. The first element is `data[0]`, not `data[1]`. In other languages, such as BASIC, the first element of an array is 1; this is not true in C.

Each element of this array is equivalent to a normal integer variable and can be used the same way. The subscript of an array can be another C variable, as in this example:

```
int data[1000];
int count;
count = 100;
data[count] = 12;      /* The same as data[100] = 12 */
```

This has been a quick introduction to arrays. However, you should now be able to understand how arrays are used in the program examples later today. If every detail of arrays isn't clear to you, don't worry. You will learn more about arrays on Day 7.

Do	Don't
	DON'T declare arrays with subscripts larger than you will need. It wastes memory.
	DON'T forget that in C, arrays are referenced starting with subscript 0, not 1.

Controlling Program Execution

The default order of execution in a C program is top-down. Execution starts at the beginning of the main() function and progresses, statement by statement, until the end of main() is reached. However, this order is rarely encountered in real C programs. The C language includes a variety of program control statements that let you control the order of program execution. You have already learned how to use C's fundamental decision operator, the if statement, so now it's time to explore three additional control statements you will find useful:

- The for statement
- The while statement
- The do...while statement

The for Statement

The for statement is a C programming construct that executes a block of one or more statements a certain number of times. It is sometimes called the for *loop* because program execution typically loops through the statement more than once. You've seen a few for statements used in programming examples earlier in this book. Now you're ready to see how the for statement works.

A for statement has the following structure:

```
for ( initial; condition; increment )
    statement;
```

initial, *condition*, and *increment* are all C expressions, and *statement* is a single or compound C statement. When a for statement is encountered during program execution, the following events occur:

1. The expression *initial* is evaluated. *initial* is usually an assignment statement that sets a variable to a particular value.

2. The expression *condition* is evaluated. *condition* is typically a relational expression.

3. If *condition* evaluates to false (that is, to zero), the for statement terminates, and execution passes to the first statement following *statement*.

4. If *condition* evaluates to true (that is, to nonzero), the C statement(s) in *statement* is executed.

5. The expression *increment* is evaluated, and execution returns to step 2.

5

Figure 5.1 shows the operation of a for statement. Note that *statement* never executes if *condition* is false the first time it's evaluated.

FIGURE 5.1.

A schematic representation of a for statement.

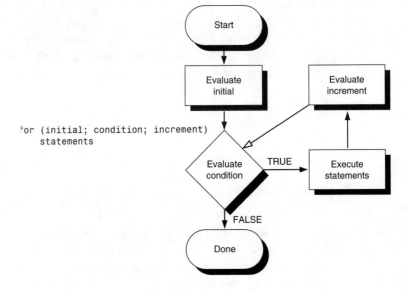

```
for (initial; condition; increment)
     statements
```

Listing 5.1 presents a simple example by using a for statement to print the numbers 1 through 20. You can see that the resulting code is much more compact than it would be if a separate printf() statement were used for each of the 20 values.

LISTING 5.1. A simple for statement.

```
 1:   /* Demonstrates a simple for statement */
 2:
 3:   #include <stdio.h>
 4:
 5:   int count;
 6:
 7:   int main(void)
 8:   {
 9:       /* Print the numbers 1 through 20 */
10:
11:       for (count = 1; count <= 20; count++)
12:           printf("%d\n", count);
13:
14:       return 0;
15:   }
```

OUTPUT
```
1
2
3
4
5
6
7
8
9
10
11
12
13
14
15
16
17
18
19
20
```

Figure 5.2 illustrates the operation of the for loop in Listing 5.1.

FIGURE 5.2.

How the for *loop in Listing 5.1 operates.*

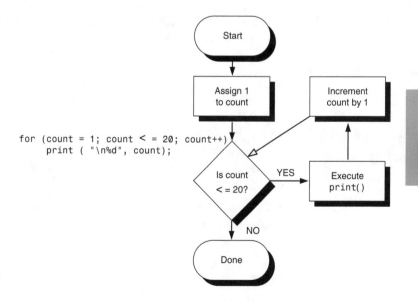

```
for (count = 1; count < = 20; count++)
      print ( "\n%d", count);
```

5

ANALYSIS   Line 3 includes the standard input/output header file. Line 5 declares a type int variable, named count, that will be used in the for loop. Lines 11 and 12 are the for loop. When the for statement is reached, the initial statement is executed first. In this listing, the initial statement is count = 1. This initializes count so that it can be used by the rest of the loop. The second step in executing this for statement is the evaluation of the condition count <= 20. Because count was just initialized to 1, you know that it is less than 20, so the statement in the for command, the printf(), is executed. After executing the printing function, the increment expression, count++, is evaluated. This adds 1 to count, making it 2. Now the program loops back and checks the condition again. If it is true, the printf() re-executes, the increment adds to count (making it 3), and the condition is checked. This loop continues until the condition evaluates to false, at which point the program exits the loop and continues to the next line (line 14), which returns 0 before ending the program.

The for statement is frequently used, as in the previous example, to "count up," incrementing a counter from one value to another. You also can use it to "count down," decrementing (rather than incrementing) the counter variable.

```
for (count = 100; count > 0; count—)
```

You can also "count by" a value other than 1, as in this example:

```
for (count = 0; count < 1000; count += 5)
```

The for statement is quite flexible. For example, you can omit the initialization expression if the test variable has been initialized previously in your program. (You still must use the semicolon separator as shown, however.)

```
count = 1;
for ( ; count < 1000; count++)
```

The initialization expression doesn't need to be an actual initialization; it can be any valid C expression. Whatever it is, it is executed once when the for statement is first reached. For example, the following prints the statement Now sorting the array...:

```
count = 1;
for (printf("Now sorting the array...") ; count < 1000; count++)
    /* Sorting statements here */
```

You can also omit the increment expression, performing the updating in the body of the for statement. Again, the semicolon must be included. To print the numbers from 0 to 99, for example, you could write

```
for (count = 0; count < 100; )
    printf("%d", count++);
```

The test expression that terminates the loop can be any C expression. As long as it evaluates to true (nonzero), the for statement continues to execute. You can use C's logical operators to construct complex test expressions. For example, the following for statement prints the elements of an array named array[], stopping when all elements have been printed or an element with a value of 0 is encountered:

```
for (count = 0; count < 1000 && array[count] != 0; count++)
    printf("%d", array[count]);
```

You could simplify this `for` loop even further by writing it as follows. (If you don't understand the change made to the test expression, you need to review Day 3.)

```
for (count = 0; count < 1000 && array[count]; )
    printf("%d", array[count++]);
```

You can follow the `for` statement with a null statement, allowing all the work to be done in the `for` statement itself. Remember, the null statement is a semicolon alone on a line. For example, to initialize all elements of a 1,000-element array to the value 50, you could write

```
for (count = 0; count < 1000; array[count++] = 50)
    ;
```

In this `for` statement, 50 is assigned to each member of the array by the increment part of the statement.

Day 3 mentioned that C's comma operator is most often used in `for` statements. You can create an expression by separating two subexpressions with the comma operator. The two subexpressions are evaluated (in left-to-right order), and the entire expression evaluates to the value of the right subexpression. By using the comma operator, you can make each part of a `for` statement perform multiple duties.

Imagine that you have two 1,000-element arrays, a[] and b[]. You want to copy the contents of a[] to b[] in reverse order so that after the copy operation, b[0] = a[999], b[1] = a[998], and so on. The following `for` statement does the trick:

```
for (i = 0, j = 999; i < 1000; i++, j—)
    b[j] = a[i];
```

The comma operator is used to initialize two variables, i and j. It is also used to increment part of these two variables with each loop.

The `for` Statement

▼ SYNTAX

```
for (initial; condition; increment)
    statement(s)
```

initial is any valid C expression. It is usually an assignment statement that sets a variable to a particular value.

condition is any valid C expression. It is usually a relational expression. When *condition* evaluates to false (zero), the `for` statement terminates, and execution passes to the first statement following *statement(s)*; otherwise, the C statement(s) in *statement(s)* is executed.

▼

▼ *increment* is any valid C expression. It is usually an expression that increments a variable initialized by the initial expression.

statement(s) are the C statements that are executed as long as the condition remains true.

A for statement is a looping statement. It can have an initialization, test condition, and increment as parts of its command. The for statement executes the initial expression first. It then checks the condition. If the condition is true, the statements execute. After the statements are completed, the increment expression is evaluated. The for statement then rechecks the condition and continues to loop until the condition is false.

Example 1

```
/* Prints the value of x as it counts from 0 to 9 */
int x;
for (x = 0; x <10; x++)
    printf( "\nThe value of x is %d", x );
```

Example 2

```
/*Obtains values from the user until 99 is entered */
int nbr = 0;
for ( ; nbr != 99; )
   scanf( "%d", &nbr );
```

Example 3

```
/* Lets user enter up to 10 integer values      */
/* Values are stored in an array named value. If 99 is */
/* entered, the loop stops                      */
int value[10];
int ctr,nbr=0;
for (ctr = 0; ctr < 10 && nbr != 99; ctr++)
{
    puts("Enter a number, 99 to quit ");
    scanf("%d", &nbr);
    value[ctr]  = nbr;
▲ }
```

Nesting for Statements

A for statement can be executed within another for statement. This is called *nesting*. (You saw nesting on Day 3 with the if statement.) By nesting for statements, you can do some complex programming. Listing 5.2 is not a complex program, but it illustrates the nesting of two for statements.

LISTING 5.2. Nested for statements.

```
 1:    /* Demonstrates nesting two for statements */
 2:
 3:    #include <stdio.h>
 4:
 5:    void draw_box( int, int);
 6:
 7:    int main(void)
 8:    {
 9:        draw_box( 8, 35 );
10:
11:        return 0;
12:    }
13:
14:    void draw_box( int row, int column )
15:    {
16:        int col;
17:        for ( ; row > 0; row—)
18:        {
19:            for (col = column; col > 0; col—)
20:                printf("X");
21:
22:            printf("\n");
23:        }
24:    }
```

OUTPUT

```
XXXXXXXXXXXXXXXXXXXXXXXXXXXXXXXXXXX
XXXXXXXXXXXXXXXXXXXXXXXXXXXXXXXXXXX
XXXXXXXXXXXXXXXXXXXXXXXXXXXXXXXXXXX
XXXXXXXXXXXXXXXXXXXXXXXXXXXXXXXXXXX
XXXXXXXXXXXXXXXXXXXXXXXXXXXXXXXXXXX
XXXXXXXXXXXXXXXXXXXXXXXXXXXXXXXXXXX
XXXXXXXXXXXXXXXXXXXXXXXXXXXXXXXXXXX
XXXXXXXXXXXXXXXXXXXXXXXXXXXXXXXXXXX
```

5

ANALYSIS The main work of this program is accomplished on line 20. When you run this program, 280 Xs are printed onscreen, forming an 8×35 square. The program has only one command to print an X, but it is nested in two loops.

In this listing, a function prototype for draw_box() is declared on line 5. This function takes two type int variables, row and column, which contain the dimensions of the box of Xs to be drawn. In line 9, main() calls draw_box() and passes the value 8 as the row and the value 35 as the column.

Looking closely at the draw_box() function, you might see a couple things you don't readily understand. The first is why the local variable col was declared. The second is why the second printf() in line 22 was used. Both of these will become clearer after you look at the two for loops.

Line 17 starts the first for loop. The initialization is skipped because the initial value of row was passed to the function. Looking at the condition, you see that this for loop is executed until the row is 0. On first executing line 17, row is 8; therefore, the program continues to line 19.

Line 19 contains the second for statement. Here the passed parameter, column, is copied to a local variable, col, of type int. The value of col is 35 initially (the value passed via column), and column retains its original value. Because col is greater than 0, line 20 is executed, printing an X. col is then decremented, and the loop continues. When col is 0, the for loop ends, and control goes to line 22. Line 22 causes the onscreen printing to start on a new line. (Printing is covered in detail on Day 6, "Fundamentals of Input and Output.") After moving to a new line on the screen, control reaches the end of the first for loop's statements, thus executing the increment expression, which subtracts 1 from row, making it 7. This puts control back at line 19. Notice that the value of col was 0 when it was last used. If column had been used instead of col, it would fail the condition test, because it will never be greater than 0. Only the first line would be printed. Take the initializer out of line 19 and change the two col variables to column to see what actually happens.

Do	Don't

DO remember the semicolon if you use a for with a null statement. Put the semicolon placeholder on a separate line or place a space between it and the end of the for statement. It's clearer to put it on a separate line.
 	
`    for (count = 0; count < 1000;`
`    array[count] = 50) ;`
`        /* note space! */`
	DON'T put too much processing in the for statement. Although you can use the comma separator, it is often clearer to put some of the functionality into the body of the loop.

The while Statement

The while statement, also called the while *loop,* executes a block of statements as long as a specified condition is true. The while statement has the following form:

```
while (condition)
    statement
```

condition is any C expression, and *statement* is a single or compound C statement. When program execution reaches a while statement, the following events occur:

1. The expression *condition* is evaluated.

2. If *condition* evaluates to false (that is, zero), the while statement terminates, and execution passes to the first statement following *statement*.

3. If *condition* evaluates to true (that is, nonzero), the C statement(s) in *statement* is executed.

4. Execution returns to step 1.

The operation of a while statement is shown in Figure 5.3.

FIGURE 5.3.

The operation of a
while *statement.*

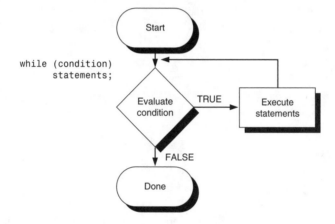

Listing 5.3 is a simple program that uses a while statement to print the numbers 1 through 20. (This is the same task that is performed by a for statement in Listing 5.1.)

5

LISTING 5.3. A simple while statement.

```
1:    /* Demonstrates a simple while statement */
2:
3:    #include <stdio.h>
4:
5:    int count;
6:
7:    int main(void)
8:    {
9:        /* Print the numbers 1 through 20 */
10:
11:       count = 1;
12:
13:       while (count <= 20)
14:       {
15:           printf("%d\n", count);
```

continues

LISTING 5.3. continued

```
16:           count++;
17:        }
18:  return 0;
19:  }
```

OUTPUT
```
1
2
3
4
5
6
7
8
9
10
11
12
13
14
15
16
17
18
19
20
```

ANALYSIS   Examine Listing 5.3 and compare it with Listing 5.1, which uses a for statement
to perform the same task. In line 11, count is initialized to 1. Because the while
statement doesn't contain an initialization section, you must take care of initializing any
variables before starting the while. Line 13 is the actual while statement, and it contains
the same condition statement from Listing 5.1, count <= 20. In the while loop, line 16
takes care of incrementing count. What do you think would happen if you forgot to put
line 16 in this program? Your program wouldn't know when to stop because count would
always be 1, which is always less than 20.

You might have noticed that a while statement is essentially a for statement without the
initialization and increment components. Thus,

```
for ( ; condition ; )
```

is equivalent to

```
while (condition)
```

Because of this equality, anything that can be done with a for statement can also be done
with a while statement. When you use a while statement, any necessary initialization
must first be performed in a separate statement, and the updating must be performed by a
statement that is part of the while loop.

When initialization and updating are required, most experienced C programmers prefer to use a `for` statement rather than a `while` statement. This preference is based primarily on source code readability. When you use a `for` statement, the initialization, test, and increment expressions are located together and are easy to find and modify. With a `while` statement, the initialization and update expressions are located separately and might be less obvious.

The `while` Statement

▼ SYNTAX

```
while (condition)
    statement(s)
```

condition is any valid C expression, usually a relational expression. When *condition* evaluates to false (zero), the `while` statement terminates, and execution passes to the first statement following *statement(s)*; otherwise, the first C statement in *statement(s)* is executed.

statement(s) is the C statement(s) that is executed as long as *condition* remains true.

A `while` statement is a C looping statement. It allows repeated execution of a statement or block of statements as long as the condition remains true (nonzero). If the condition is not true when the `while` command is first executed, *statement(s)* is never executed.

Example 1

```
int x = 0;
while (x < 10)
{
    printf("\nThe value of x is %d", x );
    x++;
}
```

Example 2

```
/* get numbers until you get one greater than 99 */
int nbr=0;
while (nbr <= 99)
    scanf("%d", &nbr );
```

Example 3

```
/* Lets user enter up to 10 integer values      */
/* Values are stored in an array named value. If 99 is */
/* entered, the loop stops                       */
int value[10];
int ctr = 0;
int nbr;
while (ctr < 10 && nbr != 99)
    {
```

```
       puts("Enter a number, 99 to quit ");
       scanf("%d", &nbr);
       value[ctr] = nbr;
       ctr++;
   }
```

Nesting `while` Statements

Just like the `for` and `if` statements, `while` statements can also be nested. Listing 5.4 shows an example of nested `while` statements. Although this isn't the best use of a `while` statement, the example does present some new ideas.

LISTING 5.4. Nested `while` statements.

```
 1:    /* Demonstrates nested while statements */
 2:
 3:    #include <stdio.h>
 4:
 5:    int array[5];
 6:
 7:    int main(void)
 8:    {
 9:       int ctr = 0,
10:           nbr = 0;
11:
12:       printf("This program prompts you to enter 5 numbers\n");
13:       printf("Each number should be from 1 to 10\n");
14:
15:       while ( ctr < 5 )
16:       {
17:           nbr = 0;
18:           while (nbr < 1 || nbr > 10)
19:           {
20:               printf("\nEnter number %d of 5: ", ctr + 1 );
21:               scanf("%d", &nbr );
22:           }
23:
24:           array[ctr] = nbr;
25:           ctr++;
26:       }
27:
28:       for (ctr = 0; ctr < 5; ctr++)
29:           printf("Value %d is %d\n", ctr + 1, array[ctr] );
30:
31:       return 0;
32:    }
```

INPUT/
OUTPUT

```
This program prompts you to enter 5 numbers
Each number should be from 1 to 10

Enter number 1 of 5: 3

Enter number 2 of 5: 6

Enter number 3 of 5: 3

Enter number 4 of 5: 9

Enter number 5 of 5: 2

Value 1 is 3
Value 2 is 6
Value 3 is 3
Value 4 is 9
Value 5 is 2
```

ANALYSIS

As in previous listings, line 1 contains a comment with a description of the program and line 3 contains an #include statement for the standard input/output header file. Line 5 contains a declaration for an array (named array) that can hold five integer values. The function main() contains two additional local variables, ctr and nbr (lines 9 and 10). Notice that these variables are initialized to 0 at the same time they are declared. Also notice that the comma operator is used as a separator at the end of line 9, allowing nbr to be declared as an int without restating the int type command. Stating declarations in this manner is a common practice for many C programmers. Lines 12 and 13 print messages stating what the program does and what is expected of the user. Lines 15 through 26 contain the first while command and its statements. Lines 18 through 22 also contain a nested while loop with its own statements that are all part of the outer while.

5

This outer loop continues to execute while ctr is less than 5 (line 15). As long as ctr is less than 5, line 17 sets nbr to 0, lines 18 through 22 (the nested while statement) gather a number in variable nbr, line 24 places the number in array, and line 25 increments ctr. Then the loop starts again. Therefore, the outer loop gathers five numbers and places each into array, indexed by ctr.

The inner loop is a good use of a while statement. Only the numbers from 1 to 10 are valid, so until the user enters a valid number, there is no point continuing the program. Lines 18 through 22 prevent continuation. This while statement states that while the number is less than 1 or greater than 10, the program should print a message to enter a number, and then get the number.

Lines 28 and 29 print the values that are stored in `array`. Notice that because the `while` statements are done with the variable `ctr`, the `for` command can reuse it. Starting at zero and incrementing by one, the `for` loops five times, printing the value of `ctr` plus one (because the count started at zero) and printing the corresponding value in `array`.

For additional practice, there are two things you can change in this program. The first is the values that the program accepts. Instead of 1 to 10, try making it accept from 1 to 100. You can also change the number of values that it accepts. Currently, it allows for five numbers. Try making it accept 10.

Do	Don't

DO use the `for` statement instead of the `while` statement if you need to initialize and increment within your loop. The `for` statement keeps the initialization, condition, and increment statements together. The `while` statement does not.	**DON'T** use the following convention if it isn't necessary:
	
	`while (x)`
	
	Instead, use this convention:
	
	`while (x != 0)`
	
	Although both conventions work, the second is clearer when you're debugging (trying to find problems in) the code. When compiled, these lines produce virtually the same code.

The do...while Loop

C's third loop construct is the `do...while` loop, which executes a block of statements as long as a specified condition is true. The `do...while` loop tests the condition at the end of the loop rather than at the beginning, as is done by the `for` loop and the `while` loop.

The structure of the `do...while` loop is as follows:

```
do
    statement
while (condition);
```

`condition` is any C expression and `statement` is a single or compound C statement. When program execution reaches a `do...while` statement, the following events occur:

1. The statements in `statement` are executed.

2. `condition` is evaluated. If it's true, execution returns to step 1. If it's false, the loop terminates.

The operation of a `do...while` loop is shown in Figure 5.4.

FIGURE 5.4.

The operation of a
do...while *loop.*

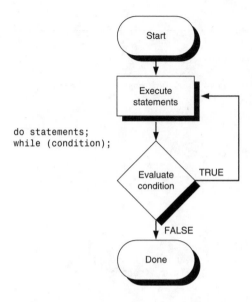

```
do statements;
while (condition);
```

The statements associated with a do...while loop are always executed at least once. This is because the test condition is evaluated at the end of the loop, instead of the beginning. In contrast, for loops and while loops evaluate the test condition at the start of the loop, so the associated statements are not executed at all if the test condition is initially false.

The do...while loop is used less frequently than while and for loops. It is most appropriate when the statement(s) associated with the loop must be executed at least once. You could, of course, accomplish the same thing with a while loop by making sure that the test condition is true when execution first reaches the loop. A do...while loop probably would be more straightforward, however.

Listing 5.5 shows an example of a do...while loop.

LISTING 5.5. A simple do...while loop.

```
1:    /* Demonstrates a simple do...while statement */
2:
3:    #include <stdio.h>
4:
5:    int get_menu_choice( void );
6:
7:    int main(void)
8:    {
9:        int choice;
```

continues

LISTING 5.5. continued

```
10:
11:        choice = get_menu_choice();
12:
13:        printf("You chose Menu Option %d\n", choice );
14:
15:        return 0;
16:  }
17:
18:  int get_menu_choice( void )
19:  {
20:        int selection = 0;
21:
22:        do
23:        {
24:            printf("\n" );
25:            printf("\n1 - Add a Record" );
26:            printf("\n2 - Change a record");
27:            printf("\n3 - Delete a record");
28:            printf("\n4 - Quit");
29:            printf("\n" );
30:            printf("\nEnter a selection: " );
31:
32:            scanf("%d", &selection );
33:
34:        }while ( selection < 1 || selection > 4 );
35:
36:        return selection;
37:  }
```

INPUT/
OUTPUT

```
1 - Add a Record
2 - Change a record
3 - Delete a record
4 - Quit

Enter a selection: 8

1 - Add a Record
2 - Change a record
3 - Delete a record
4 - Quit

Enter a selection: 4
You chose Menu Option 4
```

ANALYSIS   This program provides a menu with four choices. The user selects one of the four choices, and then the program prints the number selected. Programs later in this book use and expand on this concept. For now, you should be able to follow most of the listing. The main() function (lines 7 through 16) adds nothing to what you already know.

Note

The body of `main()` could have been written on one line like this:

`printf( "You chose Menu Option %d", get_menu_option() );`

If you were to expand this program and act on the selection, you would need the value returned by `get_menu_choice()`, so it is wise to assign the value to a variable (such as `choice`).

Lines 18 through 37 contain `get_menu_choice()`. This function displays a menu onscreen (lines 24 through 30) and then gets a selection. Because you have to display a menu at least once to get an answer, it is appropriate to use a `do...while` loop. In the case of this program, the menu is displayed until a valid choice is entered. Line 34 contains the `while` part of the `do...while` statement and validates the value of the selection, appropriately named `selection`. If the value entered is not between 1 and 4, the menu is redisplayed and the user is prompted for a new value. When a valid selection is entered, the program continues to line 36, which returns the value in the variable selection.

The `do...while` Statement

▼ SYNTAX

```
do
{
    statement(s)
}while (condition);
```

`condition` is any valid C expression, usually a relational expression. When `condition` evaluates to false (zero), the `while` statement terminates and execution passes to the first statement following the `while` statement; otherwise, the program loops back to the `do` and the C statement(s) in `statement(s)` is executed.

`statement(s)` is either a single C statement or a block of statements that are executed the first time through the loop and then as long as `condition` remains true.

A `do...while` statement is a C looping statement. It allows repeated execution of a statement or block of statements as long as the condition remains true (nonzero). Unlike the `while` statement, a `do...while` loop executes its statements at least once.

Example 1

```
/* prints even though condition fails! */
int x = 10;
do
{
    printf("\nThe value of x is %d", x );
}while (x != 10);
```

▼

5

▼ **Example 2**

```
/* gets numbers until the number is greater than 99 */
int nbr;
do
{
    scanf("%d", &nbr );
}while (nbr <= 99);
```

Example 3

```
/* Enables user to enter up to 10 integer values      */
/* Values are stored in an array named value. If 99 is */
/* entered, the loop stops                             */
int value[10];
int ctr = 0;
int nbr;
do
{
    puts("Enter a number, 99 to quit ");
    scanf( "%d", &nbr);
    value[ctr] = nbr;
    ctr++;
}while (ctr < 10 && nbr != 99);
```

Nested Loops

The term *nested loop* refers to a loop that is contained within another loop. You have seen examples of some nested statements. C places no limitations on the nesting of loops, except that each inner loop must be enclosed completely in the outer loop; you can't have overlapping loops. Thus, the following is not allowed:

```
for ( count = 1; count < 100; count++)
{
    do
    {
        /* the do...while loop */
} /* end of for loop */
    }while (x != 0);
```

If the do...while loop is placed entirely in the for loop, there is no problem:

```
for (count = 1; count < 100; count++)
{
    do
    {
        /* the do...while loop */
    }while (x != 0);
} /* end of for loop */
```

When you use nested loops, remember that changes made in the inner loop might affect the outer loop as well. Note, however, that the inner loop might be independent from any variables in the outer loop; in this example, they are not. In the previous example, if the inner `do...while` loop modifies the value of `count`, the number of times the outer `for` loop executes is affected.

Good indenting style makes code with nested loops easier to read. Each level of loop should be indented one step further than the last level. This clearly labels the code associated with each loop.

Do	Don't
DO use the `do...while` loop when you know that a loop should be executed at least once.	DON'T try to overlap loops. You can nest them, but they must be entirely within each other.

Summary

After today's lesson, you are now almost ready to start writing real C programs on your own.

C has three loop statements that control program execution: `for`, `while`, and `do...while`. Each of these constructs lets your program execute a block of statements zero times, one time, or more than one time, based on the condition of certain program variables. Many programming tasks are well served by the repetitive execution allowed by these loop statements.

Although all three statements can be used to accomplish the same task, each is different. The `for` statement lets you initialize, evaluate, and increment all in one command. The `while` statement operates as long as a condition is true. The `do...while` statement always executes its statements at least once and continues to execute them until a condition is false.

Nesting is the placing of one command within another. C allows for the nesting of any of its commands. Nesting the `if` statement was demonstrated on Day 3. In today's lesson, the `for`, `while`, and `do...while` statements were nested.

5

Q&A

Q How do I know which programming control statement to use—the `for`, the `while`, or the `do...while`?

A If you look at the syntax boxes provided, you can see that any of the three can be used to solve a looping problem. Each has a small twist to what it can do, however. The `for` statement is best when you know that you need to initialize and increment in your loop. If you only have a condition that you want to meet, and you aren't dealing with a specific number of loops, `while` is a good choice. If you know that a set of statements needs to be executed at least once, a `do...while` might be best. Because all three can be used for most problems, the best course is to learn them all and then evaluate each programming situation to determine which is best.

Q How deep can I nest my loops?

A You can nest as many loops as you want. If your program requires you to nest more than two loops deep, consider using a function instead. You might find sorting through all those braces difficult, so perhaps a function would be easier to follow in code.

Q Can I nest different loop commands?

A You can nest `if`, `for`, `while`, `do...while`, or any other command. You will find that many of the programs you try to write will require that you nest at least a few of these.

Workshop

The Workshop provides quiz questions to help you solidify your understanding of the material covered and exercises to provide you with experience in using what you've learned. The answers to the quiz and exercises are provided in Appendix C, "Answers."

Quiz

1. What is the index value of the first element in an array?
2. What is the difference between a `for` statement and a `while` statement?
3. What is the difference between a `while` statement and a `do...while` statement?
4. Is it true that a `while` statement can be used and still get the same results as coding a `for` statement?
5. What must you remember when nesting statements?
6. Can a `while` statement be nested in a `do...while` statement?

7. What are the four parts of a `for` statement?

8. What are the two parts of a `while` statement?

9. What are the two parts of a `do...while` statement?

Exercises

1. Write a declaration for an array that will hold 50 type `long` values.

2. Show a statement that assigns the value of 123.456 to the 50th element in the array from exercise 1.

3. What is the value of x when the following statement is complete?

```
for (x = 0; x < 100, x++) ;
```

4. What is the value of `ctr` when the following statement is complete?

```
for (ctr = 2; ctr < 10; ctr += 3) ;
```

5. How many Xs does the following print?

```
for (x = 0; x < 10; x++)
    for (y = 5; y > 0; y—)
        puts("X");
```

6. Write a `for` statement to count from 1 to 100 by 3s.

7. Write a `while` statement to count from 1 to 100 by 3s.

8. Write a `do...while` statement to count from 1 to 100 by 3s.

9. **BUG BUSTER:** What is wrong with the following code fragment?

```
record = 0;
while (record < 100)
{
    printf( "\nRecord %d ", record );
    printf( "\nGetting next number..." );
}
```

10. **BUG BUSTER:** What is wrong with the following code fragment? (`MAXVALUES` is not the problem!)

```
for (counter = 1; counter < MAXVALUES; counter++);
    printf("\nCounter = %d", counter );
```

5

DAY 6

Fundamentals of Input and Output

In most programs you create, you will have to display information on the screen or read information from the keyboard. Many of the programs presented in earlier days perform these tasks, but you might not have understood exactly how. Today you will learn

- The basics of C's input and output statements
- How to display information onscreen with the printf() and puts() library functions
- How to format the information that is displayed onscreen
- How to read data from the keyboard with the scanf() library function

Today's lesson isn't intended to be a complete treatment of these topics, but it provides enough information so that you can start writing real programs. These topics are covered in greater detail later in this book.

Displaying Information Onscreen

You will want most of your programs to display information onscreen. The two most frequently used ways to do this are with C's library functions `printf()` and `puts()`.

The `printf()` Function

The `printf()` function is part of the standard C library. It is perhaps the most versatile way for a program to display data onscreen. You've already seen `printf()` used in many of the examples in this book. Now you will see how `printf()` works.

Printing a text message onscreen is simple. Call the `printf()` function, passing the desired message enclosed in double quotation marks. For example, to display An error has occurred! on the screen, you write

```
printf("An error has occurred!");
```

In addition to text messages, however, you frequently have to display the value of program variables. This is a little more complicated than displaying only a message. For example, suppose that you want to display the value of the numeric variable x onscreen, along with some identifying text. Furthermore, you want the information to start at the beginning of a new line. You could use the `printf()` function as follows:

```
printf("\nThe value of x is %d", x);
```

The resulting screen display, assuming that the value of x is 12, would be

```
The value of x is 12
```

In this example, two arguments are passed to `printf()`. The first argument is enclosed in double quotation marks and is called the *format string*. The second argument is the name of the variable (x) containing the value to be printed.

The `printf()` Format Strings

A `printf()` format string specifies how the output is to be formatted. Here are the three possible components of a format string:

- *Literal text* is displayed exactly as entered in the format string. In the preceding example, the characters starting with the T (in The) and up to, but not including, the % compose a literal string.

- An *escape sequence* provides special formatting control. An escape sequence consists of a backslash (\) followed by a single character. In the preceding example, \n is an escape sequence. It is called the *newline character* and it means "move to the start of the next line." Escape sequences are also used to print certain characters. Common escape sequences are listed in Table 6.1. A full list appears in Day 14, "Pointers: Beyond the Basics."

- A *conversion specifier* consists of the percent sign (%) followed by a character. In the example, the conversion specifier is %d. A conversion specifier tells `printf()` how to interpret the variable(s) being printed. The %d tells `printf()` to interpret the variable x as a signed decimal integer.

TABLE 6.1. The most frequently used escape sequences.

Sequence	Meaning
\a	Bell (alert)
\b	Backspace
\n	Newline
\t	Horizontal tab
\\	Backslash
\?	Question mark
\'	Single quotation

The `printf()` Escape Sequences

Escape sequences are used to control the location of output by moving the screen cursor. They are also used to print characters that would otherwise have a special meaning to `printf()`. For example, to print a single backslash character, include a double backslash (\\) in the format string. The first backslash tells `printf()` that the second backslash is to be interpreted as a literal character, not as the start of an escape sequence. In general, the backslash tells `printf()` to interpret the next character in a special manner. Here are some examples.

Sequence	Meaning
n	The character n
\n	Newline
\"	The double quotation character
"	The start or end of a string

6

Listing 6.1 demonstrates some of the frequently used escape sequences.

LISTING 6.1. Using `printf()` escape sequences.

```
1:   /* Demonstration of frequently used escape sequences */
2:
3:   #include <stdio.h>
4:
5:   #define QUIT  3
6:
7:   int  get_menu_choice( void );
8:   void print_report( void );
9:
10:  int main(void)
11:  {
12:      int choice = 0;
13:
14:      while (choice != QUIT)
15:      {
16:         choice = get_menu_choice();
17:
18:         if (choice == 1)
19:             printf("\nBeeping the computer\a\a\a" );
20:         else
21:         {
22:             if (choice == 2)
23:                 print_report();
24:         }
25:      }
26:      printf("You chose to quit!\n");
27:
28:      return 0;
29:  }
30:
31:  int get_menu_choice( void )
32:  {
33:      int selection = 0;
34:
35:      do
36:      {
37:          printf( "\n" );
38:          printf( "\n1 - Beep Computer" );
39:          printf( "\n2 - Display Report");
40:          printf( "\n3 - Quit");
41:          printf( "\n" );
42:          printf( "\nEnter a selection:" );
43:
44:          scanf( "%d", &selection );
45:
46:        }while ( selection < 1 || selection > 3 );
```

```
47:
48:        return selection;
49:  }
50:
51:  void print_report( void )
52:  {
53:        printf( "\nSAMPLE REPORT" );
54:        printf( "\n\nSequence\tMeaning" );
55:        printf( "\n=========\t=======" );
56:        printf( "\n\\a\t\tbell (alert)" );
57:        printf( "\n\\b\t\tbackspace" );
58:        printf( "\n...\t\t...");
59:  }
```

INPUT/
OUTPUT

```
1 - Beep Computer
2 - Display Report
3 - Quit

Enter a selection:1

Beeping the computer

1 - Beep Computer
2 - Display Report
3 - Quit

Enter a selection:2

SAMPLE REPORT
Sequence        Meaning
=========       =======
\a              bell (alert)
\b              backspace
...             ...
1 - Beep Computer
2 - Display Report
3 - Quit

Enter a selection:3
You chose to quit!
```

6

ANALYSIS Listing 6.1 seems long compared with previous examples, but it offers some additions that are worth noting. The stdio.h header is included in line 3 because printf() is used in this listing. In line 5, a constant named QUIT is defined. From "Storing Data: Variables and Constants," in Day 2, you know that #define makes using the constant QUIT equivalent to using the value 3. Lines 7 and 8 are function prototypes. This program has two functions: get_menu_choice() and print_report(). The get_menu_choice() function is defined in lines 31 through 49. This is similar to the menu function in Listing 5.5. Lines 37 and 41 contain calls to printf() that print the newline escape sequence. Lines 38, 39, 40, and 42 also use the newline escape character and they print text. Line 37 could have been eliminated by changing line 38 to the following:

```
printf( "\n\n1 - Beep Computer" );
```

However, leaving line 37 makes the program easier to read.

Looking at the `main()` function, you see the start of a `while` loop on line 14. The `while` loop's statements will keep looping as long as `choice` is not equal to `QUIT`. Because `QUIT` is a constant, you could have replaced it with 3; however, the program wouldn't be as clear. Line 16 gets the variable `choice`, which is then analyzed in lines 18 through 25 in an `if` statement. If the user chooses 1, line 19 prints the newline character, a message, and then three beeps. If the user selects 2, line 23 calls the function `print_report()`.

The `print_report()` function is defined on lines 51 through 59. This simple function shows the ease of using `printf()` and the escape sequences to print formatted information to the screen. You've already seen the newline character. Lines 54 through 58 also use the tab escape character, `\t`. The tab character aligns the columns of the report vertically. Lines 56 and 57 might seem confusing at first, but if you start at the left and work to the right, they make sense. Line 56 prints a newline (`\n`), then a backslash (`\`), then the letter a, and then two tabs (`\t\t`). The line ends with some descriptive text, (`bell (alert)`). Line 57 follows the same format.

This program prints the first two lines of Table 6.1, along with a report title and column headings. In exercise 9 at the end of this lesson, you will complete this program by making it print the rest of the table.

The `printf()` Conversion Specifiers

The format string must contain one conversion specifier for each printed variable. The `printf()` function then displays each variable as directed by its corresponding conversion specifier. You will learn more about this process on Day 15, "Using Disk Files." For now, be sure to use the conversion specifier that corresponds to the type of variable being printed.

Exactly what does this mean? If you're printing a variable that is a signed decimal integer (types `int` and `long`), use the `%d` conversion specifier. For an unsigned decimal integer (types `unsigned int` and `unsigned long`), use `%u`. For a floating-point variable (types `float` and `double`), use the `%f` specifier. The conversion specifiers you need most often are listed in Table 6.3.

TABLE 6.3. The most commonly needed conversion specifiers.

Specifier	Meaning	Types Converted
%c	Single character	char
%d	Signed decimal integer	int, short
%ld	Signed long decimal integer	long
%f	Decimal floating-point number	float, double
%s	Character string	char arrays
%u	Unsigned decimal integer	unsigned int, unsigned short
%lu	Unsigned long decimal integer	unsigned long

> **Note** Any program that uses printf() should include the header file stdio.h.

The literal text of a format specifier is anything that doesn't qualify as either an escape sequence or a conversion specifier. Literal text is simply printed as is, including all spaces.

What about printing the values of more than one variable? A single printf() statement can print an unlimited number of variables, but the format string must contain one conversion specifier for each variable. The conversion specifiers are paired with variables in left-to-right order. If you write

```
printf("Rate = %f, amount = %d", rate, amount);
```

the variable rate is paired with the %f specifier, and the variable amount is paired with the %d specifier. The positions of the conversion specifiers in the format string determine the position of the output. If there are more variables passed to printf() than there are conversion specifiers, the unmatched variables aren't printed. If there are more specifiers than variables, the unmatched specifiers print "garbage."

You aren't limited to printing the value of variables with printf(). The arguments can be any valid C expression. For example, to print the sum of x and y, you could write

```
z = x + y;
printf("%d", z);
```

You also could write

```
printf("%d", x + y);
```

6

Listing 6.2 demonstrates the use of printf(). Day 15 gives more details on printf().

LISTING 6.2. Using printf() to display numerical values.

```
 1:   /* Demonstration using printf() to display numerical values. */
 2:
 3:   #include <stdio.h>
 4:
 5:   int a = 2, b = 10, c = 50;
 6:   float f = 1.05, g = 25.5, h = -0.1;
 7:
 8:   int main(void)
 9:   {
10:       printf("\nDecimal values without tabs: %d %d %d", a, b, c);
11:       printf("\nDecimal values with tabs: \t%d \t%d \t%d", a, b, c);
12:
13:       printf("\nThree floats on 1 line: \t%f\t%f\t%f", f, g, h);
14:       printf("\nThree floats on 3 lines: \n\t%f\n\t%f\n\t%f", f, g, h);
15:
16:       printf("\nThe rate is %f%%", f);
17:       printf("\nThe result of %f/%f = %f\n", g, f, g / f);
18:
19:       return 0;
20:   }
```

OUTPUT
```
Decimal values without tabs: 2 10 50
Decimal values with tabs:       2       10      50
Three floats on 1 line:         1.050000        25.500000          -
➥0.100000
Three floats on 3 lines:
        1.050000
        25.500000
        -0.100000
The rate is 1.050000%
The result of 25.500000/1.050000 = 24.285715
```

ANALYSIS Listing 6.2 prints six lines of information. Lines 10 and 11 each print three deci-
mals: a, b, and c. Line 10 prints them without tabs and line 11 prints them with
tabs. Lines 13 and 14 each print three float variables: f, g, and h. Line 13 prints them
on one line and line 14 prints them on three lines. Line 16 prints a float variable, f, followed by a percent sign. Because a percent sign is normally a message to print a variable, you must place two in a row to print a single percent sign. This is exactly like the
backslash escape character. Line 17 shows one final concept. When printing values in
conversion specifiers, you don't have to use variables. You can also use expressions such
as g / f, or even constants.

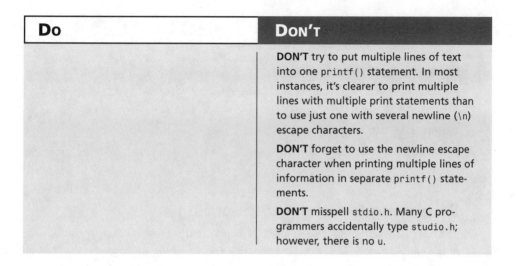

Do	Don't
	DON'T try to put multiple lines of text into one `printf()` statement. In most instances, it's clearer to print multiple lines with multiple print statements than to use just one with several newline (`\n`) escape characters. **DON'T** forget to use the newline escape character when printing multiple lines of information in separate `printf()` statements. **DON'T** misspell `stdio.h`. Many C programmers accidentally type `studio.h`; however, there is no u.

The `printf()` Function

▼ SYNTAX

```
#include <stdio.h>
printf( format-string[,arguments,...]);
```

`printf()` is a function that accepts a series of *arguments*, each applying to a conversion specifier in the given format string. `printf()` prints the formatted information to the standard output device, usually the display screen. When using `printf()`, you must include the standard input/output header file, stdio.h.

The *format-string* is required; however, arguments are optional. For each argument, there must be a conversion specifier. Table 6.3 lists the most commonly used conversion specifiers.

The *format-string* can also contain escape sequences. Table 6.1 lists the most frequently used escape sequences.

The following are examples of calls to `printf()` and their output:

Example 1 Input

```
#include <stdio.h>
int main(void)
{
    printf("This is an example of something printed!\n");
    return 0;
▼ }
```

6

▼ **Example 1 Output**

```
This is an example of something printed!
```

Example 2 Input

```
printf("This prints a character, %c\na number, %d\na floating \
point, %f\n", 'z', 123, 456.789 );
```

Example 2 Output

```
This prints a character, z
a number, 123
```
▲ ```
a floating point, 456.789
```

# Displaying Messages with puts()

The puts() function can also be used to display text messages onscreen, but it can't display numeric variables. The puts() function takes a single string as its argument and displays it, automatically adding a newline at the end. For example, the statement

```
puts("Hello, world.");
```

performs the same action as

```
printf("Hello, world.\n");
```

You can include escape sequences (including \n) in a string passed to puts(). They have the same effect as when they are used with printf() (see Table 6.1 for the most common escape sequences).

Just like printf(), any program that uses puts() should include the header file stdio.h. Note that stdio.h should be included only once in a program.

Do	**Don't**
DO use the puts() function instead of the printf() function whenever you want to print text but don't need to print any variables.	**DON'T** try to use conversion specifiers with the puts() statement.

▼ SYNTAX

The puts() Function

```
#include <stdio.h>
puts( string );
```

puts() is a function that copies a string to the standard output device, usually the display screen. When you use puts(), include the standard input/output header file (stdio.h).
```

▼ `puts()` also appends a newline character to the end of the string that is printed. The format string can contain escape sequences. Table 6.1 lists the most frequently used escape sequences.

The following are examples of calls to `puts()` and their output:

Example 1 Input

```
puts("This is printed with the puts() function!");
```

Example 1 Output

```
This is printed with the puts() function!
```

Example 2 Input

```
puts("This prints on the first line. \nThis prints on the second line.");
puts("This prints on the third line.");
puts("If these were printf()s, all four lines would be on two lines!");
```

Example 2 Output

```
This prints on the first line.
This prints on the second line.
This prints on the third line.
```
▲ `If these were printf()s, all four lines would be on two lines!`

Inputting Numeric Data with `scanf()`

Just as most programs need to output data to the screen, they also have to input data from the keyboard. The most flexible way your program can read numeric data from the keyboard is by using the `scanf()` library function.

The `scanf()` function reads data from the keyboard according to a specified format and assigns the input data to one or more program variables. Like `printf()`, `scanf()` uses a format string to describe the format of the input. The format string utilizes the same conversion specifiers as the `printf()` function. For example, the statement

```
scanf("%d", &x);
```

reads a decimal integer from the keyboard and assigns it to the integer variable x. Likewise, the following statement reads a floating-point value from the keyboard and assigns it to the variable rate:

```
scanf("%f", &rate);
```

What is that ampersand (&) before the variable's name? The & symbol is C's *address of* operator, which is fully explained on Day 8, "Understanding Pointers." For now, all you

6

have to remember is that scanf() requires the & symbol before each numeric variable name in its argument list (unless the variable is a pointer, which is also explained on Day 8).

A single scanf() can input more than one value if you include multiple conversion specifiers in the format string and variable names (again, each preceded by & in the argument list). The following statement inputs an integer value and a floating-point value and assigns them to the variables x and rate, respectively:

```
scanf("%d %f", &x, &rate);
```

When multiple variables are entered, scanf() uses whitespace to separate input into fields. Whitespace can be spaces, tabs, or new lines. Each conversion specifier in the scanf() format string is matched with an input field; the end of each input field is identified by whitespace.

This gives you considerable flexibility. In response to the preceding scanf(), you could enter

```
10 12.45
```

You also could enter this

```
10                    12.45
```

or this

```
10
12.45
```

As long as there's some whitespace between values, scanf() can assign each value to its variable.

As with the other functions discussed in today's lesson, programs that use scanf() must include the stdio.h header file. Although Listing 6.3 gives an example of using scanf(), a more complete description is presented on Day 15.

LISTING 6.3. Using scanf() to obtain numerical values.

```
1:    /* Demonstration of using scanf() */
2:
3:    #include <stdio.h>
4:
5:    #define QUIT 4
6:
7:    int get_menu_choice( void );
8:
9:    int main(void)
10:   {
```

```
11:        int    choice    = 0;
12:        int    int_var   = 0;
13:        float float_var = 0.0;
14:        unsigned unsigned_var = 0;
15:
16:        while (choice != QUIT)
17:        {
18:            choice = get_menu_choice();
19:
20:            if (choice == 1)
21:            {
22:                puts("\nEnter a signed decimal integer (i.e. -123)");
23:                scanf("%d", &int_var);
24:            }
25:            if (choice == 2)
26:            {
27:                puts("\nEnter a floating-point number        (e.g., 1.23)");
28:
29:                scanf("%f", &float_var);
30:            }
31:            if (choice == 3)
32:            {
33:                puts("\nEnter an unsigned decimal integer \
34                     (e.g. 123)" );
35:                scanf( "%u", &unsigned_var );
36:            }
37:        }
38:        printf("\nYour values are: int: %d  float: %f  unsigned: %u \n",
39:                                    int_var, float_var, unsigned_var );
40:
41:        return 0;
42:    }
43:
44:    int get_menu_choice( void )
45:    {
46:        int selection = 0;
47:
48:        do
49:        {
50:            puts( "\n1 - Get a signed decimal integer" );
51:            puts( "2 - Get a decimal floating-point number" );
52:            puts( "3 - Get an unsigned decimal integer" );
53:            puts( "4 - Quit" );
54:            puts( "\nEnter a selection:" );
55:
56:            scanf( "%d", &selection );
57:
58:        }while ( selection < 1 || selection > 4 );
59:
60:        return selection;
61:    }
```

continues

LISTING 6.3. continued

OUTPUT

```
1 - Get a signed decimal integer
2 - Get a decimal floating-point number
3 - Get an unsigned decimal integer
4 - Quit

Enter a selection:
1

Enter a signed decimal integer (e.g. -123)
-123

1 - Get a signed decimal integer
2 - Get a decimal floating-point number
3 - Get an unsigned decimal integer
4 - Quit

Enter a selection:
3

Enter an unsigned decimal integer (e.g. 123)
321

1 - Get a signed decimal integer
2 - Get a decimal floating-point number
3 - Get an unsigned decimal integer
4 - Quit

Enter a selection:
2

Enter a decimal floating point number (e.g. 1.23)
1231.123

1 - Get a signed decimal integer
2 - Get a decimal floating-point number
3 - Get an unsigned decimal integer
4 - Quit

Enter a selection:
4

Your values are: int: -123  float: 1231.123047 unsigned: 321
```

ANALYSIS   Listing 6.3 uses the same menu concepts used in Listing 6.1. The differences in get_menu_choice() (lines 44 through 61) are minor but should be noted. First, puts() is used instead of printf(). Because no variables are printed, there is no need to use printf(). Because puts() is being used, the newline escape characters have been removed from lines 51 through 53. Line 58 was also changed to allow values from 1 to 4 because there are now four menu options. Notice that line 56 has not changed; however, now it should make a little more sense. `scanf()` gets a decimal value and places it in the variable selection. The function returns `selection` to the calling program in line 60.

Listings 6.1 and 6.3 use the same `main()` structure. An `if` statement evaluates `choice`, the return value of `get_menu_choice()`. Based on `choice`'s value, the program prints a message, asks for a number to be entered, and reads the value using `scanf()`. Notice the difference between lines 23, 29, and 35. Each is set up to get a different type of variable. Lines 12 through 14 declare variables of the appropriate types.

When the user selects Quit, the program prints the last-entered number for all three types. If the user didn't enter a value, `0` is printed, because lines 12, 13, and 14 initialized all three types. One final note on lines 20 through 36: The `if` statements used here are not structured well. If you're thinking that an `if...else` structure would have been better, you're correct. Day 13, "Working with the Screen and Keyboard," introduces a new control statement, `switch`. This statement offers an even better option.

Do	Don't
DO use `printf()` or `puts()` in conjunction with `scanf()`. Use the printing functions to display a prompting message for the data you want `scanf()` to get.	DON'T forget to include the address of operator (&) when using `scanf()` variables.

The `scanf()` Function

▼ SYNTAX

```
#include <stdio.h>
scanf( format-string[,arguments,...]);
```

`scanf()` is a function that uses a conversion specifier in a given format-string to place values into variable arguments. The arguments should be the addresses of the variables instead of the actual variables themselves. For numeric variables, you can pass the address by putting the address of (&) operator at the beginning of the variable name. When using `scanf()`, you should include the stdio.h header file.

`scanf()` reads input fields from the standard input stream, usually the keyboard. It places each of these read fields into an argument. When it places the information, it converts it to the format of the corresponding specifier in the format string. For each argument, there must be a conversion specifier. Table 6.3 lists the most commonly needed conversion specifiers.

Example 1

```
int x, y, z;
scanf( "%d %d %d", &x, &y, &z );
```

6

▼ **Example 2**

```
#include <stdio.h>
int main(void)
{
    float y;
    int x;
    puts( "Enter a float, then an int" );
    scanf( "%f %d", &y, &x);
    printf( "\nYou entered %f and %d ", y, x );
    return 0;
▲ }
```

Summary

With the completion of today's lesson, you are ready to write your own C programs. By combining the printf(), puts(), and scanf() functions and the programming control statements you learned about in earlier days, you have the tools necessary to write simple programs.

Screen display is performed with the printf() and puts() functions. The puts() function can display text messages only, whereas printf() can display text messages and variables. Both functions use escape sequences for special characters and printing controls.

The scanf() function reads one or more numeric values from the keyboard and interprets each one according to a conversion specifier. Each value is assigned to a program variable.

Q&A

Q Why should I use puts() if printf() does everything puts() does and more?

A Because printf() does more, it has additional overhead. When you're trying to write a small, efficient program, or when your programs grow large and resources become valuable, you will want to take advantage of the smaller overhead of puts(). In general, you should use the simplest available resource.

Q Why do I have to include stdio.h when I use printf(), puts(), or scanf()?

A stdio.h contains the prototypes for the standard input/output functions. printf(), puts(), and scanf() are three of these standard functions. Try running a program without the stdio.h header, and see the errors and warnings you get.

Q What happens if I omit the address of operator (&) from a scanf() variable?

A This is an easy mistake to make. Unpredictable results can occur if you forget the address of operator. When you read about pointers on Days 9 and 13, you will

understand this better. For now, know that if you omit the address of operator, `scanf()` doesn't place the entered information in your variable, but in some other place in memory instead. This could do anything from apparently having no effect to making your program exit with an error. Fortunately, if you tell gcc to display all warning messages, it will tell you when you have forgotten to use the address of operator in a call to `scanf()`.

Workshop

The Workshop provides quiz questions to help you solidify your understanding of the material covered and exercises to provide you with experience in using what you've learned. The answers to the quiz and exercises are provided in Appendix C, "Answers."

Quiz

1. What is the difference between `puts()` and `printf()`?

2. What header file should you include when you use `printf()`?

3. What do the following escape sequences do?

    a. \\

    b. \b

    c. \n

    d. \t

    e. \a

4. What conversion specifiers should be used to print the following?

    a. A character string

    b. A signed decimal integer

    c. A decimal floating-point number

5. What is the difference between using each of the following in the literal text of `puts()`?

    a. b

    b. \b

    c. \

    d. \\

6

Exercises

Note

Starting with today's lesson, some of the exercises ask you to write complete programs that perform a particular task. Because there is always more than one way to do things in C, the answers provided at the back of the book shouldn't be interpreted as the only correct ones. If you can write your own code that performs what's required, great! If you have trouble, refer to the answer for help. The answers are presented with minimal comments because it's good practice for you to figure out how they operate.

1. Write both a `printf()` and a `puts()` statement to start a new line.

2. Write a `scanf()` statement that could be used to get a character, an unsigned decimal integer, and another single character.

3. Write the statements to get an integer value and print it.

4. Modify exercise 3 so that it accepts only even values (2, 4, 6, and so on).

5. Modify exercise 4 so that it returns values until the number 99 is entered, or until six even values have been entered. Store the numbers in an array. (Hint: You need a loop.)

6. Turn exercise 5 into an executable program. Add a function that prints the values, separated by tabs, in the array on a single line. (Print only the values that were entered into the array.)

7. **BUG BUSTER:** Find the error(s) in the following code fragment:

   ```
   printf( "Jack said, "Peter Piper picked a peck of pickled peppers."");
   ```

8. **BUG BUSTER:** Find the error(s) in the following program:

   ```
   int get_1_or_2( void )
   {
       int answer = 0;
       while (answer < 1 ¦¦ answer > 2)
       {
           printf(Enter 1 for Yes, 2 for No);
           scanf( "%f", answer );
       }
       return answer;
   }
   ```

9. Using Listing 6.1, complete the `print_report()` function so that it prints the rest of Table 6.1.

10. Write a program that inputs two floating-point values from the keyboard and then displays their product.

11. Write a program that inputs 10 integer values from the keyboard and then displays their sum.

12. Write a program that inputs integers from the keyboard, storing them in an array. Input should stop when a zero is entered or when the end of the array is reached. Then, find and display the array's largest and smallest values. (Note: This is a tough problem because arrays haven't been completely covered in this book yet. If you have difficulty, try solving this problem again after reading Day 7, "Using Numeric Arrays.")

6

DAY 7

Using Numeric Arrays

Arrays are a type of data storage that you often use in C programs. You had a brief introduction to arrays on Day 5, "Basic Program Control." Today you will learn

- What an array is
- The definition of single-dimensional and multidimensional numeric arrays
- How to declare and initialize arrays

What Is an Array?

NEW TERM An *array* is a collection of data storage locations, each having the same data type and the same name. Each storage location in an array is called an *array element*. Why do you need arrays in your programs? This question can be answered with an example. If you're keeping track of your business expenses for 2001 and filing your receipts by month, you could have a separate folder for each month's receipts, but it would be more convenient to have a single folder with 12 compartments.

Extend this example to computer programming. Imagine that you're designing a program to keep track of your business expenses. The program could declare 12 separate variables, one for each month's expense total. This approach is analogous to having 12 separate folders for your receipts. Good programming practice, however, would utilize an array with 12 elements, storing each month's total in the corresponding array element. This approach is comparable to filing your receipts in a single folder with 12 compartments. Figure 7.1 illustrates the difference between using individual variables and an array.

FIGURE 7.1.

Variables are like individual folders, whereas an array is like a single folder with many compartments.

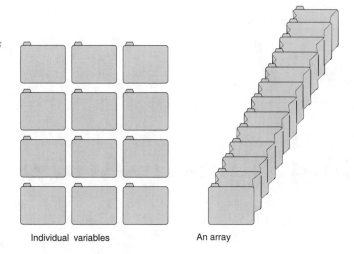

Individual variables   An array

Single-Dimensional Arrays

NEW TERM A *single-dimensional array* has only a single subscript. A *subscript* is a number in brackets that follows an array's name. This number can identify the number of individual elements in the array. An example should make this clear. For the business expenses program, you could use the following line to declare an array of type `float`:

```
float expenses[12];
```

The array is named `expenses`, and it contains 12 elements. Each of the 12 elements is the exact equivalent of a single `float` variable. All of C's data types can be used for arrays. C array elements are always numbered starting at 0, so the 12 elements of expenses are numbered 0 through 11. In the preceding example, January's expense total would be stored in `expenses[0]`, February's in `expenses[1]`, and so on.

When you declare an array, the compiler sets aside a block of memory large enough to hold the entire array. Individual array elements are stored in sequential memory locations, as shown in Figure 7.2.

FIGURE 7.2.

Array elements are stored in sequential memory locations.

`int array[10];`

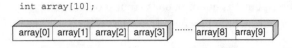

The location of array declarations in your source code is important. As with nonarray variables, the declaration's location affects how your program can use the array. The effect of a declaration's location is covered in more detail on Day 11, "Understanding Variable Scope." For now, place your array declarations with other variable declarations.

An array element can be used in your program anywhere a nonarray variable of the same type can be used. Individual elements of the array are accessed by using the array name followed by the element subscript enclosed in square brackets. For example, the following statement stores the value 89.95 in the second array element (remember, the first array element is expenses[0], not expenses[1]):

```
expenses[1] = 89.95;
```

Likewise, the statement

```
expenses[10] = expenses[11];
```

assigns a copy of the value that is stored in array element expenses[11] into array element expenses[10]. When you refer to an array element, the array subscript can be a literal constant, as in these examples. However, your programs might often use a subscript that is a C integer variable or expression, or even another array element. Here are some examples:

```
float expenses[100];
int a[10];
/* additional statements go here */
expenses[i] = 100;          /* i is an integer variable */
expenses[2 + 3] = 100;      /* equivalent to expenses[5] */
expenses[a[2]] = 100;       /* a[] is an integer array */
```

That last example might need an explanation. If, for instance, you have an integer array named a[] and the value 8 is stored in element a[2], writing

```
expenses[a[2]]
```

has the same effect as writing

```
expenses[8];
```

When you use arrays, keep the element numbering scheme in mind: In an array of *n* elements, the allowable subscripts range from 0 to *n*–1. If you use the subscript value *n,* you might get program errors. The C compiler doesn't recognize whether your program uses

7

an array subscript that is out of bounds. Your program compiles and links, but out-of-range subscripts generally produce erroneous results.

 Caution   Remember that array elements start with 0, not 1. Also remember that the last element is one less than the number of elements in the array. For example, an array with 10 elements contains elements 0 through 9.

Sometimes you might want to treat an array of *n* elements as if its elements were numbered 1 through *n*. For instance, in the previous example, a more natural method might be to store January's expense total in expenses[1], February's in expenses[2], and so on. The simplest way to do this is to declare the array with one more element than needed and ignore element 0. In this case, you would declare the array as follows. You could also store some related data in element 0 (the yearly expense total, perhaps).

```
float expenses[13];
```

The program expenses.c in Listing 7.1 demonstrates the use of an array. This is a simple program with no real practical use; however, it helps demonstrate the use of an array.

LISTING 7.1. expenses.c demonstrates the use of an array.

```
1:    /* expenses.c - Demonstrates use of an array */
2:
3:    #include <stdio.h>
4:
5:    /* Declare an array to hold expenses, and a counter variable */
6:
7:    float expenses[13];
8:    int count;
9:
10:   int main(void)
11:   {
12:       /* Input data from keyboard into array */
13:
14:       for (count = 1; count < 13; count++)
15:       {
16:           printf("Enter expenses for month %d: ", count);
17:           scanf("%f", &expenses[count]);
18:       }
19:
20:       /* Print array contents */
21:
22:       for (count = 1; count < 13; count++)
23:       {
24:           printf("Month %d = $%.2f\n", count, expenses[count]);
```

```
25:        }
26:      return 0;
27:  }
```

```
Enter expenses for month 1: 100
Enter expenses for month 2: 200.12
Enter expenses for month 3: 150.50
Enter expenses for month 4: 300
Enter expenses for month 5: 100.50
Enter expenses for month 6: 34.25
Enter expenses for month 7: 45.75
Enter expenses for month 8: 195.00
Enter expenses for month 9: 123.45
Enter expenses for month 10: 111.11
Enter expenses for month 11: 222.20
Enter expenses for month 12: 120.00
Month 1 = $100.00
Month 2 = $200.12
Month 3 = $150.50
Month 4 = $300.00
Month 5 = $100.50
Month 6 = $34.25
Month 7 = $45.75
Month 8 = $195.00
Month 9 = $123.45
Month 10 = $111.11
Month 11 = $222.20
Month 12 = $120.00
```

ANALYSIS When you run expenses.c, the program prompts you to enter expenses for months 1 through 12. The values you enter are stored in an array. You must enter a value for each month. After the twelfth value is entered, the array contents are displayed onscreen.

The flow of the program is similar to listings you've seen before. Line 1 starts with a comment that describes what the program does. Notice that the name of the program, expenses.c, is included. When the name of the program is included in a comment, you know which program you're viewing. This is helpful when you're reviewing printouts of a listing.

Line 5 contains an additional comment explaining the variables that are being declared. In line 7, an array of 13 elements is declared. In this program, only 12 elements are needed, one for each month, but 13 have been declared. The for loop in lines 14 through 18 ignores element 0. This lets the program use elements 1 through 12, which relate directly to the 12 months. Going back to line 8, a variable, count, is declared and is used throughout the program as a counter and an array index.

7

The program's main() function begins on line 10. As stated earlier, this program uses a for loop to print a message and accept a value for each of the 12 months. Notice that in line 17, the scanf() function uses an array element. In line 7, the expenses array is declared as float, so %f is used. The address-of operator (&) also is placed before the array element, just as if it were a regular type float variable and not an array element.

Lines 22 through 25 contain a second for loop that prints the values just entered. An additional formatting command has been added to the printf() function so that the expenses values print in a more orderly fashion. For now, know that %.2f prints a floating number with two digits to the right of the decimal. Additional formatting commands are covered in more detail on Day 13, "Working with the Screen and Keyboard."

Do	Don't
DO use arrays instead of creating several variables that store the same thing. For example, if you want to store total sales for each month of the year, create an array with 12 elements to hold sales rather than creating a sales variable for each month.	DON'T forget that array subscripts start at element 0.

Multidimensional Arrays

A multidimensional array has more than one subscript. A two-dimensional array has two subscripts, a three-dimensional array has three subscripts, and so on. There is no limit to the number of dimensions a C array can have. (There *is* a limit on total array size, as discussed later in today's lesson.)

For example, you might write a program that plays checkers. The checkerboard contains 64 squares arranged in eight rows and eight columns. Your program could represent the board as a two-dimensional array, as follows:

```
int checker[8][8];
```

The resulting array has 64 elements: checker[0][0], checker[0][1], checker[0][2],...,checker[7][6], checker[7][7]. The structure of this two-dimensional array is illustrated in Figure 7.3.

FIGURE 7.3.

A two-dimensional array has a row-and-column structure.

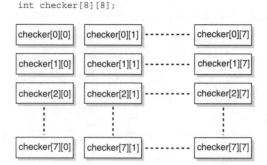

```
int checker[8][8];
```

Similarly, a three-dimensional array could be thought of as a cube. Four-dimensional arrays (and higher) are probably best left to your imagination. All arrays, no matter how many dimensions they have, are stored sequentially in memory. More detail on array storage is presented on Day 14, "Pointers: Beyond the Basics."

Naming and Declaring Arrays

The rules for assigning names to arrays are the same as for variable names, covered in the section "Storing Data: Variables and Constants" on Day 2, "The Components of a C Program: Code and Data." An array name must be unique. It can't be used for another array or for any other identifier (variable, constant, and so on). As you have probably realized, array declarations follow the same form as declarations of nonarray variables, except that the number of elements in the array must be enclosed in square brackets immediately following the array name.

When you declare an array, you can specify the number of elements with a literal constant (as was done in the earlier examples) or with a symbolic constant created with the #define directive. Thus the following:

```
#define MONTHS 12
int array[MONTHS];
```

is equivalent to this statement:

```
int array[12];
```

Unlike many compilers, gcc allows you to declare an array's elements with a symbolic constant created with the const keyword:

```
const int MONTHS = 12;
int array[MONTHS];          /* Dangerous! */
```

7

Since this feature may not work on other compilers, you should use care if you want to compile your code on a compiler other than gcc. You might tell gcc to issue warning messages about the use of non-standard gcc features by using the -pedantic option (see the section on gcc in Day 1, "Introduction to Linux and the C Programming Language").

Listing 7.2, grades.c, is another program demonstrating the use of a single-dimensional array. The grades.c program uses an array to store 10 grades.

LISTING **7.2**. grades.c stores 10 grades in an array.

```
 1:    /*grades.c - Sample program with array */
 2:    /* Get 10 grades and then average them */
 3:
 4:    #include <stdio.h>
 5:
 6:    #define MAX_GRADE 100
 7:    #define STUDENTS   10
 8:
 9:    int grades[STUDENTS];
10:
11:    int idx;
12:    int total = 0;              /* used for average */
13:
14:    int main(void)
15:    {
16:        for( idx=0;idx< STUDENTS;idx++)
17:        {
18:            printf( "Enter Person %d's grade: ", idx +1);
19:            scanf( "%d", &grades[idx] );
20:
21:            while ( grades[idx] > MAX_GRADE )
22:            {
23:                printf( "\nThe highest grade possible is %d",
24                     MAX_GRADE );
25:                printf( "\nEnter correct grade: " );
26:                scanf( "%d", &grades[idx] );
27:            }
28:
29:            total += grades[idx];
30:        }
31:
32:        printf( "\n\nThe average score is %d\n", ( total / STUDENTS) );
33:
34:        return (0);
35:    }
```

```
Enter Person 1's grade: 95
Enter Person 2's grade: 100
Enter Person 3's grade: 60
Enter Person 4's grade: 105

The highest grade possible is 100
Enter correct grade: 100
Enter Person 5's grade: 25
Enter Person 6's grade: 0
Enter Person 7's grade: 85
Enter Person 8's grade: 85
Enter Person 9's grade: 95
Enter Person 10's grade: 85

The average score is 73
```

ANALYSIS   Like expenses.c, this listing prompts the user for input. It prompts for 10 people's grades. Instead of printing each grade, it prints the average score.

As you learned earlier, arrays are named like regular variables. On line 9, the array for this program is named grades. It should be safe to assume that this array holds grades. On lines 6 and 7, two constants, MAX_GRADE and STUDENTS, are defined. These constants can be changed easily. Knowing that STUDENTS is defined as 10, you then know that the grades array has 10 elements. Two other variables are declared, idx and total. An abbreviation of *index,* idx is used as a counter and array subscript. A running total of all grades is kept in total.

The heart of this program is the for loop in lines 16 through 30. The for statement initializes idx to 0, the first subscript for an array. It then loops as long as idx is less than the number of students. Each time it loops, it increments idx by 1. For each loop, the program prompts for a person's grade (lines 18 and 19). Notice that in line 18, 1 is added to idx in order to count the people from 1 to 10 instead of from 0 to 9. Because arrays start with subscript 0, the first grade is put in grade[0]. Instead of confusing users by asking for Person 0's grade, they are asked for Person 1's grade.

Lines 21 through 27 contain a while loop nested within the for loop. This is an edit check that ensures that the grade isn't higher than the maximum grade, MAX_GRADE. Users are prompted to enter a correct grade if they enter a grade that is too high. You should check program data whenever you can.

Line 29 adds the entered grade to a total counter. In line 32, this total is used to print the average score (total/STUDENTS).

7

Do	Don't
DO use #define statements to create constants that can be used when declaring arrays. Then you can easily change the number of elements in the array. In grades.c, for example, you could change the number of students in the #define, and you wouldn't have to make any other changes in the program.	
DO avoid multidimensional arrays with more than three dimensions. Remember, multidimensional arrays can become very big very quickly.	

Initializing Arrays

You can initialize all or part of an array when you first declare it. Follow the array declaration with an equal sign and a list of values enclosed in braces and separated by commas. The listed values are assigned in order to array elements starting at number 0.

Consider the following code:

```
int array[4] = { 100, 200, 300, 400 };
```

For this example, the value 100 is assigned to array[0], the value 200 is assigned to array[1], the value 300 is assigned to array[2], and the value 400 is assigned to array[3].

If you omit the array size, the compiler creates an array just large enough to hold the initialization values. Thus, the following statement would have exactly the same effect as the previous array declaration statement:

```
int array[] = { 100, 200, 300, 400 };
```

You can, however, include too few initialization values, as in this example:

```
int array[10] = { 1, 2, 3 };
```

If you don't explicitly initialize an array element, you can't be sure what value it holds when the program runs. If you include too many initializers (more initializers than array elements), the compiler detects an error.

Initializing Multidimensional Arrays

Multidimensional arrays can also be initialized. The list of initialization values is assigned to array elements in order, with the last array subscript changing first. For example,

```
int array[4][3] = { 1, 2, 3, 4, 5, 6, 7, 8, 9, 10, 11, 12 };
```

results in the following assignments:

```
array[0][0] is equal to 1
array[0][1] is equal to 2
array[0][2] is equal to 3
array[1][0] is equal to 4
array[1][1] is equal to 5
array[1][2] is equal to 6
...
array[3][1] is equal to 11
array[3][2] is equal to 12
```

When you initialize multidimensional arrays, you can make your source code clearer by using extra braces to group the initialization values and also by spreading them over several lines. The following initialization is equivalent to the one just given:

```
int array[4][3] = { { 1, 2, 3 } , { 4, 5, 6 } ,
{ 7, 8, 9 } , { 10, 11, 12 } };
```

Remember, initialization values must be separated by a comma—even when there is a brace between them. Also, be sure to use braces in pairs—a closing brace for every opening brace—or the compiler becomes confused.

Now look at an example that demonstrates the advantages of arrays. Listing 7.3, random.c, creates a 1,000-element, three-dimensional array and fills it with random numbers. The program then displays the array elements onscreen. Imagine how many lines of source code you would need to perform the same task with nonarray variables.

You see a new library function, getchar(), in this program. The getchar() function reads a single character from the keyboard. In Listing 7.3, getchar() pauses the program until the user presses the Enter key. The getchar() function is covered in detail on Day 13.

LISTING 7.3. random.c creates a multidimensional array.

```
1:   /* random.c - Demonstrates using a multidimensional array */
2:
3:   #include <stdio.h>
4:   #include <stdlib.h>
5:   /* Declare a three-dimensional array with 1000 elements */
6:
```

7

continues

LISTING 7.3. continued

```
7:    int random_array[10][10][10];
8:    int a, b, c;
9:
10:   int main(void)
11:   {
12:       /* Fill the array with random numbers. The C library */
13:       /* function rand() returns a random number. Use one */
14:       /* for loop for each array subscript. */
15:
16:       for (a = 0; a < 10; a++)
17:       {
18:           for (b = 0; b < 10; b++)
19:           {
20:               for (c = 0; c < 10; c++)
21:               {
22:                   random_array[a][b][c] = rand();
23:               }
24:           }
25:       }
26:
27:       /* Now display the array elements 10 at a time */
28:
29:       for (a = 0; a < 10; a++)
30:       {
31:           for (b = 0; b < 10; b++)
32:           {
33:               for (c = 0; c < 10; c++)
34:               {
35:                   printf("\nrandom_array[%d][%d][%d] = ", a, b, c);
36:                   printf("%d", random_array[a][b][c]);
37:               }
38:               printf("\nPress Enter to continue, CTRL-C to quit.");
39:
40:               getchar();
41:           }
42:       }
43:       return 0;
44:   }   /* end of main() */
```

OUTPUT
```
random_array[0][0][0] = 346
random_array[0][0][1] = 130
random_array[0][0][2] = 10982
random_array[0][0][3] = 1090
random_array[0][0][4] = 11656
random_array[0][0][5] = 7117
random_array[0][0][6] = 17595
random_array[0][0][7] = 6415
random_array[0][0][8] = 22948
random_array[0][0][9] = 31126
Press Enter to continue, CTRL-C to quit.
```

```
random_array[0][1][0] = 9004
random_array[0][1][1] = 14558
random_array[0][1][2] = 3571
random_array[0][1][3] = 22879
random_array[0][1][4] = 18492
random_array[0][1][5] = 1360
random_array[0][1][6] = 5412
random_array[0][1][7] = 26721
random_array[0][1][8] = 22463
random_array[0][1][9] = 25047
Press Enter to continue, CTRL-C to quit
...        ...
random_array[9][8][0] = 6287
random_array[9][8][1] = 26957
random_array[9][8][2] = 1530
random_array[9][8][3] = 14171
random_array[9][8][4] = 6951
random_array[9][8][5] = 213
random_array[9][8][6] = 14003
random_array[9][8][7] = 29736
random_array[9][8][8] = 15028
random_array[9][8][9] = 18968
Press Enter to continue, CTRL-C to quit.

random_array[9][9][0] = 28559
random_array[9][9][1] = 5268
random_array[9][9][2] = 20182
random_array[9][9][3] = 3633
random_array[9][9][4] = 24779
random_array[9][9][5] = 3024
random_array[9][9][6] = 10853
random_array[9][9][7] = 28205
random_array[9][9][8] = 8930
random_array[9][9][9] = 2873
Press Enter to continue, CTRL-C to quit.
```

ANALYSIS On Day 5 you saw a program that used a nested for statement; this program has two nested for loops. Before you look at the for statements in detail, note that lines 7 and 8 declare four variables. The first is an array named random_array, which is used to hold random numbers. random_array is a three-dimensional type int array that is 10-by-10-by-10, giving a total of 1,000 type int elements (10×10×10). Imagine coming up with 1,000 unique variable names if you couldn't use arrays! Line 8 then declares three variables, a, b, and c, which are used to control the for loops.

This program also includes the header file stdlib.h (for standard library) on line 4. It is included to provide the prototype for the rand() function used on line 22.

7

The bulk of the program is contained in two nests of `for` statements. The first is in lines 16 through 25, and the second is in lines 29 through 42. Both `for` nests have the same structure. They work just like the loops in Listing 5.2, but they go one level deeper. In the first set of `for` statements, line 22 is executed repeatedly. Line 22 assigns the return value of a function, `rand()`, to an element of the `random_array` array, where `rand()` is a library function that returns a random number.

Going backward through the listing, you can see that line 20 changes variable c from 0 to 9. This loops through the farthest right subscript of the `random_array` array. Line 18 loops through b, the middle subscript of the random array. Each time b changes, it loops through all the c elements. Line 16 increments variable a, which loops through the farthest left subscript. Each time this subscript changes, it loops through all 10 values of subscript b, which in turn loop through all 10 values of c. This loop initializes every value in `random_array` to a random number.

Lines 29 through 42 contain the second nest of `for` statements. These work like the previous `for` statements, but this loop prints each of the values assigned previously. After 10 are displayed, line 38 prints a message and waits for Enter to be pressed. Line 40 takes care of the keypress by using `getchar()`. If Enter hasn't been pressed, `getchar()` waits until it is. Run this program and watch the displayed values.

Maximum Array Size

The maximum size of an array under Linux is limited only by the amount of space you have in your computer. As a programmer, you do not need to concern yourself with how this works; the operating system does whatever is required without any intervention from you.

The size of an array in bytes depends on the number of elements it has, as well as each element's size. Element size depends on the data type of the array and your computer. The sizes for each numeric data type, given in Table 3.2, are repeated in Table 7.1 for your convenience. These are the data type sizes for many PCs.

TABLE 7.1. Storage space requirements for numeric data types for many PCs.

Element Data Type	Element Size (Bytes)
int	4
short	2
long	4
float	4
double	8

To calculate the storage space required for an array, multiply the number of elements in the array by the element size. For example, a 500-element array of type float requires storage space of 500×4 = 2000 bytes.

You can determine storage space within a program by using C's sizeof() operator; sizeof() is a unary operator, not a function. It takes as its argument a variable name or the name of a data type and returns the size, in bytes, of that argument. The use of sizeof() is illustrated in Listing 7.4.

LISTING 7.4. Using the sizeof() operator to determine storage space requirements for an array.

```
11 : /* Demonstrates the sizeof() operator */
2 : #include <stdio.h>
3 :
4 : /* Declare several 100 element arrays */
5 :
6 : int intarray[100];
7 : long longarray[100];
8 : float floatarray[100];
9 : double doublearray[100];
10:
11: int main(void)
12: {
13:     /* Display the sizes of numeric data types */
14:
15:     printf("\nSize of short = %d bytes", (int) sizeof(short));
16:     printf("\nSize of int = %d bytes", (int) sizeof(int));
17:     printf("\nSize of long = %d bytes", (int) sizeof(long));
18:     printf("\nSize of float = %d bytes", (int) sizeof(float));
19:     printf("\nSize of double = %d bytes", (int) sizeof(double));
20:
21:     /* Display the sizes of the three arrays */
22:
23:     printf("\nSize of intarray = %d bytes", (int) sizeof(intarray));
24:     printf("\nSize of longarray = %d bytes", (int) sizeof(longarray));
25:     printf("\nSize of floatarray = %d bytes",
26:             (int) sizeof(floatarray));
27:     printf("\nSize of doublearray = %d bytes\n",
28:             (int) sizeof(doublearray));
29:
30:     return 0;
31: }
```

The following output is from a 32-bit Linux machine using an Intel Pentium processor:

OUTPUT
```
Size of short = 2 bytes
Size of int = 4 bytes
Size of long = 4 bytes
```

7

```
Size of float = 4 bytes
Size of double = 8 bytes
Size of intarray = 400 bytes
Size of longarray = 400 bytes
Size of floatarray = 400 bytes
Size of doublearray = 800 bytes
```

A 64-bit Linux machine using a DEC/Compaq Alpha processor produces the following output:

OUTPUT
```
Size of short = 2 bytes
Size of int = 4 bytes
Size of long = 8 bytes
Size of float = 4 bytes
Size of double = 8 bytes
Size of intarray = 400 bytes
Size of longarray = 800 bytes
Size of floatarray = 400 bytes
Size of doublearray = 800 bytes
```

ANALYSIS Enter and compile the program in this listing by using the procedures you learned on Day 1. When the program runs, it displays the sizes—in bytes—of the three arrays and five numeric data types.

This program is similar to the program sizeof.c you ran on Day 2. However, this listing uses sizeof() to determine the storage size of arrays. Lines 7, 8, and 9 declare three arrays, each of a different type. Lines 23 through 27 print the size of each array. The size should equal the size of the array's variable type times the number of elements. For example, if an int is 4 bytes, intarray should be 4×100, or 400 bytes. Run the program and check the values. As you can see from the output, different machines or operating systems might have different-sized data types.

Summary

Today's lesson introduced numeric arrays, a powerful data storage method that lets you group a number of same-type data items under the same group name. Individual items, or elements, in an array are identified using a subscript after the array name. Computer programming tasks that involve repetitive data processing lend themselves to array storage.

Like nonarray variables, arrays must be declared before they can be used. Optionally, array elements can be initialized when the array is declared.

Q&A

Q What happens if I use a subscript on an array that is larger than the number of elements in the array?

A If you use a subscript that is out of bounds with the array declaration, the program will probably compile and even run. However, the results of such a mistake can be unpredictable. This can be a difficult error to find after it starts causing problems, so make sure you're careful when initializing and accessing array elements.

Q What happens if I use an array without initializing it?

A This mistake doesn't produce a compiler error. If you don't initialize an array, there can be any value in the array elements. You might get unpredictable results. You should always initialize variables and arrays so that you know exactly what's in them. Day 11 introduces you to one exception to the need to initialize. For now, play it safe.

Q How many dimensions can an array have?

A As stated in today's lesson, you can have as many dimensions as you want. As you add more dimensions, you use more data storage space. You should declare an array only as large as you need to avoid wasting storage space.

Q Is there an easy way to initialize an entire array at once?

A Each element of an array must be initialized. The safest way for a beginning C programmer to initialize an array is either with a declaration, as shown today, or with a `for` statement. There are other ways to initialize an array, but they are beyond the scope of this book.

Q Can I add two arrays together (or multiply, divide, or subtract them)?

A If you declare two arrays, you can't add the two together. Each element must be added individually. Exercise 10 illustrates this point.

Q Why is it better to use an array instead of individual variables?

A With arrays, you can group like values with a single name. In Listing 7.3, 1,000 values were stored. Creating 1,000 variable names and initializing each to a random number would have taken a tremendous amount of typing. By using an array, you made the task easy.

Q What do I do if I don't know how big the array needs to be when I'm writing the program?

A There are functions within C that let you allocate space for variables and arrays on-the-fly. These functions are covered on Day 14.

7

Workshop

The Workshop provides quiz questions to help you solidify your understanding of the material covered and exercises to provide you with experience in using what you've learned. The answers to the quiz and exercises are provided in Appendix C, "Answers."

Quiz

1. Which of C's data types can be used in an array?

2. If an array is declared with 10 elements, what is the subscript of the first element?

3. In a one-dimensional array declared with *n* elements, what is the subscript of the last element?

4. What happens if your program tries to access an array element with an out-of-range subscript?

5. How do you declare a multidimensional array?

6. An array is declared with the following statement. How many total elements does the array have?

    ```
    int array[2][3][5][8];
    ```

7. What would be the name of the tenth element in the array in question 6?

Exercises

1. Write a C program line that would declare three one-dimensional integer arrays, named one, two, and three, with 1,000 elements each.

2. Write the statement that would declare a 10-element integer array and initialize all its elements to 1.

3. Given the following array, write code to initialize all the array elements to 88:

    ```
    int eightyeight[88];
    ```

4. Given the following array, write code to initialize all the array elements to 0:

    ```
    int stuff[12][10];
    ```

5. **BUG BUSTER:** What is wrong with the following code fragment?

    ```
    int x, y;
    int array[10][3];
    int main(void)
    {
        for ( x = 0; x < 3; x++ )
            for ( y = 0; y < 10; y++ )
                array[x][y] = 0;
        return 0;
    }
    ```

6. **BUG BUSTER:** What is wrong with the following?

```
int array[10];
int x = 1;

int main(void)
{
   for ( x = 1; x <= 10; x++ )
      array[x] = 99;
   .
   return 0;
}
```

7. Write a program that puts random numbers into a two-dimensional array that is 5-by-4. Print the values in columns onscreen. (Hint: Use the rand() function from Listing 7.3.)

8. Rewrite Listing 7.3 to use a single-dimensional array of type short. Print the average of the 1,000 variables before printing the individual values. (Note: Don't forget to pause after every 10 values are printed.)

9. Write a program that initializes an array of 10 elements. Each element should be equal to its subscript. The program should then print each of the 10 elements.

10. Modify the program from exercise 9. After printing the initialized values, the program should copy the values to a new array and add 10 to each value. The new array values should be printed.

11. You have now seen a number of features of the GNU C compiler that are not part of the ANSI C Standard. Using your GNU info viewer of choice, read more about these features in the "C Extensions" section of the gcc info pages.

WEEK 1

In Review

After finishing your first week of learning to program in C, you should feel comfortable entering programs and using your editor and compiler. The following program pulls together many of the topics from the first week.

You will find that this section is different from the Type & Run programs you have done before. After you look through the listing, you will see that analysis has been included. You will find that every topic in this listing has been covered in the preceding days. You will find similar Weeks in Review after Week 2 and Week 3.

```
1 : /* Program Name: week1.c
➥*/
2 : /*                program to enter the ages and
➥incomes of up */
3 : /*                to 100 people.  The program prints
➥a report */
4 : /*                based on the numbers entered.
*/
5 : /*-------------------------------------------------
➥----------*/
6 : /*-------------------*/
7 : /* included files    */
8 : /*-------------------*/
9 : #include <stdio.h>
10:
11: /*-------------------*/
12: /* defined constants */
13: /*-------------------*/
14:
15: #define MAX    100
16: #define YES    1
17: #define NO     0
18:
19: /*-------------------*/
20: /* variables         */
21: /*-------------------*/
```

```
22:
23: long    income[MAX]; /* to hold incomes      */
24: int     month[MAX], day[MAX], year[MAX]; /* to hold birthdays */
25: int        ctr;   /* For counting         */
26:
27: /*-------------------*/
28: /* function prototypes*/
29: /*-------------------*/
30:
31: int display_instructions(void);
32: void get_data(void);
33: void display_report(void);
34: int continue_function(void);
35:
36: /*-------------------*/
37: /* start of program   */
38: /*-------------------*/
39:
40: int main(void)
41: {
42:     int cont; /* For program control */
43:
44:     cont = display_instructions();
45:
46:     if ( cont == YES )
47:     {
48:         get_data();
49:         display_report();
50:     }
51:     else
52:         printf( "\nProgram Aborted by User!\n\n");
53:
54:     return 0;
55: }
56: /*------------------------------------------------------------*
57:  * Function:  display_instructions()                         *
58:  * Purpose:   This function displays information on how to    *
59:  *            use this program and asks the user to enter 0   *
60:  *            to quit, or 1 to continue.                      *
61:  * Returns:   NO  - if the user enters 0                      *
62:  *            YES - if the user enters any number other than 0*
63:  *------------------------------------------------------------*/
64:
65: int display_instructions( void )
66: {
67:     int cont;
68:
69:     printf("\n\n");
70:     printf("\nThis program enables you to enter up to 99 people\'s ");
71:     printf("\nincomes and birthdays.  It then prints the incomes by");
```

```
72:      printf("\nmonth along with the overall income and overall average.");
73:      printf("\n");
74:
75:      cont = continue_function();
76:
77:      return cont;
78: }
79: /*------------------------------------------------------------*
80:  *  Function:  get_data()                                     *
81:  *  Purpose: This function gets the data from the user. It    *
82:  *           continues to get data until either 100 people are *
83:  *           entered, or until the user enters 0 for the month.*
84:  *  Returns: nothing                                          *
85:  *  Notes:   This allows 0/0/0 to be entered for birthdays in *
86:  *           case the user is unsure.  It also allows for 31   *
87:  *           days in each month.                              *
88:  *------------------------------------------------------------*/
89:
90: void get_data(void)
91: {
92:      int cont;
93:
94:      for ( cont = YES, ctr = 0; ctr < MAX && cont == YES; ctr++ )
95:      {
96:          printf("\nEnter information for Person %d.", ctr+1 );
97:          printf("\n\tEnter Birthday:");
98:
99:          do
100:          {
101:              printf("\n\tMonth (0 - 12): ");
102:              scanf("%d", &month[ctr]);
103:          } while (month[ctr] < 0 || month[ctr] > 12 );
104:
105:          do
106:          {
107:              printf("\n\tDay (0 - 31): ");
108:              scanf("%d", &day[ctr]);
109:          } while ( day[ctr] <  0 || day[ctr] > 31 );
110:
111:          do
112:          {
113:              printf("\n\tYear (0 - 1997): ");
114:              scanf("%d", &year[ctr]);
115:          } while ( year[ctr] < 0 || year[ctr] > 1997 );
116:
117:          printf("\nEnter Yearly Income (whole dollars): ");
118:          scanf("%ld", &income[ctr]);
119:
120:          cont = continue_function();
121:      }
```

```
122:      /* ctr equals the number of people that were entered.    */
123:
124:      return;
125: }
126: /*------------------------------------------------------------*
127:  * Function: display_report()                                 *
128:  * Purpose:  This function displays a report to the screen     *
129:  * Returns:  nothing                                          *
130:  * Notes:    More information could be printed.               *
131:  *------------------------------------------------------------*/
132:
133: void display_report()
134: {
135:      int    x, y;   /* For counting */
136:      int    month_total, grand_total;  /* For totals        */
137:
138:
139:      grand_total = 0;
140:      printf("\n\n\n");                        /* skip a few lines   */
141:      printf("\n        SALARY SUMMARY");
142:      printf("\n        ==============");
143:
144:      for( x = 0; x <= 12; x++ )   /* for each month, including 0*/
145:      {
146:          month_total = 0;
147:          for( y = 0; y < ctr; y++ )
148:          {
149:              if( month[y] == x )
150:                  month_total += income[y];
151:          }
152:          printf("\nTotal for month %d is %d", x, month_total);
153:          grand_total += month_total;
154:      }
155:      printf("\n\nReport totals:");
156:      printf("\nTotal Income is %d", grand_total);
157:      printf("\nAverage Income is %d", grand_total/ctr );
158:
159:      printf("\n\n* * * End of Report * * *\n");
160: }
161: /*------------------------------------------------------------*
162:  * Function: continue_function()                              *
163:  * Purpose:  This function asks the user if they wish to continue.*
164:  * Returns:  YES - if user wishes to continue                 *
165:  *           NO - if user wishes to quit                      *
166:  *------------------------------------------------------------*/
167:
168: int continue_function( void )
169: {
170:      int x;
171:
```

```
172:    printf("\n\nDo you wish to continue? (0=NO/1=YES): ");
173:    scanf( "%d", &x );
174:
175:    while( x < 0 || x > 1 )
176:    {
177:        printf("\n%d is invalid!", x);
178:        printf("\nPlease enter 0 to Quit or 1 to Continue: ");
179:        scanf("%d", &x);
180:    }
181:    if(x == 0)
182:        return NO;
183:    else
184:        return YES;
185: }
```

After completing the quizzes and exercises on Day 1, "Introduction to Linux and the C Programming Language," you should be able to enter and compile this program. The program contains more comments than the other listings throughout this book. These comments are typical of a "real-world" C program. In particular, you should notice the comments at the beginning of the program and before each major function. The comments on lines 1 through 5 give an overview of the entire program, including the program name. Some programmers also include information such as the author of the program, its copyright, licensing information, compiling information, the libraries required, the date it was created, and the dates and details of any modifications. The comments before each function describe the purpose of the function, possible return values, the function's calling conventions, and anything else relating specifically to that function.

The comments on lines 1 through 5 specify that you can enter information for up to 100 people. Before you can enter the data, the program calls display_instructions() on line 44. This function displays instructions for using the program, asking whether you want to continue or quit. On lines 65 through 77, you can see that this function uses the printf() function from Day 6, "Fundamentals of Input and Output," to display the instructions.

On lines 157 through 172, continue_function() uses some of the features covered towards the end of the week. This function asks whether you want to continue (line 172). Using a while control statement from Day 5, "Basic Program Control," the function verifies that the answer entered was a 0 or a 1. As long as the answer isn't one of these two values, the function keeps prompting for a response. After the program receives an appropriate answer, an if..else statement (covered on Day 3, "Statements, Expressions, and Operators") returns a constant variable of either YES or NO.

The heart of this program lies in two functions: get_data() and display_report(). The get_data() function prompts the user to enter data, placing the information into the arrays declared near the beginning of the program. Using a for statement on line 94, you are prompted to enter data until the variable cont is not equal to the defined constant YES (returned from the continue_function()) or until ctr is greater than or equal to the maximum number of array elements, MAX. The program checks each piece of information as it is entered to ensure it is appropriate. For example, lines 99 through 103 prompt you to enter a month. The only values the program accepts are 0 through 12. If you enter a number greater than 12, the program again prompts for the month. Line 120 calls continue_function() to check whether you want to continue entering data.

When the user responds to continue_function() with a 0, or the maximum number of sets of information is entered (MAX sets), the program returns to line 49 in the main() function, where it calls display_report(). The display_report() function on lines 133 through 160 prints a report to the screen. This report uses a nested for loop to total incomes for each month and a grand total for all the months. This report might seem complicated; if so, review Day 5 for coverage of nested statements. Many of the reports you will create as a programmer are more complicated than this one.

This program uses what you learned during your first week of teaching yourself C programming for Linux. This was a large amount of material to cover in just one week, but you did it! If you use everything you learned this week, you can write programs in C. There are, however, still limits to what you can do.

WEEK 2

At a Glance

You have now finished your first week of learning how to program Linux using the C language. By now, you should feel comfortable entering programs and using your editor and compiler.

Where You're Going

This week covers a large amount of material. You will learn about many of the features that make up the heart of C. You will learn how to use character arrays and how to expand character variables types into arrays and strings and how to group different variable types into structures.

The second week builds on subjects you learned in the first week, introduces additional program control statements, provides detailed explanations of their function, and presents alternative functions. Day 8, "Understanding Pointers," and Day 11, "Understanding Variable Scope," focus on concepts that are extremely important to capitalizing on C's assets. You should spend extra time working with pointers and their basic functions.

By the end of the first week, you learned to write many simple C programs. By the end of the second week, you should be able to write complex programs that can accomplish almost any task.

8

9

10

11

12

13

14

Day 8

Understanding Pointers

Today's lesson introduces you to pointers, an important part of the C language. Pointers provide a powerful and flexible method of manipulating data in your programs. Today you will learn

- The definition of a pointer
- The uses of pointers
- How to declare and initialize pointers
- How to use pointers with simple variables and arrays
- How to use pointers to pass arrays to functions
- How to pass values and pointers to functions

As you read through today's lesson, the advantages of using pointers might not be clear immediately. The advantages fall into two categories: things that can be done better with pointers, and things that can be done only with pointers. The specifics should become clear as you read this and subsequent chapters. At present, just know that you must understand pointers if you want to be a proficient C programmer.

What Is a Pointer?

To understand pointers, you need a basic knowledge of how your computer stores information in memory. The following is a somewhat simplified account of PC memory storage.

Your Computer's Memory

A PC's RAM consists of many millions of sequential storage locations, and each location is identified by a unique address. The memory addresses in a given computer range from 0 to a maximum value that depends on the amount of memory installed.

When you're using your computer, the operating system uses some of the system's memory. When you're running a program, the program's code (the machine-language instructions for the program's various tasks) and data (the information the program is using) also use some of the system's memory. This section examines the memory storage for program data.

When you declare a variable in a C program, the compiler sets aside a memory location with a unique address to store that variable. The compiler associates that address with the variable's name. When your program uses the variable name, it automatically accesses the proper memory location. The location's address is used, but it is hidden from you, and you need not be concerned with it.

Figure 8.1 shows this schematically. A variable named rate has been declared and initialized to 100. The compiler has set aside storage at address 1004 for the variable and has associated the name rate with the address 1004.

FIGURE 8.1.

A program variable is stored at a specific memory address.

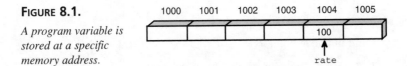

Creating a Pointer

You should note that the address of the variable rate (or any other variable) is a number and can be treated like any other number in C. If you know a variable's address, you can create a second variable in which to store the address of the first. The first step is to declare a variable to hold the address of rate. Give it the name p_rate, for example. At first, p_rate is uninitialized. Storage has been allocated for p_rate, but its value is undetermined as shown in Figure 8.2.

FIGURE 8.2.

Memory storage space has been allocated for the variable p_rate.

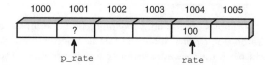

The next step is to store the address of the variable rate in the variable p_rate. Because p_rate now contains the address of rate, it indicates the location where rate is stored in memory. In C parlance, p_rate points to rate or is a pointer to rate. This is shown in Figure 8.3.

FIGURE 8.3.

The variable p_rate *contains the address of the variable* rate *and is therefore a pointer to* rate.

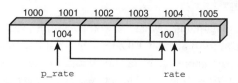

To summarize, a pointer is a variable that contains the address of another variable. Now you can get down to the details of using pointers in your C programs.

Pointers and Simple Variables

In the example just given, a pointer variable pointed to a simple (that is, nonarray) variable. This section shows you how to create and use pointers to simple variables.

Declaring Pointers

A pointer is a numeric variable and, like all variables, must be declared before it can be used. Pointer variable names follow the same rules as other variables and must be unique. Today's lesson uses the convention that a pointer to the variable name is called p_name. This isn't necessary, however; you can name pointers anything you want as long as they follow C's naming rules.

A pointer declaration takes the following form:

typename **ptrname;

where *typename* is any of C's variable types and indicates the type of the variable to which the pointer points. The asterisk (*) is the indirection operator, and it indicates that *ptrname* is a pointer to type *typename* and not a variable of type *typename*. Pointers can be declared along with nonpointer variables. The following are some more examples:

```
char *ch1, *ch2;        /* ch1 and ch2 both are pointers to type char */
float *value, percent;  /* value is a pointer to type float, and
                        /* percent is an ordinary float variable */
```

Note

> The * symbol is used as both the indirection operator and the multiplication operator. Don't worry about the compiler becoming confused. The context in which * is used always provides enough information so that the compiler can figure out whether you mean indirection or multiplication.

New Term   When the indirection operator is applied to a pointer we say that the pointer variable is being *dereferenced*.

Initializing Pointers

Now that you've declared a pointer, what can you do with it? You can't do anything with it until you make it point to something. Like regular variables, uninitialized pointers can be used, but the results are unpredictable and potentially disastrous. Until a pointer holds the address of a variable, it isn't useful. The address doesn't get stored in the pointer by magic; your program must put it there by using the address-of operator, the ampersand (&). When placed before the name of a variable, the address-of operator returns the address of the variable. Therefore, you initialize a pointer with a statement of the form

```
pointer = &variable;
```

Look back at the example in Figure 8.3. The program statement to initialize the variable p_rate to point at the variable rate would be

```
p_rate = &rate;     /* assign the address of rate to p_rate */
```

This statement assigns the *address of* rate to p_rate. Before the initialization, p_rate didn't point to anything in particular. After the initialization, p_rate is a pointer to rate.

Using Pointers

Now that you know how to declare and initialize pointers, you're probably wondering how to use them. The indirection operator (*) comes into play again. When the * precedes the name of a pointer, it refers to the variable pointed to.

Consider the previous example, in which the pointer p_rate has been initialized to point to the variable rate. If you write *p_rate, it refers to the variable rate. If you want to print the value of rate (which is 100 in the example), you could write

```
printf("%d", rate);
```

or you could write

```
printf("%d", *p_rate);
```

NEW TERM   In C, these two statements are equivalent. Accessing the contents of a variable by using the variable name is called *direct access*. Accessing the contents of a variable by using a pointer to the variable is called *indirect access* or *indirection*. Figure 8.4 shows that a pointer name preceded by the indirection operator refers to the value of the pointed-to variable.

FIGURE 8.4.

Use of the indirection operator with pointers.

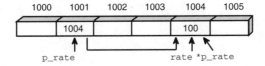

Pause a minute and think about this material. Pointers are an integral part of the C language, and it's essential that you understand them. Pointers have confused many people, so don't worry if you're feeling a bit puzzled. If you need to review, that's fine. Maybe the following summary can help.

If you have a pointer named ptr that has been initialized to point to the variable var, the following are true:

- *ptr and var both refer to the contents of var (that is, whatever value the program has stored there).

- ptr and &var refer to the address of var.

As you can see, a pointer name without the indirection operator accesses the pointer value itself, which is, of course, the address of the variable pointed to.

Listing 8.1 demonstrates basic pointer use. You should enter, compile, and run this program.

LISTING 8.1. Basic pointer use.

```
1:  /* Demonstrates basic pointer use. */
2:
3:  #include <stdio.h>
4:
5:  /* Declare and initialize an int variable */
6:
7:  int var = 1;
8:
9:  /* Declare a pointer to int */
10:
11: int *ptr;
12:
13: int main(void)
```

continues

LISTING 8.1. continued

```
14: {
15:     /* Initialize ptr to point to var */
16:
17:     ptr = &var;
18:
19:     /* Access var directly and indirectly */
20:
21:     printf("\nDirect access, var = %d", var);
22:     printf("\nIndirect access, var = %d", *ptr);
23:
24:     /* Display the address of var two ways */
25:
26:     printf("\n\nThe address of var = %lu", (unsigned long)&var);
27:     printf("\nThe address of var = %lu\n", (unsigned long)ptr);
28:
29:     return 0;
30: }
```

OUTPUT   Direct access, var = 1
             Indirect access, var = 1

             The address of var = 134518064
             The address of var = 134518064

Note | The address reported for var might not be 134518064 on your system.

ANALYSIS In this listing, two variables are declared. In line 7, var is declared as an int and initialized to 1. In line 11, a pointer to a variable of type int is declared and named ptr. In line 17, the pointer ptr is assigned the address of var using the address-of operator (&). The rest of the program prints the values from these two variables to the screen. Line 21 prints the value of var, whereas line 22 prints the value stored in the location pointed to by ptr. In this program, this value is 1. Line 26 prints the address of var using the address-of operator. This is the same value printed by line 27 using the pointer variable, ptr.

Note | The (unsigned long) in lines 26 and 27 is called a *typecast* and will be covered more fully on Day 18, "Working with Memory."

This listing is good to study. It shows the relationship between a variable, its address, a pointer, and the dereferencing of a pointer.

Do	**DON'T**
DO understand what pointers are and how they work. The mastering of C requires mastering pointers.	**DON'T** use an uninitialized pointer. Results can be disastrous if you do.

Pointers and Variable Types

The previous discussion ignores the fact that different variable types occupy different amounts of memory. On most modern operating systems, an int takes 4 bytes, a double takes 8 bytes, and so on. Each individual byte of memory has its own address, so a multi-byte variable actually occupies several addresses.

How, then, do pointers handle the addresses of multibyte variables? Here's how it works: The address of a variable is actually the address of the first (lowest) byte it occupies. This can be illustrated with an example that declares and initializes three variables:

```
int vint = 12252;
char vchar = 90;
double vfloat = 1200.156004;
```

These variables are stored in memory as shown in Figure 8.5. In this figure, the int variable occupies 4 bytes, the char variable occupies 1 byte, and the double variable occupies 8 bytes.

FIGURE 8.5.

Different types of numeric variables occupy different amounts of storage space in memory.

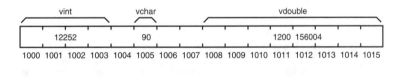

Now declare and initialize pointers to these three variables:

```
int *p_vint;
char *p_vchar;
double *p_vdouble;
/* additional code goes here */
p_vint = &vint;
p_vchar = &vchar;
p_vdouble = &vdouble;
```

Each pointer is equal to the address of the first byte of the pointed-to variable. Thus, p_vint equals 1000, p_vchar equals 1005, and p_vdouble equals 1008. Remember, however, that each pointer was declared to point to a certain type of variable. The compiler knows that a pointer to type int points to the first of four bytes, a pointer to type double points to the first of eight bytes, and so on. This is illustrated in Figure 8.6.

FIGURE 8.6.

The compiler knows the size of the variable that a pointer points to.

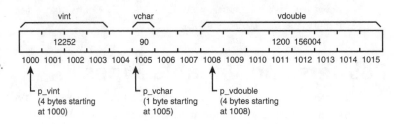

Note

Figures 8.5 and 8.6 show some empty memory storage locations among the three variables. This is for the sake of visual clarity. In practice, the C compiler may or may not place the three variables in adjacent memory locations depending on what is most efficient.

Pointers and Arrays

Pointers can be useful when you're working with simple variables, but they are more helpful with arrays. There is a special relationship between pointers and arrays in C. In fact, when you use the array subscript notation that you learned on Day 7, "Using Numeric Arrays," you're really using pointers without knowing it. The following sections explain how this works.

The Array Name as a Pointer

An array name without brackets is a pointer to the array's first element. Thus, if you've declared an array data[ ], data is the address of the first array element.

"Wait a minute," you might be saying. "Don't you need the address-of operator to get an address?" Yes. You can also use the expression &data[0] to obtain the address of the array's first element. In C, the relationship (data == &data[0]) is always true.

You've seen that the name of an array is a pointer to the array. The name of an array is a pointer constant; it can't be changed and remains fixed for the duration of program execution. This makes sense: If you changed its value, it would point elsewhere and not to the array (which remains at a fixed location in memory).

You can, however, declare a pointer variable and initialize it to point at the array. For example, the following code initializes the pointer variable p_array with the address of the first element of array[ ]:

```
int array[100], *p_array;
/* additional code goes here */
p_array = array;
```

Because p_array is a pointer variable, it can be modified to point elsewhere. Unlike array, p_array isn't locked into pointing at the first element of array[]. For example, it could be pointed at other elements of array[]. How would you do this? First, you need to look at how array elements are stored in memory.

Array Element Storage

As you might remember from Day 7, the elements of an array are stored in sequential memory locations with the first element in the lowest address. Subsequent array elements (those with an index greater than 0) are stored in higher addresses. How much higher depends on the array's data type (char, int, double, and so forth).

Take an array of type int. As you learned on Day 2, "The Components of a C Program: Code and Data," a single int variable will occupy four bytes of memory. Each array element is therefore located four bytes above the preceding element, and the address of each array element is four higher than the address of the preceding element. A type double, on the other hand, will occupy eight bytes. In an array of type double, each array element is located eight bytes above the preceding element, and the address of each array element is eight higher than the address of the preceding element.

Figure 8.7 illustrates the relationship between array storage and addresses for a three-element int array and a two-element double array.

FIGURE 8.7.

Array storage for different array types.

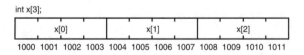

By looking at Figure 8.7, you should be able to see why the following relationships are true:

```
1: x == 1000
2: &x[0] == 1000
3: &x[1] = 1004
4: expenses == 1240
5: &expenses[0] == 1240
6: &expenses[1] == 1248
```

x without the array brackets is the address of the first element (x[0]). You can also see that x[0] is at the address of 1000. Line 2 shows this too. It can be read like this: "The address of the first element of the array x is equal to 1000." Line 3 shows that the address of the second element (subscripted as 1 in an array) is 1004. Again, Figure 8.7 can confirm this. Lines 4, 5, and 6 are virtually identical to 1, 2, and 3, respectively. They vary in the difference between the addresses of the two array elements. In the type short array x, the difference is two bytes, and in the type double array expenses, the difference is eight bytes.

How do you access these successive array elements using a pointer? You can see from these examples that a pointer must be increased by four to access successive elements of a type int array, and by eight to access successive elements of a type double array. You can generalize and say that to access successive elements of an array of a particular data type, a pointer must be increased by sizeof(datatype). Remember from Day 2 that the sizeof() operator returns the size in bytes of a C data type.

Listing 8.2 illustrates the relationship between addresses and the elements of different type arrays by declaring arrays of type short, int, float, and double and by displaying the addresses of successive elements.

LISTING 8.2. Displaying the addresses of successive array elements.

```
 1: /* Demonstrates the relationship between addresses and */
 2: /* elements of arrays of different data types. */
 3:
 4: #include <stdio.h>
 5:
 6: /* Declare three arrays and a counter variable. */
 7:
 8: short s[10];
 9: int i[10], x;
10: float f[10];
11: double d[10];
12:
13: int main(void)
14: {
15:     /* Print the table heading */
16:
17:     printf("%19s %10s %10s %10s", "Short", "Integer",
18:             "Float", "Double");
19:
20:     printf("\n=================================");
21:     printf("=====================");
22:
23:     /* Print the addresses of each array element. */
24:
25:     for (x = 0; x < 10; x++)
```

8

```
26:     printf("\nElement %d: %lu  %lu  %lu  %lu", x,
27:         (unsigned long)&s[x], (unsigned long)&i[x],
28:         (unsigned long)&f[x], (unsigned long)&d[x]);
29:
30:     printf("\n=================================");
31:     printf("=====================\n");
32:
33:     return 0;
34: }
```

OUTPUT

```
              Short    Integer    Float    Double
         ===================================================
         Element 0: 134518864  134518720  134518656  134518784
         Element 1: 134518866  134518724  134518660  134518792
         Element 2: 134518868  134518728  134518664  134518800
         Element 3: 134518870  134518732  134518668  134518808
         Element 4: 134518872  134518736  134518672  134518816
         Element 5: 134518874  134518740  134518676  134518824
         Element 6: 134518876  134518744  134518680  134518832
         Element 7: 134518878  134518748  134518684  134518840
         Element 8: 134518880  134518752  134518688  134518848
         Element 9: 134518882  134518756  134518692  134518856
         ===================================================
```

ANALYSIS The exact addresses that your system displays will be different from these, but the relationships are the same. In this output, there are 2 bytes between short elements, 4 bytes between int and float elements, and 8 bytes between double elements.

> **Note**
>
> Some machines use different sizes for variable types. If your machine differs, the preceding output might have differently sized gaps; however, they will be consistent gaps.

Looking more closely at Listing 8.2, you can see that four arrays are created in lines 8, 9, 10 and 11. Line 8 declares array s of type short, line 9 declares array i of type int, line 10 declares array f of type float, and line 11 declares array d of type double. Lines 17 and 18 print the column headers for the table that will be displayed. Lines 20 and 21, along with lines 30 and 31, print dashed lines across the top and bottom of the table data. This is a nice touch for a report. Lines 25 through 28 are a for loop that prints each of the table's rows. The number of the element x is printed first. This is followed by the address of the element in each of the four arrays. As in Listing 8.1, (unsigned long) is used to avoid compiler warning messages and can be disregarded.

Pointer Arithmetic

You have a pointer to the first array element; the pointer must increment by an amount equal to the size of the data type stored in the array. How do you access array elements using pointer notation? You use *pointer arithmetic*.

"Just what I don't need," you might be thinking, "another kind of arithmetic to learn!" Don't worry. Pointer arithmetic is simple, and it makes using pointers in your programs much easier. You have to be concerned with only two pointer operations: incrementing and decrementing.

Incrementing Pointers

When you *increment* a pointer, you are increasing its value. For example, when you increment a pointer by 1, pointer arithmetic automatically increases the pointer's value so that it points to the next array element, irrespective of how big that array element is. In other words, C knows the data type that the pointer points to (from the pointer declaration) and increases the address stored in the pointer by the size of the data type.

Suppose that `ptr_to_int` is a pointer variable to some element of an `int` array. If you execute the statement

```
ptr_to_int++;
```

the value of `ptr_to_int` is increased by the size of type `int` (4 bytes), and `ptr_to_int` now points to the next array element. Likewise, if `ptr_to_double` points to an element of a type `double` array, the statement

```
ptr_to_double++;
```

increases the value of `ptr_to_double` by the size of type `double` (8 bytes).

The same holds true for increments greater than 1. If you add the value *n* to a pointer, C increments the pointer by *n* array elements of the associated data type. Therefore,

```
ptr_to_int += 4;
```

increases the value stored in `ptr_to_int` by 16 (assuming that an integer is 4 bytes), so it points four array elements ahead. Likewise,

```
ptr_to_double += 10;
```

increases the value stored in `ptr_to_double` by 80 (assuming that a double is 8 bytes), so it points 10 array elements ahead.

Decrementing Pointers

The same concepts that apply to incrementing pointers hold true for decrementing pointers. *Decrementing* a pointer is actually a special case of incrementing by adding a negative value. If you decrement a pointer with the `--` or `-=` operators, pointer arithmetic automatically adjusts for the size of the array elements.

Listing 8.3 presents an example of how pointer arithmetic can be used to access array elements. By incrementing pointers, the program can step through all the elements of the arrays efficiently.

LISTING 8.3. Using pointer arithmetic and pointer notation to access array elements.

```
1:  /* Demonstrates using pointer arithmetic to access */
2:  /* array elements with pointer notation. */
3:
4:  #include <stdio.h>
5:  #define MAX 10
6:
7:  /* Declare and initialize an integer array. */
8:
9:  int i_array[MAX] = { 0,1,2,3,4,5,6,7,8,9 };
10:
11: /* Declare a pointer to int and an int variable. */
12:
13: int *i_ptr, count;
14:
15: /* Declare and initialize a float array. */
16:
17: float f_array[MAX] = { .0, .1, .2, .3, .4, .5, .6, .7, .8, .9 };
18:
19: /* Declare a pointer to float. */
20:
21: float *f_ptr;
22:
23: int main(void)
24: {
25:     /* Initialize the pointers. */
26:
27:     i_ptr = i_array;
28:     f_ptr = f_array;
29:
30:     /* Print the array elements. */
31:
32:     for (count = 0; count < MAX; count++)
33:         printf("%d\t%f\n", *i_ptr++, *f_ptr++);
34:
35:     return 0;
36: }
```

OUTPUT

```
0    0.000000
1    0.100000
2    0.200000
```

```
3        0.300000
4        0.400000
5        0.500000
6        0.600000
7        0.700000
8        0.800000
9        0.900000
```

ANALYSIS   In this program, a defined constant named MAX is set to 10 in line 5; it is used throughout the listing. In line 9, MAX is used to set the number of elements in an array of ints named i_array. The elements in this array are initialized at the same time that the array is declared. Line 13 declares two additional int variables. The first is a pointer named i_ptr. You know this is a pointer because an indirection operator (*) is used. The other variable is a simple type int variable named count. In line 17, a second array is defined and initialized. This array is of type float, contains MAX values, and is initialized with float values. Line 21 declares a pointer to a float named f_ptr.

The main() function is on lines 23 through 36. The program assigns the beginning address of the two arrays to the pointers of their respective types in lines 27 and 28. Remember, an array name without a subscript is the same as the address of the array's beginning. A for statement in lines 32 and 33 uses the int variable count to count from 0 to the value of MAX. For each count, line 33 dereferences the two pointers and prints their values in a printf() function call. The increment operator then increments each of the pointers so that each points to the next element in the array before continuing with the next iteration of the for loop.

You might be thinking that this program could just as well have used array subscript notation and dispensed with pointers altogether. This is true, and in simple programming tasks like this, the use of pointer notation doesn't offer any major advantages. As you start to write more complex programs, however, you should find the use of pointers advantageous.

Remember that you can't perform incrementing and decrementing operations on pointer constants. (An array name without brackets is a *pointer constant*.) Also remember that when you're manipulating pointers to array elements, the C compiler doesn't keep track of the start and finish of the array. If you're not careful, you can increment or decrement the pointer so that it points somewhere in memory before or after the array. Something is stored there, but it isn't an array element. You should keep track of pointers and where they're pointing.

Other Pointer Manipulations

The only other pointer arithmetic operation is called *differencing,* which refers to subtracting two pointers. If you have two pointers to different elements of the same array,

8

you can subtract them and find out how far apart they are. Again, pointer arithmetic auto-matically scales the answer so that it refers to array elements. Thus, if ptr1 and ptr2 point to elements of an array (of any type), the following expression tells you how far apart the elements are:

```
ptr1 - ptr2
```

You can also compare pointers. Pointer comparisons are valid only between pointers that point to the same array. Under these circumstances, the relational operators ==, !=, >, <, >=, and <= work properly. Lower array elements (that is, those having a lower subscript) always have a lower address than higher array elements. Thus, if ptr1 and ptr2 point to elements of the same array, the comparison

```
ptr1 < ptr2
```

is true if ptr1 points to an earlier member of the array than ptr2 does.

This covers all allowed pointer operations. Many arithmetic operations that can be per-formed with regular variables, such as multiplication and division, don't make sense with pointers. The C compiler doesn't allow them. For example, if ptr is a pointer, the statement

```
ptr *= 2;
```

generates an error message. As Table 8.1 indicates, you can do a total of six operations with a pointer, all of which have been covered in today's lesson.

TABLE 8.1. Pointer operations.

Operation	Description
Assignment	You can assign a value to a pointer. The value should be an address obtained with the address-of operator (&) or from a pointer constant (array name).
Indirection	The indirection operator (*) gives the value stored in the pointed-to location.
Address of	You can use the address-of operator to find the address of a pointer, so you can have pointers to pointers. This is an advanced topic and is covered on Day 14, "Pointers: Beyond the Basics."
Incrementing	You can add an integer to a pointer to point to a different memory location.
Decrementing	You can subtract an integer from a pointer to point to a different memory location.
Differencing	You can subtract one pointer from another pointer to deter-mine how far apart they are.
Comparison	Valid only with two pointers that point to the same array.

Pointer Cautions

When you're writing a program that uses pointers, you must avoid one serious error: using an uninitialized pointer on the left side of an assignment statement. For example, the following statement declares a pointer to type `int`:

```
int *ptr;
```

This pointer isn't yet initialized, so it doesn't point to anything. To be more exact, it doesn't point to anything *known*. An uninitialized pointer has some value; you just don't know what it is. In many cases, it is zero. We'll talk about this in tomorrow's lesson.

If you use an uninitialized pointer in an assignment statement, the following happens:

```
*ptr = 12;
```

The value 12 is assigned to whatever address `ptr` points to. That address can be almost anywhere in memory—where the operating system is stored or somewhere in the program's code. The 12 that is stored there might overwrite some important information, and the result can be anything from strange program errors to a full system crash. The left side of an assignment statement is the most dangerous place to use an uninitialized pointer. Other errors, although less serious, can also result from using an uninitialized pointer anywhere in your program, so be sure your program's pointers are properly initialized before you use them. You must do this yourself. The compiler won't do this for you.

Do	Don't
DO understand the size of variable types on your computer. As you can begin to see, you need to know variable sizes when working with pointers and memory.	**DON'T** try to perform mathematical operations such as division, multiplication, and modulus on pointers. Adding (incrementing) and subtracting (differencing) pointers are acceptable.
	DON'T forget that subtracting from or adding to a pointer changes the pointer based on the size of the data type it points to. It doesn't change it by 1 or by the number being added (unless it's a pointer to a 1-byte character).
	DON'T try to increment or decrement an array variable. Assign a pointer to the beginning address of the array and increment it (see Listing 8.3).

Array Subscript Notation and Pointers

An array name without brackets is a pointer to the array's first element. Therefore, you can access the first array element using the indirection operator. If array[] is a declared array, the expression *array is the array's first element, *(array + 1) is the array's second element, and so on. If you generalize for the entire array, the following relationships always hold true irrespective of the array type:

```
*(array) == array[0]
*(array + 1) == array[1]
*(array + 2) == array[2]
...
*(array + n) == array[n]
```

This illustrates the equivalence of array subscript notation and array pointer notation. You can use either in your programs; the C compiler sees them as two different ways of accessing array data using pointers.

Passing Arrays to Functions

Today's lesson has already discussed the special relationship that exists in C between pointers and arrays. This relationship comes into play when you need to pass an array as an argument to a function. The only way you can pass an array to a function is by means of a pointer.

As you learned on Day 4, "Functions: The Basics," an argument is a value that the calling program passes to a function. It can be an int, a float, or any other simple data type, but it must be a single numerical value. It can be a single array element, but it can't be an entire array. What if you need to pass an entire array to a function? Well, you can have a pointer to an array, and that pointer is a single numeric value (the address of the array's first element). If you pass that value to a function, the function knows the address of the array and can access the array elements using pointer notation.

Consider another problem. If you write a function that takes an array as an argument, you want a function that can handle arrays of different sizes. For example, you could write a function that finds the largest element in an array of integers. The function wouldn't be much use if it were limited to dealing with arrays of one fixed size.

How does the function know the size of the array whose address it was passed? Remember, the value passed to a function is a pointer to the first array element. It could be the first of 10 elements or the first of 10,000. There are two methods of letting a function know an array's size.

You can identify the last array element by storing a special value there. As the function processes the array, it looks for that value in each element. When the value is found, the end of the array has been reached. The disadvantage of this method is that it forces you to reserve a value as the end-of-array indicator, reducing the flexibility you have for storing real data in the array.

The other method is more flexible and straightforward, and it's the one used in this book: Pass the function the array size as an argument. This can be a simple type int argument. Thus, the function is passed two arguments: a pointer to the first array element and an integer specifying the number of elements in the array.

Listing 8.4 accepts a list of values from the user and stores them in an array. It then calls a function named largest(), passing the array (both pointer and size). The function finds the largest value in the array and returns it to the calling program.

LISTING 8.4. Passing an array to a function.

```
 1:  /* Passing an array to a function. */
 2:
 3:  #include <stdio.h>
 4:
 5:  #define MAX 10
 6:
 7:  int array[MAX], count;
 8:
 9:  int largest(int x[], int y);
10:
11:  int main(void)
12:  {
13:      /* Input MAX values from the keyboard. */
14:
15:      for (count = 0; count < MAX; count++)
16:      {
17:          printf("Enter an integer value: ");
18:          scanf("%d", &array[count]);
19:      }
20:
21:      /* Call the function and display the return value. */
22:      printf("\n\nLargest value = %d\n", largest(array, MAX));
23:
24:      return 0;
25:  }
26:  /* Function largest() returns the largest value */
27:  /* in an integer array */
28:
29:  int largest(int x[], int y)
30:  {
```

8

```
31:     int count, biggest = -12000;
32:
33:     for ( count = 0; count < y; count++)
34:     {
35:         if (x[count] > biggest)
36:             biggest = x[count];
37:     }
38:
39:     return biggest;
40: }
```

**INPUT/
OUTPUT**

```
Enter an integer value: 1
Enter an integer value: 2
Enter an integer value: 3
Enter an integer value: 4
Enter an integer value: 5
Enter an integer value: 10
Enter an integer value: 9
Enter an integer value: 8
Enter an integer value: 7
Enter an integer value: 6

Largest value = 10
```

ANALYSIS The function used in this example to accept a pointer to an array is called largest(). The function prototype is in line 9 and, with the exception of the semicolon, it is identical to the function header in line 29.

Most of what is presented in the function header in line 29 should make sense to you: largest() is a function that returns an int to the calling program; its second argument is an int represented by the parameter y. The only new thing is the first parameter, int x[], indicates that the first argument is a pointer to type int, represented by the parameter x. You also could write the function declaration and header as follows:

```
int largest(int *x, int y);
```

This is equivalent to the first form; both int x[] and int *x mean "pointer to int." The first form might be preferable, because it reminds you that the parameter represents a pointer to an array. Of course, the pointer doesn't know that it points to an array, but the function uses it that way.

Now look at the function largest(). When it is called, the parameter x holds the value of the first argument and is therefore a pointer to the first element of the array. You can use x anywhere an array pointer can be used. In largest(), the array elements are accessed using subscript notation in lines 35 and 36. You also could use pointer notation, rewriting the if loop as shown in the following:

```
for (count = 0; count < y; count++)
{
   if (*(x+count) > biggest)
      biggest = *(x+count);
}
```

Listing 8.5 shows the other way of passing arrays to functions.

LISTING 8.5. An alternative way of passing an array to a function.

```
1:  /* Passing an array to a function. Alternative way. */
2:
3:  #include <stdio.h>
4:
5:  #define MAX 10
6:
7:  int array[MAX+1], count;
8:
9:  int largest(int x[]);
10:
11: int main(void)
12: {
13:     /* Input MAX values from the keyboard. */
14:
15:     for (count = 0; count < MAX; count++)
16:     {
17:         printf("Enter an integer value: ");
18:         scanf("%d", &array[count]);
19:
20:         if ( array[count] == 0 )
21:             count = MAX;                    /* will exit for loop */
22:     }
23:     array[MAX] = 0;
24:
25:     /* Call the function and display the return value. */
26:     printf("\n\nLargest value = %d\n", largest(array));
27:
28:     return 0;
29: }
30: /* Function largest() returns the largest value */
31: /* in an integer array */
32:
33: int largest(int x[])
34: {
35:     int count, biggest = -12000;
36:
37:     for ( count = 0; x[count] != 0; count++)
38:     {
39:         if (x[count] > biggest)
40:             biggest = x[count];
```

```
41:     }
42:
43:     return biggest;
44: }
```

```
Enter an integer value: 1
Enter an integer value: 2
Enter an integer value: 3
Enter an integer value: 4
Enter an integer value: 5
Enter an integer value: 10
Enter an integer value: 9
Enter an integer value: 8
Enter an integer value: 7
Enter an integer value: 6

Largest value = 10
```

The following is the output from running the program a second time:

```
Enter an integer value: 10
Enter an integer value: 20
Enter an integer value: 55
Enter an integer value: 3
Enter an integer value: 12
Enter an integer value: 0

Largest value = 55
```

ANALYSIS This program uses a largest() function that has the same functionality as Listing 8.4. The difference is that only the array tag is needed. The for loop in line 37 continues looking for the largest value until it encounters a 0, at which point it knows it is done.

Looking at the early parts of this program, you can see the differences between Listing 8.4 and Listing 8.5. First, in line 7, you need to add an extra element to the array to store the value that indicates the end. In lines 20 and 21, an if statement is added to see whether the user entered 0, thus signaling that the user is done entering values. If 0 is entered, count is set to its maximum value, so the for loop can be exited cleanly. Line 23 ensures that the last element is 0 in case the user entered the maximum number of values (MAX).

By adding the extra commands when entering the data, you can make the largest() function work with any size of array; however, there is one catch. What happens if you forget to put a 0 at the end of the array? largest() continues past the end of the array, comparing values in memory until it finds a 0.

As you can see, passing an array to a function is not particularly difficult. You simply pass a pointer to the array's first element. In most situations, you also need to pass the number of elements in the array. In the function, the pointer value can be used to access the array elements with either subscript or pointer notation.

> Recall from Day 4 that when a simple variable is passed to a function, only a copy of the variable's value is passed. The function can use the value but can't change the original variable because it doesn't have access to the variable itself. When you pass an array to a function, things are different. A function is passed the array's address, not just a copy of the values in the array. The code in the function works with the actual array elements and can modify the values stored in the array.

Passing Pointers to Functions

On a related pointer note, we have to look at some of the different ways to pass an argument to a function. There are two ways, one involving the value of a parameter, the other involving the address of a variable. *Passing by value* means that the function is passed a copy of the argument's value. This method has three steps:

1. The argument expression is evaluated.
2. The result is copied onto the *stack,* a temporary storage area in memory.
3. The function retrieves the argument's value from the stack.

The main point is that if a variable is passed as the argument, code in the function cannot modify the value of the variable. Figure 8.8 illustrates passing an argument by value. In this case, the argument is a simple type `int` variable, but the principle is the same for other variable types and more complex expressions.

When a variable is passed to a function by value, the function has access to the variable's value but not to the original copy of the variable. As a result, the code in the function can't modify the original variable. This is the main reason why passing by value is the default method of passing arguments: Data outside a function is protected from inadvertent modification.

Passing arguments by value is possible with the basic data types (`char`, `int`, `long`, `float`, and `double`) and structures. There is another way to pass an argument to a function, however: passing a pointer to the argument variable rather than the value of the variable itself. This method of passing an argument is called *passing by reference*. Because the function has the address of the actual variable, the function can modify the variable's value in the calling function.

FIGURE 8.8.

Passing an argument by value. The function can't modify the original argument variable.

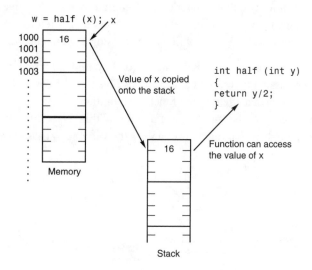

As you learned on Day 8, "Understanding Pointers," passing by reference is the only way to pass an array to a function; passing an array by value is not possible. With other data types, however, you can use either method. If your program uses large structures, passing them by value might cause your program to run out of stack space. Aside from this consideration, passing an argument by reference instead of by value offers an advantage as well as a disadvantage:

- The advantage of passing by reference is that the function can modify the value of the argument variable.

- The disadvantage of passing by reference is that the function can modify the value of the argument variable.

"What?" you might be saying. "An advantage that's also a disadvantage?" Yes. It all depends on the specific situation. If your program requires that a function modify an argument variable, passing by reference is an advantage. If there is no such need, it is a disadvantage because of the possibility of inadvertent modifications.

You might be wondering why you don't use the function's return value to modify the argument variable. You can do this, of course, as shown in the following example:

```
x = half(x);

float half(float y)
{
return y/2;
}
```

Remember, however, that a function can return only a single value. By passing one or more arguments by reference, you enable a function to "return" more than one value to the calling program. Figure 8.9 illustrates passing by reference for a single argument.

The function used in Figure 8.9 is not a good example of a real program in which you would use passing by reference, but it does illustrate the concept. When you pass by reference, you must ensure that the function definition and prototype reflect the fact that the argument passed to the function is a pointer. Within the body of the function, you must also use the indirection operator to access the variable(s) passed by reference.

FIGURE 8.9.

Passing by reference enables the function to modify the original argument's variable.

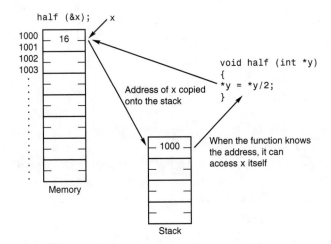

Listing 8.6 demonstrates passing by reference and the default passing by value. Its output clearly shows that a variable passed by value can't be changed by the function, whereas a variable passed by reference can be changed. Of course, a function doesn't need to modify a variable passed by reference. In such a case, there's no reason to pass by reference.

LISTING 8.6. Passing by value and passing by reference.

```
 1: /* Passing arguments by value and by reference.
 2:
 3: */ #include <stdio.h>
 4:
 5: void by_value(int a, int b, int c);
 6: void by_ref(int *a, int *b, int *c);
 7:
 8: int main(void)
 9: {
10:     int x = 2, y = 4, z = 6;
11:
12:     printf("Before calling by_value(), x = %d, y = %d, z = %d.\n",
13:         x, y, z);
```

```
14:
15:     by_value(x, y, z);
16:
17:     printf("After calling by_value(), x = %d, y = %d, z = %d.\n",
18:         x, y, z);
19:
20:     by_ref(&x, &y, &z);
21:
22:     printf("After calling by_ref(), x = %d, y = %d, z = %d.\n",
23:         x, y, z);
24:     return(0);
25: }
26:
27: void by_value(int a, int b, int c)
28: {
29:     a = 0;
30:     b = 0;
31:     c = 0;
32: }
33:
34: void by_ref(int *a, int *b, int *c)
35: {
36:     *a = 0;
37:     *b = 0;
38:     *c = 0;
39: }
```

OUTPUT

```
Before calling by_value(), x = 2, y = 4, z = 6.
After calling by_value(), x = 2, y = 4, z = 6.
After calling by_ref(), x = 0, y = 0, z = 0.
```

ANALYSIS This program demonstrates the difference between passing variables by value and passing them by reference. Lines 5 and 6 contain prototypes for the two functions call in the program. In line 5, notice that the by_value() function takes three type int arguments. In contrast, line 6 defines _by_ref() because it takes three pointers to type int variables as arguments. The function headers for these two functions on lines 27 and 34 follow the same format as the prototypes. The bodies of the two functions are similar, but not identical. Both functions assign 0 to the three variables passed to them. In the by_value() function, 0 is assigned directly to the variables. In the by_ref() function, pointers are used, so the variables must be dereferenced before the assignment is made.

Each function is called once by main(). First, the three variables to be passed are assigned values other than 0 on line 10. Line 12 prints these values to the screen. Line 15 calls the first of the two functions, by_value(). Line 17 prints the three variables again. Notice that they are not changed. The by_value() function receives the variables by value and, therefore, can't change their original content. Line 20 calls by_ref(), and line 22 prints the values again. This time, the values have all changed to 0. Passing the variables by reference gives by_ref() access to the actual contents of the variables.

You can write a function that receives some arguments by reference and others by value. Just remember to keep them straight inside the function using the indirection operator (*) to dereference arguments passed by reference.

Do	Don't
DO pass variables by value if you don't want the original value altered.	**DON'T** pass large amounts of data by value if it isn't necessary. You can run out of stack space.
	DON'T forget that a variable passed by reference should be a pointer. Also, use the indirection operator to dereference the variable in the function.

Type `void` Pointers

You've seen the `void` keyword used in a function declaration to specify that the function either doesn't take arguments or doesn't return a value. The `void` keyword can also be used to create a generic pointer—a pointer that can point to any type of data object. For example, the statement

```
void *x;
```

declares x as a generic pointer. x points to something; you just haven't yet specified what.

The most common use for type `void` pointers is in declaring function parameters. You might want to create a function that can handle different types of arguments. You can pass it a type `int` one time, a type `float` the next time, and so on. By declaring that the function takes a `void` pointer as an argument, you don't restrict it to accepting only a single data type. If you declare the function to take a `void` pointer as an argument, you can pass the function a pointer to anything.

Here's a simple example: You want to write a function that accepts a numeric variable as an argument and divides it by two, returning the answer in the argument variable. Thus, if the variable x holds the value 4, after a call to `half(x)` the variable x is equal to 2. Because you want to modify the argument, you pass it by reference. Because you want to use the function with any of C's numeric data types, you declare the function to take a `void` pointer:

```
void half(void *x);
```

Now you can call the function, passing it any pointer as an argument. There's one more thing you need, however. Although you can pass a `void` pointer without knowing what data type it points to, you can't dereference the pointer. Before the code in the function

8

can do anything with the pointer, it must know the data type. You do this with a *typecast,* which is nothing more than a way of telling the program to treat this void pointer as a pointer to a specific type. If x is a void pointer, you typecast it as follows:

```
(type *)x
```

Here, *type* is the appropriate data type. To tell the program that x is a pointer to type int, write

```
(int *)x
```

To dereference the pointer—that is, to access the int that x points to—write

```
*(int *)x
```

Typecasts are covered in more detail on Day 18. Getting back to the original topic (passing a void pointer to a function), you can see that, to use the pointer, the function must know the data type to which it points. In the case of the function you are writing that will divide its argument by two, there are four possibilities for type: int, long, float, and double. In addition to passing the void pointer to the variable to be divided by two, you must also tell the function the type of variable to which the void pointer points. You can modify the function definition as follows:

```
void half(void *x, char type);
```

Based on the argument type, the function casts the void pointer x to the appropriate type. Then the pointer can be dereferenced, and the value of the pointed-to variable can be used. The final version of the half() function is shown in Listing 8.7.

LISTING 8.7. Using a void pointer to pass different data types to a function.

```
 1: /* Using type void pointers. */
 2:
 3: #include <stdio.h>
 4:
 5: void half(void *x, char type);
 6:
 7: int main(void)
 8: {
 9:     /* Initialize one variable of each type. */
10:
11:     int i = 20;
12:     long l = 100000;
13:     float f = 12.456;
14:     double d = 123.044444;
15:
16:     /* Display their initial values. */
17:
18:     printf("%d\n", i);
```

continues

LISTING 8.7. continued

```
19:       printf("%ld\n", l);
20:       printf("%f\n", f);
21:       printf("%f\n\n", d);
22:
23:       /* Call half() for each variable. */
24:
25:       half(&i, 'i');
26:       half(&l, 'l');
27:       half(&d, 'd');
28:       half(&f, 'f');
29:
30:       /* Display their new values. */
31:       printf("%d\n", i);
32:       printf("%ld\n", l);
33:       printf("%f\n", f);
34:       printf("%f\n", d);
35:       return(0);
36: }
37:
38: void half(void *x, char type)
39: {
40:       /* Depending on the value of type, cast the */
41:       /* pointer x appropriately and divide by 2. */
42:
43:       switch (type)
44:       {
45:          case 'i':
46:             {
47:             *((int *)x) /= 2;
48:             break;
49:             }
50:          case 'l':
51:             {
52:             *((long *)x) /= 2;
53:             break;
54:             }
55:          case 'f':
56:             {
57:             *((float *)x) /= 2;
58:             break;
59:             }
60:          case 'd':
61:             {
62:             *((double *)x) /= 2;
63:             break;
64:             }
65:       }
66: }
```

OUTPUT

```
20
100000
12.456000
123.044444

10
50000
6.228000
61.522222
```

ANALYSIS   As implemented in this listing, the function `half()` on lines 38 through 66 includes no error checking (for example, if an invalid type argument is passed). This is because, in a real program, you wouldn't use a function to perform a task as simple as dividing a value by two. This is an illustrative example only.

You might think that the need to pass the type of the pointed-to variable would make the function less flexible. The function would be more general if it didn't need to know the type of the pointed-to data object, but that's not the way C works. You must always cast a `void` pointer to a specific type before you dereference it. By taking this approach, you write only one function. If you don't make use of a `void` pointer, you need to write four separate functions—one for each data type.

When you need a function that can deal with different data types, you can often write a macro to take the place of the function. The example just presented—in which the task performed by the function is relatively simple—would be a good candidate for a macro. (Day 20, "Advanced Compiler Use," covers macros.)

Do	**DON'T**
DO cast a `void` pointer when you use the value it points to.	**DON'T** try to increment or decrement a `void` pointer.

Summary

Today's lesson introduced you to pointers, a central part of C programming. A pointer is a variable that holds the address of another variable; a pointer is said to "point to" the variable whose address it holds. The two operators needed with pointers are the address-of operator (`&`) and the indirection operator (`*`). When placed before a variable name, the address-of operator returns the variable's address. When placed before a pointer name, the indirection operator returns the contents of the pointed-to variable.

Pointers and arrays have a special relationship. An array name without brackets is a pointer to the array's first element. The special features of pointer arithmetic make it easy to access array elements using pointers. Array subscript notation is in fact a special form of pointer notation.

Arrays can be passed as arguments to functions by passing a pointer to the array. Once the function knows the array's address and length, it can access the array elements using either pointer notation or subscript notation.

Normally, the value of variables passed to functions cannot be changed in the calling function. However, passing a pointer to a variable instead of the variable itself to a function overcomes this limitation.

You also saw how the void type can be used to create a generic pointer that can point to any type of C data object. Type void pointers are most commonly used with functions that can be passed arguments that aren't restricted to a single data type.

Q&A

Q Why are pointers so important in C?

A Pointers give you more control over the computer and your data. When used with functions, pointers let you change the values of variables that were passed, regardless of where they originated. On Day 14, you will learn additional uses for pointers.

Q How does the compiler know the difference between * for multiplication, for dereferencing, and for declaring a pointer?

A The compiler interprets the different uses of the asterisk based on the context in which it is used. If the statement being evaluated starts with a variable type, it can be assumed that the asterisk is for declaring a pointer. If the asterisk is used with a variable that has been declared as a pointer but not in a variable declaration, the asterisk is assumed to dereference. If it is used in a mathematical expression but not with a pointer variable, the asterisk can be assumed to be the multiplication operator.

Q What happens if I use the address-of operator on a pointer?

A You get the address of the pointer variable. Remember, a pointer is just another variable that holds the address of the variable to which it points.

Q Are variables always stored in the same location?

A No. Each time a program runs, its variables can be stored at different addresses within the computer. You should never assign a constant address value to a pointer.

Q Is passing pointers as function arguments a common practice in C programming?

A Definitely! In many instances, a function needs to change the value of multiple variables, and there are two ways this can be accomplished. The first is to declare and use global variables. The second is to pass pointers so that the function can modify the data directly. The first option is advisable only if nearly every function will use the variable; otherwise, you should avoid it (see Day 11, "Understanding Variable Scope").

Q Is it better to modify a variable by assigning a function's return value to it or by passing a pointer to the variable to the function?

A When you need to modify only one variable with a function, usually it's best to return the value from the function rather than pass a pointer to the function. The logic behind this is simple. By not passing a pointer, you don't run the risk of changing any data that you didn't intend to change, and you keep the function independent of the rest of the code.

Workshop

The Workshop provides quiz questions to help you solidify your understanding of the material covered and exercises to provide you with experience in using what you've learned. The answers to the quiz and exercises are provided in Appendix C, "Answers."

Quiz

1. What operator is used to determine the address of a variable?
2. What operator is used to determine the value at the location pointed to by a pointer?
3. What is a pointer?
4. What is indirection?
5. How are the elements of an array stored in memory?
6. Show two ways to obtain the address of the first element of the array `data[]`.
7. If an array is passed to a function, what are two ways to know where the end of that array is?
8. What are the six operations covered in this lesson that can be accomplished with a pointer?

9. Assume that you have two pointers. If the first points to the third element in an array of shorts and the second points to the fourth element, what value is obtained if you subtract the first pointer from the second? (Remember that the size of a short is 2 bytes.)

10. Assume that the array in question 9 is of float values. What value is obtained if the two pointers are subtracted? (Assume that the size of a float is 4 bytes.)

11. When passing arguments to a function, what's the difference between passing by value and passing by reference?

12. What is a type void pointer?

13. What is one reason you would use a void pointer?

14. When using a void pointer, what is meant by a typecast, and when must you use it?

Exercises

1. Show a declaration for a pointer to a type char variable. Name the pointer char_ptr.

2. If you have a type int variable named cost, how would you declare and initialize a pointer named p_cost that points to that variable?

3. Continuing with exercise 2, how would you assign the value 100 to the variable cost using both direct access and indirect access?

4. Continuing with exercise 3, how would you print the value of the pointer, plus the value being pointed to?

5. Show how to assign the address of a float value called radius to a pointer.

6. Show two ways to assign the value 100 to the third element of data[].

7. Write a function named sumarrays() that accepts two arrays as arguments, totals all values in both arrays, and returns the total to the calling program.

8. Use the function created in exercise 7 in a simple program.

9. Write a function named addarrays() that accepts two arrays that are the same size. The function should add each element in the arrays together and place the values in a third array.

DAY 9

Characters and Strings

NEW TERM   A *character* is a single letter, numeral, punctuation mark, or other such
            symbol. A *string* is any sequence of characters. Strings are used to hold
text data, which is composed of letters, numerals, punctuation marks, and other
symbols. Clearly, characters and strings are extremely useful in many programming applications. Today you will learn

- How to use C's char data type to hold single characters
- How to create arrays of type char to hold multiple-character strings
- How to initialize characters and strings
- How to use pointers with strings
- How to print and input characters and strings

The char Data Type

C uses the char data type to hold characters. You saw on Day 2, "The
Components of a C Program: Code and Data," that char is one of C's
numeric integer data types. If char is a numeric type, how can it be used to
hold characters?

The answer lies in how C stores characters. Your computer's memory stores all data in numeric form. There is no direct way to store characters. However, a numeric code exists for each character. This is called the *ASCII code* or the *ASCII character set*. (*ASCII* stands for *American Standard Code for Information Interchange*.) The code assigns values between 0 and 255 for uppercase and lowercase letters, numeric digits, punctuation marks, and other symbols. The ASCII character set is listed in Appendix A.

For example, 97 is the ASCII code for the letter *a*. When you store the character *a* in a type char variable, you're really storing the value 97. Because the allowable numeric range for type char matches the standard ASCII character set, char is ideally suited for storing characters.

At this point, you might be a bit puzzled. If C stores characters as numbers, how does your program know whether a given type char variable is a character or a number? As you'll learn later, declaring a variable as type char is not enough; you must do something else with the variable:

- If a char variable is used somewhere in a C program where a character is expected, it is interpreted as a character.

- If a char variable is used somewhere in a C program where a number is expected, it is interpreted as a number.

This gives you some understanding of how C uses a numeric data type to store character data. Now you can go on to the details.

Using Character Variables

Like other variables, you must declare chars before using them, and you can initialize them at the time of declaration. Here are some examples:

```
char a, b, c;          /* Declare three uninitialized char variables */
char code = 'x';       /* Declare the char variable named code */
                       /* and store the character x there */
code = '!';            /* Store ! in the variable named code */
```

To create literal character constants, you enclose a single character in single quotation marks. The compiler automatically translates literal character constants into the corresponding ASCII codes, and the numeric code value is assigned to the variable.

You can create symbolic character constants by using either the #define directive or the const keyword:

```
#define EX 'x'

char code = EX;        /* Sets code equal to 'x' */
const char A = 'Z';
```

9

Now that you know how to declare and initialize character variables, it's time for a demonstration. Listing 9.1 illustrates the numeric nature of character storage using the printf() function you learned on Day 6, "Fundamentals of Input and Output." The function printf() can be used to print both characters and numbers. The format string %c instructs printf() to print a character, whereas %d instructs it to print a decimal integer. Listing 9.1 initializes two type char variables and prints each one, first as a character and then as a number.

LISTING 9.1. The numeric nature of type char variables.

```
1:  /* Demonstrates the numeric nature of char variables */
2:
3:  #include <stdio.h>
4:
5:  /* Declare and initialize two char variables */
6:
7:  char c1 = 'a';
8:  char c2 = 90;
9:
10: int main(void)
11: {
12:     /* Print variable c1 as a character, then as a number */
13:
14:     printf("\nAs a character, variable c1 is %c", c1);
15:     printf("\nAs a number, variable c1 is %d", c1);
16:
17:     /* Do the same for variable c2 */
18:
19:     printf("\nAs a character, variable c2 is %c", c2);
20:     printf("\nAs a number, variable c2 is %d\n", c2);
21:
22:     return 0;
23: }
```

OUTPUT

```
As a character, variable c1 is a
As a number, variable c1 is 97
As a character, variable c2 is Z
As a number, variable c2 is 90
```

Do	Don't
DO use %c to print the character value of a number. **DO** use single quotation marks when initializing a character variable.	**DON'T** use double quotation marks when initializing a character variable.

> **Caution** When using characters, it is usually safe to assume that the values 0 to 127 are the same. However, there are many possible extensions (character values greater than 128) for dealing with the alphabet of languages other than English. Don't make any assumptions about the extended character values.

Using Strings

Variables of type char can hold only a single character, so they have limited usefulness. You also need a way to store *strings,* which are sequences of characters. A person's name and address are examples of strings. Although there is no special data type for strings, C handles this type of information with arrays of characters.

Arrays of Characters

To hold a string of six characters, for example, you need to declare an array of type char with seven elements. Arrays of type char are declared like arrays of other data types. For example, the statement

```
char string[10];
```

declares a 10-element array of type char. This array could be used to hold a string of nine or fewer characters.

"But wait," you might be saying. "It's a 10-element array, so why can it hold only nine characters?" In C, a string is defined as a sequence of characters ending with the null character, a special character represented by \0. Although it's represented by two characters (backslash and zero), the null character is interpreted as a single character and has the ASCII value of 0. It's one of C's escape sequences, covered on Day 6.

When a C program stores the string Alabama, for example, it stores the seven characters A, l, a, b, a, m, and a, followed by the null character \0, for a total of eight characters. Thus, a character array can hold a string of characters numbering one fewer than the total number of elements in the array.

Initializing Character Arrays

Like other C data types, character arrays can be initialized when they are declared. Character arrays can be assigned values element by element, as shown here:

```
char string[10] = { 'A', 'l', 'a', 'b', 'a', 'm', 'a', '\0' };
```

 It's more convenient, however, to use a *literal string,* which is a sequence of characters enclosed in double quotation marks:

```
char string[10] = "Alabama";
```

When you use a literal string in your program, the compiler automatically adds the terminating null character at the end of the string. If you don't specify the number of subscripts when you declare an array, the compiler calculates the size of the array for you. Thus, the following line creates and initializes an eight-element array:

```
char string[] = "Alabama";
```

Remember that strings require a terminating null character. The C functions that manipulate strings (covered on Day 16, "Manipulating Strings") determine string length by looking for the null character. These functions have no other way of recognizing the end of the string. If the null character is missing, your program thinks that the string extends until the next null character in memory. Pesky program bugs can result from this sort of error.

Strings and Pointers

You've seen that strings are stored in arrays of type char, with the end of the string (which might not occupy the entire array) marked by the null character. Because the end of the string is marked, all you need in order to define a given string is something that points to its beginning. (Is *points* the right word? Indeed it is!)

With that hint, you might be leaping ahead of the game. From Day 8, "Understanding Pointers," you know that the name of an array is a pointer to the first element of the array. Therefore, for a string that's stored in an array, you need only the array name in order to access it. In fact, using the array's name is C's standard method of accessing strings.

To be more precise, using the array's name to access strings is the method the C library functions expect. The C standard library includes a number of functions that manipulate strings. (These functions are covered on Day 16.) To pass a string to one of these functions, you pass the array name. The same is true of the string display functions printf() and puts(), discussed later in today's lesson.

You might have noticed that I mentioned "strings stored in an array" a moment ago. Does this imply that some strings aren't stored in arrays? Indeed it does, and the next section explains why.

Strings Without Arrays

From the preceding section, you know that a string is defined by the character array's name and a null character. The array's name is a type char pointer to the beginning of the string. The null marks the string's end. The actual space occupied by the string in an array is incidental. In fact, the only purpose the array serves is to provide allocated space for the string.

What if you could find some memory storage space without allocating an array? You could then store a string with its terminating null character there instead. A pointer to the first character could serve to specify the string's beginning just as if the string were in an allocated array. How do you go about finding memory storage space? There are two methods: One allocates space for a literal string when the program is compiled, and the other uses the `malloc()` function to allocate space while the program is executing, a process known as *dynamic allocation*.

Allocating String Space at Compilation

The start of a string, as mentioned earlier, is indicated by a pointer to a variable of type `char`. You might recall how to declare such a pointer:

```
char *message;
```

This statement declares a pointer to a variable of type `char` named `message`. It doesn't point to anything now, but what if you changed the pointer declaration to read

```
char *message = "Great Caesar\'s Ghost!";
```

When this statement executes, the string `Great Caesar's Ghost!` (with a terminating null character) is stored somewhere in memory, and the pointer `message` is initialized to point to the first character of the string. Don't worry where in memory the string is stored; it's handled automatically by the compiler. After it is defined, `message` is a pointer to the string and can be used as such.

The preceding declaration/initialization is equivalent to the following, and the two notations `*message` and `message[]` also are equivalent; they both mean "a pointer to."

```
char message[] = "Great Caesar\'s Ghost!";
```

This method of allocating space for string storage is fine when you know what you need while writing the program. What if the program has varying string storage needs, depending on user input or other factors that are unknown when you're writing the program? You use the `malloc()` function, which enables you to allocate storage space on the fly.

The `malloc()` Function

The `malloc()` function is one of C's *memory allocation* functions. When you call `malloc()`, you pass it the number of bytes of memory needed. `malloc()` finds and reserves a block of memory of the required size and returns the address of the first byte in the block. You don't need to worry about where the memory is found; it's handled automatically.

The `malloc()` function returns an address, and its return type is a pointer to type `void`. Why `void`? A pointer to type `void` is compatible with all data types. Because the memory allocated by `malloc()` can be used to store any of C's data types, the `void` return type is appropriate.

The `malloc()` Function

▼ SYNTAX

```
#include <stdlib.h>
void *malloc(size_t size);
```

`malloc()` allocates a block of memory that is the number of bytes stated in *size*. By allocating memory as needed with `malloc()` instead of all at once when a program starts, you can use a computer's memory more efficiently. When using `malloc()`, you need to include the `stdlib.h` header file.

`malloc()` returns a pointer to the allocated block of memory. If `malloc()` was unable to allocate the required amount of memory, it returns `NULL`. Whenever you try to allocate memory, you should always check the return value, even if the amount of memory to be allocated is small. We'll be discussing `NULL` and its use a little later.

Example 1

```
#include <stdlib.h>
#include <stdio.h>
int main(void)
{
   /* allocate memory for a 100-character string */
   char *str;
   if (( str = (char *) malloc(100)) == NULL)
   {
      printf( "Not enough memory to allocate buffer\n");
      exit(1);
   }
   printf( "String was allocated!\n" );
   return 0;
}
```

Example 2

```
/* allocate memory for an array of 50 integers */
int *numbers;
numbers = (int *) malloc(50 * sizeof(int));
```

Example 3

```
/* allocate memory for an array of 10 float values */
float *numbers;
numbers = (float *) malloc(10 * sizeof(float));
```

Using the `malloc()` Function

You can use `malloc()` to allocate memory to store a single type `char`. First, declare a pointer to type `char`:

```
char *ptr;
```

Next, call `malloc()` and pass the size of the desired memory block. Because a type `char` usually occupies one byte, you need a block of one byte. The value returned by `malloc()` is assigned to the pointer:

```
ptr = malloc(1);
```

This statement allocates a memory block of one byte and assigns its address to `ptr`. Unlike variables that are declared in the program, this byte of memory has no name. Only the pointer can reference the variable. For example, to store the character `'x'` there, you would write

```
*ptr = 'x';
```

Allocating storage for a string with `malloc()` is almost identical to using `malloc()` to allocate space for a single variable of type `char`. The main difference is that you need to know the amount of space to allocate—the maximum number of characters in the string. This maximum depends on the needs of your program. For this example, say you want to allocate space for a string of 99 characters, plus one for the terminating null character, for a total of 100. First you declare a pointer to type `char`, and then you call `malloc()`:

```
char *ptr;
ptr = malloc(100);
```

Now `ptr` points to a reserved block of 100 bytes that can be used for string storage and manipulation. You can use `ptr` just as though your program had explicitly allocated that space with the following array declaration:

```
char ptr[100];
```

Using `malloc()` lets your program allocate storage space as needed in response to demand. Of course, available space is not unlimited; it depends on the amount of memory installed in your computer and on the program's other storage requirements. If not enough memory is available, `malloc()` returns an uninitialized address (that is, `NULL`). Your program should test the return value of `malloc()` so that you'll know the memory requested was allocated successfully. You always should test `malloc()`'s return value against the symbolic constant `NULL`, which is defined in stdlib.h. Listing 9.2 illustrates the use of `malloc()`. Any program using `malloc()` must `#include` the header file stdlib.h.

9

> **Note**
>
> Many C programmers assign a special value to all pointers that have not yet been initialized. This is the value NULL, which is actually a special value within the system. By assigning NULL to a pointer, you direct the pointer to point nowhere. In most operating systems, including Linux, this value is usually zero and is reserved for use by the operating system; hence, it would not normally be of any use anyway.
>
> The real beauty of this scheme is that you can test whether a pointer has been initialized by testing whether it is equal to NULL. The value NULL is declared in stdio.h, so you must include this header file in order to use NULL.

LISTING 9.2. Using the `malloc()` function to allocate storage space for string data.

```
1:  /* Demonstrates the use of malloc() to allocate storage */
2:  /* space for string data. */
3:
4:  #include <stdio.h>
5:  #include <stdlib.h>
6:
7:  char count, *ptr, *p;
8:
9:  int main(void)
10: {
11:     /* Allocate a block of 35 bytes. Test for success. */
12:
13:
14:     ptr = malloc(35 * sizeof(char));
15:
16:     if (ptr == NULL)
17:     {
18:         puts("Memory allocation error.");
19:         return 1;
20:     }
21:
22:     /* Fill the string with values 65 through 90, */
23:     /* which are the ASCII codes for A-Z. */
24:
25:     /* p is a pointer used to step through the string. */
26:     /* You want ptr to remain pointed at the start */
27:     /* of the string. */
28:
29:     p = ptr;
30:
31:     for (count = 65; count < 91 ; count++)
32:         *p++ = count;
33:
34:     /* Add the terminating null character. */
```

continues

LISTING 9.2. continued

```
35:
36:    *p = '\0';
37:
38:    /* Display the string on the screen. */
39:
40:    puts(ptr);
41:
42:    return 0;
43: }
```

OUTPUT   ABCDEFGHIJKLMNOPQRSTUVWXYZ

ANALYSIS   This program uses `malloc()` in a simple way. Although the program seems long, it's filled with comments. Lines 1, 2, 11, 12, 22 through 27, 34, and 38 are all comments that detail everything the program does. Line 5 includes the stdlib.h header file needed for `malloc()`, and line 4 includes the stdio.h header file for the `puts()` functions. Line 7 declares two pointers and a character variable used later in the listing. None of these variables are initialized, so they shouldn't be used—yet!

The `malloc()` function is called in line 14 with a parameter of 35 multiplied by *the size of* a `char`. Could you have just used 35? Yes, but you're assuming that everyone running this program will be using a computer that stores `char` type variables as one byte in size. Remember from Day 2 that different compilers can use different-size variables. Using the `sizeof` operator is an easy way to create portable code.

Never assume that `malloc()` gets the memory you tell it to get. In fact, you aren't *telling* it to get memory—you're *asking* it. Line 16 shows the easiest way to check whether `malloc()` provided the memory. If the memory was allocated, `ptr` points to it; otherwise, `ptr` is `NULL`. If the program failed to get the memory, lines 18 and 19 display an error message and gracefully exit the program.

Line 29 initializes the other pointer declared in line 7, `p`. It is assigned the same address value as `ptr`. A `for` loop uses this new pointer to place values into the allocated memory. Looking at line 31, you see that `count` is initialized to 65 and incremented by 1 until it reaches 91. For each loop of the `for` statement, the value of `count` is assigned to the address pointed to by `p`. Notice that each time `count` is incremented, the address pointed to by `p` is also incremented. This means that each value is placed one after the other in memory.

You should have noticed that numbers are being assigned to `count`, which is a type `char` variable. Remember the discussion of ASCII characters and their numeric equivalents? The number 65 is equivalent to `A`, 66 equals `B`, 67 equals `C`, and so on. The `for` loop ends after the alphabet is assigned to the memory locations pointed to. Line 36 caps off the character values pointed to by putting a null at the final address pointed to by p. By appending the null, you can now use these values as a string. Remember that ptr still points to the first value, A, so if you use it as a string, it prints every character until it reaches the null. Line 40 uses puts() to prove this point and to show the results of what has been done.

Do	Don't
	DON'T allocate more memory than you need. Not everyone has a lot of memory, so you should try to use it sparingly.
	DON'T try to assign a new string to a character array that was previously allocated only enough memory to hold a smaller string. For example, in this declaration

```
char a_string[] = "NO";
```

a_string points to "NO". If you try to assign "YES" to this array, you might have serious problems. The array initially could hold only three characters—'N', 'O', and a null. "YES" is four characters—'Y', 'E', 'S', and a null. You have no idea what the fourth character, null, overwrites.

Displaying Strings and Characters

If your program uses string data, it probably needs to display the data on the screen at some time. String display is usually done with either the puts() function or the printf() function.

The puts() Function

You've seen the puts() library function in some of the programs in this book. The puts() function puts a string onscreen—hence its name. A pointer to the string to be displayed is the only argument puts() takes. Because a literal string evaluates as a pointer to a string, puts() can be used to display literal strings as well as string variables. The puts() function automatically inserts a newline character at the end of each string it displays, so each subsequent string displayed with puts() is on its own line.

Listing 9.3 illustrates the use of puts().

LISTING 9.3. Using the puts() function to display text onscreen.

```
1: /* Demonstrates displaying strings with puts(). */
2:
3: #include <stdio.h>
4:
5: char *message1 = "C";
6: char *message2 = "is the";
7: char *message3 = "best";
8: char *message4 = "programming";
9: char *message5 = "language!!";
10:
11: int main(void)
12: {
13:     puts(message1);
14:     puts(message2);
15:     puts(message3);
16:     puts(message4);
17:     puts(message5);
18:
19:     return 0;
20: }
```

OUTPUT
```
C
is the
best
programming
language!!
```

ANALYSIS This is a fairly simple listing to follow. Because puts() is a standard output function, the stdio.h header file must be included, as is done on line 3. Lines 5 through 9 declare and initialize five different message variables. Each of these variables is a character pointer, or string variable. Lines 13 through 17 use the puts() function to print each string.

The printf() Function

You can also display strings using the printf() library function. Recall from Day 6 that printf() uses a format string and conversion specifiers to shape its output. To display a string, use the conversion specifier %s.

When printf() encounters a %s in its format string, the function matches the %s with the corresponding argument in its argument list. For a string, this argument must be a pointer to the string that you want displayed. The printf() function displays the string onscreen, stopping when it reaches the string's terminating null character. For example

```
char *str = "A message to display";
printf("%s", str);
```

You can also display multiple strings and mix them with literal text and/or numeric variables:

```
char *bank = "First Federal";
char *name = "John Doe";
int balance = 1000;
printf("The balance at %s for %s is %d.", bank, name, balance);
```

The resulting output is

```
The balance at First Federal for John Doe is 1000.
```

For now, this information should be sufficient for you to be able to display string data in your programs. Complete details on using `printf()` are given on Day 13, "Working with the Screen and Keyboard."

Reading Strings from the Keyboard

In addition to displaying strings, programs must often accept inputted string data from the user via the keyboard. The C library has three functions that can be used for this purpose—`gets()`, `fgets()`, and `scanf()`. Having said that, you should avoid `gets()` because it has a serious flaw. Fortunately, `fgets()` can be safely used in place of `gets()`.

Before you can read in a string from the keyboard, however, you must have somewhere to put it. You can create space for string storage using either of the methods discussed earlier—an array declaration or the `malloc()` function.

Inputting Strings Using the `gets()` and `fgets()` Functions

The task of the `gets()` and the `fgets()` functions is to read characters from the keyboard and return them to the calling program as a string. Characters are read until the first newline character (generated by pressing the Enter key) is reached. Both of these functions terminate the string with the null character before returning it to the caller; however, `fgets()` includes the newline, whereas `gets()` does not.

The function prototypes of these two functions are defined in the stdio.h header file as follows:

```
char *gets(char *s);
```

```
char *fgets(char *s, int size, FILE *stream);
```

Don't worry about the last parameter of `fgets()`, but do notice that `fgets()` has a parameter in which you can set the size of the array s, whereas `gets()` has no such parameter. This is what makes the use of `gets()` dangerous. If you declare a char array to be 10 characters long and pass it to gets(), it will read as many characters as the user types before he or she presses Enter. This might be more than 10 characters; hence, it will overflow the end of your array. Because gets() is so potentially dangerous, we will not use it in this book. If, however, you do happen to use it in one of your own programs, you will probably find that the GNU C compiler gives you a warning message about using it.

Listing 9.4 shows an example of using fgets(). The string entered from the keyboard is stored at the location indicated by a pointer to type char passed to fgets(). The maximum allowable length of the string (including the null character) that fgets() is allowed to read is passed as the second parameter, and the external variable stdin is used as the third parameter. The external stdin variable is defined, along with fgets(), in the stdio.h header file. It is already initialized, and you should not do anything with it other than use it.

LISTING 9.4. Using fgets() to input string data from the keyboard.

```
1:  /* Demonstrates using the fgets() library function. */
2:
3:  #include <stdio.h>
4:
5:  /* Allocate a character array to hold input. */
6:
7:  char input[40];
8:
9:  int main(void)
10: {
11:     puts("Enter some text, then press Enter: ");
12:     fgets(input, 40, stdin);
13:     printf("You entered: %s\n", input);
14:
15:     return 0;
16: }
```

INPUT/
OUTPUT

```
Enter some text, then press Enter:
This is a test
You entered: This is a test
```

ANALYSIS   In this example, the first argument to fgets() is the expression input, which is the name of a type char array and, therefore, a pointer to the first array element. The array is declared with 40 elements in line 7, so the value 40 should be used as the second argument. The third argument, stdin, is explained in more detail on Day 13.

The fgets() function has a return value, which was ignored in the previous example. fgets() returns a pointer to type char with the address where the input string is stored or the NULL pointer if an error occurred. When reading from the keyboard, it is very unlikely that an error will occur, but this return value does have uses in other situations in which `fgets()` might be used. This is dealt with on Day 15, "Using Disk Files."

Do	Don't
DO use `fgets()` and do pass the length of the character array as the second parameter to the `fgets()` function.	**DON'T** use the `gets()` function because it is not always possible to know how many characters `gets()` will read and because `gets()` will continue to store characters past the end of array you passed to it.
DO make sure you pass a valid pointer that has been initialized as the first parameter to the `fgets()` function.	

Inputting Strings Using the `scanf()` Function

You saw on Day 6 that the `scanf()` library function accepts numeric data input from the keyboard. That function can also input strings. Remember that `scanf()` uses a *format string* that tells it how to read the input. To read a string, include the specifier `%s` in `scanf()`'s format string. Like `gets()`, `scanf()` is passed a pointer to the string's storage location.

How does `scanf()` decide where the string begins and ends? The beginning is the first non-whitespace character encountered. The end can be specified in one of two ways. If you use `%s` in the format string, the string runs up to (but not including) the next whitespace character (space, tab, or newline). If you use `%ns` (where n is an integer constant that specifies field width), `scanf()` inputs the next n characters or up to the next whitespace character, whichever comes first.

You can read in multiple strings with `scanf()` by including more than one `%s` in the format string. For each `%s` in the format string, `scanf()` uses the preceding rules to find the requested number of strings in the input. For example

```
scanf("%s%s%s", s1, s2, s3);
```

If, in response to this statement, you enter January February March, January is assigned to the string `s1`, February is assigned to `s2`, and March to `s3`.

What about using the field-width specifier? If you execute the statement

```
scanf("%3s%3s%3s", s1, s2, s3);
```

and, in response, you enter September, Sep is assigned to `s1`, tem is assigned to `s2`, and ber is assigned to `s3`.

Note

> Notice that, as with the dangerous function gets(), it is possible to overrun the end of your array when you use the scanf function.

What if you enter fewer or more strings than the scanf() function expects? If you enter fewer strings, scanf() continues to look for the missing strings, and the program doesn't continue until they're entered. For example, if in response to the statement

```
scanf("%s%s%s", s1, s2, s3);
```

you enter January February, the program waits for the third string specified in the scanf() format string. If you enter more strings than requested, the unmatched strings remain pending (waiting in the keyboard buffer) and are read by any subsequent scanf() or other input statements. For example, if in response to the statements

```
scanf("%s%s", s1, s2);
scanf("%s", s3);
```

you enter January February March, the result is that January is assigned to the string s1 and February is assigned to s2 in the first scanf() call. March is then automatically carried over and assigned to s3 in the second scanf() call.

The scanf() function has a return value, an integer value equaling the number of items successfully inputted. The return value is often ignored. When you're reading text only, the gets() function is usually preferable to scanf(). It's best to use the scanf() function when you're reading in a combination of text and numeric data. This is illustrated by Listing 9.5. Remember from Day 6 that you must use the address-of operator (&) when inputting numeric variables with scanf().

LISTING 9.5. Inputting numeric and text data with scanf().

```
1:  /* Demonstrates using scanf() to input numeric and text data. */
2:
3:  #include <stdio.h>
4:
5:  char lname[81], fname[81];
6:  int count, id_num;
7:
8:  int main(void)
9:  {
10:      /* Prompt the user. */
11:
12:      puts("Enter last name, first name, ID number separated");
13:      puts("by spaces, then press Enter.");
14:
```

```
15:     /* Input the three data items. */
16:
17:     count = scanf("%s%s%d", lname, fname, &id_num);
18:
19:     /* Display the data. */
20:
21:     printf("%d items entered: %s %s %d \n", count, fname, lname, id_num);
22:
23:     return 0;
24: }
```

9

INPUT/ OUTPUT
Enter last name, first name, ID number separated
by spaces, then press Enter.
Jones Bradley 12345
3 items entered: Bradley Jones 12345

ANALYSIS Remember that scanf() requires the addresses of variables for parameters. In
Listing 9.5, lname and fname are pointers (that is, addresses), so they don't need
the address-of operator (&). In contrast, id_num is a regular variable name, so it requires
the & when passed to scanf() on line 17.

Some programmers feel that data entry with scanf() is prone to errors. They prefer to
input all data, numeric and string, using fgets(), and then have the program separate the
numbers and convert them to numeric variables. Such techniques are beyond the scope of
this book, but they would make a good programming exercise. For that task, you need
the string manipulation functions covered on Day 17, "Exploring the C Function
Library."

Summary

Today's lesson covered C's char data type. One use of type char variables is to store
individual characters. You saw that characters are actually stored as numbers: The ASCII
code assigns a numerical code to each character. Therefore, you can use type char to
store small integer values as well. Both signed and unsigned char types are available.

A string is a sequence of characters terminated by the null character. Strings can be used
for text data. C stores strings in arrays of type char. To store a string of length n, you
need an array of type char with $n+1$ elements.

You can use memory allocation functions such as malloc() to make your programs more
dynamic. By using malloc(), you can allocate the right amount of memory for your program. Without such functions, you would have to guess at the amount of memory storage
the program needs. Your estimate would probably be high, so you would allocate more
memory than needed.

Q&A

Q What is the difference between a string and an array of characters?

A A string is defined as a sequence of characters ending with the null character. An array is a sequence of characters. A string, therefore, is a null-terminated array of characters.

   If you define an array of type char, the actual storage space allocated for the array is the specified size, not the size minus 1. You're limited to that size; you can't store a larger string. Here's an example:

```
char state[10]="Minneapolis";   /* Wrong! String longer than array. */
char state2[10]="MN";           /* OK, but wastes space because */
                                /* string is shorter than array. */
```

   If, on the other hand, you define a pointer to type char, these restrictions don't apply. The variable is a storage space only for the pointer. The actual strings are stored elsewhere in memory (but you don't need to worry about where in memory). There's no length restriction or wasted space. The actual string is stored elsewhere. A pointer can point to a string of any length.

Q Why shouldn't I just declare big arrays to hold values instead of using a memory allocation function such as malloc()?

A Although it might seem easier to declare large arrays, that isn't an effective use of memory. When you're writing small programs, such as those in today's lesson, it might seem trivial to use a function such as malloc() instead of arrays, but as your programs get bigger, you'll want to be able to allocate memory only as needed. When you're done with memory, you can put it back by *freeing* it. When you free memory, some other variable or array in a different part of the program can use it. (Day 18, "Working with Memory," covers freeing allocated memory.)

Q What happens if I put a string into a character array that is bigger than the array?

A This can cause a hard-to-find error. You can do this in C, but anything stored in the memory directly after the character array is overwritten. This could be an area of memory not used or some other data required by your program. Your results will depend on what you overwrite. Often, nothing happens for a while. You don't want to do this.

Q Why should I use the fgets() function instead of gets()?

A The gets() function does not allow any way to specify the length of the character array it is reading into, whereas fgets() enables you to specify a length and, therefore, prevent overrunning the end of the array.

Workshop

The Workshop provides quiz questions to help you solidify your understanding of the material covered and exercises to provide you with experience in using what you've learned. The answers to the quiz and exercises are provided in Appendix C, "Answers."

Quiz

1. What is the range of numeric values in the standard ASCII character set?

2. When the C compiler encounters a single character enclosed in single quotation marks, how is it interpreted?

3. What is C's definition of a string?

4. What is a literal string?

5. To store a string of *n* characters, you need a character array of *n*+1 elements. Why is the extra element needed?

6. When the C compiler encounters a literal string, how is it interpreted?

7. Using an ASCII character chart or a program, state the numeric values stored for each of the following:

   a. a

   b. A

   c. 9

   d. a space

8. Using an ASCII character chart or a program, translate the following ASCII values into their equivalent characters:

   a. 73

   b. 32

   c. 99

   d. 0

   e. 2

9. How many bytes of storage are allocated for each of the following variables? (Assume that a character is one byte.)

   a. `char *str1 = { "String 1" };`

   b. `char str2[] = { "String 2" };`

   c. `char string3;`

   d. `char str4[20] = { "This is String 4" };`

   e. `char str5[20];`

10. Using the following declaration,

    ```
    char *string = "A string!";
    ```

    what are the values of the following?

    a. `string[0]`

    b. `*string`

    c. `string[9]`

    d. `string[33]`

    e. `*string+8`

    f. `string`

Exercises

1. Write a line of code that declares a type `char` variable named `letter`, and initialize it to the character $.

2. Write a line of code that declares an array of type `char`, and initialize it to the string `"Pointers are fun!"`. Make the array just large enough to hold the string.

3. Write a line of code that allocates storage for the string `"Pointers are fun!"`, as in exercise 2, but without using an array.

4. Write code that allocates space for an 80-character string and then inputs a string from the keyboard and stores it in the allocated space.

5. Write a function that copies one array of characters into another. (Hint: Do this just as in the programs you wrote on Day 8.)

6. Write a function that accepts two strings. Count the number of characters in each, and return a pointer to the longer string.

7. **ON YOUR OWN:** Write a function that accepts two strings. Use the `malloc()` function to allocate enough memory to hold the two strings after they have been concatenated (linked). Return a pointer to this new string.

   For example, if I pass `"Hello "` and `"World!"`, the function returns a pointer to `"Hello World!"`. Having the concatenated value be the third string is easiest. (You might be able to use your answers from exercises 5 and 6.)

8. **BUG BUSTER:** Is anything wrong with the following?

   ```
   char a_string[10] = "This is a string";
   ```

9. **BUG BUSTER:** Is anything wrong with the following?

   ```
   char *quote[100] = { "Smile, Friday is almost here!" };
   ```

10. **BUG BUSTER:** Is anything wrong with the following?

```
char *string1;
char *string2 = "Second";
string1 = string2;
```

11. **BUG BUSTER:** Is anything wrong with the following?

```
char string1[];
char string2[] = "Second";
string1 = string2;
```

12. **ON YOUR OWN:** Using the ASCII chart, write a program that prints a box onscreen using the minus sign, the logical or vertical bar, and the plus sign at each corner.

Caution

> Today's lesson dynamically allocated memory using the `malloc()` function. When you dynamically allocate memory, you should release it back to the computer system when you are done with it. You can put dynamically allocated memory back by *freeing* it. Day 18, "Working with Memory," will cover freeing allocated memory.

9

DAY **10**

Structures

Many programming tasks are simplified by the C data constructs called *structures*. A structure is a data storage method designed by you, the programmer, to suit your programming needs exactly. Today you will learn

- What simple and complex structures are
- How to define and declare structures
- How to access data in structures
- How to create structures that contain arrays and arrays of structures
- How to declare pointers in structures and pointers to structures
- How to pass structures as arguments to functions
- How to define, declare, and use unions
- How to use type definitions with structures

Simple Structures

 A *structure* is a collection of one or more variables grouped under a single name for easy manipulation. The variables in a structure, unlike those in an array, can be of different variable types. A structure can contain any of C's data types, including arrays and other structures. Each variable within a structure is called a *member* of the structure. The next section shows a simple example.

You should start with simple structures. Note that the C language makes no distinction between simple and complex structures, but it's easier to explain structures in this way.

Defining and Declaring Structures

If you're writing a graphics program, your code needs to deal with the coordinates of points on the screen. Screen coordinates are written as an x value, giving the horizontal position, and a y value, giving the vertical position. You can define a structure named coord that contains both the x and y values of a screen location as follows:

```
struct coord {
    int x;
    int y;
};
```

The struct keyword, which identifies the beginning of a structure definition, must be followed immediately by the structure name, or *tag* (which follows the same rules as other C variable names). Within the braces following the structure name is a list of the structure's member variables. You must give a variable type and name for each member.

> **Note**
>
> It is allowable to create an unnamed structure that does not have a tag naming it, but that structure is not very useful.

The preceding statements define a structure type named coord that contains two integer variables, x and y. They do not, however, actually create any instances of the structure coord. In other words, they don't *declare* (set aside storage for) any structures. There are two ways to declare structures. One way is to follow the structure definition with a list of one or more variable names, as is done here:

```
struct coord {
    int x;
    int y;
} first, second;
```

These statements define the structure type coord and declare two structures, first and second, of type coord. first and second are each *instances* of type coord; first contains two integer members named x and y, and so does second.

This method of declaring structures combines the declaration with the definition. The second method is to declare structure variables at a different location in your source code from the definition. The following statements also declare two instances of type coord:

```
struct coord {
    int x;
    int y;
};
/* Additional code may go here */
struct coord first, second;
```

Accessing Structure Members

Individual structure members can be used like other variables of the same type. Structure members are accessed using the *structure member operator* (.), also called the *dot operator,* between the structure name and the member name. Thus, to have the structure named first refer to a screen location that has the coordinates x=50 and y=100, you could write

```
first.x = 50;
first.y = 100;
```

To display the screen locations stored in the structure second, you could write

```
printf("%d,%d", second.x, second.y);
```

At this point, you might be wondering what the advantage is of using structures rather than individual variables. One major advantage is that you can copy information between structures of the same type with a simple equation statement. Continuing with the preceding example, the statement

```
first = second;
```

is equivalent to this statement:

```
first.x = second.x;
first.y = second.y;
```

When your program uses complex structures with many members, this notation can be a great timesaver. Other advantages of structures will become apparent as you learn some advanced techniques. In general, you'll find structures to be useful whenever information of different variable types should be treated as a group. For example, in a mailing list database, each entry could be a structure, and each piece of information (name, address, city, and so on) could be a structure member.

10

The struct Keyword

▼ SYNTAX

```
struct tag {
    structure_member(s);
    /* additional statements may go here */
} instance;
```

The struct keyword is used to declare structures. A structure is a collection of one or more variables (structure_members) that have been grouped under a single name for easy manipulation. The variables don't have to be of the same variable type, nor do they have to be simple variables. Structures also can hold arrays, pointers, and other structures.

The keyword struct identifies the beginning of a structure definition. It's followed by a tag that is the name given to the structure. Following the tag are the structure members, enclosed in braces. An instance, the actual declaration of a structure, can also be defined. If you define the structure without the instance, it's just a template that can be used later in a program to declare structures. Here is a template's format:

```
struct tag {
    structure_member(s);
    /* additional statements may go here */
};
```

To use the template, you use the following format:

```
struct tag instance;
```

To use this format, you must have previously declared a structure with the given tag.

Example 1

```
/* Declare a structure template called SSN */
struct SSN {
    int first_three;
    char dash1;
    int second_two;
    char dash2;
    int last_four;
}
/* Use the structure template */
struct SSN customer_ssn;
```

Example 2

```
/* Declare a structure and instance together */
struct date {
    char month[2];
    char day[2];
    char year[4];
} current_date;
```

▼

▼ **Example 3**

```
/* Declare and initialize a structure */
struct time {
    int hours;
    int minutes;
    int seconds;
▲ } time_of_birth = { 8, 45, 0 };
```

More Complex Structures

Now that you have been introduced to simple structures, you can get to the more interesting and complex types of structures. These are structures that contain other structures as members and structures that contain arrays as members.

Structures That Contain Structures

As mentioned earlier, a C structure can contain any of C's data types. For example, a structure can contain other structures. The previous example can be extended to illustrate this.

Assume that your graphics program needs to deal with rectangles. A rectangle can be defined by the coordinates of two diagonally opposite corners. You've already seen how to define a structure that can hold the two coordinates required for a single point. You need two such structures to define a rectangle. You can define a structure as follows (assuming, of course, that you have already defined the type coord structure):

```
struct rectangle {
    struct coord topleft;
    struct coord bottomrt;
};
```

This statement defines a structure of type rectangle that contains two structures of type coord. These two type coord structures are named topleft and bottomrt.

The preceding statement defines only the type rectangle structure. To declare a structure, you must then include a statement such as

```
struct rectangle mybox;
```

You could have combined the definition and declaration, as you did before for the type coord:

```
struct rectangle {
    struct coord topleft;
    struct coord bottomrt;
} mybox;
```

10

To access the actual data locations (the type `int` members), you must apply the member operator (.) twice. Thus, the expression

```
mybox.topleft.x
```

refers to the `x` member of the `topleft` member of the type `rectangle` structure named `mybox`. To define a rectangle with the coordinates (0,10), (100,200), you would write

```
mybox.topleft.x = 0;
mybox.topleft.y = 10;
mybox.bottomrt.x = 100;
mybox.bottomrt.y = 200;
```

Maybe this is getting a bit confusing. You might understand better if you look at Figure 10.1, which shows the relationship between the type `rectangle` structure, the two type `coord` structures it contains, and the two type `int` variables each type `coord` structure contains. These structures are named as in the preceding example.

FIGURE 10.1.

The relationship among a structure, structures within a structure, and the structure members.

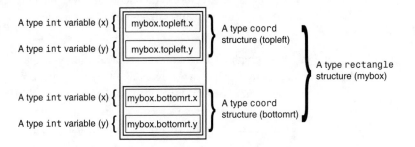

Listing 10.1 presents an example of using structures that contain other structures. This listing takes input from the user for the coordinates of a rectangle and then calculates and displays the rectangle's area. Note the program's assumptions, given in comments near the start of the program (lines 3 through 8).

LISTING 10.1. A demonstration of structures that contain other structures.

```
1:  /* Demonstrates structures that contain other structures. */
2:
3:  /* Receives input for corner coordinates of a rectangle and
4:      calculates the area. Assumes that the y coordinate of the
5:      lower-right corner is greater than the y coordinate of the
6:      upper-left corner, that the x coordinate of the lower-
7:      right corner is greater than the x coordinate of the upper-
8:      left corner, and that all coordinates are positive. */
9:
10: #include <stdio.h>
11:
12: int length, width;
```

```
13: long area;
14:
15: struct coord{
16:     int x;
17:     int y;
18: };
19:
20: struct rectangle{
21:     struct coord topleft;
22:     struct coord bottomrt;
23: } mybox;
24:
25: int main(void)
26: {
27:     /* Input the coordinates */
28:
29:     printf("\nEnter the top left x coordinate: ");
30:     scanf("%d", &mybox.topleft.x);
31:
32:     printf("\nEnter the top left y coordinate: ");
33:     scanf("%d", &mybox.topleft.y);
34:
35:     printf("\nEnter the bottom right x coordinate: ");
36:     scanf("%d", &mybox.bottomrt.x);
37:
38:     printf("\nEnter the bottom right y coordinate: ");
39:     scanf("%d", &mybox.bottomrt.y);
40:
41:     /* Calculate the length and width */
42:
43:     width = mybox.bottomrt.x - mybox.topleft.x;
44:     length = mybox.bottomrt.y - mybox.topleft.y;
45:
46:     /* Calculate and display the area */
47:
48:     area = width * length;
49:     printf("\nThe area is %ld units.\n", area);
50:
51:     return 0;
52: }
```

INPUT/ OUTPUT

```
Enter the top left x coordinate: 1

Enter the top left y coordinate: 1

Enter the bottom right x coordinate: 10

Enter the bottom right y coordinate: 10

The area is 81 units.
```

10

ANALYSIS   The coord structure is defined in lines 15 through 18 with its two members, x
           and y. Lines 20 through 23 declare and define an instance, called mybox, of the
rectangle structure. The two members of the rectangle structure are topleft and bottomrt, both structures of type coord.

Lines 29 through 39 fill in the values in the mybox structure. Because mybox has only two
members, it might seem at first that there are only two values to fill. However, each of
mybox's members has its own members. topleft and bottomrt have two members each,
x and y from the coord structure. This gives a total of four members to be filled. After
the members are filled with values, the area is calculated using the structure and member
names. When using the x and y values, you must include the structure instance name.
Because x and y are in a structure within a structure, you must use the instance names of
both structures—mybox.bottomrt.x, mybox.bottomrt.y, mybox.topleft.x, and
mybox.topleft.y—in the calculations.

C places no limits on the nesting of structures. While memory allows it, you can define
structures that contain structures that contain structures that contain structures—well, you
get the idea! Of course, there's a limit beyond which nesting becomes unproductive.
Rarely are more than three levels of nesting used in any C program.

Structures That Contain Arrays

You can define a structure that contains one or more arrays as members. The array can be
of any C data type (int, char, and so on). For example, the statements

```
struct data{
    int  x[4];
    char y[10];
};
```

define a structure of type data that contains a four-element integer array member named
x and a 10-element character array member named y. You can then declare a structure
named record of type data as follows:

```
struct data record;
```

The organization of this structure is shown in Figure 10.2. Note that, in this figure, the
elements of array x are shown to take up much more space than the elements of array y.
This is because a type int typically requires 4 bytes of storage, whereas a type char usually requires only 1 byte (as you learned on Day 2, "The Components of a C Program:
Code and Data").

FIGURE 10.2.

The organization of a structure that contains arrays as members.

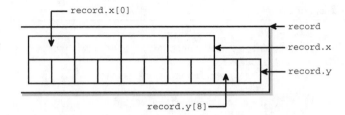

You access individual elements of arrays that are structure members by using a combination of the member operator and array subscripts:

```
record.x[2] = 100;
record.y[1] = 'x';
```

You probably remember that character arrays are most frequently used to store strings. You should also remember (from Day 8, "Understanding Pointers") that the name of an array, without brackets, is a pointer to the array. Because this holds true for arrays that are structure members, the expression

```
record.y
```

is a pointer to the first element of array y[] in the structure record. Therefore, you could print the contents of y[] onscreen by using the statement

```
puts(record.y);
```

Now look at another example. Listing 10.2 uses a structure that contains a type float variable and two type char arrays.

Listing 10.2. A structure that contains array members.

```
1:  /* Demonstrates a structure that has array members. */
2:
3:  #include <stdio.h>
4:
5:  /* Define and declare a structure to hold the data. */
6:  /* It contains one float variable and two char arrays. */
7:
8:  struct data{
9:      float amount;
10:      char fname[30];
11:      char lname[30];
12: } rec;
13:
14: int main(void)
15: {
16:      /* Input the data from the keyboard. */
```

continues

10

LISTING 10.2. continued

```
17:
18:        printf("Enter the donor's first and last names,\n");
19:        printf("separated by a space: ");
20:        scanf("%s %s", rec.fname, rec.lname);
21:
22:        printf("\nEnter the donation amount: ");
23:        scanf("%f", &rec.amount);
24:
25:        /* Display the information. */
26:        /* Note: %.2f specifies a floating-point value */
27:        /* to be displayed with two digits to the right */
28:        /* of the decimal point. */
29:
30:        /* Display the data on the screen. */
31:
32:        printf("\nDonor %s %s gave $%.2f.\n", rec.fname, rec.lname,
33:               rec.amount);
34:
35:        return 0;
36: }
```

| INPUT/ OUTPUT |

Enter the donor's first and last names,
separated by a space: **Bradley Jones**

Enter the donation amount: **1000.00**

Donor Bradley Jones gave $1000.00.

| ANALYSIS | This program includes a structure that contains array members named fname[30] and lname[30]. Both are arrays of characters that hold a person's first name and last name, respectively. The structure declared in lines 8 through 12 is called data. It contains the fname and lname character arrays with a type float variable called amount. This structure is ideal for holding a person's name (in two parts, first name and last name) and a value, such as the amount the person donated to a charitable organization.

An instance of the array, called rec, has also been declared in line 12. The rest of the program uses rec to get values from the user (lines 18 through 23) and then print them (lines 32 and 33).

Arrays of Structures

If you can have structures that contain arrays, can you also have arrays of structures? You bet you can! In fact, arrays of structures are very powerful programming tools. Here's how it's done.

You've seen how a structure definition can be tailored to fit the data your program needs to work with. Usually a program needs to work with more than one instance of the data. For example, in a program to maintain a list of phone numbers, you can define a structure to hold each person's name and number:

```
struct entry{
    char fname[10];
    char lname[12];
    char phone[8];
};
```

A phone list must hold many entries, however, so a single instance of the entry structure isn't of much use. What you need is an array of structures of type entry. After the structure has been defined, you can declare an array as follows:

```
struct entry list[1000];
```

This statement declares an array named list that contains 1,000 elements. Each element is a structure of type entry and is identified by a subscript, as with other array element types. Each of these structures has three elements, each of which is an array of type char. This entire complex creation is diagrammed in Figure 10.3.

FIGURE 10.3.

The organization of the array of structures defined in the text.

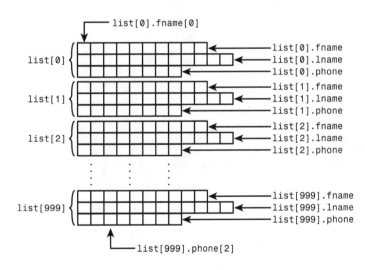

When you have declared the array of structures, you can manipulate the data in many ways. For example, to assign the data in one array element to another array element, you would write

```
list[1] = list[5];
```

This statement assigns to each member of the structure list[1] the values contained in the corresponding members of list[5]. You can also move data between individual structure members. The statement

```
strcpy(list[1].phone, list[5].phone);
```

copies the string in list[5].phone to list[1].phone. (The strcpy() library function copies one string to another string. You'll learn the details of this on Day 16, "Manipulating Strings.") If you want to, you can also move data between individual elements of the structure member arrays:

```
list[5].phone[1] = list[2].phone[3];
```

This statement moves the second character of list[5]'s phone number to the fourth position in list[2]'s phone number. (Don't forget that subscripts start at offset 0.)

Listing 10.3 demonstrates the use of arrays of structures. Moreover, it demonstrates arrays of structures that contain arrays as members.

LISTING 10.3. Arrays of structures.

```
1:   /* Demonstrates using arrays of structures. */
2:
3:   #include <stdio.h>
4:
5:   /* Define a structure to hold entries. */
6:
7:   struct entry {
8:       char fname[20];
9:       char lname[20];
10:      char phone[10];
11: };
12:
13: /* Declare an array of structures. */
14:
15: struct entry list[4];
16:
17: int i;
18:
19: int main(void)
20: {
21:
22:     /* Loop to input data for four people. */
23:
24:     for (i = 0; i < 4; i++)
25:     {
26:         printf("\nEnter first name: ");
27:         scanf("%s", list[i].fname);
```

```
28:          printf("Enter last name: ");
29:          scanf("%s", list[i].lname);
30:          printf("Enter phone in 123-4567 format: ");
31:          scanf("%s", list[i].phone);
32:      }
33:
34:      /* Print two blank lines. */
35:
36:      printf("\n\n");
37:
38:      /* Loop to display data. */
39:
40:      for (i = 0; i < 4; i++)
41:      {
42:          printf("Name: %s %s", list[i].fname, list[i].lname);
43:          printf("\t\tPhone: %s\n", list[i].phone);
44:      }
45:
46:      return 0;
47: }
```

**INPUT/
OUTPUT**

```
Enter first name: Bradley
Enter last name: Jones
Enter phone in 123-4567 format: 555-1212

Enter first name: Peter
Enter last name: Aitken
Enter phone in 123-4567 format: 555-3434

Enter first name: Melissa
Enter last name: Jones
Enter phone in 123-4567 format: 555-1212

Enter first name: Deanna
Enter last name: Townsend
Enter phone in 123-4567 format: 555-1234

Name: Bradley Jones          Phone: 555-1212
Name: Peter Aitken           Phone: 555-3434
Name: Melissa Jones          Phone: 555-1212
Name: Deanna Townsend        Phone: 555-1234
```

ANALYSIS This listing follows the same general format as most of the other listings. It starts with the comment in line 1 and, for the input/output functions, the #include file stdio.h in line 3. Lines 7 through 11 define a template structure called entry that contains three character arrays: fname, lname, and phone. Line 15 uses the template to define an array of four entry structure variables called list. Line 17 defines a variable of type int to be used as a counter throughout the program. main() starts in line 19. The first function of main() is to perform a loop four times with a for statement. This loop is used to get information for the array of structures. This can be seen in lines 24 through 32. Notice that list is being used with a subscript in the same way that the array variables were subscripted on Day 7, "Using Numeric Arrays."

Line 36 provides a break from the input before starting with the output. It prints two new lines in a manner that shouldn't be new to you. Lines 40 through 44 display the data that the user entered in the preceding step. The values in the array of structures are printed with the subscripted array name followed by the member operator (.) and the structure member name.

Familiarize yourself with the techniques used in Listing 10.3. Many real-world programming tasks are best accomplished by using arrays of structures containing arrays as members.

Do	Don't
DO declare structure instances with the same scope rules as other variables. (Day 11, "Understanding Variable Scope," covers this topic fully.)	DON'T forget the structure instance name and member operator (.) when using a structure's members.
	DON'T confuse a structure's tag with its instances! The tag is used to declare the structure's template, or format. The instance is a variable declared using the tag.
	DON'T forget the struct keyword when declaring an instance from a previously defined structure.

Initializing Structures

Like other C variable types, structures can be initialized when they're declared. This procedure is similar to that for initializing arrays. The structure declaration is followed by an equal sign and a list of initialization values separated by commas and enclosed in braces. For example, look at the following statements:

```
1: struct sale {
2:     char customer[20];
3:     char item[20];
4:     float amount;
5: } mysale = { "Acme Industries",
6:              "Left-handed widget",
7:                1000.00
8:            };
```

When these statements are executed, they perform the following actions:

1. Define a structure type named `sale` (lines 1 through 5).

2. Declare an instance of structure type `sale` named `mysale` (line 5).

3. Initialize the structure member `mysale.customer` to the string `"Acme Industries"` (line 5).

4. Initialize the structure member `mysale.item` to the string `"Left-handed widget"` (line 6).

5. Initialize the structure member `mysale.amount` to the value `1000.00` (line 7).

For a structure that contains structures as members, list the initialization values in order. They are placed in the structure members in the order in which the members are listed in the structure definition. Here's an example that expands on the previous one:

```
1:  struct customer {
2:      char firm[20];
3:      char contact[25];
4:  }
5:
6:  struct sale {
7:      struct customer buyer;
8:      char item[20];
9:      float amount;
10: } mysale = { { "Acme Industries", "George Adams"},
11:              "Left-handed widget",
12:              1000.00
13:           };
```

These statements perform the following initializations:

1. The structure member `mysale.buyer.firm` is initialized to the string `"Acme Industries"` (line 10).

2. The structure member `mysale.buyer.contact` is initialized to the string `"George Adams"` (line 10).

3. The structure member `mysale.item` is initialized to the string `"Left-handed widget"` (line 11).

4. The structure member `mysale.amount` is initialized to the amount `1000.00` (line 12).

You can also initialize arrays of structures. The initialization data that you supply is applied, in order, to the structures in the array. For example, to declare an array of structures of type `sale` and initialize the first two array elements (that is, the first two structures), you could write

```
1:  struct customer {
2:      char firm[20];
3:      char contact[25];
4:  };
5:
6:  struct sale {
7:      struct customer buyer;
8:      char item[20];
9:      float amount;
10: };
11:
12:
13: struct sale y1990[100] = {
14:      { { "Acme Industries", "George Adams"},
15:          "Left-handed widget",
16:            1000.00
17:      },
18:      { { "Wilson & Co.", "Ed Wilson"},
19:          "Type 12 gizmo",
20:            290.00
21:      }
22: };
```

This is what occurs in this code:

1. The structure member y1990[0].buyer.firm is initialized to the string "Acme Industries" (line 14).

2. The structure member y1990[0].buyer.contact is initialized to the string "George Adams" (line 14).

3. The structure member y1990[0].item is initialized to the string "Left-handed widget" (line 15).

4. The structure member y1990[0].amount is initialized to the amount 1000.00 (line 16).

5. The structure member y1990[1].buyer.firm is initialized to the string "Wilson & Co." (line 18).

6. The structure member y1990[1].buyer.contact is initialized to the string "Ed Wilson" (line 18).

7. The structure member y1990[1].item is initialized to the string "Type 12 gizmo" (line 19).

8. The structure member y1990[1].amount is initialized to the amount 290.00 (line 20).

Structures and Pointers

Given that pointers are such an important part of C, you shouldn't be surprised to find that they can be used with structures. You can use pointers as structure members, and you can also declare pointers to structures. These topics are covered in the following sections.

Pointers as Structure Members

You have complete flexibility in using pointers as structure members. Pointer members are declared in the same manner as pointers that aren't members of structures—that is, by using the indirection operator (*). Here's an example:

```
struct data {
    int *value;
    int *rate;
} first;
```

These statements define and declare a structure whose two members are both pointers to type int. As with all pointers, declaring them is not enough; you must also initialize them to point to something. Remember, this can be done by assigning them the address of a variable. If cost and interest have been declared to be type int variables, you could write

```
first.value = &cost;
first.rate = &interest;
```

Now that the pointers have been initialized, you can use the indirection operator (*), as explained on Day 8, to evaluate the values stored in each of these. The expression *first.value evaluates to the value of cost, and the expression *first.rate evaluates to the value of interest.

Perhaps the type of pointer most frequently used as a structure member is a pointer to type char. Recall from Day 9, "Characters and Strings," that a string is a sequence of characters delineated by a pointer that points to the string's first character and a null character that indicates the end of the string. To refresh your memory, you can declare a pointer to type char and initialize it to point at a string as follows:

```
char *p_message;
p_message = "Teach Yourself C In 21 Days";
```

You can do the same thing with pointers to type char that are structure members:

```
struct msg {
    char *p1;
    char *p2;
} myptrs;
myptrs.p1 = "Teach Yourself C In 21 Days";
myptrs.p2 = "By SAMS Publishing";
```

Figure 10.4 illustrates the result of executing these statements. Each pointer member of
the structure points to the first byte of a string, stored elsewhere in memory. Contrast this
with Figure 10.3, which shows how data is stored in a structure that contains arrays of
type char.

FIGURE 10.4.

*A structure that con-
tains pointers to type
char.*

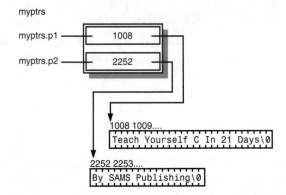

You can use pointer structure members anywhere a pointer can be used. For example, to
print the pointed-to strings, you would write

```
printf("%s %s", myptrs.p1, myptrs.p2);
```

What's the difference between using an array of type char as a structure member and
using a pointer to type char? These are both methods for "storing" a string in a structure,
as shown here in the structure msg, which uses both methods:

```
struct msg {
    char p1[30];
    char *p2;      /* caution: uninitialized */
} myptrs;
```

Recall that an array name without brackets is a pointer to the first array element.
Therefore, you can use these two structure members in similar fashion (note that p2
should be initialized before you copy a value to it):

```
strcpy(myptrs.p1, "Teach Yourself C In 21 Days");
strcpy(myptrs.p2, "By SAMS Publishing");
/* additional code goes here */
puts(myptrs.p1);
puts(myptrs.p2);
```

What's the difference between these methods? It is this: If you define a structure that
contains an array of type char, every instance of that structure type contains storage
space for an array of the specified size. Furthermore, you're limited to the specified size;
you can't store a larger string in the structure. Here's an example:

```
struct msg {
    char p1[10];
    char p2[10];
} myptrs;
...
strcpy(p1, "Minneapolis"); /* Wrong! String longer than array.*/
strcpy(p2, "MN");          /* OK, but wastes space because    */
                           /* string shorter than array.      */
```

If, on the other hand, you define a structure that contains pointers to type char, these restrictions don't apply. Each instance of the structure contains storage space for only the pointer. The actual strings are stored elsewhere in memory (but you don't need to worry about *where* in memory). There's no length restriction or wasted space. The actual strings aren't stored as part of the structure. Each pointer in the structure can point to a string of any length. That string becomes part of the structure, even though it isn't stored in the structure.

Caution

> If you do not initialize the pointer, you could inadvertently overwrite memory being used for something else. When using a pointer instead of an array, you must remember to initialize the pointer. This can be done by assigning it to another variable or by allocating memory dynamically.

Pointers to Structures

A C program can declare and use pointers to structures, just as it can declare pointers to any other data storage type. As you'll see later in today's lesson, pointers to structures are often used when passing a structure as an argument to a function. Pointers to structures are also used in a very powerful data storage method known as *linked lists*. Linked lists are explored on Day 14, "Pointers: Beyond the Basics."

For now, take a look at how your program can create and use pointers to structures. First, define a structure:

```
struct part {
    int number;
    char name[10];
};
```

Now declare a pointer to type part:

```
struct part *p_part;
```

Remember, the indirection operator (*) in the declaration says that p_part is a pointer to type part, not an instance of type part.

Can the pointer be initialized now? No, because even though the structure part has been defined, no instances of it have been declared. Remember that it's a declaration, not a definition, that sets aside storage space in memory for a data object. Because a pointer needs a memory address to point to, you must declare an instance of type part before anything can point to it. Here's the declaration:

```
struct part gizmo;
```

Now you can perform the pointer initialization:

```
p_part = &gizmo;
```

This statement assigns the address of gizmo to p_part. (Recall the address-of operator, &.) Figure 10.5 shows the relationship between a structure and a pointer to the structure.

FIGURE 10.5.

A pointer to a structure points to the structure's first byte.

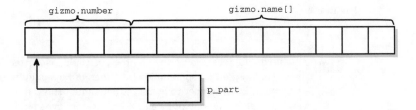

Now that you have a pointer to the structure gizmo, how do you make use of it? One method uses the indirection operator (*). If ptr is a pointer to a data object, the expression *ptr refers to the object pointed to.

Applying this to the current example, you know that p_part is a pointer to the structure gizmo, so *p_part refers to gizmo. You then apply the structure member operator (.) to access individual members of gizmo. To assign the value 100 to gizmo.number, you could write

```
(*p_part).number = 100;
```

*p_part must be enclosed in parentheses because the structure member operator (.) has a higher precedence than the indirection operator (*).

A second way to access structure members using a pointer to the structure is to use the *indirect membership operator*, which consists of the characters -> (a hyphen followed by the greater-than symbol). (Note that when they are used together in this way, C treats them as a single operator, not two.) This symbol is placed between the pointer name and the member name. For example, to access the number member of gizmo with the p_part pointer, you would write

```
p_part->number
```

Looking at another example, if `str` is a structure, `p_str` is a pointer to `str`, and `memb` is a member of `str`, you can access `str.memb` by writing

`p_str->memb`

Therefore, there are three ways to access a structure member:

- Using the structure name
- Using a pointer to the structure with the indirection operator (`*`)
- Using a pointer to the structure with the indirect membership operator (`->`)

If `p_str` is a pointer to the structure `str`, the following three expressions are all equivalent:

`str.memb`

`(*p_str).memb`

`p_str->memb`

Pointers and Arrays of Structures

You've seen that arrays of structures can be a very powerful programming tool, as can pointers to structures. You can combine the two, using pointers to access structures that are array elements.

To illustrate, here is a structure definition from an earlier example:

```
struct part {
    int number;
    char name[10];
};
```

After the `part` structure is defined, you can declare an array of type `part`:

```
struct part data[100];
```

Next you can declare a pointer to type `part` and initialize it to point to the first structure in the array `data`:

```
struct part *p_part;
p_part = &data[0];
```

Recall that the name of an array without brackets is a pointer to the first array element, so the second line could also have been written as

```
p_part = data;
```

You now have an array of structures of type `part` and a pointer to the first array element (that is, the first structure in the array). For example, you could print the contents of the first element using the statement

```
printf("%d %s", p_part->number, p_part->name);
```

What if you wanted to print all the array elements? You would probably use a `for` loop, printing one array element with each iteration of the loop. To access the members using pointer notation, you must change the pointer p_part so that with each iteration of the loop it points to the next array element (that is, the next structure in the array). How do you do this?

C's pointer arithmetic comes to your aid. The unary increment operator (++) has a special meaning when applied to a pointer: It means "increment the pointer by the size of the object it points to." Put another way, if you have a pointer `ptr` that points to a data object of type `obj`, the statement

```
ptr++;
```

has the same effect as

```
ptr += sizeof(obj);
```

This aspect of pointer arithmetic is particularly relevant to arrays because array elements are stored sequentially in memory. If a pointer points to array element n, incrementing the pointer with the (++) operator causes it to point to element n + 1. This is illustrated in Figure 10.6, which shows an array named `x[]` that consists of 4-byte elements (for example, a structure containing two type `short` members, each 2 bytes long). The pointer `ptr` was initialized to point to `x[0]`; each time `ptr` is incremented, it points to the next array element.

FIGURE 10.6.

With each increment, a pointer steps to the next array element.

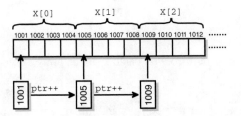

This means that your program can step through an array of structures (or an array of any other data type, for that matter) by incrementing a pointer. This sort of notation is usually easier to use and more concise than using array subscripts to perform the same task. Listing 10.4 shows how you do this.

LISTING 10.4. Accessing successive array elements by incrementing a pointer.

```
1 : /* Demonstrates stepping through an array of structures */
2 : /* using pointer notation. */
3 :
```

```
 4 : #include <stdio.h>
 5 :
 6 : #define MAX 4
 7 :
 8 : /* Define a structure, then declare and initialize */
 9 : /* an array of 4 structures. */
10:
11: struct part {
12:      int number;
13:      char name[10];
14: } data[MAX] = { {1, "Smith"},
15:                 {2, "Jones"},
16:                 {3, "Adams"},
17:                 {4, "Wilson"}
18:                 };
19:
20: /* Declare a pointer to type part, and a counter variable. */
21:
22: struct part *p_part;
23: int count;
24:
25: int main()
26: {
27:      /* Initialize the pointer to the first array element. */
28:
29:      p_part = data;
30:
31:      /* Loop through the array, incrementing the pointer */
32:      /* with each iteration. */
33:
34:      for (count = 0; count < MAX; count++)
35:      {
36:          printf("At address %lu: %d %s\n",
37:                  (unsigned long)p_part, p_part->number,
38:                    p_part->name);
39:          p_part++;
40:      }
41:
42:      return 0;
43: }
44:
```

OUTPUT

```
At address 134517984: 1 Smith
At address 134518000: 2 Jones
At address 134518016: 3 Adams
At address 134518032: 4 Wilson
```

ANALYSIS First, in lines 11 through 18, this program declares and initializes an array of part structures called data. Notice that each structure in the array must be enclosed within a set of braces ({}). A pointer called p_part is then defined in line 22 to be used to point to the data structure. The main() function's first task in line 29 is to set the pointer, p_part, to point to the part structure that was declared. All the elements are then printed using a for loop in lines 34 through 39 that increments the pointer to the array with each iteration. The program also displays the address of each element.

Look closely at the addresses displayed. The precise values might differ on your system, but they are in equal-sized increments—16 bytes. The increment size is always greater than or equal to the size of the structure. In this case, the structure consists of an int— 4 bytes—and a 10-character char array, which comes to a total of 14 bytes. So where are the extra 2 bytes going? Well, the C compiler arranges things in memory to make accessing the data easier and more efficient for the CPU. The CPU prefers to have 4-byte int variables arranged at memory addresses that are divisible by four. Therefore, it arranges the 14-byte structures so that 2 bytes are left between each one.

Passing Structures as Arguments to Functions

Like other data types, a structure can be passed as an argument to a function. Listing 10.5 shows how to do this. This program is a modification of the program shown in Listing 10.2. Listing 10.5 uses a function to display data on the screen, whereas Listing 10.2 uses statements that are part of main().

LISTING **10.5**. Passing a structure as a function argument.

```
 1:  /* Demonstrates passing a structure to a function. */
 2:
 3:  #include <stdio.h>
 4:
 5:  /* Declare and define a structure to hold the data. */
 6:
 7:  struct data {
 8:      float amount;
 9:      char fname[30];
10:      char lname[30];
11:  } rec;
12:
13:  /* The function prototype. The function has no return value, */
14:  /* and it takes a structure of type data as its one argument. */
15:
16:  void print_rec(struct data x);
17:
18:  int main(void)
19:  {
20:      /* Input the data from the keyboard. */
21:
22:      printf("Enter the donor's first and last names,\n");
23:      printf("separated by a space: ");
24:      scanf("%s %s", rec.fname, rec.lname);
```

```
25:
26:     printf("\nEnter the donation amount: ");
27:     scanf("%f", &rec.amount);
28:
29:     /* Call the display function. */
30:     print_rec( rec );
31:
32:     return 0;
33: }
34: void print_rec(struct data x)
35: {
36:     printf("\nDonor %s %s gave $%.2f.\n", x.fname, x.lname,
37:             x.amount);
38: }
```

**INPUT/
OUTPUT**

Enter the donor's first and last names,
separated by a space: **Bradley Jones**

Enter the donation amount: **1000.00**

Donor Bradley Jones gave $1000.00.

ANALYSIS Looking at line 16, you see the function prototype for the function that is to receive the structure. As you would with any other data type that is going to be passed, you need to include the proper arguments. In this case, it is a structure of type data. This is repeated in the header for the function in line 34. When calling the function, you need to pass only the structure instance name—in this case, rec (line 30). That's all there is to it. Passing a structure to a function isn't very different from passing a simple variable.

You can also pass a structure to a function by passing the structure's address (that is, a pointer to the structure). In fact, in older versions of C, this was the only way to pass a structure as an argument. It's not necessary now, but you might see older programs that still use this method. If you pass a pointer to a structure as an argument, remember that you must use the indirect membership operator (->) to access structure members in the function.

Do	Don't
DO take advantage of declaring a pointer to a structure—especially when using arrays of structures. **DO** use the indirect membership operator (->) when working with a pointer to a structure.	**DON'T** confuse arrays with structures! **DON'T** forget that when you increment a pointer, it moves a distance equivalent to the size of the data to which it points. In the case of a pointer to a structure, this is the size of the structure.

10

Unions

Unions are similar to structures. A union is declared and used in the same ways that a structure is. A union differs from a structure in that only one of its members can be used at a time. The reason for this is simple. All the members of a union occupy the same area of memory—they are laid on top of each other.

Defining, Declaring, and Initializing Unions

Unions are defined and declared in the same fashion as structures. The only difference in the declarations is that the keyword `union` is used instead of `struct`. To define a simple union of a `char` variable and an integer variable, you would write the following:

```
union shared {
    char c;
    int i;
};
```

This union, `shared`, can be used to create instances of a union that can hold either a character value c or an integer value i. This is an OR condition. Unlike a structure that would hold both values, the union can hold only one value at a time. Figure 10.7 illustrates how the `shared` union would appear in memory.

FIGURE 10.7.

The union can hold only one value at a time.

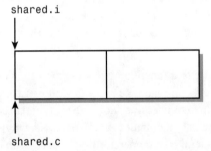

shared.i

shared.c

A union can be initialized on its declaration. Because only one member can be used at a time, only one can be initialized. To avoid confusion, only the first member of the union can be initialized. The following code shows an instance of the `shared` union being declared and initialized:

```
union shared generic_variable = {'@'};
```

Notice that the generic_variable union was initialized just as the first member of a structure would be initialized.

Accessing Union Members

Individual union members can be used in the same way that structure members can be used—by using the member operator (.). However, there is an important difference in accessing union members. Only one union member should be accessed at a time. Because a union stores its members on top of one another, it's important to access only one member at a time. Listing 10.6 presents an example.

LISTING 10.6. An example of the wrong use of unions.

```
1:    /* Example of using more than one union member at a time */
2:    #include <stdio.h>
3:
4:    int main(void)
5:    {
6:        union shared_tag {
7:            char  c;
8:            int   i;
9:            long  l;
10:           float f;
11:           double d;
12:       } shared;
13:
14:       shared.c = '$';
15:
16:       printf("\nchar c   = %c",  shared.c);
17:       printf("\nint i    = %d",  shared.i);
18:       printf("\nlong l   = %ld", shared.l);
19:       printf("\nfloat f  = %f",  shared.f);
20:       printf("\ndouble d = %f",  shared.d);
21:
22:       shared.d = 123456789.8765;
23:
24:       printf("\n\nchar c   = %c",  shared.c);
25:       printf("\nint i    = %d",  shared.i);
26:       printf("\nlong l   = %ld", shared.l);
27:       printf("\nfloat f  = %f",  shared.f);
28:       printf("\ndouble d = %f\n", shared.d);
29:
30:       return 0;
31:   }
```

OUTPUT

```
char c   = $
int i    = 36
long l   = 36
float f  = 0.000000
double d = -1.998047

char c   = 7
```

```
int i    = 1468107063
long l   = 1468107063
float f  = 284852666499072.000000
double d = 123456789.876500
```

ANALYSIS In this listing, you can see that a union named `shared` is defined and declared in lines 6 through 12. `shared` contains five members, each of a different type. Lines 14 and 22 initialize individual members of `shared`. Lines 16 through 20 and 24 through 28 then present the values of each member using `printf()` statements.

Note that, with the exceptions of `char c = $` and `double d = 123456789.876500`, the output might not be the same on your computer. Because the character variable, `c`, was initialized in line 14, it is the only value that should be used until a different member is initialized. The results of printing the other union member variables (`i`, `l`, `f`, and `d`) can be unpredictable (lines 16 through 20). Line 22 puts a value into the `double` variable, `d`. Notice that printing the variables again is unpredictable for all but `d`. The value entered into `c` in line 14 has been lost because it was overwritten when the value of `d` in line 22 was entered. This is evidence that the members all occupy the same space.

The union Keyword

▼ SYNTAX

```
union tag {
    union_member(s);
    /* additional statements may go here */
}instance;
```

The `union` keyword is used for declaring unions. A union is a collection of one or more variables (*union_members*) that have been grouped under a single name. In addition, each of these union members occupies the same area of memory.

The keyword `union` identifies the beginning of a union definition. It's followed by a tag that is the name given to the union. Following the tag are the union members enclosed in braces. An *instance*, the actual declaration of a union, also can be defined. If you define a structure without an instance, it's just a template that can be used later in a program to declare structures. The following is a template's format:

```
union tag {
    union_member(s);
    /* additional statements may go here */
};
```

To use the template, you would use the following format:

▼   `union tag instance;`

▼ To use this format, you must have previously declared a union with the given tag.

Example 1

```
/* Declare a union template called tag */
union tag {
    int nbr;
    char character;
};
/* Use the union template */
union tag mixed_variable;
```

Example 2

```
/* Declare a union and instance together */
union generic_type_tag {
    char c;
    int i;
    float f;
    double d;
} generic;
```

Example 3

```
/* Initialize a union. */
union date_tag {
    char full_date[9];
    struct part_date_tag {
        char month[2];
        char break_value1;
        char day[2];
        char break_value2;
        char year[2];
    } part_date;
▲ }date = {"01/01/97"};
```

Listing 10.7 shows a more practical use of a union. Although this use is simplistic, it's one of the more common uses of a union.

LISTING 10.7. A practical use of a union.

```
1:   /* Example of a typical use of a union */
2:
3:   #include <stdio.h>
4:
5:   #define CHARACTER   'C'
6:   #define INTEGER     'I'
7:   #define FLOAT       'F'
8:
9:   struct generic_tag{
10:      char type;
```

continues

LISTING **10.7**. continued

```
11:      union shared_tag {
12:          char    c;
13:          int     i;
14:          float   f;
15:      } shared;
16:  };
17:
18:  void print_function( struct generic_tag generic );
19:
20:  int main(void)
21:  {
22:      struct generic_tag var;
23:
24:      var.type = CHARACTER;
25:      var.shared.c = '$';
26:      print_function( var );
27:
28:      var.type = FLOAT;
29:      var.shared.f = (float) 12345.67890;
30:      print_function( var );
31:
32:      var.type = 'x';
33:      var.shared.i = 111;
34:      print_function( var );
35:      return 0;
36:  }
37:  void print_function( struct generic_tag generic )
38:  {
39:      printf("\nThe generic value is...");
40:      switch( generic.type )
41:      {
42:          case CHARACTER: printf("%c\n",  generic.shared.c);
43:                          break;
44:          case INTEGER:   printf("%d\n",  generic.shared.i);
45:                          break;
46:          case FLOAT:     printf("%f\n",  generic.shared.f);
47:                          break;
48:          default:        printf("an unknown type: %c\n",
49:                                  generic.type);
50:                          break;
51:      }
52:  }
```

OUTPUT

```
The generic value is...$

The generic value is...12345.678711

The generic value is...an unknown type: x
```

ANALYSIS This program is a very simplistic version of what could be done with a union. This program provides a way of storing multiple data types in a single storage space. The `generic_tag` structure lets you store a character, an integer, or a floating-point number within the same area. This area is a union called `shared` that operates just like the examples in Listing 10.6. Notice that the `generic_tag` structure also adds an additional field called `type`. This field is used to store information on the type of variable contained in `shared`. `type` helps prevent `shared` from being used in the wrong way, thus helping to avoid erroneous data such as that presented in Listing 10.6.

A formal look at the program shows that lines 5, 6, and 7 define constants `CHARACTER`, `INTEGER`, and `FLOAT`. These are used later in the program to make the listing more readable. Lines 9 through 16 define a `generic_tag` structure that will be used later. Line 18 presents a prototype for the `print_function()`. The structure var is declared in line 22 and is first initialized to hold a character value in lines 24 and 25. A call to `print_function()` in line 26 lets the value be printed. Lines 28 through 30 and 32 through 34 repeat this process with other values.

The `print_function()` is the heart of this listing. Although this function is used to print the value from a `generic_tag` variable, a similar function could have been used to initialize it. `print_function()` will evaluate the `type` variable in order to print a statement with the appropriate variable type. This prevents getting erroneous data such as that in Listing 10.6.

Do	**DON'T**
DO remember which union member is being used. If you fill in a member of one type and then try to use a different type, you can get unpredictable results.	**DON'T** try to initialize more than the first union member.
DO note that unions are an advanced C topic.	**DON'T** forget that the size of a union is equal to its largest member.

Creating Synonyms for Structures with `typedef`

You can use the `typedef` keyword to create a synonym for a structure or union type. For example, the following statements define `coord` as a synonym for the indicated structure:

```
typedef struct {
    int x;
    int y;
} coord;
```

You can then declare instances of this structure using the `coord` identifier:

```
coord topleft, bottomright;
```

Note that a `typedef` is different from a structure tag, as described earlier in today's lesson. If you write

```
struct coord {
    int x;
    int y;
};
```

the identifier `coord` is a tag for the structure. You can use the tag to declare instances of the structure, but unlike a `typedef`, you must include the `struct` keyword:

```
struct zcoord topleft, bottomright;
```

Whether you use `typedef` or a structure tag to declare structures makes little difference. Using `typedef` results in slightly more concise code because the `struct` keyword doesn't need to be used. On the other hand, using a tag and having the `struct` keyword explicit makes it clear that a structure is being declared.

Summary

Today's lesson shows you how to use structures, a data type that you design to meet the needs of your program. A structure can contain any of C's data types, including other structures, pointers, and arrays. Each data item within a structure, called a *member,* is accessed using the structure member operator (`.`) between the structure name and the member name. Structures can be used individually, and they can also be used in arrays.

Unions are similar to structures. The main difference between a union and a structure is that a union stores all its members in the same area. This means that only one member of a union can be used at a time.

Q&A

Q Is there any reason to declare a structure without an instance?

A Today you saw three ways of declaring a structure. The first way is to declare a structure body, tag, and instance all at once. The second way is to declare a structure body and an instance with no tag, and the third way is to declare the structure and tag without an instance. An instance can then be declared later by using the `struct` keyword, the tag, and a name for the instance. It's common programming practice to use either the second or the third method. Many programmers declare the structure body and tag without any instances. The instances are then declared later in the program. Day 11 describes variable scope. Scope will apply to the instance, but not to the tag or structure body.

Q Is it more common to use a `typedef` or a structure tag?

A Many programmers use `typedef`s to make their code easier to read, but it makes little practical difference. Many of the libraries distributed with Linux use a lot of `typedef`s to make the life of the library maintainer easier.

Q Can I simply assign one structure to another with the assignment operator?

A Yes and no. Newer versions of C compilers, including the GNU C compiler, let you assign one structure (or union) to another of the same type. In older versions of C, you might need to assign each member of the structures individually! If you want your code to be portable to older compilers, you might want to think twice before using this feature.

Q How big is a union?

A Because each of the members in a union is stored in the same memory location, the amount of room required to store the union is equal to that of its largest member.

Workshop

The Workshop provides quiz questions to help you solidify your understanding of the material covered and exercises to provide you with experience in using what you've learned. The answers to the quiz and exercises are provided in Appendix C, "Answers."

Quiz

1. How is a structure different from an array?

2. What is the structure member operator, and what purpose does it serve?

3. What keyword is used in C to create a structure?

4. What is the difference between a structure tag and a structure instance?

5. What does the following code fragment do?

```
struct address {
    char name[31];
    char add1[31];
    char add2[31];
    char city[11];
    char state[3];
    char zip[11];
} myaddress = { "Bradley Jones",
                "RTSoftware",
                "P.O. Box 1213",
                "Carmel", "IN", "46082-1213"};
```

6. Assume that you have declared an array of structures and that `ptr` is a pointer to the first array element (that is, the first structure in the array). How would you change `ptr` to point to the second array element?

Exercises

1. Write code that defines a structure named `time`, which contains three `int` members.

2. Write code that performs two tasks: defines a structure named `data` that contains one type `int` member and two type `float` members, and declares an instance of type `data` named `info`.

3. Continuing with exercise 2, how would you assign the value `100` to the integer member of the structure `info`?

4. Write code that declares and initializes a pointer to `info`.

5. Continuing with exercise 4, show two ways of using pointer notation to assign the value `5.5` to the first `float` member of `info`.

6. Write the definition for a structure type named `data` that can hold a single string of up to 20 characters.

7. Create a structure containing five strings: `address1`, `address2`, `city`, `state`, and `zip`. Create a `typedef` called `RECORD` that can be used to create instances of this structure.

8. Using the `typedef` from exercise 7, allocate and initialize an element called `myaddress`.

9. **BUG BUSTER:** What is wrong with the following code?

```
struct {
    char zodiac_sign[21];
    int month;
} sign = "Leo", 8;
```

10. **BUG BUSTER:** What is wrong with the following code?

```
/* setting up a union */
union data{
    char a_word[4];
    long a_number;
}generic_variable = { "WOW", 1000 };
```

DAY **11**

Understanding Variable Scope

On Day 4, "Functions: The Basics," you saw that a variable defined within a function is different from a variable defined outside a function. Without knowing it, you were being introduced to the concept of *variable scope*, an important aspect of C programming. Today you will learn

- About variable scope and why it's important
- What external variables are and why you should usually avoid them
- The ins and outs of local variables
- The difference between static and automatic variables
- About local variables and blocks
- How to select a storage class

What Is Scope?

NEW TERM The *scope* of a variable refers to the extent to which different parts of a program have access to the variable—in other words, where the variable is *visible*. When referring to C variables, the terms *accessibility* and *visibility* are used interchangeably. When speaking about scope, the term *variable* refers to all C data types: simple variables, arrays, structures, pointers, and so forth. It also refers to symbolic constants defined with the const keyword.

NEW TERM Scope also affects a variable's *lifetime*: how long the variable persists in memory or, in other words, when the variable's storage is allocated and deallocated. After a quick demonstration of scope, this lesson examines visibility and scope in more detail.

A Demonstration of Scope

Look at the program in Listing 11.1. It defines the variable x in line 5, uses printf() to display the value of x in line 11, and then calls the function print_value() to display the value of x again. Note that the function print_value() is not passed the value of x as an argument; it simply uses x as an argument to printf() in line 19.

LISTING 11.1. The variable x is accessible within the function print_value().

```
1:  /* Illustrates variable scope. */
2:
3:  #include <stdio.h>
4:
5:  int x = 999;
6:
7:  void print_value(void);
8:
9:  int main(void)
10: {
11:     printf("%d\n", x);
12:     print_value();
13:
14:     return 0;
15: }
16:
17: void print_value(void)
18: {
19:     printf("%d\n", x);
20: }
```

OUTPUT
```
999
999
```

This program compiles and runs with no problems. Now make a minor modification in the program, moving the definition of the variable x to a location within the main() function. The new source code is shown in Listing 11.2, with the definition of x now on line 9.

LISTING 11.2. The variable x is not accessible within the function print_value().

```
 1:  /* Illustrates variable scope. */
 2:
 3:  #include <stdio.h>
 4:
 5:  void print_value(void);
 6:
 7:  int main(void)
 8:  {
 9:      int x = 999;
10:
11:      printf("%d\n", x);
12:      print_value();
13:
14:      return 0;
15: }
16:
17: void print_value(void)
18: {
19:      printf("%d\n", x);
20: }
```

ANALYSIS If you try to compile Listing 11.2, the compiler generates an error message similar to the following:

```
list1102.c: In function `print_value':

list1102.c:19: `x' undeclared (first use in this function)

list1102.c:19: (Each undeclared identifier is reported only once

list1102.c:19: for each function it appears in.)
```

Remember that in an error message, the number after the first colon in each line refers to the program line where the error was found. Line 19 is the call to printf() within the print_value() function.

This error message tells you that in the print_value() function at line 19, the variable x has not been declared or, in other words, was not visible. Note, however, that the call to printf() in line 11 doesn't generate an error message; in this part of the program, outside print_value(), the variable x *is* visible.

The only difference between Listings 11.1 and 11.2 is where the variable x is defined. By moving the definition of x, you change its scope. In Listing 11.1, x is defined outside

11

`main()` and is therefore an *external variable,* and its scope is the entire program. It is accessible within both the `main()` function and the `print_value()` function. In Listing 11.2, x is defined inside a function, the `main()` function, and is therefore a *local variable* with its scope limited to within the `main()` function. As far as `print_value()` is concerned, x doesn't exist, and that is why the compiler generated an error message. Later today, you'll learn more about local and external variables, but first you need to understand the importance of scope.

Why Is Scope Important?

To understand the importance of variable scope, you need to recall the discussion of structured programming on Day 4. The structured approach, you might remember, divides the program into independent functions that perform a specific task. The key word here is *independent*. For true independence, it's necessary for each function's variables to be isolated from possible interference caused by code in other functions. Only by isolating each function's data can you make sure that the function goes about its job without some other part of the program throwing a monkey wrench into the works. By defining variables within functions, as you will learn soon, you can "hide" those variables from other parts of the program.

If you're thinking that complete data isolation between functions isn't always desirable, you are correct. You will soon realize that by specifying the scope of variables, a programmer has a great deal of control over the degree of data isolation.

External Variables

 NEW TERM An *external variable* is a variable defined outside of any function. This means outside of `main()` as well because `main()` is a function, too. Until now, most of the variable definitions in this book have been external, placed in the source code before the start of `main()`. External variables are sometimes referred to as *global variables.*

> **Note** If you don't explicitly initialize an external variable (assign a value to it) when it's defined, the compiler initializes it to 0.

External Variable Scope

The scope of an external variable is the entire program. This means that an external variable is visible throughout `main()` and throughout every other function in the program.

For example, the variable x in Listing 11.1 is an external variable. As you saw when you compiled and ran the program, x is visible within both functions, main() and print_value(), and would also be visible in any other functions you might add to the program.

Strictly speaking, it's not accurate to say that the scope of an external variable is the entire program. Instead, the scope is the entire source code file that contains the variable definition. If the entire program is contained in one source code file, the two scope definitions are equivalent. Most small-to-medium-sized C programs are contained in one file, and that's certainly true of the programs you're writing now.

It's possible, however, for a program's source code to be contained in two or more separate files. You'll learn how and why this is done on Day 20, "Advanced Compiler Use," and you'll see what special handling is required for external variables in these situations.

When to Use External Variables

NEW TERM   Although the sample programs to this point have used external variables, in actual practice you should use them rarely. Why? Because when you use external variables, you are violating the principle of *modular independence* that is central to structured programming. Modular independence is the idea that each function, or module, in a program contains all the code and data it needs to do its job. With the relatively small programs you're writing now, this might not seem important, but as you progress to larger and more complex programs, over-reliance on external variables can start to cause problems.

When should you use external variables? Make a variable external only when all or most of the program's functions need access to the variable. Symbolic constants defined with the const keyword are often good candidates for external status. If only some of your functions need access to a variable, pass the variable to the functions as an argument rather than making it external.

The extern Keyword

When a function uses an external variable, it is good programming practice to declare the variable within the function using the extern keyword. The declaration takes the form

```
extern type name;
```

in which *type* is the variable type and *name* is the variable name. For example, you would add the declaration of x to the functions main() and print_value() in Listing 11.1. The resulting program is shown in Listing 11.3.

LISTING 11.3. The external variable x is declared as `extern` within the functions `main()` and `print_value()`.

```
 1:  /* Illustrates declaring external variables. */
 2:
 3:  #include <stdio.h>
 4:
 5:  int x = 999;
 6:
 7:  void print_value(void);
 8:
 9:  int main(void)
10: {
11:      extern int x;
12:
13:      printf("%d\n", x);
14:      print_value();
15:
16:      return 0;
17: }
18:
19: void print_value(void)
20: {
21:      extern int x;
22:      printf("%d\n", x);
23: }
```

OUTPUT

```
999
999
```

ANALYSIS This program prints the value of x twice, first in line 13 as a part of `main()`, and then in line 21 as a part of `print_value()`. Line 5 defines x as a type `int` variable equal to 999. Lines 11 and 21 declare x as an `extern int`. Note the distinction between a variable definition, which sets aside storage for the variable, and an `extern` declaration. The latter says: "This function uses an external variable with such-and-such a name and type that is defined elsewhere." In this case, the `extern` declaration isn't needed, strictly speaking—the program will work the same without lines 11 and 21. However, if the function `print_value()` were in a different code module than the global declaration of the variable x (in line 5), the `extern` declaration would be required.

Local Variables

NEW TERM A *local variable* is one that is defined within a function. The scope of a local variable is limited to the function in which it is defined. Day 4 describes local variables within functions, how to define them, and what their advantages are. Local variables aren't automatically initialized to 0 by the compiler. If you don't initialize a local variable when it's defined, it has an undefined or *garbage* value. You must explicitly assign a value to local variables before they're used for the first time.

A variable can be local to the main() function as well. This is the case for x in Listing 11.2. It is defined within main(), and as compiling and executing that program illustrates, it's also only visible within main().

Do	Don't
DO use local variables for items such as loop counters. DO use local variables to isolate the values the variables contain from the rest of the program.	DON'T use external variables if they aren't needed by a majority of the program's functions.

Static Versus Automatic Variables

Local variables are *automatic* by default. That means local variables are created anew each time the function is called, and they are destroyed when execution leaves the function. What this means, in practical terms, is that an automatic variable doesn't retain its value between calls to the function in which it is defined.

Suppose your program has a function that uses a local variable x. Also suppose that the first time it is called, the function assigns the value 100 to x. Execution returns to the calling program, and the function is called again later. Does the variable x still hold the value 100? No, it does not. The first instance of variable x was destroyed when execution left the function after the first call. When the function was called again, a new instance of x was created. The old x is gone.

What if the function needs to retain the value of a local variable between calls? For example, a printing function might need to remember the number of lines already sent to the printer to determine when it is necessary to start a new page. In order for a local variable to retain its value between calls, it must be defined as *static* with the static keyword. For example

```
void func1(int x)
{
    static int a;
    /* Additional code goes here */
}
```

Listing 11.4 illustrates the difference between automatic and static local variables.

LISTING 11.4. The difference between automatic and static local variables.

```
1:  /* Demonstrates automatic and static local variables. */
2:  #include <stdio.h>
3:  void func1(void);
4:  int main(void)
5:  {
6:      int count;
7:
8:      for (count = 0; count < 20; count++)
9:      {
10:          printf("At iteration %d: ", count);
11:          func1();
12:      }
13:
14:      return 0;
15: }
16:
17: void func1(void)
18: {
19:      static int x = 0;
20:      int y = 0;
21:
22:      printf("x = %d, y = %d\n", x++, y++);
23: }
```

OUTPUT

```
At iteration 0: x = 0, y = 0
At iteration 1: x = 1, y = 0
At iteration 2: x = 2, y = 0
At iteration 3: x = 3, y = 0
At iteration 4: x = 4, y = 0
At iteration 5: x = 5, y = 0
At iteration 6: x = 6, y = 0
At iteration 7: x = 7, y = 0
At iteration 8: x = 8, y = 0
At iteration 9: x = 9, y = 0
At iteration 10: x = 10, y = 0
At iteration 11: x = 11, y = 0
At iteration 12: x = 12, y = 0
At iteration 13: x = 13, y = 0
At iteration 14: x = 14, y = 0
At iteration 15: x = 15, y = 0
At iteration 16: x = 16, y = 0
At iteration 17: x = 17, y = 0
At iteration 18: x = 18, y = 0
At iteration 19: x = 19, y = 0
```

ANALYSIS This program has a function, func1(), that defines and initializes one static local variable and one automatic local variable. This function is shown in lines 17 through 23. Each time the function is called, both variables are displayed onscreen and incremented (line 22). The `main()` function in lines 4 through 15 contains a `for` loop (lines 8 through 12) that prints a message (line 10) and then calls `func1()` (line 11). The `for` loop iterates 20 times.

In the output, note that x, the static variable, increases with each iteration because it retains its value between calls. The automatic variable y, on the other hand, is reinitialized to 0 with each call and, therefore, does not increment.

This program also illustrates a difference in the way explicit variable initialization is handled (that is, when a variable is initialized at the time of definition). A static variable is initialized only the first time the function is called. At later calls, the program remembers that the variable has already been initialized and therefore doesn't reinitialize. Instead, the variable retains the value it had when execution last exited the function. In contrast, an automatic variable is initialized to the specified value every time the function is called.

If you experiment with automatic variables, you might get results that disagree with what you've read here. For example, if you modify Listing 11.4 so that the two local variables aren't initialized when they're defined, the function `func1()` in lines 17 through 23 reads

```
17: void func1(void)
18: {
19:     static int x;
20:     int y;
21:
22:     printf("x = %d, y = %d\n", x++, y++);
23: }
```

When you run the modified program, you might find that the value of y increases by one with each iteration. This means that y is keeping its value between calls to the function even though it is an automatic local variable. Is what you've read here about automatic variables losing their value a bunch of malarkey?

No, what you read is true (have faith!). If you find that an automatic variable keeps its value during repeated calls to the function, it's only by chance. Here's what happens: Each time the function is called, a new y is created. The compiler might use the same memory location for the new y that was used for y the preceding time the function was called. If y isn't explicitly initialized by the function, the storage location might contain the value that y had during the preceding call. The variable seems to have kept its old value, but it's just a chance occurrence; you definitely can't count on it happening every time.

Because automatic is the default for local variables, it doesn't need to be specified in the variable definition. If you want to, you can include the `auto` keyword in the definition before the `type` keyword, as shown here:

11

```
void func1(int y)
{
    auto int count;
    /* Additional code goes here */
}
```

The Scope of Function Parameters

NEW TERM A variable that is contained in a function heading's parameter list has *local scope*. For example, look at the following function:

```
void func1(int x)
{
    int y;
    /* Additional code goes here */
}
```

Both x and y are local variables with a scope that is the entire function func1(). Of course, x initially contains whatever value was passed to the function by the calling program. After you've made use of that value, you can use x like any other local variable.

Because parameter variables always start with the value passed as the corresponding argument, it's meaningless to think of them as being either static or automatic.

External Static Variables

You can make an external variable static by including the static keyword in its definition:

```
static float rate;

int main(void)
{
    /* Additional code goes here */
}
```

The difference between an ordinary external variable and a static external variable is one of scope. An ordinary external variable is visible to all functions in the file and can be used by functions in other files. A static external variable is visible only to functions in its own file and below the point of definition.

These distinctions obviously apply mostly to programs with source code that is contained in two or more files. This topic is covered on Day 20.

Register Variables

The register keyword is used to suggest to the compiler that an automatic local variable be stored in a *processor register* rather than in regular memory. What is a processor register, and what are the advantages of using it?

The central processing unit (CPU) of your computer contains a few data storage locations called *registers*. It is in the CPU registers that actual data operations, such as addition and division, take place. To manipulate data, the CPU must move the data from memory to its registers, perform the manipulations, and then move the data back to memory. Moving data to and from memory takes a finite amount of time. If a particular variable could be kept in a register to begin with, manipulations of the variable would proceed much faster.

By using the `register` keyword in the definition of an automatic variable, you ask the compiler to store that variable in a register. Look at the following example:

```
void func1(void)
{
    register int x;
    /* Additional code goes here */
}
```

Note that I said *ask,* not *tell*. Depending on the program's needs, a register might not be available for the variable. If no register is available, the compiler treats the variable as an ordinary automatic variable. In other words, the `register` keyword is a suggestion, not an order. The benefits of the `register` storage class are greatest for variables that the function uses frequently, such as the counter variable for a loop.

The `register` keyword can be used only with simple numeric variables, not arrays or structures. Also, it can't be used with either static or external storage classes. You can't define a pointer to a register variable.

11

Do	Don't
DO initialize local variables, or you won't know what value they will contain.	**DON'T** use register variables for nonnumeric values, structures, or arrays.
DO initialize global variables even though they're initialized to 0 by default. If you always initialize your variables, you'll avoid problems such as forgetting to initialize local variables.	
DO pass data items as function parameters instead of declaring them as global if they're needed in only a few functions.	

Local Variables and the `main()` Function

Everything said so far about local variables applies to `main()` as well as to all other functions. Strictly speaking, `main()` is a function like any other. The `main()` function is called when the program is started from your operating system, and control is returned to the operating system from `main()` when the program terminates.

This means that local variables defined in `main()` are created when the program begins, and their lifetime is over when the program ends. The notion of a static local variable retaining its value between calls to `main()` really makes no sense: A variable can't remain in existence between program executions. Within `main()`, therefore, there is no difference between automatic and static local variables. You can define a local variable in `main()` as being static, but that has no effect.

Do	Don't
DO remember that `main()` is a function similar in most respects to any other function.	**DON'T** declare static variables in `main()` because doing so gains nothing.

Which Storage Class Should You Use?

When you're deciding which storage class to use for particular variables in your programs, it might be helpful to refer to Table 11.1, which summarizes the five storage classes available in C.

TABLE 11.1. C's five variable storage classes.

Storage Class	Keyword	Lifetime	Where It's Defined	Scope
Automatic	None[1]	Temporary	In a function	Local
Static	static	Temporary	In a function	Local
Register	register	Temporary	In a function	Local
External	None[2]	Permanent	Outside a function	Global (all files)
External	static	Permanent	Outside a function	Global (one file)

[1] *The auto keyword is optional.*
[2] *The extern keyword is used in functions to declare a static external variable that is defined elsewhere.*

When you're deciding on a storage class, you should use an automatic storage class whenever possible and use other classes only when needed. Here are some guidelines to follow:

- To begin with, give each variable an automatic local storage class.
- If a variable will be manipulated frequently, such as a loop counter, add the `register` keyword to its definition.
- In functions other than `main()`, make a variable static if its value must be retained between calls to the function.
- If a variable is used by most or all of the program's functions, define it with the external storage class.

Local Variables and Blocks

So far, today's lesson has discussed only variables that are local to a function. That is the primary way local variables are used, but you can define variables that are local to any program block (any section enclosed in braces). When declaring variables within the block, you must remember that the declarations must be first. Listing 11.5 shows an example.

LISTING 11.5. Defining local variables within a program block.

```
 1:   /* Demonstrates local variables within blocks. */
 2:
 3:   #include <stdio.h>
 4:
 5:   int main(void)
 6:   {
 7:       /* Define a variable local to main(). */
 8:
 9:       int count = 0;
10:
11:       printf("\nOutside the block, count = %d", count);
12:
13:       /* Start a block. */
14:       {
15:         /* Define a variable local to the block. */
16:
17:         int count = 999;
18:         printf("\nWithin the block, count = %d", count);
19:       }
20:
21:       printf("\nOutside the block again, count = %d\n", count);
22:       return 0;
23:   }
```

OUTPUT
```
Outside the block, count = 0
Within the block, count = 999
Outside the block again, count = 0
```

ANALYSIS From this program, you can see that the count defined within the block is independent of the count defined outside the block. Line 9 defines count as a type int variable equal to 0. Because it is declared at the beginning of main(), it can be used throughout the entire main() function. The code in line 11 shows that the variable count has been initialized to 0 by printing its value. A block is declared in lines 14 through 19, and within the block, another count variable is defined as a type int variable. This count variable is initialized to 999 in line 17. Line 18 prints the block's count variable value of 999. Because the block ends on line 19, the print statement in line 21 uses the original count initially declared in line 9 of main().

The use of this type of local variable isn't common in C programming, and you might never find a need for it. Its most common use is probably when a programmer tries to isolate a problem within a program. You can temporarily isolate sections of code in braces and establish local variables to assist in tracking down the problem. Another advantage is that the variable declaration/initialization can be placed closer to the point where it's used, which can help in understanding the program.

Do	Don't
DO use variables at the beginning of a block (temporarily) to help track down problems.	**DON'T** try to put variable definitions anywhere other than at the beginning of a function or at the beginning of a block.
	DON'T define variables at the beginning of a block unless it makes the program clearer.

Summary

Today's discussion covered the concept of scope and lifetime as related to C's variable storage classes. Every C variable, whether a simple variable, an array, a structure, or whatever, has a specific storage class that determines two things: its scope (where in the program it's visible) and its lifetime (how long the variable persists in memory).

Proper use of storage classes is an important aspect of structured programming. By keeping most variables local to the function that uses them, you enhance functions' independence from each other. A variable should be given automatic storage class unless there is a specific reason to make it external or static.

Q&A

Q **If global variables can be used anywhere in the program, why not make all variables global?**

A As your programs get bigger, they will contain more and more variables. Global variables take up memory as long as the program is running, whereas automatic local variables take up memory only while the function they are defined in is executing. Hence, the use of local variables reduces memory usage. More important, however, is that the use of local variables greatly decreases the chance of unwanted interactions between different parts of the program; therefore, their use decreases the number of program bugs and follows the principles of structured programming.

Q **Day 10, "Structures," stated that scope affects a structure instance but not a structure tag or body. Why doesn't scope affect the structure tag or body?**

A When you declare a structure without instances, you are creating a template but not actually declaring any variables. It isn't until you create an instance of the structure that you declare a variable that occupies memory and has scope. For this reason, you can leave a structure body external to any functions with no real effect on memory. Many programmers put commonly used structure bodies with tags into header files and then include these header files when they need to create an instance of the structure. (Header files are covered on Day 20.)

Q **How does the computer know the difference between a global variable and a local variable that has the same name?**

A The answer to this question is beyond the scope of this chapter. The important thing to know is that when a local variable is declared with the same name as a global variable, the program temporarily ignores the global variable when the local variable is in scope (inside the function where it is defined). It continues to ignore the global variable until the local variable goes out of scope.

Q **Can I declare a local variable and a global variable that have the same name, as long as they have different variable types?**

A Yes. When you declare a local variable with the same name as a global variable, it is a completely different variable. That means you can make it whatever type you want. You should be careful, however, when declaring global and local variables that have the same name. Some programmers prefix all global variable names with "g" (for example, gCount instead of Count). This makes it clear in the source code which variables are global and which are local.

11

Workshop

The Workshop provides quiz questions to help you solidify your understanding of the material covered and exercises to provide you with experience in using what you've learned. The answers to the quiz and exercises are provided in Appendix C, "Answers."

Quiz

1. What does scope refer to?

2. What is the most important difference between local storage class and external storage class?

3. How does the location of a variable definition affect its storage class?

4. When defining a local variable, what are the two options for the variable's lifetime?

5. Your program can initialize both automatic and static local variables when they are defined. When do the initializations take place?

6. True or false: A register variable will always be placed in a register.

7. What value does an uninitialized global variable contain?

8. What value does an uninitialized local variable contain?

9. What will line 21 of Listing 11.5 print if lines 9 and 12 are removed? Think about this, and then try the program to see what happens.

10. If a function needs to remember the value of a local type `int` variable between calls, how should the variable be declared?

11. What does the `extern` keyword do?

12. What does the `static` keyword do?

Exercises

1. Write a declaration for a variable to be placed in a CPU register.

2. Change Listing 11.2 to prevent the error. Do this without using any external variables.

3. Write a program that declares a global variable of type `int` called `var`. Initialize `var` to any value. The program should print the value of `var` in a function (not `main()`). Do you need to pass `var` as a parameter to the function?

4. Change the program in exercise 3. Instead of declaring `var` as a global variable, change it to a local variable in `main()`. The program should still print `var` in a separate function. Do you need to pass `var` as a parameter to the function?

5. Can a program have a global and a local variable with the same name? Write a program that uses a global and a local variable with the same name to prove your answer.

6. **BUG BUSTER:** Can you spot the problem in this code? (Hint: It has to do with where a variable is declared.)

```
void a_sample_function( void )
{
    int ctr1;

    for ( ctr1 = 0; ctr1 < 25; ctr1++ )
        printf( "*" );

    puts( "\nThis is a sample function" );
    {
        char star = '*';
        puts( "\nIt has a problem\n" );
        for ( int ctr2 = 0; ctr2 < 25; ctr2++ )
        {
            printf( "%c", star);
        }
    }
}
```

7. **BUG BUSTER:** What is wrong with the following code?

```
/*Count the number of even numbers between 0 and 100. */

#include <stdio.h>

int main(void)
{
    int x = 1;
    static int tally = 0;

    for (x = 0; x < 101; x++)
    {
        if (x % 2 == 0)   /*if x is even...*/
        tally++;..  /*add 1 to tally.*/

    }

    printf("There are %d even numbers.\n", tally);
    return 0;
}
```

11

8. **BUG BUSTER:** Is anything wrong with the following program?

```c
#include <stdio.h>

void print_function( char star );

int ctr;

int main(void)
{
    char star;

    print_function( star );
    return 0;
}

void print_function( char star )
{
    char dash;

    for ( ctr = 0; ctr < 25; ctr++ )
    {
        printf( "%c%c", star, dash );
    }
}
```

9. What does the following program print? Don't run the program—try to figure it out by reading the code.

```c
#include <stdio.h>
void print_letter2(void);               /* function prototype */

int ctr;
char letter1 = 'X';
char letter2 = '=';

int main(void)
{
    for( ctr = 0; ctr < 10; ctr++ )
    {
        printf( "%c", letter1 );
        print_letter2();
    }
    return 0;
}

void print_letter2(void)
{
    for( ctr = 0; ctr < 2; ctr++ )
        printf( "%c", letter2 );
}
```

10. **BUG BUSTER:** Will the preceding program run? If not, what's the problem? Rewrite it so that it is correct.

DAY 12

Advanced Program Control

Day 5, "Basic Program Control," introduced some of C's program control statements that govern the execution of other statements in your program. Today's discussion covers more advanced aspects of program control, including the goto statement and some of the more interesting things you can do with loops. Today you will learn

- How to use the break and continue statements
- What infinite loops are and why you might use them
- What the goto statement is and why you should avoid it
- How to use the switch statement
- How to control program exits
- How to execute functions automatically upon program completion
- How to execute system commands in your program

Ending Loops Early

On Day 5, you learned how the for loop, the while loop, and the do...while loop can control program execution. These loop constructions execute a block of C statements never, once, or more than once, depending on conditions in the program. In all three cases, termination of or exit from the loop occurs only when a certain condition occurs.

At times, however, you might want to exert more control over loop execution. The break and continue statements provide that control.

The break Statement

The break statement can be placed only in the body of a for loop, while loop, or do...while loop. (It's valid in a switch statement too, but that topic isn't covered until later today.) When a break statement is encountered, execution immediately exits the loop. The following is an example:

```
for ( count = 0; count < 10; count++ )
{
    if ( count == 5 )
        break;
}
```

Left to itself, the for loop would execute 10 times. On the sixth iteration, however, count is equal to 5, and the break statement executes causing the for loop to terminate. Execution then passes to the statement immediately following the for loop's closing brace. When a break statement is encountered inside a nested loop, it causes the program to exit the innermost loop only.

Listing 12.1 demonstrates the use of the break statement.

LISTING 12.1. Using the break statement.

```
1:  /* Demonstrates the break statement. */
2:
3:  #include <stdio.h>
4:
5:  char s[] = "This is a test string. It contains two sentences.";
6:
7:  int main(void)
8:  {
9:      int count;
10:
11:     printf("\nOriginal string: %s", s);
12:
13:     for (count = 0; s[count]!='\0'; count++)
14:     {
```

```
15:        if (s[count] == '.')
16:        {
17:            s[count+1] = '\0';
18:            break;
19:        }
20:    }
21:    printf("\nModified string: %s\n", s);
22:
23:    return 0;
24: }
```

OUTPUT Original string: This is a test string. It contains two sentences.
Modified string: This is a test string.

ANALYSIS This program extracts the first sentence from a string. It searches the string, character by character, for the first period (which should mark the end of a sentence). This is done in the for loop in lines 13 through 20. Line 13 starts the for loop, incrementing count to go from character to character in the string, s. Line 15 checks to see whether the current character in the string is a period. If it is, a null character is inserted immediately after the period (line 17). This, in effect, trims the string. After you trim the string, you no longer need to continue the loop, so a break statement (line 18) quickly terminates the loop and sends control to the first line after the loop (line 21). If no period is found, the string isn't altered.

A loop can contain multiple break statements, but only the first break executed (if any) has any effect. If no break is executed, the loop terminates normally (according to its test condition). Figure 12.1 shows the operation of the break statement.

FIGURE 12.1.

The operation of the break *and* continue *statements.*

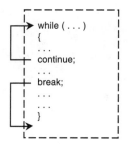

12

The break Statement

▼ SYNTAX

break;

break is used inside a loop or switch statement. It causes the control of a program to immediately exit the current loop (for, while, or do...while) or switch statement. No further iterations of the loop execute; the first statement following the loop or switch statement executes.

▼ **Example**

```
int x;
printf ( "Counting from 1 to 10\n" );
/* having no condition in the for loop will cause it to loop forever */

for( x = 1; ; x++ )
{
   if( x == 10  )   /* This checks for the value of 10 */
      break;        /* This ends the loop */
   printf( "\n%d", x );
▲ }
```

The continue Statement

Like the break statement, the continue statement can be placed only in the body of a for loop, a while loop , or a do...while loop. When a continue statement executes, the next iteration of the enclosing loop begins immediately. The statements between the continue statement and the end of the loop aren't executed. The operation of continue is also shown in Figure 12.1. Notice how it differs from the operation of a break statement.

Listing 12.2 uses the continue statement. This program accepts a line of input from the keyboard and then displays it with all lowercase vowels removed.

LISTING 12.2. Using the continue statement.

```
1:   /* Demonstrates the continue statement. */
2:
3:   #include <stdio.h>
4:
5:   int main(void)
6:   {
7:      /* Declare a buffer for input and a counter variable. */
8:
9:      char buffer[81];
10:      int ctr;
11:
12:      /* Input a line of text. */
13:
14:      puts("Enter a line of text:");
15:      fgets(buffer,81,stdin);
16:
17:      /* Go through the string, displaying only those */
18:      /* characters that are not lowercase vowels. */
19:
20:      for (ctr = 0; buffer[ctr] !='\0'; ctr++)
21:      {
22:
```

```
23:        /* If the character is a lowercase vowel, loop back */
24:        /* without displaying it. */
25:
26:        if (buffer[ctr] == 'a' || buffer[ctr] == 'e'
27:           || buffer[ctr] == 'i' || buffer[ctr] == 'o'
28:           || buffer[ctr] == 'u')
29:            continue;
30:
31:        /* If not a vowel, display it. */
32:
33:        putchar(buffer[ctr]);
34:    }
35:    return 0;
36: }
```

INPUT/
OUTPUT

Enter a line of text:
This is a line of text
Ths s ln f txt

ANALYSIS
Although this isn't the most practical program, it does use a continue statement effectively. Lines 9 and 10 declare the program's variables. buffer[] holds the string that the user enters in line 15. The other variable, ctr, increments through the elements of the array buffer[], while the for loop in lines 20 through 34 searches for vowels. For each letter in the loop, an if statement in lines 26 through 28 checks the letter against lowercase vowels. If there is a match, a continue statement executes, sending control back to line 20, the for statement. If the letter isn't a vowel, control passes to the if statement and line 33 is executed. Line 33 contains a new library function, putchar(), which displays a single character onscreen.

The continue Statement

SYNTAX

continue;

continue is used inside a loop. It causes the control of a program to skip the rest of the current iteration of a loop and start the next iteration.

Example

```
int x;
printf("Printing only the even numbers from 1 to 10\n");
for( x = 1; x <= 10; x++ )
{
   if( x % 2 != 0 )    /* See if the number is NOT even */
      continue;        /* Get next instance x */
   printf( "\n%d", x );
}
```

12

The goto Statement

The goto statement is one of C's *unconditional jump,* or *branching,* statements. When program execution reaches a goto statement, execution immediately jumps, or branches, to the location specified by the goto statement. This statement is unconditional because execution always branches when a goto statement is encountered; the branch doesn't depend on any program conditions (unlike if statements, for example).

The target of a goto statement is identified by a text label followed by a colon at the start of a line. A target label can be on a line by itself, or at the beginning of a line that contains a C statement. In a program, each target must be unique.

A goto statement and its target must be in the same function, but they can be in different blocks. Take a look at Listing 12.3, a simple program that uses a goto statement.

LISTING 12.3. Using the goto statement.

```
 1: /* Demonstrates the goto statement */
 2:
 3: #include <stdio.h>
 4:
 5: int main(void)
 6: {
 7:     int n;
 8:
 9: start:
10:
11:     puts("Enter a number between 0 and 10: ");
12:     scanf("%d", &n);
13:
14:     if (n < 0 ||n > 10 )
15:         goto start;
16:     else if (n == 0)
17:         goto location0;
18:     else if (n == 1)
19:         goto location1;
20:     else
21:         goto location2;
22:
23: location0:
24:     puts("You entered 0.\n");
25:     goto end;
26:
27: location1:
28:     puts("You entered 1.\n");
29:     goto end;
30:
```

```
31: location2:
32:     puts("You entered something between 2 and 10.\n");
33:
34: end:
35:     return 0;
36: }
```

**INPUT/
OUTPUT**
```
Enter a number between 0 and 10:
1
You entered 1.
```

**INPUT/
OUTPUT**
```
Enter a number between 0 and 10:
9
You entered something between 2 and 10.
```

ANALYSIS   This is a simple program that accepts a number between 0 and 10. If the number isn't between 0 and 10, the program uses a goto statement on line 15 to go to start, which is on line 9. Otherwise, the program checks, on line 16, to see whether the number equals 0. If it does, a goto statement on line 17 sends control to location0 (line 23), which prints a statement on line 24 and executes another goto. The goto on line 25 sends control to end at the end of the program. The program executes the same logic for the value of 1 and all values between 2 and 10 as a whole.

The target of a goto statement can come either before or after that statement in the code. The only restriction, as mentioned earlier, is that both the goto and the target must be in the same function. They can be in different blocks, however. You can use goto to transfer execution both into and out of loops, such as a for statement, but you should never do this. In fact, I strongly recommend that you never use the goto statement anywhere in your programs. There are two reasons:

- You don't need it—no programming task requires the goto statement. You can always write the needed code using C's other branching statements.

- It's dangerous—the goto statement might seem like an ideal solution for certain programming problems, but it's easy to abuse. When program execution branches with a goto statement, no record is kept of where the execution came from, so execution can weave through the program willy-nilly. This type of programming is known as *spaghetti code*.

Some careful programmers can write perfectly fine programs that use goto. There might be situations in which judicious use of goto is the simplest solution to a programming problem. It's never the only solution, however. If you're going to ignore this warning, at least be careful!

12

Do	**Don't**
DO avoid using the goto statement if possible (and it's always possible!).	**DON'T** confuse break and continue. break ends a loop, whereas continue starts the next iteration of the loop.

The goto Statement

▼ SYNTAX

```
goto location;
```

location is a label statement that identifies the program location where execution is to branch. A *label statement* consists of an identifier followed by a colon and, optionally, a C statement:

```
location: a C statement;
```

You can also put a label by itself on a line. When this is done, some programmers like to follow it with the null statement (a semicolon by itself), although that is not required:

▲
```
location: ;
```

Infinite Loops

What is an infinite loop, and why would you want one in your program? An infinite loop is one that, if left to its own devices, would run forever. It can be a for loop, a while loop, or a do...while loop. For example, if you write

```
while (1)
{
    /* additional code goes here */
}
```

you create an infinite loop. The condition that the while tests is the constant 1, which is always true and can't be changed by the program. Because 1 can never be changed on its own, the loop never terminates.

In the preceding section, you saw that the break statement can be used to exit a loop. Without the break statement, infinite loops would be useless. With break, you can take advantage of infinite loops.

You can also create an infinite for loop or an infinite do...while loop, as follows:

```
for (;;)
{
    /* additional code goes here */
}
do
```

```
{
    /* additional code goes here */
} while (1);
```

The principle remains the same for all three loop types. This section's examples use the `while` loop.

An infinite loop can be used to test many conditions and determine whether the loop should terminate. It might be difficult to include all the test conditions in parentheses after the `while` statement. It might be easier to test the conditions individually in the body of the loop, and then exit by executing a `break` as needed.

An infinite loop can also create a menu system that directs your program's operation. You might remember from Day 4, "Functions: The Basics," that a program's `main()` function often serves as a sort of "traffic cop," directing execution among the various functions that do the real work of the program. This is often accomplished by a menu of some kind: The user is presented with a list of choices and makes an entry by selecting one of them. One of the available choices should be to terminate the program. After a choice is made, one of C's decision statements is used to direct program execution accordingly.

Listing 12.4 demonstrates a menu system.

LISTING 12.4. Using an infinite loop to implement a menu system.

```
1:  /* Demonstrates using an infinite loop to implement */
2:  /* a menu system. */
3:  #include <stdio.h>
4:  #define DELAY  1500000       /* Used in delay loop. */
5:
6:  int menu(void);
7:  void delay(void);
8:
9:  int main(void)
10: {
11:     int choice;
12:
13:     while (1)
14:     {
15:
16:       /* Get the user's selection. */
17;
18:       choice = menu();
19:
20:       /* Branch based on the input. */
21:
22;       if (choice == 1)
```

continues

LISTING **12.4**. continued

```
23:      {
24:          puts("\nExecuting task A.");
25:          delay();
26:      }
27:      else if (choice == 2)
28:          {
29:              puts("\nExecuting task B.");
30:              delay();
31:          }
32;      else if (choice == 3)
33:          {
34:              puts("\nExecuting task C.");
35:              delay();
36:          }
37:      else if (choice == 4)
38:          {
39:              puts("\nExecuting task D.");
40:              delay();
41:          }
42:      else if (choice == 5)         /* Exit program. */
43:          {
44:              puts("\nExiting program now...\n");
45:              delay();
46:              break;
47:          }
48:          else
49:          {
50:              puts("\nInvalid choice, try again.");
51:              delay();
52:          }
53:      }
54:      return 0;
55: }
56:
57: /* Displays a menu and inputs user's selection. */
58: int menu(void)
59: {
60:      int reply;
61:
62:      puts("\nEnter 1 for task A.");
63:      puts("Enter 2 for task B.");
64:      puts("Enter 3 for task C.");
65:      puts("Enter 4 for task D.");
66:      puts("Enter 5 to exit program.");
67:
68:      scanf("%d", &reply);
69:
70:      return reply;
```

```
71: }
72:
73: void delay( void )
74: {
75:     long x;
76:     for ( x = 0; x < DELAY; x++ )
77:         ;
78: }
```

INPUT/
OUTPUT

```
Enter 1 for task A.
Enter 2 for task B.
Enter 3 for task C.
Enter 4 for task D.
Enter 5 to exit program.
1

Executing task A.

Enter 1 for task A.
Enter 2 for task B.
Enter 3 for task C.
Enter 4 for task D.
Enter 5 to exit program.
6

Invalid choice, try again.

Enter 1 for task A.
Enter 2 for task B.
Enter 3 for task C.
Enter 4 for task D.
Enter 5 to exit program.
5

Exiting program now...
```

ANALYSIS In Listing 12.4, a function named menu() is called on line 18 and defined on lines 58 through 71. menu() displays a menu onscreen, accepts user input, and returns the input to the main program. In main(), a series of nested if statements tests the returned value and directs execution accordingly. The only thing this program does is display messages onscreen. In a real program, the code would call various functions to perform the selected task.

This program also uses a second function named delay(). delay() is defined on lines 73 through 78 and really doesn't do much. Simply stated, the for statement on line 76 loops, doing nothing (line 77). The statement loops DELAY times.

12

Note

This kind of delay is often called a busy-wait as the computer's CPU is busy for the duration of the delay. On a multitasking, multiuser operating system such as Linux, it is silly make the CPU work hard doing nothing when it could be doing useful work.

A better way to generate a delay on Linux and other UNIX-like systems is with the `sleep()` function. This function passes control of the CPU back to the operating system for the number of seconds that is passed as its argument. To use `sleep()`, a program must include the header file unistd.h. Because `sleep()` passes control of the CPU back to the operating system where it can do something useful, you should use it instead of `delay()`.

The `switch` Statement

C's most flexible program control statement is the `switch` statement, which lets your program execute different statements based on an expression that can have more than two values. Earlier control statements, such as `if`, were limited to evaluating an expression that could have only one of two values: true or false. To control program flow based on more than two values, you had to use multiple nested `if` statements, as shown in Listing 12.4. The `switch` statement makes such nesting unnecessary.

The general form of the `switch` statement is as follows:

```
switch (expression)
{
    case  template_1: statement(s);
    case  template_2: statement(s);
    ...
    case  template_n: statement(s);
    default: statement(s);
}
```

In this statement, *expression* is any expression that evaluates to an integer value: type `long`, `int`, or `char`. The `switch` statement evaluates *expression* and compares the value against the templates following each `case` label, and then one of the following happens:

- If a match is found between *expression* and one of the templates, execution is transferred to the statement that follows the `case` label.

- If no match is found, execution is transferred to the statement following the optional `default` label.

- If no match is found and there is no `default` label, execution passes to the first statement following the `switch` statement's closing brace.

The `switch` statement is demonstrated in Listing 12.5, which displays a message based on the user's input.

LISTING 12.5. Using the `switch` statement.

```
 1:  /* Demonstrates the switch statement. */
 2:
 3:  #include <stdio.h>
 4:
 5:  int main(void)
 6:  {
 7:      int reply;
 8:
 9:      puts("Enter a number between 1 and 5:");
10:      scanf("%d", &reply);
11:
12:      switch (reply)
13:      {
14:          case 1:
15:              puts("You entered 1.");
16:          case 2:
17:              puts("You entered 2.");
18:          case 3:
19:              puts("You entered 3.");
20:          case 4:
21:              puts("You entered 4.");
22:          case 5:
23:              puts("You entered 5.");
24:          default:
25:              puts("Out of range, try again.");
26:      }
27:
28:      return 0;
29: }
```

INPUT/ OUTPUT
```
Enter a number between 1 and 5:
2
You entered 2.
You entered 3.
You entered 4.
You entered 5.
Out of range, try again.
```

ANALYSIS Well, that's certainly not right, is it? It looks as though the `switch` statement finds the first matching template and then executes everything that follows (not just the statements associated with the template). That's exactly what does happen, though. That's how `switch` is supposed to work. In effect, it performs a `goto` to the matching template. To ensure that only the statements associated with the matching template are executed, include a `break` statement where needed. Listing 12.6 shows the program rewritten with `break` statements. Now it functions properly.

12

LISTING 12.6. Correct use of switch, including break statements as needed.

```c
 1: /* Demonstrates the switch statement correctly. */
 2:
 3: #include <stdio.h>
 4:
 5: int main(void)
 6: {
 7:     int reply;
 8:
 9:     puts("\nEnter a number between 1 and 5:");
10:     scanf("%d", &reply);
11:
12:     switch (reply)
13:     {
14:       case 0:
15:           break;
16       case 1:
17:         {
18:             puts("You entered 1.\n");
19:             break;
20:         }
21:       case 2:
22:         {
23:             puts("You entered 2.\n");
24:             break;
25:         }
26:       case 3:
27:         {
28:             puts("You entered 3.\n");
29:             break;
30:         }
31:       case 4:
32:         {
33:             puts("You entered 4.\n");
34:             break;
35:         }
36:       case 5:
37:         {
38:             puts("You entered 5.\n");
39:             break;
40:         }
41:       default:
42:         {
43:             puts("Out of range, try again.\n");
44:         }
45:     }               /* End of switch */
46:     return 0;
47: }
```

INPUT/
OUTPUT

```
Enter a number between 1 and 5:
1
You entered 1.
```

INPUT/
OUTPUT

```
Enter a number between 1 and 5:
6
Out of range, try again.
```

Compile and run this version; it runs correctly.

One common use of the switch statement is to implement the sort of menu shown in Listing 12.4. Listing 12.7 uses switch instead of if to implement a menu. Using switch is much better than using nested if statements, which were used in the earlier version of the menu program, shown in Listing 12.4.

LISTING 12.7. Using the switch statement to execute a menu system.

```c
1 : /* Demonstrates using an infinite loop and the switch */
2 : /* statement to implement a menu system. */
3 : #include <stdio.h>
4 : #include <stdlib.h>
5 : #include <unistd.h>
6 :
7 : int menu(void);
8 :
9 : int main(void)
10: {
11:
12:     while (1)
13:     {
14:         /* Get user's selection and branch based on the input. */
15:
16:         switch(menu())
17:         {
18:           case 1:
19:           {
20:                    puts("\nExecuting task A.");
21:             sleep(1);
22:             break;
23:           }
24:           case 2:
25:           {
26:                    puts("\nExecuting task B.");
27:             sleep(1);
28:             break;
29:           }
30:           case 3:
31:           {
32:                    puts("\nExecuting task C.");
```

12

continues

LISTING 12.7. continued

```
33:          sleep(1);
34:          break;
35:        }
36:        case 4:
37:        {
38:                  puts("\nExecuting task D.");
39:          sleep(1);
40:          break;
41:        }
42:        case 5:     /* Exit program. */
43:        {
44:          puts("\nExiting program now...\n");
45:          sleep(1);
46:          exit(0);
47:        }
48:        default:
49:        {
50:          puts("\nInvalid choice, try again.");
51:          sleep(1);
52:        }
53:     }  /* End of switch */
54:   }        /* End of while  */
55:     return 0;
56: }
57:
58: /* Displays a menu and inputs user's selection. */
59: int menu(void)
60: {
61:     int reply;
62:
63:     puts("\nEnter 1 for task A.");
64:     puts("Enter 2 for task B.");
65:     puts("Enter 3 for task C.");
66:     puts("Enter 4 for task D.");
67:     puts("Enter 5 to exit program.");
68:
69:     scanf("%d", &reply);
70:
71:     return reply;
72: }
```

**INPUT/
OUTPUT**

```
Enter 1 for task A.
Enter 2 for task B.
Enter 3 for task C.
Enter 4 for task D.
Enter 5 to exit program.
1

Executing task A.
```

```
Enter 1 for task A.
Enter 2 for task B.
Enter 3 for task C.
Enter 4 for task D.
Enter 5 to exit program.
6

Invalid choice, try again.

Enter 1 for task A.
Enter 2 for task B.
Enter 3 for task C.
Enter 4 for task D.
Enter 5 to exit program.
5

Exiting program now...
```

ANALYSIS   One other new statement is used in this program: the exit() library function in the statements associated with case 5: on line 46. You can't use break here, as you did in Listing 12.4. Executing a break would merely break out of the switch statement; it wouldn't break out of the infinite while loop. As you'll learn in the next section, the exit() function terminates the program.

However, having execution "fall through" parts of a switch construction can be useful at times. Say, for example, that you want the same block of statements executed if one of several values is encountered. Simply omit the break statements and list all the case templates before the statements. If the test expression matches any of the case conditions, execution will "fall through" the following case statements until it reaches the block of code you want executed. This is illustrated by Listing 12.8.

12

LISTING 12.8. Another way to use the switch statement.

```
1:  /* Another use of the switch statement. */
2:
3:  #include <stdio.h>
4:  #include <stdlib.h>
5:
6:  int main(void)
7:  {
8:      int reply;
9:
10:     while (1)
11:     {
12:         puts("\nEnter a value between 1 and 10, 0 to exit: ");
13:         scanf("%d", &reply);
```

continues

LISTING 12.8. continued

```
14:
15:          switch (reply)
16:          {
17:              case 0:
18:                  exit(0);
19:              case 1:
20:              case 2:
21:              case 3:
22:              case 4:
23:              case 5:
24:                  {
25:                      puts("You entered 5 or below.\n");
26:                      break;
27:                  }
28:              case 6:
29:              case 7:
30:              case 8:
31:              case 9:
32:              case 10:
33:                  {
34:                      puts("You entered 6 or higher.\n");
35:                      break;
36:                  }
37:              default:
38:                      puts("Between 1 and 10, please!\n");
39:          } /* end of switch */
40:      }     /*end of while */
41:      return 0;
42: }
```

INPUT/OUTPUT

```
Enter a value between 1 and 10, 0 to exit:
11
Between 1 and 10, please!

Enter a value between 1 and 10, 0 to exit:
1
You entered 5 or below.

Enter a value between 1 and 10, 0 to exit:
6
You entered 6 or higher.

Enter a value between 1 and 10, 0 to exit:
0
```

ANALYSIS This program accepts a value from the keyboard and then states whether the value is 5 or below, 6 or higher, or not between 1 and 10. If the value is 0, line 18 executes a call to the exit() function, thus ending the program.

The `switch` Statement

▼ SYNTAX

```
switch  (expression)
{
    case  template_1: statement(s);
    case  template_2: statement(s);
    ...
    case  template_n: statement(s);
    default: statement(s);
}
```

The `switch` statement allows for multiple branches from a single expression. It's more efficient and easier to follow than a multileveled `if` statement. A `switch` statement evaluates an expression and then branches to the `case` statement that contains the template matching the expression's result. If no template matches the expression's result, control goes to the `default` statement. If there is no `default` statement, control goes to the end of the `switch` statement.

Program flow continues from the `case` statement down unless a `break` statement is encountered. In that case, control goes to the end of the `switch` statement.

Example 1

```
switch( letter )
{
    case 'A':
    case 'a':
        printf( "You entered A" );
        break;
    case 'B':
    case 'b':
        printf( "You entered B");
        break;
    ...
    ...
    default:
        printf( "I don't have a case for %c", letter );
}
```

Example 2

```
switch( number )
{
    case 0:    puts( "Your number is 0 or less.");
    case 1:    puts( "Your number is 1 or less.");
    case 2:    puts( "Your number is 2 or less.");
    case 3:    puts( "Your number is 3 or less.");
    ...
    ...
    case 99:   puts( "Your number is 99 or less.");
```

12

▼

▼
```
                break;
    default:    puts( "Your number is greater than 99.");
}
```

Because there are no break statements for the first case statements, this example finds the case that matches the number and prints every case from that point down to the break in case 99. If the number was 3, you would be told that your number is equal to 3 or less, 4 or less, 5 or less, up to 99 or less. The program continues printing until it

▲ reaches the break statement in case 99.

Do	Don't
DO use a default case in a switch statement, even if you think you've covered all possible cases.	**DON'T** forget to use break statements if your switch statements need them.
DO use a switch statement instead of an if statement if more than two conditions are being evaluated for the same variable.	
DO line up your case statements so that they're easy to read.	
DO use the sleep() function instead of a busy-wait loop to temporarily suspend the execution of your program.	

Exiting the Program

A C program normally terminates when execution reaches the closing brace of the main() function. However, you can terminate a program at any time by calling the library function exit(). You can also specify one or more functions to be automatically executed at termination.

The exit() Function

The exit() function terminates program execution and returns control to the operating system. This function takes a single type int argument that is passed back to the operating system to indicate the program's success or failure. The syntax of the exit() function is

```
exit(status);
```

If status has a value of 0, it indicates that the program terminated normally. A value other than 0 indicates that the program terminated with some sort of error. This can be useful if your C program is being run by some other program, for instance by the `system()` function we're about to deal with in the next section.

To use the `exit()` function, a program must include the header file stdlib.h. This header file also defines two symbolic constants for use as arguments to the `exit()` function:

```
#define EXIT_SUCCESS   0
#define EXIT_FAILURE   1
```

Thus, to exit with a return value of 0, call `exit(EXIT_SUCCESS)`; for a return value of 1, call `exit(EXIT_FAILURE)`.

Do	**Don't**
DO use the `exit()` command to get out of the program if there's a problem.	
DO pass meaningful values to the `exit()` function.	

Executing Commands from Within a Program

The C standard library includes a function, `system()`, that lets you execute operating system commands in a running C program. This can be useful, allowing you to read a disk's directory listing or format a disk without exiting the program. To use the `system()` function, a program must include the header file stdlib.h. The format of `system()` is

```
system(command);
```

The argument *command* can be either a string constant or a pointer to a string. For example, to obtain a directory listing in a Linux system, you could write either

```
system("ls");
```

or

```
char *command = "ls";
system(command);
```

After the operating system command is executed, execution returns to the program at the location immediately following the call to `system()`. If the command you pass to `system()` isn't a valid operating system command, you get a `command not found` error message before returning to the program. The use of `system()` is illustrated in Listing 12.9.

12

LISTING 12.9. Using the `system()` function to execute system commands.

```
1:  /* Demonstrates the system() function. */
2:  #include <stdio.h>
3:  #include <stdlib.h>
4:
5:  int main(void)
6:  {
7:      /* Declare a buffer to hold input. */
8:
9:      char input[40];
10:
11:     while (1)
12:     {
13:         /* Get the user's command. */
14:
15:         puts("\nInput the desired system command, blank to exit");
16:         fgets(input, 40, stdin);
17:
18:         /* Exit if a blank line was entered. */
19:
20:         if (input[0] == '\n')
21:             exit(0);
22:
23:         /* Execute the command. */
24:
25:         system(input);
26:     }
27:     return 0;
28: }
```

INPUT/
OUTPUT

```
Input the desired system command, blank to exit
ls *.c

als
list1201.c  list1203.c  list1205.c  list1207.c  list1209.c
list1202.c  list1204.c  list1206.c  list1208.c

Input the desired system command, blank to exit
```

ANALYSIS   Listing 12.9 illustrates the use of `system()`. Using a while loop in lines 11 through 26, this program enables operating system commands. Lines 15 and 16 prompt the user to enter the operating system command. If the user presses Enter without entering a command, lines 20 and 21 call `exit()` to end the program. Line 25 calls `sys-tem()` with the command entered by the user. If you run this program on your system, you'll get different output, of course.

The commands you can pass to `system()` aren't limited to simple operating commands, such as listing directories or formatting disks. You can also pass the name of any executable file or batch file—and that program is executed normally. For example, if you passed the argument `list1208`, you would execute the program called list1208. When you exit the program, execution passes back to where the `system()` call was made.

The only restrictions on using `system()` have to do with memory. When `system()` is executed, the original program remains loaded in your computer's RAM, and a new copy of the command shell (usually bash on a Linux system) and any program you run are loaded as well. This works only if the computer has sufficient memory. If not, you get an error message.

Summary

Today's discussion covered a variety of topics related to program control. You learned about the `goto` statement and why you should avoid using it in your programs. You saw that the `break` and `continue` statements give additional control over the execution of loops and that these statements can be used in conjunction with infinite loops to perform useful programming tasks. You also learned how to use the `exit()` function to control program termination. Finally, you saw how to use the `system()` function to execute system commands from within your program.

Q&A

Q Is it better to use a `switch` statement or a nested loop?

A If you're checking a variable that can take on more than two values, the `switch` statement is almost always better. The resulting code is easier to read, too. If you're checking a true/false condition, go with an `if` statement.

Q Why should I avoid a `goto` statement?

A When you first see a `goto` statement, it's easy to believe that it could be useful. However, `goto` can cause you more problems than it fixes. A `goto` statement is an unstructured command that takes you to another point in a program. Many debuggers (software that helps you trace program problems) can't interrogate a `goto` properly. `goto` statements also lead to spaghetti code—code that goes all over the place.

Q Why don't all compilers have the same functions?

A In today's discussion, you saw that certain C functions aren't available with all compilers or all computer systems.

Although there are standards that all ANSI compilers follow, these standards don't prohibit compiler manufacturers from adding additional functionality. They do this by creating and including new functions. Each compiler manufacturer usually adds a number of functions that it believes will be helpful to its users.

12

Q Isn't C supposed to be a standardized language?

A C is, in fact, highly standardized. The American National Standards Institute (ANSI) has developed the ANSI C Standard, which specifies almost all details of the C language, including the functions that are provided. Some compiler vendors have added more functions—ones that aren't part of the ANSI standard—to their C compilers in an effort to one-up the competition. In addition, you sometimes come across a compiler that doesn't claim to meet the ANSI standard. If you limit yourself to ANSI-standard compilers, however, you'll find that 99% of program syntax and functions are common among them.

Q Is it good to use the `system()` function to execute system functions?

A The `system()` function might appear to be an easy way to do such things as list the files in a directory, but you should be cautious. Most operating system commands are specific to a particular operating system. If you use a `system()` call, your code probably won't be portable. If you want to run another program (not an operating system command), you shouldn't have portability problems.

Workshop

The Workshop provides quiz questions to help you solidify your understanding of the material covered and exercises to provide you with experience in using what you've learned. The answers to the quiz and exercises are provided in Appendix C, "Answers."

Quiz

1. When is it advisable to use the `goto` statement in your programs?
2. What's the difference between the `break` statement and the `continue` statement?
3. What is an infinite loop, and how do you create one?
4. What two events cause program execution to terminate?
5. What variable types can a `switch` evaluate to?
6. What does the `default` statement do?
7. What does the `exit()` function do?
8. What does the `system()` function do?

Exercises

1. Write a statement that causes control of the program to go to the next iteration in a loop.
2. Write the statement(s) that sends control of a program to the end of a loop.

3. Write a line of code that displays a listing of all the files in the current directory.

4. **BUG BUSTER:** Is anything wrong with the following code?

```c
switch( answer )
{
    case 'Y': printf("You answered yes");
              break;
    case 'N': printf( "You answered no");
}
```

5. **BUG BUSTER:** Is anything wrong with the following code?

```c
switch( choice )
{
    default:
        printf("You did not choose 1 or 2");
    case 1:
        printf("You answered 1");
        break;
    case 2:
        printf( "You answered 2");
        break;
}
```

6. Rewrite exercise 5 using `if` statements.

7. Write an infinite `do...while` loop.

Because of the multitude of possible answers for the following exercises, answers are not provided. These are exercises for you to try on your own.

8. **ON YOUR OWN:** Write a program that works like a calculator. The program should allow for addition, subtraction, multiplication, and division.

9. **ON YOUR OWN:** Write a program that provides a menu with five different options. The fifth option should quit the program. Each of the other options should execute a system command using the `system()` function.

12

DAY 13

Working with the Screen and Keyboard

Almost every program must perform input and output. How well a program handles input and output is often the best indicator of the program's usefulness. You've already learned how to perform some basic input and output. Today you will learn

- How C uses streams for input and output
- Various ways of accepting input from the keyboard
- Methods of displaying text and numeric data onscreen
- How to send output to the printer
- How to redirect program input and output

Streams and C

Before you get to the details of program input/output, you need to learn about streams. All C input/output is done with streams, no matter where input is coming from or where output is going to. As you will see later, this standard way of handling all input and output has definite advantages for the programmer. Of course, this makes it essential that you understand what streams are and how they work. First, however, you need to know exactly what the terms *input* and *output* mean.

What Exactly Is Program Input/Output?

As you learned earlier in this book, a C program keeps data in random access memory (RAM) while executing. This data is in the form of variables, structures, and arrays that have been declared by the program. Where did this data come from, and what can the program do with it?

- Data can come from some location external to the program. Data moved from an external location into RAM, where the program can access it, is called *input*. The keyboard and disk files are the most common sources of program input.

- Data can also be sent to a location external to the program; this is called *output*. The most common destinations for output are the screen, a printer, and disk files.

Input sources and output destinations are collectively referred to as *devices*. The keyboard is a device, the screen is a device, and so on. Some devices (the keyboard) are for input only, others (the screen) are for output only, and still others (disk files) are for both input and output. This is illustrated in Figure 13.1.

FIGURE 13.1.

Input and output can take place between your program and a variety of external devices.

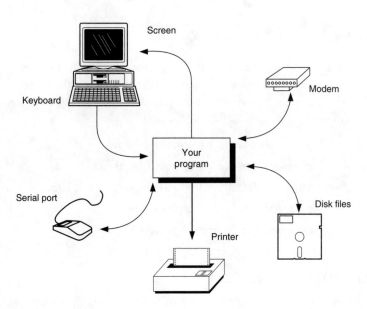

Whatever the device, and whether it's performing input or output, C carries out all input and output operations by means of streams.

What Is a Stream?

NEW TERM   A *stream* is a sequence of characters. More exactly, a stream is a sequence of bytes of data. A sequence of bytes flowing into a program is an input stream; a sequence of bytes flowing out of a program is an output stream. By focusing on streams, you don't have to worry as much about where they're going or where they originated. The major advantage of streams, therefore, is that input/output programming is *device independent*. Programmers don't need to write special input/output functions for each device (keyboard, disk, and so on). The program sees input/output as a continuous stream of bytes no matter where the input is coming from or going to.

NEW TERM   Every C stream is connected to a file. In this context, the term *file* doesn't refer to a disk file. Rather, it is an intermediate step between the stream that your program deals with and the actual physical device being used for input or output. For the most part, the beginning C programmer doesn't need to be concerned with these files because the details of interactions between streams, files, and devices are taken care of automatically by the C library functions and the operating system.

Predefined Streams

ANSI C has three predefined streams, also referred to as the *standard input/output files*, and all three are available on Linux. These streams are automatically opened when a C program starts executing and are closed when the program terminates. The programmer doesn't need to take any special action to make these streams available. Table 13.1 lists the standard streams and the devices they normally are connected with.

TABLE 13.1. The three standard streams.

Name	Streams	Device
stdin	Standard input	Keyboard
stdout	Standard output	Screen
stderr	Standard error	Screen

Whenever you use the `printf()` or `puts()` function to display text onscreen, you use the `stdout` stream. Likewise, when you use `gets()` or `scanf()` to read keyboard input, you use the `stdin` stream. You might remember using `stdin` as the third argument passed to the `fgets()` function in Day 9, "Characters and Strings." The standard streams are opened automatically, but other streams, such as those used to manipulate information stored on disk, must be opened explicitly. You'll learn how to do this on Day 15, "Using Disk Files." The remainder of today's discussion deals with the standard streams.

13

C's Stream Functions

The C standard library has a variety of functions that deal with stream input and output. Most of these functions come in two varieties: one that always uses one of the standard streams and one that requires the programmer to specify the stream. These functions are listed in Table 13.2. This table doesn't list all of C's input/output functions, nor are all of the functions in the table covered today.

TABLE 13.2. The standard library's stream input/output functions.

Uses One of the Standard Streams	Requires a Stream Name	Description
printf()	fprintf()	Formatted output
puts()	fputs()	String output
putchar()	putc(), fputc()	Character output
scanf()	fscanf()	Formatted input
gets()	fgets()	String input
getchar()	getc(), fgetc()	Character input
perror()		String output to stderr only

All these functions require that you include stdio.h, and the functions vprintf() and vfprintf() also require stdargs.h. On some systems other than Linux, the function perror() might require stdlib.h, and vprintf() and vfprintf() might require varargs.h. Your compiler's library reference or the local man pages will state whether any additional or alternative header files are needed.

An Example

The short program in Listing 13.1 demonstrates the equivalence of streams.

LISTING 13.1. The equivalence of streams.

```
1:  /* Demonstrates the equivalence of stream input and output. */
2:  #include <stdio.h>
3:
4:  main(void)
5:  {
6:      char buffer[256];
7:
8:      /* Input a line, then immediately output it. */
9:
10:     puts(fgets(buffer, 256, stdin));
```

```
11:
12:     return 0;
13: }
```

On line 10, the fgets() function is used to input a line of text from the keyboard (stdin). Because fgets() returns a pointer to the string, it can be used as the argument to puts(), which displays the string onscreen (stdout). When run, this program inputs a line of text from the user and then immediately displays the string onscreen.

Do	Don't
DO take advantage of the standard input/output streams that C provides.	DON'T rename or change the standard streams unnecessarily.
	DON'T try to use an input stream such as stdin for an output function such as fprintf().

Accepting Keyboard Input

Most C programs require some form of input from the keyboard (that is, from stdin). Input functions are divided into a hierarchy of three levels: character input, line input, and formatted input.

Character Input

The character input functions read input from a stream one character at a time. When called, each of these functions returns the next character in the stream, or EOF if the end of the file has been reached or an error has occurred. EOF is a symbolic constant defined in stdio.h as -1. Character input functions differ in terms of buffering and echoing.

- Some character input functions are *buffered*. That means the operating system holds all characters in a temporary storage space until you press Enter, and then the system sends the characters to the stdin stream. Others are *unbuffered*, meaning that each character is sent to stdin as soon as the key is pressed.

- Some input functions automatically *echo* each character to stdout as it is received. Others don't echo; the character is sent to stdin and not stdout. Because stdout is assigned to the screen, that's where input is echoed.

The stdin and stdout are, by default, buffered streams under Linux and other UNIX-like operating systems. The standard error stream stderr is unbuffered. There is a way to change the default behavior of stdin and stdout, but that is beyond the scope of this book. The rest of today's lesson assumes that both stdin and stdout are buffered streams.

13

The `getchar()` Function

The function `getchar()` obtains the next character from the stream `stdin`. It provides buffered character input with echo, and its prototype is

```
int getchar(void);
```

The use of `getchar()` is demonstrated in Listing 13.2. Notice that the `putchar()` function, explained in detail later today, simply displays a single character onscreen.

LISTING **13.2**. The `getchar()` function.

```
1:  /* Demonstrates the getchar() function. */
2:
3:  #include <stdio.h>
4:
5:  int main(void)
6:  {
7:      int ch;
8:
9:      while ((ch = getchar()) != '\n')
10:         putchar(ch);
11:
12:     return 0;
13: }
```

INPUT/
OUTPUT

This is what's typed in.
This is what's typed in.

ANALYSIS

On line 9, the `getchar()` function is called and waits to receive a character from `stdin`. Because `getchar()` is a buffered input function, no characters are received until you press Enter. However, each key you press is echoed immediately on the screen.

When you press Enter, all the characters you entered, including the newline, are sent to `stdin` by the operating system. The `getchar()` function returns the characters one at a time, assigning each in turn to `ch`.

Each character is compared to the newline character `'\n'` and, if not equal, displayed onscreen with `putchar()`. When a newline is returned by `getchar()`, the `while` loop terminates.

The `getchar()` function can be used to input entire lines of text, as shown in Listing 13.3. However, other input functions are better suited for this task, as you'll learn later today.

LISTING 13.3. Using the getchar() function to input an entire line of text.

```
1: /* Using getchar() to input strings. */
2:
3: #include <stdio.h>
4:
5: #define MAX 80
6:
7: int main(void)
8: {
9:     char ch, buffer[MAX+1];
10:    int x = 0;
11:
12:    while ((ch = getchar()) != '\n' && x < MAX)
13:        buffer[x++] = ch;
14:
15:    buffer[x] = '\0';
16:
17:    printf("%s\n", buffer);
18:
19:    return 0;
20: }
```

OUTPUT

```
This is a string
This is a string
```

ANALYSIS This program is similar to Listing 13.2 in the way that it uses getchar(). An extra condition has been added to the loop. This time the while loop accepts characters from getchar() until either a newline character is reached or 80 characters are read. Each character is assigned to an array called buffer. When the characters have been input, line 15 puts a null on the end of the array so that the printf() function on line 17 can print the entered string.

On line 9, why was buffer declared with a size of MAX + 1 instead of just MAX? If you declare buffer with a size of MAX + 1, the string can be 80 characters plus a null terminator. Don't forget to include a place for the null terminator at the end of your strings.

The getc() and fgetc() Functions

The getc() and fgetc() character input functions don't automatically work with stdin. Instead, they let the program specify the input stream. In fact, on Linux and most UNIX-like systems, getchar is equivalent to getc(stdin). getc() and fgetc() are used primarily to read characters from disk files. See Day 15 for more details.

13

Do	Don't
DO understand the difference between echoed and nonechoed input.	**DON'T** use non-ANSI standard functions if portability is a concern.
DO understand the difference between buffered and unbuffered input.	

"Ungetting" a Character with `ungetc()`

What does "ungetting" a character mean? An example should help you understand. Suppose that your program is reading characters from an input stream and can detect the end of input only by reading one character too many. For example, you might be inputting digits only, so you know that input has ended when the first nondigit character is encountered. That first nondigit character might be an important part of subsequent data, but it has been removed from the input stream. Is it lost? No, it can be returned to the input stream, where it is then the first character read by the next input operation on that stream.

To "unget" a character, you use the `ungetc()` library function. Its prototype is

```
int ungetc(int ch, FILE *fp);
```

The argument `ch` is the character to be returned. The argument `*fp` specifies the stream that the character is to be returned to, which can be any input stream. For now, simply specify `stdin` as the second argument: `ungetc(ch, stdin);`. The notation `FILE *fp` is used with streams associated with disk files; you'll learn about that on Day 15.

You can unget only a single character to a stream between reads, and you can't unget `EOF` at any time. The function `ungetc()` returns `ch` on success and `EOF` if the character can't be returned to the stream.

Line Input

The line-input functions read a line from an input stream—they read all characters up to the next newline character. The standard library has two line input functions, `gets()` and `fgets()`.

The `gets()` Function

You were introduced to the `gets()` function on Day 9 and the dangers of using it were explained. It will not be dealt with in any more detail here.

The `fgets()` Function

The `fgets()` library function is similar to `gets()` in that it reads a line of text from an input stream. It's more flexible because it lets the programmer specify the input stream to use and the maximum number of characters to be input. The `fgets()` function is often used to input text from disk files, as covered on Day 15. To use it for input from `stdin`, you specify `stdin` as the input stream. The prototype of `fgets()` is

```
char *fgets(char *str, int n, FILE *fp);
```

The last parameter, `FILE *fp`, is used to specify the input stream. As you have been doing since it was first introduced on Day 9, simply specify the standard input stream, `stdin`, as the stream argument.

The pointer `str` indicates where the input string is stored. The argument n specifies the maximum number of characters to be input. The `fgets()` function reads characters from the input stream until a newline or end-of-line is encountered or n - 1 characters have been read. The newline is included in the string and terminated with a \0 before it is stored. The return values of `fgets()` are the same as described earlier for `gets()`.

Strictly speaking, `fgets()` doesn't input a single line of text (if you define a line as a sequence of characters ending with a newline). It can read less than a full line if the line contains more than n - 1 characters. When used with `stdin`, execution doesn't return from `fgets()` until you press Enter, but only the first n - 1 characters are stored in the string. The newline is included in the string only if it falls within the first n - 1 characters. Listing 13.4 demonstrates the `fgets()` function.

LISTING 13.4. Using the `fgets()` function for keyboard input.

```
 1:  /* Demonstrates the fgets() function. */
 2:
 3:  #include <stdio.h>
 4:
 5:  #define MAXLEN 10
 6:
 7:  int main(void)
 8:  {
 9:      char buffer[MAXLEN];
10:
11:      puts("Enter text a line at a time; enter a blank to exit.");
12:
13:      while (1)
14:      {
15:          fgets(buffer, MAXLEN, stdin);
16:
17:          if (buffer[0] == '\n')
18:              break;
19:
20:          puts(buffer);
21:      }
```

13

continues

LISTING **13.4**. continued

```
22:     return 0;
23: }
```

Enter text a line at a time; enter a blank to exit.
Roses are red
Roses are
 red
Violets are blue
Violets a
re blue

Programming in C
Programmi
ng in C

Is for people like you!
Is for pe
ople like
 you!

Line 15 contains the `fgets()` function. When running the program, enter lines of lengths less than and greater than MAXLEN to see what happens. If a line of length greater than MAXLEN is entered, the first MAXLEN `- 1` characters are read by the first call to `fgets()`; the remaining characters remain in the keyboard buffer and are read by the next call to `fgets()` or any other function that reads from `stdin`. The program exits when a blank line is entered (lines 17 and 18).

Formatted Input

The input functions covered up to this point have simply taken one or more characters from an input stream and put them somewhere in memory. No interpretation or formatting of the input has been done, and you still have no way to input numeric variables. For example, how would you input the value `12.86` from the keyboard and assign it to a type `float` variable? Enter the `scanf()` and `fscanf()` functions. You were introduced to `scanf()` on Day 6, "Fundamentals of Input and Output." This section explains its use in more detail.

These two functions are identical, except that `scanf()` always uses `stdin`, whereas the user can specify the input stream in `fscanf()`. This section covers `scanf()`; `fscanf()` generally is used with disk file input and is covered on Day 15.

The `scanf()` Function's Arguments

The `scanf()` function takes a variable number of arguments; it requires a minimum of two. The first argument is a format string that uses special characters to tell `scanf()` how to interpret the input. The second and additional arguments are the addresses of the variable(s) to which the input data is assigned. Here's an example:

```
scanf("%d", &x);
```

The first argument, "%d", is the format string. In this case, %d tells scanf() to look for one signed integer value. The second argument uses the address-of operator (&) to tell scanf() to assign the input value to the variable x. Now you can look at the format string details.

The scanf() format string can contain the following:

- Spaces and tabs, which are ignored (they can be used to make the format string more readable).
- Characters (but not %), which are matched against non-whitespace characters in the input.
- One or more *conversion specifications,* which consist of the % character followed by special characters. Generally, the format string contains one conversion specification for each variable.

NEW TERM   The only required part of the format string is the conversion specifications. Each conversion specification begins with the % character and contains optional and required components in a certain order. The scanf() function applies the conversion specifications in the format string, in order, to the input fields. An *input field* is a sequence of non-whitespace characters that ends when the next whitespace is encountered or when the field width, if specified, is reached. The conversion specification components include the following:

- The optional assignment suppression flag (*) immediately follows the %. If present, this character tells scanf() to perform the conversion corresponding to the current conversion specifier, but to ignore the result (not assign it to any variable).
- The next component, the field width, is also optional. The field width is a decimal number specifying the width, in characters, of the input field. In other words, the field width specifies how many characters from stdin scanf() should examine for the current conversion. If a field width isn't specified, the input field extends to the next whitespace.
- The next component is the optional precision modifier, a single character that can be h, l, or L. If present, the precision modifier changes the meaning of the type specifier that follows it. Details are given later today.
- The only required component of the conversion specifier (besides the %) is the type specifier. The type specifier is one or more characters that tell scanf() how to interpret the input. These characters are listed and described in Table 13.3. The

13

Argument column lists the required type of the corresponding variable. For example, the type specifier d requires `int *` (a pointer to type `int`).

TABLE 13.3. The type specifier characters used in `scanf()` conversion specifiers.

Type	Argument	Meaning of Type
d	int *	A decimal integer.
i	int *	An integer in decimal, octal (with leading 0), or hexadecimal (with leading 0X or 0x) notation.
o	int *	An integer in octal notation with or without the leading 0.
u	unsigned int *	An unsigned decimal integer.
x	int *	A hexadecimal integer with or without the leading 0X or 0x.
c	char *	One or more characters are read and assigned sequentially to the memory location indicated by the argument. No terminating \0 is added. If a field width argument isn't given, one character is read. If a field width argument is given, that number of characters, including whitespace (if any), is read.
s	char *	A string of non-whitespace characters is read into the specified memory location, and a terminating \0 is added.
e,f,g	float *	A floating-point number. Numbers can be input in decimal or scientific notation.
[...]	char *	A string. Only the characters listed between the brackets are accepted. Input ends as soon as a nonmatching character is encountered, the specified field width is reached, or Enter is pressed. To accept the] character, list it first:[]...]. A \0 is added at the end of the string.
[^...]	char *	The same as [...], except that only characters not listed between the brackets are accepted.
%	None	Literal %. Reads the % character. No assignment is made.

Before seeing some examples of `scanf()`, you need to understand the precision modifiers, which are listed in Table 13.4.

TABLE 13.4. The precision modifiers.

Precision Modifier	Meaning
h	When placed before the type specifier d, i, o, u, or x, the modifier h specifies that the argument is a pointer to type short instead of type int.
l	When placed before the type specifier d, i, o, u, or x, the modifier l specifies that the argument is a pointer to type long. When placed before the type specifier e, f, or g, the modifier l specifies that the argument is a pointer to type double.
L	When placed before the type specifier e, f, or g, the modifier L specifies that the argument is a pointer to type long double.

Handling Extra Characters

Input from scanf() is buffered; no characters are actually received from stdin until the user presses Enter. The entire line of characters then "arrives" from stdin and is processed, in order, by scanf(). Execution returns from scanf() only when enough input has been received to match the specifications in the format string. Also, scanf() processes only enough characters from stdin to satisfy its format string. Extra, unneeded characters, if any, remain waiting in stdin. These characters can cause problems. Take a closer look at the operation of scanf() to see how.

When a call to scanf() is executed and the user has entered a single line, you can have three situations. For these examples, assume that scanf("%d %d", &x, &y); is being executed; in other words, scanf() is expecting two decimal integers. Here are the possibilities:

- The line the user inputs matches the format string. For example, suppose the user enters 12 14 followed by Enter. In this case, there are no problems. scanf() is satisfied, and no characters are left over in stdin.

- The line that the user inputs has too few elements to match the format string. For example, suppose the user enters 12 followed by Enter. In this case, scanf() continues to wait for the missing input. After the input is received, execution continues, and no characters are left over in stdin.

- The line that the user enters has more elements than required by the format string. For example, suppose the user enters 12 14 16 followed by Enter. In this case, scanf() reads the 12 and the 14 and then returns. The extra characters, the 1 and the 6, are left waiting in stdin.

It is this third situation (specifically, those leftover characters) that can cause problems. They remain waiting for as long as your program is running, until the next time the program reads input from stdin. Then the leftover characters are the first ones read, ahead of any input the user makes at the time. It's clear how this could cause errors. For example, the following code asks the user to input an integer and then a string:

```
puts("Enter your age.");
scanf("%d", &age);
puts("Enter your first name.");
scanf("%s", name);
```

Say, for example, that in response to the first prompt, the user decides to be precise and enters 29.00 and then presses Enter. The first call to scanf() is looking for an integer, so it reads the characters 29 from stdin and assigns the value 29 to the variable age. The characters .00 are left waiting in stdin. The next call to scanf() is looking for a string. It goes to stdin for input and finds .00 waiting there. The result is that the string .00 is assigned to name.

How can you avoid this problem? If the people who use your programs never make mistakes when entering information, that's one solution—but it's rather impractical.

A better solution is to make sure that no extra characters are waiting in stdin before prompting the user for input. You can do this by calling fgets(), which reads any remaining characters from stdin, up to and including the end of the line. Rather than call fgets() directly from the program, you can put it in a separate function with the descriptive name of clear_kb(). This function is shown in Listing 13.7.

LISTING 13.5. Clearing stdin of extra characters to avoid errors.

```
1: /* Clearing stdin of extra characters. */
2:
3: #include <stdio.h>
4:
5: void clear_kb(void);
6:
7: int main(void)
8: {
9:     int age;
10:     char name[20];
11:
12:     /* Prompt for user's age. */
13:
14:     puts("Enter your age.");
15:     scanf("%d", &age);
16:
17:     /* Clear stdin of any extra characters. */
18:
19:     clear_kb();
20:
21:     /* Now prompt for user's name. */
22:
23:     puts("Enter your first name.");
```

```
24:     scanf("%s", name);
25:     /* Display the data. */
26:
27:     printf("Your age is %d.\n", age);
28:     printf("Your name is %s.\n", name);
29:
30:     return 0;
31: }
32:
33: void clear_kb(void)
34:
35: /* Clears stdin of any waiting characters. */
36: {
37:     char junk[80];
38:     fgets(junk,80,stdin);
39: }
```

INPUT/
OUTPUT

Enter your age.
29 and never older!
Enter your first name.
Bradley
Your age is 29.
Your name is Bradley.

ANALYSIS
When you run Listing 13.5, enter some extra characters after your age before pressing Enter. Make sure that the program ignores them and correctly prompts you for your name. Then modify the program by removing the call to clear_kb(), and run it again. Any extra characters entered on the same line as your age are assigned to name.

Handling Extra Characters with `fflush()`

There is a second way you can clear the extra characters that were typed in. The fflush() function flushes the information in a stream—including the standard input stream. fflush() is generally used with disk files (which are covered on Day 15); however, it can also be used to make Listing 13.5 even simpler. Listing 13.6 uses the fflush() function instead of the clear_kb() function that was created in Listing 13.5.

LISTING 13.6. Clearing stdin of extra characters using fflush().

```
1:  /* Clearing stdin of extra characters. */
2:  /* Using the fflush() function        */
3:  #include <stdio.h>
4:
5:  int main(void)
6:  {
7:      int age;
8:      char name[20];
9:
10:     /* Prompt for user's age. */
```

continues

13

LISTING 13.6. continued

```
11:     puts("Enter your age.");
12:     scanf("%d", &age);
13:
14:     /* Clear stdin of any extra characters. */
15:     fflush(stdin);
16:
17:     /* Now prompt for user's name. */
18:     puts("Enter your first name.");
19:     scanf("%s", name);
20:
21:     /* Display the data. */
22:     printf("Your age is %d.\n", age);
23:     printf("Your name is %s.\n", name);
24:
25:     return 0;
26: }
```

**INPUT/
OUTPUT**

```
Enter your age.
29 and never older!
Enter your first name.
Bradley
Your age is 29.
Your name is Bradley.
```

ANALYSIS   As you can see in line 15, the fflush() function is being used. The prototype
for the fflush() function is as follows:

```
int fflush( FILE *stream);
```

The *stream* is the stream to be flushed. In Listing 13.6, the standard input stream, stdin,
is being passed for *stream*.

scanf() Examples

The best way to become familiar with the operation of the scanf() function is to use it.
It's a powerful function, but it can be a bit confusing at times. Try it and see what happens. Listing 13.7 demonstrates some of the unusual ways to use scanf(). You should
compile and run this program and then experiment by making changes to the scanf()
format strings.

LISTING 13.7. Some ways to use scanf() for keyboard input.

```
1:  /* Demonstrates some uses of scanf(). */
2:
3:  #include <stdio.h>
4:
5:
6:
7:  int main(void)
```

```
 8:  {
 9:      int i1, i2;
10:      long l1;
11:
12:      double d1;
13:      char buf1[80], buf2[80];
14:
15:      /* Using the l modifier to enter long integers and doubles.*/
16:
17:      puts("Enter an integer and a floating point number.");
18:      scanf("%ld %lf", &l1, &d1);
19:      printf("\nYou entered %ld and %f.\n",l1, d1);
20:      puts("The scanf() format string used the l modifier to store");
21:      puts("your input in a type long and a type double.\n");
22:
23:      fflush(stdin);
24:
25:      /* Use field width to split input. */
26:
27:      puts("Enter a 5 digit integer (for example, 54321).");
28:      scanf("%2d%3d", &i1, &i2);
29:
30:      printf("\nYou entered %d and %d.\n", i1, i2);
31:      puts("Note how the field width specifier in the scanf() format");
32:      puts("string split your input into two values.\n");
33:
34:      fflush(stdin);
35:
36:      /* Using an excluded space to split a line of input into */
37:      /* two strings at the space. */
38:
39:      puts("Enter your first and last names separated by a space.");
40:      scanf("%[^ ]%s", buf1, buf2);
41:      printf("\nYour first name is %s\n", buf1);
42:      printf("Your last name is %s\n", buf2);
43:      puts("Note how [^ ] in the scanf() format string, by excluding");
44:      puts("the space character, caused the input to be split.");
45:
46:      return 0;
47:  }
```

**INPUT/
OUTPUT**

```
Enter an integer and a floating point number.
123 45.6789

You entered 123 and 45.678900.
The scanf() format string used the l modifier to store
your input in a type long and a type double.

Enter a 5 digit integer (for example, 54321).
54321
```

13

```
You entered 54 and 321.
Note how the field width specifier in the scanf() format
string split your input into two values.

Enter your first and last names separated by a space.
```
Gayle Johnson

```
Your first name is Gayle
Your last name is Johnson
Note how [^ ] in the scanf() format string, by excluding
the space character, caused the input to be split.
```

ANALYSIS This listing starts by defining several variables in lines 9 through 13 for data input. The program then walks you through the steps of entering various types of data. Lines 17 through 21 have you enter and print long integers and a double. Line 23 calls the fflush() function to clear any unwanted characters from the standard input stream. Lines 27 and 28 get the next value, a five-character integer. Because there are width specifiers, the five-digit integer is split into two integers—one that is two characters, and one that is three characters. Line 34 calls fflush() to clear the keyboard again. The final example, in lines 36 through 44, uses the exclude character. Line 40 uses "%[^]", which tells scanf() to get a string but to stop at any spaces. This effectively splits the input.

Take the time to modify this listing and enter additional values to see what the results are.

The scanf() function can be used for most of your input needs, particularly those involving numbers (strings can be input more easily with fgets()). It is often worthwhile, however, to write your own specialized input functions.

Do	Don't
DO use the width-specifier when reading strings with scanf() to avoid buffer overruns.	DON'T use gets().
	DON'T forget to check the input stream for extra characters.
DO use the scanf() functions instead of the fscanf() functions if you're using the standard input file (stdin) only.	

Screen Output

Screen output functions are divided into three general categories along the same lines as the input functions: character output, line output, and formatted output. You were introduced to some of these functions in earlier days. This section covers them all in detail.

Character Output with `putchar()`, `putc()`, and `fputc()`

The C library's character output functions send a single character to a stream. The function `putchar()` sends its output to `stdout` (normally the screen). The functions `fputc()` and `putc()` send their output to a stream specified in the argument list.

Using the `putchar()` Function

The prototype for `putchar`, which is located in stdio.h, is as follows:

```
int putchar(int c);
```

This function writes the character stored in `c` to `stdout`. Although the prototype specifies a type `int` argument, you pass `putchar()` a type `char`. You can also pass it a type `int` as long as its value is appropriate for a character (that is, in the range 0 to 255). The function returns the character that was just written, or `EOF` if an error has occurred.

You saw `putchar()` demonstrated in Listing 13.2. Listing 13.8 displays the characters with ASCII values between 14 and 127.

LISTING 13.8. The `putchar()` function.

```
1: /* Demonstrates putchar(). */
2:
3: #include <stdio.h>
4: int main(void)
5: {
6:     int count;
7:
8:     for (count = 14; count < 128; )
9:         putchar(count++);
10:
11:    return 0;
12: }
```

You can also display strings with the `putchar()` function (as shown in Listing 13.9), although other functions are better suited for this purpose.

LISTING 13.9. Displaying a string with `putchar()`.

```
1: /* Using putchar() to display strings. */
2:
3: #include <stdio.h>
4:
5: #define MAXSTRING 80
6:
7: char message[] = "Displayed with putchar().";
8: int main(void)
9: {
```

continues

13

Listing 13.9. continued

```
10:     int count;
11:
12:     for (count = 0; count < MAXSTRING; count++)
13:     {
14:
15:         /* Look for the end of the string. When it's found, */
16:         /* write a newline character and exit the loop. */
17:
18:         if (message[count] == '\0')
19:         {
20:             putchar('\n');
21:             break;
22:         }
23:         else
24:
25:         /* If end of string not found, write the next character. */
26:
27:             putchar(message[count]);
28:     }
29:     return 0;
30: }
```

OUTPUT   Displayed with putchar().

Using the `putc()` and `fputc()` Functions

These two functions perform the same action—sending a single character to a specified stream. `putc()` is a macro implementation of `fputc()`. You'll learn about macros on Day 20, "Advanced Compiler Use." For now, just stick to `fputc()`. Its prototype is

```
int fputc(int c, FILE *fp);
```

The `FILE *fp` part might puzzle you. You pass `fputc()` the output stream in this argument. (You'll learn more about this on Day 15.) If you specify `stdout` as the stream, `fputc()` behaves exactly the same as `putchar()`. Thus, the following two statements are equivalent:

```
putchar('x');
fputc('x', stdout);
```

Using `puts()` and `fputs()` for String Output

Your programs display strings onscreen more often than they display single characters. The library function `puts()` displays strings. The function `fputs()` sends a string to a specified stream; otherwise, it is identical to `puts()`. The prototype for `puts()` is

```
int puts(char *cp);
```

*cp is a pointer to the first character of the string that you want displayed. The puts() function displays the entire string up to, but not including, the terminating null character, adding a newline at the end. Then puts() returns a positive value if successful or EOF on error. (Remember, EOF is a symbolic constant with the value -1; it is defined in stdio.h.)

The puts() function can be used to display any type of string, as demonstrated in Listing 13.10.

LISTING 13.10. Using the puts() function to display strings.

```
1: /* Demonstrates puts(). */
2:
3: #include <stdio.h>
4:
5: /* Declare and initialize an array of pointers. */
6:
7: char *messages[5] = { "This", "is", "a", "short", "message." };
8:
9: int main(void)
10: {
11:     int x;
12:
13:     for (x=0; x<5; x++)
14:         puts(messages[x]);
15:
16:     puts("And this is the end!");
17:
18:     return 0;
19: }
```

OUTPUT
```
This
is
a
short
message.
And this is the end!
```

ANALYSIS This listing declares an array of pointers, a subject not covered yet.(It will be covered tomorrow.) Lines 13 and 14 print each of the strings stored in the message array.

Using printf() and fprintf() for Formatted Output

So far, the output functions have displayed characters and strings only. What about numbers? To display numbers, you must use the C library's formatted output functions, printf() and fprintf(). These functions can also display strings and characters. You were officially introduced to printf() on Day 6, and you've used it in almost every lesson. This section provides the remainder of the details.

13

The two functions `printf()` and `fprintf()` are identical, except that `printf()` always sends output to `stdout`, whereas `fprintf()` specifies the output stream. `fprintf()` is generally used for output to disk files. It's covered on Day 15.

The `printf()` function takes a variable number of arguments, with a minimum of one. The first and only required argument is the format string, which tells `printf()` how to format the output. The optional arguments are variables and expressions whose values you want to display. Take a look at these few simple examples, which give you a feel for `printf()`, before you really get into the nitty-gritty:

- The statement `printf("Hello, world.");` displays the message `Hello, world.` onscreen. This is an example of using `printf()` with only one argument, the format string. In this case, the format string contains only a literal string to be displayed onscreen.

- The statement `printf("%d", i);` displays the value of the integer variable `i` onscreen. The format string contains only the format specifier `%d`, which tells `printf()` to display a single decimal integer. The second argument, `i`, is the name of the variable whose value is to be displayed.

- The statement `printf("%d plus %d equals %d.", a, b, a+b);` displays `2 plus 3 equals 5` onscreen (assuming that a and b are integer variables with the values of 2 and 3, respectively). This use of `printf()` has four arguments: a format string that contains literal text, as well as format specifiers, and two variables and an expression whose values are to be displayed.

Now look at the `printf()` format string in more detail. It can contain the following:

- Zero, one, or more conversion commands that tell `printf()` how to display a value in its argument list. A conversion command consists of `%` followed by one or more characters.

- Characters that are not part of a conversion command and are displayed as-is.

The third example's format string is `%d plus %d equals %d`. In this case, the three `%d`s are conversion commands, and the remainder of the string, including the spaces, is literal characters that are displayed directly.

Now you can dissect the conversion command. The components of the command are given here and explained next. Components in brackets are optional.

`%[flag][field_width][.[precision]][l]conversion_char`

The `conversion_char` is the only required part of a conversion command (other than the `%`). Table 13.5 lists the conversion characters and their meanings.

TABLE 13.5. The `printf()` and `fprintf()` conversion characters.

Conversion Character	Meaning
d, i	Display a signed integer in decimal notation.
u	Display an unsigned integer in decimal notation.
o	Display an integer in unsigned octal notation.
x, X	Display an integer in unsigned hexadecimal notation. Use x for lowercase output and X for uppercase output.
c	Display a single character (the argument gives the character's ASCII code).
e, E	Display a `float` or `double` in scientific notation (for example, `123.45` is displayed as `1.234500e+002`). Six digits are displayed to the right of the decimal point unless another precision is specified with the f specifier. Use e or E to control the case of output.
f	Display a `float` or `double` in decimal notation (for example, `123.45` is displayed as `123.450000`). Six digits are displayed to the right of the decimal point unless another precision is specified.
g, G	Use e, E, or f format. The e or E format is used if the exponent is less than -3 or greater than the precision (which defaults to 6). f format is used otherwise. Trailing zeros are truncated.
n	Nothing is displayed. The argument corresponding to an n conversion command is a pointer to type `int`. The `printf()` function assigns to this variable the number of characters output so far.
s	Display a string. The argument is a pointer to `char`. Characters are displayed until a null character is encountered or the number of characters specified by precision (which defaults to `32767`) is displayed. The terminating null character is not output.
%	Display the % character.

13

You can place the l modifier just before the conversion character. This modifier applies only to the conversion characters o, u, x, X, i, d, and b. When applied, this modifier specifies that the argument is a type `long` rather than a type `int`. If the l modifier is applied to the conversion characters e, E, f, g, or G, it specifies that the argument is a type `double`. If an l is placed before any other conversion character, it is ignored.

The precision specifier consists of a decimal point (.) by itself or followed by a number. A precision specifier applies only to the conversion characters e, E, f, g, G, and s. It specifies the number of digits to display to the right of the decimal point or, when used with s, the number of characters to output. If the decimal point is used alone, it specifies a precision of `0`.

The field-width specifier determines the minimum number of characters output. The field-width specifier can be the following:

- A decimal integer not starting with 0. The output is padded on the left with spaces to fill the designated field width.
- A decimal integer starting with 0. The output is padded on the left with zeros to fill the designated field width.
- The * character. The value of the next argument (which must be an int) is used as the field width. For example, if w is a type int with a value of 10, the statement printf("%*d", w, a); prints the value of a with a field width of 10.

If no field width is specified, or if the specified field width is narrower than the output, the output field is just as wide as needed.

The last optional part of the printf() format string is the flag, which immediately follows the % character. There are four available flags:

-	This means that the output is left-justified in its field rather than right-justified, which is the default.
+	This means that signed numbers are always displayed with a leading + or -.
' '	A space means that positive numbers are preceded by a space.
#	This applies only to x, X, and o conversion characters. It specifies that nonzero numbers are displayed with a leading 0X or 0x (for x and X) or a leading 0 (for o).

When you use printf(), the format string can be a string literal enclosed in double quotes in the printf() argument list. It can also be a null-terminated string stored in memory, in which case you pass a pointer to the string to printf(). For example, this statement

```
char *fmt = "The answer is %f.";
printf(fmt, x);
```

is equivalent to this statement:

```
printf("The answer is %f.", x);
```

As explained on Day 6, the printf() format string can contain escape sequences that provide special control over the output. Table 13.6 lists the most frequently used escape sequences. For example, including the newline sequence (\n) in a format string causes subsequent output to appear starting on the next screen line.

TABLE **13.6**. The most frequently used escape sequences.

Sequence	Meaning
\a	Bell (alert)
\b	Backspace
\n	Newline
\t	Horizontal tab
\\	Backslash
\?	Question mark
\'	Single quote
\"	Double quote

printf() is somewhat complicated. The best way to learn how to use it is to look at examples and then experiment on your own. Listing 13.11 demonstrates many of the ways you can use printf().

LISTING **13.11**. Some ways to use the printf() function.

```
1: /* Demonstration of printf(). */
2:
3: #include <stdio.h>
4:
5: char *m1 = "Binary";
6: char *m2 = "Decimal";
7: char *m3 = "Octal";
8: char *m4 = "Hexadecimal";
9:
10: int main(void)
11: {
12:     float d1 = 10000.123;
13:     int n, f;
14:
15:
16:     puts("Outputting a number with different field widths.\n");
17:
18:     printf("%5f\n", d1);
19:     printf("%10f\n", d1);
20:     printf("%15f\n", d1);
21:     printf("%20f\n", d1);
22:     printf("%25f\n", d1);
23:
24:     puts("\n Press Enter to continue...");
25:     fflush(stdin);
26:     getchar();
```

13

continues

Listing 13.11. continued

```
27:
28:     puts("\nUse the * field width specifier to obtain field width");
29:     puts("from a variable in the argument list.\n");
30:
31:     for (n=5;n<=25; n+=5)
32:         printf("%*f\n", n, d1);
33:
34:     puts("\n Press Enter to continue...");
35:     fflush(stdin);
36:     getchar();
37:
38:     puts("\nInclude leading zeros.\n");
39:
40:     printf("%05f\n", d1);
41:     printf("%010f\n", d1);
42:     printf("%015f\n", d1);
43:     printf("%020f\n", d1);
44:     printf("%025f\n", d1);
45:
46:     puts("\n Press Enter to continue...");
47:     fflush(stdin);
48:     getchar();
49:
50:     puts("\nDisplay in octal, decimal, and hexadecimal.");
51:     puts("Use # to precede octal and hex output with 0 and 0X.");
52:     puts("Use - to left-justify each value in its field.");
53:     puts("First display column labels.\n");
54:
55:     printf("%-15s%-15s%-15s", m2, m3, m4);
56:
57:     for (n = 1;n< 20; n++)
58:         printf("\n%-15d%-#15o%-#15X", n, n, n);
59:
60:     puts("\n Press Enter to continue...");
61:     fflush(stdin);
62:     getchar();
63:
64:     puts("\n\nUse the %n conversion command to count characters.\n");
65:
66:     printf("%s%s%s%s%n", m1, m2, m3, m4, &n);
67:
68:     printf("\n\nThe last printf() output %d characters.\n", n);
69:
70:     return 0;
71: }
```

OUTPUT Outputting a number with different field widths.

```
10000.123047
10000.123047
   10000.123047
```

```
    10000.123047
        10000.123047

Press Enter to continue...


Use the * field width specifier to obtain field width
from a variable in the argument list.

10000.123047
10000.123047
   10000.123047
       10000.123047
           10000.123047


Press Enter to continue...


Include leading zeros.

10000.123047
10000.123047
00010000.123047
0000000010000.123047
000000000000010000.123047


Press Enter to continue...


Display in octal, decimal, and hexadecimal.
Use # to precede octal and hex output with 0 and 0X.
Use - to left-justify each value in its field.
First display column labels.

Decimal          Octal           Hexadecimal
1                01              0X1
2                02              0X2
3                03              0X3
4                04              0X4
5                05              0X5
6                06              0X6
7                07              0X7
8                010             0X8
9                011             0X9
10               012             0XA
11               013             0XB
12               014             0XC
13               015             0XD
14               016             0XE
15               017             0XF
16               020             0X10
```

13

```
17                021              0X11
18                022              0X12
19                023              0X13
```

```
Press Enter to continue...
```

```
Use the %n conversion command to count characters.
```

```
BinaryDecimalOctalHexadecimal
```

```
The last printf() output 29 characters.
```

Redirecting Input and Output

A program that uses stdin and stdout can utilize an operating system feature called *redirection*. Redirection allows you to do the following:

- Output sent to stdout can be sent to a disk file or the stdin stream of some other program rather than to the screen.

- Program input from stdin can come from a disk file or the stdout of some other program rather than from the keyboard.

You don't code redirection into your programs; you specify it on the command line when you run the program. In Linux (and most other UNIX-like operating systems), the symbols for file redirection are < and >; whereas for piping the output into the stdin of another program, the symbol [pipe-symbol-vertical bar] is used. First up, we'll look at redirection.

Remember your first C program, hello.c? It used the printf() library function to display the message Hello, world onscreen. As you now know, printf() sends output to stdout, so it can be redirected. When you enter the program name at the command-line prompt, follow it with the > symbol and the name of the new destination:

```
hello > destination
```

Thus, if you enter hello > hello.txt, the output is placed in a disk file with the name hello.txt.

When you redirect output to a disk file, be careful. If the file already exists, the old copy is deleted and replaced with the new file. If the file doesn't exist, it is created. When redirecting output to a file, you can also use the >> symbol. If the specified destination file already exists, the program output is appended to the end of the file. Listing 13.12 demonstrates redirection.

LISTING **13.12**. The redirection of input and output.

```
1: /* Can be used to demonstrate redirection of stdin and stdout. */
2:
3: #include <stdio.h>
4:
5: int main(void)
6: {
7:    char buf[80];
8:
9:    fgets(buf,80,stdin);
10:   printf("The input was: %s\n", buf);
11:   return 0;
12: }
```

ANALYSIS   This program accepts a line of input from stdin and then sends the line to
           stdout, preceding it with The input was:. After compiling and linking the
program, run it without redirection (assuming that the program is named list1314) by
entering ./list1314 at the command-line prompt. If you then enter I can program
Linux using C, the program displays the following onscreen:

```
The input was: I can program Linux using C
```

If you run the program by entering ./list1314 >test.txt and make the same entry,
nothing is displayed onscreen. Instead, a file named test.txt is created on the disk. If you
use the cat command to display the contents of the file,

```
cat test.txt
```

you'll see that the file contains only the line The input was: I can program Linux
using C.

Run the program again, this time redirecting output to test.txt with the >> symbol.
Instead of replacing the file, the new output is appended to the end of test.txt.

Redirecting Input

Now let's look at redirecting input. First, you need a source file. Use your editor to create
a file named input.txt that contains the single line William Shakespeare. Now run
Listing 13.12 by entering the following at the command-line prompt:

```
./list1314 < input.txt
```

The program doesn't wait for you to make an entry at the keyboard. Instead, it immediately displays the following message onscreen:

```
The input was: William Shakespeare
```

13

The stream `stdin` was redirected to the disk file input.txt, so the program's call to `fgets()` reads one line of text from the file rather than the keyboard.

You can redirect input and output at the same time. Try running the program with the following command to redirect `stdin` to the file input.txt and redirect `stdout` to junk.txt:

```
./list1314 < input.txt > junk.txt
```

Redirecting `stdin` and `stdout` can be useful in certain situations. A sorting program, for example, could sort either keyboard input or the contents of a disk file. Likewise, a mailing list program could display addresses onscreen, send them to the printer for mailing labels, or place them in a file for some other use.

Piping Between Programs

Now let's look at piping data out of the `stdout` of one program into the `stdin` of another program. We still use the same program Listing 13.12 again. At the command-line prompt, type

```
./list1314 ¦ ./list1314
```

The program waits for you to type something. If you then enter `Hello there!`, you will get the following output:

```
The input was: The input was: Hello there!.
```

Notice how there are two occurrences of `The input was:`? What has happened is that the first program on the command line writes the string `The input was: Hello there!` to its `stdout`, which is connected to the `stdin` of the second program on the command line. The second program received the full string `The input was: Hello there!` as its input, so it prints `The input was:`, followed by the string it received as its input.

When using pipes, you are able to string many commands together, with each program reading its own `stdin` and writing to its `stdout`, and only the output of the final program is actually printed to the screen.

Note

Remember that redirecting and piping stdin and stdout are features of the operating system and not of the C language itself. However, it does provide another example of the flexibility of streams.

When to Use `fprintf()`

As mentioned earlier, the library function `fprintf()` is identical to `printf()`, except that you can specify the stream to which output is sent. The main use of `fprintf()` involves disk files, as explained on Day 15. There are two other uses, as explained here.

Using `stderr`

One of C's predefined streams is `stderr` (standard error). A program's error messages traditionally are sent to the stream `stderr` and not to `stdout`. Why is this?

As you just learned, output to `stdout` can be redirected to a destination other than the display screen. If `stdout` is redirected, the user might not be aware of any error messages the program sends to `stdout`. On Linux and other UNIX-like systems, `stderr` can also be redirected, but that is not normal practice. By directing error messages to `stderr`, you can be sure that the user always sees them. You do this with `fprintf()`:

```
fprintf(stderr, "An error has occurred.");
```

You can write a function to handle error messages and then call the function when an error occurs, rather than call `fprintf()`:

```
error_message("An error has occurred.");

void error_message(char *msg)
{
    fprintf(stderr, msg);
}
```

By using your own function instead of directly calling `fprintf()`, you provide additional flexibility (one of the advantages of structured programming). For example, in special circumstances you might want a program's error messages to go to the printer or a disk file. All you need to do is modify the `error_message()` function so that the output is sent to the desired destination.

Do	Don't
DO use `fprintf()` to create programs that can send output to `stdout`, `stderr`, or any other stream.	**DON'T** use `stderr` for purposes other than printing error messages or warnings.
DO use `fprintf()` with `stderr` to print error messages to the screen.	
DO create functions such as `error_message` to make your code more structured and maintainable.	

13

Summary

This was a long day full of important information on program input and output. You learned how C uses streams, treating all input and output as a sequence of bytes. You also learned that C has three predefined streams:

stdin	The keyboard
stdout	The screen
stderr	The screen

Input from the keyboard arrives from the stream stdin. Using C's standard library functions, you can accept keyboard input character by character, a line at a time, or as formatted numbers and strings. Character input can be buffered or unbuffered, echoed or unechoed.

Output to the display screen is normally done with the stdout stream. Like input, program output can be by character, by line, or as formatted numbers and strings.

When you use stdin and stdout, you can redirect program input and output. Input can come from a disk file rather than the keyboard, and output can go to a disk file or to the printer rather than to the display screen.

Finally, you learned why error messages should be sent to the stream stderr instead of stdout. Because stderr is usually connected to the display screen, you are assured of seeing error messages even when the program output is redirected.

Q&A

Q What happens if I try to get input from an output stream?

A You can write a C program to do this, but it won't work. For example, if you try to use stderr with fscanf(), the program compiles into an executable file, but stderr is incapable of sending input, so your program doesn't operate as intended.

Q What happens if I redirect one of the standard streams?

A Doing this might cause problems later in the program. If you redirect a stream, you must put it back if you need it again in the same program. Many of the functions described in this chapter use the standard streams. They all use the same streams, so if you change the stream in one place, you change it for all the functions. For example, assign stdout equal to stderr in one of today's listings and see what happens.

Q Why shouldn't I always use `fprintf()` instead of `printf()`? Or `fscanf()` instead of `scanf()`?

A If you're using the standard output or input streams, you should use `printf()` and `scanf()`. By using these simpler functions, you don't have to bother with any other streams.

Workshop

The Workshop provides quiz questions to help you solidify your understanding of the material covered and exercises to provide you with experience in using what you've learned. The answers to the quiz and exercises are provided in Appendix C, "Answers."

Quiz

1. What is a stream, and what does a C program use streams for?

2. Are the following input devices or output devices?

   a. Printer

   b. Keyboard

   c. Modem

   d. Monitor

   e. Disk drive

3. List the three predefined streams and the devices with which they are associated.

4. What stream do the following functions use?

   a. `printf()`

   b. `puts()`

   c. `scanf()`

   d. `fgets()`

   e. `fprintf()`

5. What is the difference between buffered and unbuffered character input from `stdin`?

6. Can you "unget" more than one character at a time with `ungetc()`? Can you "unget" the `EOF` character?

7. When you use C's line input functions, how is the end of a line determined?

13

8. Which of the following are valid type specifiers?

    a. `"%d"`

    b. `"%4d"`

    c. `"%3i%c"`

    d. `"%q%d"`

    e. `"%%%I"`

    f. `"%9ld"`

9. What is the difference between `stderr` and `stdout`?

Exercises

1. Write a statement to print "`Hello World`" to the screen.

2. Use two different C functions to do the same thing the function in exercise 1 did.

3. Write a statement to print "`Hello Standard Error`" to `stderr`.

4. Write a statement that gets a string 30 characters or shorter. If an asterisk is encountered, truncate the string.

5. Write a single statement that prints the following:

```
Jack asked, "What is a backslash?"
Jill said, "It is '\'"
```

Because of the multitude of possibilities, answers are not provided for the following exercises; however, you should attempt to do them.

6. **ON YOUR OWN:** Write a program that uses redirection to accept input from a disk file, counts the number of times each letter occurs in the file, and then displays the results onscreen.

7. **ON YOUR OWN:** Write a "typing" program that accepts keyboard input, echoes it to the screen, and then reproduces that input on the printer. The program should count lines and advance the paper in the printer to a new page when necessary. Use a function key to terminate the program.

DAY 14

Pointers: Beyond the Basics

On Day 8, "Understanding Pointers," you were introduced to the basics of pointers, which are an important part of the C programming language. Today you'll go further, exploring some advanced pointer topics that can add flexibility to your programming. Today you will learn

- How to declare a pointer to a pointer
- How to use pointers with multidimensional arrays
- How to declare arrays of pointers
- How to declare pointers to functions
- How to use pointers to create linked lists for data storage
- How to return a pointer from a function

Pointers to Pointers

As you learned on Day 8, a *pointer* is a numeric variable with a value that is the address of another variable. You declare a pointer using the indirectin operator (*). For example, the declaration

```
int *ptr;
```

declares a pointer named `ptr` that can point to a type `int` variable. You then use the address-of operator (&) to make the pointer point to a specific variable of the corresponding type. Assuming that x has been declared as a type `int` variable, the statement

```
ptr = &x;
```

assigns the address of x to `ptr` and makes `ptr` point to x. Again, using the indirection operator, you can access the pointed-to variable by using its pointer. Both of the following statements assign the value 12 to x:

```
x = 12;
*ptr = 12;
```

Because a pointer is itself a numeric variable, it is stored in your computer's memory at a particular address. Therefore, you can create a pointer to a pointer, a variable whose value is the address of a pointer. Here's how:

```
int x = 12;                /* x is a type int variable. */
int *ptr = &x;             /* ptr is a pointer to x. */
int **ptr_to_ptr = &ptr;   /* ptr_to_ptr is a pointer to a */
                           /* pointer to type int. */
```

Note the use of a double indirection operator (**) when declaring a pointer to a pointer. You also use the double indirection operator when accessing the pointed-to variable with a pointer to a pointer. Thus, the statement

```
**ptr_to_ptr = 12;
```

assigns the value 12 to the variable x, and the statement

```
printf("%d", **ptr_to_ptr);
```

displays the value of x onscreen. If you mistakenly use a single indirection operator, you get errors. The statement

```
*ptr_to_ptr = 12;
```

assigns the value 12 to `ptr`, which results in `ptr` pointing to whatever happens to be stored at address 12. This clearly is a mistake.

Declaring and using a pointer to a pointer is called *multiple indirection*. Figure 14.1 shows the relationship between a variable, a pointer, and a pointer to a pointer. There's really no limit to the level of multiple indirection possible—you can have a pointer to a pointer to a pointer *ad infinitum,* but there's rarely any advantage to going beyond two levels; the complexities involved are an invitation to mistakes.

FIGURE 14.1.

A pointer to a pointer.

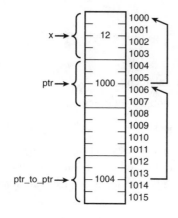

How can you use pointers to pointers? The most common use involves arrays of pointers, which are covered later today. Listing 17.5 on Day 17, "Exploring the C Function Library," presents an example of using multiple indirection.

Pointers and Multidimensional Arrays

Day 7, "Using Numeric Arrays," covers the special relationship between pointers and arrays. Specifically, the name of an array without its following brackets is a pointer to the first element of the array. As a result, it's easier to use pointer notation when you're accessing certain types of arrays. These earlier examples, however, were limited to single-dimensional arrays. What about multidimensional arrays?

Remember that a multidimensional array is declared with one set of brackets for each dimension. For example, the following statement declares a two-dimensional array that contains eight type `int` variables:

```
int multi[2][4];
```

You can visualize an array as having a row and column structure—in this case, two rows and four columns. There's another way to visualize a multidimensional array, however, and this way is closer to the manner in which C actually handles arrays. You can consider `multi` to be a two-element array, with each of those two elements being an array of four integers.

In case this isn't clear to you, Figure 14.2 dissects the array declaration statement into its component parts.

14

FIGURE 14.2.

The components of a multidimensional array declaration.

Here's how to interpret the components of the declaration:

1. Declare an array named `multi`.
2. The array `multi` contains two elements.
3. Each of those two elements contains *four* elements.
4. Each of the four elements is a type `int`.

You read a multidimensional array declaration starting with the array name and moving to the right, one set of brackets at a time. When the last set of brackets (the last dimension) has been read, you jump to the beginning of the declaration to determine the array's basic data type.

Under the array-of-arrays scheme, you can visualize a multidimensional array as shown in Figure 14.3.

FIGURE 14.3.

A two-dimensional array can be visualized as an array of arrays.

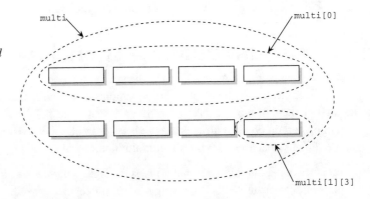

Now, let's get back to the topic of array names as pointers. (This is a discussion about pointers, after all!) As with a one-dimensional array, the name of a multidimensional array is a pointer to the first array element. Continuing with our example, `multi` is a pointer to the first element of the two-dimensional array that was declared as `int multi[2][4]`. What exactly is the first element of `multi`? It isn't the type `int` variable `multi[0][0]`, as you might think. Remember that `multi` is an array of arrays, so its first element is `multi[0]`, which is an array of four type `int` variables (one of the two such arrays contained in `multi`).

Now, if `multi[0]` is also an array, does it point to anything? Yes, indeed! `multi[0]` points to its first element, `multi[0][0]`. You might wonder why `multi[0]` is a pointer. Remember that the name of an array without brackets is a pointer to the first array element. The term `multi[0]` is the name of the array `multi[0][0]` with the last pair of brackets missing, so it qualifies as a pointer.

If you're a bit confused at this point, don't worry. This material is difficult to grasp. It might help if you remember the following rules for any array of *n* dimensions used in code:

- The array name followed by *n* pairs of brackets (each pair containing an appropriate index, of course) evaluates as array data (that is, the data stored in the specified array element).

- The array name followed by fewer than *n* pairs of brackets evaluates as a pointer to an array element.

In the example, therefore, `multi` evaluates as a pointer, `multi[0]` evaluates as a pointer, and `multi[0][0]` evaluates as array data.

Now look at what all these pointers actually point to. Listing 14.1 declares a two-dimensional array—similar to those you've been using in the examples—and then prints the values of the associated pointers. It also prints the address of the first array element.

LISTING 14.1. The relationship between a multidimensional array and pointers.

```
1: /* Demonstrates pointers and multidimensional arrays. */
2:
3: #include <stdio.h>
4:
5: int multi[2][4];
6:
7: int main(void)
8: {
9:     printf("multi = %lu\n", (unsigned long)multi);
10:    printf("multi[0] = %lu\n", (unsigned long)multi[0]);
11:    printf("&multi[0][0] = %lu\n",
12:                    (unsigned long)&multi[0][0]);
13:    return(0);
14: }
```

OUTPUT
```
multi = 134518272
multi[0] = 134518272
&multi[0][0] = 134518272
```

14

ANALYSIS The actual value might not be 134518272 on your system, but all three values will be the same. The address of the array `multi` is the same as the address of the array multi[0], and both are equal to the address of the first integer in the array, multi[0][0].

If all three pointers have the same value, what is the practical difference between them in terms of your program? Remember from Day 8 that the C compiler knows what a pointer points to. To be more exact, the compiler knows the size of the item a pointer is pointing to.

What are the sizes of the elements you've been using? Listing 14.2 uses the operator sizeof() to display the sizes, in bytes, of these elements.

LISTING 14.2. Determining the sizes of elements.

```
 1: /* Demonstrates the sizes of multidimensional array elements. */
 2:
 3: #include <stdio.h>
 4:
 5: int multi[2][4];
 6:
 7: int main(void)
 8: {
 9:     printf("The size of multi = %u\n", sizeof(multi));
10:     printf("The size of multi[0] = %u\n", sizeof(multi[0]));
11:     printf("The size of multi[0][0] = %u\n", sizeof(multi[0][0]));
12:     return(0);
13: }
```

The output of this program (this assumes that your Linux machine uses 4-byte integers) is as follows:

OUTPUT
```
The size of multi = 32
The size of multi[0] = 16
The size of multi[0][0] = 4
```

ANALYSIS Remember that on Linux using an Intel Pentium-family processor, a type int requires four bytes. On a Linux machine using a DEC/Compaq Alpha processor or some other 64-bit processor, the output might be slightly different.

Think about these size values. The array multi contains two arrays, each of which contains four integers. Each integer requires two bytes of storage. With a total of eight integers, the size of 16 bytes makes sense.

Next, multi[0] is an array containing four integers. Each integer takes 4 bytes, so the size of 16 bytes for multi[0] also makes sense.

Finally, multi[0][0] is an integer, so its size is, of course, 4 bytes.

Now, keeping those sizes in mind, recall the discussion on Day 8 about pointer arithmetic. The C compiler knows the size of the object being pointed to, and pointer arithmetic takes this size into account. When you increment a pointer, its value is increased by the amount needed to make it point to the "next" of whatever it's pointing to. In other words, it's incremented by the size of the object to which it points.

When you apply this to the example, multi is a pointer to a four-element integer array with a size of 16. If you increment multi, its value should increase by 16 (the size of a four-element integer array). If multi points to multi[0], therefore, (multi + 1) should point to multi[1]. Listing 14.3 tests this theory.

LISTING 14.3. Pointer arithmetic with multidimensional arrays.

```
 1: /* Demonstrates pointer arithmetic with pointers */
 2: /* to multidimensional arrays. */
 3: #
 4:  #include <stdio.h>
 5:
 6: int multi[2][4];
 7:
 8: int main(void)
 9: {
10:     printf("The value of (multi) = %lu\n",
11:                 (unsigned long)multi);
12:     printf("The value of (multi + 1) = %lu\n",
13:                 (unsigned long)(multi+1));
14:     printf("The address of multi[1] = %lu\n",
15:                 (unsigned long)&multi[1]);
16:     return(0);
17: }
```

OUTPUT
```
The value of (multi) = 134518304
The value of (multi + 1) = 134518320
The address of multi[1] = 134518320
```

ANALYSIS The precise values will probably be different on your system, but the relationships are the same. Incrementing multi by 1 increases its value by 16 (on a 32-bit system) and makes it point to the next element of the array, multi[1].

In this example, you've seen that multi is a pointer to multi[0]. You've also seen that multi[0] is itself a pointer (to multi[0][0]). Therefore, multi is a pointer to a pointer. To use the expression multi to access array data, you must use double indirection. To print the value stored in multi[0][0], you could use any of the following three statements:

```
printf("%d", multi[0][0]);
```

```
printf("%d", *multi[0]);
```

```
printf("%d", **multi);
```

14

These concepts apply equally to arrays with three or more dimensions. Thus, a three-dimensional array is an array with elements that are each a two-dimensional array; each of these elements is itself an array of one-dimensional arrays.

This material on multidimensional arrays and pointers might seem a bit confusing. When you work with multidimensional arrays, keep this point in mind: An array with n dimensions has elements that are arrays with $n-1$ dimensions. When n becomes 1, that array's elements are variables of the data type specified at the beginning of the array declaration line.

So far, you've been using array names that are pointer constants and that can't be changed. How would you declare a pointer variable that points to an element of a multidimensional array? Let's continue with the previous example, which declared a two-dimensional array as follows:

```
int multi[2][4];
```

To declare a pointer variable `ptr` that can point to an element of `multi` (that is, can point to a four-element integer array), you write

```
int (*ptr)[4];
```

You then make `ptr` point to the first element of `multi` by writing

```
ptr = multi;
```

You might wonder why the parentheses are necessary in the pointer declaration. Brackets ([ ]) have a higher precedence than *. If you wrote

```
int *ptr[4];
```

you would be declaring an array of four pointers to type `int`. Indeed, you can declare and use arrays of pointers. That isn't what you want to do now, however.

How can you use pointers to elements of multidimensional arrays? As with single-dimensional arrays, pointers must be used to pass an array to a function. This is illustrated for a multidimensional array in Listing 14.4, which uses two methods of passing a multidimensional array to a function.

LISTING 14.4. Passing a multidimensional array to a function using a pointer.

```
1: /* Demonstrates passing a pointer to a multidimensional */
2: /* array to a function. */
3:
4: #include <stdio.h>
5:
6: void printarray_1(int (*ptr)[4]);
```

```
 7: void printarray_2(int (*ptr)[4], int n);
 8:
 9: int main(void)
10: {
11:     int  multi[3][4] = { { 1, 2, 3, 4 },
12:                          { 5, 6, 7, 8 },
13:                          { 9, 10, 11, 12 } };
14:
15:     /* ptr is a pointer to an array of 4 ints. */
16:
17:     int (*ptr)[4], count;
18:
19:     /* Set ptr to point to the first element of multi. */
20:
21:     ptr = multi;
22:
23:     /* With each loop, ptr is incremented to point to the next */
24:     /* element (that is, the next 4-element integer array) of multi. */
25:
26:     for (count = 0; count < 3; count++)
27:         printarray_1(ptr++);
28:
29:     puts("\n\nPress Enter...");
30:     getchar();
31:     printarray_2(multi, 3);
32:     printf("\n");
33:     return(0);
34: }
35:
36: void printarray_1(int (*ptr)[4])
37: {
38: /* Prints the elements of a single four-element integer array. */
39: /* p is a pointer to type int. You must use a type cast */
40: /* to make p equal to the address in ptr. */
41:
42:     int *p, count;
43:     p = (int *)ptr;
44:
45:     for (count = 0; count < 4; count++)
46:         printf("\n%d", *p++);
47: }
48:
49: void printarray_2(int (*ptr)[4], int n)
50: {
51: /* Prints the elements of an n by four-element integer array. */
52:
53:     int *p, count;
54:     p = (int *)ptr;
55:
56:     for (count = 0; count < (4 * n); count++)
57:         printf("\n%d", *p++);
58: }
```

14

OUTPUT

```
1
2
3
4
5
6
7
8
9
10
11
12

Press Enter...

1
2
3
4
5
6
7
8
9
10
11
12
```

ANALYSIS On lines 11 through 13, the program declares and initializes an array of integers, `multi[3][4]`. Lines 6 and 7 are the prototypes for the functions `printarray_1()` and `printarray_2()`, which print the contents of the array.

The function `printarray_1()` (lines 36 through 47) is passed only one argument, a pointer to an array of four integers. This function prints all four elements of the array. The first time `main()` calls `printarray_1()` on line 27, it passes a pointer to the first element (the first four-element integer array) in `multi`. It then calls the function two more times, incrementing the pointer each time to point to the second, and then to the third, element of `multi`. After all three calls are made, the 12 integers in `multi` are displayed onscreen.

The second function, `printarray_2()`, takes a different approach. It too is passed a pointer to an array of four integers, but in addition, it is passed an integer variable that specifies the number of elements (the number of arrays of four integers) that the multidimensional array contains. With a single call from line 31, `printarray_2()` displays the entire contents of `multi`.

Both functions use pointer notation to step through the individual integers in the array. The notation `(int *)ptr` in both functions (lines 43 and 54) might not be clear. The (int *) is a typecast, which temporarily changes the variable's data type from its declared data type to a new one. The typecast is required when assigning the value of ptr to p because they are pointers to different types (p is a pointer to type int, whereas ptr is a pointer to an array of four integers). C doesn't let you assign the value of one pointer to a pointer of a different type. In effect, the typecast tells the compiler, "For this statement only, treat ptr as a pointer to type int." Day 18, "Working with Memory," covers typecasts in more detail.

Do	Don't

DO remember to use parentheses when declaring pointers to arrays.
 	
To declare a pointer to an array of characters, use this format:
 	
`char (*letters)[26];`
 	
To declare an array of pointers to characters, use this format:
 	
`char *letters[26];`
	DON'T forget to use the double indirection operator (**) when declaring a pointer to a pointer.
	
	DON'T forget that a pointer increments by the size of the pointer's type (usually what is being pointed to).

Arrays of Pointers

Recall from Day 7 that an array is a collection of data storage locations that have the same data type and are referred to by the same name. Because pointers are one of C's data types, you can declare and use arrays of pointers. This type of program construct can be very powerful in certain situations.

Perhaps the most common use of an array of pointers is with strings. A string, as you learned on Day 9, "Characters and Strings," is a sequence of characters stored in memory. The start of the string is indicated by a pointer to the first character (a pointer to type char), and the end of the string is marked by a null character. By declaring and initializing an array of pointers to type char, you can access and manipulate a large number of strings using the pointer array. Each element in the array points to a different string, and by looping through the array, you can access each of them in turn.

Strings and Pointers: A Review

This is a good time to review some material from Day 9 regarding string allocation and initialization. One way to allocate and initialize a string is to declare an array of type char as follows:

```
char message[] = "This is the message.";
```

14

You could accomplish the same thing by declaring a pointer to type `char`:

```
char *message = "This is the message.";
```

Both declarations are equivalent. In each case, the compiler allocates enough space to hold the string along with its terminating null character, and the expression `message` is a pointer to the start of the string. But what about the following two declarations?

```
char message1[20];
```

```
char *message2;
```

The first line declares an array of type `char` that is 20 characters long, with `message1` being a pointer to the first array position. Although the array space is allocated, it isn't initialized, and the array contents are undetermined. The second line declares `message2`, a pointer to type `char`. No storage space for a string is allocated by this statement—only space to hold the pointer. If you want to create a string and then have `message2` point to it, you must allocate space for the string first. On Day 9, you learned how to use the `malloc()` memory allocation function for this purpose. Remember that any string must have space allocated for it, whether at compilation in a declaration or at runtime with `malloc()` or a related memory allocation function.

Array of Pointers to Type char

Now that you're done with the review, how do you declare an array of pointers? The following statement declares an array of 10 pointers to type `char`:

```
char *message[10];
```

Each element of the array `message[]` is an individual pointer to type `char`. As you might have guessed, you can combine the declaration with initialization and allocation of storage space for the strings:

```
char *message[10] = { "one", "two", "three" };
```

This declaration does the following:

- It allocates a 10-element array named `message`; each element of `message` is a pointer to type `char`.
- It allocates space somewhere in memory (exactly where doesn't concern you) and stores the three initialization strings, each with a terminating null character.
- It initializes `message[0]` to point to the first character of the string `"one"`, `message[1]` to point to the first character of the string `"two"`, and `message[2]` to point to the first character of the string `"three"`.

This is illustrated in Figure 14.4, which shows the relationship between the array of pointers and the strings. Note that in this example, the array elements message[3] through message[9] aren't initialized to point at anything.

FIGURE 14.4.

An array of pointers to type char.

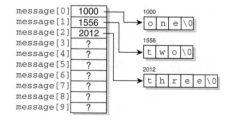

Now look at Listing 14.5, which is an example of using an array of pointers.

LISTING 14.5. Initializing and using an array of pointers to type char.

```
 1: /* Initializing an array of pointers to type char. */
 2:
 3: #include <stdio.h>
 4:
 5: int main(void)
 6: {
 7:     char *message[8] = { "Four", "score", "and", "seven",
 8:                     "years", "ago,", "our", "forefathers" };
 9:     int count;
10:
11:     for (count = 0; count < 8; count++)
12:         printf("%s ", message[count]);
13:     printf("\n");
14:     return(0);
15: }
```

OUTPUT Four score and seven years ago, our forefathers

ANALYSIS This program declares an array of eight pointers to type char and initializes them to point to eight strings (lines 7 and 8). It then uses a for loop on lines 11 and 12 to display each element of the array onscreen.

You probably can see how manipulating the array of pointers is easier than manipulating the strings themselves. This advantage is obvious in more complicated programs, such as the one presented later today. As you'll see in that program, the advantage is greatest when you're using functions. It's much easier to pass an array of pointers to a function than to pass several strings. This can be illustrated by rewriting the program in Listing 14.5 so that it uses a function to display the strings. The modified program is shown in Listing 14.6.

14

LISTING **14.6**. Passing an array of pointers to a function.

```
1: /* Passing an array of pointers to a function. */
2:
3: #include <stdio.h>
4:
5: void print_strings(char *p[], int n);
6:
7: int main(void)
8: {
9:     char *message[8] = { "Four", "score", "and", "seven",
10:                        "years", "ago,", "our", "forefathers" };
11:
12:     print_strings(message, 8);
13:     printf ("\n");
14:     return(0);
15: }
16:
17: void print_strings(char *p[], int n)
18: {
19:     int count;
20:
21:     for (count = 0; count < n; count++)
22:         printf("%s ", p[count]);
23: }
```

OUTPUT Four score and seven years ago, our forefathers

ANALYSIS Looking at line 17, you see that the function `print_strings()` takes two arguments. One is an array of pointers to type `char`, and the other is the number of elements in the array. Thus, `print_strings()` could be used to print the strings pointed to by any array of pointers.

You might remember that in the section on pointers to pointers, you were told that you would see a demonstration later. Well, you've just seen it. Listing 14.6 declared an array of pointers, and the name of the array is a pointer to its first element. When you pass that array to a function, you're passing a pointer (the array name) to a pointer (the first array element).

An Example

Now it's time for a more complicated example. Listing 14.7 uses many of the programming skills you've learned, including arrays of pointers. This program accepts lines of input from the keyboard, allocating space for each line as it is entered and keeping track of the lines by means of an array of pointers to type `char`. When you signal the end of an entry by entering a blank line, the program sorts the strings alphabetically and displays them onscreen.

If you were writing this program from scratch, you would approach the design of this program from a structured programming perspective. First, make a list of the things the program must do:

1. Accept lines of input from the keyboard one at a time until a blank line is entered.
2. Sort the lines of text into alphabetical order.
3. Display the sorted lines onscreen.

This list suggests that the program should have at least three functions: one to accept input, one to sort the lines, and one to display the lines. Now you can design each function independently. What do you need the input function—called get_lines()—to do? Again, make a list:

1. Keep track of the number of lines entered, and return that value to the calling program after all lines have been entered.
2. Don't allow input of more than a preset maximum number of lines.
3. Allocate storage space for each line.
4. Keep track of all lines by storing pointers to strings in an array.
5. Return to the calling program when a blank line is entered.

Now think about the second function, the one that sorts the lines. It could be called sort(). (Really original, right?) The sort technique used is a simple, brute-force method that compares adjacent strings and swaps them if the second string is less than the first string. More exactly, the function compares the two strings whose pointers are adjacent in the array of pointers and swaps the two pointers if necessary.

To be sure that the sorting is complete, you must go through the array from start to finish, comparing each pair of strings and swapping if necessary. For an array of n elements, you must go through the array $n-1$ times. Why is this necessary?

Each time you go through the array, a given element can be shifted by, at most, one position. For example, if the string that should be first is actually in the last position, the first pass through the array moves it to the next-to-last position, the second pass through the array moves it up one more position, and so on. It requires $n-1$ passes to move it to the first position, where it belongs.

Note that this is a very inefficient and inelegant sorting method. However, it's easy to implement and understand, and it's more than adequate for the short lists that the sample program sorts.

14

The final function displays the sorted lines onscreen. It is, in effect, already written in Listing 14.6; it requires only minor modification for use in Listing 14.7.

LISTING 14.7. A program that reads lines of text from the keyboard, sorts them alphabetically, and displays the sorted list.

```
1: /* Inputs a list of strings from the keyboard, sorts them, */
2: /* and then displays them on the screen. */
3: #include <stdlib.h>
4: #include <stdio.h>
5: #include <string.h>
6:
7: #define MAXLINES 25
8:
9: int get_lines(char *lines[]);
10: void sort(char *p[], int n);
11: void print_strings(char *p[], int n);
12:
13: char *lines[MAXLINES];
14:
15: int main(void)
16: {
17:     int number_of_lines;
18:
19:     /* Read in the lines from the keyboard. */
20:
21:     number_of_lines = get_lines(lines);
22:
23:     if ( number_of_lines < 0 )
24:     {
25:         puts(" Memory allocation error");
26:         exit(-1);
27:     }
28:
29:     sort(lines, number_of_lines);
30:     print_strings(lines, number_of_lines);
31:     return(0);
32: }
33:
34: int get_lines(char *lines[])
35:{
36:      int n = 0, slen;
37:     char buffer[80];  /* Temporary storage for each line. */
38:
39:     puts("Enter one line at time; enter a blank when done.");
40:
41:     while ((n < MAXLINES) && (fgets(buffer,80,stdin) != 0))
42:     {
43:         slen = strlen (buffer);
44:         if (slen < 2)
45:             break;
46:         buffer [slen-1] = 0;
47:         if ((lines[n] = (char *)malloc(strlen(buffer)+1)) == NULL)
```

```
48:            return -1;
49:        strcpy( lines[n++], buffer );
50:    }
51:    return n;
52:
53: } /* End of get_lines() */
54:
55: void sort(char *p[], int n)
56: {
57:    int a, b;
58:    char *x;
59:
60:    for (a = 1; a < n; a++)
61:    {
62:        for (b = 0; b < n-1; b++)
63:        {
64:            if (strcmp(p[b], p[b+1]) > 0)
65:            {
66:                x = p[b];
67:                p[b] = p[b+1];
68:                p[b+1] = x;
69:            }
70:        }
71:    }
72: }
73:
74: void print_strings(char *p[], int n)
75: {
76:    int count;
77:
78:    for (count = 0; count < n; count++)
79:        printf("%s\n ", p[count]);
80: }
```

INPUT/
OUTPUT

```
Enter one line at time; enter a blank when done.
dog
apple
zoo
program
merry

apple
dog
merry
program
zoo
```

ANALYSIS   It is worthwhile for you to examine some of the details of this program. Several new library functions are used for various types of string manipulation. They are explained briefly here and in more detail on Day 16, "Manipulating Strings." The header file string.h must be included in a program that uses these functions.

14

In the `get_lines()` function, input is controlled by the `while` statement on line 41, which reads as follows:

```
while ((n < MAXLINES) && (fgets(buffer,80,stdin) != 0))
```

The condition tested by the `while` has two parts. The first part, `n < MAXLINES`, ensures that the maximum number of lines has not been input yet. The second part, `fgets(buffer,80,stdin) != 0`, calls the `fgets()` library function to read a line from the keyboard into `buffer` and verifies that end-of-file or some other error has not occurred. Remember from Day 9 that `fgets()` returns the line read from the keyboard and includes the newline character. On line 43, the library function `strlen()` (included from string.h) returns the length of the string—not including the null character—and assigns that value to the variable `slen`. The variable `slen` is tested on line 44 and if the length of the string is less than 2 (that is, only a newline), the program breaks out of the `while` loop using `break` on line 45. On line 46, the newline character at the end of the string is overwritten with the null character. Remember that arrays are indexed from position 0 so that the index of the last character is `length-1`.

If either of the two test conditions of the `while` returns false or the length of the input string is less than 2, the loop terminates, and execution returns to the calling program, with the number of lines entered as the return value. Otherwise, the following `if` statement on line 47 is executed:

```
if ((lines[n] = (char *)malloc(strlen(buffer)+1)) == NULL)
```

This statement calls `malloc()` to allocate space for the string that was just input. The `strlen()` function returns the length of the string passed as an argument; the value is incremented by 1 so that `malloc()` allocates space for the string plus its terminating null character. The `(char *)`, just before `malloc()` on line 47, is a *typecast* that specifies the type of pointer to be returned by `malloc()`, in this case a pointer to type `char`. You'll learn more about typecasts on Day 18.

The library function `malloc()`, you might remember, returns a pointer. The statement assigns the value of the pointer returned by `malloc()` to the corresponding element of the array of pointers. If `malloc()` returns `NULL`, the `if` loop returns execution to the calling program with a return value of `-1`. The code in `main()` tests the return value of `get_lines()` and checks whether a value less than zero is returned; lines 23 through 27 report a memory allocation error and terminate the program.

If the memory allocation was successful, the program uses the `strcpy()` function on line 48 to copy the string from the temporary storage location `buffer` to the storage space just allocated by `malloc()`. The `while` loop then repeats, getting another line of input.

After execution returns from get_lines() to main(), the following items have been accomplished (assuming that a memory allocation error didn't occur):

- A number of lines of text have been read from the keyboard and stored in memory as null-terminated strings.
- The array lines[] contains pointers to all the strings. The order of pointers in the array is the order in which the strings were input.
- The variable number_of_lines holds the number of lines that were input.

Now it's time to sort. Remember, you're not actually moving the strings around, only the order of the pointers in the array lines[]. Look at the code in the function sort(). It contains one for loop nested inside another (lines 60 through 71). The outer loop executes number_of_lines - 1 times. Each time the outer loop executes, the inner loop steps through the array of pointers, comparing (string n) with (string n+1) for n = 0 to n = number_of_lines - 1. The comparison is performed by the library function strcmp() on line 64, which is passed pointers to two strings. The function strcmp() returns one of the following:

- A value greater than zero if the first string is greater than the second string.
- Zero if the two strings are identical.
- A value less than zero if the second string is greater than the first string.

In the program, a return value from strcmp() that is greater than zero means that the first string is greater than the second string, and the strings must be swapped (that is, their pointers in lines[] must be swapped). This is done using a temporary variable x. Lines 66 through 68 perform the swap.

When program execution returns from sort(), the pointers in lines[] are ordered properly: A pointer to the "lowest" string is in lines[0], a pointer to the "next-lowest" is in lines[1], and so on. Suppose, for example, that you entered the following five lines, in this order:

```
dog
apple
zoo
program
merry
```

The situation before calling sort() is illustrated in Figure 14.5, and the situation after the return from sort() is illustrated in Figure 14.6.

14

FIGURE 14.5.

Before sorting, the pointers are in the same order in which the strings were entered.

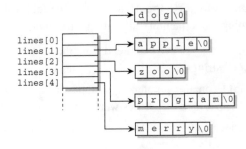

FIGURE 14.6.

After sorting, the pointers are ordered according to the alphabetical order of the strings.

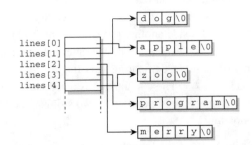

Finally, the program calls the function `print_strings()` to display the sorted list of strings onscreen. This function should be familiar to you from examples earlier today.

The program in Listing 14.7 is the most complex you have yet encountered in this book. It uses many of the C programming techniques that were covered on previous days. With the aid of the preceding explanation, you should be able to follow the program's operation and understand each step. If you find areas that are unclear to you, review the related sections of this book until you understand.

Pointers to Functions

Pointers to functions provide another way of calling functions. "Hold on," you might be thinking. "How can you have a pointer to a function? Doesn't a pointer hold the address where a variable is stored?"

Well, yes and no. It's true that a pointer holds an address, but it doesn't have to be the address where a variable is stored. When your program runs, the code for each function is loaded into memory starting at a specific address. A pointer to a function holds the starting address of a function—its entry point.

Why use a pointer to a function? As I mentioned earlier, it provides a more flexible way of calling a function. It lets the program choose from among several functions, selecting the one that is appropriate for the current circumstances.

Declaring a Pointer to a Function

As with all C variables, you must declare a pointer to a function before using it. The general form of the declaration is as follows:

```
type (*ptr_to_func)(parameter_list);
```

This statement declares ptr_to_func as a pointer to a function that returns *type* and is passed the parameters in *parameter_list*. Here are some more concrete examples:

```
int (*func1)(int x);

void (*func2)(double y, double z);

char (*func3)(char *p[]);

void (*func4)();
```

The first line declares func1 as a pointer to a function that takes one type int argument and returns a type int. The second line declares func2 as a pointer to a function that takes two type double arguments and has a void return type (no return value). The third line declares func3 as a pointer to a function that takes an array of pointers to type char as its argument and returns a type char. The final line declares func4 as a pointer to a function that doesn't take any arguments and has a void return type.

Why do you need parentheses around the pointer name? Why can't you write, for the first example

```
int *func1(int x);
```

The reason has to do with the precedence of the indirection operator, *. It has a relatively low precedence, lower than the parentheses surrounding the parameter list. The declaration just given, without the first set of parentheses, declares func1 as a function that returns a pointer to type int. (Functions that return pointers are covered a little later today.) When you declare a pointer to a function, always remember to include a set of parentheses around the pointer name and indirection operator, or you will get into trouble.

Initializing and Using a Pointer to a Function

A pointer to a function must not only be declared, but also initialized to point to something. That "something" is, of course, a function. There's nothing special about a function that is pointed to. The only requirement is that its return type and parameter list match the return type and parameter list of the pointer declaration. For example, the following code declares and defines a function and a pointer to that function:

14

```
float square(float x);      /* The function prototype.  */
float (*p)(float x);        /* The pointer declaration. */
float square(float x)       /* The function definition. */
{
return x * x;
}
```

Because the function square() and the pointer p have the same parameter and return types, you can initialize p to point to square as follows:

```
p = square;
```

You can then call the function using the pointer as follows:

```
answer = p(x);
```

It's that simple. For a real example, compile and run Listing 14.8, which declares and initializes a pointer to a function and then calls the function twice, using the function name the first time and the pointer the second time. Both calls produce the same result.

Listing 14.8. Using a pointer to a function to call the function.

```
 1: /* Demonstration of declaring and using a pointer to a function.*/
 2:
 3: #include <stdio.h>
 4:
 5: /* The function prototype. */
 6:
 7: double square(double x);
 8:
 9: /* The pointer declaration. */
10:
11: double (*p)(double x);
12:
13: int main(void)
14: {
15:     /* Initialize p to point to square(). */
16:
17:      p = square;
18:
19:     /* Call square() two ways. */
20:     printf("%f  %f\n", square(6.6), p(6.6));
21:     return(0);
22: }
23:
24: double square(double x)
25: {
26:     return x * x;
27: }
```

OUTPUT 43.560000   43.560000

ANALYSIS Line 7 declares the function square(), and line 11 declares the pointer p to a function containing a double argument and returning a double value, matching the declaration of square(). Line 17 sets the pointer p equal to square. Notice that parentheses aren't used with square or p. Line 20 prints the return values from calls to square() and p().

A function name without parentheses is a pointer to the function (sounds similar to the situation with arrays, doesn't it?). What's the point of declaring and using a separate pointer to the function? Well, the function name itself is a pointer constant and can't be changed (again, a parallel to arrays). A pointer variable, in contrast, can be changed. Specifically, it can be made to point to different functions as the need arises.

Listing 14.9 calls a function, passing it an integer argument. Depending on the value of the argument, the function initializes a pointer to point to one of three other functions and then uses the pointer to call the corresponding function. Each of these three functions displays a specific message onscreen.

LISTING 14.9. Using a pointer to a function to call different functions depending on program circumstances.

```
1: /* Using a pointer to call different functions. */
2:
3: #include <stdio.h>
4:
5:/* The function prototypes. */
6:
7: void func1(int x);
8: void one(void);
9: void two(void);
10: void other(void);
11:
12:  int main(void)
13: {
14:      int a;
15:
16:      for (;;)
17:      {
18:          puts("\nEnter an integer between 1 and 10, 0 to exit: ");
19:          scanf("%d", &a);
20:
21:          if (a == 0)
22:              break;
23:          func1(a);
24:      }
```

14

continues

LISTING 14.9. continued

```
25:        return(0);
26: }
27:
28: void func1(int x)
29: {
30:      /* The pointer to function. */
31:
32:      void (*ptr)(void);
33:
34:      if (x == 1)
35:          ptr = one;
36:      else if (x == 2)
37:          ptr = two;
38:      else
39:          ptr = other;
40:
41:      ptr();
42: }
43:
44: void one(void)
45: {
46:      puts("You entered 1.");
47: }
48:
49: void two(void)
50: {
51:      puts("You entered 2.");
52: }
53:
54: void other(void)
55: {
56:      puts("You entered something other than 1 or 2.");
57: }
```

INPUT/
OUTPUT

```
Enter an integer between 1 and 10, 0 to exit:
2
You entered 2.

Enter an integer between 1 and 10, 0 to exit:
9
You entered something other than 1 or 2.

Enter an integer between 1 and 10, 0 to exit:
0
```

ANALYSIS
This program employs an infinite loop starting on line 16 to continue execution until a value of 0 is entered. When a nonzero value is entered, it's passed to func1(). Note that line 32, in func1(), contains a declaration for a pointer ptr to a function. Being declared within a function makes ptr local to func1(), which is appropriate

because no other part of the program needs access to it. func1() then uses this value to set ptr equal to the appropriate function (lines 34 through 39). Line 41 then makes a single call to ptr(), which calls the appropriate function.

Of course, this program is for illustration purposes only. You could have easily accomplished the same result without using a pointer to a function.

Now you can learn another way to use pointers to call different functions: passing the pointer as an argument to a function. Listing 14.10 is a revision of Listing 14.9.

LISTING 14.10. Passing a pointer to a function as an argument.

```
1: /* Passing a pointer to a function as an argument. */
2:
3: #include <stdio.h>
4:
5: /* The function prototypes. The function func1() takes as */
6: /* its one argument a pointer to a function that takes no */
7: /* arguments and has no return value. */
8:
9: void func1(void (*p)(void));
10: void one(void);
11: void two(void);
12: void other(void);
13:
14: int main(void)
15: {
16:     /* The pointer to a function. */
18:     void (*ptr)(void);
19:     int  a;
20:
21:     for (;;)
22:     {
23:         puts("\nEnter an integer between 1 and 10, 0 to exit: ");
24:         scanf("%d", &a);
25:
26:         if (a == 0)
27:             break;
28:         else if (a == 1)
29:             ptr = one;
30:         else if (a == 2)
31:             ptr = two;
32:         else
33:             ptr = other;
34:         func1(ptr);
35:     }
36:     return(0);
37: }
38:
```

continues

14

LISTING 14.10. continued

```
39: void func1(void (*p)(void))
40: {
41:     p();
42: }
43:
44: void one(void)
45: {
46:     puts("You entered 1.");
47: }
48:
49: void two(void)
50: {
51:     puts("You entered 2.");
52: }
53:
54: void other(void)
55: {
56:     puts("You entered something other than 1 or 2.");
57: }
```

INPUT/
OUTPUT

```
Enter an integer between 1 and 10, 0 to exit:
2
You entered 2.

Enter an integer between 1 and 10, 0 to exit:
11
You entered something other than 1 or 2.

Enter an integer between 1 and 10, 0 to exit:
0
```

ANALYSIS   Notice the differences between Listing 14.9 and Listing 14.10. The declaration of the pointer to a function has been moved to line 18 in main(), where it is needed. Code in main() now initializes the pointer to point to the correct function, depending on the value the user entered (lines 26 through 33), and then passes the initialized pointer to func1(). func1() really serves no purpose in Listing 14.10; all it does is call the function pointed to by ptr. Again, this program is for illustration purposes. The same principles can be used in real-world programs, such as the example in the next section.

One programming situation in which you might use pointers to functions is one in which sorting is required. Sometimes you might want different sorting rules used. For example, you might want to sort in alphabetical order one time and in reverse alphabetical order another time. By using pointers to functions, your program can call the correct sorting function. More precisely, it's usually a different comparison function that's called.

Look back at Listing 14.7. In the sort() function, the actual sort order is determined by the value returned by the strcmp() library function, which tells the program whether a given string is less than or greater than another string. What if you wrote two comparison functions—one that sorts alphabetically (where A is less than Z), and another that sorts in reverse alphabetical order (where Z is less than A)? The program can ask the user what order he wants and, by using pointers, the sorting function can call the proper comparison function. Listing 14.11 modifies Listing 14.7 to incorporate this feature.

LISTING 14.11. Using pointers to functions to control sort order.

```
 1:  /* Inputs a list of strings from the keyboard, sorts them */
 2:  /* in ascending or descending order, and then displays them */
 3:  /* on the screen. */
 4:  #include <stdlib.h>
 5:  #include <stdio.h>
 6:  #include <string.h>
 7:
 8:  #define MAXLINES 25
 9:
10:  int get_lines(char *lines[]);
11:  void sort(char *p[], int n, int sort_type);
12:  void print_strings(char *p[], int n);
13:  int alpha(char *p1, char *p2);
14:  int reverse(char *p1, char *p2);
15:
16:  char *lines[MAXLINES];
17:
18:   int main(void)
19:  {
20:     int number_of_lines, sort_type;
21:
22:     /* Read in the lines from the keyboard. */
23:
24:     number_of_lines = get_lines(lines);
25:
26:     if ( number_of_lines < 0 )
27:     {
28:        puts("Memory allocation error");
29:        exit(-1);
30:     }
31:
32:     puts("Enter 0 for reverse order sort, 1 for alphabetical:" );
33:     scanf("%d", &sort_type);
34:
35:     sort(lines, number_of_lines, sort_type);
36:     print_strings(lines, number_of_lines);
37:     return(0);
38:  }
39:
40:  int get_lines(char *lines[])
```

14

continues

LISTING **14.11**. continued

```
41:  {
42:      int n = 0;
43:      char buffer[80];  /* Temporary storage for each line. */
44:
45:      puts("Enter one line at time; enter a blank when done.");
46:
47:      while (n < MAXLINES && fgets(buffer,80,stdin) != 0 &&
                          [ic:ccc]buffer[0] != '\n')
48:      {
49:          if ((lines[n] = (char *)malloc(strlen(buffer)+1)) == NULL)
50:          return -1;
51:          strcpy( lines[n++], buffer );
52:      }
53:      return n;
54:
55:  } /* End of get_lines() */
56:
57:  void sort(char *p[], int n, int sort_type)
58:  {
59:      int a, b;
60:       char *x;
61:
62:      /* The pointer to function.  */
63:
64:      int (*compare)(char *s1, char *s2);
65:
66:      /* Initialize the pointer to point to the proper comparison */
67:      /* function depending on the argument sort_type. */
68:
69:      compare = (sort_type) ? reverse : alpha;
70:
71:      for (a = 1; a < n; a++)
72:      {
73:          for (b = 0; b < n-1; b++)
74:          {
75:              if (compare(p[b], p[b+1]) > 0)
76:              {
77:                  x = p[b];
78:                  p[b] = p[b+1];
79:                  p[b+1] = x;
80:              }
81:          }
82:      }
83:  }  /* end of sort() */
84:
85:  void print_strings(char *p[], int n)
86:  {
87:      int count;
88:
89:      for (count = 0; count < n; count++)
```

```
90:            printf("%s", p[count]);
91:  }
92:
93:  int alpha(char *p1, char *p2)
94:  /* Alphabetical comparison. */
95:  {
96:      return(strcmp(p2, p1));
97:  }
98:
99:  int reverse(char *p1, char *p2)
100: /* Reverse alphabetical comparison. */
101: {
102:      return(strcmp(p1, p2));
103: }
```

INPUT/
OUTPUT

```
Enter one line at time; enter a blank when done.
Roses are red
Violets are blue
C has been around,
But it is new to you!

Enter 0 for reverse order sort, 1 for alphabetical:
0

Violets are blue
Roses are red
C has been around,
But it is new to you!
```

ANALYSIS   Lines 32 and 33 in main() prompt the user for the desired sort order. The value entered is placed in sort_type. This value is passed to the sort() function along with the other information described for Listing 14.7. The sort() function contains a couple of changes. Line 64 declares a pointer to a function called compare() that takes two character pointers (strings) as arguments. Line 69 sets compare() equal to one of the two new functions added to the listing based on the value of sort_type. The two new functions are alpha() and reverse(). alpha() uses the strcmp() library function just as it was used in Listing 14.7; reverse() does not. reverse() switches the parameters passed so that a reverse-order sort is done.

14

Do	**Don't**
DO use structured programming.	**DON'T** forget to use parentheses when declaring pointers to functions.
DO initialize a pointer before using it.	Here's how you declare a pointer to a function that takes no arguments and returns a character:
	`char (*func)();`
	Here's how you declare a function that returns a pointer to a character:
	`char *func();`
	DON'T use a function pointer that has been declared with a different return type or different arguments than you need.

Functions That Return a Pointer

In previous days, you saw several functions from the C standard library whose return value is a pointer. You can write your own functions that return a pointer. As you might expect, the indirection operator (*) is used in both the function declaration and the function definition. The general form of the declaration is

```
type *func(parameter_list);
```

This statement declares a function `func()` that returns a pointer to `type`. Here are two concrete examples:

```
double *func1(parameter_list);
```

```
struct address *func2(parameter_list);
```

The first line declares a function that returns a pointer to type `double`. The second line declares a function that returns a pointer to type `address` (which you assume is a user-defined structure).

Don't confuse a function that returns a pointer with a pointer to a function. If you include an additional pair of parentheses in the declaration, you declare a pointer to a function, as shown in these two examples:

```
double (*func)(...);    /* Pointer to a function that returns a double. */

double *func(...);      /* Function that returns a pointer to a double. */
```

Now that you have the declaration format straight, how do you use a function that returns a pointer? There's nothing special about such functions—you use them just as you do any other function, assigning their return value to a variable of the appropriate type (in this case, a pointer). Because the function call is a C expression, you can use it anywhere you would use a pointer of that type.

Listing 14.12 presents a simple example, a function that is passed two arguments and determines which is larger. The listing shows two ways of doing this: One function returns an `int`, and the other returns a pointer to `int`.

LISTING 14.12. Returning a pointer from a function.

```
 1: /* Function that returns a pointer. */
 2:
 3: #include <stdio.h>
 4:
 5: int larger1(int x, int y);
 6: int *larger2(int *x, int *y);
 7:
 8: int main(void)
 9: {
10:     int a, b, bigger1, *bigger2;
11:
12:     printf("Enter two integer values: ");
13:     scanf("%d %d", &a, &b);
14:
15:     bigger1 = larger1(a, b);
16:     printf("The larger value is %d.\n", bigger1);
17:     bigger2 = larger2(&a, &b);
18:     printf("The larger value is %d.\n", *bigger2);
19:     return(0);
20: }
21:
22: int larger1(int x, int y)
23: {
24:     if (y > x)
25:         return y;
26:     return x;
27: }
28:
29: int *larger2(int *x, int *y)
30: {
31:     if (*y > *x)
32:         return y;
33:
34:     return x;
35: }
```

INPUT/
OUTPUT

```
Enter two integer values: 1111 3000

The larger value is 3000.
The larger value is 3000.
```

14

ANALYSIS This is a relatively easy program to follow. Lines 5 and 6 contain the prototypes for the two functions. The first, `larger1()`, receives two `int` variables and returns an `int`. The second, `larger2()`, receives two pointers to `int` variables and returns a pointer to an `int`. The `main()` function on lines 8–20 is straightforward. Line 10 declares four variables. `a` and `b` hold the two variables to be compared. `bigger1` and `bigger2` hold the return values from the `larger1()` and `larger2()` functions, respectively. Notice that `bigger2` is a pointer to an `int`, and `bigger1` is just an `int`.

Line 15 calls `larger1()` with the two `int`s, `a` and `b`. The value returned from the function is assigned to `bigger1`, which is printed on line 16. Line 17 calls `larger2()` with the address of the two `int`s. The value returned from `larger2()`, a pointer, is assigned to `bigger2`, also a pointer. This value is dereferenced and printed on the following line.

The two comparison functions are very similar. They both compare the two values and return the larger one. The difference between the functions is that `larger2()` works with pointers, whereas `larger1()` does not. In `larger2()`, notice that the dereference operator is used in the comparisons, but not in the `return` statements on lines 32 and 34.

In many cases, as in Listing 14.12, it is equally feasible to write a function to return a value or a pointer. Which one you select depends on the specifics of your program—mainly on how you intend to use the return value.

Do	**Don't**
DO use all the elements described today when writing functions that have variable arguments. This is true even if your compiler doesn't require all the elements.	DON'T confuse pointers to functions with functions that return pointers.

Linked Lists

A *linked list* is a useful method of data storage that can easily be implemented in C. Why are we covering linked lists in a discussion of pointers? Because, as you will soon see, pointers are central to linked lists.

There are several kinds of linked lists, including single-linked lists, double-linked lists, and binary trees. Each type is suited for certain types of data storage. The one thing that these lists have in common is that the links between data items are defined by information that is contained in the items themselves, in the form of pointers. This is distinctly different from arrays, in which the links between data items result from the layout and storage of the array. This section explains the most fundamental kind of linked list: the single-linked list (which I refer to as simply a linked list).

Basics of Linked Lists

Each data item in a linked list is contained in a structure. (You learned about structures on Day 10, "Structures.") The structure contains the data elements needed to hold the data being stored; these depend on the needs of the specific program. In addition, there is one more data element—a pointer. This pointer provides the links in a linked list. Here's a simple example:

```
struct person {
char name[20];
struct person *next;
};
```

This code defines a structure named person. For the data, person contains only a 20-element array of characters. You generally wouldn't use a linked list for such simple data, but this will serve as an example. The person structure also contains a pointer to type person—in other words, a pointer to another structure of the same type. That means each structure of type person can not only contain a chunk of data, but also can point to another person structure. Figure 14.7 shows how this lets the structures be linked together in a list.

FIGURE 14.7.

Links in a linked list.

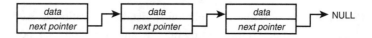

Notice that in Figure 14.7, each person structure points to the next person structure. The last person structure doesn't point to anything. The last element in a linked list is identified by the pointer element being assigned the value of NULL.

 Note

The structures that make up a link in a linked list can be referred to as *links, nodes,* or *elements* of a linked list.

You have seen how the last link in a linked list is identified. What about the first link? This is identified by a special pointer (not a structure) called the *head pointer*. The head pointer always points to the first element in the linked list. The first element contains a pointer to the second element; the second element contains a pointer to the third, and so on, until you encounter an element whose pointer is NULL. If the entire list is empty (contains no links), the head pointer is set to NULL. Figure 14.8 illustrates the head pointer before the list is started and after the first list element is added.

14

FIGURE 14.8.

*A linked list's head
pointer.*

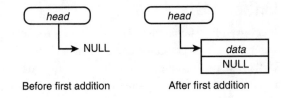

Before first addition | After first addition

Note

> The *head pointer* is a pointer to the first element in a linked list. The head
> pointer is sometimes referred to as the *first element pointer* or *top pointer*.

Working with Linked Lists

When you're working with a linked list, you can add, delete, or modify elements or links.
Modifying an element presents no real challenge; however, adding and deleting elements
can. As I stated earlier, elements in a list are connected with pointers. Much of the work
of adding and deleting elements consists of manipulating these pointers. Elements can be
added to the beginning, middle, or end of a linked list; this determines how the pointers
must be changed.

Later today, you'll find a simple linked list demonstration, as well as a more complex
working program. Before getting into the nitty-gritty of code, however, it's a good idea to
examine some of the actions you need to perform with linked lists. For these sections, we
will continue using the person structure that was introduced earlier.

Preliminaries

Before you start a linked list, you must define the data structure that will be used for the
list, and you also need to declare the head pointer. Because the list starts out empty, the
head pointer should be initialized to NULL. You will also need an additional pointer to
your list structure type for use in adding records. (You might need more than one pointer,
as you'll soon see.) Here's how you do it:

```
struct person {
  char name[20];
  struct person *next;
};
struct person *new;
struct person *head;
head = NULL;
```

Adding an Element to the Beginning of a List

If the head pointer is NULL, the list is empty, and the new element will be its only member.
If the head pointer is not NULL, the list already contains one or more elements. In either
case, however, the procedure for adding a new element to the start of the list is the same:

1. Create an instance of your structure, allocating memory space using `malloc()`.

2. Set the next pointer of the new element to the current value of the head pointer. The current value will be NULL if the list is empty, or the address of the current first element otherwise.

3. Make the head pointer point to the new element.

Here is the code to perform this task:

```
new = (person*)malloc(sizeof(struct person));
new->next = head;
head = new;
```

Note that `malloc()` is typecast so that its return value is the proper type—a pointer to the person data structure. Also remember that in the second line, the value of head is NULL.

 Caution

> It's important to switch the pointers in the correct order. If you reassign the head pointer first, you will lose the list!

Figure 14.9 illustrates the procedure for adding a new element to an empty list, and Figure 14.10 illustrates adding a new first element to an existing list.

FIGURE 14.9.

Adding a new element to an empty linked list.

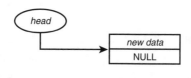

Before addition

After addition

14

FIGURE 14.10.

Adding a new first element to an existing list.

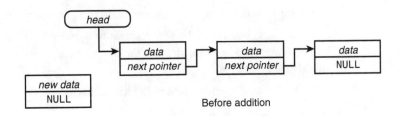

Before addition

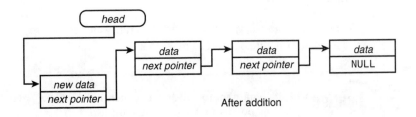

After addition

Notice that `malloc()` is used to allocate the memory for the new element. As each new element is added, only the memory needed for it is allocated. The `calloc()` function could also be used. You should be aware of the differences between these two functions. The main difference is that `calloc()` will initialize the new element; `malloc()` will not.

Caution

In these code fragments, the return value of `malloc()` in the preceding code fragment is not checking to ensure that the memory was successfully allocated. In a real program, you should always check the return value of a memory allocation function.

Tip

When possible, you should always initialize pointers to NULL when you declare them. Never leave a pointer uninitialized. Doing so is just asking for trouble.

Adding an Element to the End of the List

To add an element to the end of a linked list, you need to start at the head pointer and go through the list until you find the last element. After you've found it, follow these steps:

1. Create an instance of your structure, allocating memory space using `malloc()`.

2. Set the next pointer in the last element to point to the new element (whose address is returned by `malloc()`).

3. Set the next pointer in the new element to NULL to signal that it is the last item in the list.

Here is the code:

```
person *current;
...
current = head;
while (current->next != NULL)
    current = current->next;
new = (person*)malloc(sizeof(struct person));
current->next = new;
new->next = NULL;
```

Figure 14.11 illustrates the procedure for adding a new element to the end of a linked list.

FIGURE 14.11.

Adding a new element to the end of a linked list.

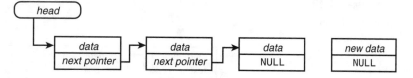

Before addition

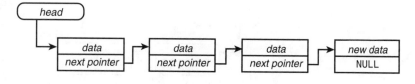

After addition

Adding an Element to the Middle of the List

When you're working with a linked list, most of the time you will be adding elements somewhere in the middle of the list. Exactly where the new element is placed depends on how you're keeping the list—for example, if it is sorted on one or more data elements. This process, then, requires that you first locate the position in the list where the new element will go, and then add it. Here are the steps to follow:

1. In the list, locate the existing element that the new element will be placed after. Let's call this the *marker element*.

2. Create an instance of your structure, allocating memory space using malloc().

14

3. Set the next pointer of the marker element to point to the new element (whose address is returned by `malloc()`).

4. Set the next pointer of the new element to point to the element that the marker element used to point to.

Here's how the code might look:

```
person *marker;
/* Code here to set marker to point to the desired list location. */
...
new = (person*)malloc(sizeof(PERSON));
new->next = marker->next;
marker->next = new;
```

Figure 14.12 illustrates this process.

FIGURE 14.12.

Adding a new element to the middle of a linked list.

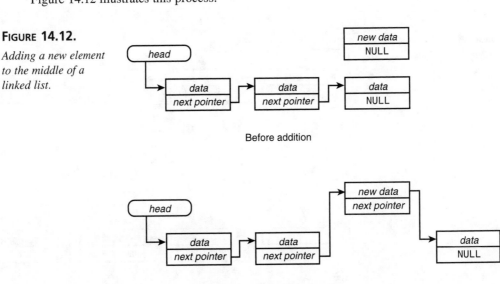

Before addition

After addition

Deleting an Element from the List

Deleting an element from a linked list is a simple matter of manipulating pointers. The exact process depends on where in the list the element is located:

- To delete the first element, set the head pointer to point to the second element in the list.

- To delete the last element, set the next pointer of the next-to-last element to NULL.

- To delete any other element, set the next pointer of the element before the one being deleted to point to the element after the one being deleted.

In addition, the memory of the element that is removed from the list should be freed so the program does not claim more memory than it needs (this is called a *memory leak*). Freeing memory is done with the `free()` function. Here's the code to delete the first element in a linked list:

```
free(head);
head = head->next;
```

This code deletes the last element in a list with two or more elements:

```
person *current1, *current2;
current1 = head;
current2= current1->next;
while (current2->next != NULL)
{
    current1 = current2;
    current2= current1->next;
}
free(current1->next);
current1->next = NULL;
if (head == current1)
    head = NULL;
```

Finally, the following code deletes an element from within the list:

```
person *current1, *current2;
/* Code goes here to have current1 point to the */
/* element just before the one to be deleted. */
current2 = current1->next;
free(current1->next);

current1->next = current2->next;
```

After any of these procedures, the deleted element still exists in memory, but it is removed from the list because there is no pointer in the list pointing to it. In a real-world program, you would want to reclaim the memory occupied by the deleted element. This is accomplished with the `free()` function.

A Simple Linked List Demonstration

Listing 14.13 demonstrates the basics of using a linked list. This program is clearly for demonstration purposes only; it doesn't accept user input and doesn't do anything useful other than show the code required for the most basic linked list tasks. The program does the following:

1. It defines a structure and the required pointers for the list.

2. It adds the first element to the list.

3. It adds an element to the end of the list.

14

4. It adds an element to the middle of the list.

5. It displays the list contents onscreen.

LISTING 14.13. The basics of a linked list.

```
1: /* Demonstrates the fundamentals of using */
2: /* a linked list. */
3:
4: #include <stdlib.h>
5: #include <stdio.h>
6: #include <string.h>
7:
8: /* The list data structure. */
9: struct data {
10:     char name[20];
11:     struct data *next;
12:     };
13:
14: /* Define typedefs for the structure */
15: /* and a pointer to it. */
16: typedef struct data PERSON;
17: typedef PERSON *LINK;
18:
19: int main(void)
20: {
21:     /* Head, new, and current element pointers. */
22:     LINK head = NULL;
23:     LINK new = NULL;
24:     LINK current = NULL;
25:
26:     /* Add the first list element. We do not */
27:     /* assume the list is empty, although in */
28:     /* this demo program it always will be. */
29:
30:     new = (LINK)malloc(sizeof(PERSON));
31:     new->next = head;
32:     head = new;
33:     strcpy(new->name, "Abigail");
34:
35:     /* Add an element at the end of the list. */
36:     /* We assume the list contains at least one element. */
37:
38:     current = head;
39:     while (current->next != NULL)
40:     {
41:         current = current->next;
42:     }
43:
44:     new = (LINK)malloc(sizeof(PERSON));
```

```
45:     current->next = new;
46:     new->next = NULL;
47:     strcpy(new->name, "Catherine");
48:
49:     /* Add a new element at the second position in the list. */
50:     new = (LINK)malloc(sizeof(PERSON));
51:     new->next = head->next;
52:     head->next = new;
53:     strcpy(new->name, "Beatrice");
54:
55:     /* Print out all data items in order. */
56:     current = head;
57:     while (current != NULL)
58:     {
59:         printf("%s\n", current->name);
60:         current = current->next;
61:     }
62:
63:     printf("\n");
64:     return(0);
65: }
```

OUTPUT

```
Abigail
Beatrice
Catherine
```

ANALYSIS You can probably figure out at least some of the code. Lines 9 through 12 declare the data structure for the list. Lines 16 and 17 define typedefs for both the data structure and for a pointer to the data structure. Strictly speaking, this isn't necessary, but it simplifies coding by enabling you to write PERSON in place of struct data and LINK in place of struct data *.

Lines 22 through 24 declare a head pointer and a couple pointers that will be used when manipulating the list. All these pointers are initialized to NULL.

Lines 30 through 33 add a new link to the start of the list. Line 30 allocates a new data structure. Note that the successful operation of malloc() is assumed—something you would never do in a real program!

Line 31 sets the next pointer in this new structure to point to whatever the head pointer contains. Why not simply assign NULL to this pointer? That works only if you know that the list is empty. As it is written, the code will work even if the list already contains some elements. The new first element will point to the element that used to be first, which is just what you want.

Line 32 makes the head pointer point to the new record, and line 33 stores some data in the record.

14

Adding an element to the end of the list is a bit more complicated. Although in this case you know that the list contains only one element, you can't assume that in a real program. Therefore, it's necessary to loop through the list, starting with the first element, until you find the last element (as indicated by the next pointer's being NULL). Then you know you have found the end of the list. This task is accomplished in lines 38 through 42. After you have found the last element, it is a simple matter to allocate a new data structure, have the old last element point to it, and set the new element's next pointer to NULL because it is now the last element in the list. This is done in lines 44 through 47. Note that the return type from malloc() is typecast to be type LINK. (You learn more about typecasts on Day 18.)

The next task is to add an element to the middle of the list—in this case, at the second position. After a new data structure is allocated (line 50), the new element's next pointer is set to point to the element that used to be second and is now third in the list (line 51), and the first element's next pointer is made to point to the new element (line 52).

Finally, the program prints all the records in the linked list. This is a simple matter of starting with the element that the head pointer points to and then progressing through the list until the last list element is found, as indicated by a NULL pointer. Lines 56 through 61 perform this task.

Implementing a Linked List

Now that you have seen the ways to add links to a list, it's time to see them in action. Listing 14.14 is a rather long program that uses a linked list to hold a list of five characters. The characters are stored in memory using a linked list. These characters just as easily could have been names, addresses, or any other data. To keep the example as simple as possible, only a single character is stored in each link.

What makes this linked list program complicated is the fact that it sorts the links as they are added. Of course, this also is what makes this program so valuable. Each link is added to the beginning, middle, or end, depending on its value. The link is always sorted. If you were to write a program that simply added the links to the end, the logic would be much simpler. However, the program also would be less useful.

LISTING 14.14. Implementing a linked list of characters.

```
1: /*================================================================*
2: * Program:  list1413.c                                          *
3: * Book:     Teach Yourself C Programming for Linux in 21 Days *
4: * Purpose:  Implementing a linked list                          *
5: *================================================================*/
6: #include <stdio.h>
7: #include <stdlib.h>
```

```
8:
9: #ifndef NULL
10:    #define NULL 0
11: #endif
12:
13: /* List data structure */
14: struct list
15: {
16:    int     ch;        /* using an int to hold a char */
17:    struct list *next_rec;
18: };
19:
20: /* Typedefs for the structure and pointer. */
21: typedef struct list LIST;
22: typedef LIST *LISTPTR;
23:
24: /* Function prototypes. */
25: LISTPTR add_to_list( int, LISTPTR );
26: void show_list(LISTPTR);
27: void free_memory_list(LISTPTR);
28:
29: int main( void )
30: {
31:    LISTPTR first = NULL;  /* head pointer */
32:    int i = 0;
33:    int ch;
34:    char trash[256];        /* to clear stdin buffer. */
35:
36:    while ( i++ < 5 )      /* build a list based on 5 items given */
37:    {
38:       ch = 0;
39:       printf("\nEnter character %d, ", i);
40:
41:       do
42:       {
43:          printf("\nMust be a to z: ");
44:          ch = getc(stdin); /* get next char in buffer  */
45:          fgets(trash,256,stdin);   /* remove trash from buffer */
46:       } while( (ch < 'a' ¦¦ ch > 'z') && (ch < 'A' ¦¦ ch > 'Z'));
47:
48:       first = add_to_list( ch, first );
49:    }
50:
51:    show_list( first );          /* Dumps the entire list */
52:    free_memory_list( first );   /* Release all memory */
53:    return(0);
54: }
55:
56: /*========================================================*
57:  * Function: add_to_list()
58:  * Purpose : Inserts new link in the list
```

14

continues

LISTING 14.14. continued

```
59:  * Entry   : int ch = character to store
60:  *                LISTPTR first = address of original head pointer
61:  * Returns : Address of head pointer (first)
62:  *=========================================================*/
63:
64: LISTPTR add_to_list( int ch, LISTPTR first )
65: {
66:    LISTPTR new_rec = NULL;        /* Holds address of new rec */
67:    LISTPTR tmp_rec = NULL;        /* Hold tmp pointer         */
68:    LISTPTR prev_rec = NULL;
69:
70:    /* Allocate memory. */
71:    new_rec = (LISTPTR)malloc(sizeof(LIST));
72:    if (new_rec == NULL)       /* Unable to allocate memory */
73:    {
74:       printf("\nUnable to allocate memory!\n");
75:       exit(1);
76:    }
77:
78:    /* set new link's data */
79:    new_rec->ch = ch;
80:    new_rec->next_rec = NULL;
81:
82:    if (first == NULL)    /* adding first link to list */
83:    {
84:       first = new_rec;
85:       new_rec->next_rec = NULL;  /* redundant but safe */
86:    }
87:    else    /* not first record */
88:    {
89:       /* see if it goes before the first link */
90:       if ( new_rec->ch < first->ch)
91:       {
92:          new_rec->next_rec = first;
93:          first = new_rec;
94:       }
95:       else   /* it is being added to the middle or end */
96:       {
97:          tmp_rec = first->next_rec;
98:          prev_rec = first;
99:
100:          /* Check to see where link is added. */
101:
102:          if ( tmp_rec == NULL )
103:          {
104:             /* we are adding second record to end */
105:             prev_rec->next_rec = new_rec;
106:          }
107:          else
```

```
108:          {
109:              /* check to see if adding in middle */
110:              while (( tmp_rec->next_rec != NULL))
111:              {
112:                 if( new_rec->ch < tmp_rec->ch )
113:                 {
114:                    new_rec->next_rec = tmp_rec;
115:                    if (new_rec->next_rec != prev_rec->next_rec)
116:                    {
117:                       printf("ERROR");
118:                       getc(stdin);
119:                       exit(0);
120:                    }
121:                    prev_rec->next_rec = new_rec;
122:                    break;    /* link is added; exit while */
123:                 }
124:                 else
125:                 {
126:                    tmp_rec = tmp_rec->next_rec;
127:                    prev_rec = prev_rec->next_rec;
128:                 }
129:              }
130:
131:              /* check to see if adding to the end */
132:              if (tmp_rec->next_rec == NULL)
133:              {
134:                 if (new_rec->ch < tmp_rec->ch ) /* 1 b4 end */
135:                 {
136:                    new_rec->next_rec = tmp_rec;
137:                    prev_rec->next_rec = new_rec;
138:                 }
139:                 else  /* at the end */
140:                 {
141:                    tmp_rec->next_rec = new_rec;
142:                    new_rec->next_rec = NULL;  /* redundant */
143:                 }
144:              }
145:          }
146:       }
147:    }
148:    return(first);
149: }
150:
151: /*========================================================*
152:  * Function: show_list
153:  * Purpose : Displays the information current in the list
154:  *========================================================*/
155:
156: void show_list( LISTPTR first )
157: {
158:    LISTPTR cur_ptr;
```

continues

LISTING 14.14. continued

```
159:    int counter = 1;
160:
161:    printf("\n\nRec addr  Position  Data  Next Rec addr\n");
162:    printf("========  ========  ====  =============\n");
163:
164:    cur_ptr = first;
165:    while (cur_ptr != NULL )
166:    {
167:       printf("  %X   ", cur_ptr );
168:       printf("     %2i      %c", counter++, cur_ptr->ch);
169:       printf("       %X  \n",cur_ptr->next_rec);
170:       cur_ptr = cur_ptr->next_rec;
171:    }
172: }
173:
174: /*=======================================================*
175:  * Function: free_memory_list
176:  * Purpose : Frees up all the memory collected for list
177:  *=======================================================*/
178:
179: void free_memory_list(LISTPTR first)
180: {
181:    LISTPTR cur_ptr, next_rec;
182:    cur_ptr = first;                   /* Start at beginning */
183:
184:    while (cur_ptr != NULL)            /* Go while not end of list */
185:    {
186:       next_rec = cur_ptr->next_rec; /* Get address of next record */
187:       free(cur_ptr);                 /* Free current record */
188:       cur_ptr = next_rec;            /* Adjust current record*/
189:    }
190: }
```

**INPUT/
OUTPUT**

```
Enter character 1,
Must be a to z: q

Enter character 2,
Must be a to z: b

Enter character 3,
Must be a to z: z

Enter character 4,
Must be a to z: c

Enter character 5,
Must be a to z: a
```

Rec addr	Position	Data	Next Rec addr
=========	========	====	==============
0x8049ae8	1	f	0x8049b18
0x8049b18	2	g	0x8049af8
0x8049af8	3	h	0x8049b08
0x8049b08	4	t	0x8049b28
0x8049b28	5	v	(nil)

Note

Your output will probably show different address values.

ANALYSIS This program demonstrates adding a link to a linked list. It isn't the easiest listing to understand; however, if you walk through it, you'll see that it's a combination of the three methods of adding links that were discussed earlier. This listing can be used to add links to the beginning, middle, or end of a linked list. Additionally, this listing takes into consideration the special cases of adding the first link (the one that is added to the beginning) and the second link (the one that is added to the middle).

Tip

The easiest way to fully understand this listing is to step through it line by line using DDD and to read the following analysis. By seeing the logic executed, you will better understand the listing. By using the View Data Window command, you will be able to view a visual representation of your linked list as shown in Figure 14.13.

FIGURE 14.13.

DDD showing the first pointer and a two-element linked list in the Data Window.

14

Several items at the beginning of Listing 14.14 should be familiar or easy to understand. Lines 9 through 11 check to see whether the value of NULL is already defined. If it isn't, line 10 defines it to be 0. Lines 14 through 22 define the structure for the linked list and also declare the type definitions to make working with the structure and pointers easier.

The main() function should be easy to follow. A head pointer called first is declared in line 31. Notice that this is initialized to NULL. Remember that you should never let a pointer go uninitialized. Lines 36 through 49 contain a while loop that is used to get five characters from the user. Within this outer while loop, which repeats five times, a do...while is used to ensure that each character entered is a letter. The isalpha() function could have been used just as easily.

After a piece of data is obtained, add_to_list() is called. The pointer to the beginning of the list and the data being added to the list are passed to the function.

The main() function ends by calling show_list() to display the list's data and then free_memory_list() to release all the memory that was allocated to hold the links in the list. Both these functions operate in a similar manner. Each starts at the beginning of the linked list using the head pointer first. A while loop is used to go from one link to the next using the next_ptr value. When next_ptr is equal to NULL, the end of the linked list has been reached, and the functions return.

The most important (and most complicated!) function in this listing is add_to_list() in lines 56 through 149. Lines 66 through 68 declare three pointers that will be used to point to three different links. The new_rec pointer will point to the new link that is to be added. The tmp_rec pointer will point to the current link in the list being evaluated. If there is more than one link in the list, the prev_rec pointer will be used to point to the previous link that was evaluated.

Line 71 allocates memory for the new link that is being added. The new_rec pointer is set to the value returned by malloc(). If the memory can't be allocated, lines 74 and 75 print an error message and exit the program. If the memory is allocated successfully, the program continues.

Line 79 sets the data in the structure to the data passed to this function. This simply consists of assigning the character passed to the function ch to the new record's character field (new_rec->ch). In a more complex program, this could entail assigning several fields. Line 80 sets the next_rec in the new record to NULL so that it doesn't point to some random location.

Line 82 starts the "add a link" logic by checking to see whether there are any links in the list. If the link being added is the first link in the list, as indicated by the head pointer first being NULL, the head pointer is simply set equal to the new pointer, and you're done.

If this link isn't the first, the function continues within the else at line 87. Line 90 checks to see whether the new link goes at the beginning of the list. As you should remember, this is one of the three cases for adding a link. If the link does go first, line 92 sets the next_rec pointer in the new link to point to the previous "first" link. Line 93 then sets the head pointer, first, to point to the new link. This results in the new link being added to the beginning of the list.

If the new link isn't the first link to be added to an empty list, and if it's being added at the first position in an existing list, you know it must be in the middle or at the end of the list. Lines 97 and 98 set up the tmp_rec and prev_rec pointers that were declared earlier. The pointer tmp_rec is set to the address of the second link in the list, and prev_rec is set to the first link in the list.

You should note that if there is only one link in the list, tmp_rec will be equal to NULL. This is because tmp_rec is set to the next_ptr in the first link, which will be equal to NULL. Line 102 checks for this special case. If tmp_rec is NULL, you know that this is the second link being added to the list. Because you know the new link doesn't come before the first link, it can only go at the end. To accomplish this, you simply set prev_rec->next_ptr to the new link, and then you're done.

If the tmp_rec pointer isn't NULL, you know that you already have more than two links in your list. The while statement in lines 110 through 129 loops through the rest of the links to determine where the new link should be placed. Line 112 checks to see whether the new link's data value is less than the link currently being pointed to. If it is, you know this is where you want to add the link. If the new data is greater than the current link's data, you need to look at the next link in the list. Lines 126 and 127 set the pointers tmp_rec and next_rec to the next links.

If the character is less than the current link's character, you would follow the logic presented earlier in this chapter for adding to the middle of a linked list. This process can be seen in lines 114 through 122. In line 114, the new link's next pointer is set to equal the current link's address (tmp_rec). Line 121 sets the previous link's next pointer to point to the new link. After this, you're done. The code uses a break statement to get out of the while loop.

Note

Lines 115 through 120 contain debugging code that was left in the listing for you to see. These lines could be removed; however, as long as the program is running correctly, they will never be called. After the new link's next pointer is set to the current pointer, it should be equal to the previous link's next pointer, which also points to the current record. If they aren't equal, something went wrong!

14

The previously covered logic takes care of links being added to the middle of the list. If the end of the list is reached, the `while` loop in lines 110 through 129 will end without adding the link. Lines 132 through 144 take care of adding the link to the end.

If the last link in the list was reached, `tmp_rec->next_rec` will equal `NULL`. Line 132 checks for this condition. Line 134 checks to see whether the link goes before or after the last link. If it goes after the last link, the last link's `next_rec` is set to the new link (line 132), and the new link's next pointer is set to `NULL` (line 142).

Improving Listing 14.14

Linked lists are not the easiest thing to learn. As you can see from Listing 14.14, however, they are an excellent way of storing data in a sorted order. Because it's easy to add new data items anywhere in a linked list, the code for keeping a list of data items in sorted order with a linked list is a lot simpler that it would be if you used, say, an array. This listing could easily be converted to sort names, phone numbers, or any other data. Additionally, although this listing sorted in ascending order (A to Z), it just as easily could have sorted in descending order (Z to A).

Deleting from a Linked List

The ability to add information to a linked list is essential, but there will be times when you will want to remove information too. Deleting links, or elements, is similar to adding them. You can delete links from the beginning, middle, or end of linked lists. In each case, the appropriate pointers need to be adjusted. Also, the memory used by the deleted link needs to be freed.

> **Note**   Don't forget to free memory when deleting links!

Do	**Don't**
DO understand the difference between `calloc()` and `malloc()`. Most important, remember that `malloc()` doesn't initialize allocated memory—`calloc()` does.	**DON'T** forget to free any memory allocated for links when deleting them.

Summary

Today's lesson covered some of the advanced uses of pointers. As you probably realize by now, pointers are a central part of the C language. C programs that don't use pointers are rare. You saw how to use pointers to pointers and how arrays of pointers can be very useful when dealing with strings. You also learned how C treats multidimensional arrays as arrays of arrays, and you saw how to use pointers with such arrays. You learned how to declare and use pointers to functions, an important and flexible programming tool. Finally, you learned how to implement linked lists, a powerful and flexible data storage method.

This has been a long and involved discussion. Although some of its topics are a bit complicated, they're exciting as well. With today's lesson, you're really getting into some of the sophisticated capabilities of the C language. Power and flexibility are among the main reasons C is such a popular language.

Q&A

Q How many levels deep can I go with pointers to pointers?

A The GNU C compiler does not make any limitation on how many levels deep your pointers may be. It's usually impractical to go more than three levels deep with pointers (pointers to pointers to pointers). Most programs rarely go over two levels.

Q Is there a difference between a pointer to a string and a pointer to an array of characters?

A No. A string can be considered an array of characters.

Q Is it necessary to use the concepts presented today to take advantage of C?

A You can use C without ever using any advanced pointer concepts; however, you won't take advantage of the power that C offers. By using pointer manipulations such as those shown today, you should be able to perform virtually any programming task in a quick, efficient manner.

Q Are there other times when function pointers are useful?

A Yes. Pointers to functions also are used with menus. Based on a value returned from a menu, a pointer is set to an appropriate function that should be called based on the menu choice.

Q What are two major advantages of linked lists?

A One advantage is that the size of a linked list can be increased or decreased while the program is running, and it doesn't have to be predefined when you write the code. A second advantage is that it's easy to keep a linked list in sorted order because elements can easily be added or deleted anywhere in the list.

14

Workshop

The Workshop provides quiz questions to help you solidify your understanding of the material covered and exercises to provide you with experience in using what you've learned. The answers to the quiz and exercises are provided in Appendix C, "Answers."

Quiz

1. Write code that declares a type `float` variable, declares and initializes a pointer to the variable, and declares and initializes a pointer to the pointer.

2. Continuing with the example in question 1, say that you want to use the pointer to a pointer to assign the value `100` to the variable x. What, if anything, is wrong with the following assignment statement?

   ```
   *ppx = 100;
   ```

   If it isn't correct, how should it be written?

3. Assume that you have declared an array as follows:

   ```
   int array[2][3][4];
   ```

   What is the structure of this array, as seen by the C compiler?

4. Continuing with the array declared in question 3, what does the expression `array[0][0]` mean?

5. Again using the array from question 3, which of the following comparisons is true?

   ```
   array[0][0] == &array[0][0][0];
   array[0][1] == array[0][0][1];
   array[0][1] == &array[0][1][0];
   ```

6. Write the prototype for a function that takes an array of pointers to type `char` as its one argument and returns `void`.

7. How would the function that you wrote a prototype for in question 6 know how many elements are in the array of pointers passed to it?

8. What is a pointer to a function?

9. Write a declaration of a pointer to a function that returns a type `char` and takes an array of pointers to type `char` as an argument.

10. You might have answered question 9 with

    ```
    char *ptr(char *x[]);
    ```

    What is wrong with this declaration?

11. What value is added to a `void` pointer when it's incremented?

12. Can a function return a pointer?

13. When defining a data structure to be used in a linked list, what is the one element that must be included?

14. What does it mean if the head pointer is equal to `NULL`?

15. How are single-linked lists connected?

16. What do the following declare?

    a. `int *var1;`

    b. `int var2;`

    c. `int **var3;`

17. What do the following declare?

    a. `int a[3][12];`

    b. `int (*b)[12];`

    c. `int *c[12];`

18. What do the following declare?

    a. `char *z[10];`

    b. `char *y(int field);`

    c. `char (*x)(int field);`

Exercises

1. Write a declaration for a pointer to a function that takes an integer as an argument and returns a type `float` variable.

2. Write a declaration for an array of pointers to functions. The functions should take a character string as a parameter and return an integer. What could such an array be used for?

3. Write a statement to declare an array of 10 pointers to type `char`.

4. **BUG BUSTER:** Is anything wrong with the following code?

```
int x[3][12];
int *ptr[12];
ptr = x;
```

5. Write a structure that is to be used in a single-linked list. This structure should hold your friends' names and addresses.

Because of the many possible solutions, answers are not provided for exercises 6–8.

6. Write a program that declares a 12×12 array of characters. Place an X in every other element. Use a pointer to the array to print the values to the screen in a grid format.

7. Write a program that uses pointers to type `double` variables to accept 10 numbers from the user, sort them, and print them to the screen. (Hint: Refer to Listing 14.10.)

8. Write the prototype for a function that returns an integer. It should take a pointer to a character array as its argument.

14

9. Write a prototype for a function called `numbers` that takes three integer arguments. The integers should be passed by reference.

10. Show how you would call the `numbers` function in exercise 9 with the three integers `int1`, `int2`, and `int3`.

11. **BUG BUSTER:** Is anything wrong with the following?

```
void squared(void *nbr)
{
*nbr *= *nbr;
}
```

12. **BUG BUSTER:** Is anything wrong with the following?

```
float total( int num, ...)
{
int count, total = 0;
for ( count = 0; count < num; count++ )
total += va_arg( arg_ptr, int );
return ( total );
}
```

Because of the many possible solutions, answers are not provided for the following exercises.

13. Write a function that (a) is passed a variable number of strings as arguments; (b) concatenates the strings, in order, into one longer string; and (c) returns a pointer to the new string to the calling program.

14. Write a function that (a) is passed an array of any numeric data type as an argument; (b) finds the largest and smallest values in the array; and (c) returns pointers to these values to the calling program. (Hint: You need some way to tell the function how many elements are in the array.)

15. Write a function that accepts a string and a character. The function should look for the first occurrence of the character in the string and return a pointer to that location.

16. Modify the program in exercise 7.10 to allow the user to specify whether the sort order is ascending or descending.

17. Load the program in Listing 14.14 into the DDD debugger and run the program until you have one or two elements in the linked list. Then turn on the Data Window from the View menu item. To display the value of the `first` pointer, highlight the variable name and right-click it with your mouse. That will bring up a small pop-up menu; then click on `Display first`. Experiment with this feature of DDD; it can be very useful for understanding the operation of linked lists and how to debug them.

WEEK 2

In Review

You have now finished your second week of learning how to program Linux using the C language. By now, you should feel comfortable with the language and you have covered almost all the basic C commands. The following program pulls together many of the topics from the past week.

```
1 : /*-------------------------------------------------*/
2 : /* Program Name:  week2.c                          */
3 : /* program to enter information for up to 100      */
4 : /* people.  The program prints a report            */
5 : /*          based on the numbers entered.          */
6 : /*-------------------------------------------------*/
7 : /*--------------------*/
8 : /* included files     */
9 : /*--------------------*/
10: #include <stdio.h>
11: #include <stdlib.h>
12:
13: /*--------------------*/
14: /* defined constants  */
15: /*--------------------*/
16: #define MAX    100
17: #define YES    1
18: #define NO     0
19:
20: #define FNAME_LEN  20
21: #define LNAME_LEN  24
22: #define PHONE_LEN  10
23:
24: /*--------------------*/
25: /* variables          */
26: /*--------------------*/
27:
```

```
28: struct record
29: {
30:     char fname[FNAME_LEN];          /* first name + NULL   */
31:     char lname[LNAME_LEN];          /* last name + NULL    */
32:     char phone[PHONE_LEN];          /* phone number + NULL */
33:     int  income;                    /* incomes             */
34:     int  month;                     /* birthday month      */
35:     int  day;                       /* birthday day        */
36:     int  year;                      /* birthday year       */
37: };
38:
39: struct record list[MAX];       /* declare actual structure */
40:
41: int last_entry = 0;               /* total number of entries  */
42:
43: /*--------------------*/
44: /* function prototypes */
45: /*--------------------*/
46: void get_data(void);
47: void display_report(void);
48: int  continue_function(void);
49: void clear_kb(void);
50: void new_gets(char*str, int len);
51:
52: /*--------------------*/
53: /* start of program    */
54: /*--------------------*/
55:
56: int main(void)
57: {
58:     int cont = YES;
59:     int ch;
60:
61:     while( cont == YES )
62:     {
63:         printf( "\n");
64:         printf( "\n     MENU");
65:         printf( "\n   ========\n");
66:         printf( "\n1.  Enter names");
67:         printf( "\n2.  Print report");
68:         printf( "\n3.  Quit");
69:         printf( "\n\nEnter Selection ==> ");
70:
71:         ch = getchar();
72:
73:         clear_kb() ; /* remove extra characters from keyboard buffer */
74:
75:         switch( ch )
76:         {
77:             case '1': get_data();
```

```
78:                          break;
79:              case '2': display_report();
80:                          break;
81:              case '3': printf("\n\nThank you for using this program!\n");
82:                          cont = NO;
83:                          break;
84:              default: printf("\n\nInvalid choice, Please select 1 to 3!");
85:                          break;
86:          }
87:       }
88:
89:      return 0;
90: }
91:
92: /*------------------------------------------------------------*
93:  *  Function:  get_data()                                     *
94:  *  Purpose: This function gets the data from the user. It    *
95:  *           continues to get data until either 100 people are *
96:  *           entered, or the user chooses not to continue.    *
97:  *  Returns: nothing                                          *
98:  *  Notes: This allows 0/0/0 to be entered for birthdates in  *
99:  *         case the user is unsure.  It also allows for 31 days *
100:  *         in each month.                                     *
101:  *------------------------------------------------------------*/
102:
103: void get_data(void)
104: {
105:      int cont;
106:
107:      for ( cont = YES; last_entry < MAX && cont == YES;last_entry++ )
108:      {
109:          printf("\n\nEnter information for Person %d.",last_entry+1 );
110:
111:          printf("\n\nEnter first name: ");
112:          new_gets(list[last_entry].fname, FNAME_LEN);
113:
114:          printf("\nEnter last name: ");
115:          new_gets(list[last_entry].lname, LNAME_LEN);
116:
117:          printf("\nEnter phone in 123-4567 format: ");
118:          new_gets(list[last_entry].phone, PHONE_LEN);
119:
120:          printf("\nEnter Yearly Income (whole dollars): ");
121:          scanf("%d", &list[last_entry].income);
122:
123:          printf("\nEnter Birthday:");
124:
125:          do
126:          {
127:              printf("\n\tMonth (0 - 12): ");
```

```
128:                scanf("%d", &list[last_entry].month);
129:            } while ( list[last_entry].month < 0 ¦¦
130:                list[last_entry].month > 12 );
131:
132:        do
133:        {
134:            printf("\n\tDay (0 - 31): ");
135:            scanf("%d", &list[last_entry].day);
136:        } while ( list[last_entry].day <  0 ¦¦
137:            list[last_entry].day > 31 );
138:
139:        do
140:        {
141:            printf("\n\tYear (1800 - 1996): ");
142:            scanf("%d", &list[last_entry].year);
143:        } while (list[last_entry].year != 0 &&
144:            (list[last_entry].year < 1800 ¦¦
145:                list[last_entry].year > 1996 ));
146:
147:        cont = continue_function();
148:    }
149:
150:    if( last_entry == MAX)
151:        printf("\n\nMaximum Number of Names has been entered!\n");
152: }
153:
154: /*-----------------------------------------------------------*
155:  * Function:   display_report()                              *
156:  * Purpose:    This function displays a report to the screen *
157:  * Returns:    nothing                                       *
158:  * Notes:      More information could be displayed.          *
159:  *             Change stdout to stdprn to Print report       *
160:  *-----------------------------------------------------------*/
161:
162: void display_report()
163: {
164:     int   month_total = 0,
165:           grand_total = 0;        /* For totals */
166:     int   x, y;
167:
168:     printf("\n\n");         /* skip a few lines */
169:     printf("\n          REPORT");
170:     printf("\n          ========");
171:
172:     for( x = 0; x <= 12; x++ )   /* for each month, including 0 */
173:     {
174:         month_total = 0;
175:         for( y = 0; y < last_entry; y++ )
176:         {
177:             if( list[y].month == x )
```

```
178:              {
179:                   printf("\n\t%s %s %s %d",list[y].fname,
180:                        list[y].lname, list[y].phone,list[y].income);
181:                   month_total += list[y].income;
182:              }
183:          }
184:          printf("\nTotal for month %d is %d",x,month_total);
185:          grand_total += month_total;
186:      }
187:      printf("\n\nReport totals:");
188:      printf("\nTotal Income is %d", grand_total);
189:      printf("\nAverage Income is %d", grand_total/last_entry );
190:
191:      printf("\n\n* * * End of Report * * *");
192: }
193:
194: /*-------------------------------------------------------------------*
195:  *  Function:  continue_function()                                   *
196:  *  Purpose:   This function asks the user if they wish to continue. *
197:  *  Returns:   YES - if user wishes to continue                      *
198:  *             NO  - if user wishes to quit                          *
199:  *-------------------------------------------------------------------*/
200:
201: int continue_function( void )
202: {
203:      int ch;
204:
205:      printf("\n\nDo you wish to continue? (Y)es/(N)o: ");
206:
207:      clear_kb();
208:      ch = getchar();
209:
210:      while( ch != 'n' && ch != 'N' && ch != 'y' && ch != 'Y' )
211:      {
212:          printf("\n%c is invalid!", ch);
213:          printf("\n\nPlease enter \'N\' to Quit or \'Y\' to Continue: ");
214:
215:          fflush(stdin);      /* clear keyboard buffer (stdin) */
216:          ch = getchar();
217:      }
218:
219:      clear_kb();  /* this function is similar to fflush(stdin) */
220:
221:      if(ch == 'n' || ch == 'N')
222:          return NO;
223:       else
224:          return YES;
225: }
226:
227: /*-------------------------------------------------------------------*
```

```
228:   *  Function:   clear_kb()                                              *
229:   *  Purpose:    This function clears the keyboard of extra characters.  *
230:   *  Returns:    Nothing                                                 *
231:   *  Note:       This function could be replaced by fflush(stdin);       *
232:   *................................................................*/
233: void clear_kb(void)
234: {
235:     char junk[80];
236:     fgets(junk, 80, stdin);
237: }
238:
239: /*................................................................*
240:   *  Function:   new_gets()                                              *
241:   *  Purpose:    This function gets a string from the keyboard using     *
242:   *              fgets() and removes the trailing newline character.     *
243:   *  Returns:    Nothing                                                 *
244:   *................................................................*/
245: void new_gets(char*str, int len)
246: {
247:     int index;
248:
249:     fgets(str, len, stdin);
250:
251:     for(index = 0; index < len; index++)
252:         if (str[index] == '\n')
253:         {
254:             str[index] = 0;
255:             return;
256:         }
257: }
```

It appears that, as you learn more about C, your programs grow larger. Although this program resembles the one presented after your first week of programming in C, it changes a few of the tasks and adds a few more. Like Week 1's review, you can enter up to 100 sets of information. The data entered is information about people. You should notice that this program can display the report while you enter information. With the other program, you couldn't print the report until you finished entering the data.

You should also notice that the addition of a structure used to save the data. The structure is defined on lines 28 through 37. Structures often are used to group similar or related data, as discussed on Day 10, "Structures." This program groups all the data for each person into a structure named record. Much of this data should look familiar; however, a few new items are being tracked. Lines 30 through 32 contain three arrays, or strings, of characters to hold the first name, last name, and phone number. Notice that the length of these strings is declared using the symbolic constants FNAME_LEN, LNAME_LEN, and PHONE_LEN. The actual lengths of these strings will be one fewer than these values because the last space in the array must be left for the null character.

This program demonstrates proper use of variable scope (see Day 11, "Understanding Variable Scope"). Lines 39 and 41 contain two global variables. Line 41 uses an `int` called `last_entry` to hold the index of the number of people who have been entered. This is similar to the variable `ctr` used in Week 1 in Review. The other global variable is `list[MAX]`, an array of record structures. Local variables are used in each function throughout the program. Of special note here are the variables `month_total`, `grand_total`, `x`, and `y` on lines 164 through 166 in the function `display_report()`.

An additional program control statement, the `switch` statement (see Day 12, "Advanced Program Control"), is used on lines 75 through 86. Using a `switch` statement instead of several `if..else` statements makes the code easier to follow. Lines 74 through 84 execute various tasks based on a menu choice. Notice that the `default` statement is also included in case you enter a value that isn't a valid menu option.

Looking at the `get_data()` function, you should notice that there are some additional changes from Week 1 in Review. Lines 111 and 112 prompt for a string and line 112 uses the function `new_gets()` function defined on lines 245 through 257. The `new_gets()` function uses the `fgets()` library function examined on Day 13, "Working with the Screen and Keyboard," to retrieve a string from the keyboard and removes the newline at the end of the string. The `new_gets()` function gets a string and places the value in `list[last_entry].name`. You should remember from Day 10 that this places the first name in `fname`, a member of the structure `list`.

The function `continue_function()` on lines 201 through 225 has been modified. You now respond to the question with `y` or `n` instead of `0` or `1`. This is much more user-friendly. Also notice that the `clear_kb()` function from Listing 14.7 has been added on line 219 to remove any extra characters that the user has entered. Additionally, the `fflush()` function is used to clear any characters that might be left in the buffer.

This program uses what you learned in your first two weeks of teaching yourself C programming for Linux. Week 3 continues to build on these concepts.

WEEK 3

At a Glance

You have now finished your second week of learning to program Linux using the C language. You should feel comfortable with the language now, having touched on the most important areas of the language.

Where You're Going

In the third week, you'll complete your study of C. You'll learn some aspects of C that are new to you, as well as return to some topics from the first and second weeks to cover more advanced techniques.

When you complete the third week, you should have a thorough knowledge of C. Day 15, "Using Disk Files," covers a subject that is necessary for most applications—disk files. You will learn how to use disk files for data storage and retrieval. Day 16, "Manipulating Strings," discusses all the tools C provides for working with text strings. Day 17, "Exploring the C Function Library," provides details on a variety of useful functions in the standard C library. Day 18, "Working with Memory," covers memory management in greater detail. Day 19, "Processes and Signals," covers the starting and stopping processes. Day 20, "Advanced Compiler Use," covers the odds and ends of C, explaining such issues as command-line arguments and preprocessor directives. The final lesson serves as an introduction to graphical user interface programming.

DAY **15**

Using Disk Files

Most of the programs you write will use disk files for one purpose or another: data storage, configuration information, and so on. Today you will learn about

- Relating streams to disk files
- Opening a file
- Writing data to a file
- Reading data from a file
- Closing a file
- Managing disk files
- Using temporary files

Streams and Disk Files

As you learned on Day 13, "Working with the Screen and Keyboard," C performs most of its input and output, including disk files, by means of streams. You saw how to use C's predefined streams that are connected to specific devices such as the keyboard and screen. Disk file streams work essentially the same way. This is one of the advantages of stream input/output—techniques for using one stream can be used with little or no change for other streams. The major difference with disk file streams is that your program must explicitly create a stream associated with a specific disk file.

Types of Disk Files

Unlike some other operating systems, Linux (and the other members of the UNIX family) makes no distinction between text and binary files. The functions used to operate on streams do not need to know whether they are operating on one kind of stream or another. However, as the programmer, you need to decide how you want to operate on streams—whether you want to read the file as lines of text or whether the data is binary and should be read as blocks of memory data. The distinction is important when trying to port code that works correctly on Linux to something such as Microsoft Windows. Unless specifically told otherwise, Windows assumes files are opened in text mode. Porting code from Linux to Windows without taking that factor into account can cause trouble. These traps will be pointed out when we deal with binary files later in today's lesson.

Filenames

Every disk file has a name, and you must use filenames when dealing with disk files. Filenames are stored as strings, just like other text data. Linux and UNIX allow just about any ASCII character to be part of a valid filename. Taking advantage of this fact is probably not very sensible and filenames should be limited to the alphanumeric characters, +, -, underscores, and as many dots as required.

A filename in a C program also can contain path information. The *path* specifies the directory (or folder) where the file is located. If you specify a filename without a path, it will be assumed that the file is located at whatever location Linux currently designates as the default. It's good programming practice to always be aware of paths when dealing with files.

On Linux, a forward-slash character is used to separate directory names in a path. For example, the name

```
/tmp/list.txt
```

refers to the file named list.txt in the directory /tmp.

Opening a File

The process of creating a stream linked to a disk file is called *opening* the file. When you open a file, it becomes available for reading (meaning that data is input from the file to the program), writing (meaning that data from the program is saved in the file), or both. When you're done using the file, you must close it. Closing a file is covered later today.

To open a file, you use the `fopen()` library function. The prototype of `fopen()` is located in stdio.h and reads as follows:

```
FILE *fopen(const char *filename, const char *mode);
```

This prototype tells you that `fopen()` returns a pointer to type `FILE`, which is a structure declared in stdio.h. The members of the `FILE` structure are used by the program in the various file access operations, and it is not a good idea to try to modify them. However, for each file that you want to open, you must declare a pointer to type `FILE`. When you call `fopen()`, that function creates an instance of the `FILE` structure and returns a pointer to that structure. You use this pointer in all subsequent operations on the file. If `fopen()` fails, it returns `NULL`. Such a failure can be caused, for example, by a hardware error or by trying to open a file with an invalid path.

The argument `filename` is the name of the file to be opened. As noted earlier, `filename` can—and should—contain a path specification. The `filename` argument can be a literal string enclosed in double quotation marks or a pointer to a string variable.

The argument `mode` specifies the mode in which to open the file. In this context, `mode` controls whether the file is being opened for reading, writing, or both. The permitted values for `mode` are listed in Table 15.1.

TABLE 15.1. Values of *mode* for the `fopen()` function.

mode	Meaning
r	Opens the file for reading. If the file doesn't exist, `fopen()` returns `NULL`.
w	Opens the file for writing. If a file of the specified name doesn't exist, it is created. If a file of the specified name does exist, it is deleted without warning, and a new, empty file is created.
a	Opens the file for appending. If a file of the specified name doesn't exist, it is created. If the file does exist, new data is appended to the end of the file.
r+	Opens the file for reading and writing. If a file of the specified name doesn't exist, it is created. If the file does exist, new data is added to the beginning of the file, overwriting existing data.
w+	Opens the file for reading and writing. If a file of the specified name doesn't exist, it is created. If the file does exist, it is overwritten.
a+	Opens a file for reading and appending. If a file of the specified name doesn't exist, it is created. If the file does exist, new data is appended to the end of the file.

> **Caution**
>
> If your programs are only ever going to run on Linux, the list of modes in Table 15.1 is all you'll ever need. If, however, you want to write code that runs on Linux and Windows, you need to be aware of the following.
>
> - Windows makes a distinction between text and binary files.
> - Windows defaults to text mode operation.
> - If you want to write a program that deals with non-text data and also runs on Windows, you must add a b to the mode string. The b is ignored by Linux and other systems that don't make a distinction between text and binary files.

Remember that fopen() returns NULL if an error occurs. Error conditions that can cause a return value of NULL include the following:

- Using an invalid filename
- Trying to open a file on a disk that isn't ready (the drive door isn't closed or the disk isn't formatted, for example)
- Trying to open a file in a nonexistent directory or on a nonexistent disk drive
- Trying to open a nonexistent file in mode r

Whenever you use fopen(), you need to test for the occurrence of an error. If an error occurs, the extern variable errno will be set to an appropriate value and perror() may then be used to print an error message explaining what happened. The function perror() is defined in stdio.h and is covered more fully in Day 17, "Exploring the C Function Library."

Listing 15.1 demonstrates fopen().

LISTING 15.1. Using fopen() to open disk files in various modes.

```
1 :  /* Demonstrates the fopen() function. */
2 : #include <stdlib.h>
3 : #include <stdio.h>
4 :
5 : int main(void)
6 : {
7 :     FILE *fp;
8 :     char ch, filename[40], mode[5];
9 :
10:     while (1)
11:     {
12:
13:         /* Input filename and mode. */
14:
```

15

```
15:        printf("\nEnter a filename: ");
16:        fgets(filename,40,stdin);
17:        filename [strlen(filename)-1] = 0 ;
18:        printf("\nEnter a mode (max 3 characters): ");
19:        fgets(mode,5,stdin);
20:        mode [strlen(mode)-1] = 0 ;
21:
22:        /* Try to open the file. */
23:
24:        if ( (fp = fopen( filename, mode )) != NULL )
25:        {
26:            printf("\nSuccessful opening %s in mode %s.\n",
27:                    filename, mode);
28:            fclose(fp);
29:            puts("Enter x to exit, any other to continue.");
30:            if ( (ch = getc(stdin)) == 'x')
31:                break;
32:            else
33:                continue;
34:        }
35:        else
36:        {
37:            fprintf(stderr, "\nError opening file %s in mode %s.\n",
38:                    filename, mode);
39:            perror("list1501");
40:            puts("Enter x to exit, any other to try again.");
41:            if ( (ch = getc(stdin)) == 'x')
42:                break;
43:            else
44:                continue;
45:        }
46:    }
47:    return 0 ;
48: }
```

INPUT/
OUTPUT

Enter a filename: **junk.txt**

Enter a mode (max 3 characters): **w**

Successful opening junk.txt in mode w.
Enter x to exit, any other to continue.
j

Enter a filename: **morejunk.txt**

Enter a mode (max 3 characters): **r**

Error opening morejunk.txt in mode r.
list1501: No such file or directory
Enter x to exit, any other to try again.
x

ANALYSIS   This program prompts you for both the filename and the mode specifier on lines 15 through 20. Lines 17 and 20 remove the newline at the end of each string by overwriting it with a null character. After getting a name, line 24 attempts to open the file and assign its file pointer to fp. As an example of good programming practice, the if statement on line 24 checks to see that the opened file's pointer isn't equal to NULL. If fp isn't equal to NULL, a message is printed stating that the open was successful and that the user can continue. If the file pointer is NULL, the else condition of the if loop executes. The else condition on lines 35 through 45 prints a message stating that there is a problem. It then prompts the user to determine whether the program should continue.

You can experiment with different names and modes to see which ones give you an error. In the output just shown, you can see that trying to open morejunk.txt in mode r resulted in an error because the file didn't exist on the disk. If an error occurs, you're given the choice of entering the information again or quitting the program. You might also like to see what characters are acceptable in a filename. To delete files with problematic characters in them, you should enclose the filename in quotation marks when using the rm (delete) command.

Writing and Reading File Data

A program that uses a disk file can write data to a file, read data from a file, or a combination of the two. You can write data to a disk file in three ways:

- You can use formatted output to save formatted text data to a file. The primary use of formatted output is to create files containing text and numeric data to be read by other programs, such as spreadsheets or databases.
- You can use character output to save single characters or lines of characters to a file.
- You can use direct output to save the contents of a section of memory directly to a disk file. This method is for binary files only.

When you want to read data from a file, you have the same three options: formatted input, character input, or direct input. The type of input you use in a particular case depends almost entirely on the nature of the file being read. Generally, you will read data in the same mode it was saved in, but that is not a requirement.

Formatted File Input and Output

Formatted file input/output (I/O) deals with text and numeric data that is formatted in a specific way. It is directly analogous to formatted keyboard input and screen output done with the printf() and scanf() functions, as described on Day 13. I'll discuss formatted file output first, followed by input.

Formatted File Output

Formatted file output is done with the library function fprintf(). The prototype of fprintf() is in the header file stdio.h, and it reads as follows:

```
int fprintf(FILE *fp, char *fmt, ...);
```

The first argument is a pointer to type FILE. To write data to a particular disk file, you pass the pointer that was returned when you opened the file with fopen().

The second argument is the format string. You learned about format strings in the discussion of printf() on Day 13. The format string used by fprintf() follows exactly the same rules as printf(). Refer to Day 13 for details.

The final argument is .... What does that mean? In a function prototype, ellipses represent a variable number of arguments. In other words, in addition to the file pointer and the format string arguments, fprintf() takes zero, one, or more additional arguments. This is just like printf(). These arguments are the names of the variables to be output to the specified stream.

Remember, fprintf() works just like printf(), except that it sends its output to the stream specified in the argument list. In fact, if you specify a stream argument of stdout, fprintf() is identical to printf().

Listing 15.2 demonstrates the use of fprintf().

LISTING 15.2. The equivalence of fprintf() formatted output to both a file and to stdout.

```
 1 : /* Demonstrates the fprintf() function. */
 2 :
 3 : #include <stdio.h>
 4 : #include <stdlib.h>
 5 : void clear_kb(void);
 6 :
 7 : int main(void)
 8 : {
 9 :     FILE *fp;
10:     float data[5];
11:     int count;
12:     char filename[20];
13:
14:     puts("Enter 5 floating point numerical values.");
15:
16:     for (count = 0; count < 5; count++)
17:         scanf("%f", &data[count]);
18:
19:     /* Get the filename and open the file. First clear stdin */
20:     /* of any extra characters. */
```

continues

LISTING 15.2. continued

```
21:
22:        clear_kb();
23:
24:        puts("Enter a name for the file.");
25:        scanf("%s", filename);
26:
27:        if ( (fp = fopen(filename, "w")) == NULL)
28:        {
29:            fprintf(stderr, "Error opening file %s.\n", filename);
30:            exit(1);
31:        }
32:
33:        /* Write the numerical data to the file and to stdout. */
34:
35:        for (count = 0; count < 5; count++)
36:        {
37:            fprintf(fp, "data[%d] = %f\n", count, data[count]);
38:            fprintf(stdout, "data[%d] = %f\n", count, data[count]);
39:        }
40:        fclose(fp);
41:        printf("\n");
42:        return(0);
43: }
44:
45: void clear_kb(void)
46: /* Clears stdin of any waiting characters. */
47: {
48:        char junk[80];
49:        fgets(junk,80,stdin);
50: }
```

INPUT/
OUTPUT

```
Enter 5 floating-point numerical values.
3.14159
9.99
1.50
3.
1000.0001
Enter a name for the file.
numbers.txt

data[0] = 3.141590
data[1] = 9.990000
data[2] = 1.500000
data[3] = 3.000000
data[4] = 1000.000122
```

ANALYSIS You might wonder why the program displays 1000.000122 when the value you entered was 1000.0001. This isn't an error in the program. It's a normal consequence of the way C stores numbers internally. Some floating-point values can't be stored exactly, so minor inaccuracies such as this one sometimes result.

This program uses `fprintf()` on lines 37 and 38 to send some formatted text and numeric data to `stdout` and to the disk file whose name you specified. The only difference between the two lines is the first argument—that is, the stream to which the data is sent. After running the program, use your editor to look at the contents of the file numbers.txt (or whatever name you assigned to it), which will be in the same directory as the program files. You'll see that the text in the file is an exact copy of the text that was displayed onscreen.

Note that Listing 15.2 uses the `clear_kb()` function discussed on Day 13. This is necessary to remove from `stdin` any extra characters that might be left over from the call to `scanf()`. If you don't clear `stdin`, these extra characters (specifically, the newline) are read by the `fgets()` that inputs the filename, and the result is a file creation error.

Formatted File Input

For formatted file input, use the `fscanf()` library function, which is used like `scanf()` (refer to Day 13), except that input comes from a specified stream instead of from `stdin`. The prototype for `fscanf()` is

```
int fscanf(FILE *fp, const char *fmt, ...);
```

The argument `fp` is the pointer to type `FILE` returned by `fopen()`, and `fmt` is a pointer to the format string that specifies how `fscanf()` is to read the input. The components of the format string are the same as for `scanf()`. Finally, the ellipses (...) indicate one or more additional arguments: the addresses of the variables where `fscanf()` is to assign the input.

Before getting started with `fscanf()`, you might want to review the section on `scanf()` on Day 13. The function `fscanf()` works exactly the same as `scanf()`, except that characters are taken from the specified stream rather than from `stdin`.

To demonstrate `fscanf()`, you need a text file containing some numbers or strings in a format that can be read by the function. Use your editor to create a file named input.txt, and enter five floating-point numbers with some space between them (spaces or newlines). For example, your file might look like this:

```
123.45     87.001
100.02
0.00456    1.0005
```

Now, compile and run Listing 15.3.

LISTING 15.3. Using `fscanf()` to readformatted data from a disk file.

```
1: /* Reading formatted file data with fscanf(). */
2: #include <stdlib.h>
3: #include <stdio.h>
4:
5: int main(void)
6: {
7:     float f1, f2, f3, f4, f5;
8:     FILE *fp;
9:
10:     if ( (fp = fopen("input.txt", "r")) == NULL)
11:     {
12:         fprintf(stderr, "Error opening file.\n");
13:         exit(1);
14:     }
15:
16:     fscanf(fp, "%f %f %f %f %f", &f1, &f2, &f3, &f4, &f5);
17:     printf("The values are %f, %f, %f, %f, and %f\n.",
18:             f1, f2, f3, f4, f5);
19:
20:     fclose(fp);
21:     return(0);
22: }
```

OUTPUT   The values are 123.449997, 87.000999, 100.019997, 0.004560, and
1.000500.

Note   The precision of the values might cause some numbers to not display as the exact values you entered. For example, `100.02` might appear as `100.01999`.

ANALYSIS   This program reads the five values from the file you created and then displays them onscreen. The `fopen()` call on line 10 opens the file for read mode. It also checks to see that the file opened correctly. If the file wasn't opened, an error message is displayed on line 12, and the program exits (line 13). Line 16 demonstrates the use of the `fscanf()` function. With the exception of the first parameter, `fscanf()` is identical to `scanf()`, which you have been using throughout this book. The first parameter points to the file that you want the program to read. You can do further experiments with `fscanf()`, creating input files with your programming editor and seeing how `fscanf()` reads the data.

Character Input and Output

When used with disk files, the term *character I/O* refers to single characters as well as lines of characters. Remember, a line is a sequence of zero or more characters terminated by the newline character. Use character I/O with text-mode files. The following sections describe character input/output functions, and then you'll see a demonstration program.

Character Input

There are three character input functions: getc() and fgetc() for single characters, and fgets() for lines.

The getc() and fgetc() Functions

The functions getc() and fgetc() are identical and can be used interchangeably. They input a single character from the specified stream. Here is the prototype of getc(), which is in stdio.h:

```
int getc(FILE *fp);
```

The argument fp is the pointer returned by fopen() when the file was opened. The function returns the character that was input or EOF on error.

You've seen getc() used in earlier programs to input a character from the keyboard. This is another example of the flexibility of C's streams—the same function can be used for keyboard or file input.

If getc() and fgetc() return a single character, why are they prototyped to return a type int? The reason is that when reading files, you must be able to read in the end-of-file marker; on some systems, the end-of-file marker isn't a type char, but a type int. You'll see getc() in action later in Listing 15.10.

The fgets() Function

To read a line of characters from a file, use the fgets() library function. The prototype is

```
char *fgets(char *str, int n, FILE *fp);
```

The argument str is a pointer to a buffer in which the input is to be stored. n is the maximum number of characters to be input. fp is the pointer to type FILE that was returned by fopen() when the file was opened.

When called, fgets() reads characters from fp into memory, starting at the location pointed to by str. Characters are read until a newline is encountered or until n-1 characters have been read, whichever occurs first. By setting n equal to the number of bytes allocated for the buffer str, you prevent input from overwriting memory beyond the allocated space. (The n-1 is to allow space for the terminating \0 that fgets() adds to the end of the string.) If successful, fgets() returns str. Two types of errors can occur, as indicated by the return value of NULL:

- If a read error or EOF is encountered before any characters have been assigned to str, NULL is returned and the memory pointed to by str is unchanged.

- If a read error or EOF is encountered after one or more characters have been assigned to str, NULL is returned and the memory pointed to by str contains garbage.

You can see that fgets() doesn't necessarily input an entire line (that is, everything up to the next newline character). If n-1 characters are read before a newline is encountered, fgets() stops. The next read operation from the file starts where the last one leaves off. To be sure that fgets() reads in entire strings, stopping only at newlines, be sure the size of your input buffer and the corresponding value of n passed to fgets() are large enough.

Character Output

You need to know about two character output functions: putc() and fputs().

The putc() Function

The library function putc() writes a single character to a specified stream. Its prototype, in stdio.h, reads

```
int putc(int ch, FILE *fp);
```

The argument ch is the character to output. As with other character functions, it is formally called a type int, but only the lower-order byte is used. The argument fp is the pointer associated with the file (the pointer returned by fopen() when the file was opened). The function putc() returns the character just written (if successful) or EOF (if an error occurs). The symbolic constant EOF is defined in stdio.h, and it has the value -1. Because no real character has that numeric value, EOF can be used as an error indicator (with text-mode files only).

The fputs() Function

To write a line of characters to a stream, use the library function fputs(). This function works just like puts(), covered on Day 13. The only difference is that with fputs(), you can specify the output stream. Also, fputs() doesn't add a newline to the end of the string; if you want it, you must explicitly include it. Its prototype in stdio.h is

```
char fputs(char *str, FILE *fp);
```

The argument str is a pointer to the null-terminated string to be written, and fp is the pointer to type FILE returned by fopen() when the file was opened. The string pointed to by str is written to the file, minus its terminating \0. The function fputs() returns a nonnegative value if successful or EOF on error.

Direct File Input and Output

You use direct file I/O most often when you save data to be read later by the same or a different C program. Direct file I/O is normally used only with binary-mode files. With direct output, blocks of data are written from memory to disk. Direct file input reverses the process: A block of data is read from a disk file into memory. For example, a single direct-output function call can write an entire array of type `double` to disk, and a single direct-input function call can read the entire array from disk back into memory. The direct file I/O functions are `fread()` and `fwrite()`.

The `fwrite()` Function

The `fwrite()` library function writes a block of data from memory to a file. `fwrite()` is usually used to write binary data and its prototype, in stdio.h, is

```
int fwrite(void *buf, int size, int count, FILE *fp);
```

The argument *buf* is a pointer to the region of memory holding the data to be written to the file. The pointer type is `void`; it can be a pointer to anything.

The argument *size* specifies the size, in bytes, of the individual data items, and *count* specifies the number of items to be written. For example, if you wanted to save a 100-element integer array, *size* would be 2 (because each `int` occupies 2 bytes), and *count* would be 100 (because the array contains 100 elements). To obtain the *size* argument, you can use the `sizeof()` operator.

The argument `fp` is, of course, the pointer to type `FILE`, returned by `fopen()` when the file was opened. The `fwrite()` function returns the number of items written on success; if the value returned is less than `count`, it means that an error has occurred. To check for errors, you usually program `fwrite()` as follows:

```
if( (fwrite(buf, size, count, fp)) != count)
fprintf(stderr, "Error writing to file.");
```

Here are some examples of using `fwrite()`. To write a single type `double` variable x to a file, use the following:

```
fwrite(&x, sizeof(double), 1, fp);
```

To write an array `data[]` of 50 structures of type `address` to a file, you have two choices:

```
fwrite(data, sizeof(address), 50, fp);
```

```
fwrite(data, sizeof(data), 1, fp);
```

The first method writes the array as 50 elements, with each element having the size of a single type `address` structure. The second method treats the array as a single element. The two methods accomplish exactly the same thing.

The following section explains `fread()` and then presents a program demonstrating `fread()` and `fwrite()`.

The `fread()` Function

The `fread()` library function reads a block of data from a file into memory. `fread()` is usually used to read binary data and its prototype in stdio.h is

```
int fread(void *buf, int size, int count, FILE *fp);
```

The argument *buf* is a pointer to the region of memory that receives the data read from the file. As with `fwrite()`, the pointer type is `void`.

The argument *size* specifies the size, in bytes, of the individual data items being read, and *count* specifies the number of items to read. Note how these arguments parallel the arguments used by `fwrite()`. Again, the `sizeof()` operator is typically used to provide the *size* argument. The argument fp is (as always) the pointer to type `FILE` that was returned by `fopen()` when the file was opened. The `fread()` function returns the number of items read; this can be less than *count* if end-of-file was reached or an error occurred.

Listing 15.4 demonstrates the use of `fwrite()` and `fread()`.

LISTING 15.4. Using `fwrite()` and `fread()` for direct file access.

```
 1: /* Direct file I/O with fwrite() and fread(). */
 2: #include <stdlib.h>
 3: #include <stdio.h>
 4:
 5: #define SIZE 20
 6:
 7: int main(void)
 8: {
 9:     int count, array1[SIZE], array2[SIZE];
10:     FILE *fp;
11:
12:     /* Initialize array1[]. */
13:
14:     for (count = 0; count < SIZE; count++)
15:         array1[count] = 2 * count;
16:
17:     /* Open the file, making sure to our. */
18:     /* code will also run on Windows.     */
19:     if ( (fp = fopen("direct.txt", "wb")) == NULL)
20:     {
21:         fprintf(stderr, "Error opening file.\n");
22:         exit(1);
23:     }
24:     /* Save array1[] to the file. */
25:
26:     if (fwrite(array1, sizeof(int), SIZE, fp) != SIZE)
27:     {
28:         fprintf(stderr, "Error writing to file.");
29:         exit(1);
```

15

```
30:    }
31:
32:    fclose(fp);
33:
34:    /* Now open the same file for reading in binary mode. */
35:
36:    if ( (fp = fopen("direct.txt", "rb")) == NULL)
37:    {
38:        fprintf(stderr, "Error opening file.");
39:        exit(1);
40:    }
41:
42:    /* Read the data into array2[]. */
43:
44:    if (fread(array2, sizeof(int), SIZE, fp) != SIZE)
45:    {
46:        fprintf(stderr, "Error reading file.");
47:        exit(1);
48:    }
49:
50:    fclose(fp);
51:
52:    /* Now display both arrays to show they're the same. */
53:
54:    for (count = 0; count < SIZE; count++)
55:        printf("%d\t%d\n", array1[count], array2[count]);
56:    return(0);
57: }
```

OUTPUT

```
0       0
2       2
4       4
6       6
8       8
10      10
12      12
14      14
16      16
18      18
20      20
22      22
24      24
26      26
28      28
30      30
32      32
34      34
36      36
38      38
```

ANALYSIS Listing 15.4 demonstrates the use of the `fwrite()` and `fread()` functions. This program initializes an array on lines 14 and 15. It then uses `fwrite()` on line 26 to save the array to disk. The program uses `fread()` on line 44 to read the data into a different array. Finally, it displays both arrays onscreen to show that they now hold the same data (lines 54 and 55).

When you save data with `fwrite()`, not much can go wrong except some type of disk error. With `fread()`, be careful, however. As far as `fread()` is concerned, the data on the disk is just a sequence of bytes. The function has no way of knowing what the data represents. For example, a block of 100 bytes could be 100 `char` variables, 50 `short` variables, 25 `int` variables, or 25 `float` variables. If you ask `fread()` to read that block into memory, it obediently does so. However, if the block is saved from an array of type `int` and you retrieve it into an array of type `float`, no error occurs, but you get strange results. When writing programs, you must be sure that `fread()` is used properly, reading data into the appropriate types of variables and arrays. Notice that in Listing 15.4, all calls to `fopen()`, `fwrite()`, and `fread()` are checked to ensure that they worked correctly.

File Buffering: Closing and Flushing Files

When you're finished using a file, you should close it using the `fclose()` function. You saw `fclose()` used in programs presented earlier today. Its prototype is

```
int fclose(FILE *fp);
```

The argument `fp` is the `FILE` pointer associated with the stream; `fclose()` returns `0` on success or `-1` on error. When you close a file, the file's buffer is flushed (written to the file).

When a program terminates (either by reaching the end of `main()` or by executing the `exit()` function), all streams are automatically flushed and closed. However, it's a good idea to close streams explicitly—particularly those linked to disk files—as soon as you're finished with them. The reason has to do with stream buffers.

When you create a stream linked to a disk file, a buffer is automatically created and associated with the stream. A buffer is a block of memory used for temporary storage of data being written to and read from the file. Buffers are needed because disk drives are block-oriented devices, which means they operate most efficiently when data is read and written in blocks of a certain size. The size of the ideal block differs, depending on the specific hardware in use. It's typically on the order of a few hundred to a thousand bytes. You don't need to be concerned about the exact block size, however.

The buffer associated with a file stream serves as an interface between the stream (which is character-oriented) and the disk hardware (which is block-oriented). As your program writes data to the stream, the data is saved in the buffer until the buffer is full, and then the entire contents of the buffer are written, as a block, to the disk. An analogous process occurs when reading data from a disk file. The creation and operation of the buffer is handled by the operating system and is entirely automatic; you don't have to be concerned with it. (C does offer some functions for buffer manipulation, but they are beyond the scope of this book.)

In practical terms, this buffer operation means that during program execution, data that your program wrote to the disk might still be in the buffer, not on the disk. If your program hangs up, if there's a power failure, or if some other problem occurs, the data still in the buffer might be lost, and you won't know what's contained in the disk file.

You can flush a stream's buffers without closing it by using the `fflush()` library functions. Use `fflush()` when you want a file's buffer to be written to disk while you are still using the file. Use `flushall()` to flush the buffers of all open streams. The prototype of `fflush()` is as follows:

```
int fflush(FILE *fp);
```

The argument `fp` is the `FILE` pointer returned by `fopen()` when the file was opened. If a file was opened for writing, `fflush()` writes its buffer to disk. If the file was opened for reading, the buffer is cleared. The function `fflush()` returns 0 on success or `EOF` if an error occurred.

Do	Don't
DO open a file before trying to read or write to it.	**DON'T** assume that a file access is okay. Always check after doing a read, write, or open to ensure that the function worked.
DO use the `sizeof()` operator with the `fwrite()` and `fread()` functions.	
DO close all files that you've opened.	
DO use b as part of the mode string if you are opening or closing binary files and you care about portability to Windows.	

Sequential Versus Random File Access

Every open file has a file position indicator associated with it. The position indicator specifies where read and write operations take place in the file. The position is always given in terms of bytes from the beginning of the file. When a new file is opened, the position indicator is always at the beginning of the file, position 0. (Because the file is new and has a length of 0, there's no other location to indicate.) When an existing file is opened, the position indicator is at the end of the file if the file is opened in append mode, or at the beginning of the file if the file is opened in any other mode.

The file input/output functions, covered earlier today, make use of the position indicator, although the manipulations go on behind the scenes. Writing and reading operations occur at the location of the position indicator and update the position indicator as well. For example, if you open a file for reading, and 10 bytes are read, you input the first 10 bytes in the file (the bytes at positions 0 through 9). After the read operation, the position indicator is at position 10, and the next read operation begins there. Thus, if you want to read all the data in a file sequentially or write data to a file sequentially, you don't need to be concerned about the position indicator. The stream I/O functions take care of it automatically.

When you need more control, use the C library functions that enable you to determine and change the value of the file position indicator. By controlling the position indicator, you can perform random file access. Here, *random* means that you can read data from or write data to any position in a file without reading or writing all the preceding data.

The `ftell()` and `rewind()` Functions

To set the position indicator to the beginning of the file, use the library function `rewind()`. Its prototype, in stdio.h, is

```
void rewind(FILE *fp);
```

The argument `fp` is the `FILE` pointer associated with the stream. After `rewind()` is called, the file's position indicator is set to the beginning of the file (byte 0). Use `rewind()` if you've read some data from a file and you want to start reading from the beginning of the file again without closing and reopening the file.

To determine the value of a file's position indicator, use `ftell()`. This function's prototype, located in stdio.h, reads

```
long ftell(FILE *fp);
```

The argument `fp` is the `FILE` pointer returned by `fopen()` when the file was opened. The function `ftell()` returns a type `long` that gives the current file position in bytes from the start of the file (the first byte is at position 0). If an error occurs, `ftell()` returns `-1L` (a type `long` `-1`).

To get a feel for the operation of `rewind()` and `ftell()`, look at Listing 15.5.

LISTING 15.5. Using `ftell()` and `rewind()`.

```
1: /* Demonstrates ftell() and rewind(). */
2: #include <stdlib.h>
3: #include <stdio.h>
4:
5: #define BUFLEN 6
6:
7: char msg[] = "abcdefghijklmnopqrstuvwxyz";
8:
9: int main(void)
10: {
11:     FILE *fp;
12:     char buf[BUFLEN];
13:
14:     if ( (fp = fopen("text.txt", "w")) == NULL)
15:     {
16:         fprintf(stderr, "Error opening file.");
17:         exit(1);
18:     }
19:
20:     if (fputs(msg, fp) == EOF)
21:     {
22:         fprintf(stderr, "Error writing to file.");
23:         exit(1);
24:     }
25:
26:     fclose(fp);
27:
28:     /* Now open the file for reading. */
29:
30:     if ( (fp = fopen("text.txt", "r")) == NULL)
31:     {
32:         fprintf(stderr, "Error opening file.");
33:         exit(1);
34:     }
35:     printf("\nImmediately after opening, position = %ld", ftell(fp));
36:
37:     /* Read in 5 characters. */
38:
39:     fgets(buf, BUFLEN, fp);
40:     printf("\nAfter reading in %s, position = %ld", buf, ftell(fp));
41:
42:     /* Read in the next 5 characters. */
43:
44:     fgets(buf, BUFLEN, fp);
45:     printf("\n\nThe next 5 characters are %s, and position now = %ld",
46:             buf, ftell(fp));
47:
48:     /* Rewind the stream. */
49:
```

continues

LISTING 15.5. continued

```
50:      rewind(fp);
51:
52:      printf("\n\nAfter rewinding, the position is back at %ld",
53:              ftell(fp));
54:
55:      /* Read in 5 characters. */
56:
57:      fgets(buf, BUFLEN, fp);
58:      printf("\nand reading starts at the beginning again: %s\n", buf);
59:      fclose(fp);
60:      return(0);
61: }
```

OUTPUT

```
Immediately after opening, position = 0
After reading in abcde, position = 5

The next 5 characters are fghij, and position now = 10

After rewinding, the position is back at 0
and reading starts at the beginning again: abcde
```

ANALYSIS This program writes a string, msg, to a file called text.txt. The message consists of the 26 letters of the alphabet, in order. Lines 14 through 18 open text.txt for writing and test to ensure that the file was opened successfully. Lines 20 through 24 write msg to the file using fputs() and check to ensure that the write was successful. Line 26 closes the file with fclose(), completing the process of creating a file for the rest of the program to use.

Lines 30 through 34 open the file again, only this time for reading. Line 35 prints the return value of ftell(). Notice that this position is at the beginning of the file. Line 39 performs a gets() to read five characters. The five characters and the new file position are printed on line 40. Notice that ftell() returns the correct offset. Line 50 calls rewind() to put the pointer back at the beginning of the file before line 52 prints the file position again. This should confirm for you that rewind() resets the position. An additional read on line 57 further confirms that the program is indeed back at the beginning of the file. Line 59 closes the file before ending the program.

The fseek() Function

More precise control over a stream's position indicator is possible with the fseek() library function. By using fseek(), you can set the position indicator anywhere in the file. The function prototype, in stdio.h, is

```
int fseek(FILE *fp, long offset, int origin);
```

The argument fp is the FILE pointer associated with the file. The distance that the position indicator is to be moved is given by *offset* in bytes. The argument *origin* specifies the move's relative starting point. There can be three values for *origin*, with symbolic constants defined in io.h, as shown in Table 15.2.

TABLE 15.2. Possible origin values for fseek().

Constant	Value	Description
SEEK_SET	0	Moves the indicator *offset* bytes from the beginning of the file
SEEK_CUR	1	Moves the indicator *offset* bytes from its current position
SEEK_END	2	Moves the indicator *offset* bytes from the end of the file

The function fseek() returns 0 if the indicator was successfully moved or nonzero if an error occurred. Listing 15.6 uses fseek() for random file access.

LISTING 15.6. Random file access with fseek().

```
1: /* Random access with fseek(). */
2:
3:  #include <stdlib.h>
4: #include <stdio.h>
5:
6: #define MAX 50
7:
8: int main(void)
9: {
10:     FILE *fp;
11:     int data, count, array[MAX];
12:     long offset;
13:
14:     /* Initialize the array. */
15:
16:     for (count = 0; count < MAX; count++)
17:         array[count] = count * 10;
18:
19:     /* Open a binary file for writing. */
20:
21:     if ( (fp = fopen("random.dat", "wb")) == NULL)
22:     {
23:         fprintf(stderr, "\nError opening file.");
24:         exit(1);
25:     }
26:
27:     /* Write the array to the file, then close it. */
28:
29:     if ( (fwrite(array, sizeof(int), MAX, fp)) != MAX)
```

continues

LISTING **15.6**. continued

```
30:      {
31:          fprintf(stderr, "\nError writing data to file.");
32:          exit(1);
33:      }
34:
35:      fclose(fp);
36:
37:      /* Open the file for reading. */
38:
39:      if ( (fp = fopen("random.dat", "rb")) == NULL)
40:      {
41:          fprintf(stderr, "\nError opening file.");
42:          exit(1);
43:      }
44:
45:      /* Ask user which element to read. Input the element */
46:      /* and display it, quitting when -1 is entered. */
47:
48:      while (1)
49:      {
50:          printf("\nEnter element to read, 0-%d, -1 to quit: ",MAX-1);
51:          scanf("%ld", &offset);
52:
53:          if (offset < 0)
54:              break;
55:          else if (offset > MAX-1)
56:              continue;
57:
58:          /* Move the position indicator to the specified element. */
59:
60:          if ( (fseek(fp, (offset*sizeof(int)), SEEK_SET)) != 0)
61:          {
62:              fprintf(stderr, "\nError using fseek().");
63:              exit(1);
64:          }
65:
66:          /* Read in a single integer. */
67:
68:          fread(&data, sizeof(int), 1, fp);
69:
70:          printf("\nElement %ld has value %d.", offset, data);
71:      }
72:
73:      fclose(fp);
74:      return(0);
75: }
```

**INPUT/
OUTPUT**

```
Enter element to read, 0-49, -1 to quit: 5

Element 5 has value 50.
Enter element to read, 0-49, -1 to quit: 6

Element 6 has value 60.
Enter element to read, 0-49, -1 to quit: 49

Element 49 has value 490.
Enter element to read, 0-49, -1 to quit: 1

Element 1 has value 10.
Enter element to read, 0-49, -1 to quit: 0

Element 0 has value 0.
Enter element to read, 0-49, -1 to quit: -1
```

ANALYSIS Lines 14 through 35 are similar to Listing 15.5. Lines 16 and 17 initialize an array called data with 50 type int values. The value stored in each array element is equal to 10 times the index. Then the array is written to a binary file called random.dat.

Line 39 reopens the file in binary read mode before going into an infinite while loop. The while loop prompts the user to enter the number of the array element that he wants to read. Notice that lines 53 through 56 check that the entered element is within the range of the file. Does C let you read an element that is beyond the end of the file? Yes. Like going beyond the end of an array with values, C also lets you read beyond the end of a file. If you do read beyond the end (or before the beginning), your results are unpredictable. It's always best to check what you're doing (as lines 53 through 56 do in this listing).

After you have input the element to find, line 60 jumps to the appropriate offset with a call to fseek(). Because SEEK_SET is being used, the seek is done from the beginning of the file. Notice that the distance into the file is not just *offset*, but *offset* multiplied by the size of the elements being read. Line 68 then reads the value, and line 70 prints it.

Detecting the End of a File

Sometimes you know exactly how long a file is, so there's no need to be able to detect the file's end. For example, if you used fwrite() to save a 100-element integer array, you know the file is 400 bytes long. At other times, however, you don't know how long the file is, but you still want to read data from the file, starting at the beginning and proceeding to the end. There are two ways to detect end-of-file.

When reading from a text file character-by-character, you can look for the end-of-file character. The symbolic constant EOF is defined in stdio.h as -1, a value never used by a real character. When a character input function reads EOF from a text-mode stream, you can be sure that you've reached the end of the file. For example, you could write the following:

```
while ( (c = fgetc( fp )) != EOF )
```

With a binary file, you can't detect the end-of-file by looking for -1 because a byte of data from a binary stream could have that value, which would result in premature end of input. Instead, you can use the library function feof():

```
int feof(FILE *fp);
```

Listing 15.7 demonstrates the use of feof(). When you're prompted for a filename, enter the name of any text file—one of your C source files, for example, or a header file such as stdio.h. Just be sure that the file is in the current directory, or else enter a path as part of the filename. The program reads the file one line at a time, displaying each line on stdout, until feof() detects end-of-file.

The argument fp is the FILE pointer returned by fopen() when the file was opened. The function feof() returns 0 if the end of file fp hasn't been reached, or a nonzero value if end-of-file has been reached. If a call to feof() detects end-of-file, no further read operations are permitted until a rewind() has been done, fseek() is called, or the file is closed and reopened.

LISTING 15.7. Using feof() to detect the end of a file.

```
1: /* Detecting end-of-file. */
2: #include <stdlib.h>
3: #include <stdio.h>
4:
5: #define BUFSIZE 100
6:
7: int main(void)
8: {
9:     char buf[BUFSIZE];
10:     char filename[60];
11:     FILE *fp;
12:
13:     puts("Enter name of text file to display: ");
14:     fgets(filename,60,stdin);
15:     filename[strlen(filename)-1] = 0;
16:
17:     /* Open the file for reading. */
```

15

```
18:     if ( (fp = fopen(filename, "r")) == NULL)
19:     {
20:         fprintf(stderr, "Error opening file.\n");
21:         exit(1);
22:     }
23:
24:     /* If end of file not reached, read a line and display it. */
25:
26:     while ( !feof(fp) )
27:     {
28:         fgets(buf, BUFSIZE, fp);
29:         printf("%s",buf);
30:     }
31:     printf("\n");
32:     fclose(fp);
33:     return(0);
34: }
```

INPUT/ OUTPUT

```
Enter name of text file to display:
hello.c
#include <stdio.h>
int main(void)
{
    printf("Hello, world.");
    return(0);
}
```

ANALYSIS   The while loop in this program (lines 26 through 30) is typical of a while used in more complex programs that do sequential processing. As long as the end of the file hasn't been reached, the code within the while statement (lines 28 and 29) continues to execute repeatedly. When the call to feof() returns a nonzero value, the loop ends, the file is closed, and the program ends.

Note

Linux and other members of the UNIX family provide another set of functions for reading, writing, and seeking within files. These functions, which include open(), creat(), read(), write(), lseek(), and close(), are known as *system functions* (as opposed to the C library functions we have been looking at in today's lesson). They are defined by the operating system itself instead of by the C library. In fact, the C library functions such as fread(), fgets(), and fwrite() were written using the lower-level system functions. Unfortunately, the use of the lower-level system functions is beyond the scope of this book.

Do	Don't
DO check your position within a file so that you don't read beyond the end or before the beginning of a file.	**DON'T** use EOF with binary files.
DO use either `rewind()` or `fseek( fp, SEEK_SET, 0 )` to reset the file position to the beginning of the file.	
DO use `feof()` to check for the end of the file when working with binary files.	

File Management Functions

The term *file management* refers to dealing with existing files—not reading from or writing to them, but deleting, renaming, and copying them. The C standard library contains functions for deleting and renaming files, and you can also write your own file-copying program.

Deleting a File

To delete a file, you use the library function `remove()`. Its prototype is in stdio.h, as follows:

```
int remove( const char *filename );
```

The variable `*filename` is a pointer to the name of the file to be deleted. (See the section on filenames earlier in this lesson.) The specified file must not be open. If the file exists, it is deleted (just as if you used the `rm` command), and `remove()` returns 0. If the file doesn't exist, if it's read-only, if you don't have sufficient access rights, or if some other error occurs, `remove()` returns -1.

Listing 15.8 demonstrates the use of `remove()`. Be careful: If you `remove()` a file, it's gone forever.

LISTING 15.8. Using the `remove()` function to delete a disk file.

```
1: /* Demonstrates the remove() function. */
2:
3: #include <stdio.h>
4:
5: int main(void)
6: {
7:     char filename[80];
8:
9:     printf("Enter the filename to delete: ");
```

```
10:     fgets(filename,80,stdin);
11:     filename[strlen(filename)-1] = 0;
12:
13:     if ( remove(filename) == 0)
14:         printf("The file %s has been deleted.\n", filename);
15:     else
16:         fprintf(stderr, "Error deleting the file %s.\n", filename);
17:     return(0);
18: }
```

INPUT/OUTPUT

```
Enter the filename to delete: *.bak
Error deleting the file *.bak.
Enter the filename to delete: list1414.bak
The file list1414.bak has been deleted.
```

ANALYSIS Line 9 prompts the user for the name of the file to be deleted. Line 13 then calls remove() to delete the entered file. If the return value is 0, the file is removed, and a message is displayed stating this fact. If the return value is not zero, an error occurs, and the file is not removed.

Renaming a File

The rename() functionchanges the name of an existing disk file. The function prototype, in stdio.h, is as follows:

```
int rename( const char *oldname, const char *newname );
```

The filenames pointed to by *oldname* and *newname* follow the rules given earlier today. The only restriction is that both names must refer to the same disk drive; you can't rename a file to a different disk drive. The function rename() returns 0 on success, or -1 if an error occurs. Errors can be caused by the following conditions (among others):

- The file *oldname* does not exist.
- A file with the name *newname* already exists.
- You try to rename to another disk.

Listing 15.9 demonstrates the use of rename().

LISTING 15.9. Using rename() to change the name of a disk file.

```
1: /* Using rename() to change a filename. */
2:
3: #include <stdio.h>
4:
5: int main(void)
6: {
7:     char oldname[80], newname[80];
8:
```

continues

LISTING 15.9. continued

```
 9:        printf("Enter current filename: ");
10:        scanf("%80s",oldname);
11:        printf("Enter new name for file: ");
12:        scanf("%80s",newname);
13:
14:        if ( rename( oldname, newname ) == 0 )
15:            printf("%s has been renamed %s.\n", oldname, newname);
16:        else
17:            fprintf(stderr, "An error has occurred renaming %s.\n", oldname);
18:        return(0);
19: }
```

INPUT/
OUTPUT

Enter current filename: **list1509.c**
Enter new name for file: **rename.c**
list1509.c has been renamed rename.c.

ANALYSIS Listing 15.9 shows how powerful C can be. With only 18 lines of code, this program replaces an operating system command, and it's a much friendlier function.
Line 9 prompts for the name of the file to be renamed. Line 11 prompts for the new filename. The call to the rename() function is wrapped in an if statement on line 14. The
if statement checks to ensure that the renaming of the file was carried out correctly. If
so, line 15 prints an affirmative message; otherwise, line 17 prints a message stating that
there was an error.

Copying a File

It's frequently necessary to make a copy of a file—an exact duplicate with a different
name (or with the same name but in a different drive or directory). You could do this
with the cp command, but how do you copy a file in C? There's no library function, so
you need to write your own.

This might sound a bit complicated, but it's really quite simple thanks to C's use of
streams for input and output. Here are the steps you follow:

1. Open the source file for reading in binary mode. (Using binary mode ensures that
   the function can copy all sorts of files, not just text files.)

2. Open the destination file for writing in binary mode.

3. Read a character from the source file. Remember, when a file is first opened, the
   pointer is at the start of the file, so there's no need to position the file pointer
   explicitly.

4. If the function feof() indicates that you've reached the end of the source file,
   you're finished and can close both files and return to the calling program.

5. If you haven't reached end-of-file, write the character to the destination file, and
   then loop back to step 3.

Listing 15.10 contains a function, `copy_file()`, that is passed the names of the source and destination files and then performs the copy operation just as the preceding steps outlined. If there's an error opening either file, the function doesn't attempt the copy operation and returns -1 to the calling program. When the copy operation is complete, the program closes both files and returns 0.

LISTING 15.10. A function that copies a file.

```
1: /* Copying a file. */
2:
3: #include <stdio.h>
4:
5: int file_copy( char *oldname, char *newname );
6:
7: int main(void)
8: {
9:     char source[80], destination[80];
10:
11:     /* Get the source and destination names. */
12:
13:     printf("\nEnter source file: ");
14:     scanf("%80s",source);
15:     printf("\nEnter destination file: ");
16:     scanf("%80s",destination);
17:
18:     if ( file_copy( source, destination ) == 0 )
19:         puts("Copy operation successful");
20:     else
21:         fprintf(stderr, "Error during copy operation");
22:     return(0);
23: }
24: int file_copy( char *oldname, char *newname )
25: {
26:     FILE *fold, *fnew;
27:     int c;
28:
29:     /* Open the source file for reading in binary mode. */
30:
31:     if ( ( fold = fopen( oldname, "rb" ) ) == NULL )
32:         return -1;
33:
34:     /* Open the destination file for writing in binary mode. */
35:
36:     if ( ( fnew = fopen( newname, "wb" ) ) == NULL  )
37:     {
38:         fclose ( fold );
39:         return -1;
40:     }
41:
```

continues

LISTING **15.10**. continued

```
42:     /* Read one byte at a time from the source; if end of file */
43:     /* has not been reached, write the byte to the */
44:     /* destination. */
45:
46:     while (1)
47:     {
48:         c = fgetc( fold );
49:
50:         if ( !feof( fold ) )
51:             fputc( c, fnew );
52:         else
53:             break;
54:     }
55:
56:     fclose ( fnew );
57:     fclose ( fold );
58:
59:     return 0;
60: }
```

INPUT/ OUTPUT

Enter source file: **list1510.c**

Enter destination file: **tmpfile.c**
Copy operation successful

| ANALYSIS | The function copy_file() works perfectly well, letting you copy anything from a small text file to a huge program file. It does have limitations, however. If the destination file already exists, the function deletes it without asking. A good programming exercise for you is to modify copy_file() to check whether the destination file already exists, and then query the user as to whether the old file should be overwritten.

main() in Listing 15.10 should look very familiar. It's nearly identical to the main() in Listing 15.9, with the exception of line 14. Instead of rename(), this function uses copy(). Because C doesn't have a copy function, lines 24 through 60 create a copy function. Lines 31 and 32 open the source file, fold, in binary read mode. Lines 36 through 40 open the destination file, fnew, in binary write mode. Notice that line 38 closes the source file if there is an error opening the destination file. The while loop in lines 46 through 54 does the actual copying of the file. Line 48 gets a character from the source file, fold. Line 50 checks to see whether the end-of-file marker was read. If the end of the file has been reached, a break statement is executed in order to get out of the while loop. If the end of the file has not been reached, the character is written to the destination file, fnew. Lines 56 and 57 close the two files before returning to main().

Using Temporary Files

15

Some programs make use of one or more temporary files during execution. A temporary file is a file that is created by the program, used for some purpose during program execution, and then deleted before the program terminates. When you create a temporary file, you don't really care what its name is because the file is deleted. All that is necessary is that you use a name that isn't already in use for another file. The C standard library includes a function, tmpnam(), that creates a valid filename that doesn't conflict with any existing file. Its prototype in stdio.h is as follows:

```
char *tmpnam(char *s);
```

The argument s must be a pointer to a buffer large enough to hold the filename. You can also pass a null pointer (NULL), in which case the temporary name is stored in a buffer internal to tmpnam(), and the function returns a pointer to that buffer. Listing 15.11 demonstrates both methods of using tmpnam() to create temporary filenames.

LISTING **15.11**. Using tmpnam() to create temporary filenames.

```
1: /* Demonstration of temporary filenames. */
2:
3: #include <stdio.h>
4:
5: int main(void)
6: {
7:     char buffer[10], *c;
8:
9:     /* Get a temporary name in the defined buffer. */
10:
11:     tmpnam(buffer);
12:
13:     /* Get another name, this time in the function's */
14:     /* internal buffer. */
15:
16:     c = tmpnam(NULL);
17:
18:     /* Display the names. */
19:
20:     printf("Temporary name 1: %s", buffer);
21:     printf("\nTemporary name 2: %s\n", c);
22: }
```

OUTPUT
```
Temporary name 1: /tmp/filefWM714
Temporary name 2: /tmp/fileW53KxY
```

Note | The temporary names created in your system will probably be different from these.

ANALYSIS This program only generates and prints the temporary names; it doesn't actually create any files. Line 11 stores a temporary name in the character array, `buffer`. Line 15 assigns the character pointer to the name returned by `tmpnam()` to c. Your program must use the generated name to open the temporary file and then delete the file before program execution terminates. The following code fragment illustrates this:

```
char tempname[80];
FILE *tmpfile;
tmpnam(tempname);
tmpfile = fopen(tempname, "w");   /* Use appropriate mode */
fclose(tmpfile);
remove(tempname);
```

Do	Don't
	DON'T remove a file that you might need again.
	DON'T try to rename files across different file paths.
	DON'T forget to remove temporary files that you create. They aren't deleted automatically.

Summary

Today, you learned how C programs can use disk files. C treats a disk file like a stream (a sequence of characters), just like the predefined streams you learned about on Day 13. A stream associated with a disk file must be opened before it can be used, and it must be closed after use. A disk file stream can be opened in either text or binary mode.

After a disk file has been opened, you can read data from the file into your program, write data from the program to the file, or both. There are three general types of file I/O: formatted, character, and direct. Each type of I/O is best used for certain types of data storage and retrieval tasks.

Each open disk file has a file position indicator associated with it. This indicator specifies the position in the file, measured as the number of bytes from the start of the file, where subsequent read and write operations occur. With some types of file access, the position indicator is updated automatically, and you don't have to be concerned with it. For random file access, the C standard library provides functions for manipulating the position indicator.

Finally, C provides some rudimentary file management functions, letting you delete and rename disk files. In today's lesson, you developed your own function for copying a file.

Q&A

Q **Windows makes a distinction between binary and text files. How do I know what kind of file I'm dealing with?**

A Binary files are usually operated on by using `fread()` and `fwrite()`. If you are using the character or formatted input/output, you're probably dealing with a text file.

Q **Can I use paths with filenames when using `remove()`, `rename()`, `fopen()`, and the other file functions?**

A Yes. You can use a full filename with a path or just the filename by itself. If you use the filename by itself, the function looks for the file in the current directory.

Q **Can I read beyond the end of a file?**

A Yes. You can also read before the beginning of a file. Results from such reads can be disastrous. Reading files is just like working with arrays. You're looking at offsets within memory. If you're using `fseek()`, you should make sure you don't go beyond the end of the file.

Q **What happens if I don't close a file?**

A It's good programming practice to close any files you open. By default, the file should be closed when the program exits; however, you should never count on this. If the file isn't closed, you might not be able to access it later because the operating system will think that the file is already in use.

Q **How many files can I open at once?**

A This question can't be answered with a simple number. The limitation on the number of files that can be opened is based on variables set within your operating system. Linux systems can typically have 1,024 files open at any time.

Q **Can I read a file sequentially with random-access functions?**

A When reading a file sequentially, there is no need to use such functions as `fseek()`. Because the file pointer is left at the last position it occupied, it is always where you want it for sequential reads. You can use `fseek()` to read a file sequentially; however, you gain nothing.

Workshop

The Workshop provides quiz questions to help you solidify your understanding of the material covered and exercises to provide you with experience in using what you've learned. The answers to the quiz and exercises are provided in Appendix C, "Answers."

Quiz

1. What's the difference between a text-mode stream and a binary-mode stream?
2. What do you have to do to make sure your program that reads binary data is portable to Windows?
3. What must your program do before it can access a disk file?
4. When you open a file with fopen(), what information must you specify, and what does this function return?
5. What are the three general methods of file access?
6. What are the two general methods of reading a file's information?
7. What is the value of EOF and when is it used?
8. How do you detect the end of a file in text and binary modes?
9. What is the file position indicator, and how can you modify it?
10. When a file is first opened, where does the file position indicator point to? (If you're unsure, refer to Listing 15.5.)

Exercises

1. Write code to close all file streams.
2. Show two different ways to reset the file position pointer to the beginning of the file.
3. **BUG BUSTER:** Is anything wrong with the following?

```
FILE *fp;
int c;

if ( ( fp = fopen( oldname, "rb" ) ) == NULL )
    return -1;

while (( c = fgetc( fp)) != EOF )
    fprintf( stdout, "%c", c );

fclose ( fp );
```

15

Because of the many possible solutions, answers are not provided for the following exercises.

4. Write a program that displays a file to the screen.

5. Write a program that opens a file and counts the number of characters. The program should print the number of characters when finished.

6. Write a program that opens an existing text file and copies it to a new text file with all lowercase letters changed to uppercase and all other characters unchanged.

7. Write a program that opens any disk file, reads it in 128-byte blocks, and displays the contents of each block onscreen in both hexadecimal and ASCII formats.

8. Write a function that opens a new temporary file with a specified mode. All temporary files created by this function should automatically be closed and deleted when the program terminates. (Hint: Use the `atexit()` library function.)

DAY **16**

Manipulating Strings

Text data, which C stores in strings, is an important part of many programs. So far, you have learned how a C program stores strings and how you can input and output strings. C offers a variety of functions for other types of string manipulations as well. Today you will learn

- How to determine the length of a string
- How to copy and join strings
- Functions that compare strings
- How to search strings
- How to convert strings
- How to test characters

String Length and Storage

You should remember from previous days that, in C programs, a string is a sequence of characters with its beginning indicated by a pointer and its end marked by the null character \0. At times, you need to know the length of a string—the number of characters it contains. This length is obtained with the library function `strlen()`. Its prototype, in string.h, is

```
size_t strlen(char *str);
```

You might be puzzling over the `size_t` return type. This type is defined `unsigned int` on most systems, but it may also be of type `unsigned long` on computers based on 64-bit processors. The `size_t` type is used with many of the string functions. Just remember that it is an `unsigned` type.

The argument passed to `strlen` is a pointer to the string whose length you want to know. The function `strlen()` returns the number of characters between `str` and the next null character, not counting the null character. Listing 16.1 demonstrates `strlen()`.

LISTING 16.1. Using the `strlen()` function to determine the length of a string.

```
1: /* Using the strlen() function. */
2:
3: #include <stdio.h>
4: #include <string.h>
5:
6: int main(void)
7: {
8:     size_t length;
9:     char buf[80];
10:
11:    while (1)
12:    {
13:        puts("\nEnter a line of text, a blank line to exit.");
14:        fgets(buf,80,stdin);
15:
16:        length = strlen(buf);
17:
18:        if (length > 1)
19:            printf("That line is %u characters long.\n", length-1);
20:        else
21:            break;
22:    }
23:     return(0);
24: }
```

INPUT/
OUTPUT

```
Enter a line of text, a blank line to exit.
Just do it!

That line is 11 characters long.
Enter a line of text, a blank line to exit.
```

ANALYSIS This program does little more than demonstrate the use of `strlen()`. Lines 13 and 14 display a message and get a string called `buf`. Line 16 uses `strlen()` to assign the length of `buf` to the variable `length`. Line 18 checks whether the string was blank by checking for a length of more than 1. Remember that the `fgets()` function returns the line entered from the keyboard including the newline character. A blank line, therefore, would contain one character: the newline. If the string is not blank, line 19 prints the string's size.

Copying Strings

The C library has three functions for copying strings. Because of the way C handles strings, you can't simply assign one string to another, as you can in some other computer languages. You must copy the source string from its location in memory to the memory location of the destination string. The string-copying functions are `strcpy()`, `strncpy()`, and `strdup()`. All the string-copying functions require the header file string.h.

The `strcpy()` Function

The library function `strcpy()` copies an entire string to another memory location. Its prototype is as follows:

```c
char *strcpy( char *destination, char *source );
```

The function `strcpy()` copies the string (including the terminating null character \0) pointed to by `source` to the location pointed to by `destination`. The return value is a pointer to the new string, `destination`.

When using `strcpy()`, you must first allocate storage space for the destination string. The function has no way of knowing whether `destination` points to allocated space. If space hasn't been allocated, the function will probably cause a segmentation fault because your program tried to access memory that didn't belong to it. The use of `strcpy()` is illustrated in Listing 16.2.

 Note

When a program uses malloc( ) to allocate memory, as Listing 16.2 does, good programming practice requires the use of the free( ) function to free up the memory when the program is finished with it. You'll learn about free( ) on Day 18, "Working with Memory."

LISTING 16.2. Before using `strcpy()`, you must allocate storage space for the destination string.

```
 1: /* Demonstrates strcpy(). */
 2: #include <stdlib.h>
 3: #include <stdio.h>
 4: #include <string.h>
 5:
 6: char source[] = "The source string.";
 7:
 8: int main(void)
 9: {
10:     char dest1[80];
11:     char *dest2, *dest3;
12:
13:     printf("source: %s\n", source );
14:
15:     /* Copy to dest1 is okay because dest1 points to */
16:     /* 80 bytes of allocated space. */
17:
18:     strcpy(dest1, source);
19:     printf("dest1:  %s\n", dest1);
20:
21:     /* To copy to dest2, you must allocate space. */
22:
23:     dest2 = (char *)malloc(strlen(source) +1);
24:     strcpy(dest2, source);
25:     printf("dest2:  %s\n", dest2);
26:
27:     /* Copying without allocating destination space is a no-no. */
28:     /* The following could cause serious problems. */
29:
30:     /* strcpy(dest3, source); */
31:     return(0);
32: }
```

OUTPUT
```
source: The source string.
dest1:  The source string.
dest2:  The source string.
```

ANALYSIS This program demonstrates copying strings both to character arrays such as `dest1` (declared on line 10) and to character pointers such as `dest2` (declared along with `dest3` on line 11). Line 13 prints the original source string. This string is then copied to `dest1` with `strcpy()` on line 18. Line 24 copies source to `dest2`. Both `dest1` and `dest2` are printed to show that the function was successful. Notice that line 23 allocates the appropriate amount of space for `dest2` with the `malloc()` function. If you copy a string to a character pointer that hasn't been allocated memory, you will not get the results you expected.

The strncpy() Function

The strncpy() function is similar to strcpy(), except that strncpy() lets you specify how many characters to copy. Its prototype is

```
char *strncpy(char *destination, char *source, size_t n);
```

The arguments destination and source are pointers to the destination and source strings. The function copies, at most, the first n characters of source to destination. If source is shorter than n characters, enough null characters are added at the end of source to make a total of n characters copied to destination. If source is longer than n characters, no terminating \0 is added to destination. The function's return value is destination.

Listing 16.3 demonstrates the use of strncpy().

LISTING 16.3. The strncpy() function.

```
1: /* Using the strncpy() function. */
2:
3: #include <stdio.h>
4: #include <string.h>
5:
6: char dest[] = ".........................";
7: char source[] = "abcdefghijklmnopqrstuvwxyz";
8:
9: int main(void)
10: {
11:     size_t n;
12:
13:     while (1)
14:     {
15:         puts("Enter the number of characters to copy (1-26)");
16:         scanf("%d", &n);
17:
18:         if (n > 0 && n< 27)
19:             break;
20:     }
21:
22:     printf("Before strncpy destination = %s\n", dest);
23:
24:     strncpy(dest, source, n);
25:
26:     printf("After  strncpy destination = %s\n", dest);
27:     return(0);
28: }
```

INPUT/
OUTPUT

```
Enter the number of characters to copy (1-26)
15
Before strncpy destination = .........................
After  strncpy destination = abcdefghijklmno..........
```

In addition to demonstrating the strncpy() function, this program also illustrates an effective way to ensure that only correct information is entered by the
user. Lines 13 through 20 contain a while loop that prompts the user for a number from
1–26. The loop continues until a valid value is entered, so the program can't continue
until the user enters a valid value. When a number between 1 and 26 is entered, line 22
prints the original value of dest, line 24 copies the number of characters specified by the
user from source to dest, and line 26 prints the final value of dest.

> **Caution**
>
> Be sure that the number of characters copied doesn't exceed the allocated
> size of the destination. Remember that you have to make room for the null
> character at the end of the string.

The strdup() Function

The library function strdup() is similar to strcpy(), except that strdup() performs its
own memory allocation for the destination string with a call to malloc(). In effect, it
does what you did in Listing 16.2 by allocating space with malloc() and then calling
strcpy(). The prototype for strdup() is

```
char *strdup( char *source );
```

The argument source is a pointer to the source string. The function returns a pointer to
the destination string—the space allocated by malloc()—or NULL if the needed memory
can't be allocated. Listing 16.4 demonstrates the use of strdup(). Note that strdup() is
not an ANSI/ISO-standard function, but it is available on Linux and many other operating
systems.

LISTING 16.4. Using strdup() to copy a string with automatic memory allocation.

```
1: /* The strdup() function. */
2: #include <stdlib.h>
3: #include <stdio.h>
4: #include <string.h>
5:
6: char source[] = "The source string.";
7:
8: int main(void)
9: {
10:     char *dest;
11:
12:     if ( (dest = strdup(source)) == NULL)
13:     {
14:         fprintf(stderr, "Error allocating memory.\n");
```

```
15:          exit(1);
16:      }
17:
18:      printf("The destination = %s\n", dest);
19:      return(0);
20: }
```

OUTPUT The destination = The source string.

ANALYSIS In this listing, `strdup()` allocates the appropriate memory for `dest`. It then makes a copy of the passed string, `source`. Line 18 prints the duplicated string.

16

Concatenating Strings

If you're not familiar with the term *concatenation,* you might be asking, "What is it?" and "Is it legal?" Well, it means to join two strings—to tack one string onto the end of another—and, in most places in the world, it is legal. The C standard library contains two string concatenation functions—`strcat()` and `strncat()`—both of which require the header file string.h.

The `strcat()` Function

The prototype of `strcat()` is

```
char *strcat(char *str1, char *str2);
```

The function appends a copy of `str2` to the end of `str1`, moving the terminating null character to the end of the new string. You must allocate enough space for `str1` to hold the resulting string. The return value of `strcat()` is a pointer to `str1`. Listing 16.5 demonstrates `strcat()`.

LISTING 16.5. Using `strcat()` to concatenate strings.

```
1: /* The strcat() function. */
2:
3: #include <stdio.h>
4: #include <string.h>
5:
6: char str1[27] = "a";
7: char str2[2];
8:
9: int main(void)
10: {
11:     int n;
12:
13:     /* Put a null character at the end of str2[]. */
```

continues

LISTING 16.5. continued

```
14:
15:     str2[1] = '\0';
16:
17:     for (n = 98; n< 123; n++)
18:     {
19:         str2[0] = n;
20:         strcat(str1, str2);
21:         puts(str1);
22:     }
23:      return(0);
24: }
```

OUTPUT

```
ab
abc
abcd
abcde
abcdef
abcdefg
abcdefgh
abcdefghi
abcdefghij
abcdefghijk
abcdefghijkl
abcdefghijklm
abcdefghijklmn
abcdefghijklmno
abcdefghijklmnop
abcdefghijklmnopq
abcdefghijklmnopqr
abcdefghijklmnopqrs
abcdefghijklmnopqrst
abcdefghijklmnopqrstu
abcdefghijklmnopqrstuv
abcdefghijklmnopqrstuvw
abcdefghijklmnopqrstuvwx
abcdefghijklmnopqrstuvwxy
abcdefghijklmnopqrstuvwxyz
```

ANALYSIS The ASCII codes for the letters b–z are 98–122. This program uses these ASCII codes in its demonstration of strcat(). The for loop on lines 17 through 22 assigns these values, in turn, to str2[0]. Because str2[1] is already the null character (line 15), the effect is to assign the strings "b", "c", and so on, to str2. Each of these strings is concatenated with str1 (line 20), and then str1 is displayed onscreen (line 21).

The strncat() Function

The library function strncat() also performs string concatenation, but it lets you specify how many characters of the source string are appended to the end of the destination string. The prototype is

```
char *strncat(char *str1, char *str2, size_t n);
```

If str2 contains more than n characters, the first n characters are appended to the end of str1. If str2 contains fewer than n characters, all of str2 is appended to the end of str1. In either case, a terminating null character is added at the end of the resulting string. You must allocate enough space for str1 to hold the resulting string. The function returns a pointer to str1. Listing 16.6 uses strncat() to produce the same output as Listing 16.5.

LISTING 16.6. Using the strncat() function to concatenate strings.

```
1: /* The strncat() function. */
2:
3: #include <stdio.h>
4: #include <string.h>
5:
6: char str2[] = "abcdefghijklmnopqrstuvwxyz";
7:
8: int main(void)
9: {
10:     char str1[27];
11:     int n;
12:
13:     for (n=1; n< 27; n++)
14:     {
15:         strcpy(str1, "");
16:         strncat(str1, str2, n);
17:         puts(str1);
18:     }
19: }
```

OUTPUT

```
a
ab
abc
abcd
abcde
abcdef
abcdefg
abcdefgh
abcdefghi
abcdefghij
abcdefghijk
abcdefghijkl
abcdefghijklm
abcdefghijklmn
abcdefghijklmno
abcdefghijklmnop
abcdefghijklmnopq
abcdefghijklmnopqr
abcdefghijklmnopqrs
abcdefghijklmnopqrst
```

```
abcdefghijklmnopqrstu
abcdefghijklmnopqrstuv
abcdefghijklmnopqrstuvw
abcdefghijklmnopqrstuvwx
abcdefghijklmnopqrstuvwxy
abcdefghijklmnopqrstuvwxyz
```

ANALYSIS You might wonder about the purpose of line 15, strcpy(str1, "");. This line copies to str1 an empty string consisting of only a single null character. The result is that the first character in str1—str1[0]—is set equal to 0 (the null character). The same thing could have been accomplished with the statement str1[0] = 0; or str1[0] = '\0';.

Comparing Strings

Strings are compared to determine whether they are equal or unequal. If they are unequal; one string is greater than or less than the other. Determinations of greater and less are made with the numeric values of the ASCII codes for the characters. In the case of letters, this is equivalent to alphabetical order, with the one seemingly strange exception that all uppercase letters are less than the lowercase letters. This is true because the uppercase letters have ASCII codes 65–90 for A–Z, whereas lowercase a–z are represented by 97–122. Thus, "ZEBRA" would be considered to be less than "apple" by evaluating these C functions.

The ANSI/ISO C library contains functions for two types of string comparisons: comparing two entire strings and comparing a certain number of characters in two strings.

Comparing Two Entire Strings

The function strcmp() compares two strings, character by character. Its prototype is

```
int strcmp(char *str1, char *str2);
```

The arguments str1 and str2 are pointers to the strings being compared. The function's return values are given in Table 16.1. Listing 16.7 demonstrates strcmp().

TABLE 16.1. The values returned by strcmp().

Return Value	Meaning
< 0	str1 is less than str2.
0	str1 is equal to str2.
> 0	str1 is greater than str2.

LISTING 16.7. Using strcmp() to compare strings.

```
1: /* The strcmp() function. */
2:
3: #include <stdio.h>
4: #include <string.h>
5:
6: int main(void)
7: {
8:     char str1[80], str2[80];
9:     int x;
10:
11:    while (1)
12:    {
13:        /* Input two strings. */
14:
15:        printf("\n\nInput the first string, a blank to exit: ");
16:        fgets(str1,80,stdin);
17:        str1[strlen(str1)-1] = 0;
18:
19:        if ( strlen(str1) < 2 )
20:            break;
21:
22:        printf("\nInput the second string: ");
23:        fgets(str2,80,stdin);
24:        str2[strlen(str2)-1] = 0;
25:
26:        /* Compare them and display the result. */
27:
28:        x = strcmp(str1, str2);
29:
30:        printf("\nstrcmp(%s,%s) returns %d", str1, str2, x);
31:    }
32:    return(0);
33: }
```

16

INPUT/
OUTPUT

```
Input the first string, a blank to exit: First string

Input the second string: Second string

strcmp(First string,Second string) returns -13

Input the first string, a blank to exit: test string

Input the second string: test string

strcmp(test string,test string) returns 0

Input the first string, a blank to exit: zebra

Input the second string: aardvark

strcmp(zebra,aardvark) returns 25

Input the first string, a blank to exit:
```

Note On some systems, such as Windows, string comparison functions return -1, 0, or 1 rather than the values shown in the output here. They will, however, always return a nonzero value for unequal strings.

ANALYSIS This program demonstrates strcmp(), prompting the user for two strings (lines 16, 22, and 23) and displaying the result returned by strcmp() on line 28. Lines 17 and 24 remove the newline character from the end of the string returned by the fgets() function.

Experiment with this program to get a feel for how strcmp() compares strings. Try entering two strings that are identical except for case, such as Smith and SMITH. You learn that strcmp() is case sensitive, meaning that the program considers uppercase and lowercase letters to be different.

Comparing Partial Strings

The library function strncmp() compares a specified number of characters of one string to another string. Its prototype is

```
int strncmp(char *str1, char *str2, size_t n);
```

The function strncmp() compares n characters of str2 to str1. The comparison proceeds until n characters have been compared or the end of str1 has been reached. The method of comparison and return values are the same as for strcmp(). The comparison is case sensitive. Listing 16.8 demonstrates strncmp().

LISTING 16.8. Comparing parts of strings with strncmp().

```
 1: /* The strncmp() function. */
 2:
 3: #include <stdio.h>
 4: #include <string.h>
 5:
 6: char str1[] = "The first string.";
 7: char str2[] = "The second string.";
 8:
 9: int main(void)
10: {
11:     size_t n, x;
12:
13:     puts(str1);
14:     puts(str2);
15:
16:     while (1)
17:     {
18:         puts("Enter number of characters to compare, 0 to exit.");
```

```
19:          scanf("%d", &n);
20:
21:          if (n <= 0)
22:              break;
23:
24:          x = strncmp(str1, str2, n);
25:
26:          printf("Comparing %d characters, strncmp() returns %d.\n\n", n, x);
27:      }
28:      return(0);
29: }
```

16

<table>
<tr><td>INPUT/
OUTPUT</td><td>The first string.
The second string.</td></tr>
</table>

```
Enter number of characters to compare, 0 to exit.
3

Comparing 3 characters, strncmp() returns 0.

Enter number of characters to compare, 0 to exit.
6

Comparing 6 characters, strncmp() returns -13.

Enter number of characters to compare, 0 to exit.
0
```

ANALYSIS   This program compares the two strings defined on lines 6 and 7. Lines 13 and 14
print the strings to the screen so that the user can see what they are. The program
executes a while loop on lines 16 through 27 so that multiple compares can be done. If
the user asks to compare zero characters on lines 18 and 19, the program breaks on line
22; otherwise, a strncmp() executes on line 24, and the result is printed on line 26.

Comparing Two Strings While Ignoring Case

Unfortunately, the ANSI/ISO C library doesn't include any functions for case-insensitive
string comparison. Linux, however, has the function strcasecmp()—of course, this function might not be available on other systems. When you use a function that isn't case
sensitive, the strings Smith and SMITH compare as equal. Modify line 27 in Listing 16.7
to use strcasecmp(), and try the program again.

Searching Strings

The C library contains a number of functions that search strings. To put it another way,
these functions determine whether one string occurs within another string and, if so,
where. You can choose from six string searching functions, all of which require the header
file string.h.

The strchr() Function

The strchr() function finds the first occurrence of a specified character in a string. The prototype is

```
char *strchr(char *str, int ch);
```

The function strchr() searches str from left to right until the character ch is found or the terminating null character is found. If ch is found, a pointer to it is returned. If not, NULL is returned.

When strchr() finds the character, it returns a pointer to that character. Knowing that str is a pointer to the first character in the string, you can obtain the position of the found character by subtracting str from the pointer value returned by strchr(). Listing 16.9 illustrates this. Remember that the first character in a string is at position 0. Like many of C's string functions, strchr() is case sensitive and will, therefore, report that the character F isn't found in the string "raffle".

LISTING 16.9. Using strchr() to search a string for a single character.

```
1: /* Searching for a single character with strchr(). */
2:
3: #include <stdio.h>
4: #include <string.h>
5:
6: int main(void)
7: {
8:     char *loc, buf[80];
9:     int ch;
10:
11:     /* Input the string and the character. */
12:
13:     printf("Enter the string to be searched: ");
14:     fgets(buf,80,stdin);
15:     printf("Enter the character to search for: ");
16:     ch = getchar();
17:
18:     /* Perform the search. */
19:
20:     loc = strchr(buf, ch);
21:
22:     if ( loc == NULL )
23:         printf("The character %c was not found.\n", ch);
24:     else
25:         printf("The character %c was found at position %d.\n",
26:                 ch, (int)loc-buf);
27:     return(0);
28: }
```

INPUT/
OUTPUT

```
Enter the string to be searched: How now Brown Cow?
Enter the character to search for: C
The character C was found at position 14.
```

ANALYSIS

This program uses strchr() on line 20 to search for a character within a string. strchr() returns a pointer to the location where the character is first found or NULL if the character isn't found. Line 22 checks whether the value of loc is NULL and prints an appropriate message. As described in the section "The strchr() Function," the position of the character within the string is determined by subtracting the string pointer from the value returned by the function.

The strrchr() Function

The library function strrchr() is identical to strchr(), except that it searches a string for the last occurrence of a specified character in a string. In other words, it searches in reverse. Its prototype is

```
char *strrchr(char *str, int ch);
```

The function strrchr() returns a pointer to the last occurrence of ch in str and NULL if it finds no match. To see how this function works, modify line 20 in Listing 16.9 to use strrchr() instead of strchr().

The strcspn() Function

The library function strcspn() searches one string for the first occurrence of any of the characters in a second string. Its prototype is

```
size_t strcspn(char *str1, char *str2);
```

The function strcspn() starts searching at the first character of str1, looking for any of the individual characters contained in str2. This is important to remember: The function doesn't look for the string str2, but only the characters it contains. If the function finds a match, it returns the offset from the beginning of str1 where the matching character is located. If it finds no match, strcspn()returns the value of strlen(str1). This indicates that the first match was the null character, terminating the string. Listing 16.10 shows you how to use strcspn().

LISTING **16.10**. Searching for a set of characters with strcspn().

```
1: /* Searching with strcspn(). */
2:
3: #include <stdio.h>
4: #include <string.h>
5:
6: int main(void)
```

continues

LISTING 16.10. continued

```
7: {
8:     char  buf1[80], buf2[80];
9:     size_t loc;
10:
11:     /* Input the strings. */
12:
13:     printf("Enter the string to be searched: ");
14:     fgets(buf1,80,stdin);
15:     printf("Enter the string containing target characters: ");
16:     fgets(buf2,80,stdin);
17:     buf2[strlen(buf2)-1] = 0;   /* Strip the newline char. */
18:
19:     /* Perform the search. */
20:     loc = strcspn(buf1, buf2);
21:
22:     if ( loc ==  strlen(buf1) )
23:         printf("No match was found.\n");
24:     else
25:         printf("The first match was found at position %d.\n", loc);
26:     return(0);
27: }
```

**INPUT/
OUTPUT**

Enter the string to be searched: **How now Brown Cow?**
Enter the string containing target characters: **Cat**
The first match was found at position 14.

ANALYSIS   This listing is similar to Listing 16.10. Instead of searching for the first occurrence of a single character, it searches for the first occurrence of any of the characters entered in the second string. The program calls strcspn() on line 20 with buf1 and buf2. If any of the characters in buf2 are in buf1, strcspn() returns the offset from the beginning of buf1 to the location of the first occurrence. Line 22 checks the return value to determine whether it is NULL. If the value is NULL, no characters were found and an appropriate message is displayed on line 23. If a value was found, a message is displayed stating the character's position in the string.

The strspn() Function

This function is related to the preceding one, strcspn(), as the following paragraph explains. Its prototype is

```
size_t strspn(const char *str, char *accept);
```

The function strspn() searches str, comparing it character by character with the characters contained in accept. It returns the position of the first character in str that doesn't match a character in accept. In other words, strspn() returns the length of the initial segment of str that consists entirely of characters found in accept. The return is 0 if no characters match. Listing 16.11 demonstrates strspn().

LISTING **16.11**. Searching for the first nonmatching character with strspn().

```
 1: /* Searching with strspn(). */
 2:
 3: #include <stdio.h>
 4: #include <string.h>
 5:
 6: int main(void)
 7: {
 8:     char  buf1[80], buf2[80];
 9:     size_t loc;
10:
11:     /* Input the strings. */
12:
13:     printf("Enter the string to be searched: ");
14:     fgets(buf1,80,stdin);
15:     printf("Enter the string containing target characters: ");
16:     fgets(buf2,80,stdin);
17:     buf2[strlen(buf2)-1] = 0;   /* Strip the newline char. */
18:
19:     /* Perform the search. */
20:     loc = strspn(buf1, buf2);
21:
22:     if ( loc ==  0 )
23:         printf("No match was found.\n");
24:     else
25:         printf("Characters match up to position %d.\n", loc-1);
26:
27: }
```

INPUT/ OUTPUT

```
Enter the string to be searched: How now Brown Cow?
Enter the string containing target characters: How now what?
Characters match up to position 7.
```

ANALYSIS

This program is identical to the previous example, except that it calls strspn() instead of strcspn() on line 20. The function returns the offset into buf1 where the first character not in buf2 is found. Lines 22 through 25 evaluate the return value and print an appropriate message.

The strpbrk() Function

The library function strpbrk() is similar to strcspn(), searching one string for the first occurrence of any character contained in another string. It differs in that it doesn't include the terminating null characters in the search. The function prototype is

```
char *strpbrk(char *str, char *accept);
```

The function strpbrk() returns a pointer to the first character in str that matches any of the characters in accept. If it doesn't find a match, the function returns NULL. As previously explained for the function strchr(), you can obtain the offset of the first match in str by subtracting the pointer str from the pointer returned by strpbrk() (if it isn't NULL, of course). For example, replace strcspn() on line 20 of Listing 16.10 with strpbrk().

The strstr() Function

The final and, perhaps, most useful C string searching function is strstr(). This function searches for the first occurrence of one string within another, and it searches for the entire string, not just for individual characters within the string. Its prototype is

```
char *strstr(char *haystack, char *needle);
```

The function strstr() returns a pointer to the first occurrence of needle within haystack. If it finds no match, the function returns NULL. If the length of needle is 0, the function returns haystack. When strstr() finds a match, you can obtain the offset of needle within haystack by pointer subtraction, as explained earlier for strchr(). The matching procedure that strstr() uses is case sensitive. Listing 16.12 demonstrates how to use strstr().

LISTING **16.12**. Using strstr() to search for one string within another.

```
 1: /* Searching with strstr(). */
 2:
 3: #include <stdio.h>
 4: #include <string.h>
 5:
 6: int main(void)
 7: {
 8:     char *loc, buf1[80], buf2[80];
 9:
10:     /* Input the strings. */
11:
12:     printf("Enter the string to be searched: ");
13:     fgets(buf1,80,stdin);
14:     printf("Enter the target string: ");
15:     fgets(buf2,80,stdin);
16:     buf2[strlen(buf2)-1] = 0;  /* Strip the newline char. */
17:
18:     /* Perform the search. */
19:     loc = strstr(buf1, buf2);
20:
21:     if ( loc ==  NULL )
22:         printf("No match was found.\n");
23:     else
24:         printf("%s was found at position %d.\n", buf2, loc-buf1);
25:     return(0);
26: }
```

Enter the string to be searched: **How now brown cow?**
Enter the target string: **cow**
Cow was found at position 14.

This function provides an alternative way to search a string. This time you can search for an entire string within another string. Lines 12 through 15 prompt for two strings. Line 19 uses `strstr()` to search for the second string, `buf2`, within the first string, `buf1`. A pointer to the first occurrence is returned, or `NULL` is returned if the string isn't found. Lines 21 through 24 evaluate the returned value, `loc`, and print an appropriate message.

16

Do	**Don't**
DO remember that for many of the string functions, there are equivalent functions that enable you to specify a number of characters to manipulate. The functions that allow specification of the number of characters are usually named `strnxxx()`, where *xxx* is specific to the function.	**DON'T** forget that C is case sensitive. A and a are different.

String-to-Number Conversions

Sometimes, you will need to convert the string representation of a number to an actual numeric variable. For example, the string `"123"` can be converted to a type `int` variable with the value 123. Three functions can be used to convert a string to a number. They are explained in the following paragraphs, and their prototypes are in stdlib.h.

The `atoi()` Function

The library function `atoi()` converts a string to an integer. The prototype is

```
int atoi(char *ptr);
```

The function `atoi()` converts the string pointed to by `ptr` to an integer. Besides digits, the string can contain leading whitespace and a + or - sign. Conversion starts at the beginning of the string and proceeds until an unconvertible character (for example, a letter or punctuation mark) is encountered. The resulting integer is returned to the calling program. If it finds no convertible characters, `atoi()` returns 0. Table 16.2 lists some examples.

TABLE 16.2. String-to-number conversions with `atoi()`.

String	Value Returned by atoi()
"157"	157
"-1.6"	-1
"+50x"	50
"twelve"	0
"x506"	0

The first example is straightforward. In the second example, you might be confused about why the ".6" didn't translate. Remember that this is a string-to-integer conversion. The third example is also straightforward; the function understands the plus sign and considers it a part of the number. The fourth example uses "twelve". The `atoi()` function can't translate words; it sees only characters. Because the string didn't start with a number, `atoi()` returns 0. This is true of the last example, also.

The `atol()` Function

The library function `atol()` works exactly like `atoi()`, except that it returns a type `long`. The function prototype is

```
long atol(char *ptr);
```

The values returned by `atol()` would be the same as shown for `atoi()` in Table 16.2, except that each return value would be a type `long` instead of a type `int`.

The `atof()` Function

The function `atof()` converts a string to a type `double`. The prototype is

```
double atof(char *str);
```

The argument `str` points to the string to be converted. This string can contain leading whitespace and a + or - character. The number can contain the digits 0–9, the decimal point, and the exponent indicator E or e. If there are no convertible characters, `atof()` returns 0. Table 16.3 lists some examples of using `atof()`.

TABLE 16.3. String-to-number conversions with `atof()`.

String	Value Returned by atof()
"12"	12.000000
"-0.123"	-0.123000
"123E+3"	123000.000000
"123.1e-5"	0.001231

Listing 16.13 lets you enter your own strings for conversion.

LISTING 16.13. Using `atof()` to convert strings to type `double` numeric variables.

```
1: /* Demonstration of atof(). */
2:
3: #include <string.h>
4: #include <stdio.h>
5: #include <stdlib.h>
6:
7: int main(void)
8: {
9:     char buf[80];
10:    double d;
11:
12:    while (1)
13:    {
14:        printf("\nEnter the string to convert (blank to exit):    ");
15:        fgets(buf,80,stdin);
16:
17:        if ( strlen(buf) < 2 )
18:            break;
19:
20:        d = atof( buf );
21:
22:        printf("The converted value is %f.\n", d);
23:    }
24:    return(0);
25:}
```

INPUT/
OUTPUT

```
Enter the string to convert (blank to exit):    1009.12
The converted value is 1009.120000.
Enter the string to convert (blank to exit):    abc
The converted value is 0.000000.
Enter the string to convert (blank to exit):    3
The converted value is 3.000000.
Enter the string to convert (blank to exit):
```

ANALYSIS   The `while` loop on lines 12 through 23 lets you keep running the program until you enter a blank line. Lines 14 and 15 prompt for the value. Line 17 checks whether a blank line is entered. If it is, the program breaks out of the `while` loop and ends. Line 20 calls `atof()`, converting the value entered (`buf`) to a type `double`, `d`. Line 22 prints the final result.

Character Test Functions

The header file ctype.h contains the prototypes for a number of functions that test characters, returning TRUE or FALSE depending on whether the character meets a certain condition. For example, is it a letter or is it a numeral? The is*xxxx*() functions are actually macros, defined in ctype.h. You learn about macros on Day 20, "Advanced Compiler Use." At that time, you might want to look at the definitions in ctype.h to see how they work. For now, you only need to see how they're used.

The isxxxx() macros all have the same prototype.

```
int isxxxx(int ch);
```

In the preceding line, ch is the character being tested. The return value is TRUE (nonzero) if the condition is met or FALSE (zero) if it isn't. Table 16.4 lists the complete set of isxxxx() macros.

TABLE 16.4. The isxxxx() macros.

Macro	Action
isalnum()	Returns TRUE if ch is a letter or a digit
isalpha()	Returns TRUE if ch is a letter
isascii()	Returns TRUE if ch is a standard ASCII character(between 0 and 127)
iscntrl()	Returns TRUE if ch is a control character
isdigit()	Returns TRUE if ch is a digit
isgraph()	Returns TRUE if ch is a printing character (other than a space)
islower()	Returns TRUE if ch is a lowercase letter
isprint()	Returns TRUE if ch is a printing character (including a space)
ispunct()	Returns TRUE if ch is a punctuation character
isspace()	Returns TRUE if ch is a whitespace character (space, tab, vertical tab, line feed, form feed, or carriage return)
isupper()	Returns TRUE if ch is an uppercase letter
isxdigit()	Returns TRUE if ch is a hexadecimal digit (0–9, a–f, A–F)

You can do many interesting things with the character-test macros. One example is the function get_int() in Listing 16.14. This function inputs an integer from stdin and returns it as a type int variable. The function skips over leading whitespace and returns 0 if the first nonspace character isn't a numeric character.

LISTING 16.14. Using the isxxxx() macros to implement a function that inputs an integer.

```
1: /* Using character test macros to create an integer */
2: /* input function. */
3: #include <stdio.h>
4: #include <ctype.h>
5:
6: int get_int(void);
```

```
7:
8: int main(void)
9: {
10:     int x;
11:     printf("Enter an integer: ") ;
12:     x =  get_int();
13:     printf("You entered %d.\n", x);
14:     return 0;
15: }
16:
17: int get_int(void)
18: {
19:     int ch, i, sign = 1;
20:
21:     /* Skip over any leading white space. */
22:
23:     while ( isspace(ch = getchar()) )
24:         ;
25:
26:     /* If the first character is nonnumeric, unget */
27:     /* the character and return 0. */
28:
29:     if (ch != '-' && ch != '+' && !isdigit(ch) && ch != EOF)
30:     {
31:         ungetc(ch, stdin);
32:         return 0;
33:     }
34:
35:     /* If the first character is a minus sign, set */
36:     /* sign accordingly. */
37:
38:     if (ch == '-')
39:         sign = -1;
40:
41:     /* If the first character was a plus or minus sign, */
42:     /* get the next character. */
43:
44:     if (ch == '+' || ch == '-')
45:         ch = getchar();
46:
47:     /* Read characters until a nondigit is input. Assign */
48:     /* values, multiplied by proper power of 10, to i. */
49:
50:     for (i = 0; isdigit(ch); ch = getchar() )
51:         i = 10 * i + (ch - '0');
52:
53:     /* Make result negative if sign is negative. */
54:
55:     i *= sign;
56:
57:     /* If EOF was not encountered, a nondigit character */
```

16

continues

LISTING 16.14. continued

```
58:       /* must have been read in, so unget it. */
59:
60:       if (ch != EOF)
61:           ungetc(ch, stdin);
62:
63:       /* Return the input value. */
64:
65:       return i;
66: }
```

INPUT/
OUTPUT

```
-100
You entered -100.
abc3.145
You entered 0.
9 9 9
You entered 9.
2.5
You entered 2.
```

ANALYSIS   This program uses the library function ungetc() on lines 31 and 61, which you learned about on Day 13, "Working with the Screen and Keyboard." Remember that this function "ungets," or returns, a character to the specified stream. This returned character is the first one input the next time the program reads a character from that stream. This is necessary because when the function get_int() reads a nonnumeric character from stdin, you want to put that character back in case the program needs to read it later.

In this program, main() is simple. An integer variable, x, is declared (line 10), assigned the value of the get_int() function (line 11), and printed to the screen (line 13). The get_int() function makes up the rest of the program.

The get_int() function isn't as simple. To remove leading whitespace that might be entered, line 23 loops with a while command. The isspace() macro tests a character, ch, obtained with the getchar() function. If ch is a space, another character is retrieved until a nonwhitespace character is received. Line 29 checks whether the character is one that can be used. Line 29 could be read, "If the character input isn't a negative sign, a plus sign, a digit, or the end of the file(s)". If this is true, ungetc() is used on line 31 to put the character back, and the function returns to main(). If the character is usable, execution continues.

Lines 38 through 45 handle the sign of the number. Line 38 checks whether the character entered is a negative sign. If it is, a variable (sign) is set to -1. sign is used to make the final number either positive or negative (line 55). Because positive numbers are the default, after you have taken care of the negative sign, you are almost ready to continue. If a sign is entered, the program must get another character. Lines 44 and 45 take care of this.

The heart of the function is the for loop on lines 50 and 51, which continues to get characters as long as the characters received are digits. Line 51 might be a little confusing at first. This line takes the individual character entered and turns it into a number. Subtracting the character '0' from your number changes a character number to a real number. (Remember the ASCII values.) When the correct numerical value is obtained, the numbers are multiplied by the proper power of 10. The for loop continues until a nondigit number is entered. At that point, line 55 applies the sign to the number, making it complete.

Before returning, the program needs to do a little cleanup. If the last number wasn't the end of file, it needs to be put back (in case it's needed elsewhere). Line 61 does this before line 65 returns.

tolower() and toupper()

The header file ctype.h also contains two useful functions for converting characters from uppercase to lowercase and lowercase to uppercase. These functions are defined as

```
int toupper (int c);
int tolower (int c);
```

Each of these functions takes an int as its argument and returns an int. Each of these functions returns the letter unchanged if the case is already correct or it is a nonalphabetic character. Listing 16.15 gives an example of the use of these functions.

LISTING 16.15. Using the tolower() function to change the case of a string.

```
1:  /* Using the function tolower() */
2:  #include <stdio.h>
3:  #include <ctype.h>
4:
5:  char* strlwr(char *str);
6:
7:  int main(void)
8:  {
9:      char buffer[80];
10:
11:     printf("Enter a string to convert: ");
12:     fgets(buffer,80,stdin);
13:
14:     strlwr (buffer);
15:
16:     printf (buffer);
17:
18:     return 0;
19: }
```

continues

LISTING 16.15. continued

```
20:
21: char* strlwr(char *str)
22: {
23:     int k ;
24:
25:     for (k = 0 ; str [k] ; k++)
26:         str[k] = tolower(str[k]);
27:
28:     return str ;
29: }
```

INPUT/
OUTPUT

Enter a string to convert: **MiXeD CaSE**
mixed case

ANALYSIS
Very little is new here. Lines 11 and 12 prompt for and read a line of text into a
character array buffer. The character array is passed to the function strlwr()
and printed to the screen in line 16. The strlwr() is defined in lines 21 through 29. It
takes a pointer to a character array as its argument and returns a pointer to the same array
when it's finished. The main work of this function is carried out in lines 25 and 26. Line
25 is a for loop that is terminated when the character at position k in the array str is the
null character \0. For each value of k that fails to meet the test condition in the for loop,
the statement on line 26 converts the character to lowercase. Notice that no test is
required to make sure that the character being converted is a letter of the alphabet.

Do	**DON'T**
DO take advantage of the string functions that are available.	**DON'T** use non-ANSI/ISO functions if you plan to port your application to other platforms.
	DON'T confuse characters with numbers. It's easy to forget that the character 1 isn't the same thing as the number 1.

Summary

Today's discussion shows the various ways you use C to manipulate strings. By using C
standard library functions, you can copy, concatenate, compare, and search strings. These
are all necessary tasks in most programming projects. The standard library also contains
functions for converting the case of characters in strings and for converting strings to
numbers. Finally, C provides a variety of character-test functions or, more accurately,
macros that perform a variety of tests on individual characters. By using these macros to
test characters, you can create your own custom input functions.

Q&A

Q How do I know whether a function is ANSI/ISO compatible?

A If you look at the manual or man page for the function, it will usually have a section titled "CONFORMING TO." That section will state which standards it is conformant to. ANSI/ISO conformance will only be listed if you have an old version of the man pages. Remember from Day 1, "Introduction to Linux and the C Programming Language," that the ISO standards have taken over from ANSI. On other platforms, you will have to consult the relevant reference manuals for that system.

Q Were all the available string functions presented today?

A No. However, the string functions presented today should cover virtually all your needs. Consult the man pages to see what other functions are available.

Q Does `strcat()` ignore trailing spaces when doing a concatenation?

A No. `strcat()` looks at a space as just another character.

Q Can I convert numbers to strings?

A Yes. You can write a function similar to the one in Listing 16.16, or you can check your library reference for available functions. Some functions available include `itoa()`, `ltoa()`, and `ultoa()`. `sprintf()` can also be used.

Workshop

The Workshop provides quiz questions to help you solidify your understanding of the material covered and exercises to provide you with experience in using what you've learned. The answers to the quiz and exercises are provided in Appendix C, "Answers."

Quiz

1. What is the length of a string, and how can the length be determined?

2. Before copying a string, what must you be sure to do?

3. What does the term *concatenate* mean?

4. When comparing strings, what is meant by "One string is greater than another string"?

5. What is the difference between `strcmp()` and `strncmp()`?

6. What is the difference between `strcmp()` and `strcasecmp()`?

7. What values does `isascii()` test for?

8. Using Table 16.4, which macros would return `TRUE` for `var`?

```
int var = 1;
```

9. Using Table 16.4, which macros would return TRUE for x?

```
char x = 65;
```

10. What are the character-test functions used for?

Exercises

1. What values do the test functions return?

2. What would the `atoi()` function return if passed the following values?

    a. `"65"`

    b. `"81.23"`

    c. `"-34.2"`

    d. `"ten"`

    e. `"+12hundred"`

    f. `"negative100"`

3. What would the `atof()` function return if passed the following?

    a. `"65"`

    b. `"81.23"`

    c. `"-34.2"`

    d. `"ten"`

    e. `"+12hundred"`

    f. `"1e+3"`

4. **BUG BUSTER:** Is anything wrong with the following?

```
char *string1, string2;
string1 = "Hello World";
strcpy( string2, string1);
printf( "%s %s", string1, string2 );
```

Because of the many possible solutions, answers aren't provided for the following exercises.

5. Write a program that prompts for the user's last name, first name, and middle name individually. Then store the name in a new string as first initial, period, space, middle initial, period, space, last name. For example, if Bradley, Lee, and Jones are entered, store B. L. Jones. Display the new name to the screen.

6. Write a program to prove your answers to quiz questions 8 and 9.

7. The function `strstr()` finds the first occurrence of one string within another, and it is case sensitive. Write a function that performs the same task without case sensitivity.

8. Write a function that determines the number of times one string occurs within another.

9. Write a program that searches a text file for occurrences of a user-specified target string and then reports the line numbers where the target is found. For example, if you search one of your C source code files for the string "printf", the program should list all the lines where the printf() function is called by the program.

10. Listing 16.14 demonstrates a function that inputs an integer from stdin. Write a function get_float() that inputs a floating-point value from stdin.

16

DAY 17

Exploring the C Function Library

As you've seen throughout this book, much of C's power comes from the functions in the C standard library. In today's lesson, you'll explore some of the functions that don't fit into the subject matter of other days. Today you will learn about

- Mathematical functions
- Functions that deal with time
- Error-handling functions
- Functions for searching and sorting data

Mathematical Functions

The C standard library contains a variety of functions that perform mathematical operations. Prototypes for the mathematical functions are in the header file math.h. The math functions all return a type double. For the trigonometric functions, angles are expressed in radians rather than degrees, which you might be more used to. Remember, one radian equals 57.296 degrees, and a full circle (360 degrees) contains 2π radians.

Trigonometric Functions

The trigonometric functions perform calculations that are used in some graphical and engineering applications.

Function	Prototype	Description
acos()	double acos(double x)	Returns the arccosine of its argument. The argument must be in the range -1 <= x <= 1, and the return value is in the range 0 <= acos <= π.
asin()	double asin(double x)	Returns the arcsine of its argument. The argument must be in the range -1 <= x <= 1, and the return value is in the range -π/2 <= asin <= π/2.
atan()	double atan(double x)	Returns the arctangent of its argument. The return value is in the range -π/2 <= atan <= π/2.
atan2()	double atan2 (double x, double y)	Returns the arctangent of x/y. The value returned is in the range -π <= atan2 <= π.
cos()	double cos(double x)	Returns the cosine of its argument.
sin()	double sin(double x)	Returns the sine of its argument.
tan()	double tan(double x)	Returns the tangent of its argument.

Exponential and Logarithmic Functions

The exponential and logarithmic functions are needed for certain types of mathematical calculations.

Function	Prototype	Description
exp()	double exp(double x)	Returns the natural exponent of its argument— that is, e^x, where e equals 2.7182818284590452354.
log()	double log(double x)	Returns the natural logarithm of its argument. The argument must be greater than zero.
log10()	double log10(double x)	Returns the base-10 logarithm of its argument. The argument must be greater than zero.

Function	Prototype	Description
frexp()	double frexp (double x, int *y)	The function calculates the normalized fraction representing the value x. The function's return value r is a fraction in the range $0.5 <= r <= 1.0$. The function assigns to y an integer exponent such that $x = r * 2^y$. If the value passed to the function is 0, both r and y are 0.
ldexp()	double ldexp (double x, int y)	Returns $x * 2^y$.

Hyperbolic Functions

The hyperbolic functions perform hyperbolic trigonometric calculations.

Function	Prototype	Description
cosh()	double cosh(double x)	Returns the hyperbolic cosine of its argument.
sinh()	double sinh(double x)	Returns the hyperbolic sine of its argument.
tanh()	double tanh(double x)	Returns the hyperbolic tangent of its argument.

Other Mathematical Functions

The standard C library contains the following miscellaneous mathematical functions:

Function	Prototype	Description
sqrt()	double sqrt(double x)	Returns the square root of its argument. The argument must be zero or greater.
ceil()	double ceil(double x)	Returns the smallest integer not less than its argument. For example, ceil(4.5) returns 5.0, and ceil(-4.5) returns -4.0. Although ceil() returns an integer value, it is returned as a type double.
abs()	int abs(int x)	Returns the absolute labs()long labs (long x)value of the arguments.
floor()	double floor(double x)	Returns the largest integer not greater than its argument. For example, floor(4.5) returns 4.0, and floor(-4.5) returns -5.0.

continues

Function	Prototype	Description
modf()	double modf (double x, double *y)	Splits x into integral and fractional parts, each with the same sign as x. The fractional part is returned by the function, and the integral part is assigned to *y.
pow()	double pow (double x, double y)	Returns x^y. An error occurs if x == 0 and y <= 0 or if x < 0 and y is not an integer.
fmod()	double fmod (double x, double y)	Returns the floating-point remainder of x/y, with the same sign as x. The function returns 0 if x == 0.

A Demonstration of the Math Functions

An entire book could be filled with programs demonstrating all the math functions. Listing 17.1 contains a single program that demonstrates several of these functions. Please note that to compile this program, you must tell gcc that you want to use the maths functions, which are kept in a separate library. To compile this program, you should use

```
gcc -Wall -ggdb list1701.c -lm -o list1701
```

The -l parameter asks gcc to link in a library; in the case of the maths library, the library is simply called m. We will be exploring libraries further on Day 20, "Advanced Compiler Usage."

LISTING 17.1. Using the C library math functions.

```
1: /* Demonstrates some of C's math functions */
2:
3: #include <stdio.h>
4: #include <math.h>
5:
6: int main(void)
7: {
8:
9:     double x;
10:
11:     printf("Enter a number: ");
12:     scanf( "%lf", &x);
13:
14:     printf("\n\nOriginal value: %lf", x);
15:
16:     printf("\nCeil: %lf", ceil(x));
17:     printf("\nFloor: %lf", floor(x));
```

```
18:     if( x >= 0 )
19:         printf("\nSquare root: %lf", sqrt(x) );
20:     else
21:        printf("\nNegative number" );
22:
23:     printf("\nCosine: %lf\n", cos(x));
24:     return(0);
25: }
```

**INPUT/
OUTPUT**

```
Enter a number: 100.95

Original value: 100.950000
Ceil: 101.000000
Floor: 100.000000
Square root: 10.047388
Cosine: 0.913482
```

ANALYSIS   This listing uses just a few of the math functions that are available in the C standard library. Line 12 inputs a number from the user, which is then printed. Next, that value is passed to four of the C library math functions—`ceil()`, `floor()`, `sqrt()`, and `cos()`. Notice that `sqrt()` is called only if the number isn't negative because, by definition, negative numbers don't have square roots. You can add any of the other math functions to a program such as this to test its functionality.

17

Dealing with Time

The C library contains several functions that let your program work with times. In C, the term *times* refers to dates as well as times. The function prototypes and the definition of the structure used by many of the time functions are in the header file time.h.

Representing Time

The C time functions represent time in two ways. The more basic method is the number of seconds elapsed since midnight on January 1, 1970. Negative values are used to represent times before that date. These time values are stored as type `long` integers. In time.h, the symbols `time_t` and `clock_t` are defined with a `typedef` statement as `long`. These symbols are used in the time function prototypes rather than `long`.

The second method represents a time broken down into its components: year, month, day, and so on. For this kind of time representation, the time functions use the structure `tm`, defined in time.h as follows:

```
struct tm {
int tm_sec;      /* seconds after the minute - [0,59]  */
int tm_min;      /* minutes after the hour - [0,59]    */
int tm_hour;     /* hours since midnight - [0,23]  */
int tm_mday;     /* day of the month - [1,31]      */
```

```
int tm_mon;     /* months since January - [0,11]     */
int tm_year;    /* years since 1900             */
int tm_wday;    /* days since Sunday - [0,6]    */
int tm_yday;    /* days since January 1 - [0,365] */
int tm_isdst;   /* daylight savings time flag   */
};
```

The Time Functions

This section describes the various C library functions that deal with time. Remember that the term *time* refers to the date, as well as hours, minutes, and seconds. A demonstration program follows the descriptions.

Obtaining the Current Time

To obtain the current time as set on your system's internal clock, use the time() function. The prototype is

```
time_t time(time_t *timeptr);
```

Remember, time_t is defined in time.h as a synonym for long. The function time() returns the number of seconds elapsed since midnight, January 1, 1970. If it is passed a non-NULL pointer, time() also stores this value in the type time_t variable pointed to by timeptr. Thus, to store the current time in the type time_t variable now, you could write

```
time_t now;
```

```
now = time(0);
```

You also could write

```
time_t now;
time_t *ptr_now = &now;
time(ptr_now);
```

Converting Between Time Representations

Knowing the number of seconds since January 1, 1970, is not often useful. Therefore, C provides the capability to convert time represented as a time_t value to a tm structure, using the localtime()function. A tm structure contains day, month, year, and other time information in a format more appropriate for display and printing. The prototype of this function is

```
struct tm *localtime(time_t *ptr);
```

This function returns a pointer to a static type tm structure, so you don't need to declare a type tm structure to use—only a pointer to type tm. This static structure is reused and overwritten each time localtime() is called; if you want to save the value returned, your program must declare a separate type tm structure and copy the values from the static structure.

The reverse conversion—from a type tm structure to a type time_t value—is performed by the function mktime(). The prototype is

```
time_t mktime(struct tm *ntime);
```

This function returns the number of seconds between midnight, January 1, 1970, and the time represented by the type tm structure pointed to by ntime.

Displaying Times

To convert times into formatted strings appropriate for display, use the functions ctime() and asctime(). Both of these functions return the time as a string with a specific format. They differ because ctime() is passed the time as a type time_t value, whereas asctime() is passed the time as a type tm structure. Their prototypes are

```
char *asctime(struct tm *ptr);
char *ctime(time_t *ptr);
```

Both functions return a pointer to a static, null-terminated, 26-character string that gives the time of the function's argument in the following format:

```
Thu Jun 13 10:22:23 1991
```

The time is formatted in 24-hour military time. Both functions use a static string, overwriting it each time they're called.

For more control over the format of the time, use the strftime() function. This function is passed a time as a type tm structure. It formats the time according to a format string. The function prototype is

```
size_t strftime(char *s, size_t max, char *fmt, struct tm *ptr);
```

This function takes the time in the type tm structure pointed to by ptr, formats it according to the format string fmt, and writes the result as a null-terminated string to the memory location pointed to by s. The argument max should specify the amount of space allocated at s. If the resulting string (including the terminating null character) has more than max characters, the function returns 0, and the string s is invalid. Otherwise, the function returns the number of characters written—strlen(s).

The format string consists of one or more conversion specifiers from Table 17.1.

Caution The now infamous Y2K bug happened because programmers selected a two-digit year specifier when a four-digit one was required. Some of the following format specifiers display years with only two digits; that is, 1999 is shown as 99. For dates after December 31, 1999, they might show a year of 00 or 100, depending on the implementation. Always use care when selecting date specifiers.

17

TABLE 17.1. Conversion specifiers that can be used with `strftime()`.

Specifier	What It's Replaced By
%a	Abbreviated weekday name.
%A	Full weekday name.
%b	Abbreviated month name.
%B	Full month name.
%c	Date and time representation (for example, 10:41:50 30-Jun-91).
%d	Day of month as a decimal number 01 through 31.
%H	The hour (24-hour clock) as a decimal number 00 through 23.
%I	The hour (12-hour clock) as a decimal number 00 through 11.
%j	The day of the year as a decimal number 001 through 366.
%m	The month as a decimal number 01 through 12.
%M	The minute as a decimal number 00 through 59.
%p	AM or PM.
%S	The second as a decimal number 00 through 59.
%U	The week of the year as a decimal number 00 through 53. Sunday is considered the first day of the week.
%w	The weekday as a decimal number 0 through 6 (Sunday = 0).
%W	The week of the year as a decimal number 00 through 53. Monday is considered the first day of the week.
%x	The date representation (for example, 30-Jun-91).
%X	The time representation (for example, 10:41:50).
%y	The year, without century, as a decimal number 00 through 99.
%Y	The year, with century, as a decimal number.
%Z	The time zone name if the information is available or blank if not.
%%	A single percent sign %.

Calculating Time Differences

You can calculate the difference, in seconds, between two times with the `difftime()` macro, which subtracts two `time_t` values and returns the difference. The prototype is

```
double difftime(time_t later, time_t earlier);
```

This function subtracts `earlier` from `later` and returns the difference, the number of seconds between the two times. A common use of `difftime()` is to calculate elapsed time, as demonstrated (along with other time operations) in Listing 17.2.

You can determine duration of a different sort using the clock() function, which returns the amount of time that has passed since the program started execution, in units of 1 millionth of a second. The prototype is

```
clock_t clock(void);
```

To determine the duration of some portion of a program, call clock() twice—before and after the process occurs—and subtract the two return values.

Using the Time Functions

Listing 17.2 demonstrates how to use the C library time functions.

LISTING 17.2. Using the C library time functions.

```
 1: /* Demonstrates the time functions. */
 2:
 3: #include <stdio.h>
 4: #include <time.h>
 5:
 6: int main(void)
 7: {
 8:     time_t start, finish, now;
 9:     struct tm *ptr;
10:     char *c, buf1[80];
11:     double duration;
12:
13:     /* Record the time the program starts execution. */
14:
15:     start = time(0);
16:
17:     /* Record the current time, using the alternate method of */
18:     /* calling time(). */
19:
20:     time(&now);
21:
22:     /* Convert the time_t value into a type tm structure. */
23:
24:     ptr = localtime(&now);
25:
26:     /* Create and display a formatted string containing */
27:     /* the current time. */
28:
29:     c = asctime(ptr);
30:     puts(c);
31:     getc(stdin);
32:
33:     /* Now use the strftime() function to create several different */
34:     /* formatted versions of the time. */
```

continues

LISTING 17.2. continued

```
35:
36:         strftime(buf1, 80, "This is week %U of the year %Y", ptr);
37:         puts(buf1);
38:         getc(stdin);
39:
40:         strftime(buf1, 80, "Today is %A, %m/%d/%Y", ptr);
41:         puts(buf1);
42:         getc(stdin);
43:
44:         strftime(buf1, 80, "It is %M minutes past hour %I.", ptr);
45:         puts(buf1);
46:         getc(stdin);
47:
48:         /* Now get the current time and calculate program duration. */
49:
50:         finish = time(0);
51:         duration = difftime(finish, start);
52:         printf("Execution time using time() = %f seconds.\n", duration);
53:
54:         /* Also display program duration in hundredths of seconds */
55:         /* using clock(). */
56:
57:         printf("Execution time using clock() = %ld hundredths of sec.\n",
58:             clock());
59:         return(0);
60: }
```

OUTPUT

```
Wed Sep 15 12:21:27 1999

This is week 37 of the year 1999

Today is Wednesday, 09/15/1999

It is 21 minutes past hour 12.

Execution time using time() = 11.000000 seconds.
Execution time using clock() = 10000 hundredths of sec.
```

ANALYSIS
This program has numerous comment lines, so it should be easy to follow. Because the time functions are being used, the time.h header file is included on line 4. Line 8 declares three variables of type time_t—start, finish, and now. These variables can hold the time as an offset from January 1, 1970, in seconds. Line 9 declares a pointer to a tm structure. The tm structure was described earlier. The rest of the variables have types that should be familiar to you.

The program records its starting time on line 15. This is done with a call to time(). The program then does virtually the same thing in a different way. Instead of using the value returned by the `time()` function, line 20 passes `time()` a pointer to the variable now. Line 24 does exactly what the comment on line 22 states: It converts the `time_t` value of now to a type `tm` structure. The next few sections of the program print the value of the current time to the screen in various formats. Line 29 uses the `asctime()` function to assign the information to a character pointer, `c`. Line 30 prints the formatted information. The program then waits for the user to press Enter.

Lines 36 through 46 use the `strftime()` function to print the date in three formats. Using Table 17.1, you should be able to determine what these lines print. Do take note of the warnings about some of the format specifiers.

The program then determines the time again on line 50. This is the program-ending time. Line 51 uses the ending time and the starting time to calculate the program's duration by means of the `difftime()` function. This value is printed on line 52. The program concludes by printing the program execution time from the `clock()` function.

17

Error-Handling Functions

The C standard library contains a variety of functions and macros that help you deal with program errors.

The `assert()` Function

The macro `assert()` can diagnose program bugs. It is defined in assert.h, and its prototype is

```
void assert(int expression);
```

The argument *expression* can be anything you want to test—a variable or any C expression. If *expression* evaluates to TRUE, `assert()` does nothing. If *expression* evaluates to FALSE, `assert()` displays an error message on stderr and aborts program execution.

How do you use `assert()`? It is most frequently used to track down program bugs (which are distinct from compilation errors). A bug doesn't prevent a program from compiling, but it causes the program to give incorrect results or to run improperly (locking up, for example). For instance, a financial analysis program you're writing might occasionally give incorrect answers. You suspect that the problem is caused by the variable interest_rate taking on a negative value, which should never happen. To check this, place the statement

```
assert(interest_rate >= 0);
```

at locations in the program where interest_rate is used. If the variable ever does become negative, the `assert()` macro alerts you. You can then examine the relevant code to locate the cause of the problem.

To see how assert() works, run Listing 17.3. If you enter a nonzero value, the program displays the value and terminates normally. If you enter zero, the assert() macro forces abnormal program termination. The exact error message you see will depend on your compiler, but here's a typical example:

```
Assertion failed: x, file list1703.c, line 13
```

Note that, in order for assert() to work, your program must be compiled in debug mode. Refer to your compiler documentation for information on enabling debug mode (as explained in a moment). When you later compile the final version in release mode, the assert() macros are disabled.

LISTING 17.3. Using the assert() macro.

```
1: /* The assert() macro. */
2:
3: #include <stdio.h>
4: #include <assert.h>
5:
6: int main(void)
7: {
8:     int x;
9:
10:     printf("\nEnter an integer value: ");
11:     scanf("%d", &x);
12:
13:     assert(x >= 0);
14:
15:     printf("You entered %d.\n\n", x);
16:     return(0);
17: }
```

INPUT/
OUTPUT
```
Enter an integer value: 10
You entered 10.
Enter an integer value: -1

list1703: list1703.c:13: main: Assertion `x >= 0' failed.
Aborted (core dumped)
```

Your error message might differ, depending on your system and compiler, but the general idea is the same. In this example, it gives you both the C source code filename, list1703.c, and the line number. Notice that the error message states that it has core dumped. That means all the memory belonging to your program has been written to a disk file named core, which can be loaded into in a debugger and examined.

ANALYSIS Run this program to see that the error message displayed by assert() on line 13 includes the expression whose test failed, the name of the file, and the line number where the assert() is located.

The action of assert() depends on another macro named NDEBUG (which stands for "no debugging"). If the macro NDEBUG isn't defined (the default), assert() is active. If NDEBUG is defined, assert() is turned off and has no effect. If you place assert() in various program locations to help with debugging and then solve the problem, you can define NDEBUG to turn assert() off. This is much easier than going through the program and removing the assert() statements (only to discover later that you want to use them again). To define the macro NDEBUG, use the #define directive. You can demonstrate this by adding the line

```
#define NDEBUG
```

to Listing 17.3, on line 2. Now the program prints the value entered and then terminates normally, even if you enter -1.

Note that NDEBUG doesn't need to be defined as anything in particular, as long as it's included in a #define directive. You'll learn more about the #define directive on Day 20.

The errno.h Header File

The header file errno.h defines several macros used to define and document runtime errors. These macros are used in conjunction with the perror() function, which is used for the first time in Day 15, "Using Disk Files." We will study it more fully here.

The errno.h definitions include an external integer named errno. Many C library functions assign a value to this variable if an error occurs during function execution. The file errno.h also defines a group of symbolic constants for these errors, listed in Table 17.2.

TABLE 17.2. The symbolic error constants defined in errno.h.

Name	Value	Message and Meaning
E2BIG	1000	Argument list too long (list length exceeds 128 bytes).
EACCES	5	Permission denied (for example, trying to write to a file opened for read only).
EBADF	6	Bad file descriptor.
EDOM	1002	Math argument out of domain (an argument passed to a math function is outside the allowable range).
EEXIST	80	File exists.
EMFILE	4	Too many open files.
ENOENT	2	No such file or directory.
ENOEXEC	1001	Exec format error.

continues

TABLE 17.2. continued

Name	Value	Message and Meaning
ENOMEM	8	Not enough core (for example, not enough memory to execute the exec() function).
ENOPATH	3	Path not found.
ERANGE	1003	Result out of range (for example, result returned by a math function is too large or too small for the return data type).

You can use errno two ways. Some functions signal, by means of their return values, that an error has occurred. If this happens, you can test the value of errno to determine the nature of the error and take appropriate action. Otherwise, when you have no specific indication that an error occurred, you can test errno. If it's nonzero, an error has occurred, and the specific value of errno indicates the nature of the error. Be sure to reset errno to zero after handling the error. The next section explains perror(), and Listing 17.4 illustrates the use of errno.

The perror() Function

The perror() function is another of C's error-handling tools. When called, perror() displays a message on stderr describing the most recent error that occurred during a library function call or system call. The prototype, in stdio.h, is

```
void perror(char *msg);
```

The argument msg points to an optional, user-defined message. This message is printed first, followed by a colon and the implementation-defined message that describes the most recent error. If you call perror() when no error has occurred, the message displayed is no error.

A call to perror() does nothing to deal with the error condition. It's up to the program to take action. The action might consist of prompting the user to do something such as terminate the program. The action the program takes can be determined by testing the value of errno and by the nature of the error. Note that a program need not include the header file errno.h to use the external variable errno. That header file is required only if your program uses the symbolic error constants listed in Table 17.2. Listing 17.4 illustrates the use of perror() and errno for handling runtime errors.

LISTING 17.4. Using `perror()` and `errno` to deal with runtime errors.

```
1: /* Demonstration of error handling with perror() and errno. */
2:
3: #include <stdio.h>
4: #include <stdlib.h>
5: #include <errno.h>
6:
7: int main(void)
8: {
9:     FILE *fp;
10:    char filename[80];
11:
12:    printf("Enter filename: ");
13:    fgets(filename,80,stdin);
14:    filename[strlen(filename)-1] = 0;
15:
16:    if (( fp = fopen(filename, "r")) == NULL)
17:    {
18:        perror("You goofed!");
19:        printf("errno = %d.\n", errno);
20:        exit(1);
21:    }
22:    else
23:    {
24:        puts("File opened for reading.");
25:        fclose(fp);
26:    }
27:    return(0);
28: }
```

**INPUT/
OUTPUT**
```
Enter file name: list1904.c
File opened for reading.

Enter file name: notafile.xxx
You goofed!: No such file or directory
errno = 2.
```

ANALYSIS This program prints one of two messages, based on whether a file can be opened for reading. Line 15 tries to open a file. If the file opens, the `else` part of the `if` loop executes, printing the following message:

```
File opened for reading.
```

If there is an error when the file is opened, such as the file not existing, lines 18–20 of the `if` loop execute. Line 18 calls the `perror()` function with the string `"You goofed!"`. The error number is then printed. The result of entering a file that does not exist is

```
You goofed!: No such file or directory.
errno = 2
```

Do	Don't
DO include the errno.h header file if you're going to use the symbolic errors listed in Table 17.2. **DO** check for possible errors in your programs. Never assume that everything is okay.	**DON'T** include the errno.h header file if you aren't going to use the symbolic error constants listed in Table 17.2.

Functions That Have Variable Numbers of Arguments

You have used several library functions, such as `printf()` and `scanf()`, that take a variable number of arguments. You can write your own functions that take a variable argument list. Programs that have functions with variable argument lists must include the header file stdarg.h.

When you declare a function that takes a variable argument list, you first list the fixed parameters—those that are always present (there must be at least one fixed parameter). You then include an ellipsis (. . .) at the end of the parameter list to indicate that zero or more additional arguments are passed to the function. During this discussion, please remember the distinction between a parameter and an argument, as explained on Day 4, "Functions: The Basics."

How does the function know how many arguments have been passed to it on a specific call? You tell it. One of the fixed parameters informs the function of the total number of arguments. For example, when you use the `printf()` function, the number of conversion specifiers in the format string tells the function how many additional arguments to expect. More directly, one of the function's fixed arguments can be the number of additional arguments. The example you'll see in a moment uses this approach, but first you need to look at the tools that C provides for dealing with a variable argument list.

The function must also know the type of each argument in the variable list. In the case of `printf()`, the conversion specifiers indicate the type of each argument. In other cases, such as the following example, all arguments in the variable list are of the same type, so there's no problem. To create a function that accepts different types in the variable argument list, you must devise a method of passing information about the argument types. For example, you could use a character code, as was done in the function `half()` in Listing 14.13.

The tools for using a variable argument list are defined in stdarg.h. These tools are used within the function to retrieve the arguments in the variable list. They are as follows:

va_list	A pointer data type
va_start()	A macro used to initialize the argument list
va_arg()	A macro used to retrieve each argument, in turn, from the variable list
va_end()	A macro used to clean up when all arguments have been retrieved

I've outlined how these macros are used in a function, and then I've included an example. When the function is called, the code in the function must follow these steps to access its arguments:

1. Declare a pointer variable of type va_list. This pointer is used to access the individual arguments. It is common practice, although certainly not required, to call this variable arg_ptr.

2. Call the macro va_start(), passing it the pointer arg_ptr and the name of the last fixed argument. The macro va_start() has no return value; it initializes the pointer arg_ptr to point at the first argument in the variable list.

3. To retrieve each argument, call va_arg(), passing it the pointer arg_ptr and the data type of the next argument. The return value of va_arg() is the value of the next argument. If the function has received n arguments in the variable list, call va_arg() n times to retrieve the arguments in the order listed in the function call.

4. When all the arguments in the variable list have been retrieved, call va_end(), passing it the pointer arg_ptr. In some implementations, this macro performs no action, but in others, it performs necessary clean-up actions. You should get in the habit of calling va_end() in case you use a C implementation that requires it.

Now for that example: The function average() in Listing 17.5 calculates the arithmetic average of a list of integers. This program passes the function a single fixed argument, indicating the number of additional arguments followed by the list of numbers.

LISTING 17.5. Using a variable-size argument list.

```
1: /* Functions with a variable number of arguments. */
2:
3: #include <stdio.h>
4: #include <stdarg.h>
5:
6: float average(int num, ...);
```

continues

LISTING 17.5. continued

```
 7:
 8: int main(void)
 9: {
10:     float x;
11:
12:     x = average(10, 1, 2, 3, 4, 5, 6, 7, 8, 9, 10);
13:     printf("The first average is %f.\n", x);
14:     x = average(5, 121, 206, 76, 31, 5);
15:     printf("The second average is %f.\n", x);
16:     return(0);
17: }
18:
19: float average(int num, ...)
20: {
21:     /* Declare a variable of type va_list. */
22:
23:     va_list arg_ptr;
24:     int count, total = 0;
25:
26:     /* Initialize the argument pointer. */
27:
28:     va_start(arg_ptr, num);
29:
30:     /* Retrieve each argument in the variable list. */
31:
32:     for (count = 0; count < num; count++)
33:         total += va_arg( arg_ptr, int );
34:
35:     /* Perform clean-up. */
36:
37:     va_end(arg_ptr);
38:
39:     /* Divide the total by the number of values to get the */
40:     /* average. Cast the total to type float so the value */
41:     /* returned is type float. */
42:
43:     return ((float)total/num);
44: }
```

OUTPUT
The first average is 5.500000.
The second average is 87.800003.

ANALYSIS
The function average() is first called on line 19. The first argument passed, the only fixed argument, specifies the number of values in the variable argument list. In the function, as each argument in the variable list is retrieved on lines 32–33, it is added to the variable total. After all arguments have been retrieved, line 43 casts total as type float and then divides total by num to obtain the average.

Two other things should be pointed out in this listing. Line 28 calls va_start() to initialize the argument list. This must be done before the values are retrieved. Line 37 calls va_end() to clean up because the function is done with the values. You should use both these functions in your programs whenever you write a function with a variable number of arguments.

Strictly speaking, a function that accepts a variable number of arguments doesn't need to have a fixed parameter informing it of the number of arguments being passed. For example, you could mark the end of the argument list with a special value not used elsewhere. This method places limitations on the arguments that can be passed, however, so it's best avoided.

Searching and Sorting

17

Among the most common tasks that programs perform are searching and sorting data. The C standard library contains general-purpose functions that you can use for each task.

Searching with `bsearch()`

The library function bsearch() performs a binary search of a data array, looking for an array element that matches a key. To use bsearch(), the array must be sorted into ascending order. Also, the program must provide the comparison function used by bsearch() to determine whether one data item is greater than, less than, or equal to another item. The prototype of bsearch() is in stdlib.h:

```
void *bsearch(const void *key, const void *base, size_t num, size_t width,
int (*cmp)(void *element1, void *element2));
```

This is a fairly complex prototype, so go through it carefully. The argument key is a pointer to the data item being searched for, and base is a pointer to the first element of the array being searched. Both are declared as type void pointers, so they can point to any of C's data objects.

The argument num is the number of elements in the array, and width is the size (in bytes) of each element. The type specifier size_t refers to the data type returned by the sizeof() operator, which is unsigned. The sizeof() operator is usually used to obtain the values for num and width.

The final argument, cmp, is a pointer to the comparison function. This can be a user-written function or, when searching string data, it can be the library function strcmp(). The comparison function must meet the following two criteria:

- It is passed pointers to two data items.
- It returns a type `int` as follows:

  < 0   Element 1 is less than element 2.

  0   Element 1 is equal to element 2.

  > 0   Element 1 is greater than element 2.

The return value of `bsearch()` is a type `void` pointer. The function returns a pointer to the first array element it finds that matches the key, or `NULL` if no match is found. You must cast the returned pointer to the proper type before using it.

The `sizeof()` operator can provide the `num` and `width` arguments as follows. If `array[]` is the array to be searched, the statement

```
sizeof(array[0]);
```

returns the value of `width`—the size (in bytes) of one array element. Because the expression `sizeof(array)` returns the size, in bytes, of the entire array, the following statement obtains the value of `num`, the number of elements in the array:

```
sizeof(array)/sizeof(array[0])
```

The binary search algorithm is very efficient; it can search a large array quickly. Its operation is dependent on the array elements being arranged in ascending order. Here's how the algorithm works:

1. The key is compared to the element at the middle of the array. If there's a match, the search is done. Otherwise, the key must be either less than or greater than the array element.

2. If the key is less than the array element, the matching element, if any, must be located in the first half of the array. Likewise, if the key is greater than the array element, the matching element must be located in the second half of the array.

3. The search is restricted to the appropriate half of the array, and then the algorithm returns to step 1.

You can see that each comparison performed by a binary search eliminates half of the array being searched. For example, a 1,000-element array can be searched with only 10 comparisons, and a 16,000-element array can be searched with only 14 comparisons. In general, a binary search requires n comparisons to search an array of 2^n elements.

Sorting with `qsort()`

The library function `qsort()` is an implementation of the quicksort algorithm, invented by C.A.R. Hoare. This function sorts an array into order. Usually the result is in ascending order, but qsort() can be used for descending order as well. The function prototype, defined in stdlib.h, is

```
void qsort(void *base, size_t num, size_t size,
int (*cmp)(void *element1, void *element2));
```

The argument base points at the first element in the array, num is the number of elements in the array, and size is the size (in bytes) of one array element. The argument cmp is a pointer to a comparison function. The rules for the comparison function are the same as for the comparison function used by bsearch(), described in the preceding section: You often use the same comparison function for both bsearch() and qsort(). The function qsort() has no return value.

Searching and Sorting: Two Demonstrations

Listing 17.6 demonstrates the use of qsort() and bsearch(). The program sorts and searches an array of values.

17

LISTING 17.6. Using the qsort() and bsearch() functions with values.

```
 1: /* Using qsort() and bsearch() with values.*/
 2:
 3: #include <stdio.h>
 4: #include <stdlib.h>
 5:
 6: #define MAX 20
 7:
 8: int intcmp(const void *v1, const void *v2);
 9:
10: int main(void)
11: {
12:     int arr[MAX], count, key, *ptr;
13:
14:     /* Enter some integers from the user. */
15:
16:     printf("Enter %d integer values; press Enter after each.\n", MAX);
17:
18:     for (count = 0; count < MAX; count++)
19:         scanf("%d", &arr[count]);
20:
21:     puts("Press Enter to sort the values.");
22:     getc(stdin);
23:
24:     /* Sort the array into ascending order. */
25:
26:     qsort(arr, MAX, sizeof(arr[0]), intcmp);
27:
28:     /* Display the sorted array. */
```

continues

LISTING 17.6. continued

```
29:
30:         for (count = 0; count < MAX; count++)
31:             printf("\narr[%d] = %d.", count, arr[count]);
32:
33:         puts("\nPress Enter to continue.");
34:         getc(stdin);
35:
36:         /* Enter a search key. */
37:
38:         printf("Enter a value to search for: ");
39:         scanf("%d", &key);
40:
41:         /* Perform the search. */
42:
43:         ptr = (int *)bsearch(&key, arr, MAX, sizeof(arr[0]),intcmp);
44:
45:         if ( ptr != NULL )
46:             printf("%d found at arr[%d].\n", key, (ptr - arr));
47:         else
48:             printf("%d not found.\n", key);
49:         return(0);
50: }
51:
52: int intcmp(const void *v1, const void *v2)
53: {
54:         return (*(int *)v1 - *(int *)v2);
55: }
```

INPUT/ OUTPUT	Enter 20 integer values; press Enter after each.

```
45
12
999
1000
321
123
2300
954
1968
12
2
1999
1776
1812
1456
1
9999
3
76
200
```

```
Press Enter to sort the values.

arr[0] = 1.
arr[1] = 2.
arr[2] = 3.
arr[3] = 12.
arr[4] = 12.
arr[5] = 45.
arr[6] = 76.
arr[7] = 123.
arr[8] = 200.
arr[9] = 321.
arr[10] = 954.
arr[11] = 999.
arr[12] = 1000.
arr[13] = 1456.
arr[14] = 1776.
arr[15] = 1812.
arr[16] = 1968.
arr[17] = 1999.
arr[18] = 2300.
arr[19] = 9999.
Press Enter to continue.

Enter a value to search for:
1776
1776 found at arr[14]
```

17

ANALYSIS Listing 17.6 incorporates everything described previously about sorting and searching. This program lets you enter up to MAX values (20 in this case). It sorts the values and prints them in order. Then it lets you enter a value to search for in the array. A printed message states the search's status.

Familiar code is used to obtain the values for the array on lines 18 and 19. Line 26 contains the call to qsort() to sort the array. The first argument is a pointer to the array's first element. This is followed by MAX, the number of elements in the array. The size of the first element is then provided so that qsort() knows the width of each item. The call is finished with the argument for the sort function, intcmp.

The function intcmp() is defined on lines 52–55. It returns the difference of the two values passed to it. This might seem too simple at first, but remember what values the comparison function is supposed to return. If the elements are equal, 0 should be returned. If element one is greater than element two, a positive number should be returned. If element one is less than element two, a negative number should be returned. That is exactly what intcmp() does.

The searching is done with bsearch(). Notice that its arguments are virtually the same as those of qsort(). The difference is that the first argument of bsearch() is the key to be searched for. bsearch() returns a pointer to the location of the found key or NULL if the key isn't found. On line 43, ptr is assigned the returned value of bsearch(). ptr is used in the if loop on lines 45–48 to print the status of the search.

Listing 17.7 has the same functionality as Listing 17.6; however, Listing 17.7 sorts and searches strings.

LISTING **17.7**. Using qsort() and bsearch() with strings.

```
1: /* Using qsort() and bsearch() with strings. */
2:
3: #include <stdio.h>
4: #include <stdlib.h>
5: #include <string.h>
6:
7: #define MAX 20
8:
9: int comp(const void *s1, const void *s2);
10:
11: int main(void)
12: {
13:     char *data[MAX], buf[80], *ptr, *key, **key1;
14:     int count;
15:
16:     /* Input a list of words. */
17:
18:     printf("Enter %d words, pressing Enter after each.\n",MAX);
19:
20:     for (count = 0; count < MAX; count++)
21:     {
22:         printf("Word %d: ", count+1);
23:         fgets(buf,80,stdin);
24:         buf[strlen(buf)-1] = 0;
25:         data[count] = malloc(strlen(buf)+1);
26:         strcpy(data[count], buf);
27:     }
28:
29:     /* Sort the words (actually, sort the pointers). */
30:
31:     qsort(data, MAX, sizeof(data[0]), comp);
32:
33:     /* Display the sorted words. */
34:
35:     for (count = 0; count < MAX; count++)
36:         printf("\n%d: %s", count+1, data[count]);
37:
38:     /* Get a search key. */
39:
40:     printf("\n\nEnter a search key: ");
41:     fgets(buf,80,stdin);
```

```
42:        buf[strlen(buf)-1] = 0;
43:
44:        /* Perform the search. First, make key1 a pointer */
45:        /* to the pointer to the search key.*/
46:
47:        key = buf;
48:        key1 = &key;
49:        ptr = bsearch(key1, data, MAX, sizeof(data[0]), comp);
50:
51:        if (ptr != NULL)
52:            printf("%s found.\n", buf);
53:        else
54:            printf("%s not found.\n", buf);
55:        return(0);
56: }
57:
58: int comp(const void *s1, const void *s2)
59: {
60:        return (strcmp(*(char **)s1, *(char **)s2));
61: }
```

17

```
Enter 20 words, pressing Enter after each.
Word 1: apple
Word 2: orange
Word 3: grapefruit
Word 4: peach
Word 5: plum
Word 6: pear
Word 7: cherries
Word 8: banana
Word 9: lime
Word 10: lemon
Word 11: tangerine
Word 12: star
Word 13: watermelon
Word 14: cantaloupe
Word 15: musk melon
Word 16: strawberry
Word 17: blackberry
Word 18: blueberry
Word 19: grape
Word 20: cranberry

1: apple
2: banana
3: blackberry
4: blueberry
5: cantaloupe
6: cherries
7: cranberry
8: grape
```

```
9: grapefruit
10: lemon
11: lime
12: musk melon
13: orange
14: peach
15: pear
16: plum
17: star
18: strawberry
19: tangerine
20: watermelon

Enter a search key: orange
orange found.
```

ANALYSIS A couple of points about Listing 17.7 bear mentioning. This program makes use of an array of pointers to strings, a technique introduced on Day 14, "Pointers: Beyond the Basics." As you saw in that day, you can sort the strings by sorting the array of pointers. However, this method requires a modification to the comparison function. This function is passed pointers to the two items in the array that are compared. However, you want to sort the array of pointers based not on the values of the pointers themselves but on the values of the strings they point to.

Because of this, you must use a comparison function that is passed pointers to pointers. Each argument to comp() is a pointer to an array element, and because each element itself is a pointer (to a string), the argument is, therefore, a pointer to a pointer. Within the function itself, you dereference the pointers so that the return value of comp() depends on the values of the strings pointed to.

The fact that the arguments passed to comp() are pointers to pointers creates another problem. You store the search key in buf[], and you also know that the name of an array (buf in this case) is a pointer to the array. However, you need to pass not buf itself, but a pointer to buf. The problem is that buf is a pointer constant, not a pointer variable. buf itself has no address in memory; it's a symbol that evaluates to the address of the array. Because of this, you can't create a pointer that points to buf by using the address-of operator in front of buf, as in &buf.

What to do? First, create a pointer variable and assign the value of buf to it. In the program, this pointer variable has the name key. Because key is a pointer variable, it has an address, and you can create a pointer that contains that address—in this case, key1. When you finally call bsearch(), the first argument is key1, a pointer to a pointer to the key string. The function bsearch() passes that argument on to comp(), and everything works properly.

Do	Don't
	DON'T forget to put your search array into ascending order before using `bsearch()`.

Summary

Today we explored some of the more useful functions supplied in the C function library. There are functions that perform mathematical calculations, deal with time, and assist your program with error handling. The functions for sorting and searching data are particularly useful; they can save you considerable time when you're writing your programs.

Q&A

Q Why do nearly all of the math functions return `doubles`?

A The answer to this question is to achieve precision, not consistency. A `double` is more precise than the other variable types; therefore, your answers are more accurate. On Day 18, "Working with Memory," you will learn the specifics of casting variables and variable promotion. These topics are also applicable to precision.

Q Are `bsearch()` and `qsort()` the only ways in C to sort and search?

A These two functions are provided in the standard library; however, you don't have to use them. Many computer-programming textbooks teach you how to write your own searching and sorting programs. C contains all the commands you need to write your own. You can purchase especially written searching and sorting routines. The biggest benefits of `bsearch()` and `qsort()` are that they are already written, and they are provided with any ANSI/ISO-compatible compiler.

Q Do the math functions validate bad data?

A Never assume that data entered is correct. Always validate user-entered data. For example, if you pass a negative value to `sqrt()`, the function generates an error. If you're formatting the output, you probably don't want this error displayed as it is. Remove the `if` statement in Listing 17.1 and enter a negative number to see what I mean.

Workshop

The Workshop provides quiz questions to help you solidify your understanding of the material covered and exercises to provide you with experience in using what you've learned. The answers to the quiz and exercises are provided in Appendix C, "Answers."

Quiz

1. What is the return data type for all of C's mathematical functions?

2. What C variable type is `time_t` equivalent to?

3. What are the differences between the `time()` function and the `clock()` function?

4. When you call the `perror()` function, what does it do to correct an existing error condition?

5. Can you write a function that takes a variable argument list only, with no fixed arguments?

6. What macros should be used when you write functions with variable argument lists?

7. Before you search an array with `bsearch()`, what must you do?

8. Using `bsearch()`, how many comparisons would be required to find an element if the array had 16,000 items?

9. Using `bsearch()`, how many comparisons would be required to find an element if an array had only 10 items?

10. Using `bsearch()`, how many comparisons would be required to find an element if an array had 2,000,000 items?

11. What values must a comparison function for `bsearch()` and `qsort()` return?

12. What does `bsearch()` return if it can't find an element in an array?

Exercises

1. Write a call to `bsearch()`. The array to be searched is called `names`, and the values are characters. The comparison function is called `comp_names()`. Assume that all the names are the same size.

2. **BUG BUSTER:** What is wrong with the following program?

```
#include <stdio.h>
#include <stdlib.h>
int main(void)
{
int values[10], count, key, *ptr;

printf("Enter values");
for( ctr = 0; ctr < 10; ctr++ )
scanf( "%d", &values[ctr] );

qsort(values, 10, compare_function());
}
```

3. **BUG BUSTER:** Is anything wrong with the following compare function?

```
int intcmp( int element1, int element2)
{
if ( element 1 > element 2 )
return -1;
else if ( element 1 < element2 )
return 1;
else
return 0;
}
```

Answers are not provided for the following exercises:

4. Modify Listing 17.1 so that the sqrt() function works with negative numbers. Do this by taking the absolute value of x. You might need to consult the man pages to find the appropriate function for calculating the absolute value.

5. Write a program that consists of a menu that performs various math functions. Use as many of the math functions as you can.

6. Using the time functions discussed today, write a function that causes the program to pause for approximately five seconds.

7. Add the assert() function to the program in exercise 4. The program should print a message if a negative value is entered.

8. Write a program that accepts 30 names and sorts them using qsort(). The program should print the sorted names.

9. Modify the program in exercise 8 so that if the user enters QUIT, the program stops accepting input and sorts the entered values.

10. Refer to Day 14 for a brute-force method of sorting an array of pointers to strings based on the string values. Write a program that measures the time required to sort a large array of pointers with that method and then compares that time with the time required to perform the same sort with the library function qsort().

17

DAY **18**

Working with Memory

Today's lesson covers some of the more advanced aspects of managing memory within your C programs. Today you will learn

- About type conversions
- How to allocate and free memory storage
- How to manipulate memory blocks
- How to manipulate individual bits

Type Conversions

All of C's data objects have a specific type. A numeric variable can be an `int` or a `float`, a pointer can be a pointer to a `double` or `char`, and so on. Programs often require that different types be combined in expressions and statements. What happens in such cases? Sometimes C automatically handles the different types, so you don't need to be concerned. Other times, you must explicitly convert one data type to another to avoid erroneous results. You've seen this in earlier lessons when you had to convert or cast a type `void` pointer to a specific type before using it. In this and other situations, you need a clear understanding of when explicit type conversions are necessary and what types of errors can result when the proper conversion isn't applied. The following sections cover C's automatic and explicit type conversions.

Automatic Type Conversions

As the name implies, automatic type conversions are performed automatically by the C compiler without any action on your part. However, you should be aware of what's going on so that you can understand how C evaluates expressions.

Type Promotion in Expressions

When a C expression is evaluated, the resulting value has a particular data type. If all the components in the expression have the same type, the resulting type is that type as well. For example, if x and y are both type int, the following expression is type int also:

```
x + y
```

What if the components of an expression have different types? In that case, the expression has the same type as its most comprehensive component. From least-comprehensive to most-comprehensive, the numerical data types are

```
char

int

long

float

double
```

Thus, an expression containing an int and a char evaluates to type int, an expression containing a long and a float evaluates to type float, and so on.

Within expressions, individual operands are promoted as necessary to match the associated operands in the expression. Operands are promoted, in pairs, for each binary operator in the expression. Of course, promotion isn't needed if both operands are the same type. If they aren't, promotion follows these rules:

- If either operand is a double, the other operand is promoted to type double.
- If either operand is a float, the other operand is promoted to type float.
- If either operand is a long, the other operand is converted to type long.

For example, if x is an int and y is a float, evaluating the expression x/y causes x to be promoted to type float before the expression is evaluated. That doesn't mean the type of variable x is changed. It means a type float copy of x is created and used in the expression evaluation. The value of the expression is, as you just learned, type float. Likewise, if x is a type double and y is a type float, y will be promoted to double.

Conversion by Assignment

Promotions also occur with the assignment operator. The expression on the right side of an assignment statement is always promoted to the type of the data object on the left side of the assignment operator. Note that this might cause a "demotion" rather than a promotion. If f is a type float and i is a type int, i is promoted to type float in this assignment statement:

```
f = i;
```

In contrast, the assignment statement

```
i = f;
```

causes f to be demoted to type int. Its fractional part is lost on assignment to i. Remember that f itself isn't changed at all; promotion affects only a copy of the value. Thus, after the following statements are executed

```
float f = 1.23;
int i;
i = f;
```

the variable i has the value 1, and f still has the value 1.23. As this example illustrates, the fractional part is lost when a floating-point number is converted to an integer type.

You should be aware that when an integer type is converted to a floating-point type, the resulting floating-point value might not exactly match the integer value. That is because the floating-point format used internally by the computer can't accurately represent every possible integer number, so keep integer values in type int or type long variables.

Explicit Conversions Using Typecasts

A *typecast* uses the cast operator to explicitly control type conversions in your program. A typecast consists of a type name, in parentheses, before an expression. Casts can be performed on arithmetic expressions and pointers. The result is that the expression is converted to the type specified by the cast. In this manner, you can control the type of expressions in your program rather than relying on C's automatic conversions.

Casting Arithmetic Expressions

Casting an arithmetic expression tells the compiler to represent the value of the expression in a certain way. In effect, a cast is similar to a promotion, which was discussed earlier. However, a cast is under your control, not the compiler's. For example, if i is a type int, the expression

```
(float)i
```

18

casts i to type float. In other words, the program makes an internal copy of the value of i in floating-point format.

When would you use a typecast with an arithmetic expression? The most common use is to avoid losing the fractional part of the answer in an integer division. Listing 18.1 illustrates this. You should compile and run this program.

LISTING 18.1. When one integer is divided by another, any fractional part of the answer is lost.

```
 1: #include <stdio.h>
 2:
 3: int main(void)
 4: {
 5:     int i1 = 100, i2 = 40;
 6:     float f1;
 7:
 8:     f1 = i1/i2;
 9:     printf("%f\n", f1);
10:     return(0);
11: }
```

OUTPUT   `2.000000`

ANALYSIS   The answer displayed by the program is `2.000000`, but 100/40 evaluates to 2.5. What happened? The expression i1/i2 on line 8 contains two type int variables. Following the rules explained earlier today, the value of the expression i1/i2 is type int itself. As such, it can represent only whole numbers, so the fractional part of the answer is lost.

You might think that assigning the result of i1/i2 to a type float variable promotes it to type float. That is correct, but now it's too late; the fractional part of the answer is already gone.

To avoid this sort of inaccuracy, you must cast one of the type int variables to type float. If one of the variables is cast to type float, the previous rules tell you that the other variable is promoted automatically to type float, and the value of the expression is also type float. The fractional part of the answer is thus preserved. To demonstrate this, change line 8 in the source code so that the assignment statement reads as follows:

```
f1 = (float)i1/i2;
```

The program will then display the correct answer.

Casting Pointers

You have already been introduced to the casting of pointers. A type void pointer is a generic pointer; it can point to anything. Before you can use a void pointer, you must cast it to the proper type. Note that you don't need to cast a pointer in order to assign a value to it or to compare it with NULL. However, you must cast it before dereferencing it or performing pointer arithmetic with it.

Do	Don't
DO use a cast to promote or demote variable values when necessary.	DON'T use a cast just to prevent a compiler warning. You might find that using a cast gets rid of a warning, but before removing the warning this way, be sure you understand why you're getting the warning.

Allocating Memory Storage Space

The C library contains functions for allocating memory storage space at runtime, a process called *dynamic memory allocation*. This technique can have significant advantages over explicitly allocating memory in the program source code by declaring variables, structures, and arrays. The latter method, called *static memory allocation,* requires you to know, when you're writing the program, exactly how much memory you need. Dynamic memory allocation enables the program to react, while it's executing, to demands for memory such as user input. All the functions for handling dynamic memory allocation require the header file stdlib.h; with some compilers, malloc.h is required as well. Note that all allocation functions return a type void pointer. A type void pointer must be cast to the appropriate type before being used.

Before we move on to the details, a few words are in order about memory allocation. What exactly does it mean? Each computer has a certain amount of memory (random access memory, or RAM) installed. This amount varies from system to system. When you run a program, whether a word processor, a graphics program, or a C program you wrote yourself, the program is loaded from disk into the computer's memory. The memory space the program occupies includes the program code, as well as space for all the program's static data—that is, data items that are declared in the source code. The memory left over is what's available for allocation using the functions in this section.

How much memory is available for allocation? It depends. If you're running a large program on a system with only a modest amount of memory installed, the amount of free memory will be small. Conversely, when a small program is running on a multi-megabyte system, plenty of memory will be available. That means your programs can't make any assumptions about memory availability. When a memory allocation function is

18

called, you must check its return value to ensure that the memory was allocated successfully. In addition, your programs must be able to gracefully handle the situation when a
memory allocation request fails. Unfortunately, Linux is a multiuser, multitasking operating system that makes use of virtual memory (disk space used as temporary memory), so
there is no general, reliable way of determining exactly how much memory is available.
This is usually not a problem.

Also note that your operating system might have an effect on memory availability. Linux
and other members of the UNIX family basically behave in the same way. Some other
operating systems might handle memory in a slightly different way, but in general, these
operating system differences in memory allocation should be transparent to you. If you
use one of the C functions to allocate memory, the call either succeeds or fails, and you
don't need to worry about the details of what's happening.

The `malloc()` Function

In previous days, you learned how to use the `malloc()` library functionto allocate storage
space for strings. The `malloc()` function isn't limited to allocating memory for strings,
of course; it can allocate space for any storage need. This function allocates memory by
the byte. Recall that `malloc()`'s prototype is

```
void *malloc(size_t num);
```

The argument `size_t` is defined in stdlib.h as `unsigned_int` or `unsigned long`. The
`malloc()` function allocates *num* bytes of storage space and returns a pointer to the first
byte. This function returns NULL if the requested storage space couldn't be allocated.
According to the ISO standard, if *num* `== 0`, the library might do a number of things
depending on the system. It might return a NULL pointer or a valid pointer to some area
of memory, as the library sees fit. The GNU C library, which is part of the GNU/Linux
system, takes the second approach. Even though a valid pointer has been returned, no
guarantees can be made as to the size of the memory area the pointer points to; therefore,
it is not safe to use it.

The `calloc()` Function

The `calloc()` function also allocates memory. Rather than allocating a group of bytes as
`malloc()` does, `calloc()` allocates a group of objects. The function prototype is

```
void *calloc(size_t num, size_t size);
```

The argument *num* is the number of objects to allocate, and *size* is the size (in bytes) of
each object. If allocation is successful, all the allocated memory is cleared (set to 0), and
the function returns a pointer to the first byte. If allocation fails or if either `num` or `size` is
0, the function returns NULL.

Listing 18.2 illustrates the use of `calloc()`.

LISTING 18.2. Using the `calloc()` function to allocate memory storage space dynamically.

```
 1: /* Demonstrates calloc(). */
 2:
 3: #include <stdlib.h>
 4: #include <stdio.h>
 5:
 6: int main(void)
 7: {
 8:     unsigned num;
 9:     int *ptr;
10:
11:     printf("Enter the number of type int to allocate: ");
12:     scanf("%d", &num);
13:
14:     ptr = (int*)calloc(num, sizeof(int));
15:
16:     if (ptr != NULL)
17:         puts("Memory allocation was successful.");
18:     else
19:         puts("Memory allocation failed.");
20:     return(0);
21: }
```

```
Enter the number of type int to allocate: 100
Memory allocation was successful.
```

Caution

> Don't be tempted to enter ridiculously large values at the prompt. Requesting amounts of memory significantly larger than physical memory can cause Linux to swap all the currently running applications to virtual memory on disk. Swapping other applications to disk can take a number of minutes. While this is being done, your Linux machine will respond very sluggishly to mouse and keyboard commands. Eventually, the program will terminate and print out one of the two messages. It might, however, take a number of minutes for Linux to terminate your program and swap the applications back from virtual memory into physical memory.

This program prompts for a value on lines 11 and 12. This number determines how much space the program will attempt to allocate. The program attempts to allocate enough memory (line 14) to hold the specified number of `int` variables. If the allocation fails, the return value from `calloc()` is `NULL`; otherwise, it's a pointer to the allocated memory. In the case of this program, the return value from `calloc()` is placed in the `int` pointer, `ptr`. An `if` statement on lines 16–19 checks the status of the allocation based on `ptr`'s value and prints an appropriate message.

The `realloc()` Function

The `realloc()` function changes the size of a block of memory that was previously allocated with `malloc()` or `calloc()`. The function prototype is

```
void *realloc(void *ptr, size_t size);
```

The `ptr` argument is a pointer to the original block of memory. The new size, in bytes, is specified by `size`. There are several possible outcomes with `realloc()`:

- If sufficient space exists to expand the memory block pointed to by `ptr`, the additional memory is allocated and the function returns `ptr`.
- If sufficient space does not exist to expand the current block in its current location, a new block of the size for `size` is allocated, and existing data is copied from the old block to the beginning of the new block. The old block is freed, and the function returns a pointer to the new block.
- If the `ptr` argument is `NULL`, the function acts like `malloc()`, allocating a block of `size` bytes and returning a pointer to it.
- If the argument size is 0, the memory that `ptr` points to is freed, and the function returns `NULL`.
- If memory is insufficient for the reallocation (either expanding the old block or allocating a new one), the function returns `NULL`, and the original block is unchanged.

Listing 18.3 demonstrates the use of `realloc()`.

LISTING 18.3. Using `realloc()` to increase the size of a block of dynamically allocated memory.

```
 1: /* Using realloc() to change memory allocation. */
 2:
 3: #include <stdio.h>
 4: #include <stdlib.h>
 5: #include <string.h>
 6:
 7: int main(void)
 8: {
 9:     char buf[80], *message;
10:
11:     /* Input a string. */
12:
13:     puts("Enter a line of text.");
14:     fgets(buf,80,stdin);
15:     buf[strlen(buf)-1] = 0;   /* Strip off newline char. */
16:
```

```
17:     /* Allocate the initial block and copy the string to it. */
18:     message = realloc(NULL, strlen(buf)+1);
19:     strcpy(message, buf);
20:
21:     /* Display the message. */
22:
23:     puts(message);
24:
25:     /* Get another string from the user. */
26:
27:     puts("Enter another line of text.");
28:     fgets(buf,80,stdin);
29:     buf[strlen(buf)-1] = 0;   /* Strip off newline char. */
30:
31:     /* Increase the allocation, then concatenate the string to it. */
32:
33:     message = realloc(message,(strlen(message) + strlen(buf)+1));
34:     strcat(message, buf);
35:
36:     /* Display the new message. */
37:     puts(message);
38:     return(0);
39: }
```

OUTPUT

```
Enter a line of text.
This is the first line of text.
This is the first line of text.
Enter another line of text.
This is the second line of text.
This is the first line of text.This is the second line of text.
```

18

ANALYSIS   This program gets an input string on line 14, reading it into an array of characters called buf. The string is then copied into a memory location pointed to by message (line 19). message was allocated using realloc() on line 18. realloc() was called even though there was no previous allocation. By passing NULL as the first parameter, realloc() knows that this is a first allocation.

Line 28 gets a second string in the buf buffer. This string is concatenated to the string already held in message. Because message is just big enough to hold the first string, it must be reallocated to make room to hold both the first and second strings. This is exactly what line 33 does. The program concludes by printing the final concatenated string.

The free() Function

When you allocate memory with either malloc() or calloc(), it is taken from the dynamic memory pool that is available to your program. This pool is sometimes called the *heap,* and it is finite. When your program finishes using a particular block of dynamically allocated memory, you should deallocate, or free, the memory to make it available for future use. To free memory that was allocated dynamically, use free(). Its prototype is

```
void free(void *ptr);
```

The free() function releases the memory pointed to by ptr. This memory must have been allocated with malloc(), calloc(), or realloc(). If ptr is NULL, free() does nothing. Listing 18.4 demonstrates the free() function.

LISTING 18.4. Using free() to release previously allocated dynamic memory.

```
1: /* Using free() to release allocated dynamic memory. */
2:
3: #include <stdio.h>
4: #include <stdlib.h>
5: #include <string.h>
6:
7: #define BLOCKSIZE 30000
8:
9: int main(void)
10: {
11:     void *ptr1, *ptr2;
12:
13:     /* Allocate one block. */
14:
15:     ptr1 = malloc(BLOCKSIZE);
16:
17:     if (ptr1 != NULL)
18:         printf("First allocation of %d bytes successful.\n",BLOCKSIZE);
19:     else
20:     {
21:         printf("Attempt to allocate %d bytes failed.\n",BLOCKSIZE);
22:         exit(1);
23:     }
24:
25:     /* Try to allocate another block. */
26:
27:     ptr2 = malloc(BLOCKSIZE);
28:
29:     if (ptr2 != NULL)
30:     {
31:         /* If allocation successful, print message and exit. */
32:
33:         printf("Second allocation of %d bytes successful.\n",
34:                 BLOCKSIZE);
35:         exit(0);
36:     }
37:
38:     /* If not successful, free the first block and try again.*/
```

```
39:
40:     printf("Second attempt to allocate %d bytes failed.\n",BLOCKSIZE);
41:     free(ptr1);
42:     printf("\nFreeing first block.\n");
43:
44:     ptr2 = malloc(BLOCKSIZE);
45:
46:     if (ptr2 != NULL)
47:         printf("After free(), allocation of %d bytes successful.\n",
48:                 BLOCKSIZE);
49:     return(0);
50: }
```

OUTPUT
```
First allocation of 30000 bytes successful.
Second allocation of 30000 bytes successful.
```

ANALYSIS This program tries to dynamically allocate two blocks of memory. It uses the defined constant BLOCKSIZE to determine how much to allocate. Line 15 does the first allocation using malloc(). Lines 17 through 23 check the status of the allocation by determining whether the return value was equal to NULL. A message is displayed, stating the status of the allocation. If the allocation failed, the program exits. Line 27 tries to allocate a second block of memory, again checking to see whether the allocation was successful (lines 29 through 36). If the second allocation was successful, a call to exit() ends the program. If it was not successful, a message states that the attempt to allocate memory failed. The first block is then freed with free() (line 41), and a new attempt is made to allocate the second block.

On systems, such as Linux, with large amounts of virtual memory, these two allocations should always succeed. The output you will see is

```
First allocation of 30000 bytes successful.
Second attempt to allocate 30000 bytes failed.

Freeing first block.

After free(), allocation of 30000 bytes successful.
```

Do	**Don't**
DO free allocated memory when you're done with it.	**DON'T** assume that a call to malloc(), calloc(), or realloc() was successful. In other words, always check to see that the memory was indeed allocated.

Manipulating Memory Blocks

So far today, you've seen how to allocate and free blocks of memory. The C library also contains functions that can be used to manipulate blocks of memory—setting all bytes in a block to a specified value, copying, and moving information from one location to another.

The `memset()` Function

To set all the bytes in a block of memory to a particular value, use `memset()`. The function prototype is

```
void * memset(void *dest, int c, size_t count);
```

The argument `dest` points to the block of memory. `c` is the value to set, and `count` is the number of bytes, starting at `dest`, to be set. Note that although `c` is a type `int`, it is treated as a type `char`. In other words, only the low-order byte is used, and you can specify values of `c` only in the range 0 through 255.

Use `memset()` to initialize a block of memory to a specified value. Because this function can use only a type `char` as the initialization value, it is not useful for working with blocks of data types other than type `char`, except when you want to initialize to 0. In other words, it wouldn't be efficient to use `memset()` to initialize an array of type `int` to the value 99, but you could initialize all array elements to the value 0. `memset()` will be demonstrated in Listing 18.5.

The `memcpy()` Function

`memcpy()` copies bytes of data between memory blocks, sometimes called *buffers*. This function doesn't care about the type of data being copied—it simply makes an exact byte-for-byte copy. The function prototype is

```
void *memcpy(void *dest, void *src, size_t count);
```

The arguments `dest` and `src` point to the destination and source memory blocks, respectively. `count` specifies the number of bytes to be copied. The return value is `dest`. If the two blocks of memory overlap, the function might not operate properly—some of the data in `src` might be overwritten before being copied. Use the `memmove()` function, discussed next, to handle overlapping memory blocks. `memcpy()` will be demonstrated in Listing 18.5.

The `memmove()` Function

`memmove()` is much like `memcpy()`, copying a specified number of bytes from one memory block to another. It's more flexible, however, because it can handle overlapping memory blocks properly. Because `memmove()` can do everything `memcpy()` can do (with the added flexibility of dealing with overlapping blocks), you rarely, if ever, have a reason to use memcpy(). The prototype is

```
void *memmove(void *dest, void *src, size_t count);
```

dest and src point to the destination and source memory blocks, and count specifies the number of bytes to be copied. The return value is dest. If the blocks overlap, this function ensures that the source data in the overlapped region is copied before being overwritten. Listing 18.5 demonstrates memset(), memcpy(), and memmove().

LISTING 18.5. A demonstration of memset(), memcpy(), and memmove().

```
1 : /* Demonstrating memset(), memcpy(), and memmove(). */
2 :
3 : #include <stdio.h>
4 : #include <string.h>
5 :
6 : char message1[60] = "Four score and seven years ago ...";
7 : char message2[60] = "abcdefghijklmnopqrstuvwxyz";
8 : char temp[60];
9 :
10: int main(void)
11: {
12:     printf("message1[] before memset():\t%s\n", message1);
13:     memset(message1 + 5, '@', 10);
14:     printf("\nmessage1[] after memset():\t%s\n", message1);
15:
16:     strcpy(temp, message2);
17:     printf("\nOriginal message: %s\n", temp);
18:     memcpy(temp + 4, temp + 16, 10);
19:     printf("After memcpy() without overlap:\t%s\n", temp);
20:     strcpy(temp, message2);
21:     memcpy(temp + 6, temp + 4, 10);
22:     printf("After memcpy() with overlap:\t%s\n", temp);
23:
24:     strcpy(temp, message2);
25:     printf("\nOriginal message: %s\n", temp);
26:     memmove(temp + 4, temp + 16, 10);
27:     printf("After memmove() without overlap:\t%s\n", temp);
28:     strcpy(temp, message2);
29:     memmove(temp + 6, temp + 4, 10);
30:     printf("After memmove() with overlap:\t%s\n", temp);
31:     return (0);
32: }
```

OUTPUT

```
message1[] before memset():    Four score and seven years ago ...
message1[] after memset():     Four @@@@@@@@@@seven years ago ...

Original message: abcdefghijklmnopqrstuvwxyz
After memcpy() without overlap: abcdqrstuvwxyzopqrstuvwxyz
```

18

```
After memcpy() with overlap:     abcdefefefefefefqrstuvwxyz

Original message: abcdefghijklmnopqrstuvwxyz
After memmove() without overlap:         abcdqrstuvwxyzopqrstuvwxyz
After memmove() with overlap:    abcdefefghijklmnqrstuvwxyz
```

ANALYSIS The operation of `memset()` is straightforward. Note how the pointer notation `message1 + 5` is used to specify that `memset()` is to start setting characters at the sixth character in `message1[]` (remember, arrays are zero-based). As a result, the sixth through fifteenth characters in `message1[]` have been changed to @.

When source and destination do not overlap, `memcpy()` works fine. The 10 characters of `temp[]` starting at position 17 (the letters q through z) have been copied to positions 5 though 14, where the letters e though n were originally located. If, however, the source and destination overlap, things are different. When the function tries to copy 10 characters starting at position 4 to position 6, an overlap of 8 positions occurs. You might expect the letters e through n to be copied over the letters g through p. Instead, the letters e and f are repeated five times.

If there's no overlap, `memmove()` works just like `memcpy()`. With overlap, however, `memmove()` copies the original source characters to the destination.

Do	**Don't**
DO use `memmove()` instead of `memcpy()`, in case you're dealing with overlapping memory regions.	**DON'T** try to use `memset()` to initialize type `int`, `float`, or `double` arrays to any value other than 0.

Working with Bits

As you might know, the most basic unit of computer data storage is the bit. There are times when being able to manipulate individual bits in your C program's data is very useful. C has several tools that let you do this.

The C bitwise operators let you manipulate the individual bits of integer variables. Remember, a *bit* is the smallest possible unit of data storage, and it can have only one of two values: 0 or 1. The bitwise operators can be used only with integer types: `char`, `int`, and `long`. Before continuing with this section, you should be familiar with binary notation—the way the computer internally stores integers.

The bitwise operators are most frequently used when your C program interacts directly with your system's hardware—a topic that is beyond the scope of this book. They do have other uses, however, which this chapter introduces.

The Shift Operators

Two shift operators shift the bits in an integer variable by a specified number of positions. The << operator shifts bits to the left and the >> operator shifts bits to the right. The syntax for these binary operators is

x << n

and

x >> n

Each operator shifts the bits in x by n positions in the specified direction. For a right shift, zeros are placed in the n high-order bits of the variable; for a left shift, zeros are placed in the n low-order bits of the variable. Here are a few examples:

Binary 00001100 (decimal 12) right-shifted by 2 evaluates to binary 00000011 (decimal 3).

Binary 00001100 (decimal 12) left-shifted by 3 evaluates to binary 01100000 (decimal 96).

Binary 00001100 (decimal 12) right-shifted by 3 evaluates to binary 00000001 (decimal 1).

Binary 00110000 (decimal 48) left-shifted by 3 evaluates to binary 10000000 (decimal 128).

Under certain circumstances, the shift operators can be used to multiply and divide an integer variable by a power of 2. Left-shifting an integer by n places has the same effect as multiplying it by 2^n, and right-shifting an integer has the same effect as dividing it by 2^n. The results of a left-shift multiplication are accurate only if there is no overflow—that is, if no bits are "lost" by being shifted out of the high-order positions. A right-shift division is an integer division, in which any fractional part of the result is lost. For example, if you right-shift the value 5 (binary 00000101) by one place, intending to divide by 2, the result is 2 (binary 00000010) instead of the correct 2.5, because the fractional part (the .5) is lost. Listing 18.6 demonstrates the shift operators.

LISTING 18.6. Using the shift operators.

```
1 : /* Demonstrating the shift operators. */
2 :
3 : #include <stdio.h>
4 :
5 : int main(void)
6 : {
7 :     unsigned char y, x = 255;
```

continues

18

LISTING 18.6. continued

```
8 :     int count;
9 :
10:     printf("%s %15s %13s\n", "Decimal", "shift left by", "result");
11:
12:     for (count = 1; count < 8; count++)
13:     {
14:         y = x << count;
15:         printf("%6d %12d %16d\n", x, count, y);
16:     }
17:     printf("%s %16s %13s\n", "Decimal", "shift right by", "result");
18:
19:     for (count = 1; count < 8; count++)
20:     {
21:         y = x >> count;
22:         printf("%6d %12d %16d\n", x, count, y);
23:     }
24:     return(0);
25: }
```

OUTPUT

```
Decimal    shift left by        result
   255            1              254
   255            2              252
   255            3              248
   255            4              240
   255            5              224
   255            6              192
   255            7              128
Decimal    shift right by       result
   255            1              127
   255            2              63
   255            3              31
   255            4              15
   255            5              7
   255            6              3
   255            7              1
```

The Bitwise Logical Operators

Three bitwise logical operators are used to manipulate individual bits in an integer data type, as shown in Table 18.1. These operators have names similar to the TRUE/FALSE logical operators you learned about in previous days, but their operations differ.

TABLE 18.1. The bitwise logical operators.

Operator	Action
&	AND
¦	Inclusive OR
^	Exclusive OR

These are all binary operators, setting bits in the result to 1 or 0 depending on the bits in the operands. They operate as follows:

- Bitwise AND sets a bit in the result to 1 only if the corresponding bits in both operands are 1; otherwise, the bit is set to 0. The AND operator is used to turn off, or clear, one or more bits in a value.

- Bitwise inclusive OR sets a bit in the result to 0 only if the corresponding bits in both operands are 0; otherwise, the bit is set to 1. The OR operator is used to turn on, or set, one or more bits in a value.

- Bitwise exclusive OR sets a bit in the result to 1 if the corresponding bits in the operands are different (if one is 1 and the other is 0); otherwise, the bit is set to 0.

The following are examples of how these operators work:

Operation	Example
AND	11110000
	& 01010101
	01010000
Inclusive OR	11110000
	¦ 01010101
	11110101
Exclusive OR	11110000
	^ 01010101
	10100101

18

You just read that bitwise AND and bitwise inclusive OR can be used to clear or set, respectively, specified bits in an integer value. Here's an explanation of what that means. Suppose you have a type char variable, and you want to ensure that the bits in positions 0 and 4 are cleared (that is, equal to 0) and that the other bits stay at their original values. If you AND the variable with a second value that has the binary value 11101110, you'll obtain the desired result. Here's how this works.

In each position where the second value has a 1, the result will have the same value, 0 or 1, as was present in that position in the original variable:

```
0 & 1 == 0
1 & 1 == 1
```

In each position where the second value has a 0, the result will have a 0 regardless of the value that was present in that position in the original variable:

```
0 & 0 == 0
1 & 0 == 0
```

Setting bits with OR works in a similar way. In each position where the second value has a 1, the result will have a 1, and in each position where the second value has a 0, the result will be unchanged:

```
0 | 1 == 1
1 | 1 == 1
0 | 0 == 0
1 | 0 == 1
```

The Complement Operator

The final bitwise operator is the complement operator, ~. This is a unary operator. Its action is to reverse every bit in its operand, changing all 0s to 1s, and vice versa. For example, ~254 (binary 11111110) evaluates to 1 (binary 00000001).

All the examples in this section have used type char variables containing 8 bits. For larger variables, such as type int and type long, things work exactly the same.

Bit Fields in Structures

The final bit-related topic is the use of bit fields in structures. On Day 10, "Structures," you learned how to define your own data structures, customizing them to fit your program's data needs. By using bit fields, you can accomplish even greater customization and save memory space as well.

A *bit field* is a structure member that contains a specified number of bits. You can declare a bit field to contain one bit, two bits, or whatever number of bits are required to hold the data stored in the field. What advantage does this provide?

Suppose that you're programming an employee database program that keeps records on your company's employees. Many of the items of information that the database stores are of the yes/no variety, such as "Is the employee enrolled in the dental plan?" or "Did the employee graduate from college?" Each piece of yes/no information can be stored in a single bit, with 1 representing yes and 0 representing no.

Using C's standard data types, the smallest type you could use in a structure is a type char. You could indeed use a type char structure member to hold yes/no data, but seven of the char's eight bits would be wasted space. By using bit fields, you can store eight yes/no values in a single char.

Bit fields aren't limited to yes/no values. Continuing with this database example, imagine that your firm has three different health insurance plans. Your database needs to store data about the plan in which each employee is enrolled (if any). You could use 0 to represent no health insurance and use the values 1, 2, and 3 to represent the three plans. A bit field containing two bits is sufficient because two binary bits can represent values of 0 through 3. Likewise, a bit field containing three bits could hold values in the range 0 through 7, four bits could hold values in the range 0 through 15, and so on.

Bit fields are named and accessed in the same way as regular structure members. All bit fields have type unsigned int, and you specify the size of the field (in bits) by following the member name with a colon and the number of bits. To define a structure with a one-bit member named dental, another one-bit member named college, and a two-bit member named health, you write the following:

```
struct emp_data {
unsigned dental     : 1;
unsigned college    : 1;
unsigned health     : 2;
...
};
```

The ellipsis (. . .) indicates space for other structure members. The members can be bit fields or fields made up of regular data types. To access the bit fields, use the structure member operator just as you do with any structure member. For example, you can expand the structure definition to something more useful:

```
struct emp_data {
unsigned dental     : 1;
unsigned college    : 1;
unsigned health     : 2;
char fname[20];
char lname[20];
char ssnumber[10];
};
```

You can then declare an array of structures:

```
struct emp_data workers[100];
```

To assign values to the first array element, write something like this:

```
workers[0].dental = 1;
workers[0].college = 0;
workers[0].health = 2;
strcpy(workers[0].fname, "Mildred");
```

Your code would be clearer, of course, if you used the symbolic constants YES and NO with values of 1 and 0 when working with one-bit fields. In any case, you treat each bit field as a small, unsigned integer with the given number of bits. The range of values that can be assigned to a bit field with n bits is from 0 to 2^{n-1}. If you try to assign an out-of-range value to a bit field, the compiler won't report an error, but you will get unpredictable results.

Do	Don't
DO use the defined constants YES and NO or TRUE and FALSE when working with bits. They are much easier to read and understand than 1 and 0.	**DON'T** define a bit field that takes 8 or 32 bits. These are the same as other available variables such as type char or int.

Summary

Today's discussion covered a variety of C programming topics. You learned how to allocate, reallocate, and free memory at runtime, and you saw commands that give you flexibility in allocating storage space for program data. You also saw how and when to use typecasts with variables and pointers. Forgetting about typecasts, or using them improperly, is a common cause of hard-to-find program bugs, so this is a topic worth reviewing! You also learned how to use the memset(), memcpy(), and memmove() functions to manipulate blocks of memory. Finally, you saw the ways in which you can manipulate and use individual bits in your programs.

Q&A

Q What's the advantage of dynamic memory allocation? Why can't I just declare the storage space I need in my source code?

A If you declare all your data storage in your source code, the amount of memory available to your program is fixed. You have to know ahead of time, when you write the program, how much memory will be needed. Dynamic memory allocation lets your program control the amount of memory used to suit the current conditions and user input. The program can use as much memory as it needs, up to the limit of what's available in the computer.

Q Why would I ever need to free memory?

A When you're first learning to use C, your programs aren't very big. As your programs grow, their use of memory also grows. You should try to write your programs to use memory as efficiently as possible. When you're done with memory, you should release it. If you write programs that work in a multitasking environment, other applications might need memory that you aren't using.

Q **What happens if I reuse a string without calling `realloc()`?**

A You don't need to call `realloc()` if the string you're using was allocated enough room. Call `realloc()` when your current string isn't big enough. Remember, the C compiler lets you do almost anything, even things you shouldn't! You can over-write one string with a bigger string as long as the new string's length is equal to or smaller than the original string's allocated space. However, if the new string is bigger, you will also overwrite whatever came after the string in memory. This could be nothing, or it could be vital data. If you need a bigger allocated section of memory, call `realloc()`.

Q **What's the advantage of the `memset()`, `memcpy()`, and `memmove()` functions? Why can't I just use a loop with an assignment statement to initialize or copy memory?**

A You can use a loop with an assignment statement to initialize memory in some cases. In fact, sometimes this is the only way to do it—for example, setting all elements of a type `float` array to the value `1.23`. In other situations, however, the memory will not have been assigned to an array or list, and the `mem...()` functions are your only choice. There are also times when a loop and assignment statement work, but the `mem...()` functions are simpler and faster.

Q **When would I use the shift operators and the bitwise logical operators?**

A The most common use for these operators is when a program is interacting directly with the computer hardware—a task that often requires specific bit patterns to be generated and interpreted. This topic is beyond the scope of this book. Even if you never need to manipulate hardware directly, you can use the shift operators, in certain circumstances, to divide or multiply integer values by powers of two.

Q **Do I really gain that much by using bit fields?**

A Yes, you can gain quite a bit with bit fields. (Pun intended!) Consider a circumstance similar to today's example in which a file contains information from a survey. People are asked to answer TRUE or FALSE to the questions asked. If you ask 100 questions of 10,000 people and store each answer as a type `char` as T or F, you will need 10,000 × 100 bytes of storage (because a character is 1 byte). This is 1 million bytes of storage. If you use bit fields instead and allocate one bit for each answer, you will need 10,000 × 100 bits. Because 1 byte holds 8 bits, this amounts to 130,000 bytes of data, which is significantly less than 1 million bytes.

18

Workshop

The Workshop provides quiz questions to help you solidify your understanding of the material covered and exercises to provide you with experience in using what you've learned. The answers to the quiz and exercises are provided in Appendix C, "Answers."

Quiz

1. What is the difference between the `malloc()` and `calloc()` memory-allocation functions?

2. What is the most common reason for using a typecast with a numeric variable?

3. What variable type do the following expressions evaluate to? Assume that `c` is a type `char` variable, `i` is a type `int` variable, `l` is a type `long` variable, and `f` is a type `float` variable.

   a. `( c + i + l )`

   b. `( i + 32 )`

   c. `( c + 'A')`

   d. `( i + 32.0 )`

   e. `( 100 + 1.0 )`

4. What is meant by dynamically allocating memory?

5. What is the difference between the `memcpy()` function and the `memmove()` function?

6. Imagine that your program uses a structure that must (as one of its members) store the day of the week as a value between 1 and 7. What's the most memory-efficient way to do so?

7. What is the smallest amount of memory in which the current date can be stored? (Hint: month/day/year—think of year as an offset from 1900.)

8. What does `1000 << 4` evaluate to?

9. What does `8000 >> 4` evaluate to?

10. Describe the difference between the results of the following two expressions (assuming all the numbers are binary):

    ```
    (01010101 ^ 11111111 )
    ( ~01010101 )
    ```

Exercises

1. Write a `malloc()` command that allocates memory for 1,000 `long`s.

2. Write a `calloc()` command that allocates memory for 1,000 `long`s.

3. Assume that you have declared an array as follows:

   ```
   float data[1000];
   ```

   Show two ways to initialize all elements of the array to 0. Use a loop and an assignment statement for one method, and the `memset()` function for the other.

4. **BUG BUSTER:** Is anything wrong with the following code?

   ```
   void func()
   {
   int number1 = 100, number2 = 3;
   float answer;
   answer = number1 / number2;
   printf("%d/%d = %lf", number1, number2, answer)
   }
   ```

5. **BUG BUSTER:** What, if anything, is wrong with the following code?

   ```
   void *p;
   p = (float*) malloc(sizeof(float));
   *p = 1.23;
   ```

6. **BUG BUSTER:** Is the following structure allowed?

   ```
   struct quiz_answers {
   char student_name[15];
   unsigned answer1    : 1;
   unsigned answer2    : 1;
   unsigned answer3    : 1;
   unsigned answer4    : 1;
   unsigned answer5    : 1;
   }
   ```

   Answers are not provided for the following exercises.

7. Write a program that uses each of the bitwise logical operators. The program should apply the bitwise operator to a number and then reapply it to the result. You should observe the output to be sure you understand what's going on.

8. Write a program that displays the binary value of a number. For instance, if the user enters 3, the program should display `00000011`. (Hint: You will need to use the bitwise operators.)

18

DAY 19

Processes and Signals

You might have heard Linux referred to as a multitasking and multiuser operating system. These two concepts are fundamental to the operation of Linux as both a server and a client computer. In today's lesson, you will learn about

- Processes and how to control them
- Starting new processes with fork()
- Signals and how they relate to processes

Processes

When people say Linux is a multitasking operating system, they mean that it can carry out many different tasks at once. For instance, when you are working through the exercises in this book, you would be using a text editor to edit your source code, an xterm to compile and run your programs, and maybe also something like the gnome-help-browser to read documentation. Each of these programs behaves as if it were the only program running on the computer.

Linux does this by switching very quickly—100 times a second or more—between the programs. This gives you, the user, the illusion that many programs are running at once. To see some of the programs running, you can type the command ps u at the command prompt. You'll probably see something like

```
[erik@coltrane erikd]$ ps u
USER         PID %CPU %MEM   VSZ   RSS TTY       STAT START    TIME COMMAND
erik         914  0.0  0.2  1776   652 pts/5     S    Sep24    0:01 -bash
erik       11359  0.0  1.1  4516  2928 pts/5     S    Sep25    0:00 nedit list1901.c
erik       11362  0.0  0.9  4516  2928 pts/5     S    Sep25    0:00 nedit list1902.c
erik       11368  0.0  0.3  2528   908 pts/5     R    Sep25    0:00 ps u
```

It is extremely unlikely that you will get identical results. My user ID, erik, will be replaced with your user ID, and most of the values in the other columns will also be different. In this particular instance, the ps command shows three programs but four processes: bash (the command line interpreter), two instances of the nedit text editor, and the ps process itself. The difference between a program and a process is that a program is an executable file stored on disk, whereas a process is an instance of that program currently being executed by the operating system.

The list of processes shown in the preceding listing is really only a small proportion of the programs running on your machine. For a full list of all the programs, type the command ps aux. This might show 50 or more programs.

Ignoring the larger list for the moment, notice that there are a number of columns in the preceding short list. The column we are most interested in at the moment is the second column, marked PID, which stands for *process identifier*. When a program is run on Linux, it is given a unique process ID or number in the range 1 to 32767. Rather than use something ambiguous like the program name—there may be more than one program with the same name running—the process ID is used by the operating system whenever it refers to a running program. When a program finishes and exits, the process ID it used is free to be used by some other program at a later time.

On Day 12, "Advanced Program Control," we looked at the system() function, which allows one program to run another program. In a situation like this, the program that calls system() is called the *parent process*, and the program that is run is called the *child process*. These two processes will have unique process IDs.

Linux and other operating systems in the UNIX family provide a function to allow a process to find out its PID. There is also a function to allow a child process to find out the PID of its parent. These functions are defined in the header file unistd.h as follows:

```
pid_t getpid(void);
```

```
pid_t getppid(void);
```

The first function, getpid(), returns the process ID of the process that calls getpid(). The second function, getppid(), returns the PID of the parent process. The return value is of type pid_t, which is defined as int in one of the header files included by stdlib.h.

Listing 19.1 gives a very simple demonstration of these two functions.

LISTING 19.1. Retrieving the process ID and the process ID of the parent process.

```
1 : /* Using getpid() and getppid(). */
2 : #include <stdio.h>
3 : #include <stdlib.h>
4 : #include <unistd.h>
5 :
6 : int main(void)
7 : {
8 :     pid_t  pid;
9 :
10:     pid = getpid();
11:     printf ("My pid = %d\n", pid) ;
12:
13:     pid = getppid();
14:     printf ("My parent's pid = %d\n", pid) ;
15:
16:     return 0;
17: }
```

OUTPUT

```
My pid = 12179
My parent's pid = 914
```

ANALYSIS The program in this listing defines a variable of type pid_t on line 8 and first calls getpid() on line 10 and then getppid() on line 13. The values returned by the functions are printed out on lines 11 and 14. Remember that the type pid_t is really an int, so the two printf function calls use the %d conversion specifier.

Each time you run this program in the same terminal window, you will get a different number for the process ID; however, the parent process will stay the same. If you run the ps command, you should notice that the process ID of the parent process is the same as the process ID of the bash command interpreter in the terminal window, which ran both the ps command and the program in Listing 19.1.

So how does a program like the bash command interpreter start the execution of another program but still continue execution itself? Well, we're working up to that. To work as a command interpreter, a program must be able to do two things: start another process and replace one process with another.

The capability of the bash command interpreter to start another process but continue running itself can be demonstrated by using the program in Listing 19.2. When this program

19

is compiled, it should be run first without the ampersand (&) symbol and then with the ampersand symbol at the end of the command line. When you run a program with the ampersand symbol, you are asking the command interpreter to run the given program in the background. This allows the interpreter to return immediately so that you can enter another command. Without the ampersand character, the interpreter waits for the program to terminate before allowing further commands to be entered. In both cases—with and without the ampersand—you should try executing other commands such as ls. Look for differences in behavior and try to figure out what they mean.

LISTING **19.2**. A program that can be run in the background.

```
1 : /* A program which can be run in the background. */
2 : #include <stdio.h>
3 : #include <unistd.h>
4 :
5 : int main(void)
6 : {
7 :     int count;
8 :
9 :     for(count = 0; count < 10; count ++)
10:     {
11:         sleep(2);
12:         puts("I'm still running!");
13:     }
14:
15:     puts("I've finished now!");
16:     return 0;
17: }
18:
```

INPUT/
OUTPUT

```
[erik@coltrane day19]$ ./list1902
I'm still running!
I'm still running!
ls
I'm still running!
I'm still running!
I'm still running!
I'm still running!
I'm still running!
I'm still running!
I'm still running!
I'm still running!
I'm finished now!
[erik@coltrane day19]$ ls
list1901.c  list1902    list1902.c  list1903.c list1904.c
[erik@coltrane day19]$
[erik@coltrane day19]$
[erik@coltrane day19]$ ./list1902 &
```

```
[1] 12345
[erik@coltrane day19]$ I'm still running!
I'm still running!
I'm still running!
I'm still running!
[erik@coltrane day19]$ ls
list1901.c  list1902    list1902.c  list1903.c list1904.c
[erik@coltrane day19]$ I'm still running!
I'm still running!
I'm still running!
I'm still running!
I'm still running!
I've finished now!
[1]+  Done                        ./list1902
```

ANALYSIS   The program itself is very simple and uses nothing that has not been dealt with in earlier lessons. The thing we are interested in here is the output of the program. From the output shown, you can see that the program was run without the ampersand first. After the program printed out its message twice, the user typed the ls command and then pressed Enter. Normally this command would execute immediately, but our program is running, and the ls command doesn't execute until our program has terminated. As you can see, the output from the ls command doesn't appear until after our program prints its I'm finished now! message.

When our program is run with an ampersand on the command line, the behavior is quite different. First, the bash command interpreter prints out a message consisting of two numbers, the first being enclosed in brackets. The number in brackets is the number of processes currently running in the background, whereas the other number is the process ID of the process that has just been started. The bash command line interpreter then prints out its prompt, but our program—running in the background—prints out its message. When the user enters the ls command, the bash interpreter executes it immediately and our program continues in the background, printing out its I'm still running! message until it finishes. At this time, the interpreter notifies the user that the program has terminated with the Done message.

Starting Another Process Using fork()

Linux and other members of the UNIX family have a standard method of starting another process by means of the fork() function. Like the getpid() function, fork() returns a process ID and is defined in the unistd.h header file. It looks like this:

```
pid_t fork(void);
```

If fork() fails because of some error, it returns a value of -1. If no error occurs, fork() creates a new process that is identical to the calling process. Both the old and the new process then continue execution from the instruction after the call to fork(). Although they are both executing the same program, each process has its own private copy of all the data and variables. One of the these variables, the variable of type pid_t returned by the fork() function, is 0 in the child process, and in the parent process, its value is the process ID of the child process. After the fork() function, neither the child nor the parent is able to change values of any variables or data in the other process. Listing 19.3 gives a demonstration of the fork() function.

LISTING 19.3. Creating a new process using fork().

```
1 : /* Starting another process using fork(). */
2 : #include <stdio.h>
3 : #include <stdlib.h>
4 : #include <unistd.h>
5 :
6 : int main(void)
7 : {
8 :     pid_t   pid;
9 :     int     x=13;
10:
11:     pid = fork();
12:
13:     if (pid < 0)
14:     {
15:         printf("Error : fork () returned %u.\n", pid);
16:         exit(1);
17:     }
18:
19:     if (pid == 0)
20:     {
21:         printf("Child : pid = %u. Parent's pid = %u\n",
22:                 getpid(), getppid());
23:         printf("Child : x = %d, ", x);
24:         x = 10;
25:         printf("new x = %d\n", x);
26:         sleep(2);
27:         puts ("Child : about to exit.");
28:         exit(42);
29:         puts ("Child : You'll never see this.");
30:     }
31:     else
32:     {
33:         printf("Parent: pid = %u. Child's  pid = %u\n",
34:                 getpid(), pid);
35:         puts("Parent: going to sleep for 60 seconds.");
36:         sleep(60);
37:         puts("Parent: waking up.");
38:         printf("Parent: x = %d\n", x);
```

```
39:    }
40:
41:    return 0;
42: }
```

OUTPUT

```
Parent: pid = 16525. Child's  pid = 16526

Parent: going to sleep for 60 seconds.
Child : pid = 16526. Parent's pid = 16525
Child : x = 13, new x = 10
Child : about to exit.
Parent: waking up.
Parent: x = 13
```

ANALYSIS   Apart from the fork() function call, this listing contains nothing new. Lines 2 to 4 include the necessary header files, and lines 8 and 9 define two variables, one of which, x, is set to 13. The fork() function is called on line 11, and its return value is tested for an error condition on line 13. If no error occurred, two processes will be executing the code from line 12 on. In the child process, the value of pid will be 0; in the parent process, the value will be a process ID in the range 1 to 32767. The if statement on line 21 is evaluated by both processes, and the child process will execute the block of statements from lines 21 to 29. The parent process will execute lines 33 to 38.

From the program output, you will see that after the fork() call, the parent process prints out its own PID and the child's PID on lines 33 and 34. It then prints a message, and using the sleep() function we dealt with on Day 12, the parent goes to sleep for 60 seconds.

When the parent process goes to sleep, the child process continues to run. The first thing it does is print out its own PID and that of its parent on lines 21 and 22. Notice from the output that these values agree with the values in the parent process —the child's parent's PID *is* the PID of the parent. The child process then prints out the value of the variable x, changes the value, and then prints out the new value. It then calls the sleep() function to sleep for 2 seconds, but the parent process is sleeping for 60 seconds, so the child process wakes up before its parent prints out a message on line 27. It then calls exit() with a value of 42 on line 28. Notice that the placement of the exit() statement prevents the message on line 29 from ever being printed. You should remember from Day 12 that the exit() function terminates a program and returns the value of the integer argument to the operating system. 60 seconds later, the parent process wakes up from its own sleep() call, prints out the value of the variable x, and exits by executing the return at line 41.

Notice that the variable x was originally set equal to 13 in the parent process before fork() was called. The child then set x equal to 10, but after the child process terminated, the value of x in the parent process was still equal to 13. This is because after the fork() function call, both processes have their own copy of the variable x.

19

Note

> Until the fork() function, the predefined functions we have been dealing with have been library functions—part of the standard C library. The fork() function and some other functions we will be dealing with today are more correctly referred to as *system functions* rather than as part of the C library; that is, functions defined by and intended for interaction with the operating system.

Zombie Processes

The program in Listing 19.3 is the simplest possible use of the fork() function. It does, however, have a flaw that in some cases could cause problems. To see the results of this flaw, run the program in Listing 19.3 with an ampersand character (&) to run the process in the background. When you see the Child: about to exit. message, run ps u and you should see something like this:

INPUT/OUTPUT

```
[erik@coltrane day19]$ ./list1902 &
Parent: going to sleep for 60 seconds.
Child : pid = 16714. Parent's pid = 16713
Child : x = 13, new x = 10
Child : about to exit.

[erik@coltrane day19]$ ps u
USER      PID %CPU %MEM   VSZ  RSS TTY     STAT START   TIME COMMAND
erik      914  0.0  0.2  1784  708 pts/5   S    Sep24  0:01 -bash
erik    16490  0.0  1.2  4640 3184 pts/5   S    Sep27  0:00 nedit
➥list1902.c
erik    16713  0.0  0.1  1052  332 pts/5   S    Sep27  0:00 ./list1902
erik    16714  0.0  0.0     0    0 pts/5   Z    Sep27  0:00 [list1902
➥<defunct>]
erik    16715  0.0  0.3  2556  936 pts/5   R    Sep27  0:00 ps u
```

Notice the fourth item in the output of the ps command. It's a copy of the program list1902, which is defunct. In the STAT column for that process is a Z, which means that the process is what is known as a *zombie process*.

When a process terminates, it either uses the return statement or calls exit() with a value that is returned to the operating system. The operating system keeps the process in its internal data tables until the parent of the process reads the value returned by the child or the parent process terminates. A *zombie process*, therefore, is a process that has terminated, but whose parent has not read the exit value set by the child. When the parent process terminates, the zombie process will be removed from the operating system's process table.

Why are zombie processes so bad? Well, one of the most common uses of the fork() system function is in a server application that communicates with client programs over a network connection. Good examples of this kind of server are a mail server and a World Wide Web server. Server applications are usually started when a machine boots and are usually stopped only when the machine is shut down, which might be weeks, months, or even years later. Every time a client program connects to the server over the network, the server uses fork() to create a child process to deal with the communicating client. When the client is finished communicating with the server, it disconnects and the server's child process terminates. Obviously, a server must ensure that none of its child processes become zombies, or the operating system would quickly run out of space in its process table. Cleaning up zombie child processes is often referred to as *reaping*—an allusion to the grim reaper.

There are two (and possibly more) ways to prevent zombie processes. The most common is to use the system function wait(), which is defined in the header file sys/wait.h as follows:

```
pid_t wait(int *status);
```

This function has an int pointer as a parameter and returns a type pid_t. When called, it suspends execution of the parent process until a child process terminates. When a child process terminates or if a child process is in a zombie state, wait() returns the process ID of the child and copies the child's exit value to the address pointed to by the pointer argument *status. If you are not interested in the return value of the child process, the value NULL should be passed to wait(). If there is no child process, wait() returns -1. Listing 19.4 demonstrates the use of the wait() function on a child that has already terminated.

LISTING 19.4. Preventing zombie processes using wait().

```
 1 : /* Using wait() to wait for a child process. */
 2 : #include <stdio.h>
 3 : #include <stdlib.h>
 4 : #include <unistd.h>
 5 : #include <sys/types.h>
 6 : #include <sys/wait.h>
 7 :
 8 : int main(void)
 9 : {
10:     pid_t  pid;
11:     int    status;
12:
13:     pid = fork();
14:
15:     if (pid < 0)
16:     {
17:         printf("Error : fork () returned %u.\n", pid);
```

continues

LISTING 19.4. continued

```
18:            exit(1);
19:       }
20:
21:       if (pid == 0)
22:       {
23:           printf("Child : pid = %u. Parent's pid = %u\n",
24:                       getpid(), getppid());
25:           sleep(1);
26:           puts ("Child : about to exit.");
27:           exit(42);
28:       }
29:       else
30:       {
31:           printf("Parent: pid = %u. Child's  pid = %u\n",
32:                       getpid(), pid);
33:           puts("Parent: going to sleep for 10 seconds.");
34:           sleep(10);
35:           puts("Parent: waking up.");
36:
37:           pid = wait(&status);
38:           printf("Parent: child with pid %u ", pid);
39:           if (WIFEXITED(status)  != 0)
40:               printf("exited with status %d\n", WEXITSTATUS(status));
41:           else
42:               printf("exited abnormally.\n");
43:           puts("Parent: going to sleep for another 30 seconds.");
44:           sleep(30);
45:       }
46:
47:       return 0;
48: }
```

OUTPUT

```
Parent: pid = 19301. Child's  pid = 19302
Parent: going to sleep for 10 seconds.
Child : pid = 19302. Parent's pid = 19301
Child : about to exit.
Parent: waking up.
Parent: child with pid 19302 exited with status 42
Parent: going to sleep for another 30 seconds.
```

ANALYSIS This listing is much like Listing 19.4. The main difference is that when the parent process wakes up, it calls wait() on line 37. Because the child process has already terminated, wait() returns immediately with the variable pid set to the process ID of the child process that has terminated. It also copies data into the variable status, the address of which was passed into the wait() function. The parent process then prints out the process ID of the child and uses the macros WIFEXITED() and WEXITSTATUS(), which are defined in sys/wait.h, to retrieve the return status of the child process. If you read the man page for the wait() function, you will notice that these macros allow only an 8-bit exit status value—1 to 255—to be returned.

If you run this in the background by placing an ampersand on the command line, you will be able to run the command ps u. If you run it after the child calls exit() on line 27, but before the parent process wakes up from the sleep() function on line 34, you will see the child process is a zombie, just as it was before. If you run the ps u command again after the parent process calls the sleep() function once more on line 43, you will see that the zombie process has been destroyed by the operating system.

The wait() function is obviously useful if you know that the child process has already terminated. If the child process has not terminated, the wait() function will stop execution of the parent process until the child process terminates. When this behavior is not acceptable, the waitpid() function can be used. Like wait(), this system function is defined in sys/wait.h and looks like this:

```
pid_t waitpid(pid_t pid, int *status, int options);
```

This function allows you to wait for a particular process ID or for any child process if a pid of -1 is used. Like wait(), it allows the retrieval of the exit status of the child process. The final parameter, *options*, can be set to 0 to behave like wait() or WNOHANG or WUNTRACED. The first of these is the most interesting value in that it causes waitpid() to return immediately with a value of 0—an invalid process ID—if no child has terminated. This allows the parent process to continue processing and to call waitpid() again at some later time. Listing 19.5 shows the use of waitpid() to reap terminated child processes.

LISTING 19.5. Preventing zombie processes using waitpid().

```
 1 : /* Using wait() to wait for a child process. */
 2 : #include <stdio.h>
 3 : #include <stdlib.h>
 4 : #include <unistd.h>
 5 : #include <sys/types.h>
 6 : #include <sys/wait.h>
 7 :
 8 : int main(void)
 9 : {
10:     pid_t  pid;
11:     int    status;
12:
13:     pid = fork();
14:
15:     if (pid < 0)
16:     {
17:         printf("Error : fork () returned %u.\n", pid);
18:         exit(1);
19:     }
```

19

continues

LISTING **19.5**. continued

```
20:
21:     if (pid == 0)
22:     {
23:         printf("Child : pid = %u. Parent's pid = %u\n",
24:                 getpid(), getppid());
25:         sleep(10);
26:         puts ("Child : about to exit.");
27:         exit(33);
28:     }
29:     else
30:     {
31:         printf("Parent: pid = %u. Child's  pid = %u\n",
32:                 getpid(), pid);
33:
34:         while ((pid = waitpid (-1, &status,  WNOHANG)) == 0)
35:         {
36:             printf("Parent: No child has terminated.");
37:             puts(" Going to sleep for 1 second.");
38:             sleep(1);
39:         }
40:
41:         printf("Parent: child with pid %u ", pid);
42:         if (WIFEXITED(status) != 0)
43:             printf("exited with status %d\n", WEXITSTATUS(status));
44:         else
45:             printf("exited abnormally.\n");
46:     }
47:
48:     return 0;
49: }
```

OUTPUT

```
Parent: pid = 19454. Child's pid = 19455
Parent: No child has terminated. Going to sleep for 1 second.
Child : pid = 19455. Parent's pid = 19454
Parent: No child has terminated. Going to sleep for 1 second.
Parent: No child has terminated. Going to sleep for 1 second.
Parent: No child has terminated. Going to sleep for 1 second.
Parent: No child has terminated. Going to sleep for 1 second.
Parent: No child has terminated. Going to sleep for 1 second.
Parent: No child has terminated. Going to sleep for 1 second.
Parent: No child has terminated. Going to sleep for 1 second.
Parent: No child has terminated. Going to sleep for 1 second.
Parent: No child has terminated. Going to sleep for 1 second.
Child : about to exit.
Parent: child with pid 19455 exited with status 33
```

ANALYSIS This listing is much like the previous two in that fork() is used to create a child process that terminates before the parent process does. The parent process calls waitpid() on line 34. If no child process is ready for reaping, the parent process prints out a message and then sleeps for a second. When the child process terminates, the parent process prints out the child's process ID and exit status value.

Do	Don't
DO use `wait()` or `waitpid()` to clean up or reap child processes that have terminated. This is particularly important in any program that creates many child processes with `fork()` and runs for any length of time.	

Replacing One Process with Another

As you might remember, we are figuring out how the `bash` command interpreter is able to run another process while maintaining execution itself. The `fork()` function is only part of the solution; the second part is the capability to replace a running process with another. The command interpreter works by first forking a child process that is a copy of itself. The child process then replaces itself with a process that is the command that you, the user, have asked the command interpreter to execute.

There is a family of system functions, called the `exec` family, that allow a process to switch from one program to another while maintaining the same process ID. You can read about the other members of the family in the `exec` man page. The function we will be dealing with is `execl()`, which is defined in the unistd.h header file as follows:

```
int execl( const char *path, const char *arg, ...);
```

This function returns only if an error occurs. If no error occurs, the calling process is replaced completely by the new process. The process that is to replace the calling process is specified by giving the program name as the `path` parameter and as many command-line parameters as required. The difference between `execl()` and a function such as `printf()`, which can also take a variable list of arguments, is that `execl()` must be passed a `NULL` pointer as the last argument so that it can tell where the last argument is.

The `execl()` function can also cause first-time users some confusion because the second argument passed to `execl()` is not the first command-line argument passed to the program specified by the `path` argument. It is, in fact, the name that will be given to the new process in the process list produced by the `ps` command. The first argument passed to the program specified by the `path` argument is actually the *third* argument passed to

19

execl(). If, for instance, you wanted to run the program /bin/ls with the -al parameter, but you want to give the program the name "dir" in the process list, you would call execl() as follows:

```
execl("/bin/ls", "dir", "-al", NULL);
```

This would replace the current process with a process that would be equivalent to running /bin/ls -al on the command line. Listing 19.6 demonstrates the execl() function, but uses the ps program to show that execl() does indeed replace the current process instead of creating a new one.

LISTING 19.6. Replacing a running process using execl().

```
 1 : /* Replacing one process with another using execl(). */
 2 : #include <stdio.h>
 3 : #include <stdlib.h>
 4 : #include <unistd.h>
 5 : #include <errno.h>
 6 :
 7 : int main(void)
 8 : {
 9 :     pid_t  pid ;
10:
11:     pid = getpid();
12:     printf ("My pid = %u\n", pid);
13:
14:     puts ("Executing /bin/ps.");
15:     execl ("/bin/ps", "** prog **", "u", NULL);
16:
17:     puts("An error occurred.");
18:     perror("list1902");
19:     return 0;
20: }
```

OUTPUT

```
My pid = 19569
Executing /bin/ps.
USER    PID   %CPU  %MEM  VSZ   RSS TTY    STAT START  TIME COMMAND
erik    914   0.0   0.2   1784  716 pts/5  S    Sep24  0:01 -bash
erik  19569   0.0   0.3   2544  924 pts/5  R    Sep27  0:00 ** prog ** u
```

ANALYSIS This listing is very simple. After including the necessary header files on lines 2 to 5, the program retrieves its process ID using the getpid() function and prints it out. It then prints a message to the screen on line 14, before calling the execl() function on line 15. The rest of this program is executed if, and only if, the call to execl() fails, in which case it prints out an error message on lines 17 and 18. As we can see from the program output, the `execl()` function did not fail; instead, it executed the command `ps u`. Notice how the second argument to the `execl()` function, `"** prog **"`, becomes the name of the process in the process listing. Also notice that the process is printed out by the original program on line 12 is the same as the process ID of the process that replaced it.

Do	Don't
DO terminate the argument list passed to `execl()` with a `NULL` pointer.	**DON'T** forget that the second argument passed to `execl()` is the name you are giving the process, not the first argument passed to the program that is being `execl()`ed.

Signals

Like the capability to start a new process and replace the current process with another, signals—also known as *software interrupts*—are an important feature of UNIX-like operating systems. *Signals* are messages sent to a running process by the operating system. Some signals are caused by an error in the program itself, or they might be requests from the user at the keyboard that the operating system routes to the running process.

Signals received by the program because of errors can be due to things such as trying to divide a number by zero or trying to access memory not belonging to the process. These signals are *synchronous* signals because they occur at the same place in the program every time the program is run.

Other signals are caused by events outside the program itself, such as the user at the terminal typing control sequence characters or the operating system sending all programs a signal that they should terminate because the operating system is about to shut down. These signals are *asynchronous* signals because it is unlikely that the program will be in the same state and at the same instruction each time it receives the signal.

All the signals that can be sent to a program have a default behavior that is determined by the operating system. Some of these signals, especially the ones that are sent to the process because of error conditions, cause the process to terminate and generate a core dump file—a file, generated by the operating system, that is the contents of memory owned by the process at the time it received the signal. This core file may be used for debugging the error that caused the program to core dump and is especially useful for programs that received a signal because of a division-by-zero error or tried to access memory it isn't allowed to use.

19

A list of common signals in UNIX-like systems is given in Table 19.1. A full list of the signals defined in Linux can be found in the header file /usr/include/bits/signum.h.

TABLE 19.1. The signals symbolic error constants defined in bits/signum.h.

Name	Value	Function
SIGHUP	1	Terminal hangup.
SIGINT	2	Interrupt (generated by Ctrl+C) from user.
SIGQUIT	3	Quit (generated by Ctrl+\) from user.
SIGFPE	8	Floating-point error, such as divide by zero.
SIGKILL	9	Kill the process.
SIGUSR1	10	User-defined signal.
SIGSEGV	11	Process has tried to access memory not belonging. to it
SIGUSR2	12	Second user-defined signal.
SIGALRM	14	Timer set with alarm() function has timed out.
SIGTERM	15	Termination request.
SIGCHLD	17	Child process termination signal.
SIGCONT	18	Continue after a SIGSTOP or SIGTSTP signal.
SIGSTOP	19	Stop the process.
SIGTSTP	20	Terminal stop; generated by Ctrl+Z.
SIGWINCH	28	Change of window size.

In addition to the default behavior, all signals other than SIGSTOP and SIGKILL can have their behavior modified by the installation of a signal handler. A *signal handler* is a function set up by the programmer that is called whenever the process receives a signal. Separate signal handlers may be set up for each of the signals in Table 19.1, other than SIGSTOP and SIGKILL. It is also possible, but probably not advisable, to set all the signals to be handled—or trapped—by one signal handler. The function used as a signal handler must have a single type int parameter and a void return type. When a signal arrives at the process, the signal handler is called with the signal number as the argument to the signal handler function.

In order to trap and act on signals with an appropriate signal handler, the programmer must instruct the operating system to call this signal handler whenever the specified signal would be sent to the process. There are two functions used to modify or examine a signal handler in UNIX, signal() and sigaction(), both of which are defined in the header file signal.h. The second function, `sigaction()`, is more recent than the first and is also more commonly used. It is defined as follows:

```
int sigaction(int signum, const struct sigaction *act,
          ➡struct sigaction *oldact);
```

This function returns `0` on success and `-1` on error. The first parameter for `sigaction()` is the signal number whose behavior you would like to modify or examine. Rather than use the actual number, it is advisable to use the symbolic constant; for instance, use `SIG-INT` instead of the number 2. The second and third parameters are pointers to a `sigac-tion` structure. The `sigaction` structure is defined in signal.h as

```
struct sigaction
{   void (*sa_handler)(int);
    sigset_t sa_mask;
    int sa_flags;
    void (*sa_restorer)(void);
}
```

By passing a pointer to a correctly constructed `sigaction` structure as the second parameter to the `sigaction()` function, it is possible to change the behavior for the given signal. Passing a pointer to a similar structure as the third parameter asks the `sigac-tion()` function to copy the values for the current behavior of the given signal into the specified `sigaction` structure. It is valid to pass the `NULL` pointer as one or the other of these parameters.

Using this scheme, it is possible to examine the current behavior without changing it, change the behavior permanently, or find out the current behavior and change it so that it may be restored later, as shown in the following three code snippets:

```
/* Examine current behavior. */
sigaction(SIGINT,NULL,&oldact);

/* Change the behavior. */
sigaction(SIGINT,&newact,NULL);

/* Retrieve a copy of the current behavior */
/* and change to the new behavior.        */
sigaction(SIGINT,&newact,&oldact);
```

Now, let's have a closer look at the `sigaction` structure. You should notice that the first field of this structure, `sa_handler`, is a pointer to a function that takes an `int` parameter. This is a pointer to the function that will act as the signal handler for the signal being modified. It is also possible to assign the symbolic constants `SIG_DFL` or `SIG_IGN` to this field; the first, `SIG_DFL`, restores handling of that signal to its default behavior, and `SIG_IGN` causes the specified signal to be ignored. The `sa_flags` field has a number of

19

possible settings, but in our examples we will set this field to zero. The sa_mask field specifies which of the other signals should be blocked during the execution of the signal handler. Usually this field is set using the function sigemptyset(), which is defined in signal.h as

```
int sigemptyset(sigset_t *set);
```

The last field in the structure sa_restorer is no longer used. Listing 19.7 demonstrates a simple program that sets up a signal handler for the SIGINT signal.

LISTING 19.7. A simple example of signal handling.

```
1 : /* A simple example of signal handling. */
2 : #include <stdio.h>
3 : #include <unistd.h>
4 : #include <signal.h>
5 :
6 : void  sig_handler(int sig);
7 :
8 : static int exit_now = 0;
9 :
10: int main(void)
11: {
12:     struct sigaction sig_struct ;
13:
14:     sig_struct.sa_handler = sig_handler;
15:     sigemptyset(&sig_struct.sa_mask);
16:     sig_struct.sa_flags = 0;
17:
18:     if (sigaction(SIGINT,&sig_struct,NULL) != 0)
19:     {
20:         perror ("error") ;
21:         exit (1);
22:     }
23:
24:     puts("Press Control-C to end processing.");
25:     while (exit_now == 0)
26:     {
27:         puts("Processing.");
28:         sleep(1);
29:     }
30:
31:     puts("Saving data to disk.");
32:
33:     return 0;
34: }
35:
36: void  sig_handler(int sig)
```

```
37: {
38:     printf("Received signal %d. Exiting soon.\n", sig);
39:     exit_now = 1;
40: }
```

OUTPUT
```
Press Control-C to end processing.
Processing.
Processing.
Processing.
Received signal 2. Exiting soon.
Saving data to disk.
```

ANALYSIS Lines 2 to 5 include the necessary header files, and line 6 defines a prototype for our signal handler, which is defined on lines 35 to 39. Note that this prototype matches the sa_handler field of the sigaction structure. Line 8 defines and sets to 0 a static variable, exit_now, that will be used for communication between the signal handler and the main program. On line 12, we define a sigaction structure that is filled in on lines 14 to 16. Line 14 sets the sa_handler field to the address of the sig_handler() function that was prototyped on line 6. Line 15 sets the sa_mask field using the sigemptyset() function, and the sa_flags field is set to 0 on line 16. After these fields are set up, we can call sigaction() on line 18—making sure to check the return value for an error condition. If an error occurs, a message is printed and the program exits on line 21.

If the signal handler is installed correctly, the program prints out a message on line 24 and executes the main program loop on lines 25 to 29. Whenever the variable exit_now is zero, the while statement prints out a message on line 27 and sleeps for 1 second on line 28. These two statements simulate a large computation.

The signal handler function, sig_handler(), is defined on lines 36 to 40. When this function is called, it prints a message to the screen stating which signal it received and setting the static variable exit_now to 1.

Looking at the output of the program, we see the message that was printed on line 24 and three lines of the message printed on line 27. The next line of the output is from the printf() statement on line 38. That's because I held down the Ctrl key and pressed C after the third Processing. message was printed. This keystroke causes the operating system to send this process a SIGINT signal, which is caught by the function sig_handler() on lines 36 to 40. The sig_handler() function then prints out its own message on line 38 and sets the exit_now variable, which is global to this file. When the signal handler finishes execution, control is passed back to the main function. The value of the variable exit_now has been changed in the signal handler, however, and is no longer equal to zero. Therefore, the while loop terminates and the code from 30 to 34 is executed, including the puts() statement on line 31.

19

So, how has the use of a signal handler changed the behavior of this program? You might like to try commenting out lines 17 to 22 by placing a /* on line 17 and an */ on line 22. This changes all the code between these markers into comments that the compiler will ignore and not place in the executable. If you now compile the code with the comments in place and run the new program as before, you will get different output, which looks like this:

```
Press Control-C to end processing.
Processing.
Processing.
Processing.
Processing.
```

This time when Ctrl+C is pressed, the program exhibits the default behavior for the SIG-INT signal; it just exits immediately. Notice how the message Saving data to disk. is not printed. Removing the comment markers on line 17 and 22 and recompiling the program restores the program to its previous operation.

Handling SIGCHLD to Prevent Zombie Child Processes

Earlier in today's lesson, we dealt with the fork() system function and the necessity of reaping zombie child processes. At that time, two methods of dealing with zombie processes were mentioned but only one was actually demonstrated. We will now deal with the other method.

Whenever a process terminates, the signal SIGCHLD is sent to the parent process of the child.

Reaping zombie child processes can also be achieved by changing the default behavior of the SIGCHLD signal handler. One common approach is to set it to SIG_IGN with code like the following snippet:

```
sig_struct.sa_handler = SIG_IGN;
sigemptyset(&sig_struct.sa_mask);
sig_struct.sa_flags = 0;
sigaction(SIGCHLD,&sig_struct,NULL);
```

This code works on Linux and might work on other members of the UNIX family, but it has two problems. First, it does not allow the exit status of the child process to be read. Second, it does not work on all members of the UNIX family. It should not be used if you care about portability.

The best way to deal with zombie child processes is to set up a SIGCHLD signal handler and call waitpid() within the handler. Listing 19.8 demonstrates this approach.

LISTING 19.8. Trapping SIGCHLD to prevent zombie child processes.

```
 1 : /* Trapping SIGCHLD to prevent zombie child processes. */
 2 : #include <stdio.h>
 3 : #include <stdlib.h>
 4 : #include <unistd.h>
 5 : #include <signal.h>
 6 : #include <sys/types.h>
 7 : #include <sys/wait.h>
 8 :
 9 : void  sigchld_handler (int);
10:
11: int main(void)
12: {
13:     pid_t  pid;
14:     struct sigaction sig_struct;
15:     int    k;
16:
17:     sig_struct.sa_handler = sigchld_handler;
18:     sigemptyset(&sig_struct.sa_mask);
19:     sig_struct.sa_flags = 0;
20:
21:     if (sigaction(SIGCHLD,&sig_struct,NULL) != 0)
22:     {
23:         perror ("error") ;
24:         exit (1);
25:     }
26:
27:     pid = fork();
28:
29:     if (pid < 0)
30:     {
31:         printf("Error : fork () returned %u.\n", pid);
32:         exit(1);
33:     }
34:
35:     if (pid == 0)
36:     {
37:         printf("Child : pid = %u. Parent's pid = %u\n",
38:                 getpid(), getppid());
39:         sleep(1);
40:         puts ("Child : about to exit.");
41:         exit(42);
42:     }
43:     else
44:     {
45:         printf("Parent: pid = %u. Child's  pid = %u\n",
46:                 getpid(), pid);
47:
48:         puts("Parent: going to sleep for 30 seconds.");
49:         for (k=0; k<30; k++)
```

19

continues

LISTING 19.8. continued

```
50:             sleep(1);
51:         puts("\nParent: Exiting.");
52:     }
53:
54:     return 0;
55: }
56:
57: void  sigchld_handler (int sig)
58: {
59:     pid_t  pid;
60:     int    status;
61:
62:     while ((pid = waitpid (-1, &status,  WNOHANG)) > 0)
63:     {
64:         printf("SIGCHLD: child with pid %u ", pid);
65:         if (WIFEXITED(status) != 0)
66:             printf("exited with status %d\n", WEXITSTATUS(status));
67:         else
68:             printf("exited abnormally.\n");
69:     }
70:
71: }
```

INPUT/OUTPUT

```
[erik@coltrane day19]$  ./list1907 &
[2] 1914
[erik@coltrane day19]$  Parent: pid = 1914. Child's  pid = 1915
Child : pid = 1915. Parent's pid = 1914
Parent: going to sleep for 30 seconds.
Child : about to exit.
SIGCHLD: child with pid 1915 exited with status 42

[erik@coltrane day19]$  ps u
USER       PID %CPU %MEM   VSZ  RSS TTY      STAT START   TIME COMMAND
erik      1110  0.0  0.3  1720  980 pts/3    S    02:24   0:00 -bash
erik      1849  0.0  1.2  4616 3136 pts/3    S    05:43   0:00 nedit
➥list1907.c
erik      1914  0.0  0.1  1052  332 pts/3    S    05:49   0:00
➥./list1907
erik      1916  0.0  0.3  2536  916 pts/3    R    05:49   0:00 ps u
[erik@coltrane day19]$
Parent: Exiting.
[2]+  Done                    ./list1907
```

ANALYSIS In this listing, lines 17 to 25 set up a signal handler similar to Listing 19.7. The difference is that instead of trapping `SIGINT` as we did in Listing 19.7, we are now trapping `SIGCHLD`. The rest of the `main()` function contains a `fork()` statement on line 27 and some code for the child process on lines 36 to 42. The parent process executes the code on lines 44 to 51. Note that the parent process does not need to use `wait()` or `waitpid()` as it does in Listings 19.4 and 19.5.

The function that will act as a signal handler is prototyped in line 9 and defined on lines 57 to 71. The signal handler has two local variables, pid and status, defined on lines 59 and 60. On line 62, a while loop is used to call waitpid() repeatedly until it returns an invalid process ID. If waitpid() does return a valid process ID—in the range 1 to 32767—the body of the while loop is executed. The body of the while loop simply prints out the process ID and exit status of the child process. If waitpid() returns anything other than a valid process ID, the body of the while statement is not executed and the signal handler returns. You might remember from the previous discussion that wait-pid() returns a negative number on error. So why aren't we checking for an error condition? Because if you call waitpid() when a process doesn't have any children, it returns -1 and the global variable errno is set to ECHILD—meaning that the process has no children. We don't check for an error condition because the most likely error—no child processes—is guaranteed to happen if there are no more children.

Another point to note about this program is that instead of using a single sleep() statement as in previous examples, this listing uses a for loop on lines 49 and 50. Why, you ask? Well, there are a number of system functions, of which sleep() is one, that terminate whenever the process receives a signal. If this listing just used a single sleep() of 30 seconds, that sleep would have been interrupted when the child process terminated, and the program would then have exited. This would have prevented you from confirming that the child process had been cleaned up.

Another potential trap in using a SIGCHLD signal handler should be mentioned. If there is more than one child process and the signal handler is called in response to one of the children terminating, it is possible for a second child to terminate before the signal handler has completed handling of the first child. In this case, a second SIGCHLD signal might not be generated. In other words, the programmer should not expect to received a SIGCHLD signal for every child process that terminates. This is why waitpid() is called inside a while loop in Listing 19.8 instead of just being called once.

19

Do	Don't
DO call waitpid() in a loop inside your SIGCHLD signal handler in case more than one child has terminated, but only one signal has been generated.	**DON'T** try to do too much inside your signal handler. The code inside the signal handler should be kept to a minimum.
	DON'T expect the termination of every child process to generate a SIGCHLD signal. If the SIGCHLD signal handler is being executed when the second child process terminates, a second signal might not occur.

Summary

In today's lesson, we looked at processes and signals on Linux and other UNIX-like systems. You learned that a process is an instance of a program on disk actually being executed by the operating system. Each process has a unique process ID, and by using the `fork()` system function, it is possible for a process to spawn a child process. You also learned how it is possible for a process to replace itself with another process using the `execl()` function. The command-line interpreter `bash` uses these two function to spawn and execute other programs. Finally, you learned about signals and how to trap them using the `sigaction` function to install a signal handler.

Q&A

Q Do all processes have a parent process?

A No, but only one process has no parent. That process is `init`, which has a process ID of 1. You might like to look for it in the process list by using the `ps u` command. The `init` process is the first process to be started when your Linux machine boots up and the last process to terminate when you shut down. There are also instances in which a child process loses its parent process but does not terminate. That child process will be inherited by the `init` process.

Q What is the main use of signals in Linux?

A There is no main use because signals are used for so many things. They are used by the command-line interpreter to control programs using the `SIGINT`, `SIGTSTOP`, `SIGSTOP`, and `SIGCONT` signals. They are used by the operating system to notify a process that a child process has terminated using the `SIGCHLD` signal. Many server applications are designed to reread their configuration files whenever they receive a `SIGHUP` signal. When a system shutdown is requested, the `init` process sends first `SIGTERM`, and later `SIGKILL`, to all other processes. `SIGSEGV`, `SIGFPE`, and `SIGILL` are sent to processes that have caused an error. The list of uses for signals goes on and on.

Workshop

The Workshop provides quiz questions to help you solidify your understanding of the material covered and exercises to provide you with experience in using what you've learned. The answers to the quiz and exercises are provided in Appendix C, "Answers."

Quiz

1. What is a process ID?

2. What is the range of valid process IDs?

3. What is the difference between the `getpid()` and `getppid()` functions?

4. Assuming that no error occurs, what is the return value of `fork()` in (a) the parent process and (b) the child process?

5. What is a zombie process?

6. What is the main difference between the `wait()` and `waitpid()` functions?

7. Why is none of the code after a successful `execl()` call executed?

8. If a process with a process ID of 1523 calls `execl()`, what is the process ID of the `execl()`ed program?

9. What are the two signals whose behavior cannot be changed by installing a signal handler?

Exercises

1. Write and test a function called `my_system()` that can replace the `system()` call. Use the `fork()` and `execl()` functions.

19

DAY 20

Advanced Compiler Use

Today's lesson covers some additional features of the C compiler. Today you will learn about

- Using the C preprocessor
- Using command-line arguments
- Programming with multiple source-code files
- Using the make utility
- Using and building libraries

The C Preprocessor

The preprocessor is a part of all C compiler packages. When you compile a C program, the preprocessor is the first compiler component that processes your program. In most C compilers, including GNU gcc, the preprocessor is part of the compiler program. When you run the compiler, it automatically runs the preprocessor.

The preprocessor changes your source code based on instructions, or *preprocessor directives,* in the source code. The output of the preprocessor is a modified source-code file that is then used as the input for the next compilation step. Normally, you never see this file because the compiler deletes it after it's used. However, later today you'll learn how to look at this intermediate file. First, you need to learn about the preprocessor directives, all of which begin with the # symbol.

The #define Preprocessor Directive

The #define preprocessor directive has two uses: creating symbolic constants and creating macros.

Simple Substitution Macros Using #define

You learned about substitution macros on Day 2, "The Components of a C Program: Code and Data," although the term used to describe them in that discussion is *symbolic constants*. You create a substitution macro by using #define to replace text with other text. For example, to replace text1 with text2, you write

```
#define text1 text2
```

This directive causes the preprocessor to go through the entire source-code file, replacing every occurrence of text1 with text2. The only exception occurs if text1 is found within double quotation marks, in which case no change is made.

The most frequent use for substitution macros is to create symbolic constants, as explained on Day 2. For example, if your program contains the following lines:

```
#define MAX 1000
x = y * MAX;
z = MAX - 12;
```

during preprocessing, the source code is changed to read as follows:

```
x = y * 1000;
z = 1000 - 12;
```

The effect is the same as using your editor's search-and-replace feature in order to change every occurrence of MAX to 1000. Your original source-code file isn't changed, of course. Instead, a temporary copy is created with the changes. Note that #define isn't limited to creating symbolic numeric constants. For example, you can write

```
#define ZINGBOFFLE printf
ZINGBOFFLE("Hello, world.");
```

although there is little reason to do so. You should also be aware that some authors consider symbolic constants defined with #define to be macros themselves. (Symbolic constants are also called *manifest constants*.) However, in this book, the word *macro* is reserved for the type of construction described next.

Creating Function Macros with #define

You can also use the #define directive to create function macros. A *function macro* is a type of shorthand, using something simple to represent something more complicated. The reason for the *function* name is that this type of macro can accept arguments, just as a real C function does. One advantage of function macros is that their arguments aren't type-sensitive. Therefore, you can pass any numeric variable type to a function macro that expects a numeric argument.

Let's look at an example. The preprocessor directive

```
#define HALFOF(value) ((value)/2)
```

defines a macro named HALFOF that takes a parameter named value. Whenever the preprocessor encounters the text HALFOF(value) in the source code, it replaces that text with the definition text and inserts the argument as needed. Thus, the source code line

```
result = HALFOF(10);
```

is replaced by this line:

```
result = ((10)/2);
```

Likewise, the program line

```
printf("%f", HALFOF(x[1] + y[2]));
```

is replaced by this line:

```
printf("%f", ((x[1] + y[2])/2));
```

A macro can have more than one parameter, and each parameter can be used more than once in the replacement text. For example, the following macro, which calculates the average of five values, has five parameters:

```
#define AVG5(v, w, x, y, z) (((v)+(w)+(x)+(y)+(z))/5)
```

The following macro, in which the conditional operator determines the larger of two values, also uses each of its parameters twice. (You learned about the conditional operator on Day 3, "Statements, Expressions, and Operators.")

```
#define LARGER(x, y) ((x) > (y) ? (x) : (y))
```

A macro can have as many parameters as needed, and when you invoke the macro, you must pass it the correct number of arguments.

When you write a macro definition, the opening parenthesis must immediately follow the macro name; there can be no whitespace. The opening parenthesis tells the preprocessor

20

that a function macro is being defined and that this isn't a simple symbolic constant type substitution. Look at the following definition:

```
#define SUM (x, y, z) ((x)+(y)+(z))
```

Because of the space between SUM and (, the preprocessor treats this like a simple substitution macro. Every occurrence of SUM in the source code is replaced with (x, y, z) ((x)+(y)+(z)), clearly not what you wanted.

Also note that in the substitution string, each parameter is enclosed in parentheses. This is necessary to avoid unwanted side effects when passing expressions as arguments to the macro. Look at the following example of a macro defined without parentheses:

```
#define SQUARE(x) x*x
```

If you invoke this macro with a simple variable as an argument, there's no problem. But what if you pass an expression as an argument?

```
result = SQUARE(x + y);
```

The resulting macro expansion is as follows, which doesn't give the proper result:

```
result = x + y * x + y;
```

If you use parentheses, you can avoid the problem, as shown in this example:

```
#define SQUARE(x) (x)*(x)
```

This definition expands to the following line, which does give the proper result:

```
result = (x + y) * (x + y);
```

You can obtain additional flexibility in macro definitions by using the *stringizing operator* (#) (sometimes called the *string-literal operator*). When a macro parameter is preceded by # in the substitution string, the argument is converted into a quoted string when the macro is expanded. Thus, if you define a macro as

```
#define OUT(x) printf(#x)
```

and you invoke it with the statement

```
OUT(Hello Mom);
```

it expands to this statement:

```
printf("Hello Mom");
```

The conversion performed by the stringizing operator takes special characters into account. Thus, if a character in the argument normally requires an escape character, the # operator inserts a backslash before the character. Continuing with the example, the invocation

```
OUT("Hello Mom");
```

expands to

```
printf("\"Hello Mom\"");
```

The # operator is demonstrated in Listing 20.1. First, you need to look at one other operator used in macros, the *concatenation operator* (##). This operator concatenates, or joins, two strings in the macro expansion. It doesn't include quotation marks or special treatment of escape characters. Its main use is to create sequences of C source code. For example, if you define and invoke a macro as

```
#define CHOP(x) func ## x
salad = CHOP(3)(q, w);
```

the macro invoked in the second line is expanded to

```
salad = func3 (q, w);
```

You can see that, by using the ## operator, you determine which function is called. You have actually modified the C source code.

Listing 20.1 shows an example of one way to use the # operator.

LISTING 20.1. Using the # operator in macro expansion.

```
1: /* Demonstrates the # operator in macro expansion. */
2:
3: #include <stdio.h>
4:
5: #define OUT(x) printf(#x " is equal to %d.\n", x)
6:
7: int main(void)
8: {
9:    int value = 123;
10:   OUT(value);
11:   return 0;
12: }
```

OUTPUT   value is equal to 123.

ANALYSIS   By using the # operator on line 5, the call to the macro expands with the variable name value as a quoted string passed to the printf() function. After expansion on line 9, the macro OUT looks like this:

```
printf("value" " is equal to %d.",  value );
```

Macros Versus Functions

You have seen that function macros can be used in place of real functions, at least in situations in which the resulting code is relatively short. Function macros can extend beyond

20

one line, but they usually become impractical beyond a few lines. When you can use either a function or a macro, which should you use? It's a trade-off between program speed and program size.

A macro's definition is expanded into the code each time the macro is encountered in the source code. If your program invokes a macro 100 times, 100 copies of the expanded macro code are in the final program. In contrast, a function's code exists only as a single copy. Therefore, in terms of program size, the better choice is a true function.

When a program calls a function, a certain amount of processing overhead is required in order to pass execution to the function code and then return execution to the calling program. There is no processing overhead in "calling" a macro because the code is right there in the program. In terms of speed, a function macro has the advantage.

These size/speed considerations aren't usually of much concern to the beginning programmer. Only with large, time-critical applications do they become important.

Viewing Macro Expansion

At times, you might want to see what your expanded macros look like, particularly when they aren't working properly. To see the expanded macros, you instruct the compiler to create a file that includes macro expansion after the compiler's first pass through the code.

For example, to precompile a program named program.c with the GNU C compiler, you would enter

```
gcc -E program.c
```

The preprocessor makes the first pass through your source code. All header files are included, #define macros are expanded, and other preprocessor directives are carried out. The output of the preprocessor stage is dumped to stdout (that is, the screen). Unfortunately, it's not at all useful to have the processed code whip by on your screen! You can use the pipe command to pipe it through the more program or redirect this output to a file.

```
gcc -E program.c ¦ more
```

```
gcc -E program.c > program.pre
```

You can then load the file into your editor for printing or viewing.

Do	**Don't**
DO use `#defines`, especially for symbolic constants. Symbolic constants make your code much easier to read. Examples of things to put into defined constants are colors, true/false, yes/no, the keyboard keys, and maximum values. Symbolic constants are used throughout this book.	DON'T overuse macro functions. Use them where needed, but be sure they are a better choice than a normal function.

The `#include` Directive

You have already learned how to use the `#include` preprocessor directive to include header files in your program. When it encounters an `#include` directive, the preprocessor reads the specified file and inserts it at the location of the directive. You can't use the * or ? wildcards to read in a group of files with one `#include` directive. You can, however, nest `#include` directives. In other words, an included file can contain `#include` directives, which can contain `#include` directives, and so on. Most compilers limit the number of levels deep that you can nest, but you usually can nest up to 10 levels.

There are two ways to specify the filename for an `#include` directive. If the filename is enclosed in angle brackets, such as `#include <stdio.h>` (as you have seen throughout this book), the preprocessor first looks for the file in the standard directory. If the file isn't found, or no standard directory is specified, the preprocessor looks for the file in the current directory.

"What is the standard directory?" you might be asking. In Linux, it's the directories /usr/include and /usr/local/include. But, if you want to add extra directories to the include path, you can do so with the `-I` command-line switch. If you wanted to add the directory /home/user/erik/include to the include path while compiling program.c you would use

```
gcc -Wall -I/home/user/erik/include program.c -o program
```

The second method of specifying the file to include is enclosing the filename in double quotation marks: `#include "myfile.h"`. In this case, the preprocessor doesn't search the standard directories; instead, it looks in the directory containing the source code file being compiled. Generally speaking, the header files you write should be kept in the same directory as the C source code files, and they are included by using double quotation marks. The standard directory is reserved for systemwide header files.

20

Using #if, #elif, #else, and #endif

These four preprocessor directives control conditional compilation. The term *conditional compilation* means that blocks of C source code are compiled only if certain conditions are met. In many ways, the #if family of preprocessor directives operates like the C language's if statement. The difference is that if controls whether certain statements are executed, whereas #if controls whether they are compiled.

The structure of an #if block is as follows:

```
#if condition_1
statement_block_1
#elif condition_2
statement_block_2
...
#elif condition_n
statement_block_n
#else
default_statement_block
#endif
```

The test expression that #if uses can be almost any expression that evaluates to a constant. You can't use the sizeof() operator, typecasts, or the float type. Most often you use #if to test symbolic constants created with the #define directive.

Each *statement_block* consists of one or more C statements of any type, including preprocessor directives. They don't need to be enclosed in braces, although they can be.

The #if and #endif directives are required, but #elif and #else are optional. You can have as many #elif directives as you want, but only one #else. When the compiler reaches an #if directive, it tests the associated condition. If the condition evaluates to TRUE (nonzero), the statements following the #if are compiled. If the condition evaluates to FALSE (zero), the compiler tests, in order, the conditions associated with each #elif directive. The statements associated with the first TRUE #elif are compiled. If none of the conditions evaluates as TRUE, the statements following the #else directive are compiled.

Note that, at most, a single block of statements within the #if...#endif construction is compiled. If the compiler finds no #else directive, it might not compile any statements.

The possible uses of these conditional compilation directives are limited only by your imagination. Here's one example. Suppose you're writing a program that uses a great deal of country-specific information. This information is contained in a header file for each country. When you compile the program for use in different countries, you can use an #if...#endif construction as follows:

```
#if ENGLAND == 1
#include "england.h"
#elif FRANCE == 1
#include "france.h"
#elif ITALY == 1
#include "italy.h"
#else
#include "usa.h"
#endif
```

Then, by using #define to define the appropriate symbolic constant, you can control which header file is included during compilation.

Using #if...#endif to Help Debug

Another common use of #if...#endif is to include conditional debugging code in the program. You could define a DEBUG symbolic constant set to either 1 or 0. Throughout the program, you can insert debugging code as follows:

```
#if DEBUG == 1
debugging code here
#endif
```

During program development, if you define DEBUG as 1, the debugging code is included to help track down any bugs. After the program is working properly, you can redefine DEBUG as 0 and recompile the program without the debugging code.

The defined() operator is useful when you write conditional compilation directives. This operator tests to see whether a particular name is defined. Thus, the expression

```
defined( NAME )
```

evaluates to TRUE or FALSE, depending on whether NAME is defined. By using defined(), you can control compilation, based on previous definitions, without regard to the specific value of a name. Referring to the previous debugging code example, you could rewrite the #if...#endif section as follows:

```
#if defined( DEBUG )
debugging code here
#endif
```

You can also use defined() to assign a definition to a name only if it hasn't been previously defined. Use the NOT operator (!) as follows:

```
#if !defined( TRUE )      /* if TRUE is not defined. */
#define TRUE 1
#endif
```

20

Notice that the `defined()` operator doesn't require that a name be defined as anything in particular. For example, after the following program line, the name RED is defined, but not as anything in particular:

```
#define RED
```

Even so, the expression `defined( RED )` still evaluates as TRUE. Of course, occurrences of RED in the source code are removed and not replaced with anything, so you must use caution.

Avoiding Multiple Inclusions of Header Files

As programs grow, or as you use header files more often, you run the risk of accidentally including a header file more than once. This can cause the compiler to balk in confusion. Using the directives that you've learned, you can easily avoid this problem. Look at the example shown in Listing 20.2.

LISTING 20.2. Using preprocessor directives with header files.

```
1: /* PROG.H - A header file with a check to prevent multiple includes! */
2:
3. #if defined( PROG_H )
4: /* the file has been included already */
5: #else
6: #define PROG_H
7:
8: /* Header file information goes here... */
9:
10:
11:
12: #endif
```

ANALYSIS   Examine what this header file does. On line 3, it checks whether PROG_H is defined. Notice that PROG_H is similar to the name of the header file. If PROG_H is defined, a comment is included on line 4, and the program looks for the #endif at the end of the header file. This means that nothing more is done.

How does PROG_H get defined? It is defined on line 6. The first time this header is included, the preprocessor checks whether PROG_H is defined. It won't be, so control goes to the #else statement. The first thing done after the #else is to define PROG_H so that any other inclusions of this file skip the body of the file. Lines 7 through 11 can contain any number of commands or declarations.

The #undef Directive

The #undef directive is the opposite of #define—it removes the definition from a name. Here's an example:

```
#define DEBUG 1
/* In this section of the program, occurrences of DEBUG    */
/* are replaced with 1, and the expression defined( DEBUG ) */
/* evaluates to TRUE. *.
#undef DEBUG
/* In this section of the program, occurrences of DEBUG   */
/* are not replaced, and the expression defined( DEBUG ) */
/* evaluates to FALSE. */
```

You can use #undef and #define to create a name that is defined only in parts of your source code. You can use this in combination with the #if directive, as explained earlier, for more control over conditional compilations.

Predefined Macros

Most compilers have a number of predefined macros. The most useful of these are __DATE__, __TIME__, __LINE__, and __FILE__. Notice that each of these is preceded and followed by double underscores. This is done to prevent you from redefining them, on the theory that programmers are unlikely to create their own definitions with leading and trailing underscores.

These macros work just like the macros described earlier today. When the precompiler encounters one of these macros, it replaces the macro with the macro's code. __DATE__ and __TIME__ are replaced with the current date and time. The "current date and time" are the date and time the source file is precompiled. This can be useful information when you're working with different versions of a program. By having a program display its compilation date and time, you can tell whether you're running the latest version of the program or an earlier one.

The other two macros are even more valuable. __LINE__ is replaced by the current source-file line number. __FILE__ is replaced with the current source-code filename. These two macros are best used when you're trying to debug a program or deal with errors. Consider the following printf() statement:

```
31:
32: printf( "Program %s: (%d) Error opening file ", __FILE__, __LINE__ );
33:
```

20

If these lines were part of a program called myprog.c, they would print

```
Program myprog.c: (32) Error opening file
```

This might not seem important at this point, but as your programs grow and spread across multiple source files, finding errors becomes more difficult. Using __LINE__ and __FILE__ makes debugging much easier.

Do	Don't
DO use the __LINE__ and __FILE__ macros to make your error messages more helpful.	**DON'T** forget the #endif when using the #if statement.

DO put parentheses around the value to be passed to a macro. This prevents errors. For example, use this:
 	
`#define CUBE(x)    (x)*(x)*(x)`
 	
instead of this:
 	
`#define CUBE(x)    x*x*x`	

Using Command-Line Arguments

Your C program can access arguments passed to the program on the command line. This refers to information entered after the program name when you start the program. If you want to start a program named progname—which is in the current directory—from the prompt, for example, you would enter

```
[erik@coltrane day20]$ ./progname smith jones
```

The two command-line arguments smith and jones can be retrieved by the program during execution. You can think of this information as arguments passed to the program's main() function. Such command-line arguments permit information to be passed to the program at startup rather than during execution, which can be convenient at times. You can pass as many command-line arguments as you like. Note that command-line arguments can be retrieved only within main(). To do so, declare main() as follows:

```
int main(int argc, char *argv[])
{
/* Statements go here */
}
```

The first parameter, argc, is an integer giving the number of command-line arguments available. This value is always at least 1 because the program name is counted as the first argument. The parameter argv[] is an array of pointers to strings. The valid subscripts for this array are 0 through argc - 1. The pointer argv[0] points to the program name (including path information), argv[1] points to the first argument that follows the program name, and so on. Note that the names argc and argv[] aren't required—you can use any valid C variable names you like to receive the command-line arguments. However, these two names are traditionally used for this purpose, so you should probably stick with them.

The command line is divided into discrete arguments by any whitespace. If you need to pass an argument that includes a space, enclose the entire argument in double quotation marks. For example, if you enter

```
./progname smith "and jones"
```

smith is the first argument (pointed to by argv[1]), and and jones is the second (pointed to by argv[2]). Listing 20.3 demonstrates how to access command-line arguments.

LISTING 20.3. Passing command-line arguments to main().

```
1: /* Accessing command-line arguments. */
2:
3: #include <stdio.h>
4:
5: int main(int argc, char *argv[])
6: {
7:     int count;
8:
9:     printf("Program name: %s\n", argv[0]);
10:
11:     if (argc > 1)
12:     {
13:         for (count = 1; count < argc; count++)
14:             printf("Argument %d: %s\n", count, argv[count]);
15:     }
16:     else
17:         puts("No command line arguments entered.");
18:     return 0;
19: }
```

OUTPUT

```
./list2003
Program name: ./list2003
No command line arguments entered.

./list2006 first second "3 4"
Program name: ./list2003
Argument 1: first
Argument 2: second
Argument 3: 3 4
```

20

ANALYSIS This program does no more than print the command-line parameters entered by the user. Notice that line 5 uses the argc and argv parameters shown previously. Line 9 prints the one command-line parameter that you always have, the program name. Notice this is argv[0]. Line 11 checks to see whether there is more than one command-line parameter. Why more than one and not more than zero? Because there is always at least one—the program name. If there are additional arguments, a for loop prints each to the screen (lines 13 and 14). Otherwise, an appropriate message is printed (line 17).

Command-line arguments generally fall into two categories: those that are required because the program can't operate without them and those that are optional, such as flags that instruct the program to act in a certain way. For example, imagine a program that sorts the data in a file. If you write the program to receive the input filename from the command line, the name is required information. If the user forgets to enter the input filename on the command line, the program must somehow deal with the situation. The program could also look for the argument /r, which signals a reverse-order sort. This argument isn't required; the program looks for it and behaves one way if it's found and another way if it isn't.

Do	Don't
DO use argc and argv as the variable names for the command-line arguments for main(). Most C programmers are familiar with these names.	**DON'T** assume users will enter the correct number of command-line parameters. Check to be sure they did, and if they did not, display a message explaining the arguments they should enter.

Command-Line Arguments Using getopt()

Reading command-line options using argc and argv[] is relatively simple as long as the options are kept to a minimum. Many programs have a huge variety of command-line options, and writing code to handle them with argc and argv[] can become quite complicated. Fortunately, Linux and most other UNIX-like operating systems have the getopt() function to help you parse command-line options. This function is defined in getopt.h as follows:

```
int getopt(int argc, char * const argv[],const char *optstring);
```

The first two parameters to getopt() are the two arguments passed into the main() function, and the third parameter is a character string. When called repeatedly, the getopt() function searches through the argv[] array to find strings in that array that begin with "-" and are followed by characters in the optstring array. For each character found in optstring, getopts() returns the character or EOF if there are no more characters in the optstring or if all the elements in argv[] have been handled. If any character in optsting is followed by a colon, the following string element of the argv[] array is considered a parameter, and the char* pointer optarg will be set to point to that parameter. When getopt() returns EOF, it sets the integer value optind equal to the first element of argv[] that getopt() did not parse. The variables optarg and optind are defined as extern in getopt.h. This all seems very complicated, but Listing 20.4 gives an example of the use of getopt() that should make things clearer.

LISTING 20.4. Passing command-line arguments using getopt().

```
 1 : /* Accessing command-line arguments using getopt(). */
 2 :
 3 : #include <stdio.h>
 4 : #include <getopt.h>
 5 :
 6 : int main(int argc, char *argv[])
 7 : {
 8 :     int option;
 9 :
10:     while ((option = getopt (argc, argv, "abi:o:z")) != EOF)
11:     {
12:         switch (option)
13:         {
14:             case 'a' :
15:             case 'b' :
16:             case 'z' :
17:                     printf("option : %c\n", option);
18:                     break;
19:
20:             case 'i' :
21:                     printf("input  : %s\n", optarg);
22:                     break;
23:
24:             case 'o' :
25:                     printf("output : %s\n", optarg);
26:                     break;
27:
28:             default :
29:                     exit(1);
30:         }
31:     }
32:
33:     for ( ; optind < argc ; optind++)
34:         printf ("opt %2d : %s\n", optind, argv [optind]);
35:
36:     return 0;
37: }
```

20

OUTPUT

```
./list2004 -za -i infile -b -o outfile -z peter brad erik
option : z
option : a
input  : infile
option : b
output : outfile
option : z
opt  8 : peter
opt  9 : brad
opt 10 : erik
```

ANALYSIS   This listing begins by including the two required header files on lines 3 and 4. In the main() function, it defines a single variable option of type int that will be used as the return value for the getopts() function. On line 10, getopt() is called within the conditional expression of the while statement on line 10. Notice that argc and argv[], the arguments to the main() function, are simply passed into getopt() without modification. The third argument to getopt() is the option string, which, in this case, specifies that getopt() should look for the single-letter options a, b, and z, as well as options i and o, both of which will both be followed by an argument that is the following element of the argv[] array.

The getopt() function returns, setting the variable option for each option character—a, b, i, o, and z—it has been asked to look for. The switch statement on line 12 then allows each of the option characters to be processed individually. The i and o options are followed by a colon in the options string passed to getopt(), so the variable optarg is set to point to the next element of the argv[] array. You should note from the preceding output that the option -i infile resulted in optarg being set to the string infile and getopt() returning the character i.

Finally, when getopt() has handled all the cases it was asked to, it returns a value of EOF, which causes the while loop to terminate. The for loop on lines 33 and 34 is then able to process the remaining arguments in the argv[] array.

As flexible and useful as the getopt() function is, two other functions defined in getopt.h, getopt_long() and getopt_long_only(), have even more features. Unfortunately they are beyond the scope of this book, but you are encouraged to consult the manual page—man 3 getopt—for further information.

Programming with Multiple Source Files

Until now, all your C programs have consisted of a single source-code file (not counting the header files, of course). A single source-code file is often all you need, particularly for small programs, but you can also divide the source code for a single program between two or more files, a practice called *modular programming*. Why would you want to do that? The following sections explain.

Advantages of Modular Programming

The primary reason to use modular programming is closely related to structured programming and its reliance on functions. As you become a more experienced programmer, you develop more general-purpose functions that you can use, not only in the program for which they were originally written, but in other programs as well. For example, you might write a collection of general-purpose functions for displaying information onscreen. By keeping these functions in a separate file, you can use them again in different programs that also display information onscreen. When you write a program that consists of multiple source-code files, each source file is called a *module*.

Modular Programming Techniques

A C program can have only one `main()` function. The module that contains the `main()` function is called the *main module,* and other modules are called *secondary modules*. A separate header file is usually associated with each secondary module (you'll learn why later today). For now, look at a few simple examples that illustrate the basics of multiple module programming. Listings 20.5, 20.6, and 20.7 show the main module, the secondary module, and the header file, respectively, for a program that inputs a number from the user and displays its square.

LISTING 20.5. list2005.c: The main module.

```
1: /* Inputs a number and displays its square. */
2:
3: #include <stdio.h>
4: #include "calc.h"
5:
6: int main(void)
7: {
8:     int x;
9:
10:     printf("Enter an integer value: ");
11:     scanf("%d", &x);
12:     printf("\nThe square of %d is %ld.\n", x, sqr(x));
13:     return 0;
14: }
```

20

Listing 20.6. calc.c: The secondary module.

```
1: /* Module containing calculation functions. */
2:
3: #include "calc.h"
4:
5: long sqr(int x)
6: {
7:    return ((long)x * x);
8: }
```

Listing 20.7. calc.h: The header file for calc.c.

```
1: /* calc.h: header file for calc.c. */
2:
3: long sqr(int x);
4:
5: /* end of calc.h */
```

INPUT/OUTPUT

```
Enter an integer value: 100

The square of 100 is 10000.
```

ANALYSIS Let's look at the components of these three files in greater detail. The header file, calc.h, contains the prototype for the sqr() function in calc.c. Because any module that uses sqr() needs to know sqr()'s prototype, the module must include calc.h.

The secondary module file, calc.c, contains the definition of the sqr() function. The #include directive is used to include the header file, calc.h. Note that the header file-name is enclosed in double quotation marks rather than angle brackets. (You'll learn the reason for this later today.)

The main module, list2005.c, contains the main() function. This module also includes the header file, calc.h. To compile these two C source code files into one program, you must issue the following command:

```
gcc -Wall -ggdb calc.c list2005.c -o list2005
```

Note that this compile command contains two C source code files. The gcc compiler allows more than one C source code file to be compiled at once.

An alternative to compiling both the C source code files at the same time is to compile each source code file separately to create intermediate files, called *object files*, with the .o extension. These object-code files are in a special format; they have been converted into machine code by the compiler, but also contain extra information that will allow them to be linked to other object files to create an executable. To create an object code from the C source code file named list2005.c, you would execute the following command:

```
gcc -Wall -ggdb -c list2005.c
```

The -c command line option tells the compiler to compile the C source code file and, assuming there are no errors, generate an object-code file—named list2005.o in this case—on disk. Similarly, the command

```
gcc -Wall -ggdb -c calc.c
```

would create an object file named calc.o. To link these two files together to create an executable file, you execute the command:

```
gcc -Wall -ggdb calc.o list2005.o -o list2005
```

This command tells the compiler to link the two object files calc.o and list2005.o together and create an executable named list2005.

Using .o Files

So why compile the C source code files separately into object files and then link them together instead of just compiling all the C source code files into an executable in one go? Consider a case in which a project consists of many C source files. Each of these source files might contain hundreds of lines of code. With a large number of source code files, compiling all the files every time you change one may take a long time. On the other hand, if you compile each source code file separately into an object file and then link the objects together, only the file that has changed must be recompiled. The new object file can then be linked with all the existing object files to create a new executable. In other words, you need to compile only the module you are currently changing into an object file. If the other source code files haven't changed, their object files can be reused.

So, if we consider the preceding case in which a change was required in the file list2005.c, creating a new program based on the existing object file and the new C file could be done with the command

```
gcc -Wall list2005.c calc.o -o list2005
```

This command compiles list2005.c, links it with the object file calc.o that was generated earlier, and generates the executable file list2005.

Module Components

As you can see, the mechanics of compiling and linking a multiple-module program are quite simple. After these mechanics are understood, the only real question is what to put in each file. This section gives you some general guidelines.

20

The secondary module should contain general utility functions—that is, functions that you might want to use in other programs. A common practice is to create one secondary module for each type of function—for example, keyboard.c for your keyboard functions, screen.c for your screen display functions, and so on.

There is usually one header file for each secondary module. Each file has the same name as the associated module, with an .h extension. In the header file, put

- Prototypes for functions in the secondary module
- `#define` directives for any symbolic constants and macros used in the module
- Definitions of any structures or external variables used in the module

Because this header file might be included in more than one source file, you want to prevent portions of it from compiling more than once. You can do this by using the preprocessor directives for conditional compilation (discussed earlier today).

External Variables and Modular Programming

In many cases, the only data communication between the main module and the secondary module is through arguments passed to and returned from the functions. In this case, you don't need to take special steps regarding data visibility, but what about an external variable that must be visible in both modules?

Recall from Day 11, "Understanding Variable Scope," that an external variable is one declared outside any function. An external variable is visible throughout the entire source code file in which it is declared. However, it is not automatically visible in other modules. To make it visible, you must declare the variable in each module, using the `extern` keyword. For example, if you have an external variable declared in the main module as

```
float interest_rate;
```

you make `interest_rate` visible in a secondary module by including the following declaration in that module (outside any function):

```
extern float interest_rate;
```

The `extern` keyword tells the compiler that the original declaration of `interest_rate` (the one that set aside storage space for it) is located elsewhere, but that the variable should be made visible in this module. All `extern` variables have static duration and are visible to all functions in the module. Figure 20.1 illustrates the use of the `extern` keyword in a multiple-module program.

FIGURE 20.1.

Using the extern *key-word to make an external variable visible across modules.*

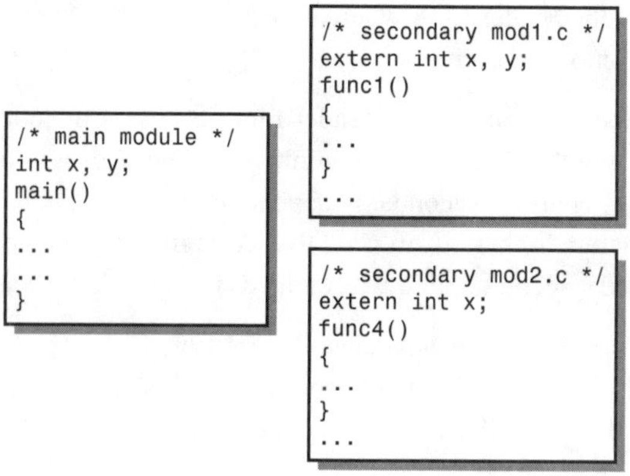

```
/* main module */
int x, y;
main()
{
...
...
}
```

```
/* secondary mod1.c */
extern int x, y;
func1()
{
...
}
...
```

```
/* secondary mod2.c */
extern int x;
func4()
{
...
}
...
```

In Figure 20.1, the variable x is visible throughout all three modules. In contrast, y is visible only in the main module and secondary module 1.

Do	Don't
DO create generic functions in their own source files. That way, they can be linked into any other programs that need them.	DON'T try to compile multiple source files together if more than one module contains a main() function. You can have only one main(). DON'T always use the C source files when compiling multiple files together. If you compile a source file into an object file, recompile only when the file changes. This saves a great deal of time.

Using the make Utility

Almost all systems that have a C compiler also come with a make utility that can simplify the task of working with multiple source-code files. Linux is no exception; it comes with GNU make, which is a very good example of this utility. The differences between make utilities on different platforms are minor and are not within the scope of this book.

So what does make do? It enables you to write a *Makefile* (usually named Makefile or makefile), so called because it helps you make your programs by removing the complications of figuring out the dependencies between files each time you change something.

Imagine a project that has a main module named program.c and a secondary module named second.c. There are also two header files, program.h and second.h. program.c

20

includes both of the header files, whereas second.c includes only second.h. Code in program.c calls functions in second.c.

program.c is dependent on the two header files because it includes them both. If you make a change to either header file, you must recompile program.c so that it will include those changes. In contrast, second.c is dependent on second.h, but not on program.h. If you change program.h, there is no need to recompile second.c—you can just link the existing object file, second.o, that was created when second.c was last compiled.

A Makefile describes the dependencies that exist in your project, such as those just discussed. Each time you edit one or more of your source code files, you use the make utility to "run" the Makefile. This utility examines the time and date stamps on the source-code file and the object files and, based on the dependencies you have defined, instructs the compiler to recompile only those files that are dependent on the modified file(s). The result is that no unnecessary compilation is done, and you can work at maximum efficiency. Listing 20.8 shows a minimal Makefile for the program in Listing 20.5.

LISTING 20.8. Makefile: A Makefile for list2005.c.

```
 1 : # Makefile for Listing 20.5
 2 :
 3 : CC = gcc
 4 : CFLAGS = -Wall -ggdb   # All warnings and debugging
 5 :
 6 : list2005 : list2005.o calc.o
 7 :      $(CC) list2005.o calc.o -o list2005
 8 :
 9 : list2005.o : list2005.c calc.h
10:      $(CC) $(CFLAGS) -c list2005.c
11:
12: calc.o : calc.c calc.h
13:      $(CC) $(CFLAGS) -c calc.c
14:
15: clean :
16:      rm -f *.o
```

Just as for the C source code throughout this book, the numbers and colon at the far left are not part of the Makefile. In fact, lines 1, 3, 4, 6, 9, and 12 should all be aligned to the far left. So, for instance, line 1 should have the hash character (#) as the first character of line 1. Also note that lines 7, 10, and 13 must not begin in character position 1 in the line. The first character must be a whitespace (tab or space) character on those lines.
Depending on the settings of your editor, the tab character might indent those lines by up to and including eight characters. In fact, eight characters is the most common tab setting.

Let's go through this Makefile and figure out what it does. As you might have guessed, the first line is a comment. In Makefiles, comments start with the hash character and extend to the end of the current line. Lines 2 and 4 set up two variables (CC and CFLAGS) that behave much like variables in C. The values of each of these variables is the string to the right of the equal sign on each line, not including any comments. When the make utility processes the Makefile, it looks for variable names enclosed in parentheses and preceded by a dollar sign and substitutes the values of those variables. For example, wherever the make utility finds $(CC) after line 3, it will replace the whole of that expression with gcc, the value of the CC variable.

Lines 6, 9, and 12 define a target on the left side of the colon and a dependency list on the right side. A target is something that make has to build, and the dependency list tells make what files are required for the target to be up-to-date. In line 6, the Makefile states that the object list2005, which is a program, depends on two object files, list2005.o and calc.o. This makes sense because if either of these two object files is newer than the program, the program must be rebuilt. Similarly, the target-dependency list pair on line 9 states that if either of the files list2005.c or calc.h has a date later than the date of the object file list2005.o, the object file must be rebuilt. Line 15 looks like a target without a dependency list, and that's exactly what it is. We'll come back to that a little later.

Along with each target-dependency list pair, there may be any number of lines telling the make utility how to build the target—in some cases, there won't even be one. For the target on line 6—the program list2005—the build instructions are on line 7. Remember that the make utility replaces $(CC) with gcc and then runs the whole line as a separate program. In this case, if either of the files list2005.o or calc.o has a later date than the program list2005, the make utility runs the following command:

```
gcc list2005.o calc.o -o list2005
```

To use the Makefile with the make utility, place the Makefile in the same directory as the C source code files list2005.c and calc.c, and type make at the prompt. Assuming there are no errors in the C source code, what you should see is the following:

```
gcc -Wall -ggdb -c list2005.c
```

```
gcc -Wall -ggdb -c calc.c
```

```
gcc list2005.o calc.o -o list2005
```

If all went according to plan, you should then have the program list2005 in the same directory. Notice, however, that if you type the make command again, you will get the message

```
make: `list2005' is up to date
```

20

This is saying that make has checked through the dependency list and found that the main target, list2005, has a file time and date that are more recent than any of its dependencies.

To explore this a little further, open the file calc.c in your editor, add a few space characters somewhere in the file, and save it. Now, run the make utility again. You should see something like this:

```
gcc -Wall -ggdb -c calc.c

gcc list2005.o calc.o -o list2005
```

The make utility saw that the file calc.c was newer than its object file calc.o, so it ran the compiler command in the first line, re-creating the object file from the new C file. make then rescans its target-dependency list pairs and sees the newly created calc.o is newer than the program list2005 that depends on it. It then executes the second compiler command. Notice, however, that make was perfectly happy to use the object file list2005.o and did not need to recompile list2005.c.

In addition to running make to make the first target in the Makefile, any of the other targets can also be built by calling make with the name of the target. The last target in the Makefile is called clean. clean has no dependencies, but typing make clean at the command line runs the build instruction for the target clean, which, in this case deletes all the object files in the current directory. Similarly, running make calc.o causes calc.o to be built if necessary.

Listing 20.9 contains a second, slightly more complicated Makefile named Makefile2.

LISTING 20.9. Makefile2: A slightly more complicated Makefile.

```
 1 : # Makefile for multiple targets.
 2 :
 3 : CC = gcc
 4 : CFLAGS = -Wall -ggdb
 5 :
 6 : all : list2004 list2005
 7 :
 8 : list2004 : list2004.c
 9 :     $(CC) $(CFLAGS) list2004.c -o list2004
10:
11: list2005 : list2005.o calc.o
12:     $(CC) list2005.o calc.o -o list2005
13:
14: list2005.o : list2005.c calc.h
15:     $(CC) $(CFLAGS) -c list2005.c
16:
17: calc.o : calc.c calc.h
```

```
18:      $(CC) $(CFLAGS) -c calc.c
19:
20: clean :
21:      rm -f $(TARGETS) *.o
```

The main difference between this Makefile and the preceding one is that the first target in line 6 is named `all` and has two dependencies, the programs list2004 and list2005, but no build instructions. That is okay because each of these two dependencies is a target as well, `list2004` in line 8 and `list2005` in line 11. The other difference is that this file is named `Makefile2`, and the `make` utility, when run, will be looking in current directory for a file named Makefile or makefile. You can override this behavior by giving `make` the name of the Makefile you want it to operate on:

```
make -f Makefile2
```

The Makefiles we have seen here are very simple indeed, but are obviously useful. The `make` utility may also be used to build projects written in languages other than C. Nearly every program for Linux that is distributed with source code contains at least one Makefile. Most of these projects will contain C source code spanning many subdirectories of the main directory. The top-level Makefile in the main directory visits each of the subdirectories and runs the Makefile of each, one by one. In projects of this size, the Makefile often spans several hundred lines and is often automatically generated by another program. The Makefiles we have dealt with here might be simple, but they can be easily modified to help you as you write larger programs and start splitting your source code into many files.

Using Shared Libraries

Linux, in common with most of the other members of the UNIX family of operating systems, allows programs to use libraries of useful functions kept in files external to the program executable file. These libraries are called *shared* or *dynamically linked* libraries. When a program using shared libraries is run, the program is dynamically linked to the shared library just before the program is run. They are called *shared* libraries because many programs can link to one shared library instead of each program having its own copy of the library. Obviously this technique reduces the memory requirements when many programs all share one copy of a library.

The programs in this book have already been using shared libraries without you, the programmer, being aware of it. That's because the C compiler automatically links C programs to a library containing all the common Standard C library functions such as `printf()`, `puts()`, `scanf()`, `fgets()`, and so on.

20

A program named ldd on all Linux systems will tell you which shared libraries a program uses. Try using ldd on some of the programs in this lesson. For instance, the executable program obtained by compiling Listing 20.5 produces the following:

```
[erik@coltrane day20]$ ldd list2005
        libc.so.6 => /lib/libc.so.6 (0x40019000)
        /lib/ld-linux.so.2 => /lib/ld-linux.so.2 (0x40000000)
```

You will see that the program list2005 uses two shared libraries. The first is libc, the standard C library, and it contains all the functions in the Standard C library. The other library contains functions required by the dynamic linker, and its details are beyond the scope of this book.

In Day 17, "Exploring the C Function Library," we looked at using the math functions such as exp(), sin(), and so on. In order to use those functions, we had to tell the compiler to link in the maths library by adding an extra argument, -lm, to the compile command. You will find a large number of libraries in the directories /lib, /usr/lib, and maybe also /usr/local/lib. They all have names beginning with *lib*. A library named libname can be linked to your program by including -lname as an argument to the link command.

To use the functions in any given library usually requires inclusion of the appropriate header file in the C source code files. When we used the math functions in Day 17, we included the header file math.h, which defines the math functions and adds the -lm argument to the compile command to dynamically link the math library to the program.

On Linux, gcc has a number of standard directories it looks in for header files and libraries. For header files, the directories are /usr/include and /usr/local/include/, whereas for libraries the directories are /lib, /usr/lib, and /usr/local/lib. gcc also allows the user to add directories to the search path for both header files and libraries. To ask gcc to include the directory named /home/erik/headers in the search path for header files, the argument -I/home/erikd/headers should be added to the command line. For extra libraries, the directory /home/erik/lib can be added to the library search path by using -L/home/erik/lib to the link command.

In Day 21, "An Introduction to GUI Programming with GTK+," the final day of this book, we will use some of these concepts when we start programming for the X Window System GUI using the GTK+ toolkit. X GUI programming requires the use of libraries and header files that are not in the standard search path.

Summary

Today's lesson covered some of the more advanced programming tools available with C compilers. First, you saw how you can use preprocessor directives to create function macros, for conditional compilation and other tasks. You also saw that the compiler provides some function macros for you. You learned how to write a program that has source code divided among multiple files or modules. This practice, called *modular programming*, makes it easy to reuse general-purpose functions in more than one program.

Q&A

Q Are all the predefined macros and preprocessor directives presented in today's lesson?

A No. The predefined macros and directives presented today are ones common to most compilers. However, most compilers, including gcc, have additional macros and constants.

Q Is the following header also acceptable when using `main()` with command-line parameters?

```
main( int argc, char **argv);
```

A You can probably answer this one on your own. This declaration uses a pointer to a character pointer instead of a pointer to a character array. Because an array is a pointer, this definition is virtually the same as the one presented today. This declaration is also commonly used. (See Day 7, "Using Numeric Arrays," and Day 9, "Characters and Strings," for more details.)

Q When compiling multiple files, how does the compiler know which filename to use for the executable file?

A You might think the compiler uses the name of the file containing the `main()` function; however, this isn't the case. On Linux and most other UNIX-like operating systems, the output file is named a.out unless the compiler is explicitly told otherwise.

Q Do header files need to have an .h extension?

A No. You can give a header file any name you want. It is standard practice to use the .h extension.

Q When including header files, can I use an explicit path?

A Yes. If you want to state the path where a file to be included is, you can. In such a case, you put the name of the include file between quotation marks.

20

Workshop

The Workshop provides quiz questions to help you solidify your understanding of the material covered and exercises to provide you with experience in using what you've learned. The answers to the quiz and exercises are provided in Appendix C, "Answers."

Quiz

1. What does the term *modular programming* mean?

2. In modular programming, what is the main module?

3. When you define a macro, why should each argument be enclosed in parentheses?

4. What are the pros and cons of using a macro in place of a regular function?

5. What does the `defined()` operator do?

6. What must always be used if `#if` is used?

7. What does `#include` do?

8. What is the difference between this line of code

   ```
   #include <myfile.h>
   ```

   and the following line of code?

   ```
   #include "myfile.h"
   ```

9. What is `__DATE__` used for?

10. What does `argv[0]` point to?

Exercises

Because many solutions are possible for the following exercises, answers are not provided.

1. Use your compiler to compile multiple source files into a single executable file. (You can use Listings 20.1, 20.2, and 20.3 or your own listings.)

2. Write an error routine that receives an error number, line number, and module name. The routine should print a formatted error message and then exit the program. Use the predefined macros for the line number and module name. (Pass the line number and module name from the location where the error occurs.) Here's a possible example of a formatted error:

   ```
   module.c (Line ##): Error number ##
   ```

3. Modify exercise 2 to make the error message more descriptive. Create a text file with your editor that contains an error number and message. Call this file errors.txt. It could contain information such as the following:

```
1    Error number 1
2    Error number 2
90   Error opening file
100  Error reading file
```

Have your error routine search this file and display the appropriate error message based on a number passed to it.

4. Some header files might be included more than once when you're writing a modular program. Use preprocessor directives to write the skeleton of a header file that compiles only the first time it is encountered during compilation.

5. Write a program that takes two filenames as command-line parameters. The program should copy the first file into the second file. (See Day 15, "Using Disk Files," if you need help working with files.)

6. This is the last exercise of the book, and its content is up to you. Select a programming task of interest to you that also meets a real need you have. For example, you could write programs to catalog your compact disc collection, keep track of your checkbook, or calculate financial figures related to a planned house purchase. There's no substitute for tackling a real-world programming problem in order to sharpen your programming skills and help you remember all the things you learned in this book.

20

DAY **21**

An Introduction to GUI Programming with GTK+

In today's lesson, you will be introduced to the complexities of GUI programming using the GTK+ programming library. You will learn

- A little about the history of the X Window System GUI
- The concepts behind GUI programming
- How to set up some of the common GUI objects such as buttons, menu bars and dialog boxes

History

Until now, all the C programming examples in this book have used the standard input and output streams to read input from the keyboard and to print messages on the screen. In today's lesson, you will look at programming Linux's GUI (Graphical User Interface). The GUI in Linux is based on the X Window System, which is often just called X.

X began development in 1984 at the Massachusetts Institute of Technology (MIT) in an attempt to provide a uniform and network-oriented graphical user interface on a large variety of workstations with high-quality graphical displays. It was written in C and released in source code form, under a license stating that anybody could copy it, modify it, and sell binary executables as long as MIT's copyright notice was attached to every copy of the source code and the executables.

X Concepts

From a user's perspective, the X Window System might seem similar to windowing environments such as those of Microsoft Windows and the Apple Macintosh. However, the underlying concepts are very different. The GUI of MS Windows and the Macintosh are tightly coupled to the machine the program is running on. In contrast, any correctly written X program can—without any extra effort on the part of the programmer—run on one machine and display its output on any other machine that uses X as its GUI and is connected to the first by a network. The two machines do not need to be using the same microprocessor or operating system, and the display machine can be in the same room or on the other side of the world. All that is required is a reliable, reasonably high-speed network connection.

The X Window System achieves network awareness by splitting the functionality into two components, the X server and the X client. The server runs on the machine that is displaying the GUI, and the client is the program that receives mouse and keyboard input events from the server and sends drawing requests to the server. Communication between the client and server is in terms of a message-based protocol system, the X Protocol. The client program should not generate these X Protocol messages itself, but should use a set of library functions defined in a library named Xlib. The Xlib library provides a C interface to the X messaging system.

The functionality of Xlib is limited in that it is able to do little more than create windows, draw simple objects, and transmit mouse and keyboard actions from the server to the client. The simple design was intentional; it allowed the building of secondary libraries that used Xlib and extended its functionality to provide a richer set of capabilities. This has allowed many libraries—or *widget toolkits,* as they are also known—with a wide range of features and interfaces to flourish. Some of those libraries are XForms, Motif, OpenLook, EZWGL, FLTK, Xaw, Qt, and GTK+.

GTK+—The Gimp Toolkit

GTK+, the Gimp Toolkit, was developed as part of an effort to develop a program called the Gimp, the GNU Image Manipulation Tool. GTK+ is written in C and provides a C programming interface to its wide variety of useful widgets such as buttons, scrollbars, text entry fields, progress meters, labels, radio buttons, menus, and more. It is relatively lightweight, freely available, portable to any machine supporting the X Window System, and licensed under the GNU Lesser General Public License. That means any kind of software, be it public domain, freeware, shareware, GPL, or commercial, can be dynamically linked to GTK+ without having to pay any royalties or license fees.

NEW TERM In X Window programming parlance, the term *widget* is used to refer to graphical user interface elements that the user may manipulate using the mouse or keyboard. These elements are self-contained functional modules that can be used as building blocks to build a graphical user interface. Some of the more commonly used widgets are buttons, menu bars, dialog boxes, and scrollbars. They have well-defined interfaces that can be exposed at runtime. Their operation can be adjusted by changing their properties (switches) and when running they respond to events. These are quite amazing little pieces of code and have revolutionized the programming industry.

Today's discussion is too short to be anything more than an introduction to the concepts of GTK+ programming. The GNU info pages contain comprehensive documentation of the GTK+ toolkit. For a more thorough understanding of those concepts, you should browser the GTK+ info pages using a program such as the gnome-help-browser or the info program. Another good source of GTK+ programming tricks and tips is the huge number of GTK+ programs distributed under the GNU General Public License that come with full source code.

Finding GTK+

Day 20, "Advanced Compiler Use," showed how to instruct gcc to look in particular directories to find header files and libraries. To write programs using the GTK+ widget set requires the use of header files and libraries that might be in different directories, depending on how the libraries were installed on the system. Fortunately, the people who wrote the GTK+ widget set have provided a simple way to find out where those files and libraries are installed. When GTK+ is installed, a program named gtk-config is also installed. gtk-config knows where the required header files and libraries are installed. If you try running gtk-config in the terminal window, you should see something like this:

```
[erik@coltrane day21]$ gtk-config
Usage: gtk-config [OPTIONS] [LIBRARIES]
Options:
        [—prefix[=DIR]]
        [—exec-prefix[=DIR]]
        [—version]
        [—libs]
        [—cflags]
Libraries:
        gtk
        gthread
```

21

Note

> If you do not see something like that and you get a command not found error, you might not have GTK+ installed on your system. In that case, you should install it from your installation CD-ROM or download it from the Web site of the distribution you are using.
>
> On some Linux distributions, such as Red Hat, Mandrake, and SuSE, GTK+ is split into two separate packages: one for the libraries themselves and another containing the header files and other GTK+-related development tools. The second package will probably have something like gtk+-devel as the first part of its name.

The gtk-config program shows a number of options, although for the moment it is really only the last two options that are of interest. The −cflags option prints out a list of include directories ready for use with gcc, and the −libs option does the same for the extra libraries required by a GTK+ program. On my system, these two options to the gtk-config command print out the following information—it might be slightly different on your system:

```
[erik@coltrane day21]$ gtk-config −cflags
-I/usr/X11R6/include -I/usr/lib/glib/include
[erik@coltrane day21]$ gtk-config −libs
-L/usr/lib -L/usr/X11R6/lib -lgtk -lgdk -rdynamic -lgmodule -lglib -ldl -lXext
-lX11 -lm
```

The gtk-config program will be used in the remainder of today's lesson to help you compile the programs that use the GTK+ library.

GUIs and Events

The programs that have been explored so far in this book have run in a primarily linear fashion from start to finish. The only exceptions were the programs that used signals on Day 19, "Processes and Signals." As you should remember, these programs set up a *signal handler*—a function that is called asynchronously by the operating system on particular events, such as terminal control sequences.

Programs that have a graphical user interface must also respond to asynchronous events from the user. If a GUI program has a number of GUI widgets, such as buttons, scrollbars, and text entry fields, the programmer cannot make any assumptions about which of those widgets will be manipulated by the user or the order in which they will be used.

Whenever a user operates a GUI widget, the X server running on the user's machine sends an X Protocol message or event to the client program. Handling these asynchronous user-generated events is usually performed by what is known as a *callback function*.

The mechanism is very similar to the signal handlers explored on Day 19. When a widget is created, an event handler or callback function is specified. When the widget is operated by the user, the X server generates an event, causing Xlib or the widget toolkit to call the specified callback function. Under this regimen, each widget will usually have its own callback function.

Because callback functions within a GUI program are called asynchronously, debugging these programs can be difficult. The programmer is often unsure of which functions are being called and in which order. Using a debugger such as DDD is often not of much help either because as stated earlier, GUI programs do not execute in a linear fashion. They do, in fact, jump from function to function in a rather unpredictable way. Often the best way to debug a GUI application is with the use of `printf()` or similar statements and to then run the GUI application from the console where the output of the `printf()` statements can be seen.

A First GTK+ Program

Let's dive in and try a simple GTK+ program. The program in Listing 21.1 does not do anything very useful, but it will allow us to explore some of the concepts behind GTK+ programming. It should be compiled with the following command:

```
gcc -Wall -ggdb `gtk-config —cflags` `gtk-config —libs` list2101.c \
-o list2101
```

Note

Unfortunately, for page layout purposes this command had to be broken into two lines using the backslash line continuation character. If you are able to fit this command on one line you may do so, but you must omit the backslash character.

The `gtk-config` command is used to supply gcc with the directories containing the extra header files and libraries it requires to compile a GTK+ program. Note that `gtk-config` `—cflags` and `gtk-config` `—libs` are contained within backward-sloping single quotation marks, not forward-sloping ones. The backward-sloping single quotation mark is usually found to the left of the number 1 key in the upper-left side of the keyboard. The normal single quotation mark character will not work for this command.

When this program is compiled and run, it should produce a small window like the one at the left of Figure 21.1 with `list2101.c` in the title bar. Clicking on the close window button—usually a box marked with a cross at the right end of the window's title bar—will close the program's window and print a message on the terminal from which the program was run.

21

FIGURE 21.1.

The first three programs today produce the windows titled list2101.c, list2102.c, and list2103.c. The window titled Quit? is a dialog box that belongs to list2103.c.

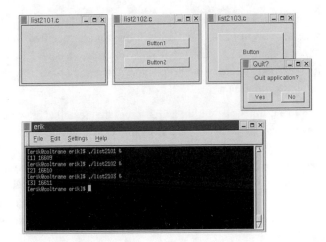

Note

Because the look and feel of the X Window System GUI is configurable, these windows might look slightly different on your system. The look and feel of the X GUI is determined by the window manager, which draws the title bar and border of each window and sets the behavior of the mouse. The window manager in this screenshot is Enlightenment with the Gnome desktop environment. Some of the other common window managers are Window Maker, KDE, AfterStep, NeXtStep, and FVWM.

LISTING 21.1. A minimal GTK+ program.

```
 1 : /* list2101.c - A minimal GTK+ program. */
 2 :
 3 : #include <gtk/gtk.h>
 4 :
 5 : void destroy_func(GtkWidget *widget, gpointer data);
 6 :
 7 : int main(int argc, char *argv[])
 8 : {
 9 :     GtkWidget *main_win;
10 :
11 :     gtk_init(&argc, &argv);
12 :
13 :     main_win = gtk_window_new(GTK_WINDOW_TOPLEVEL);
14 :     gtk_widget_set_usize(GTK_WIDGET(main_win), 180, 120);
15 :     gtk_window_set_title(GTK_WINDOW(main_win), __FILE__);
16 :
17 :     gtk_signal_connect(GTK_OBJECT(main_win), "destroy",
18 :                     GTK_SIGNAL_FUNC(destroy_func), NULL);
```

```
19:
20:     /* Make the window visible. */
21:     gtk_widget_show(main_win);
22:
23:     gtk_main();
24:
25:     g_print("About to exit main().\n");
26:     return 0;
27: }
28:
29: void destroy_func(GtkWidget *widget, gpointer pdata)
30: {
31:     g_print("Quitting : Received destroy signal.\n");
32:     gtk_main_quit();
33: }
```

ANALYSIS This listing includes only one header file, gtk/gtk.h, and does not use stdio.h, which has been used in every other program. The gtk/gtk.h header file is the main header required for GTK+ programming and defines a number of functions and types that are used in this program. The new types are GtkWidget and gpointer; their use will become clear as the program is analyzed.

At line 5, there is a function prototype for the function destroy_func(), which is defined fully on lines 29–33. The main() function starts on line 7 and uses the command-line arguments argc and argv[], but instead of operating on these arguments itself, the program passes them to the function gtk_init() on line 11, which initializes the GTK+ libraries. Note that the arguments passed to gtk_init() are pointers to argc and argv[], not the variables themselves. This trick allows the GTK+ toolkit to access and remove any of the command-line arguments it understands, and to modify the values of argc and argv[] in the main function. The main function will, therefore, not see any of the command-line arguments that were meant for the GTK+ widget set. Therefore, the program should parse the command-line arguments after the call to gtk_init().

On line 13, gtk_window_new() is called to create the top-level window. This function returns a pointer to a GtkWidget type. Just as with the FILE* pointers used in Day 15, "Using Disk Files," you do not need to know what a GtkWidget contains; you just use the pointer in further calls to the GTK+ functions. The initial size of the main window is set in a call to the function gtk_widget_set_usize() on line 14, and the name in its title bar is set in line 15 with a call to gtk_window_set_title(). The first argument in the calls to these two functions—GTK_WIDGET(main_win) in line 14 and GTK_WINDOW(main_win) in line 15—have a special purpose. These two macros are defined in the gtk/gtk.h header file and perform error checking and typecasting from the given type to the type required by the function. In the second case on line 15, the function gtk_window_set_title() requires a GtkWindow pointer as its first parameter. The

21

variable main_win was defined as a GtkWidget*, so the macro invocation
GTK_WINDOW(main_win) checks whether it is possible to cast the pointer main_win from a
GtkWidget* to a GtkWindow*, and does so if it is possible. If the typecast is not possible,
a error message will be printed. Unfortunately, there is no way for an application to
recover from such an error, and it should be killed using the Ctrl+C key combination.
Normally, this kind of error only occurs during the development and debugging of a new
program.

After the main window has been created, you need a way to close it and shut down the
application. Most of the common window managers display a button marked with a cross
in the upper-right corner of each main window. For most applications, clicking on the
close button shuts it down. As you might have guessed from the earlier discussion of
events, this action sends an asynchronous message to the application to shut down. In
GTK+ programming, these asynchronous messages are called *signals* and are referred to
by name using a string. This particular signal associated with the close button in the title
bar is named "destroy".

Associating a callback function with a particular signal in GTK+ is done by calling the
function gtk_signal_connect() as on line 17. The gtk_signal_connect() function
takes four parameters, the first of which is a pointer to a GtkObject. A GtkObject pointer is not the same as a GtkWidget pointer, but it is possible to typecast the GtkWidget
pointer to a GtkObject pointer using the GTK_OBJECT() macro. The second parameter
passed to gtk_signal_connect() is a string specifying the name of the signal, which in
this case is "destroy", and the third parameter is a pointer to the callback function,
which is typecast to the GtkSignalFunc pointer by use of the macro GTK_SIGNAL_FUNC().
The final parameter is a generic point, which in this case is set to NULL.

After the destroy event callback function has been installed, the function gtk_show() on
line 21 makes the main window visible. This is followed by the call to gtk_main() on
line 23. The gtk_main() function starts the processing of GUI events and does not return
until the program is ready to exit.

The function destroy_func(), defined on lines 29–33, is the callback function for the
"destroy" signal. When called, destroy_func() prints out a message using g_print(),
which is very similar to the printf() function that has been used throughout previous
days. It then calls the function gtk_main_quit(), which causes the function gtk_main()
in the program's main() function to return. On Day 19, the program in Listing 19.6 displayed similar behavior; the program ran in a loop until a variable was changed in a
SIGINT signal handler.

By looking at the output the program prints to the stdout stream

```
erik@coltrane day21]$ ./list2101
Quitting : Received destroy signal.
```

```
About to exit main().
erik@coltrane day21]$
```

it is possible to see that the function `destroy_func()` prints out its message on line 31. This happens before `gtk_main()` returns and prints out its message on 25 and returns on line 26.

Buttons

The GTK+ program in Listing 21.1 did not do anything very interesting, but it did demonstrate some introductory concepts. The program in Listing 21.2 should be a little more interesting and should look something like the window titled list2102.c in Figure 21.1.

LISTING 21.2. A minimal GTK+ program.

```
 1 : /* list2102.c - A GTK+ program with push buttons. */
 2 :
 3 : #include <gtk/gtk.h>
 4 :
 5 : void button_func(GtkWidget *widget, gpointer data);
 6 : void destroy_func(GtkWidget *widget, gpointer data);
 7 :
 8 : int main(int argc, char *argv[])
 9 : {
10:     GtkWidget *window;
11:     GtkWidget *button;
12:     GtkWidget *vbox;
13:     int       bdata1, bdata2;
14:
15:     gtk_init(&argc, &argv);
16:
17:     /* Create the main window. */
18:     window = gtk_window_new(GTK_WINDOW_TOPLEVEL);
19:     gtk_widget_set_usize(GTK_WIDGET(window), 180, 120);
20:     gtk_window_set_title(GTK_WINDOW(window), __FILE__);
21:
22:     gtk_signal_connect(GTK_OBJECT(window), "destroy",
23:                     GTK_SIGNAL_FUNC(destroy_func), NULL);
24:     gtk_container_set_border_width(GTK_CONTAINER(window), 20);
25:
26:     vbox = gtk_vbox_new(TRUE, 0);
27:     gtk_container_add(GTK_CONTAINER(window), vbox);
28:
29:     /* Setup first button. */
30:     bdata1 = 0;
31:     button = gtk_button_new_with_label("Button1");
32:     gtk_signal_connect(GTK_OBJECT(button), "clicked",
33:             GTK_SIGNAL_FUNC(button_func), (gpointer)&bdata1);
34:     gtk_box_pack_start(GTK_BOX(vbox), button, TRUE, FALSE, 0);
```

21

continues

LISTING 21.2. continued

```
35:      gtk_widget_show(button);
36:
37:      /* Setup second button. */
38:      bdata2 = 1;
39:      button = gtk_button_new_with_label("Button2");
40:      gtk_signal_connect(GTK_OBJECT(button), "clicked",
41:              GTK_SIGNAL_FUNC(button_func), (gpointer)&bdata2);
42:      gtk_box_pack_start(GTK_BOX(vbox), button, TRUE, FALSE, 0);
43:      gtk_widget_show(button);
44:
45:      /* Make everything visible. */
46:      gtk_widget_show(vbox);
47:      gtk_widget_show(window);
48:
49:      gtk_main();
50:
51:      return 0;
52: }
53:
54: void button_func(GtkWidget *widget, gpointer pdata)
55: {
56:      static int count [2] = { 0, 0 };
57:      int index ;
58:
59:      index = *((int*)pdata);
60:      count [index]++;
61:      g_print("Button %d click %d.\n",index+1,count [index]);
62: }
63:
64: void destroy_func(GtkWidget *widget, gpointer pdata)
65: {
66:      g_print("Quitting : Received destroy signal.\n");
67:      gtk_main_quit();
68: }
```

ANALYSIS Just like Listing 21.1, this listing includes only one header file, gtk/gtk.h. On lines 5 and 6, it defines function prototypes for the two callback functions, button_func() and destroy_func(), the second of which is identical to the function of the same name in the previous program. The main() function beginning on line 8 defines a number of local variables on lines 10–13. The first three, window, button, and vbox, are of type GtkWidget and will be used during the initialization of the GUI elements. The other two variables, bdata1 and bdata2, are of type int.

Lines 15–23 are the same as lines 11–18 of Listing 21.1. On line 24 is a new function, gtk_container_set_border_width(). In GTK+ programming, any window that can have another window within it as a child window is a *container*. The function gtk_container_set_border_width() sets the width of the border, which will prevent child windows from being placed within a specified boundary around the edge of the window. As in the previous examples, GTK_CONTAINER() is a macro that performs error checking and typecasting from the GtkWidget* to a GtkContainer* type. On line 26, a new widget is created using gtk_vbox_new() and then added to the main window as a child window using gtk_container_add(). The widget created using gtk_vbox_new() is a vertical box widget. Similarly, there is also a horizontal box widget created using gtk_hbox_new().

Box widgets are container widgets that allow other widgets to be placed inside them. When the box widgets are resized, the widgets inside the boxes are scaled appropriately. In lines 34 and 42, buttons will be added to the vertical box widget. When the window is resized, these buttons will move to keep the layout of the window uniform.

The first button is created on line 31. On line 32, the "clicked" signal is set up to call the function button_func() so that whenever the button is clicked, button_func() will be called. The last parameter to gtk_signal_connect() is a pointer to an integer that was set equal to zero in line 30. When the second button is defined in lines 38–43, it will also use button_func() as its callback function, but on the call to gtk_signal_connect(), a different pointer to a different integer will be given. That pointer is passed to the button_func() callback function as the second argument every time the button is clicked. This allows the callback function to know which button was clicked by examining the value pointed to by the pointer.

After the button callback function has been set up, the first button is packed into the vertical box on line 34 by calling gtk_box_pack_start(). This function takes a GtkBox* as its first parameter and the widget to be packed as the second parameter. The third and fourth parameters control how the child widgets fill the space within the box and they both take values of TRUE or FALSE. The final parameter to gtk_box_pack_start() is a field specifying padding, which is set to 0 in this case. You are encouraged to try all the possible combinations of the last three parameters.

The final step before calling gtk_main() is to make all the widgets visible. This is done for the buttons on line 35 and 43, for the vertical box on line 46, and for the main window on line 47.

The button_func() callback function is on lines 54–62. It defines a static array of two integers that are both initialized to zero. Remember that variables that are local to a function, but defined as static, retain their values between calls to the function. When the button_func() callback was set up on lines 22 and 32, the last argument to gtk_signal_ connect() was a pointer to an integer: bdata1 for button 1 and bdata2 for button 2, which had values of 0 and 1, respectively. Each time button_func() is called because one of the buttons was clicked, a pointer is passed into the callback function as the second parameter.

21

When button 1 is clicked, the pointer will point to bdata1, and when button 2 is clicked, it will point to bdata2. This pointer is a generic pointer—like a void pointer—which is type-cast back into a pointer to int on line 59 and then immediately dereferenced to read the value being pointed to in the variable index. The value of index is then used to increment one of the two static count array values on line 60 and then a message is printed out on line 61.

When you run this program from a terminal window, you will see that clicking on the buttons prints out the message specified on line 61. Notice that the message displays which of the two buttons was pressed and also how many times each of the buttons has been pressed.

Creating a Dialog Box

Dialog boxes are very common graphical user interface objects. They are used to retrieve input from the user for the program, such as yes/no decisions or a filename for the program to load or save data. Unlike the program's main window, which is on display for the duration of the running program, dialog boxes are usually created and destroyed as needed by the program. In the following example, a simple yes/no dialog box will be created and different actions will be taken by the program on the basis of the yes/no decision.

With the two sample programs in Listings 21.1 and 21.2, clicking in the window manager's close application box in the top right corner of the window immediately closes down the applications. This is not good in an application in which the user enters data and might want to save it before closing the application. Most GUI programs in this situation would use a dialog box to ask the user whether he wants to save any unsaved data before exiting. This program is too simple to have any data to save, so it will just give the user a yes/no choice whether to close the application.

The program consists of three separate files: The main program source code is in Listing 21.3, code for the dialog box code is in the file named yesno.c in Listing 21.4, and a header file yesno.h is in Listing 21.5. Compiling multiple source code file programs was dealt with in Day 20. These three files may be compiled into a single executable by using the following commands:

```
gcc -Wall -ggdb `gtk-config —cflags` -c list2103.c
gcc -Wall -ggdb `gtk-config —cflags` -c yesno.c
gcc -Wall -ggdb `gtk-config —libs` list2103.o yesno.o -o list2103
```

It might also be worthwhile to write a Makefile—also part of Day 20—to perform this compilation.

LISTING 21.3. A simple program with a dialog box.

```
1 : /* list2103.c - A simple program with a  */
2 : /*             quit application dialog. */
3 :
4 : #include <gtk/gtk.h>
5 : #include "yesno.h"
6 :
7 : int delete_func(GtkWidget *widget, gpointer data);
8 : void button_func(GtkWidget *widget, gpointer data);
9 :
10: int main(int argc, char *argv[])
11: {
12:     GtkWidget *window;
13:     GtkWidget *button;
14:
15:     gtk_init(&argc, &argv);
16:
17:     /* Create the main window. */
18:     window = gtk_window_new(GTK_WINDOW_TOPLEVEL);
19:     gtk_widget_set_usize(GTK_WIDGET(window), 180, 120);
20:     gtk_window_set_title(GTK_WINDOW(window), __FILE__);
21:
22:     gtk_signal_connect(GTK_OBJECT(window), "delete_event",
23:                        GTK_SIGNAL_FUNC(delete_func), NULL);
24:     gtk_container_set_border_width(GTK_CONTAINER(window), 20);
25:
26:     /* Set up first button. */
27:     button = gtk_button_new_with_label("Button1");
28:     gtk_signal_connect(GTK_OBJECT(button), "clicked",
29:             GTK_SIGNAL_FUNC(button_func), NULL);
30:
31:     gtk_container_add(GTK_CONTAINER(window), button);
32:
33:     /* Make everything visible. */
34:     gtk_widget_show_all(window);
35:
36:     gtk_main();
37:
38:     return 0;
39: }
40:
41: int delete_func(GtkWidget *widget, gpointer pdata)
42: {
43:     if (yes_no_dialog("Quit?", "Quit application?"))
44:     {
45:         gtk_main_quit();
46:         return FALSE;
47:     }
48:     return TRUE;
49: }
```

21

continues

LISTING 21.3. continued

```
50:
51: void button_func(GtkWidget *widget, gpointer pdata)
52: {
53:     g_print("Click\n");
54: }
```

LISTING 21.4. A generic yes/no option dialog box.

```
 1 : /* yesno.c - a general purpose yes/no dialog. */
 2 :
 3 : #include <gtk/gtk.h>
 4 : #include "yesno.h"
 5 :
 6 : static void yesno_func (GtkWidget *widget, gchar *yesno);
 7 :
 8 : /* A static variable for the yes/no return value. */
 9 : static gint yesno;
10:
11: int yes_no_dialog (gchar *title, gchar *labeltext)
12: {
13:     GtkWidget *dialog, *label, *ybutton, *nbutton;
14:     GtkWidget *vbox, *hbox;
15:
16:     /* Create the required widgets. */
17:     dialog  = gtk_window_new(GTK_WINDOW_TOPLEVEL);
18:     label   = gtk_label_new(labeltext);
19:     ybutton = gtk_button_new_with_label("   Yes   ");
20:     nbutton = gtk_button_new_with_label("   No    ");
21:     vbox    = gtk_vbox_new(FALSE, 0);
22:     hbox    = gtk_hbox_new(FALSE, 0);
23:
24:     /* Pack the widgets. */
25:     gtk_box_pack_start(GTK_BOX(vbox), label, TRUE, FALSE, 0);
26:     gtk_box_pack_start(GTK_BOX(hbox), ybutton, TRUE, FALSE, 0);
27:     gtk_box_pack_start(GTK_BOX(hbox), nbutton,  TRUE, FALSE, 0);
28:     gtk_box_pack_start(GTK_BOX(vbox), hbox, TRUE, FALSE, 0);
29:     gtk_container_add(GTK_CONTAINER(dialog), vbox);
30:
31:     gtk_widget_set_usize(GTK_WIDGET(dialog), 140, 80);
32:     gtk_window_set_title(GTK_WINDOW(dialog), title);
33:     gtk_window_set_modal(GTK_WINDOW(dialog), TRUE);
34:
35:     /* Connect the signals. */
36:     gtk_signal_connect(GTK_OBJECT(ybutton), "clicked",
37:                         GTK_SIGNAL_FUNC(yesno_func), "yes");
38:     gtk_signal_connect(GTK_OBJECT(nbutton),  "clicked",
39:                         GTK_SIGNAL_FUNC(yesno_func), "no");
40:     gtk_signal_connect(GTK_OBJECT(dialog), "delete_event",
```

```
41:                      GTK_SIGNAL_FUNC(gtk_main_quit), dialog);
42:
43:      /* Make everything visible. */
44:      gtk_widget_show_all(dialog);
45:
46:      /* Start gtk_main() for the dialog box. */
47:      gtk_main();
48:
49:      /* Destroy the dialog box. */
50:      gtk_widget_destroy(dialog);
51:
52:      return yesno;
53: }
54:
55: static void yesno_func (GtkWidget *widget, gchar *yesnostr)
56: {
57:      if (yesnostr [0] == 'y')
58:          yesno = TRUE;
59:      else
60:          yesno = FALSE;
61:
62:      gtk_main_quit();
63: }
```

LISTING 21.5. A generic yes/no option dialog box.

```
1 : /* yesno.h - A header file for yesno.c. */
2 :
3 : /* Create a dialog box with two buttons marked "yes"   */
4 : /* and "no" with the given label text and title.       */
5 : /* If the user clicks the "yes" button return TRUE.     */
6 : /* If the user clicks the "no" button return FALSE.     */
7 :
8 : int yes_no_dialog (gchar *title, gchar *labeltext);
```

ANALYSIS Listing 21.3 is very similar to Listing 21.2, but has one button instead of two. The button is created on line 27 and a callback function is connected to the button's "clicked" event on line 28. The button's callback function, button_func(), is defined on lines 51–54 and does nothing more than print the message Click whenever the user clicks the button.

One of the important differences between Listing 21.3 and the previous listings is on line 22, where the call to gtk_signal_connect() connects to the "delete_event" signal rather than the "destroy" signal. The difference between the "delete_event" and the "destroy" signals is subtle. When the user clicks the close window button of a window's title bar, the window manager sends as many as two signals to the program. The first is a signal called "delete_event". If there is no callback function defined for this signal or

21

the callback function returns a value of FALSE, the window manager sends a second signal—a "destroy" signal—that causes all the windows to be destroyed. If, on the other hand, the callback function that handles the "delete_event" signal returns a value of TRUE, the second "destroy" signal is not sent to the program. The callback function that is connected to the "delete_event" is defined on lines 41–49. This callback function simply calls the function yes_no_dialog() that was defined in the header file yesno.h included on line 5. As you will see when you run the program, the function yes_no_dia-log() displays a small window with Quit? in the title bar, two buttons marked Yes and No, and the text Quit application? above the buttons. The yes_no_dialog() function also returns a TRUE value if the Yes button was clicked and FALSE if the No button was clicked. If TRUE was returned, the delete_func() callback function calls gtk_main_quit() to terminate the gtk_main() function and returns FALSE.

Another interesting difference between Listing 21.3 and Listing 21.2 is the call to gtk_widget_show_all() on line 34. This function makes the specified widget—in this case, window—visible as well as all the widgets contained within window. This is a short-cut to making separate calls to gtk_widget_show() for window and all its child widgets as was done in Listing 21.2.

Listing 21.4 contains code for the function yes_no_dialog(). It includes the gtk/gtk.h header file on line 3 and its own header file on line 4. On line 6, it prototypes the function yesno_func(), which will be used as the callback function for both of the two buttons. Because the button that the user clicked can only be known in the callback function, a static variable, yesno, is defined on line 9. This variable, being global to the file but declared static, may be accessed anywhere within the file after the declaration but is not accessible outside the file.

The function yes_no_dialog() is defined on lines 11 to 58. In many ways, it is very similar to the main() functions of Listings 21.1 and 21.2. On lines 13 and 14, it declares a number of variables of type GtkWidget*. The only new widget used here is a GtkLabel widget that is created with gtk_label_new(). A GtkLabel widget does not respond to mouse clicks nor is the user able to change it using keyboard input; it is simply a widget for holding and displaying static text.

The widgets are created on lines 19–22, packed into boxes on lines 25–29 and the dialog box's size and title are set on lines 31 and 32. The call to gtk_window_set_modal() on line 33 makes the dialog box main window modal. A *modal window* is a window that stops operation of its parent's windows while it is operational. In this particular case, the programmer does not want the user to operate the parent window while the program is waiting for the user's yes/no response. This is common behavior for something like a dialog box.

This dialog box can respond to three signals, which are specified by use of the function gtk_signal_connect() on lines 36–41. The first two events are the button "clicked" events, which will be generated when the user clicks the Yes button or the No button. Both of these signals are connected to the same callback function—yesno_func()—but the callback will be called with different arguments depending on which button is clicked. If the Yes button is clicked, the second argument to yesno_func() will be a pointer to the string "yes"; if the No button is clicked, the second argument will be a pointer to "no". The other signal that is connected to a callback function is the "destroy" signal for the dialog box window, which uses gtk_main_quit() as its callback. The reason for using gtk_main_quit() as the callback function will become clearer later in this analysis.

After the signals have been connected, the various widgets are made visible with a call to gtk_widget_show_all() in line 44. Finally, the gtk_main() function is called on line 50. Remember that this function, yes_no_dialog(), is called by a callback function in the main program in Listing 21.3. For yes_no_dialog() to be called, the gtk_main() function must already have been called from the main() function in Listing 21.3. In effect, this is calling gtk_main() recursively, which is allowed but should be done with caution.

The function yesno_func() acts as the callback function for the Yes and No buttons. When this function was attached to the signal using gtk_signal_connect() on lines 36–39, the last arguments were pointers to the strings "yes" and "no" for the Yes and No buttons, respectively. When one of these buttons is clicked, the second argument to yesno_func(), the variable yesnostr, is the pointer to one of these two strings depending on which button was clicked. The if statement on line 57 then checks to see whether the first character of the string pointed to by yesnostr is the letter y. If the first character is the letter y, the static variable yesno is set to TRUE; if it is not, yesno is set to FALSE. After one or the other of the buttons has been clicked, the dialog box has served its purpose, so it can be destroyed. It is destroyed by calling gtk_main_quit() on line 62, which causes the gtk_main() function call on line 47 to return. The function yes_no_dialog() then returns the value of the variable yesno on line 52.

It is important to note here that when the function yes_no_dialog() calls gtk_main_quit() on line 62, it causes the most recently called gtk_main() function to return. It does not terminate the gtk_main() function call in Listing 21.3 unless you pressed the Yes button. If the No button was pressed, only returning from one of the gtk_main() functions allows the dialog box to be destroyed but the main window to keep running as was required.

21

> **Note** You might notice that the function `yes_no_dialog()` was written to be as general as possible. The question it is asking the user to answer yes or no to can be set simply by passing the required question as a string argument to the function. Therefore, any program that requires the user to give a yes or no answer can call `yes_no_dialog()` with appropriate arguments. This simple dialog box can now be used over and over again, in many different programs, instead of rewriting it for every particular case. This is a good example of the use of modular programming techniques.

A Simple Text Editor

The examples studied so far in this lesson have been interesting but did not really do anything useful. The next program will be a more complete example that has a menu bar and uses a dialog box for choosing a filename for the file data is saved to. The program is contained in the following three listings, beginning with Listing 21.6. Listing 21.6 contains the `main()` function and all the code required to set up the main window. Listing 21.7 is the header file for the self-contained filename selection dialog box that is defined in Listing 21.8. The filename selection dialog box code is kept separate so that it may be reused in any other project that needs a filename selection dialog box.

As you might have guessed from the heading at the start of this section, this program implements a very simple text editor. It is not complete, but it is able to do things such as cut and paste and save the entered text as a file. All this can be done in fewer than 200 lines of code due to the implementation of an even more simple text editor widget by the authors of GTK+. The missing features are things such as reading the command-line arguments to obtain a filename, the implementation of a file open dialog, and more advanced features such as text search and replace.

The text editor program can be compiled with the following commands:

```
gcc -Wall -ggdb `gtk-config —cflags` -c list2106.c
gcc -Wall -ggdb `gtk-config —cflags` -c filename.c
gcc -Wall -ggdb `gtk-config —libs` list2106.o filename.o -o list2106
```

LISTING 21.6. A simple GTK+ text editor.

```
1 : /* list2106.c - A simple (and incomplete) GTK+ text editor. */
2 : #include <gtk/gtk.h>
3 : #include <stdio.h>
4 : #include "filename.h"
5 :
6 : void destroy_func(GtkWidget *widget, gpointer data);
7 : void menu_func(GtkWidget *widget, guint number);
8 : GtkWidget *make_menu(GtkWidget  *window);
```

```
 9 : void file_save_dlg(GtkWidget *widget, gpointer pdata);
10: int save_file(char *filename);
11:
12: static GtkWidget *textbox ;
13:
14: int main(int argc, char *argv[])
15: {
16:     GtkWidget *window, *menubar, *vscrollbar;
17:     GtkWidget *vbox, *hbox;
18:     GdkFont   *textfont ;
19:     GtkStyle  *style;
20:
21:     gtk_init(&argc, &argv);
22:
23:     /* Create the main window. */
24:     window = gtk_window_new(GTK_WINDOW_TOPLEVEL);
25:     gtk_widget_set_usize(GTK_WIDGET(window), 400, 300);
26:     gtk_window_set_title(GTK_WINDOW(window), __FILE__);
27:
28:     gtk_signal_connect(GTK_OBJECT(window), "destroy",
29:                        GTK_SIGNAL_FUNC(destroy_func), NULL);
30:
31:     vbox = gtk_vbox_new(FALSE, 0);
32:     hbox = gtk_hbox_new(FALSE, 0);
33:     gtk_container_add(GTK_CONTAINER(window), vbox);
34:
35:     /* Create the menu bar. */
36:     menubar = make_menu(window);
37:     gtk_box_pack_start(GTK_BOX(vbox), menubar, FALSE, TRUE, 0);
38:     gtk_widget_show(menubar);
39:
40:     /* Create the text area. */
41:     textbox = gtk_text_new(NULL, NULL);
42:     vscrollbar = gtk_vscrollbar_new(GTK_TEXT(textbox)->vadj);
43:
44:     gtk_text_set_editable(GTK_TEXT(textbox), TRUE);
45:     gtk_text_set_line_wrap(GTK_TEXT(textbox), FALSE);
46:
47:     if ((textfont = gdk_font_load("7x13")) != NULL)
48:     {
49:         style = gtk_widget_get_style(textbox);
50:         style->font = textfont;
51:         gtk_widget_set_style(textbox, style);
52:     }
53:
54:     /* Pack the widgets in boxes. */
55:     gtk_box_pack_start(GTK_BOX(hbox), textbox, TRUE, TRUE, 0);
56:     gtk_box_pack_start(GTK_BOX(hbox), vscrollbar, FALSE, FALSE, 1);
57:     gtk_box_pack_start(GTK_BOX(vbox), hbox, TRUE, TRUE, 0);
58:
59:     /* Make everything visible. */
```

21

continues

LISTING 21.6. continued

```
60:     gtk_widget_show_all(window);
61:
62:     gtk_main();
63:
64:     return 0;
65: }
66:
67: void destroy_func(GtkWidget *widget, gpointer pdata)
68: {
69:     gtk_main_quit();
70: }
71:
72: /* Menu bar creation code. */
73:
74: static GtkItemFactoryEntry menu_array[] =
75: {
76:   { "/_File"      , NULL          , NULL          , 0, "<Branch>" },
77:   { "/File/_Open", "<control>O", menu_func     , 0, NULL },
78:   { "/File/_Save", "<control>S", file_save_dlg, 0, NULL },
79:   { "/File/sep1" , NULL          , NULL          , 0, "<Separator>" },
80:   { "/File/Quit" , "<control>Q", gtk_main_quit, 0, NULL },
81:
82:   { "/_Two"      , NULL, NULL      , 0, "<Branch>" },
83:   { "/Two/_One", NULL, menu_func,  1, NULL },
84:   { "/Two/_Two", NULL, menu_func,  2, NULL },
85:
86:   { "/_Menu3"     , NULL,  NULL, 0, "<Branch>" },
87:   { "/Menu3/Test1", NULL,  NULL, 0, "<ToggleItem>" },
88:   { "/Menu3/sep1" , NULL,  NULL, 0, "<Separator>" },
89:   { "/Menu3/Test2", NULL,  NULL, 0, "<RadioItem>" },
90:   { "/Menu3/Test3", NULL,  NULL, 0, "/Menu3/Test2" },
91:   { "/Menu3/Test4", NULL,  NULL, 0, "/Menu3/Test2" },
92:
93:   { "/_Help"      , NULL,  NULL, 0, "<LastBranch>" },
94:   { "/_Help/About", NULL,  NULL, 0, NULL },
95: };
96:
97: GtkWidget *make_menu(GtkWidget  *window)
98: {
99:     GtkWidget        *menubar;
100:    GtkItemFactory *itemfact;
101:    GtkAccelGroup  *accelgroup;
102:
103:    gint msize = sizeof(menu_array) / sizeof(menu_array[0]);
104:
105:    accelgroup = gtk_accel_group_new();
106:    gtk_accel_group_attach(accelgroup, GTK_OBJECT(window));
107:
```

```
108:     itemfact = gtk_item_factory_new(GTK_TYPE_MENU_BAR, "<main>",
109:                                     accelgroup);
110:     gtk_item_factory_create_items(itemfact, msize, menu_array, NULL);
111:
112:     menubar = gtk_item_factory_get_widget(itemfact, "<main>");
113:
114:     return menubar;
115: }
116:
117: void menu_func(GtkWidget *widget, guint number)
118: {
119:     if (number)
120:         g_print("Number : %d\n", number);
121:     else
122:         g_print("Hello!\n");
123: }
124:
125: /* File save dialog callback functions. */
126: void file_save_dlg(GtkWidget *widget, gpointer pdata)
127: {
128:     gchar filename [512];
129:
130:   if (filename_dialog("Save file as:", filename, 512))
131:         save_file (filename);
132: }
133:
134: int save_file(char *filename)
135: {
136:     FILE *file;
137:     int  length;
138:     char *cptr;
139:
140:     if ((file = fopen(filename, "w")) == NULL)
141:         return 1 ;
142:
143:     length = gtk_text_get_length(GTK_TEXT(textbox));
144:     cptr = gtk_editable_get_chars(GTK_EDITABLE(textbox),0,length);
145:
146:     if (cptr)
147:         fwrite(cptr, length, 1, file);
148:
149:     fclose(file);
150:     return 0 ;
151: }
```

21

LISTING 21.7. filename.h: the header file for the filename selection dialog box defined in Listing 21.8.

```
/* filename.h - A header file for a self contained filename   */
/*              selection dialog box.                          */

/* The title parameter sets the title of the dialog box. The  */
/* filename that the use selects is copied into the filename   */
/* provided by the called. The filename string is assumed to   */
/* at least namelen characters in length.                      */

/* On success this function returns TRUE. On failure (ie the   */
/* user clicks the cancel button) the function returns FALSE.  */

int filename_dialog(gchar *title, gchar *filename, gint namelen);
```

ANALYSIS The main part of the program is in Listing 21.6 and it begins by including the standard gtk/gtk.h header file—the header file for stdio.h required for the file open, write, and close functions—and filename.h, which contains a prototype for the file-name selection dialog box. The program then prototypes five functions on lines 6–12 and a static variable of type GtkWidget* on line 12. This GTK+ widget is the widget that will be used to do the text editing functions. The reason it must be global to the file will become apparent later.

The main() function begins on 14, defines the required variables on lines 16–19, and performs tasks similar to the previous examples up to line 35. Lines 36–38 create the menu bar for this application. The function make_menu() does most of the work, and it is defined on lines 79–114.

The text editing area of the program is defined on lines 41–52. Our work is made much easier by the availability of an easy-to-use text editor widget. This widget is created on line 41 with a call to the function gtk_text_new(); its associated vertical scrollbar is created on line 42 with a call to the function gtk_vscrollbar_new(). The argument passed to this function, GTK_TEXT(textbox)->vadj, is interesting. It takes a GtkWidget* pointer textbox, and by using the GTK_TEXT() macro, does some error checking and typecasts it into a GtkText pointer. After it has a GtkText* pointer—which is a pointer to a GtkText structure—it dereferences the pointer and points to the vadj element of the GtkText structure. If you look at the gtktext.h header file—probably located at /usr/include/gtk/gtktext.h—you will see that vadj is a GtkAdjustment* pointer. In addition, if you look at the documentation for the GtkVScrollbar widget in the gtk section of the info pages, you will see that the gtk_vscrollbar_new() function is defined as

```
GtkWidget *gtk_vscrollbar_new (GtkAdjustment* adj);
```

so, passing a GtkAdjustment pointer to gtk_vscrollbar_new() is exactly what should be done.

On lines 44 and 45, changes are made to the default behavior of the GtkText widget. When a GtkText widget is created, it starts in a mode where the programmer is able to display text, but the user is not able to modify it using the keyboard. This behavior can be modified by a call to gtk_text_set_editable(). Calling this function with an argument of TRUE enables editing, and calling it with an argument of FALSE disables editing. Similarly, the call to gtk_text_set_line_wrap() on line 45 disables line wrap mode because most text editors do not use this feature.

The standard font used in the GtkText widget is a proportionally spaced font, which means that the letter *i* takes up much less space on the line than a wide letter such as *w*. This is not good for a text editor that will be used to edit source code, so on lines 47–52, the default font of the GtkText widget is changed to a fixed-width font. As the name suggests, a fixed-width font has the same width irrespective of whether the character is narrow like an *i* or wide like a *w*. The function gdk_font_load() is used to load a font referenced by its name held in a string. The font "7x13" is a common fixed-width font that should be available on every machine. If the call to gdk_font_load() is successful—textfont is not a NULL pointer—the default font of the GtkText is changed on lines 49–51. This is done by accessing the GtkStyle widget, which is part of the GtkText widget. The GtkStyle widget keeps track of things such as the colors of the widget and the font used to draw any text associated with the widget. By using gtk_widget_get_style() on line 49, the program can retrieve a pointer in the GtkText widget's current GtkStyle structure. It then modifies the GtkStyle widget's font field on line 50 and asks the widget to reload its GtkStyle component on line 51 with a call to gtk_widget_set_style().

After the GtkText widget has been set up correctly, the widgets are packed into boxes on lines 53–55. All the widgets are made visible by calling gtk_widget_show_all() on line 58, followed by an obligatory call to gtk_main() on line 60.

The program's menu bar is created on lines 74–114. There are two ways of constructing menus using GTK+, and the method used here is the easier of the two. This code consists of a static array of type GtkItemFactoryEntry defined on line 74 and initialized on lines 76–94. The GtkItemFactoryEntry type is defined in the header file /usr/include/gtk/gtkitemfactory.h as follows:

```
struct _GtkItemFactoryEntry
{
  gchar *path;
  gchar *accelerator;

  GtkItemFactoryCallback callback;
  guint                  callback_action;
```

21

```
    /* possible values:
     * NULL                   -> "<Item>"
     * ""                     -> "<Item>"
     * "<Title>"              -> create a title item
     * "<Item>"               -> create a simple item
     * "<CheckItem>"          -> create a check item
     * "<ToggleItem>"         -> create a toggle item
     * "<RadioItem>"          -> create a radio item
     * <path>                 -> path of a radio item to link against
     * "<Separator>"          -> create a separator
     * "<Branch>"             -> create an item to hold sub items
     * "<LastBranch>"         -> create a right justified item to hold sub items
     */
    gchar           *item_type;
};
```

The structure has five fields: path, accelerator, callback, callback_action, and
item_type. Notice how the authors of GTK+ have used comments to specify the possible
values of the item_type field. The use of the rest of the fields within the
GtkItemFactoryEntry structure should be reasonably obvious if the menu_array array
that is initialized on lines 74–89 is compared to the behavior of the menu bar in the program. The first field, path, specifies the name and position of the menu item. The first
element of the array on line 76 defines the File menu item, which is at the root level of
the menu. That means it will be displayed on the menu bar itself. The second element is
defined with the path field set to "/File/_Open", which defines the Open menu item
under the File root menu item. Notice how both these path fields have an underscore
character in them. This underscore character specifies that the following character in the
path field string is a shortcut key for invoking that menu item. You can check this by
running the program and holding down the Alt key and pressing F, which should drop
down the File menu. It is then possible to move around the menu items by using the
arrow keys.

The second field of the GtkItemFactoryEntry structure is accelerator, an optional
string specifying an keyboard accelerator shortcut. For the "/File/_Save" item, the
accelerator is defined as "<control>S", which asks the GTK+ library to interpret the
user holding down the Ctrl key and pressing S as equivalent to selecting the file save
options from the menu bar. A value of NULL for the accelerator field means there is no
keyboard accelerator for that menu item.

Menus can also be defined to have callback functions. The callback function is specified by setting the third and fourth fields of the GtkItemFactoryEntry structure, callback and callback_action. The callback function is specified by name and the
callback_action field takes an integer that will become the second argument to the
callback function when it is called. Under the top-level menu labeled Two are two menu

items that specify `menu_func()` as their callback function, but specify different numbers as their `callback_action` values. If you run the program and select these two menu items one by one, you will notice that the `menu_func()` callback function is able to print out the value specified for each item.

The last field in the `GtkItemFactoryEntry` structure is `item_type`. Most of the different allowable types are used in this example. Wherever the value `NULL` is placed in this field, it means the menu item is a standard item. The use of `"<Branch>"` specifies that selecting the specified item should cause a submenu to appear. The entries with `"<Separator>"` in the `item_type` field are not selectable, but are used simply to organize the other menu items at the same level into groups. In the File menu, the Open and Save menu items are separated from the Quit menu item. Some of the other values for `item_type` are used in Menu3 submenu. Toggle buttons and radio buttons are shown, but their use is not fully explored.

The function `make_menu()` is defined on lines 97–115. The input parameter is the window to which the menu that is created should be attached. The `make_menu()` function uses the array of `GtkItemFactoryEntry` structures `menu_array` to create the menu. It sets up the required variables on lines 99–101 and uses a clever little trick on line 103 to find out how many items are in `menu_array`. It divides the size of the whole array by the size of the first element. This is better than using a constant because the value is always correct. If a constant were used, the value of the constant would have to be changed every time the menu is changed. The value calculated, `msize`, will be required later in this function.

The use of keyboard accelerators in menus was covered earlier in this section. To use a keyboard accelerator in a menu, it must be created before the menu with a call to the function `gtk_accel_group_new()`, as in line 105. It must then be attached to the main window with a call to `gtk_accel_group_attach()`, as on line 106. The accelerator is then passed as an argument to `gtk_item_factory_new()`, which returns a pointer to a `GtkItemFactory` type. This `GtkItemFactory` type is filled in from the `menu_array` defined on lines 79–94 by passing them both to the function `gtk_item_factory_create_items()`. Because the main program might want to manipulate the menu bar at a later stage, a `GtkWidget*` pointer is created with a call to `gtk_item_factory_get_widget()` on line 112 and the pointer is returned to the calling function on line 114.

The remainder of Listing 21.6 contains the definition for the callback function `menu_func()` used by the menu bar on lines 117–123. This callback has a `guint`—an unsigned `int` type defined in the GTK+ header files—as a second parameter. If this parameter is zero, the callback simply prints a `Hello!` message; if the parameter is not zero, the callback prints out the value.

21

The function `file_save_dlg()` is the callback function called when the user selects the Save item from the File menu. Most of the difficult work is done by calling `filename_dialog()`. `filename_dialog()` is prototyped in the header file filename.h and defined in filename.c, which are shown as Listings 21.7 and 21.8. If `filename_dialog()` returns a `TRUE` value, the string `filename` should contain a valid filename, which is passed to the function `save_file()` (defined on lines 134–151). This function opens the file for reading on line 140, and interrogates the `GtkText` widget `textbox`, which was defined as a static variable that is global to this file. The function `gtk_text_get_length()` returns the length of text contained in the `GtkText` widget. The function `gtk_editable_get_chars()` is then called and it returns a `char*` pointer to an array containing the text from the specified start and end points. In this case, the program is specifying all characters from the zero character to the last character. If the call to `gtk_editable_get_chars()` is successful, it returns a non-`NULL` pointer and the function `fwrite()` is used to write the complete text to the file in one go. The file is then closed and `save_file()` returns.

LISTING 21.8. filename.c: a filename selection dialog box.

```
1 : /* filename.c - A filename selection dialog. */
2 : #include <gtk/gtk.h>
3 : #include <string.h>
4 : #include "filename.h"
5 :
6 : typedef struct
7 : {   GtkWidget *filesel;
8 :     gchar     *filename;
9 :     gint      len ;
10: } FILEDATA ;
11:
12: static void filename_ok(GtkWidget *widget, FILEDATA *filedata);
13: static void filename_cancel(GtkWidget *widget, GtkWidget *filesel);
14:
15: int filename_dialog(gchar *title, gchar *filename, gint namelen)
16: {
17:     GtkWidget *filesel;
18:     FILEDATA  filedata;
19:
20:     if (filename == NULL)
21:         return FALSE;
22:     filename [0] = 0;
23:
24:     filesel = gtk_file_selection_new("Save file as :");
25:     gtk_window_set_modal(GTK_WINDOW(filesel), TRUE);
26:     gtk_widget_show(filesel);
27:
```

```
28:        filedata.filesel = filesel;
29:        filedata.filename = filename;
30:        filedata.len = namelen;
31:
32:        gtk_signal_connect(
33:                GTK_OBJECT(GTK_FILE_SELECTION(filesel)->ok_button),
34:                "clicked", (GtkSignalFunc) filename_ok, &filedata);
35:        gtk_signal_connect(
36:                GTK_OBJECT(GTK_FILE_SELECTION(filesel)->cancel_button),
37:                "clicked", (GtkSignalFunc) filename_cancel, filesel);
38:        gtk_signal_connect(GTK_OBJECT(filesel), "destroy",
39:                GTK_SIGNAL_FUNC(filename_cancel), filesel);
40:
41:        gtk_main();
42:
43:        if (strlen (filename) > 0)
44:            return TRUE;
45:
46:        return FALSE;
47: }
48:
49: static
50: void filename_ok(GtkWidget *widget, FILEDATA *filedata)
51: {
52:        gchar *selectname;
53:
54:        selectname = gtk_file_selection_get_filename(
55:                        GTK_FILE_SELECTION(filedata->filesel));
56:
57:        if (strlen (selectname) < filedata->len)
58:            strcpy (filedata->filename, selectname);
59:
60:        gtk_widget_destroy(filedata->filesel);
61:        gtk_main_quit();
62: }
63:
64: static
65: void filename_cancel(GtkWidget *widget, GtkWidget *filesel)
66: {
67:        gtk_widget_destroy(filesel);
68:        gtk_main_quit();
69: }
```

The filename selection dialog box is defined in Listing 21.8. It includes the standard gtk/gtk.h header file as well as string.h for the functions strlen() and strcpy(), and it also includes its own header file filename.h. Lines 6–10 show a structure is required later in this file, and two functions that will be used as callback functions are prototyped on lines 12 and 13.

21

The main dialog box function is `filename_dialog()`, which starts on line 15. This function is much like the yes/no dialog box of Listing 21.4. It starts by defining the variables it will need on lines 17 and 18. It then checks that the filename parameter is not a NULL pointer on line 20 before setting the first character in the `filename` string to the null character. This is done so that if the user clicks on the cancel button of the filename selection button, an empty string will be returned to the calling function. The file selection widget is created on line 24 with a call to `gtk_file_selection_new()`, made modal on line 24, and visible on line 25.

The `filedata` structure is initialized on lines 28–30. It contains a pointer to the file selection widget, the `char*` pointer that the caller provided to copy the filename into, and a maximum allowable length of the filename. This structure is passed to the `gtk_signal_connect()` function on line 32, which makes the function `filename_ok()` the callback function called when the user clicks the OK button of the file selection dialog box. When the `filename_ok()` callback function is called, it receives a pointer to the `filedata` structure and uses that to pass the filename the user has selected back to the `filename_dialog()` function. The other signals handled are the `"click"` event for the file selection's cancel button and the `"destroy"` event for the file selection widget as a whole. Both of these signals are handled by the function `filename_cancel()`.

After the callback functions have been set up, `gtk_main()` is called but returns only after one of the two file selection buttons or the close window button of the file selection widget's title bar has been clicked. If the user has actually selected a filename rather than clicking the cancel button, the string `filename` will contain the selected filename. If the user clicked the cancel button, the string `filename` will still be a zero-length string because that was how it was set on line 22. If the length of the string `filename` is greater than zero, a value of TRUE is returned on line 44. Otherwise, a value of FALSE is returned on line 46.

The `filename_ok()` callback function is defined on lines 49–62. It is called when the user clicks the OK button of the file selection widget, and receives a pointer to the `filedata` structure declared inside the function `filename_dialog()` as its second parameter. When called, this faction needs to retrieve the selected filename from the file selection widget. It does this by calling the function `gtk_file_selection_get_filename()` on line 54. If the length of the selected name is shorter than maximum allowable length, it is copied into the string provided by the caller on line 58. The file selection dialog has now done all that is required of it, so it is destroyed on line 60 with a call to `gtk_widget_destroy()`. The `gtk_main()` function inside the `filename_dialog()` function is terminated by a call to `gtk_main_quit()` on line 61.

The `filename_cancel()` callback function is defined on lines 65–69. It is called if the user clicks the file selection widget's cancel button or if he clicks the close window button of the file selection widget's title bar. This callback needs to do nothing more than destroy the widget using `gtk_widget_destroy()` and then call `gtk_main_quit()`.

Summary

Today's lesson covered the GTK+ GUI programming library. You learned a little bit about the history of X and the concepts beyond its operation. You learned about GUI events and GTK+ signals. You saw how a number of the more common GUI elements such as buttons, menu bars, and dialog boxes are created and operated. You saw how to write self-contained reusable dialog boxes, such as the yes/no dialog box and the file selection dialog box. The last program today brought many of these ideas together to create a simple, if somewhat incomplete, GUI text editor.

Unfortunately, this lesson really only brushed the surface of GUI programming using the GTK+ widget library. It would not be difficult to fill a whole book with information on and examples of how to write GTK+ programs. I encourage you to use the insight gained today to gain an understanding of GTK+ programming by looking at programs written using GTK+, reading the GTK+ info pages, and exploring this elegant GUI programming library.

Q&A

Q Why were the functions used today not explained as fully as the functions used on previous days?

A There are a number of reasons for this. First, there are space constraints. Today's discussion used more than 30 new functions. Including the function prototypes and explaining each in detail was simply not possible. These functions are also documented quite well in the info pages distributed with the GTK+ library. Finally, this is the last lesson of the book and after this you will be on your own. You need to learn to use whatever documentation you can find, experiment, and figure out how to solve programming problems for yourself.

Q Are GTK+ signals the same as the signals in Day 19?

A The ideas are similar, but the signals are not the same. Most signals in Day 19 were generated by the operating system. GTK+ signals are generated by the actions of a user manipulating the graphical user interface elements.

21

Workshop

The Workshop provides quiz questions to help you solidify your understanding of the material covered and exercises to provide you with experience in using what you've learned. The answers to the quiz and exercises are provided in Appendix C, "Answers."

Quiz

1. How do you tell the location of the GTK+ header files to gcc?
2. How do you tell the location of the GTK+ libraries to gcc?
3. What is a callback function?
4. What does the gtk_main() function do and when does it return?

Exercises

1. The yes/no dialog box in Listing 21.4 has one shortcoming. If the question passed in as the variable labeltext is too long, it will be cut off at the edges of the dialog box itself. Modify the yes_no_dialog() function so that it is able to detect the length of the labeltext parameter and resize the dialog box according to the size of the question.

2. Modify the yes_no_dialog() function in Listing 21.4 so that it does more than just resize the dialog box; it also splits the question into multiple lines if necessary.

WEEK 3

In Review

You have now finished your third week of learning how to program Linux using the C language. You started the week by covering such advanced issues as disk files and text strings. In the middle of the week, you saw a few of the many functions provided by the standard C library and some more UNIX-specific functions for process and signal handling. You ended the week by discovering the odds and ends of the C compiler and tackling the complexities of graphical user interface programming. The following program pulls together many of those topics.

```
1 : /* Program Name:  week3.c
➥*/
2 : /* Program to keep track of names and phone numbers.
➥*/
3 : /* Information is written to a disk file specified
➥*/
4 : /* with a command-line parameter.
➥*/
5 :
6 : #include <stdlib.h>
7 : #include <stdio.h>
8 : #include <time.h>
9 : #include <string.h>
10:
11: /*** defined constants ***/
12: #define YES    1
13: #define NO     0
14: #define REC_LENGTH  54
15:
16: #define NAME_LEN    24
17: #define PHONE_LEN  10
18:
19: /*** variables ***/
20:
21: struct record {
```

```
22:     char fname[NAME_LEN];              /* first name + NULL    */
23:     char lname[NAME_LEN];              /* last name + NULL     */
24:     char mname[NAME_LEN];              /* middle name + NULL   */
25:     char phone[PHONE_LEN];             /* phone number + NULL */
26: } rec;
27:
28: /*** function prototypes ***/
29:
30: void display_usage(char *filename);
31: int  display_menu(void);
32: void get_data(FILE *fp, char *progname, char *filename);
33: void display_report(FILE *fp);
34: int  continue_function(void);
35: int  look_up( FILE *fp );
36: void new_gets(char*str, int len);
37:
38: /* start of program */
39:
40: int main(int argc, char *argv[])
41: {
42:     FILE *fp;
43:     int  cont = YES;
44:
45:     if( argc < 2 )
46:     {
47:         display_usage(argv[0]);
48:         return 1;
49:     }
50:
51:     /* Open file. */
52:     if ((fp = fopen( argv[1], "a+")) == NULL)
53:     {
54:          fprintf( stderr, "%s(%d)Error opening file %s",
55:                            argv[0],__LINE__, argv[1]);
56:          return 1;
57:     }
58:
59:     while( cont == YES )
60:     {
61:         switch( display_menu() )
62:         {
63:           case '1': get_data(fp, argv[0], argv[1]); /* Day 18*/
64:                     break;
65:           case '2': display_report(fp);
66:                     break;
67:           case '3': look_up(fp);
68:                     break;
69:           case '4': printf("\n\nThank you for using this program!\n");
70:                     cont = NO;
71:                     break;
```

```
72:                default:  printf("\n\nInvalid choice, Please select 1 to 4!");
73:                    break;
74:            }
75:        }
76:        fclose(fp);        /* close file */
77:        return 0;
78: }
79:
80: /* display_menu() */
81:
82: int display_menu(void)
83: {
84:     char ch, buf[20];
85:
86:     printf( "\n");
87:     printf( "\n      MENU");
88:     printf( "\n    ========\n");
89:     printf( "\n1.  Enter names");
90:     printf( "\n2.  Print report");
91:     printf( "\n3.  Look up number");
92:     printf( "\n4.  Quit");
93:     printf( "\n\nEnter Selection ==> ");
94:     new_gets(buf, 20);
95:     ch = *buf;
96:     return ch;
97: }
98:
99: /****************************************************
100:    Function:  get_data()
101: ****************************************************/
102:
103: void get_data(FILE *fp, char *progname, char *filename)
104: {
105:     int cont = YES;
106:
107:     while( cont == YES )
108:     {
109:         printf("\n\nPlease enter information: " );
110:
111:         printf("\n\nEnter first name: ");
112:         new_gets(rec.fname, NAME_LEN);
113:         printf("\nEnter middle name: ");
114:         new_gets(rec.mname, NAME_LEN);
115:         printf("\nEnter last name: ");
116:         new_gets(rec.lname, NAME_LEN);
117:         printf("\nEnter phone in 123-4567 format: ");
118:         new_gets(rec.phone, PHONE_LEN);
119:
120:         if (fseek( fp, 0, SEEK_END ) == 0)
121:             if( fwrite(&rec, 1, sizeof(rec), fp) != sizeof(rec))
```

```
122:            {
123:                fprintf( stderr, "%s(%d) Error writing to file %s",
124:                              progname,__LINE__, filename);
125:                exit(2);
126:            }
127:          cont = continue_function();
128:      }
129: }
130:
131: /********************************************************
132: Function:  display_report()
133: Purpose:    To print out the formatted names and numbers
134:             of people in the file.
135: ********************************************************/
136:
137: void display_report(FILE *fp)
138: {
139:     time_t rtime;
140:     int num_of_recs = 0;
141:
142:     time(&rtime);
143:
144:     fprintf(stdout, "\n\nRun Time: %s", ctime( &rtime));
145:     fprintf(stdout, "\nPhone number report\n");
146:
147:     if(fseek( fp, 0, SEEK_SET ) == 0)
148:     {
149:         fread(&rec, 1, sizeof(rec), fp);
150:         while(!feof(fp))
151:         {
152:             fprintf(stdout,"\n\t%s, %s %c %s", rec.lname,
153:                                     rec.fname, rec.mname[0],
154:                                     rec.phone);
155:             num_of_recs++;
156:             fread(&rec, 1, sizeof(rec), fp);
157:         }
158:         fprintf(stdout, "\n\nTotal number of records: %d",
159:                 num_of_recs);
160:         fprintf(stdout, "\n\n* * * End of Report * * *");
161:     }
162:     else
163:         fprintf( stderr, "\n\n*** ERROR WITH REPORT ***\n");
164: }
165:
166: /************************************************
167: *  Function:  continue_function()
168: ************************************************/
169:
170: int continue_function( void )
171: {
```

```
172:      char ch, buf[20];
173:      do
174:      {
175:       printf("\n\nDo you wish to enter another? (Y)es/(N)o ");
176:          new_gets(buf, 20);
177:          ch = *buf;
178:      } while( strchr( "NnYy", ch) == NULL );
179:
180:      if(ch == 'n' || ch == 'N')
181:          return NO;
182:      else
183:          return YES;
184: }
185:
186: /***********************************************************
187: *  Function:  display_usage()
188: ***********************************************************/
189:
190: void display_usage( char *filename )
191: {
192:      char *cptr ;
193:
194:      cptr = strrchr(filename, '/');
195:      if (cptr == NULL)
196:          cptr = filename;
197:      else
198:          cptr++;
199:
200:      printf("\n\nUSAGE: %s filename", cptr );
201:      printf("\n\n   where filename is a file to store people's names");
202:      printf("\n     and phone numbers.\n\n");
203: }
204:
205: /***********************************************
206: *  Function:  look_up()
207: *  Returns:   Number of names matched
208: ***********************************************/
209:
210: int look_up( FILE *fp )
211: {
212:      char tmp_lname[NAME_LEN];
213:      int  ctr = 0;
214:
215:      fprintf(stdout, "\n\nPlease enter last name to be found: ");
216:      new_gets(tmp_lname, NAME_LEN);
217:
218:      if( strlen(tmp_lname) != 0 )
219:      {
220:         if (fseek( fp, 0, SEEK_SET ) == 0)
221:         {
```

```
222:            fread(&rec, 1, sizeof(rec), fp);
223:            while( !feof(fp))
224:            {
225:                if( strcmp(rec.lname, tmp_lname) == 0 )
226:                /* if matched */
227:                {
228:                    fprintf(stdout, "\n%s %s %s - %s", rec.fname,
229:                                                      rec.mname,
230:                                                      rec.lname,
231:                                                      rec.phone);
232:                    ctr++;
233:                }
234:                fread(&rec, 1, sizeof(rec), fp);
235:            }
236:        }
237:        fprintf( stdout, "\n\n%d names matched.", ctr );
238:    }
239:    else
240:    {
241:        fprintf( stdout, "\nNo name entered." );
242:    }
243:    return ctr;
244: }
245:
246:
247: /*------------------------------------------------------------------*
248:  * Function:  new_gets()                                            *
249:  * Purpose:   This function gets a string from the keyboard using   *
250:  *            fgets() and removes the trailing newline character.   *
251:  * Returns:   Nothing                                              *
252:  *------------------------------------------------------------------*/
253: void new_gets(char*str, int len)
254: {
255:     int index;
256:
257:     fgets(str, len, stdin);
258:
259:     for(index = 0; index < len; index++)
260:         if (str[index] == '\n')
261:         {
262:             str[index] = 0;
263:             return;
264:         }
265: }
```

In some respects, this program is similar to the programs presented in Week 1 in Review and Week 2 in Review. Fewer data items are tracked, but additional program capabilities have been added. This program lets the user keep track of names and phone numbers of friends, relatives, business contacts, and so on. As written, the program tracks only first name, middle name, last name, and phone number. It would be a simple matter to have the program record additional information, and you might like to try that as an exercise. The major difference between this program and the earlier review programs is that there is no limit to the number of people who can be entered into the program. That is because a disk file is used for data storage.

When you start the program, you enter the name of the data file on the command line. The `main()` function starts on line 38 with the `argc` and `argv` arguments used to retrieve the command-line parameters. You saw this on Day 20, "Advanced Compiler Use." Line 45 checks the value of `argc` to see how many parameters were entered on the command line. If `argc` is less than 2, only one parameter was entered (the command to run the program), which means that the user didn't specify a data filename. In this case, the program calls `display_usage()` with `argv[0]` as an argument. `argv[0]`, the first parameter entered on the command line, is the name of the program.

The `display_usage()` function is on lines 190 through 203. Whenever you write a program that takes command-line arguments, it's a good idea to include a function similar to `display_usage()` that tells the user how the program should be used. Why doesn't the program just hard code the name of the program (Week 3) instead of using the command-line argument? The answer is simple. When you obtain the program name from the command line, you don't have to worry if the user renames the program; the usage description is always correct. Also note that the `display_usage()` function strips off any path information from `argv[0]`. For instance, if the program were run from the current directory by invoking the command `./week3 names.data`, the `strrchr()` function on line 194 would find the last `'/'` character in the string and use that as the name. If there is no `'/'` character, `display_usage()` just uses the program name as it was received.

Most of the new concepts in this program come from Day 15, "Using Disk Files." Line 42 declares a file pointer `fp` that is used throughout the program to access the data file. Line 52 tries to open this file with a mode of `"+a"` (remember, `argv [1]` is the second item listed on the command line—the data filename). The `"a+"` mode is used because you want to be able to append to the current file as well as read any records that already exist. If the file open operation fails, lines 54 and 55 display an error message before the program exits on line 56. Notice that the error message contains descriptive information. Also notice that `__LINE__`, covered on Day 20, indicates the line number where the error occurred.

If the file is opened successfully, a menu is displayed. When the user chooses to exit the program, line 76 closes the file with `fclose()` before the program returns control to the operating system. Other menu options allow the user to enter a record, display all records, or search for a particular person.

The function get_data() contains are a few significant changes. Line 103 contains the function header. The function now accepts three pointers. The first is the most important; it is the handle for the file to be written to. Lines 107 through 128 contain a while loop that continues to get data until the user wants to quit. Lines 109 through 118 prompt for the data in the same format as the program in Week 2 in Review. Line 120 calls fseek() to set the file pointer to the end of the file so it can write new information there. Notice that the program doesn't do anything if the seek fails. A complete program would handle such a failure, but it has been omitted here to keep the program from becoming too long. Line 121 writes the data to the disk file with a call to fwrite().

The report feature in this program has also changed. One feature typical of most real-world reports is the inclusion of the current date and time at the top of the report. On line 139, the variable rtime is declared. This variable is passed to the time() function and then displayed using the ctime() function. These time functions were presented on Day 17, "Exploring the C Function Library."

Before the program can start printing the records in the file, it needs to reposition the file pointer at the beginning of the file. This is done on line 147 with a call to fseek(). After the file pointer is positioned, records can be read one after another. Line 149 does the first read. If the read is successful, the program begins a while loop that continues until the end of the file is reached (when feof() returns a nonzero value). If the end of the file hasn't been reached, line 152 prints the information, line 155 counts the record, and line 156 tries to read the next record. You should notice that these functions are used without checking their return values in order to keep the program at a reasonable length. To protect the program from errors, the function calls should contain checks to ensure that no errors occurred.

One function in this program is new. Lines 210 through 244 contain the function look_up(), which searches the disk file for all records that contain a certain last name. Lines 215 and 216 prompt for the name to be found and store it in a local variable called tmp_lname. If tmp_lname isn't blank (line 218), the file pointer is set to the beginning of the file. Each record is then read. Using strcmp() (line 225), the record's last name is compared to tmp_lname. If the names match, the record is printed (lines 228 through 231). This continues until the end of the file is reached. Again, you should notice that not all functions have their return values checked. You should always check return values.

You should also be able to modify this program to create your own files that can store any information. Using the functions learned during Week 3, along with the other functions in the C library, you should be able to create a program to do just about anything you want.

APPENDIX A

ASCII Character Chart

Dec	Hex	ASCII	Dec	Hex	ASCII
0	00	nul	32	20	space
1	01	soh	33	21	!
2	02	stx	34	22	"
3	03	etx	35	23	#
4	04	eot	36	24	$
5	05	enq	37	25	%
6	06	ack	38	26	&
7	07	bel	39	27	'
8	08	bs	40	28	(
9	09	ht	41	29	)
10	0A	lf	42	2A	*
11	0B	vt	43	2B	+
12	0C	ff	44	2C	'
13	0D	cr	45	2D	-
14	0E	so	46	2E	.
15	0F	si	47	2F	/
16	10	dle	48	30	0
17	11	dc1	49	31	1
18	12	dc2	50	32	2
19	13	dc3	51	33	3
20	14	dc4	52	34	4
21	15	nak	53	35	5
22	16	syn	54	36	6
23	17	etb	55	37	7
24	18	can	56	38	8
25	19	em	57	39	9
26	1A	sub	58	3A	:
27	1B	esc	59	3B	;
28	1C	fs	60	3C	<
29	1D	gs	61	3D	=
30	1E	rs	62	3E	>
31	1F	us	63	3F	?

Dec	Hex	ASCII	Dec	Hex	ASCII
64	40	@	96	60	`
65	41	A	97	61	a
66	42	B	98	62	b
67	43	C	99	63	c
68	44	D	100	64	d
69	45	E	101	65	e
70	46	F	102	66	f
71	47	G	103	67	g
72	48	H	104	68	h
73	49	I	105	69	i
74	4A	J	106	6A	j
75	4B	K	107	6B	k
76	4C	L	108	6C	l
77	4D	M	109	6D	m
78	4E	N	110	6E	n
79	4F	O	111	6F	o
80	50	P	112	70	p
81	51	Q	113	71	q
82	52	R	114	72	r
83	53	S	115	73	s
84	54	T	116	74	t
85	55	U	117	75	u
86	56	V	118	76	v
87	57	W	119	77	w
88	58	X	120	78	x
89	59	Y	121	79	y
90	5A	Z	122	7A	z
91	5B	[	123	7B	{
92	5C	\	124	7C	¦
93	5D	]	125	7D	}
94	5E	^	126	7E	~
95	5F	–	127	7F	Δ

A

APPENDIX B

C/C++ Reserved Words

The identifiers listed in Table B.1 are reserved C keywords. You shouldn't use them for any other purpose in a C program. They are allowed, of course, within double quotation marks.

Also included is a list of words that aren't reserved in C but are C++ reserved words. These C++ reserved words aren't described here, but if there's a chance your C programs might eventually be ported to C++, you must avoid these words as well.

TABLE B.1. Reserved C keywords.

Keyword	Description
asm	Keyword that denotes inline assembly language code.
auto	The default storage class.
break	Command that exits `for`, `while`, `switch`, and `do...while` statements unconditionally.
case	Command used within the `switch` statement.
char	The simplest C data type.
const	Data modifier that prevents a variable from being changed. See `volatile`.
continue	Command that resets a `for`, `while`, or `do...while` statement to the next iteration.
default	Command used within the `switch` statement to catch any instances not specified with a `case` statement.
do	Looping command used in conjunction with the `while` statement. The loop will always execute at least once.
double	Data type that can hold double-precision floating-point values.
else	Statement signaling alternative statements to be executed when an `if` statement evaluates to `FALSE`.
enum	Data type that allows variables to be declared that accept only certain values.
extern	Data modifier indicating that a variable will be declared in another area of the program.
float	Data type used for floating-point numbers.
for	Looping command that contains initialization, incrementation, and conditional sections.
goto	Command that causes a jump to a predefined label.
if	Command used to change program flow based on a `TRUE/FALSE` decision.
int	Data type used to hold integer values.
long	Data type used to hold larger integer values than `int`.
register	Storage modifier that specifies that a variable should be stored in a register if possible.
return	Command that causes program flow to exit from the current function and return to the calling function. It can also be used to return a single value.
short	Data type used to hold integers. It isn't commonly used, and it's the same size as an `int` on most computers.
signed	Modifier used to signify that a variable can have both positive and negative values. See `unsigned`.

Keyword	Description
sizeof	Operator that returns the size of the item in bytes.
static	Modifier used to signify that the compiler should retain the variable's value.
struct	Keyword used to combine C variables of any data type into a group.
switch	Command used to change program flow in a multitude of directions. Used in conjunction with the case statement.
typedef	Modifier used to create new names for existing variable and function types.
union	Keyword used to allow multiple variables to share the same memory space.
unsigned	Modifier used to signify that a variable will contain only positive values. See signed.
void	Keyword used to signify either that a function doesn't return anything or that a pointer being used is considered generic or able to point to any data type.
volatile	Modifier that signifies that a variable can be changed. See const.
while	Looping statement that executes a section of code as long as a condition remains TRUE.

B

In addition to the preceding keywords, the following are C++ reserved words:

catch	inline	template
class	new	this
delete	operator	throw
except	private	try
finally	protected	virtual
friend	public	

APPENDIX **C**

Answers

Day 1: Introduction to Linux and the C Programming Language

Quiz Answers

1. C is a powerful, popular, and portable language.

2. The compiler checks the source code and, if there are no errors, it then translates the source code into machine language that the machine can understand. If there are errors, the compiler displays messages stating where and what kind the error is.

3. Edit, compile, and test.

4. `gcc myprogram1.c -o myprog`

   If you want the compiler to show all warning messages and to include debugging information the following would be used:

   `gcc -Wall -ggdb myprogram1.c -o myprog`

5. C source code files should use the .c extension.

6. The name filename.txt is not a valid name for a C source-code file.

7. You should make changes to the source code to correct the problems. You should then recompile the program and test again.

8. Machine language is the digital or binary instructions that the computer can understand. Because the computer can't understand C source code, it must be compiled by a C compiler to create machine language.

9. The debugger allows you to step through a compiled C program line by line. This is useful for both finding errors in programs and gaining a better understanding of how they work.

10. Debugging information. Adding -ggdb to the gcc command line will tell the compiler to add debugging information that is required by the debugger.

Answers to Exercises

1. The editor might or might not display unusual characters, depending on your editor's behavior.

2. It calculates the area of a circle. First, it prompts the user for the radius and then it displays the area.

3. This program prints out a 10×10 block of X characters. A similar program is covered on Day 5, "Basic Program Control."

4. Line 3. You will probably get a set of error messages such as the following:

```
test.c:4: parse error before '{'

test.c:6: parse error before string constant

test.c:6: warning: data definition has no type or storage class
```

The first line of the error message states that the problem is on line 4 before the open brace. The open brace is the first character of line 4, so that means the problem could be with the end of line 3 as well. In fact, it is; removing the semicolon at the end of line 3 fixes the problem.

5. This produces a different error:

```
/tmp/ccyNzE2u.o: In function 'main':

/tmp/ccyNzE2u.o(.text+0x1f): undefined reference to 'do_it'

collect2: ld returned 1 exit status
```

When the compiler tried to create an executable, it could not find any reference to the function do_it(). Try changing do_it() to printf().

6. The program now prints out a 10×10 block of diamonds.

Day 2: The Components of a C Program: Code and Data

Quiz Answers

1. A group of one or more C statements enclosed in braces is called a block.

2. The one component that must be present in every C program is a `main()` function.

3. Any text occurring between `/*` and `*/` is a program comment and is ignored by the compiler. Comments are used to make notations about the program's structure and operation.

4. A function is an independent section of a program that performs a certain task and has been assigned a name. By using a function's name, a program can execute the code in the function.

5. A user-defined function is created by the programmer, whereas a library function is supplied by the compiler or the operating system.

6. A `#include` directive instructs the compiler to add the code from another file into your source code during the compilation process.

7. Comments shouldn't be nested. Some compilers allow this and others don't. To keep your code portable, you shouldn't nest comments.

8. Yes. Comments can be as long as needed. A comment starts with `/*` and doesn't end until a `*/` is encountered.

9. An include file is also known as a header file.

10. An include file is a separate disk file that contains information needed by the compiler to use various functions.

Answers to Exercises

1. Remember that only the `main()` function is required in a C program. The following is the smallest possible program, but it doesn't do anything useful:

```
int main(void)
{
    return 0;
}
```

This program could also be written as

```
int main(void) { return 0; }
```

2. Consider the following program:

```
1 : /* ex2-2.c */
2 : #include <stdio.h>
3 :
4 : void display_line(void);
5 :
6 : int main(void)
7 : {
8 :     display_line();
9 :     printf("\n Sams Teach Yourself C In 21 Days!\n");
10:     display_line();
11:     printf("\n\n");
12:      return 0;
13: }
14:
15: /* print asterisk line */
16: void display_line(void)
17: {
18:     int counter;
19:
20:     for( counter = 0; counter < 34; counter++ )
21:         printf("*" );
22: }
23: /* end of program */
```

   a. Statements are on lines 8, 9, 10, 12, 20, and 21.

   b. The only variable definition is on line 18.

   c. The only function prototype is on line 4.

   d. The function definitions are on lines 16 through 22.

   e. Comments are on lines 1, 15, and 23.

3. A comment is any text included between /* and */. Examples include the following:

```
/* This is a comment. */

/* ??? */

/*
This is a
third comment */
```

4. This program prints the alphabet of capital letters. You should understand this program better after you finish Day 9, "Characters and Strings."

   The output is ABCDEFGHIJKLMNOPQRSTUVWXYZ.

5. This program counts and prints the number of characters and spaces you enter. This program also will be clearer after you finish Day 9.

Day 3: Statements, Expressions, and Operators

Quiz Answers

1. It is an assignment statement that instructs the computer to add 5 and 8, and assign the result to the variable x.

2. An expression is anything that evaluates to a numerical expression.

3. The relative precedence of the operators.

4. After the first statement, the value of a is 10, and the value of x is 11. After the second statement, both a and x have values of 11. (The statements must be executed separately.)

5. 1, which is the remainder after 10 is divided by 3.

6. 19

7. (5 + 3) * 8 / (2 + 2)

8. 0

9. See the section "Operator Precedence Revisited" near the end of today's lesson. It shows the C operators and their precedence.

   a. < has higher precedence than ==.

   b. * has higher precedence than +.

   c. != and == have the same precedence, so they are evaluated left to right.

   d. >= and > have the same precedence. Use parentheses if you need to use more than one relational operator in a single statement or expression.

10. The compound assignment operators let you combine a binary mathematical operation with an assignment operation, thus providing a shorthand notation. The compound operator presented today are +=, -=, *=, /=, and %=.

Answers to Exercises

1. This listing should work even though it is poorly structured. The purpose of this listing is to demonstrate that whitespace is irrelevant to the program runs. You should, however, use whitespace to make your programs readable.

2. The following is a better way to structure the listing from exercise 1:

```
#include <stdio.h>

int x,y;

int main(void)
```

```
{
    printf("\nEnter two numbers");
    scanf("%d %d",&x,&y);
    printf("\n\n%d is bigger\n",(x>y)?x:y);
    return 0;
}
```

This program asks for two numbers to be entered and then prints whichever number is bigger.

3. The only changes needed in Listing 3.1 are the following:

```
17:        printf("\n%d        %d", a++, ++b);
18:        printf("\n%d        %d", a++, ++b);
19:        printf("\n%d        %d", a++, ++b);
20:        printf("\n%d        %d", a++, ++b);
21:        printf("\n%d        %d\n", a++, ++b);
```

4. The following code fragment is just one of many possible answers. It checks to see if x is greater than or equal to 1 and less than or equal to 20. If those two conditions are met, x is assigned to y; otherwise, x is not assigned to y and y remains the same.

```
if ((x >= 1) && (x <= 20))
    y = x;
```

5. The code is as follows:

```
y = (x >= 1) && (x <= 20)) ? x : y;
```

Again, if the statement is TRUE, x is assigned to y; otherwise, y is assigned to itself, thus having no effect.

6. The code is as follows:

```
if (x < 1 && x > 10 )
        statement;
```

7.

    a. 7

    b. 0

    c. 9

    d. 1

    e. 5

8.   a. TRUE

      b. FALSE

      c. TRUE. Notice that there is a single equal sign, making the if an assignment rather than a relation.

      d. TRUE

9. Write an `if` statement that determines whether someone is legally an adult (age 21), but not a senior citizen (age 65).

```
if (age < 21)
    printf("You are not an adult");
else if (age >= 65)
    printf("You are a senior citizen");
else
    printf("You are an adult");
```

10. This program has four problems. The first is on line 3 where the assignment should end with a semicolon, not a colon. The second problem is the semicolon at the end of the `if` statement on line 6. The third problem is a common one; an assignment operator (=) is used instead of a relational operator (==) in the `if` statement. The final problem is the word `otherwise` on line 8. This should be `else`. Here is the corrected code:

```
/* a program with problems... */
#include <stdio.h>
int x= 1;
int main(void)
{
   if( x == 1)
      printf(" x equals 1" );
   else
      printf(" x does not equal 1");
   return 0;
}
```

Day 4: Functions: The Basics

Quiz Answers

1. Yes (at least it should be). You should use structured programming techniques if you want to become a good C programmer.

2. Structured programming takes a complex programming problem and breaks it into a number of simpler tasks that are easier to handle one at a time.

3. After you've broken your program into a number of simpler tasks, you can write a function to perform each task.

4. The first line of a function definition must be the function header. It contains the function's name, its return type, and its parameters.

5. A function can return either one or no values. The value can be any of the C variable types. On Day 14, "Pointers: Beyond the Basics," you will see how to get more values back from a function.

6. A function that doesn't return a value should be declared as type `void`.

7. A function definition is a complete function, including the header and all the function's statements. The definition determines what actions take place when the function executes. The prototype is a single line, identical to the function header but ending in a semicolon. The prototype informs the compiler of the function's name, its return type, and parameter list.

8. A local variable is declared with a function.

9. Local variables are independent of other variables within the program.

10. The `main()` function should be the first function in your listing.

Answers to Exercises

1. `float do_it(char a, char b, char c)`

   To make this into a function prototype, add a semicolon to the end of the line. As a function header, it should be followed by the function's statements enclosed in braces.

2. `void print_a_number(int number)`

   This is a `void` function. As in exercise 1, to make this into a function prototype, add a semicolon to the end of the line. As a function header, it should be followed by the function's statements enclosed in braces.

3.   a. `int`

       b. `long`

4. There are two problems. First, the `print_msg()` function is declared as `void`, but it returns a value. The `return` statement should be removed. The second problem is on the fifth line. The call to `print_msg()` passes a parameter (a string). The function prototype states that the function has a void parameter list and, therefore, shouldn't be passed anything. The following is the correct listing.

```
#include <stdio.h>
void print_msg( void );
int main(void)
{
    print_msg();
    return 0;
}
void print_msg( void )
{
    puts( "This is a message to print" );
}
```

5. There should not be a semicolon at the end of the function header.

6. Only the `larger_of()` function needs to be changed.

```
int larger_of( int a, int b)
{
    int save;
    if (a > b)
        save = a;
    else
        save = b;
    return save;
}
```

Another perfectly valid solution is

```
int larger_of( int a, int b)
{
    return (a > b) ? a : b ;
}
```

7. The following assumes that the numbers are integers and that the function returns an integer.

```
int product(int x, int y)
{
    return (x * y);
}
```

8. Division by zero causes an error, so the following function checks whether the second value is zero before doing the division. You should never assume that the values passed are correct.

```
int divide_em(int a, int b)
{
    if (b == 0)
        return 0;
    return (a / b);
}
```

9. Although the following function uses `main()`, it could use any function.

```
#include <stdio.h>

int product(int x, int y);
int divide_em(int a, int b);

int main (void)
{
    int number1 = 10,
        number2 = 5;
    int x, y, z;

    x = product(number1, number2);
    y = divide_em(number1, number2);
    z = divide_em(number1, 0);
```

C

```
    printf("number1 is %d and number2 is %d\n", number1, number2);
    printf("number1 * number2 is %d\n", x);
    printf("number1 / number2 is %d\n", y);
    printf("number1 / 0 is %d\n", z);

    return 0;
}

int product(int x, int y)
{
    return (x * y);
}

int divide_em(int a, int b)
{
    if (b == 0)
        return 0;
    return (a / b);
}
```

10. One possible solution is as follows:

```
#include <stdio.h>

float average (float a, float b, float c, float d, float e);

int main (void)
{
    float v, w, x, y, z, answer;

    puts("Enter 5 numbers:");
    scanf("%f%f%f%f%f", &v, &w, &x, &y, &z);

    answer = average(v, w, x, y, z);

    printf("The average is %f\n", answer);

    return 0;
}

float average (float a, float b, float c, float d, float e)
{
    return ((a+b+c+d+e)/5);
}
```

11. The following is a solution using type int variables. It will only work correctly for values less than or equal to 19.

```
#include <stdio.h>

int three_powered (int power);
```

```
int main (void)
{
    int a = 4, b = 19;

    printf("3 to the power of %d is %d\n", a, three_powered(a));
    printf("3 to the power of %d is %d\n", b, three_powered(b));

    return 0;
}

int three_powered (int power)
{
    if (power < 1)
        return 1;
    else
        return 3 * three_powered (power -1);
}
```

C

Day 5: Basic Program Control

Quiz Answers

1. The first index value of an array in C is 0.

2. The for statement contains initialization, conditional, and incrementing/decrementing expressions as part of the command, whereas the while statement contains only the conditional expression.

3. A do...while statement contains the while after the block and always executes the loop at least once.

4. Yes, a while statement can accomplish the same tasks as a for statement, but you need to do two additional things. You must initialize any variables before starting the loop and you must increment or decrement any variables as part of the while loop.

5. You can't overlap the loops. A nested loop must be completely contained inside the outer loop.

6. Yes, a while statement can be nested in a do...while statement. You can nest any command within a loop block.

7. The four parts of a for statement are the initializer, the conditional, the increment, and the statement(s).

8. The two parts of a while statement are the conditional and the statement(s).

9. The two parts of a do...while statement are the conditional and the statement(s).

Answers to Exercises

1. `long array[50];`

2. Note that the 50th element in the array is indexed to 49. That is because array indexes start at 0.

   `array [49] = 123.456;`

3. When the statement is complete, x equals 100.

4. When the statement is complete, cptr equals 11. (cptr starts at 2 and is increment-ed by 3 while it is less than 10.)

5. The inner loop prints five Xs. The outer loop executes the inner loop 10 times. That means a total of 50 Xs are printed.

6. The code is as follows:
   ```
   int x;
   for(x = 1; x <= 100; x +=3);
   ```

7. The code is as follows:
   ```
   int x = 1;
   while(x <= 100)
       x += 3;
   ```

8. The code is as follows:
   ```
   int x = 1;
   do
   {
       x += 3;
   }
   while(x <= 100)
   ```

9. This program never ends. The variable program is initialized to 0. The while loop then checks whether record is less than 100. 0 is less than 100, so the loop exe-cutes, thus printing the two statements. The loop then checks the conditional again. 0 is still less than 100, so the loop runs again. To make this work correctly, record must be incremented inside the loop as follows:
   ```
   record = 0;
   while (record < 100)
   {
       printf( "\nRecord %d ", record );
       printf( "\nGetting next number..." );
       record++;
   }
   ```

10. Using a defined constant is common in looping; you'll see examples similar to this in Weeks 2 and 3. The problem with this code fragment is simple. There should not be a semicolon at the end of the for statement. This is a common bug.

Day 6: Fundamentals of Input and Output

Quiz Answers

1. There are two differences between `puts()` and `printf()`.

   `printf()` can print variable parameters.

   `puts()` always prints a newline after the string.

2. You should include stdio.h when you use `printf()`.

3.
   a. \\ prints a backslash
   b. \b prints a backspace
   c. \n prints a newline
   d. \t prints a tab
   e. \a (for alert) sounds the beep

4.
   a. `%s` is used for character string
   b. `%d` is used for signed decimal integer
   c. `%f` is used for decimal floating-point number

5.
   a. b prints the literal character b
   b. \b prints a backspace
   c. \ looks at the next character to determine an escape character (see Table 6.1)
   d. \\ prints a backslash

Answers to Exercises

1. The `puts()` statement automatically prints a newline, whereas `printf()` does not.

   ```
   puts("");
   printf("\n");
   ```

2. The code is as follows:

   ```
   char c1, c2;
   unsigned int d1;
   scanf("%c %ud %c", c1, d1, c2);
   ```

3. Your solution may be slightly different.

   ```
   #include <stdio.h>

   int main(void)
   ```

```
{
    int x;

    puts("Enter an integer value:");
    scanf("%d", &x);
    printf("The value entered was %d.\n", x);
    return 0;
}
```

4. It's typical to edit a program to allow only specific values to be accepted. The following is one way to accomplish that.

```
#include <stdio.h>

int main(void)
{
    int x;

    puts("Enter an even value:");
    scanf("%d", &x);
    while (x % 2 != 0)
    {
        printf("%d is not even.\nTry again\n", x);
        scanf("%d", &x);
    }

    printf("The value entered was %d.\n", x);

    return 0;
}
```

5. One solution is as follows:

```
#include <stdio.h>

int main(void)
{
    int array[6], x, number;

    /* Loop 6 times or until the last entered value is 99. */
    for(x = 0; x < 6 && number != 99; x++)
    {
        puts("Enter an even value or 99 to quit:");
        scanf("%d", &number);
        while (number % 2 == 1 && number != 99)
        {
            printf("%d is not even.\nTry again\n", x);
            scanf("%d", &number);
        }
        array[x] = number;
    }
```

```
    /* Now print them out. */
    for(x = 0; x < 6 && number != 99; x++)
        printf("The value entered was %d.\n", array [x]);

    return 0;
}
```

6. The previous answers are already executable programs. The only change that must be made is to the last `printf()`. To print each value separated by a tab, change the final printf() statement to the following:

```
printf ("%d\t", array [x]);
```

7. You can't have quotation marks within quotation marks. To print quotation marks within quotation marks, you must use the escape character as shown here:

```
printf( "Jack said, \"Peter Piper picked a peck of pickled peppers.\"");
```

8. This program has three errors. The first is the lack of quotation marks in the `printf()` statement, and the second is the missing address-of operator in the `scanf()` function call. The final error is also in the `scanf()` statement. The correct conversion specifier for an integer is %d—not %f—because answer is of type int, not type float. The following is correct.

```
int get_1_or_2( void )
{
    int answer = 0;
    while (answer < 1 || answer > 2)
    {
        printf("Enter 1 for Yes, 2 for No");
        scanf( "%d", &answer );
    }
    return answer;
}
```

9. Here is a completed `print_report()` function.

```
void print_report( void )
{
    printf( "\nSAMPLE REPORT" );
    printf( "\n\nSequence\tMeaning" );
    printf( "\n=========\t=======" );
    printf( "\n\\a\t\tbell (alert)" );
    printf( "\n\\b\t\tbackspace" );
    printf( "\n\\n\t\tnewline" );
    printf( "\n\\t\t\thorizontal tab" );
    printf( "\n\\\\\t\tbackslash" );
    printf( "\n\\\?\t\tquestion mark" );
    printf( "\n\\\'\t\tsingle quote" );
    printf( "\n\\\"\t\tdouble quote" );
    printf( "\n...\t\t...");
}
```

C

10. One solution is as follows:

```c
/* Inputs two floating point numbers and   */
/* displays their product.                  */
#include <stdio.h>

int main(void)
{
    float x, y;

    puts("Enter two values: ");
    scanf("%f %f", &x, &y);
    printf("The product of %f and %f is %f.\n", x, y, x*y);
    return 0;
}
```

11. The following program inputs 10 integer values from the keyboard and then displays their sum.

```c
#include <stdio.h>

int main(void)
{
    int count, temp, total = 0;

    for(count = 1; count <= 10; count++)
    {
        printf("Enter integer #%d: ", count);
        scanf("%d", &temp);
        total += temp;
    }

    printf("The total is %d.\n", total);

    return 0;
}
```

12. The following is one solution.

```c
#include <stdio.h>

#define  MAX  100

int main(void)
{
    int array [MAX];
    int count = -1, maximum, minimum, num_entered, temp;

    puts("Enter integer values one per line.");
    puts("Enter 0 when finished.");

    do
```

```
{
    scanf("%d", &temp);
    array[++count] = temp;
} while (count < (MAX-1) && temp != 0);

num_entered = count;

/* Find the largest and smallest values.     */
/* At the start, the first value is both the  */
/* maximum and the minimum.                    */
maximum = minimum = array [0];

for(count = 1; count < num_entered; count++)
{
    if (array[count] > maximum)
        maximum = array[count];
    if (array[count] < minimum)
        minimum = array[count];

}

printf("The maximum value is %d.\n", maximum);
printf("The minimum value is %d.\n", minimum);

return 0;
}
```

C

Day 7: Using Numeric Arrays

Quiz Answers

1. All of them, but arrays can only contain elements of the same type.

2. 0. Regardless of the size of the array, all C arrays start with index 0.

3. n-1.

4. The program compiles but might crash or produce unpredictable results.

5. In the declaration statement, follow the array name with one set of brackets for each dimension. Each set of brackets contains the number of elements in the corresponding dimension.

6. 240. This is determined by multiplying 2*3*5*8.

7. array [0][0][1][1]

Answers to Exercises

1.

```
int one [1000], two [1000], three [1000];
```

2.

```
int array [10] = { 1, 1, 1, 1, 1, 1, 1, 1, 1, 1 };
```

3. This can be solved in numerous ways. The first is to initialize the array when it's declared:

```
int eightyeight[88] = { 88, 88, 88, 88, 88, 88, 88, 88, 88, ...... , 88 };
```

However, this approach would require eighty-eight 88s between the braces instead of the ... used here. This is not a good method for initializing large arrays. The following is much better:

```
int eightyeight [88];
int x;

for(x = 0; x < 88 x++)
    eightyeight [x] = 88;
```

4. The code is as follows:

```
int stuff [12][10];
int sub1, sub2;

for(sub1 = 0; sub1 < 12; sub1++)
    for(sub2 = 0; sub2 < 10 ; sub2++)
        stuff [sub1][sub2] = 0;
```

5. Be careful with this fragment. This bug is easy to create. Notice that the array was declared as 10*3, but initialized as a 3*10 array. To describe this differently, the left subscript is declared as 10 but the for loop uses x as the left subscript, which is incremented three times. The right subscript is declared as 3, but the second loop uses y as a subscript and y is incremented 10 times. At best, this can cause unpredictable results; at worst, it can cause the program to crash. The program can be fixed in two ways. The first way is to switch x and y in the line that does the initialization.

```
int x, y;
int array[10][3];
int main(void)
{
    for ( x = 0; x < 3; x++ )
        for ( y = 0; y < 10; y++ )
            array[y][x] = 0;   /* changed! */
    return 0;
}
```

The second way (which is recommended) is to switch the values in the `for` loops.

```
int x, y;
int array[10][3];
int main(void)
{
    for ( x = 0; x < 10; x++ )    /* changed! */
        for ( y = 0; y < 3; y++ )   /* changed! */
            array[x][y] = 0;
    return 0;
}
```

6. This should be an easy bug to bust. This program initializes an element in the array that is out of bounds. If you have an array of 10 elements, the elements' subscripts are 0 to 9. This program initializes the array with subscripts 1 to 10. You can't initialize element `array[10]` because it doesn't exist. The `for` statement should be changed to one of the following examples:

```
for ( x = 1; x <= 9; x++ )  /* initializes 9 of the 10 elements */

for ( x = 0; x < 10; x++ )
```

Note that x `<=` 9 is the same as x `<` 10. Either is appropriate, although x `<` 10 is more common.

7. The following is one of many possible answers.

```
#include <stdio.h>
#include <stdlib.h>

int main(void)
{
    int array [5][4];
    int a, b;

    for(a = 0 ; a < 5; a++)
        for(b = 0; b < 4; b++)
            array [a][b] = rand();

    /* Now print the array elements. */
    for(a = 0 ; a < 5; a++)
    {
        for(b = 0; b < 4; b++)
            printf ("%12d\t", array [a][b]);

        printf("\n"); /* Go to a new line */
    }

    return 0;
}
```

8.

```c
#include <stdio.h>
#include <stdlib.h>

int main(void)
{
    short random [1000];
    int a;
    int total = 0;

    for(a = 0 ; a < 1000; a++)
    {
        random [a] = rand();
        total += random [a];
    }

    printf("Average is %d\n", total / 1000);

    /* Now display the elements 10 at a time. */
    for(a = 0 ; a < 1000; a++)
    {
        printf("random [%4d] = %d\n", a, random [a]);

        if (a % 10 == 0 && a > 0)
        {
            printf("Press enter to continue, CTRL-C to quit.\n");
            getchar();
        }
    }

    return 0;
}
```

9. The following are two solutions.

Solution 1

```c
#include <stdio.h>

int main(void)
{
    int elements [10] = { 0, 1, 2, 3, 4, 5, 6, 7, 8, 9 };
    int idx;

    for(idx = 0 ; idx < 10; idx++)
        printf("elements [%d] = %d\n", idx, elements [idx]);

    return 0;
}
```

Solution 2

```c
#include <stdio.h>

int main(void)
{
    int elements [10];
    int idx;

    for(idx = 0 ; idx < 10; idx++)
        elements [idx] = idx;

    for(idx = 0 ; idx < 10; idx++)
        printf("elements [%d] = %d\n", idx, elements [idx]);

    return 0;
}
```

10.

```c
#include <stdio.h>

int main(void)
{
    int elements [10] = { 0, 1, 2, 3, 4, 5, 6, 7, 8, 9 };
    int new_array [10];
    int idx;

    for(idx = 0 ; idx < 10; idx++)
        new_array [idx] = elements [idx] + 10;

    for(idx = 0 ; idx < 10; idx++)
        printf("elements [%d] = %d\nnew_array[%d] = %d\n",
        idx, elements [idx], idx, new_array [idx]);

    return 0;
}
```

C

Day 8: Understanding Pointers

Quiz Answers

1. The address-of operator is the ampersand (&) sign.

2. The indirection operator * is used. When you precede the name of the pointer with *, it refers to the value pointed to.

3. A pointer is a variable that contains the address of another variable.

4. Indirection is the act of accessing the contents of a variable by using a pointer to the variable.

5. They are stored in sequential memory locations with lower array elements stored at lower addresses.

6. `&data[0]` and data.

7. One way is to pass the length of the array as a parameter to the function. The other is to have a special value in the array, such as `NULL`, signifying the array's end.

8. Assignment, indirection, address-of, incrementing, decrementing, and comparison.

9. Subtracting two pointers returns the number of elements in between. In this case, the answer is 1. The actual size of the elements in the array is irrelevant.

10. The answer is still 1.

11. Passing by value means the called function receives a copy of the argument variable. Passing by reference means the function receives the address of the argument variable. The difference is that passing by reference allows the function to modify the original value, whereas passing by value does not.

12. A type `void` pointer can point to any type of C data object. In other words, it's a generic pointer.

13. By using a `void` pointer, you can create a generic pointer that can point to any data object. The most common use of a `void` pointer is to declare function parameters that can handle different types of arguments.

14. A typecast provides information about the type of the data object that the `void` pointer is pointing to at the moment. You must cast a `void` pointer before dereferencing it.

Answers to Exercises

1. `char *char_ptr;`

2. The following declares a pointer to an `int` and then assigns the address of cost (`&cost`) to it:

   ```
   int *p_cost;
   p_cost = &cost;
   ```

3. Direct access: `cost = 100;`

   Indirect access: `*p_cost = 100;`

4. `printf ( " Pointer value : %p, points at value : %d\n", p_cost, *p_cost);`

5. `float *variable = &radius;`

6. The code is as follows:

   ```
   data[2] = 100;
   *(data+2) = 100;
   ```

7. The following code also contains the answer for exercise 8:

```c
#include <stdio.h>

#define MAX1 5
#define MAX2 8

int array1[MAX1] = { 1, 2, 3, 4, 5 };
int array2[MAX2] = { 1, 2, 3, 4, 5, 6, 7, 8 };
int total;

int sumarrays(int x1[], int len_x1, int x2[], int len_x2);

int main(void)
{
    total = sumarrays(array1, MAX1, array2, MAX2);
    printf("The total is %d\n", total);

    return 0;
}

int sumarrays(int x1[], int len_x1, int x2[], int len_x2)
{

    int total = 0, count = 0;

    for (count = 0; count < len_x1; count++)
        total += x1[count];

    for (count = 0; count < len_x2; count++)
        total += x2[count];

    return total;
}
```

8. Refer to the answer for exercise 7.

9. The following is just one possible answer:

```c
/* Exercise 8.9 */

#include <stdio.h>

#define SIZE 10

/* function prototypes */
void addarrays( int [], int []);

int main(void)
{
    int a[SIZE] = {1, 1, 1, 1, 1, 1, 1, 1, 1, 1};
    int b[SIZE] = {9, 8, 7, 6, 5, 4, 3, 2, 1, 0};
```

```
        addarrays(a, b);

        return 0;
    }

    void addarrays( int first[], int second[])
    {
        int total[SIZE];
        int ctr = 0;

        for (ctr = 0; ctr < SIZE; ctr ++ )
        {
            total[ctr] = first[ctr] + second[ctr];
            printf("%d + %d = %d\n", first[ctr], second[ctr], total[ctr]);
        }
    }
```

Day 9: Characters and Strings

Quiz Answers

1. The range of values of the ASCII character set is 0 to 255. The standard ASCII character set ranges from 0 to 127, and the extended character set ranges from 128 to 255. The extended part of the character set changes depending on language modes and other configuration settings.

2. As the character's ASCII code.

3. A string is a sequence of characters terminated by the null character.

4. A sequence of one or more characters enclosed in double quotation marks.

5. To hold the string's terminating null character.

6. As a sequence of ASCII character values corresponding to the quotation mark characters, followed by 0 (the ASCII code for the null character).

7.

    a. 97

    b. 65

    c. 57

    d. 32

8.

    a. I

    b. A space

    c. c

    d. Null character

    e. [character value 2]

9.

    a. 9 bytes. Actually, the variable is a pointer to a string and the string requires 9 bytes of memory—8 for the string and 1 for the null terminator.

    b. 9 bytes

    c. 1 byte

    d. 20 bytes

    e. 20 bytes

10.

    a. A

    b. a

    c. 0 (null character)

    d. This is beyond the end of the string. It could be any value.

    e. !

    f. This contains the address of the first element of the string.

Answers to Exercises

1.

```
char letter = '$';
```

2.

```
char array[18] = "Pointers are fun!";
```

3.

```
char *array = "Pointers are fun!";
```

4.

```
char *ptr;
ptr = malloc(81);
fgets(ptr,81,stdin);
```

5. The following is just one possible answer. A complete program is provided:

```
/* Exercise 9.5 */

#include <stdio.h>

#define SIZE 10

/* function prototypes */
void copyarrays( int [], int []);

int main(void)
{
    int ctr=0;
    int a[SIZE] = {1, 2, 3, 4, 5, 6, 7, 8, 9, 10};
    int b[SIZE];

    /* values before copy */
    for (ctr = 0; ctr < SIZE; ctr ++ )
    {
       printf( "a[%d] = %d, b[%d] = %d\n",
               ctr, a[ctr], ctr, b[ctr]);
    }

    copyarrays(a, b);

    /* values after copy */
    for (ctr = 0; ctr < SIZE; ctr ++ )
    {
       printf( "a[%d] = %d, b[%d] = %d\n",
               ctr, a[ctr], ctr, b[ctr]);
    }

    return 0;
}

void copyarrays( int orig[], int newone[])
{
    int ctr = 0;

    for (ctr = 0; ctr < SIZE; ctr ++ )
    {
        newone[ctr] = orig[ctr];
    }
}
```

6. The following is one of many possible answers:

```
/* Exercise 9.6 */

#include <stdio.h>
#include <string.h>
```

```
/* function prototypes */
char * compare_strings( char *, char *);

int main(void)
{
    char *a = "Hello";
    char *b = "World!";
    char *longer;

    longer = compare_strings(a, b);

    printf( "The longer string is: %s\n", longer );

    return 0;
}

char * compare_strings( char * first, char * second)
{
    int x, y;

    x = strlen(first);
    y = strlen(second);

    if( x > y)
       return(first);
    else
       return(second);
}
```

7. This exercise is on your own!

8. a_string is declared as an array of 10 characters, but it's initialized with a string larger than 10 characters. a_string needs to be larger.

9. If the intent of this line of code is to initialize a string, it is wrong. You should use either *quote or quote[100].

10. No. Nothing is wrong.

11. Yes. Although you can assign one pointer to another, you can't assign one array to another. You should change the assignment to a string-copying command, such as strcpy().

12. This exercise is on your own!

Day 10: Structures

Quiz Answers

1. The data items in an array must all be of the same type. A structure can contain items of different types.

2. The structure member operator is a period. It is used to access members of a structure.

3. `struct`

4. A structure tag is tied to a template of a structure and is not an actual variable. A structure instance is an allocated structure that can hold data.

5. These statements define a structure and declare an instance called `myaddress`. That instance is then initialized. The structure member `myaddress.name` is initialized to `"Bradley Jones"`, `myaddress.addr1` is initialized to `"RTSoftware"`, `myaddress.addr2` is initialized to `"P.O. Box 1213"`, `myaddress.city` is initialized to `"Carmel"`, `myaddress.state` is initialized to `"IN"`, and `myaddress.zip` is initialized to `"46032-1213"`.

6. The following statement changes `ptr` to point to the second array element:

   ```
   ptr++;
   ```

Answers to Exercises

1. The code is as follows:
   ```
   struct time
   {      int hours;
          int minutes;
          int seconds ;
   } ;
   ```

2. The code is as follows:
   ```
   struct data
   {     int value1;
         float value2, value3;
   } info;
   ```

3. The code is as follows:
   ```
   info.value1 = 100;
   ```

4. The code is as follows:
   ```
   struct data *ptr;
   ptr = &info;
   ```

5. The code is as follows:
```
ptr->value2 = 5.5;
(*ptr).value2 = 5.5;
```

6. The code is as follows:
```
struct data
{    char name [21]
};
```

7. The code is as follows:
```
typedef struct
{    char address1[31];
     char address2[31];
     char city[11];
     char state[3];
     char zip[11];
} RECORD;
```

8. The following uses the values from quiz question 5 for initialization:
```
RECORD myaddress = { ""RTSoftware",
                     "P.O. Box 1213",
                "Carmel", "IN", "46082-1213"};
```

9. This code fragment has two problems. The first problem is that the structure should contain a tag. The second problem is the way sign is initialized. The initialization values should be in braces. Here is the correct code:
```
struct zodiac
{    char zodiac_sign [21];
     int month ;
} sign = { "Leo", 8 } ;
```

10. The union declaration has only one problem. Only one variable in a union can be used at a time. This is also true during union initialization. Here is the correct initialization:
```
/* setting up a union */
union data{
    char a_word[4];
    long a_number;
} generic_variable = { "WOW" } ;
```

C

Day 11: Understanding Variable Scope

Quiz Answers

1. The scope of a variable refers the extent to which different parts of a program have access to the variable or where the program is visible.

2. A variable with local storage class is visible only in the function in which the variable is defined. A variable with external storage class is visible throughout the program.

3. Defining a variable within a function makes it local; defining a variable outside of any function makes it external.

4. Automatic (the default) or static. An automatic variable is created each time the function is called and is destroyed when the function ends. A static local variable persists and retains its value between calls to the function that contains it.

5. An automatic variable is initialized each time the function is called. A static variable is initialized only the first time the function is called.

6. False. When declaring register variables, you're making a request. There is no guarantee that the compiler will honor the request.

7. An uninitialized global variable is automatically initialized to 0; however, it is best to initialize variables explicitly.

8. An uninitialized local variable is not automatically initialized; it could contain any value. You should never use an uninitialized variable. Always initialize a variable before using it.

9. Because the variable count is local to the block, the printf() function no longer has access to a variable called count. The compiler will give you an error message.

10. If the value must be remembered, it should be declared as static. For example, if the variable is called vari, the declaration would be

    ```
    static int vari;
    ```

11. The extern keyword is used as a storage class modifier. It indicates that the variable has been declared somewhere else in the program.

12. The static keyword is used as a storage class modifier. It tells the compiler to retain the value of a variable or function for the duration of the program. Within a function, the variable keeps its value between function calls.

Answers to Exercises

1. `register int x = 0;`

2.

```
/* Exercise 11.2 */
#include <stdio.h>
void print_value (int x);
int main(void)
{
    int x = 999;

    printf("%d\n", x);
    print_value(x);

    return 0;
}

void print_value (int x)
{
    printf("%d\n", x);
}
```

3. Because you're declaring the variable var as global, you don't need to pass it as a parameter.

```
/* Exercise 11.3 */

#include <stdio.h>

void print_value (void);

int var = 99;

int main(void)
{
    print_value();

    return 0;
}

void print_value (void)
{
    printf("The value is %d.\n", var);
}
```

4. Yes, you need to pass the variable var in order to print it in a different function.

```
/* Exercise 11.4 */
#include <stdio.h>

void print_value (int x);

int main(void)
{
    int var = 99;

    print_value(var);

    return 0;
}

void print_value (int x)
{
    printf("The value is %d.\n", x);
}
```

5. Yes, a program can have a local and a global variable of the same name. In such cases, active local variables take precedence.

```
/* Exercise 11.5 */
#include <stdio.h>

void print_value (void);

int var = 99;

int main(void)
{
    int var = 77;
    printf ("Printing in function with local and global.\n");
    printf("The value of var is %d.\n", var);
    print_value();

    return 0;
}

void print_value (void)
{
    printf("The value is %d.\n", var);
}
```

6. There is only one problem with a_sample_function(). Variables can be declared at the beginning of any block, so the declarations of ctr1 and star are fine. The other variable, ctr2, is not declared at the beginning of the block. The way it is declared is legal for the C++ language, but not for C. The following is a complete program with the corrected function.

```
/* Exercise 11.6 */
#include <stdio.h>

void a_sample_function( void );

int main(void)
{
    a_sample_function();
    puts("");

    return 0;
}

void a_sample_function( void )
{
    int ctr1;

    for ( ctr1 = 0; ctr1 < 25; ctr1++ )
       printf( "*" );

    puts( "\nThis is a sample function" );
    {
       char star = '*';
       int ctr2;   /* This is the fix. */
       puts( "\nIt has a problem\n" );
       for ( ctr2 = 0; ctr2 < 25; ctr2++ )
       {
          printf( "%c", star);
       }
    }
}
```

7. This program actually works properly, but it could be better. First, there is no need to initialize the variable x to 1 because it is initialized to 0 in the for statement. Also, declaring the variable tally as static is pointless because static keywords have no effect within the main() function.

8. What is the value of star and dash? These two variables are never initialized. Because they are both local variables, each could contain any value. Note that although this program compiles without any error or warning messages, there is still a problem.

   A second issue should be mentioned. The variable ctr is declared as global, but is used only in print_function(). This isn't a good assignment. The program would be better if ctr were a local variable to the function print_function().

9. The program prints the following pattern forever:

   X==X==X==X==X==X==X==X==X==X==X==X==X==X==X==X==...

10. The program poses a problem because of the global scope of the variable `ctr`. Both `main()` and `print_letter2()` use `ctr` in loops at the same time. Because `print_letter2()` changes the value, the `for` loop in `main()` never completes. This could be fixed in a number of ways, but the best solution is to declare a local variable `ctr` in both `main()` and `print_letter2()`.

It also makes sense to move the two other global variables `letter1` and `letter2` into the functions that use them.

```
#include <stdio.h>

void print_letter2(void);

int main(void)
{
    char letter1 = 'X';
    int  ctr;

    for( ctr = 0; ctr < 10 ; ctr++ )
    {
        printf("%c", letter1);
        print_letter2();
    }
    puts ("");
    return 0;
}

void print_letter2(void)
{
    char letter2 = '=';
    int  ctr;          /* This variable is local */
                       /* it is different from the one in main() */

    for( ctr = 0; ctr < 2 ; ctr++ )
        printf("%c", letter2);
}
```

Day 12: Advanced Program Control

Quiz Answers

1. Never. (Unless using a `goto` statement makes code far more easy to understand.)

2. When a `break` statement is encountered, execution immediately exits the `for`, `do...while`, or `while` loop that contains the `break` statement. When a `continue` statement is encountered, the next iteration of the enclosing loop begins immediately.

3. An infinite loop executes forever. You create one by writing a for, do...while, or while loop with a test condition that is always TRUE.

4. Execution terminates when the program reaches the end of the main() function or the exit() function is called.

5. The expression in a switch statement can evaluate to a long, int, or char value.

6. The default statement is a case in a switch statement. When the expression in the switch statement evaluates to a value that doesn't have a matching case, control goes to the default case.

7. The exit() function causes the program to end. A value can be passed to the exit() function, which is returned to the operating system.

8. The system() function executes an operating system command.

Answers to Exercises

1. continue;

2. break;

3.
   ```
   system ("/bin/ls");
   ```

4. This sample is correct. You do not need a break statement after the 'N' case because the switch statement ends anyway.

5. You might think that the default case must go at the bottom of the switch statement but this isn't true. The default can be placed anywhere within the switch statement. The problem with this code is that there should be a break statement at the end of the default statement.

6. The code is as follows:
   ```
   if (choice == 1)
       printf("You answered 1");
   else if (choice == 2)
       printf("You answered 2");
   else
       printf("You did not choose 1 or 2");
   ```

7. The code is as follows:

   ```
   do {
       /* any C statements. */
   } while (1);
   ```

Day 13: Working with the Screen and Keyboard

Quiz Answers

1. A stream is a sequence of bytes. A C program uses streams for all input and output.

2.

   a. A printer is an output device.

   b. A keyboard is an input device.

   c. A modem is both an input and an output device.

   d. A monitor is an output device. (If it is a touch screen, it is both an input and an output device.)

   e. A disk drive can be both an input and an output device.

3. C compilers support three predefined streams: stdin (the keyboard), stdout (the screen), and stderr (the screen).

4.

   a. stdout.

   b. stdout.

   c. stdin.

   d. stdin.

   e. fprintf() can use any output steam. It could, for instance, use stdout or stderr.

5. Buffered input is sent to the program only when the user presses Enter. Unbuffered input is sent one character at a time as soon as each key is pressed.

6. You can "unget" only one character between reads. The EOF character cannot be put back into the input stream with ungetc().

7. With a newline character, which corresponds to the user pressing the Enter key.

8.

   a. Valid.

   b. Valid.

   c. Valid.

   d. Not valid. q is not a valid format specifier.

   e. Valid.

   f. Valid.

9. The main difference is that stderr is not buffered, whereas stdout is.

Answers to Exercises

1. `printf("Hello World");`

2.

```
fprintf(stdout, "Hello World");
puts("Hello World");
```

3. `fprintf (stderr, "Hello Standard Error");`

4. The code is as follows:

```
char buffer[31];
scanf("%30[^*]s"", buffer);
```

5. The code is as follows:

```
printf("Jack asked, \"What is a backslash\?\"\nJill said, \"It is
\'\\\'\");
```

6. No specific answer.

7. Hint: Use an array of 26 integers. To count each character, increment the appropriate array element for each character read.

Day 14: Pointers: Beyond the Basics

Quiz Answers

1. The code is as follows:

```
float x;
float *px = &x;
float **px = &psx;
```

2. The error is that it uses a single direction operator and, as a result, assigns a value of `100` to px instead of x. The statement should be written with a double indirection operator:

```
**ppx = 100;
```

3. `array` is an array with two elements. Each of these elements is itself an array that contains three elements. Each of these three elements is an array that contains four type `int` variables.

4. `array[0][0]` is a pointer to the first four-element array of type `int`.

5. The first and the third comparisons are true; the second is false.

6. `void func (char *p[]);`

7. It has no way of knowing. Usually when this kind of function is used, the array's end is marked with some kind of marker such as a `NULL` pointer.

8. A pointer to a function is a pointer that contains the address where the function is stored in memory.

9. `char *(ptr)(char *x[]);`

10. If you omit the parentheses around `*ptr`, the line is a prototype of a function that returns a pointer to type `char`.

11. Trick question! A `void` pointer can't be incremented because the compiler does not know the size of the object it is pointing to.

12. A function can return a pointer to any of the C variable types. A function can also return a pointer to such storage areas as arrays, structures, and unions.

13. The structure must contain a pointer to the same type of structure.

14. If the head pointer is equal to `NULL`, it means that the list is empty.

15. Each element in the list contains a pointer that identifies the next element in the list. The first element in the list is identified by the head pointer.

16.
   a. `var1` is a pointer to an integer.
   b. `var2` is an integer.
   c. `var3` is a pointer to a pointer to an integer.

17.
   a. `a` is an array of 36 (3 * 12) integers.
   b. `b` is a pointer to an array of 12 integers.
   c. `c` is an array of 12 pointers to integers.

18. What do the following declare?
   a. `z` is an array of 12 pointers to characters.
   b. `y` is a function that takes an integer as an argument and returns a pointer to a character.
   c. `x` is a pointer to a function that takes an integer as an argument and returns a character.

Answers to Exercises

1. `float (*func)(int field);`

2. `int (*option_menu [10])(char *title);`

   An array of pointers to function can be used in conjunction with a menuing system. The number selected from the menu could correspond to the array index for the function pointer array. For example, the function pointed to by the fifth element of the array would be executed if item 5 were selected from the menu.

3. `char *ptrs [10];`

4. Yes, `ptr` is declared as an array of 12 pointers to integers, not a pointer to an array of 12 integers. The correct code is

```
int x[3][12];
int (*ptr)[12];
ptr = x;
```

5. The following is one of many solutions:

```
struct friend
{
    char name [32];
    char address [64];
    struct friend *next;
};
```

8. `int function (char *ptr[]);`

9. Assuming that the return type is `void`, the prototype for the function `numbers()` is as follows:

```
void numbers (int *a, int *b, int *c);
```

10. To call the `numbers()` function in exercise 9, you must use the address-of operator as follows:

```
numbers (&int1, &int2, &int3);
```

11. Although this looks confusing, it is correct. This function takes the value being pointed to by `nbr` and multiplies it by itself.

12. When using variable argument lists, you should use all the macro tools. This includes `va_list`, `va_start()`, `va_arg()`, and `va_end()`. See Listing 17.5 for the correct use of variable parameter lists.

Day 15: Using Disk Files

Quiz Answers

1. Linux makes no distinction between text mode and binary files. Under Microsoft Windows, a text mode stream automatically performs translation between the newline character (`'\n'`) that C uses to mark the end of a line and the carriage return linefeed combination (`"\n\r"`) that Windows uses to mark the end of a line.

2. To make sure your program that reads binary data is portable to Windows, you must use a b character as part of the mode string agreement to the `fopen()` call.

3. Open the file using `fopen()`.

4. When using `fopen()`, you must specify the name of the file to open and the mode to open in it. The function `fopen()` returns a pointer to type `FILE`; this pointer is used in subsequent file access functions to refer to the specific file.

5. Formatted, character, and direct.

6. Sequential and random.

7. The value of `EOF` is a symbolic constant equal to `-1`, and it marks the end of the file.

8. For binary files, the end of the file can be detected by using the function `feof()`, whereas for text files, you can look for the `EOF` character or use `feof()`.

9. The file position indicator indicates the position in a given file where the next read or write operation will occur. You can modify the file position indicator with `rewind()` or `fseek()`.

10. When a file is first opened, the file position indicator points to the first character or offset 0. The one exception to this is when the file is opened in append mode, in which case the position indicator points to the end of the file.

Answers to Exercises

1. `fcloseall()`

2.
   ```
   rewind(fp);

   fseek(fp, 0, SEEK_SET);
   ```

3. That depends. If the file contains binary data, this code might not work as expected because the data in the file might contain the `EOF` character. It would be better to use the `feof()` function.

Day 16: Manipulating Strings

Quiz Answers

1. The length of a string is the number of characters between the start of the string and the terminating null character (not counting the null character). You can determine the length of a string by using the `strlen()` function.

2. Before copying a string, you must be sure to allocate sufficient storage space for the new string.

3. *Concatenate* means to join together. When talking about strings, it means to append one string to another.

4. When you compare strings, "greater than" means one string's ASCII values are larger than the other's ASCII values.

5. The function `strcmp()` compares two entire strings, whereas `strncmp()` compares only a specified number of characters within the string.

6. The function `strcmp()` compares two strings considering the case of the letters (that is, `'a'` and `'A'` are considered different characters). The `strcasecmp()` function performs a case insensitive comparison. (`'a'` and `'A'` are considered to be the same.)

7. The `isascii()` function tests a character to see whether it is in the range of 0 to 127.

8. The functions `isascii()` and `iscntrl()` would both return TRUE. All the others would return FALSE.

9. The value `65` is equivalent to the character `'A'`. The following macros return TRUE: `isalnum()`, `isalpha()`, `isascii()`, `isgraph()`, `isprint()`, and `isupper()`.

10. The character-test functions determine whether a particular character meets a certain condition, such as whether it is a letter, a punctuation mark, or something else.

Answers to Exercises

1. TRUE (1) or FALSE (0).

2.
    a. `65`

    b. `81`

    c. `-34`

    d. `0`

    e. `12`

    f. `0`

3.
    a. `65.000000`

    b. `81.230000`

    c. `-34.200000`

    d. `0.000000`

    e. `12.00000`

    f. `1000.0000`

4. Storage space for `string2` wasn't allocated before it was used. There is no way to know where `strcpy()` copies the value of `string1`.

Day 17: Exploring the C Function Library

Quiz Answers

1. Type `double`.

2. On most operating systems, including Linux, it's equivalent to type `long`.

3. The `time()` function returns the number of seconds that have elapsed since midnight, January 1, 1970. The `clock()` function returns the number of one millionths of a second that have elapsed since the program started.

4. Nothing, the `perror()` function simply displays a message that describes the error.

5. A function that takes a variable argument list must have at least one fixed argument. This is done to inform the function of the number of arguments being passed each time it is called.

6. `va_start()` should be used to initialize the argument list. `va_arg()` should be used to retrieve the arguments. `va_end()` should be used to clean up after all the arguments have been retrieved.

7. Before you search an array with `bsearch()`, you must sort the array into ascending order.

8. 14

9. 4

10. 21

11. `0` if the values are equal, `>0` if the value of element 1 is greater than element 2, and `<0` if element 1 is less than element 2.

12. `NULL`

Answers to Exercises

1. The code is as follows:
   ```
   bsearch(myname, names, (sizeof(names)/sizeof(names[0])),
                   sizeof(names[0]), comp_names);
   ```

2. There are three problems. First, the field width isn't provided in the cal to `qsort()`. Second, the parentheses shouldn't be added to the end of the function name `qsort()`. Third, the program is missing its comparison function. `qsort()` uses `compare_function()`, which isn't defined in the program.

3. The compare function returns the wrong values. It should return a positive value if `element1 > element2` and a negative number if `element1 < element2`.

Day 18: Working with Memory

Quiz Answers

1. The `malloc()` function allocates a specified number of bytes, whereas `calloc()` allocates sufficient memory for a specified number of items of a specified size. `calloc()` also sets the bytes of memory to 0, whereas `malloc()` doesn't initialize them to any specific value.

2. The most common reason for using a typecast with a numeric variable is to preserve the fractional part of the answer when dividing one integer by another and assigning the result to a floating-point variable.

3.
    a. `long`
    b. `int`
    c. `char`
    d. `float`
    e. `float`

4. Dynamically allocated memory is allocated at runtime—when the program is executing. Dynamically allocating memory allows you to allocate exactly as much memory as is needed, only when it is needed.

5. The `memmove()` function operates correctly when the source and destination memory locations overlap, whereas `memmove()` does not. If the source and destination regions don't overlap, the two functions are identical.

6. By defining a bit-field member with a size of 3 bits. Because 2^3 equals 8, such a field is sufficient to hold values 1 through 7.

7. 2 bytes. Using bit fields, you could declare a structure as follows:

```
struct date
{
    unsigned month : 4;
    unsigned day   : 5;
    unsigned year  : 7;
};
```

This structure stores the date in 2 bytes (16 bits). The 4-bit `month` field can hold values from 0 to 15, which is sufficient for holding 12 months. Likewise, the 5-bit `day` field can hold values from 0 to 31 and the 7-bit `year` field can hold values form 0 to 127. We assume that the year will be added to 1900 to allow year values from 1900 to 2027.

Although this structure works for the range of years from 1900 to 2027, it is not advisable to use this structure for any piece of software that has any possibility of being used for more than 20 years.

8. `16000`

9. `500`

10. These two expressions result in the same answer. Using exclusive `OR` with a binary value of `11111111` gives the same result as using the complement operator. Each bit in the original values is reversed.

Answers to Exercises

1. The code is as follows:

```
long *ptr;
ptr = malloc (1000 * sizeof(long));
```

2.

```
long *ptr;
ptr = calloc (1000, sizeof(long));
```

3. Using a loop and assignment statement:

```
int count;
for(count = 0 ; count < 1000; count++)
    data[count] = 0;
```

Using the `memset()` function:

```
memset(data, 0, 1000 * sizeof(float));
```

4. This code will compile and run without error; however, the results will be incorrect. Because both `number1` and `number2` are integers, the result of their divisions will be an integer; thus, any fractional part of the answer is lost. In order to get the correct answer, you must cast the expression to type `float`:

```
answer = (float) number1 / number2;
```

5. Because `p` is a type `void` pointer, it must be cast to the proper type before being used in an assignment statement. The third line should be as follows:

```
*(float*)p = 1.23;
```

6. No. When using bit fields, you must place them within a structure first. The following is correct:

```
struct quiz_answers {
unsigned answer1   : 1;
unsigned answer2   : 1;
unsigned answer3   : 1;
unsigned answer4   : 1;
unsigned answer5   : 1;
char student_name[15];
};
```

Day 19: Processes and Signals

Quiz Answers

1. A process ID is a unique number that the operating system uses to identify a running process.

2. The range of valid process IDs is 1 to 32767, inclusive.

3. The function getpid() returns the process ID of the process calling it, whereas getppid() returns the process ID of the parent process.

4. (a) The process ID of the forked child process

   (b) 0

5. A zombie process is a process that has terminated, but is still in the operating systems process table waiting for its parent process to retrieve its exit code.

6. The wait() function will always wait until a child process has terminated, whereas the waitpid() function can be told to return immediately if there are no zombie child processes.

7. After a successful call to execl(), the current process is replaced by the new program, so no more code in the program that called it is executed.

8. 1523

9. SIGSTOP and SIGKILL

Answers to Exercises

1. The following code works for commands without arguments.

```c
#include <stdio.h>
#include <stdlib.h>
#include <unistd.h>
#include <sys/wait.h>

int my_system(char *command);

int main (void)
{

    my_system ("/bin/ls");

    printf ("Done\n");

    return 0;
}

int my_system(char *command)
```

```
{
    pid_t    pid;
    int      status;

    pid = fork();
    if (pid == -1)
        return -1;
    if (pid == 0)
    {
        execl(command, command, NULL);
    }

    wait (&status);

    return status;
}
```

Day 20: Advanced Compiler Use

Quiz Answers

1. The term *modular programming* refers to the program development method that breaks a program into multiple source code files.

2. The main module is the module that contains the main() function.

3. To avoid unwanted side-effects by ensuring that complex expressions passed as arguments are fully evaluated first.

4. Compared to a function, a macro results in faster program execution but large program size.

5. The defined() operator tests to see whether a particular names is defined, returning TRUE if the name is defined and FALSE if it isn't.

6. A #if must be matched with a #endif.

7. #include copied the contents of the specified file into the current file.

8. A #include in double quotes asks the compiler to look in the current directory for the include file. A #include statement with the filename enclosed in <> asks the compiler to search in the standard directories.

9. __DATE__ is used to place the date on which the program was compiled into the program.

10. argv[0] points to a string containing the name of the current program.

Answers to Exercises

Because many solutions are possible for the exercises in Day 20, answers are not provided.

Day 21: An Introduction to GUI Programming with GTK+

Quiz Answers

1. To inform gcc of the location of the GTK+ header files, you should add `gtk-config —cflags` to the compile command.

2. To inform gcc of the location of the GTK+ header files, you should add `gtk-config —libs` to the compile command.

3. A callback function performs a specific set of actions specified by the programmer. It is set up to be called whenever one or more particular GUI events occur, such as the click of a button or the selection of an item from a menu.

Answers to Exercises

There is no single correct answer to the exercise questions. In fact, the exercises are too general to give even a single specific answer.

C

TYPE & RUN 1

Printing Your Listings

Throughout this book, you will find a number of Type & Run sections. These sections present a listing that is a little longer than the listings within the chapters. The purpose of these listings is to give you a program to type in and run. The listings might contain elements not yet explained in the book.

These programs will generally do something either fun or practical. For instance, the program included here is called Print_It. In addition to printing the source code, Print_It adds line numbers just like those included in this book. This program can be used to print your listings as you work through the rest of this book.

I suggest that after you type in and run these programs, you take the time to experiment with the code. Make changes, recompile, and then rerun the programs. See what happens. There won't be explanations on how the code works, only what it does. Don't fret, though. By the time you complete this book, you should understand everything within these earlier listings. In the meantime, you will have had the chance to enter and run some listings that are a little more fun or practical!

The First Type & Run

Enter and compile the following program. If you get any errors, make sure you entered the program correctly.

The usage for this program is print_it *filename.ext*, where *filename.ext* is the source filename along with the extension. Note that this program adds line numbers to the listing. (Don't let this program's length worry you; you're not expected to understand it yet. It's included here to help you compare printouts of your programs with the ones given in the book.)

LISTING T&R 1. print_it.c.

```
1: /* print_it.c—This program prints a listing with line numbers! */
2: #include <stdlib.h>
3: #include <stdio.h>
4:
5: void do_heading(char *filename);
6:
7: int line, page;
8:
9: int main( int argv, char *argc[] )
10: {
11:     char buffer[256];
12:     FILE *fp;
13:
14:     if( argv < 2 )
15:     {
16:         printf("\nProper Usage is: " );
17:         printf("\n\nPRINT_IT filename.ext\n" );
18:         exit(1);
19:     }
20:
21:     if (( fp = fopen( argc[1], "r" )) == NULL )
22:     {
23:         fprintf( stderr, "Error opening file, %s!", argc[1]);
24:         exit(1);
25:     }
26:
27:     page = 0;
28:     line = 1;
29:     do_heading( argc[1]);
30:
31:     while( fgets( buffer, 256, fp ) != NULL )
32:     {
33:         if( line % 55 == 0 )
34:             do_heading( argc[1] );
35:
```

```
36:          printf("%4d:\t%s", line++, buffer );
37:      }
38:
39:      printf("\f" );
40:      fclose(fp);
41:      return 0;
42: }
43:
44: void do_heading( char *filename )
45: {
46:      page++;
47:
48:      if ( page > 1 )
49:          printf("\f" );
50:
51:      printf("Page: %d, %s\n\n", page, filename );
52: }
```

Note

This listing prints out the given filename to the screen. It splits the file into pages and adds line numbers. Using Linux's redirection features, you should be able to redirect the output from the screen to the printer if you have one.

On Day 13, "Working with the Screen and Keyboard," you will learn more about how this program works.

TYPE & RUN 2

Find the Number

This is the second Type & Run section. Remember, the purpose of the listings in these sections is to give you something a little more functional than what you might be getting in the daily discussions. This listing contains elements not yet explained in the book; however, I believe you will find the listing easy to follow. After you type in and run this program, take the time to experiment with the code. Make changes, recompile, and then rerun the program to see what happens. If you get any errors, make sure you entered it correctly.

LISTING T&R 2. Find_nbr.c.

```c
1 : /* Name:      Find_nbr.c
2 : * Purpose:   This program picks a random number and then
3 : *            lets the user try to guess it
4 : * Returns:   Nothing
5 : */
6 :
7 : #include <stdio.h>
8 : #include <stdlib.h>
9 : #include <time.h>
10:
11: #define NO    0
12: #define YES   1
13:
14: int main( void )
15: {
16:     int guess_value = -1;
17:     int number;
18:     int nbr_of_guesses;
19:     int done = NO;
20:
21:     printf("\n\nGetting a Random number\n");
22:
23:     /* use the time to seed the random number generator */
24:     srand( (unsigned) time( NULL ) );
25:     number = rand();
26:
27:     nbr_of_guesses = 0;
28:     while ( done == NO )
29:     {
30:         printf("\nPick a number between 0 and %d> ", RAND_MAX);
31:         scanf( "%d", &guess_value );   /* Get a number */
32:
33:         nbr_of_guesses++;
34:
35:         if ( number == guess_value )
36:         {
37:             done = YES;
38:         }
39:         else
40:         if ( number < guess_value )
41:         {
42:             printf("\nYou guessed high!");
43:         }
44:         else
45:         {
46:             printf("\nYou guessed low!");
47:         }
48:     }
```

```
49:
50:     printf("\n\nCongratulations! You guessed right in %d Guesses!",
51:              nbr_of_guesses);
52:     printf("\n\nThe number was %d\n\n", number);
53:
54:     return 0;
55: }
```

This program is a simple guessing game. You're trying to find the number that the computer randomly generates. After each guess, the program will tell you if your guess was high or low. When you guess correctly, you will be congratulated and told how many guesses it took you.

If you want to cheat, you can add a line to the program that prints the answer after the program generates it. You might want to add this cheat into the program after you first compile it:

```
26:  printf( "The random number (answer) is: %d", number ); /* cheat */
```

This lets you see that the program works correctly. If you decide to give the running program to your friends, make sure to take the cheat line out!

TYPE & RUN 3

Secret Messages

This is the third Type & Run section. Remember, the purpose of the listings in the Type & Run sections is to give you something a little more functional than the sample code presented in the daily lessons. This listing contains many elements you have already learned. This includes using disk files from Day 15, "Using Disk Files."

The following program enables you to code or decode secret messages. When you run this program, you need to include two command-line parameters:

```
coder filename action
```

The `filename` is either the name of the file you are creating to hold the new secret message or the name of a file that contains a secret message to be decoded. The `action` is either D for decode a secret message or C for encode a secret message. If you run the program without passing any parameters, you are given instructions on how to enter the correct parameters.

Because the program codes and decodes, you can give a copy to your friends or associates. You can then code a secret message and send it to them. Using the same program, they will be able to decode it. People without the program won't know what the message in the file says!

```
1 : /* Program:  Coder.c
2 : * Usage:    Coder  [filename] [action]
3 : *              where filename = filename for/with coded data
4 : *              where action = D for decode anything else for
5 : *                             coding
6 : *—————————————————————————————————*/
7 :
8 : #include <stdio.h>
9 : #include <stdlib.h>
10: #include <string.h>
11:
12: int encode_character( int ch, int val );
13: int decode_character( int ch, int val );
14:
15: int main( int argc, char *argv[])
16: {
17:     FILE *fh;              /* file handle  */
18:     int rv = 1;           /* return value */
19:     int ch = 0;           /* variable to hold a character */
20:     unsigned int ctr = 0;  /* counter */
21:     int val = 5;          /* value to code with */
22:     char buffer[256];      /* buffer */
23:
24:     if( argc != 3 )
25:     {
26:        printf("\nError:  Wrong number of parameters..." );
27:        printf("\n\nUsage:\n  %s filename action", argv[0]);
28:        printf("\n\n   Where:");
29:        printf("\n         filename = name of file to code or decode");
30:        printf("\n         action   = D for decode or C for encode\n\n");
31:        rv = -1;          /* set return error value */
32:     }
33:     else
34:     if(( argv[2][0] == 'D') || (argv [2][0] == 'd' ))  /* to decode */
35:     {
36:        fh = fopen(argv[1], "r");   /* open the file   */
37:        if( fh <= 0 )               /* check for error */
38:        {
39:            printf( "\n\nError opening file..." );
40:            rv = -2;                /* set return error value */
41:        }
42:        else
43:        {
44:            ch = getc( fh );     /* get a character */
45:            while( !feof( fh ) )  /* check for end of file */
46:            {
47:               ch = decode_character( ch, val );
48:               putchar(ch);  /* write the character to screen */
```

```
49:                    ch = getc( fh);
50:                }
51:
52:                fclose(fh);
53:                printf( "\n\nFile decoded to screen.\n" );
54:            }
55:        }
56:    else   /* assume coding to file. */
57:        {
58:
59:            fh = fopen(argv[1], "w");
60:            if( fh <= 0 )
61:            {
62:                printf( "\n\nError creating file..." );
63:                rv = -3;   /* set return value */
64:            }
65:            else
66:            {
67:                printf("\n\nEnter text to be coded. ");
68:                printf("Enter a blank line to end.\n\n");
69:
70:                while( fgets(buffer, 256, stdin) != NULL )
71:                {
72:                    if( strlen (buffer) <= 1 )
73:                        break;
74:
75:                    for( ctr = 0; ctr < strlen(buffer); ctr++ )
76:                    {
77:                        ch = encode_character( buffer[ctr], val );
78:                        ch = fputc(ch, fh);     /* write the character to file */
79:                    }
80:                }
81:                printf( "\n\nFile encoded to file.\n" );
82:                fclose(fh);
83:            }
84:
85:        }
86:    return (rv);
87: }
88:
89: int encode_character( int ch, int val )
90: {
91:     ch = ch + val;
92:     return (ch);
93: }
94:
95: int decode_character( int ch, int val )
96: {
97:     ch = ch - val;
98:     return (ch);
99: }
```

Here is an example of a secret message:

```
Ymnx%nx%f%xjhwjy%rjxxflj&
```

Decoded, this message says:

```
This is a secret message!
```

This program codes and decodes the information by simply adding and subtracting a value from the characters being entered. This is a pretty easy code to crack. You can make it even harder to crack by replacing lines 91 and 97 with the following:

```
ch = ch ^ val;
```

Suffice it to say that the ^ is a binary math operator that modifies the character at the bit level. It will make your secret messages even more secret!

If you want to give the program to a number of different people, you might want to add a third parameter to the command line. This parameter would accept the value for val. The variable val stores the value to be used to encode or decode.

TYPE & RUN 4

Counting Characters

It's time for another Type & Run. This program, called count_ch, opens the specified text file and counts the number of times each character occurs in it. All the standard keyboard characters are counted, including uppercase and lowercase letters, numerals, spaces, and punctuation marks. The results are displayed onscreen. In addition to being a potentially useful program, count_ch illustrates some interesting programming techniques. You can use the operating system's redirection operator (>) to place the output in a file. For example, the command

```
count_ch > results.txt
```

runs the program and outputs the results to a file named results.txt, instead of displaying them onscreen. You can view the output in your text editor or print it.

LISTING T&R 4. count_ch.c: A program to count characters in a file.

```
 1: /* Counts the number of occurrences   */
 2: /* of each character in a file.        */
 3: #include <stdio.h>
 4: #include <stdlib.h>
 5:
 6: int file_exists(char *filename);
 7:
 8: int main(void)
 9: {
10:     char source[80];
11:     int  ch, index;
12:     int  count[127];
13:     FILE *fp;
14:
15:     /* Get the source and destination filenames. */
16:     fprintf(stderr, "\nEnter source file name: ");
17:     fscanf(stdin, "%80s", source);
18:
19:     /* See that the source file exists. */
20:     if (!file_exists(source))
21:     {
22:         fprintf(stderr, "\n%s does not exist.\n", source);
23:         exit(1);
24:     }
25:     /* Open the file. */
26:     if ((fp = fopen(source, "rb")) == NULL)
27:     {
28:         fprintf(stderr, "\nError opening %s.\n", source);
29:         exit(1);
30:     }
31:     /* Zero the array elements. */
32:     for (index = 31; index < 127 ; index++)
33:         count[index] = 0;
34:
35:     while ( 1 )
36:     {
37:         ch = fgetc(fp);
38:         /* Done if end of file */
39:         if (feof(fp))
40:             break;
41:         /* Count only characters between 32 and 126. */
42:     if (ch > 31 && ch < 127)
43:             count[ch]++;
44:     }
45:
46:     /* Display the results. */
47:     printf("\nChar\tCount\n");
48:     for (index = 32; index < 127 ; index++)
```

```
49:          printf("[%c]\t%d\n", index, count[index]);
50:     /* Close the file and exit. */
51:     fclose(fp);
52:     return(0);
53: }
54:
55: int file_exists(char *filename)
56: {
57:     /* Returns TRUE if filename exists,
58:      * FALSE if not.
59:      */
60:     FILE *fp;
61:     if ((fp = fopen(filename, "r")) == NULL)
62:         return 0;
63:     else
64:     {
65:         fclose(fp);
66:         return 1;
67:     }
68: }
```

ANALYSIS Look first at the function `file_exists()` on lines 51–63. Passed a filename as its argument, this function returns TRUE if the file exists and FALSE if it doesn't. Code in the function checks for the file by trying to open it in read mode (line 56). This is a general-purpose function that you can use in other programs.

Next, note how screen messages are displayed with the `fprintf()` function rather than `printf()`, as in line 14, for example. Why is this? Because `printf()` always sends output to stdout, the user won't see any messages if the redirection operator is used to direct program output to a disk file. Using `fprintf()` forces the messages to stderr, which is always the screen.

Finally, observe how the numerical value of each character is used as an index to the results array (lines 40 and 41). For example, the numerical value 32 represents a space, so the array element `count[32]` is used to keep a total of spaces.

TYPE & RUN 5

Calculating Mortgage Payments

This Type & Run is called mortgage, and as the name suggests, it can calculate the payments on a mortgage or any other type of loan. When you run this program, it prompts you for the following three pieces of information:

- Amount: How much you're borrowing (also called the principal).

- Annual interest rate: The amount of interest charged per year. You need to enter the actual rate, so for 8 1/2% you enter 8.5. Do not adjust for the actual numerical value (0.085 in this case) because the program does this for you.

- The loan duration, or term, in months: This is the number of months over which you will be paying off the loan.

After you type in and run this program, you'll be able to calculate payments on mortgages and other types of loans.

LISTING T&R 5. The mortgage calculator.

```c
1 : /* mortgage.c - Calculates loan/mortgage payments. */
2 :
3 : #include <stdio.h>
4 : #include <math.h>
5 : #include <stdlib.h>
6 :
7 : int main(void)
8 : {
9 :     float principal, rate, payment;
10:     int term;
11:     char ch;
12:
13:     while (1)
14:     {
15:       /* Get loan data */
16:       puts("\nEnter the loan amount: ");
17:       scanf("%f", &principal);
18:       puts("\nEnter the annual interest rate: ");
19:       scanf("%f", &rate);
20:       /* Adjust for percent. */
21:       rate /= 100;
22:       /* Adjust for monthly interest rate. */
23:       rate /= 12;
24:
25:       puts("\nEnter the loan duration in months: ");
26:       scanf("%d", &term);
27:       payment = (principal * rate) / (1 - pow((1 + rate), -term));
28:       printf("Your monthly payment will be $%.2f.\n", payment);
29:
30:       puts("Do another (y or n)?");
31:       do
32:       {
33:       ch = getchar();
34:       } while (ch != 'n' && ch != 'y');
35:
36:       if (ch == 'n')
37:           break;
38:     }
39:     return(0);
40: }
```

Note To compile this program correctly, you will need to inform the gcc compiler to include the maths library so that it can find the function pow(). To do this, you could use a compile command like the following:

```
gcc -Wall -ggdb calc.c -lm -o calc
```

 This program assumes a standard loan, such as a typical fixed-rate car or home loan. The payment is calculated using the following standard financial formula:

$payment = (P * R) / (1 - (1 + R)^{(-T)})$

P is the principal, R is the interest rate, and T is the term. Note that the ^ symbol means "to the power of." In this formula, it is essential that the term and the rate be expressed in the same time units. Thus, if the loan term is expressed in months, the interest rate must be in months also. Because loans typically have rates expressed as annual rates, line 23 divides the annual rate by 12 to obtain the monthly interest rate. The actual payment calculation is performed on line 27, and line 28 displays the answer.

INDEX

Symbols

! (NOT operator), 76
!= (not equal to operator),
67
" " (quotation marks),
format strings, 138
(stringizing operator),
564
    code example, 565
(concatenation
operator), 565
#define directive, 47, 166
    constants, 47
    declaring arrays, 163
    symbolic character
        constants, 218
#define preprocessor
    directive, 562
    function macros,
        563-565
    symbolic constants, 562
#elif preprocessor
    directive, 568

#else preprocessor
    directive, 568
#endif preprocessor
    directive
    conditional compilation,
        568-569
    conditional debugging,
        569-570
#if preprocessor directive
    conditional compilation,
        568-569
    conditional debugging,
        569-570
#include directive, 29
#include preprocessor
    directive, 567
#undef preprocessor
    directive, conditional
    debugging, 571
% (modulus operator), 62
% (percent sign)
    conversion specifiers, 139
%d conversion specifier,
    142, 537

%f conversion specifier,
    143
%s conversion specifier,
    228
%u conversion specifier,
    142
& (address-of) operator,
    148, 352, 527, 538
    initializing pointers, 188,
        214
    on command line, 539
&& (AND operator), 76
( ) (parentheses), 89, 104
    function operator, 83
    operator precedence,
        65-66
* (asterisk) operator, 352
    passing arguments by
        reference, 208
    pointers, 187-189, 214
* (multiplication
    operator), 46, 62
** (double indirection)
    operator, 352, 255

+ (addition operator), 62
++ (increment operator), 60-62, 260
, (comma) operator, 119, 122
- (subtraction operator), 60-62
-< (indirect membership operator), 258
. (dot operator), unions, 241, 252, 265
... (ellipses), function prototypes, 421
/ (division operator), 62
//comment slashes, 32
= (assignment operator), 60
   initializing variables, 43
== (equals operator), 67
> (greater than operator), 67, 344
>= (greater than or equal to operator), 67
>> operator, 525, 344
< (less than operator), 67
<= (less than or equal to operator), 67
[ ] (square brackets) , 83, 159
\ (line continuation character, 138, 595
\t tab escape character, 142
^ (exclusive OR) operator, 527
__DATE__ predefined macro, 571
__FILE__ predefined macro, 571
__LINE__ predefined macro, 571

__TIME__ predefined macro, 571
{ } (braces), 33, 90-91, 98
   arrays, 261
   compound statements, 57
   initializing multi-dimensional arrays, 167
| (inclusive OR) operator, 527
   redirecting input/output, 346
|| (OR operator), 76

A

abs function, 483
accelerators, keyboard, 614-615
accessing
   array elements (pointers), 193-195
   bit fields, 529
   disk files
      fseek function, 434-437
      ftell function, 432-434
      random file access, 432-437
      rewind function, 432-434
      sequential file access, 431-432, 447
share libraries, 585-586
   structure members, 241
   structure pointers, 258-259
   union members, 265-266
acos function, 482

adding
   elements to linked lists, 386-387, 392
   links to linked lists, 397-400
addition operator (+), 62
address-of operator (&), 148, 352
   initializing pointers, 188, 214
addresses
   array elements, displaying
      code listing, 194-195
      pointers, 193-195
   memory, 186
      pointer constant address values, 214
      pointers, 187
   RAM, 36
   structures, passing as function arguments, 263
add_to_list function, 398
alarm function (SIGALRM signal), 550
algorithms, 500
allocating memory
   calloc function, 516-517
   characters
      malloc function, 224
   checking, 521
   dynamic memory allocation, 515, 530
   free function, 453, 519-521
   free memory, 530
   malloc function, 453, 516
   memory availability, 515-516

overestimating issues, 517
realloc function, 518-519, 531
static memory allocation, 515
strcpy function, 453
strdup function, 456
strings, 221, 361, 368
  compilation allocation, 222
  dynamic memory allocation, 222-227, 234
  malloc function, 222-227, 234
  overwriting issues, 227
alpha function, 379
American National Standards Institute (ANSI), 9, 314
American Standard Code for Information Interchange. *See* ASCII
ampersand (&) symbol, 538
  initializing pointers, 188, 214
  on command line, 539
AND operator (&&), 76, 527
ANSI (American National Standards Institute), 9, 314
ANSI C Standard, 314
ANSI/ISO compatibility, functions, 477
applications. *See also* **programs**
  external variable scope, 276
  servers, 542

argc parameter, command-line arguments, 572
arguments, 28. *See also* **variables**
  bsearch function, 499
    comparison functions, 499-500
  command argument, system function, 311
  command-line, 572
    argc parameter, 572
    argv[] parameter, 573
    getopt function, 574-576
    main function, 572-573, 587
    optional, 574
    required, 574
  comparing to parameters, 97
  double quotation mards, 138
  execl function, 549
  fopen function, 417-418
  fprintf function, 421
  fscanf function, 423
  functions, 89-90
    passing structures, 262-263
    writing, 96-98
  passing
    to functions, 104-105, 215
    to parameters, 97
  pointers, 375-376
    passing by reference, 206-210
    passing by value, 206-210
    passing to functions, 215

printf function, 145
  format strings, 338-340
scanf function, 151, 326-329
variable-argument functions
  argument data types, 496
  code example, 497-499
  declaring, 496
  process, 497
  setting number of arguments, 496
  stdarg.h header file, 496-497
argv[] parameter (command-line arguments), 573
arithmetic expressions, typecasting, 513-514
arrays, 157
  { } (braces), 261
  binary search algorithm, 500
  calculating storage space, 171-172
  cautions, 114
  character, 220, 234
    initializing, 220-221
    overwriting issues, 234
    pointers, 221
  checkerboard, 162
  declarations, 159
  declaring, 163, 165
  elements, 114, 157
    addresses, displaying, 194-195
    numbering, 158
    storing, 158

in for statements, 114
indexing, 368
initializing, 166
lines[], 369
maximum size, 170-172
multidimensional, 162,
   353-354
  cautions, 166
  dimensions, 358
  initializing, 167
  integers, 356
  names, 355
  passing to functions,
    358-361
  relationship with
    pointers, 355-356
naming, 163-165
pointers, 192, 353, 361
  array element storage,
    193-195
  array names, 192-193
  comparisons, 199
  declaraing, 362-365
  decrementing, 196
  differencing, 198
  incrementing, 196
  operations, 199-200
  passing arrays to
    functions, 201-206
  pointer arithmetic,
    196-198
  pointer constants, 198
  strings, 361
quick sort algorithm, 500
shifting elements,
  365-369
single-dimensional,
  158-162
structure members,
  246-248
structures, 248-252
  copying content, 250
  declaring, 249

initializing, 253-254
  pointers, 259-262
subscripts, 114, 158
  out-of-range, 159
  pointers comparison,
    201
  versus variables, 162
ASCII (American
Standard Code for
Information
Interchange), 12, 218
  character set, 218, 630
  comparing strings, 460
  source code files, 12
asctime function, 487, 491
asin function, 482
asm keyword, 634
assert function
  code example, 492-493
  definition, 491
  NDEBUG macro, 493
  use, 491
assigning structures (C
compilers), 271
assignment operators (=),
60
  compound, 80
  initializing variables, 43
  type conversions, 513
assignment statements
  cautions, 76
  operator precedence,
    64-65
assignment suppression
flag, 327
asterisk (*) symbol
  passing arguments by
    reference, 208
  pointers, 187-189, 214
asynchronous events, pro-
gramming GUIs, 594-595

asynchronous signals, 549
atan function, 482
atan2 function, 482
atof function, 470-471
atoi function, 469-470
atol function, 470
auto keyword, 634
automatic variables
  compared to static
    variables, 281
  keeping value between
    calls, 281
  local, 279, 282

B

backslash (\), line
continuation character,
138, 595
bash command
interpreter, 537
  replacing one process
    with another, 547-549
binary files, 447
binary operators, 62, 64
  type promotion, 512
binary search algorithm,
500
binary trees, 382. *See also*
linked lists
binary-mode files, direct
file I/O, 426
bits, 524
  bit fields, 528
    accessing, 529
    naming, 529
    structures, 528-531
  bitwise operators, 524,
    527
    complement
      operators, 528

logical operators, 526-528, 531

shift operators, 525-526, 531

blocks, 57

if statements, 68

memory

buffers, 522

manipulating, 522-524

memcyp function, 522-524, 531

memovefunction, 522-524, 531

memset function, 522-524, 531

BLOCKSIZE constant, 521

body of functions, 90-91

writing, 98, 100-103

boolean operators. *See* **logical operators**

braces { }, 33, 90-91, 98

arrays, 261

compound statements, 57

initializing multidimen-sional arrays, 167

branching statements

goto, 296-298

cautions, 297, 313

code listing, 296-297

label statements, 296-298

break keyword, 634

break statements, 292-294

switch statements, 303-308

breaking lines (literal string constants), 57

bsearch function, 499-500, 507

arguments, 499

code example (using strings), 504-506

code example (using values), 501-504

comparison functions, 499-500

buffered character input functions, 321

buffers

file streams, 430-431

memory, 522

bugs, 92, 487

busy-wait loops (sleep function comparison), 302

button_func function, 600-601, 605

C

C compilers

assigning structures, 271

#include directive, 29

pointers, 356

whitespace, 56

C extensions, 12

C language, 8

ANSI Standard C, 9, 314

C++ comparison, 8-9

flexibility, 8

history, 9

ISO standard, 9

Java comparison, 9

kernel (Linux), 8

keywords, 8

modularity, 8

name, 9

popularity, 8

portability, 8

preprocessor, 561-562

reserved keywords, 633-635

Ritchie, Dennis, 9

C++ language, reserved keywords, 635

calculating

time differences, 488

time durations, 489

callback functions

menus, 614

widgets (GUIs), 595

calling

fork function, 541

functions, 31, 90, 105-106

pointers to different functions, 374-379

pointers to functions, 370

recursion, 106-108

sigaction, 553

syntax, 91-92

waitpid, 546

signal handlers, 550

calloc function, 386, 516-517

camel notation, 38

case

characters

converting, 475

tolower function, 475-476

toupper function, 475-476

sensitivity, 17, 38

code example, 464-465

comparing strings, 463

strchr function, 464

case keyword, 634

case statements, switch statements, 309-310

casts. *See* **typecasting**

ceil function, 483

char keyword, 634
char pointers, 362-363
char type, 217-218
 bit fields, 528
 character I/O, 424-426
 fgets function, 425-426
 fputs function, 426
 getc/fgetc functions, 425
 putc function, 426
 structure member
  pointers, 255-256
**character input functions,
 321**
 buffered, 321
 echoing, 321
 fgetc function, 323-324
 fgets function, 324-326
 getc function, 323-324
 getchar function,
  322-323
 gets function, 324
 line-input functions,
  324-326
 unbuffered character
  input functions, 321
 ungetc function, 324
character output functions
 fputc function, 336
 putc function, 336
 putchar function,
  335-336
**character test functions,
 471**
 code example, 472-475
characters, 217. *See also*
 strings
 arrays, 220, 234
  initializing, 220-221
  overwriting issues,
   234
  pointers, 221
 ASCII character set, 218

case conversion, 475
 tolower function,
  475-476
 toupper function,
  475-476
char data type, 217-218
constants, 218
displaying, 227
 printf function,
  228-229
 puts function,
  227-228
line continuation (\), 595
memory allocation,
 malloc function, 224
variables, 218-220
checkerboard array, 162
**checking memory
 allocation, 521**
child processes, 536
 fork function, 540-541
 SIGCHLD signal, 550,
  554-557
 terminating, 543
 wait function, 543-544
 zombie, 543
**cleaning up zombie child
 processes, 543**
clients (X), 592
clock function, 489, 491
clocks (internal), 486
closing disk files, 430, 447
 stream buffers, 430-431
code
 listings
  arguments compared
   with parameters, 97
  declaring an external
   variable, 278
  defining local
   variables within a
   program block, 285

determining size of
 elements, 356
displaying numerical
 values with printf
 function, 144
do...while loops,
 129-130
execl function,
 replacing running
 processes, 548
expenses.c, 160-161
for statements,
 116-117
functions returning
 pointers, 381
grades.c, 164-165
if statement with else
 clause, 71
if statements, 69
implementing linked
 lists, 392
initializing an array of
 pointers to type
 char, 363
linked lists, 390
list_it.c, 34-35
local variables, 99
logical operator
 precedence, 79
multidimensional
 arrays (random.c),
 167-169
multidimensional
 arrays and pointers,
 355-356
multidimensional
 arrays, passing to
 functions, 358
multiple return state-
 ments in a function,
 101-102
multiply.c, 28-29

nested for statements, 121

nested while statements, 126-127

passing arrays of pointers to functions, 364

passing pointers to functions as arguments, 375

pointer arithmetic, multidimensional arrays, 357

pointers to functions, 372

pointers to functions to call different functions, 373

pointers to functions to control sort order, 377

preventing zombie processes, 543-545

printf function escap sequences, 140-141

process IDs, retrieving, 537

processes, creating with fork function, 540

programs, running in background, 538

reading numerical values with scanf function, 148-151

recursive functions, 107

relational expressions, 74

SIGCHLD signal, preventing zombie child processes, 555-556

signal handling, 552

sizeof operator, 171

sizeof.c, 39-40

smodulus operator, 62-63

sorting array elements (example program), 366

static versus automatic variables, 280

user-defined function, 88-89

using variables & constants, 48-49

variable scope, 274

variables (inaccessible), 275

while statement, 123-124

logical operators, 77

spaghetti code, 297, 313

whitespace, 56

comma (,) operator, 81, 119, 122

command argument (system function), 311

command interpreters, 537

command lines

& symbol, 539

command-line arguments, 572

argc parameter, 572

argv[] parameter, 573

getopt function, 574-576

getopt function code example, 575

main function, 572, 587

main function code example, 573

optional, 574

required, 574

commands

case-sensitivity, 17

conversion (printf function), 338

displaying processes, 536

gnome-help-browser, 17

gtk-config, 593-595

info, 16

kdehelp, 17

operating system commands, 311-314

comments, 31

C++ and Java, 32

including program name, 161

Makefiles, 583

nested, 31

comp function, 506

compare function, 379, 382

comparing

pointers, 199

strings, 460

case-sensitivity, 463

entire strings, 460-462

partial strings, 462-463

return values, 462

strcasecmp function, 463

strcmp function, 460-462

strncmp function, 462-463

compatibility (text editors), 23

compilation errors, 15

Hello World program, 20-21

compilers, 14
* (asterisk), 214
automatic type
  conversions, 512
compilation errors, 15
  Hello World program,
  20-21
differences in compiling
  code, 164
function standards, 313
gcc
  checking installation
    status, 14
  running, 14-15
nested comments, 32
predefined macros,
  571-572
typecasting arithmetic
  expressions, 513
variable name length, 38
warning messages, 15,
  24
compiling
conditional compilation
  defined operator,
    569-570
  preprocessor
    directives, 568
hello.c, 19
make utilities, 582
multiple files, filenames,
  587
multiply.c, 33
source code, 15
**complement operators,
  528**
complex expressions, 58-59
**compound assignment
  operators, 80**
compound statements, 57

**concatenating strings,
  457-460**
strcat function, 457-458
  trailing spaces, 477
strncat function, 458-460
condition expression, 115
conditional compilation
defined operator,
  569-570
preprocessor directives,
  568
conditional operator, 81
conditions, 119
OR, 264
const keyword, 49, 634
declaring arrays, 163
defining symbolic
  constants, 47
symbolic character
  constants, 218
constants, 36
BLOCKSIZE, 521
decimal, 46
without decimal points,
  45
floating-point, 45
hexadecimal, 46
literal, 45, 58, 218
literal string
  breaking lines, 57
  whitespace, 56
octal, 46
pointer constants, 198
symbolic, 46
  #define directive, 47
  #define preprocessor
    directive, 562
  characters, 218
  defining, 47
  defining with const
    keyword, 47, 49
  errno.h header file,
    493-494

**constructing menu bars
  (GTK+), 613-615**
continue keyword, 634
**continue statement,
  294-295**
**conversion characters
  (fprintf/printf functions),
  338-339**
**conversion commands
  (printf function), 338**
**conversion specifications,
  139**
printf function, 142
scanf function, 148,
  327-329
  assignment
    suppression flag,
    327
  field width, 327
  precision modifiers,
    327-329
  type specifiers, 328
specifiers
  %d, 142
  %f, 143
  %s (printf function),
    228
  %u, 142
  arguments, 145
  list of, 143
strftime function, 488
converting
characters
  case, 475
  tolower function,
    475-476
  toupper function,
    475-476
numbers to strings, 477
strings
  atof function, 470-471
  atoi function, 469-470

atol function, 470
numeric variables,
469-471
time representation
styles, 486-487
copying
files, 442-444
strings, 453-457
strcpy function,
453-454
strdup function,
456-457
strncpy function,
455-456
structures, arrays, 250
copy_file function, 443-444
core dump files, 549
cos function, 482
cosh function, 483
creating
compound assignment
operators, 80
cord dump files, 549
functions that return
pointers, 380
null statements, 57
processes (fork function),
540
ctime function, 487

D

data
arrays, 157
isolation, 276
linked lists, 382-383
adding elements,
384-387, 392
adding links, 397-400

deleting elements,
388-389, 400
displaying, 398
implementing, 392,
397-399
modifying, 384
reassigning head
pointers, 385
sample program,
389-392
storing, 36
registers, 283
validating math
functions, 507
data types, 512. *See also*
type conversions
arguments (variable-
argument functions),
496
arrays, 157
size of, 170
char, 217-218
bit fields, 528
structure member
pointers, 255-256
double
atof function, 470-471
math functions, 481,
507
type promotion, 512
float, type promotion,
512
GtkWidget, 597
int (atoi function),
469-470
long (atol function), 470
pointers, 191-192
void, 210-213
structures, 240
**__DATE__ predefined
macro, 571**

ddd debugger, 16
hello2.c debugging
example, 22-23
running, 22
setup, 21
debugging, 16, 92
conditional debugging,
569-570
ddd debugger, 16
hello2.c debugging
example, 22-23
running, 22
setup, 21
goto statements, 313
GUI programs, 595
hello2.c debugging
example, 22-23
source code, 15-16,
21-23
decimal integers, 45
reading with scanf
function, 147
declaring
arrays, 159, 163-165
cautiosn, 114
initializing, 166
of pointers, 362-365
character variables,
218-220
external variables, 277
function parameters
(void type pointers),
210
multidimensional arrays,
354
pointers, 187-188, 352,
386
to functions, 371
to multidimensional
array elements, 358
to pointers, 352
structures, 257-258

structures, 240-241
  arrays, 249
  instances, 270
  struct keyword,
    242-243
  synonyms
    (structure/union),
    269-270
  unions, 264-269
  variable-argument
    functions, 496
  variables, 42, 63
decrement operators, 60
decrementing
  counter variables, 118
  pointers, 196
    code example,
      197-198
    pointer constants, 198
default keyword, 634
#define directive, 47, 166
  constants, 47
  declaring arrays, 163
  symbolic character
    constants, 218
#define preprocessor
  directive, 562
  function macros,
    563-565
  symbolic constants, 562
defined operator,
  conditional compilation,
  569-570
defining
  function macros,
    563-564
    # (stringizing
      operator), 564-565
    ## (concatenation
      operator), 565
  functions, 88-92
  linked list data structure,
    384

structures, 240-241
symbolic constants, 47
synonyms
  (structure/union),
  269-270
unions, 264-269
variables, 29, 286
  static keyword, 282
degrees (trigonometric
  functions), 482
delay function, infinite
  loops, 301
deleting
  elements from linked
    lists, 388-389
  files, 440-441
  links from linked lists,
    400
demo() function, 99
dependencies (Makefiles),
  581-584
dereferencing pointers,
  188, 211
destroy_func function,
  598-600
detecting EOF, 437-439
determining string length,
  451-453
developing programs
  (ASCII format), 12
  compiling source code,
    15
  debugging source code,
    15-16, 21-22
  development tools, 12
  Hello World, 18-19
  IDEs (Integrated
    Development
    Environments), 12
  make utility, 16
  Program Development
    Cycle, 10-12

text editors, 12-13, 23
writing source code, 12
devices
  independence, 319
  input/output, 318
differencing pointers, 198
difftime function, 488, 491
dimensions (multidimen-
  sional arrays), 354
direct access (variables),
  189
direct file I/O, 426-429
  fread function, 428-430
  fwrite function, 427-430
directives
  #define, 163, 166, 562
    function macros,
      563-565
    symbolic character
      constants, 218
    symbolic constants,
      562
  #elif, 568
  #else, 568
  #endif
    conditional
      compilation,
      568-569
    conditional
      debugging, 569-570
  #if
    conditional
      compilation,
      568-569
    conditional
      debugging, 569-570
  #include, 29, 567
  #undef, 571
  preprocessor, 561
    header files, 570
disk drives, file stream
  buffers, 430

disk files
  character I/O, 424-426
    fgets function,
      425-426
    fputs function, 426
    getc/fgetc functions,
      425
    putc function, 426
  closing, 430, 447
  copying, 442-444
  deleting, 440-441
  direct file I/O, 426-429
    fread function,
      428-430
    fwrite function,
      427-430
  EOF, 437-439
  file management,
    440-444
  filenames, 416
  formatted file input,
    423-424
  formatted file output,
    421-423
  opening (open file
    limitations), 447
  random file access,
    432-437
    fseek function,
      434-437
    ftell function,
      432-434
    rewind function,
      432-434
  reading beyond EOF, 447
  reading/writing, 420
  renaming, 441-442
  sequential file access,
    431-432, 447
  stream buffers, 430-431

  streams, 415
    direct file I/O, fread
      function, 430
    file types, 416
    opening, 416-420
    temporary files, 445-446
displaying
  array element addresses,
    194-195
  linked list data, 398
  processes, 536
  strings, 227
    onscreen
      (print_strings
      function), 370
    printf function,
      228-229
    puts function,
      227-228
  time, 487
  values of program
    variables, 138
  variables
    printf function, 143
    size in bytes, 39
division operator (/), 62
do keyword, 634
**do...while loops, 128-132,
  292.** *See also* **loops**
  break statement, 292
  continue statement, 294
  listing, 129-130
  statements, 129
  structure, 128
documentation
  gnome-help-browser
    command, 17
  GTK+, 619
  info command, 16
  kdehelp command, 17
dot operator (.), 241, 252
  unions, 265

**double indirection (**)
  operator, 352**
double keyword, 634
**double quotation marks
  (""), 138**
double type
  atof function, 470-471
  math functions, 481, 507
  type promotion, 512
double-linked lists, 382.
  See also **linked lists**
draw_box function, 121
**dynamic memory
  allocation, 515, 530**
  strings, 222-227, 234
**dynamically linked
  libraries.** *See* **shared
  libraries**

E

**echoing (character input
  functions), 321**
editors (text)
  compatibility, 23
  GTK+ program, 608-619
  Linux, 12-13
  source code, 12-13
elements
  arrays
    numbering, 160
    pointers, 193-195
    shifting, 365-369
  linked lists, 384
    adding, 386-387, 392
    deleting, 388-389,
      400
  size, 356
**#elif preprocessor
  directive, 568**

#else preprocessor directive, 568
ellipses (...), function prototypes, 421
else clauses, 71-72
else keyword, 634
end-of-file. *See* EOF
#endif preprocessor directive
    conditional compilation, 568-569
    conditional debugging, 569-570
enum keyword, 634
EOF (end-of-file), 437
    detecting, 437-439
    fgets function, 425
    reading beyond, 447
equals operator (==), 67
equivalence streams, 320-321
errno variable, 493-495
errno.h header file
    errno variable, 493-495
    macros, 493
    symbolic constants, 493-494
error-handling functions, 491-496
    assert
        code example, 492-493
        definition, 491
        NDEBUG macro, 493
        use, 491
    errno.h header file
        errno variable, 493-495
        macros, 493
        symbolic constants, 493-494
    perror, 494-496

errors, 491
    compilation, 15, 20
        Hello World program, 20-21
        warning messages, 15, 24
    fgets function, 425
    initializing arrays, 166
    out-of-range subscripts, 160
    semicolons in function headers, 96
    stderr stream (fprintf function), 347
    typogrphical, 33
    undeclared variables, 275
    understanding, 275
    uninitialized pointers, 200
escape characters, tab (\t), 142
escape sequences, 139
    list of, 139
    printf function, 139, 142, 340-341
        listing, 140-141
    puts function, 146
evaluating relational operators, 73-75
events (asynchronous), 594-595
exclusive OR operator, 527
exec family (system functions), 547
execl function, 548
    argument confusion, 547
    arguments, 549
    defined, 547
executing programs
    controlling, 115
    do... while loops, 128-132

do... while statements, 131-132
for statements, 115-120
    nesting, 120-122
loops, nested, 132-133
mathematical statements, 61
while statements, 122-126
    nested, 126-127
    nesting, 128
exit function, 310-311, 541
exiting programs, 310-311
exp function, 482
expansion (macros), 566
expenses.c, 160-162
explicit variable initialization, 281
exponential functions, 482-483
expressions, 58
    arithmetic
        typecasting, 513-514
        typecasting integer division code listing, 514
    complex, 58-59
    condition, 115
    increment, 115
    initial, 115
    logical operators, 77
    multiple operators, 59
    parentheses, 66
    precedence, 64-65
    relational operators, 67
    type promotion, 512
extensions (C), 12
extern keywords, 277, 580, 634
external variables, 276
    declaring, 277
    extern keyword, 580

initializing, 276
modular programming,
  580-581
scope, 276
static, 282
when to use, 277

F

factorial function, 108
failures (fork command),
  539
false values, 77
fclose function, file
  buffering, 430
feof function, 438-439
fflush function, 431-332
fgetc function, 323-324,
  425
fgets function, 324-326,
  368, 425-426
  clearing extra characters
    (stdin), 330-331
  reading strings, 229-231,
    234
field-width specifier
  printf function, 340
  scanf function conversion
    specifications, 327
fields
  bit, 528-531
  input, 327
file extensions (C), 12
file management, 440-444
  copying files, 442-444
  deleting files, 440-441
  renaming files, 441-442
__FILE__ predefined
  macro, 571
FILE structure, 417

filenames
  compiling multiple files,
    587
  disk files, 416
  file functions, 447
  #include preprocessor
    directive, 567
  paths, 416
filename_cancel function,
  618-619
filename_dialog function,
  616-618
filename_ok function, 618
files
  binary, 447
  disk
    character I/O,
      424-426
    closing, 430, 447
    copying, 442-444
    deleting, 440-441
    direct file I/O,
      426-429
    EOF, 437-439
    file management,
      440-444
    filenames, 416, 447
    flushing, 431
    formatted file input,
      423-424
    formatted file output,
      421-423
    opening, 416-420,
      447
    random file access,
      432-437
    reading beyond EOF,
      447
    reading/writing, 420
    renaming, 441-442
    sequential file access,
      431-432, 447

    stream buffers,
      430-431
    streams, 415-416
    temporary files,
      445-446
  disk streaming, fread
    function, 430
  header
    gtk/gtk.h, 597
    modular
      programming,
      577-580
    names, 587
    preprocessor
      directives, 570
  included, 29
  Makefiles, 581, 585
    code example
      (version 1), 582
    code example
      (version 2), 584
    comments, 583
    dependencies,
      581-584
    targets, 583-584
  multiple, compiling, 587
  object, modular
    programming, 578-579
  position indicators, 431
    ftell function, 432
    rewind function, 432
  source code
    modular
      programming,
      576-581
    modules, 577
    saving, 24
  standard input/output
    files, 319
  streams, 319
  text, 447

file_save_dlg function, 616
flags (printf function), 340
float arrays, 158
float keyword, 634
float type (type promotion), 512
floating-point constants, 45
floating-point variables, 39, 42
floor function, 483
flushall function, 431
flushing disk files, 431
fmod function, 484
fopen function, 417, 420
    arguments, 417-418
    code listing, 418-419
for keyword, 634
for loops, 115-117, 292, 363. *See also* loops
    break statement, 292
    continue statement, 294
    nested, 169
for statements, 115-116, 119-120
    arrays, 114
    cautions, 122
    commas, 122
    condition, 119
    following with null statements, 119
    incrementing counter variables, 118
    initialization expression, 118
    listing, 116-117
    nesting, 120, 122
    omitting increment expressions, 118
    semicolons, 122
    structure, 115
    versus while statements, 124

fork functions, 539
    calling, 541
    failures, 539, 542
    servers, 542
    system functions, 542
format specifiers, literal text, 143
format strings, 138
    printf function, 138, 338-340
        conversion characters, 338-339
        conversion commands, 338
        field-width specifier, 340
        flags, 340
        l modifier, 339
        precision specifier, 339
    scanf function, 231
    strftime function, 487
        conversion specifiers, 488
formatted file input, 423-424
formatted file output, 421-423
formatted input functions, 326
    fscanf function, 326
    scanf function
        arguments, 326-329
        code examples, 332-334
        conversion specifications, 327-329
        format strings, 327
        handling extra characters, 329-332

formatted output functions, 337
    fprintf function, 337
        conversion characters, 338-339
    printf function, 337
        arguments, 338
        code examples, 341-343
        conversion characters, 338-339
        conversion commands, 338
        escape sequences, 340-341
        field-width specifier, 340
        flags, 340
        format strings, 338-340
        l modifier, 339
        precision specifier, 339
formatting
    source code, 56
    time, 487-488
forward slashes (//), 32
fprintf function, 337, 347, 421-423. *See also* printf function
    arguments, 421
    code listing, 421-422
    conversion characters, 338-339
    printf comparison, 349
    stderr stream, 347
fputc function, 336
fputs function, 336, 426
fread function, 428-430
free function, 389, 519-521
    freeing memory, 453
free memory, 530

frexp function, 483
fscanf function, 423-424.
See also **scanf function**
  arguments, 423
  code listing, 423-424
  scanf function
    comparison, 349
fseek function, 434-437
ftell function, 432-434
function macros
  # (stringizing operator),
    564
  ## (concatenation
    operator), 565
  #define preprocessor
    directive, 563-565
  definitions, 563-564
  functions comparison,
    565-566
  parameters, 563
function prototypes, 30
functions, 8, 28, 31
  abs, 483
  acos, 482
  ANSI/ISO compatibility,
    477
  arguments, 89-90
    multiple, 104
    passing structures,
      262-263
    passing to, 104-105
    passing to parameters,
      97
  asctime, 487, 491
  asin, 482
  assert
    code example,
      492-493
    definition, 491
    NDEBUG macro, 493
    use, 491
  atan, 482

atan2, 482
atof, 470-471
atoi, 469-470
atol, 470
body, 90-91
bsearch, 499-500, 507
  arguments, 499
  code example (using
    strings), 504-506
  code example (using
    values), 501-504
  comparison functions,
    499-500
bugs, 92
button_func, 600-601,
  605
callback
  menus, 614
  widgets (GUIs), 595
calling, 88, 90, 105-106
  recursion, 106-108
  syntax, 91-92
calloc, 516-517
cautions, 104
ceil, 483
character case
  conversion, 475-476
character test, 471
  code example,
    472-475
clock, 489, 491
comp, 506
comparing arguments
  and parameters, 97
comparison, 382
compiler standards, 313
copy_file, 443-444
cos, 482
cosh, 483
ctime, 487
data isolation, 276
defined, 88

definitions, 30, 89-92
delay (infinite loops),
  301
demo(), 99
destroy_func, 598-600
difftime, 488, 491
entries and exits, 103
error-handling, 491-496
  errno.h header file,
    493-495
  perror, 494-496
exec family, 547
exit, 310-311
exp, 482
factorial, 108
fclose, file buffering, 430
feof, 438-439
fflush, 331-332, 431
fgetc, 323-324, 425
fgets, 324-326, 425-426
  clearning extra
    characters (stdin),
    330-331
  reading strings,
    229-231, 234
file, filenames, 447
filename_cancel,
  618-619
filename_dialog,
  616-618
filename_ok, 618
file_save_dlg, 616
floor, 483
flushall, 431
fmod, 484
fopen, 417, 420
  arguments, 417-418
  code listing, 418-419
fprintf, 337, 347,
  421-423
  arguments, 421
  code listing, 421-422

printf comparison,
349
stderr stream, 347
fprintfconversion
characters, 338-339
fputc, 336
fputs, 336, 426
fread, 428-430
free, 519-521
freeing memory, 453
frexp, 483
fscanf, 326, 423-424
arguments, 423
code listing, 423-424
scanf comparison,
349
fseek, 434-437
ftell, 432-434
fwrite, 427-430, 616
gdk_font_load, 613
getc, 323-324
file I/O, 425
getchar, 167, 322-323
getopt (command-line
arguments), 574-576
getopt_long, 576
getopt_long_only, 576
gets, 324
reading strings,
229-231, 234
get_file_selection_new,
618
get_int, 474-475
get_label_new, 606
get_menu_choice, 141
gtk_accel_group_attach,
615
gtk_accel_group_new,
615
gtk_box_pack_start, 601
gtk_container_add, 601
gtk_container_set_
border_width, 600-601

gtk_editable_get_chars,
616
gtk_file_selection_get_
filename, 618
gtk_hbox_new, 601
gtk_init, 597
gtk_item_factory_
create_items, 615
gtk_item_factory_get_
widget, 615
gtk_item_factory_new,
615
gtk_main, 598, 607
gtk_main_quit, 598, 607,
618
gtk_show, 598
gtk_signal_connect, 598,
601, 605, 618
gtk_text_get_length, 616
gtk_text_new, 612
gtk_text_set_editable,
613
gtk_text_set_line_wrap,
613
gtk_vbox_new, 601
gtk_vscrollbar_new, 612
gtk_widget_destroy, 618
gtk_widget_get_style,
613
gtk_widget_set_usize,
597
gtk_widget_show_all,
606, 613
gtk_window_new, 597
gtk_window_set_modal,
606
gtk_window_set_title,
597
half, 104
half_of, 105
headers, 90-91, 96
if statement, 105
indirect recursion, 106

input/output functions,
320
intcmp, 503
isalnum, 472
isalpha, 472
isascii, 472
iscntrl, 472
isdigit, 472
isgraph, 472
islower, 472
isprint, 472
ispunct, 472
isspace, 472
isupper, 472
isxdigit, 472
keywords, 89
larger_of, 102
ldexp, 483
library, 31
line-input functions,
324-326
listing, 88-89
localtime, 486
log, 482
log10, 482
macros comparison, 565
main, 29, 474
command-line argu-
ments, 572, 587
main modules,
577-579
main(), 94, 100, 109
make_menu, 612, 615
malloc, 516
allocating memory,
453
characters, 224
pointers, 223
strings, 222-227, 234
math, 481
code example,
484-485
double type, 481, 507

exponential, 482-483
hyperbolic, 483
logarithmic, 482-483
trigonometric, 482
validating data, 507
memcpy, 522-524, 531
memory allocation, 362
checking return
values, 386
memmove, 522-524, 531
memset, 522-524, 531
menu (infinite loops),
301
menu_func, 615
mktime, 487
modf, 484
naming, 95
parameters
scope, 282
void type pointers,
210
passing
arrays of pointers to,
363
multidimensional
arrays to, 358-361
placing, 109-110
pointers
passing arguments to
functions, 206-210,
215
passing arrays to
functions, 201-206
passing as arguments,
375-376
pointers to, 370-371
calling different
functions, 374-379
initializing, 371-373
pow, 484

printf, 30, 138, 228-229,
337
arguments, 338
code examples,
341-343
conversion characters,
338-339
conversion com-
mands, 338
conversion specifiers,
142
escape sequences,
139, 142, 340-341
field-width specifier,
340
flags, 340
format strings, 138,
338-340
fprintf function, 349
l modifier, 339
precision specifier,
339
printf(), 100
print_report, 142
prototypes, 89-92
ellipses (...), 421
putc, 336, 426
putchar, 335-336
puts, 102, 146, 227-228,
336-337
qsort, 500, 507
code example (using
strings), 504-506
code example (using
values), 501-504
realloc, 518-519, 531
remove, 440-441
rename, 441-442
return keyword, 101
return statements, 90-91,
101

returning pointers,
380-382
rewind, 432-434
save_file, 616
scanf, 30, 147, 150-151,
231-233
arguments, 326-329
code examples, 332-334
conversion
specifications,
327-329
format strings, 327
fscanf comparison,
349
handling extra
characters, 329-332
searching, 499-500
searchingbinary search
algorithm, 500
shared libraries, 585-586
signal handlers, 550
sin, 482
sinh, 483
sleep, busy-wait loop
comparison, 302
sorting, 500
sqrt, 483
square, 104
statements, 90, 100-101
strcasecmp, 463
strcat, 457-458
trailing spaces, 477
strchr, 464-465
case-sensitivity, 464
code example,
464-465
strcmp, 460-462
strcpy, 453-454
allocating memory,
453
code example, 454
structure arrays, 250

strcspn, 465-466

strdup, 456

   allocating memory,
      456

   code example,
      456-457

strftime, 487, 491

   conversion specifiers,
      488

   format string, 487

string (man pages), 477

strlen, 451-453

strncat, 458-460

strncmp, 462-463

strncpy, 455-456

strpbrk, 467

strrchr, 465

strspn, 466-467

strstr, 468-469

structured programming,
   92

   advantages, 92-93

   hierarchical structure,
      94

   menus, 94

   planning, 93-94

   tasks and subtasks, 93

   top-down approach,
      94-95

system, 311-314, 439

   command argument,
      311

   fork, 542

tan, 482

tanh, 483

third, 104

time, 486, 490

   calculating time
      differences, 488

   calculating time
      durations, 489

code example,
   489-491

converting
   representation
   styles, 486-487

displaying time, 487

formatting time,
   487-488

obtaining current
   time, 486

time representation
   styles, 485-486

tmpnam, 445-446

tolower, 475-476

toupper, 475-476

ungetc, 324, 474

user-defined, 31, 87

variable-argument
   functions

   argument data types,
      496

   code example,
      497-499

   declaring, 496

   process, 497

   setting number of
      arguments, 496

   stdarg.h header file,
      496-497

variables, 89-90, 100

void return type, 106

writing, 95

   arguments, 96-98

   body, 98-103

   headers, 95-98

   local variables,
      98-100

   parameters, 96-98

   prototypes, 103-104

   return types, 95

   returning values,
      101-103

yesno_func, 606-607

yes_no_dialog, 606-608

**fwrite function, 427-430,
616**

G

garbage values, 279

gcc compiler, 14

   checking installation
      status, 14

   running, 14-15

**gdk_font_load function,
613**

**General Public License
(GPL), 593**

getc function, 323-324

   file I/O, 425

**getchar function, 167,
322-323**

**getopt function, command-
line arguments, 574-576**

getopt_long function, 576

**getopt_long_only function,
576**

getpid function, 537

gets function, 324

   reading strings, 229-231,
      234

**get_file_selection_new
function, 618**

**get_int function, character
test functions, 474-475**

**get_label_new function,
606**

get_lines function, 368

**get_menu_choice function,
141**

**Gimp (GNU Image
Manipulation Tool),
592-593**

global variables.
See **external variables**
**gnome-help-browser
command, 17**
GNU
gcc compiler, 14
checking installation
status, 14
running, 14-15
Gimp, 592-593
GPL (General Public
License), 593
goto keyword, 634
goto statements, 296-298
cautions, 297, 313
code listing, 296-297
debugger problems, 313
label statements, 298
target labels, 296
**GPL (General Public
License), 593**
grades.c, 164-165
Graphical User Interfaces.
See **GUIs**
**graphics, screen
coordinates, 240**
**greater than operator (>),
67**
**greater than or equal to
operator (>=), 67**
GTK+, 592
button_func, 600-601
button_func function,
605
constructing menu bars,
613-615
destroy_func, 600
destroy_func function,
598
filename_cancel
function, 618-619

filename_dialog
function, 616-618
filename_ok function,
618
file_save_dlg function,
616
fwrite function, 616
gdk_font_load function,
613
get_file_selection_new
function, 618
get_label_new function,
606
GTK+ program code
example, 595-599
GTK+ program code
example (buttons),
599-602
GTK+ program code
example (dialog boxes),
602-608
GTK+ program code
example (text editors),
608-619
gtk-config command,
593-595
gtk/gtk.h header file, 597
GtkWidget data type,
597
gtk_accel_group_attach
function, 615
gtk_accel_group_new
function, 615
gtk_box_pack_start, 601
gtk_container_add, 601
gtk_container_set_
border_width, 600-601
gtk_editable_get_chars
function, 616
gtk_file_selection_get_
filename function, 618
gtk_hbox_new, 601

gtk_init function, 597
gtk_item_factory_
create_items function,
615
gtk_item_factory_get_
widget function, 615
gtk_item_factory_new
function, 615
gtk_main function, 598,
607
gtk_main_quit function,
598, 607, 618
gtk_show function, 598
gtk_signal_connect, 601
gtk_signal_connect
function, 598, 605, 618
gtk_text_get_length
function, 616
gtk_text_new function,
612
gtk_text_set_editable
function, 613
gtk_text_set_line_wrap
function, 613
gtk_vbox_new, 601
gtk_vscrollbar_new
function, 612
gtk_widget_destroy
function, 618
gtk_widget_get_style
function, 613
gtk_widget_set_usize
function, 597
gtk_widget_show_all
function, 606, 613
gtk_window_new
function, 597
gtk_window_set_modal
function, 606
gtk_window_set_title
function, 597
info pages, 619

make_menu function, 612, 615

menu_func function, 615

save_file function, 616

yesno_func function, 606-607

yes_no_dialog function, 606-608

GTK+ signals, 619

GTK+s, 613-615

gtk-config command, 593-595

gtk/gtk.h header file, 597

GtkItemFactoryEntry structure, 613-615

GtkWidget data type, 597

gtk_accel_group_attach function, 615

gtk_accel_group_new function, 615

gtk_box_pack_start function, 601

gtk_container_add function, 601

gtk_container_set_ border_width function, 600-601

gtk_editable_get_chars function, 616

gtk_file_selection_get_ filename function, 618

gtk_hbox_new function, 601

gtk_init function, 597

gtk_item_factory_create_ items function, 615

gtk_item_factory_get_ widget function, 615

gtk_item_factory_new function, 615

gtk_main function, 598, 607

gtk_main_quit function, 598, 607, 618

gtk_show function, 598

gtk_signal_connect function, 598, 601, 605, 618

gtk_text_get_length function, 616

gtk_text_new function, 612

gtk_text_set_editable function, 613

gtk_text_set_line_wrap function, 613

gtk_vbox_new function, 601

gtk_vscrollbar_new function, 612

gtk_widget_destroy function, 618

gtk_widget_get_style function, 613

gtk_widget_set_usize function, 597

gtk_widget_show_all function, 606, 613

gtk_window_new function, 597

gtk_window_set_modal function, 606

gtk_window_set_title function, 597

GUIs (Graphical User Interfaces), 591

asynchronous events, 594-595

callback functions, 595

debugging programs, 595

widgets, 593-594

window managers, 596

X Window System. *See* X

H

half function, 104

half_of function, 105

head pointers, 383-385

header files

errno.h

errno variable, 493-495

macros, 493

symbolic constants, 493-494

explicit paths, 587

gtk/gtk.h, 597

modular programming, 577-580

names, 587

preprocessor directives, 570

sdarg.h, 496-497

headers, 29

functions, 90-91

writing, 95-98

stdio.h, 141

puts function, 146

heap, dynamic memory allocation, 519

Hello World program, 18

compilation errors, 20-21

compiling hello.c, 19

entering hello.c, 18-19

hello2.c debugging example, 22-23

running hello.c, 19

help

error messages (fprintf function), 347

gnome-help-browser command, 17

GTK+, 619

info command, 16

kdehelp command, 17

hexadecimal constant, 46
hierarchical structure (structured programs), 94
hyperbolic functions, 483

I

I/O, 138. *See also* input; output
    character, 424-426
        fgets function, 425-426
        fputs function, 426
        getc/fgetc functions, 425
        putc function, 426
    direct file I/O, 426-427, 429
        fread function, 428-430
        fwrite function, 427-430
IDEs (Integrated Development Environments), 12
IDs (PIDs), 536
if keyword, 634
if statements, 68-70, 105
    else clause, 71-72
    listing, 69
    nested, 73
    semicolons, 69
#if preprocessor directive
    conditional compilation, 568-569
    conditional debugging, 569-570
ignoring warning messages, 24

implementing linked lists, 392, 397-399
#include directive, 29
#include preprocessor directive, 567
included files, 29
inclusive OR operator, 527
increment expression, 115
increment operator (++), 60
    structure array pointers, 260
incrementing
    counter variables, 118
    pointers, 196, 357
        code example, 197-198
        pointer constants, 198
indenting
    statements, 71
    styles, nesting loops, 133
indexes, 114
    arrays, 368
indirect access (variables), 189
indirect membership operator (-<), 258
indirect recursion, 106
indirection (variables), 189
indirection (*) operator, 255, 352
    passing arguments by reference, 208
    pointers, 187-189, 214
infinite loops, code listing, 299-301
    creating, 298
        delay function, 301
        menu function, 301
        uses, 299
info command, 16
initial expression, 115

initializing
    arrays, 166
    character arrays, 220-221
    character variables, 218-220
    external variables, 276
    for statements
        initialization expressions, 118
        versus while statements, 125
    local variables, 279
    multidimensional arrays, 167
    pointers, 188, 386
    pointers to functions, 371-373
    strings, 361
    structure member pointer, 255-257
    structures, 252
    unions, 264
    variables, 43-44
input, 318. *See also* output; I/O
    devices, 318
    keyboard input, 321
        character input functions, 321
        fgetc function, 323-324
        fgets function, 324-326
        formatted input functions, 326
        fscanf function, 326
        getc function, 323-324
        getchar function, 322-323
        gets function, 324

line-input functions,
324-326
scanf function,
326-334
ungetc function, 324
redirecting, 344
< symbol, 345-346
| (pipes), 346
code example,
344-345
troubleshooting, 348
scanf function, 147,
150-151
streams, 317-319
equivalence, 320-321
files, 319
input/output
functions, 320
predefined streams,
319
input fields, 327
input/output functions,
320
instances, structures, 241,
270
int keyword, 634
int type
atoi function, 469-470
integer division code
listing, typecasting, 514
intcmp function, 503
integer variables, 39
reading with scanf
function, 147
integers, storage space,
356
Integrated Development
Environments (IDEs), 12
interfaces
GTK+. See GTK+
widget toolkits, 592
Xlib library (X), 592

internal clock, obtaining
current time, 486
International Standards
Organization (ISO), 9
intializing structures
arrays, 253-254
nesting, 253
isalnum function, 472
isalpha function, 472
isascii function, 472
iscntrl function, 472
isdigit function, 472
isgraph function, 472
islower function, 472
ISO (International
Standards Organization),
9
isprint function, 472
ispunct function, 472
isspace function, 472
isupper function, 472
isxdigit function, 472
iteration, 109

J - K

Java, C comparison, 9

kdehelp command, 17
keyboard input, 321
character input functions,
321
buffered character
input functions, 321
echoing, 321
fgetc function,
323-324
fgets function,
324-326
getc function,
323-324

getchar function,
322-323
gets function, 324
line-input functions,
324-326
unbuffered character
input functions, 321
ungetc function, 324
formatted input
functions, 326
fscanf function, 326
scanf function,
326-334
keyboards
accelerators, 614-615
reading strings, 229
fgets function,
229-231, 234
gets function,
229-231, 234
scanf function, 147,
150-151, 231-233
keywords, 8
asm, 634
auto, 634
break, 634
case, 634
char, 634
const, 163, 218, 634
continue, 634
default, 634
do, 634
double, 634
eise, 634
enum, 634
extern, 580, 634
float, 634
for, 634
in functions, 89
goto, 634
if, 634
int, 634

long, 634
register, 634
reserved
    C, 633-635
    C++, 635
return, 101, 634
short, 634
signed, 634
sizeof, 635
static, 635
struct, 240-243, 635
switch, 635
typedef, 635
    structure/union
        synonyms, 269-270
    tags comparison, 271
union, 264-269, 635
unsigned, 635
void, 635
volatile, 635
while, 635

L

l modifier (printf function, 339
label statements, 298
languages
    C
        ANSI Standard C, 9, 314
        flexibility, 8
        history, 9
        ISO standard, 9
        kernel (Linux), 8
        keywords, 8
        modularity, 8
        name, 9

popularity, 8
portability, 8
preprocessor, 561-562
reserved keywords, 633-635
Ritchie, Dennis, 9
C++, 8-9, 635
Java, 9
machine, 14
larger_of function, 102
ldexp function, 483
length of strings, determining, 451-453
less than operator (>), 67
less than or equal to operator (>=), 67
libraries
    GTK+. See GTK+
    shared, 585-586
    widget toolkits, 592
    Xlib (X), 592
library functions, 28, 31.
    See also functions
    abs, 483
    acos, 482
    asctime, 487, 491
    asin, 482
    assert
        code example, 492-493
        definition, 491
        NDEBUG macro, 493
    atan, 482
    atan2, 482
    atof, 470-471
    atoi, 469-470
    atol, 470
    bsearch, 499-500, 507
        arguments, 499
        code example (using strings), 504-506

code example (using values), 501-504
comparison functions, 499-500
ceil, 483
clock, 489-491
cos, 482
cosh, 483
ctime, 487
difftime, 488, 491
errno.h header file
    errno variable, 493-495
    macros, 493
    symbolic constants, 493-494
error-handling, 491-496
exp, 482
feof, 438-439
fflush, 431
fgets, 324-326, 425
floor, 483
flushall, 431
fmod, 484
fopen, 417-420
    arguments, 417-418
    code listing, 418-419
fprintf, 421-423
    arguments, 421
    code listing, 421-422
fread, 428-430
frexp, 483
fscanf
    arguments, 423
    code listing, 423-424
fseek, 434-437
ftell, 432-434
fwrite, 427-430
getchar, 167
ldexp, 483
localtime, 486
log, 482

malloc, 516
math
    code example,
        484-485
    double type, 481, 507
    exponential, 482-483
    hyperbolic
        logarithmic, 482-483
        trigonometric, 482
        validating data, 507
mktime, 487
modf, 484
perror, 494-496
pow, 484
printf, 30, 138, 228-229
puts, 227-228, 336-337
qsort, 500-507
    code example (using
        strings), 504-506
    code example (using
        values), 501-504
remove, 440-441
rename, 441-442
rewind, 432-434
scanf, 30, 147, 231-233
searching, 499-500
sin, 482
sinh, 483
sorting, 500
sqrt, 483
strcat, 457-458, 477
strchr
    case-sensitivity, 464
    code example,
        464-465
strcmp, 460-462
strcpy
    allocating memory,
        453
    code example, 454
    structure arrays, 250
strcspn, 465-466

strdup
    allocating memory,
        456
    code example,
        456-457
strftime, 491
    conversion specifiers,
        488
    format string, 487
strlen, 451-453
strncat, 458-460
strncmp, 462-463
strncpy, 455-456
strpbrk, 467
strrchr, 465
strspn, 466-467
strstr, 468-469
tan, 482
tanh, 483
time
    calculating time
        differences, 488
    calculating time
        durations, 489
    code example,
        489-491
    converting
        representation
        styles, 486-487
    displaying time, 487
    formatting time,
        487-488
    obtaining current
        time, 486
    time function, 486,
        490
    time representation
        styles, 485-486
tmpnam function,
    445-446
ungetc, 324, 474
lifetimes, 274

line continuation charac-
    ter (\), 595
line-input functions,
    324-326
__LINE__ predefined
    macro, 571
lines[] array, 369
linked lists, 382-383
    displaying data, 398
    elements
        adding, 384-387, 392
        deleting, 388-389,
            400
    empty, 383
    head pointers, 383-385
    implementing, 392,
        397-399
    links, 397-400
    modifying, 384
    sample program,
        389-392
    structure, 383-384
    structure pointers, 257
    visual representation,
        397
links, deleting from linked
    lists, 400
Linux
    commands. See
        commands
    determining element
        size, 356
    kernel, 8
    multitasking, 536
    text editors, 12-13
list0403.c, 69-70
list_it.c, 34-35
listings
    # (stringizing operator),
        565
    arguments compared
        with parameters, 97

arrays
    element addresses,
        194-195
    expenses.c, 160-161
    grades.c, 164-165
    of pointers, 363
    sizeof operator, 171
    sorting elements, 366
assert function, 492
atof function, 471
break statement, 292-293
bsearch function
    using strings, 504-506
    using values, 501-503
char variables,
    initializing, 219
character test functions,
    472-474
command-line arguments
    getopt function, 575
    main function, 573
continue statement,
    294-295
copy_file function,
    443-444
do-while loops, 129-130
element size,
    determining, 356
errno variable, 494-495
execl function, 548
external variables, 278
feof function, 438-439
fflush function, 331-332
fgets function, 325-326,
    330-331
fopen function, 418-419
for statements, 116-117
fprintf function formatted
    output, 421-422
fread/fwrite functions,
    428
fscanf function, 423-424
fseek function, 435-437

ftell function, 432-434
functions overview,
    88-89
getchar function
    single characters, 322
    text lines, 323
goto statement, 296-297
GTK+ program
    examples, 596-597
    buttons, 599-600
    dialog boxes, 603-605
    filename.c dialog box,
        616-617
    filename.h header file,
        612
    text editors, 608-611
hello.c, 18
hello.c (error version), 20
hello2.c, 22
if statements, 69-71
infinite loops, 299-301
linked lists, 390-392
list_it.c, 34-35
local variables, 285
logical operator
    precedence, 79
Makefile example
    version 1, 582
    version 2, 584
malloc function, 225-226
math functions, 484-485
memory allocation
    calloc function, 517
    free function, 520-521
    realloc function,
        518-519
memory manipulation,
    523
modular programming
    header files, 578
    main module, 577
    secondary module,
        578

modulus operator, 62-63
multidimensional arrays
    passing, 358
    pointers, 355-356
    random.c, 167-169
multiple return state-
    ments in a function,
    101-102
multiply.c, 28-29
nested for statements,
    121
nested while statements,
    126-127
numeric nature of char
    variables, 219
passing arguments to
    functions, 208-209
passing arrays to
    functions
    first example,
        202-203
    pointers example,
        364, 375
    second example,
        204-205
perror function, 494-495
pointer arithmetic,
    197-198, 357
pointer usage, 189-190
    calling different
        functions, 373
    pointers to functions,
        372
    returning pointers,
        381
    sort order, 377
preprocessor directives
    with header files, 570
printf function, 341-344
    displaying numerical
        values, 144
    escape sequences,
        140-141

process IDs, 537
processes, creating, 540
programs, running in
   background, 538
putchar function
   displaying characters,
      335
   displaying strings,
      335-336
puts function, 228, 337
qsort function
   using strings, 504-506
   using values, 501-503
recursive functions, 107
redirecting input/output,
   345
relational expressions, 74
remove function,
   440-441
rename function,
   441-442
rewind function, 432,
   434
scanf function, 148-151,
   232-233, 332, 334
shift operators, 525-526
SIGCHLD signal,
   555-556
signal handling, 552
sizeof.c, 39-40
static versus automatic
   variables, 280
strcat function, 457-458
strchr function, 464-465
strcmp function, 461
strcsp function, 465-466
strdup function, 456-457
streams, 320-321
strlen function, 452
strncat function, 459-460
strncmp function,
   462-463
strncpy function, 455

strspn function, 467
strstr function, 468-469
structures
   array members, 247
   arrays, 250-251
   nesting, 244-245
   passing as function
      argument, 262-263
   pointers, 260
switch statement, 303
   break statements,
      including, 304-305
   break statements,
      omitting, 307-308
   menu systems code
      listing, 305-307
system function, 312
time functions, 489-490
tmpnam function, 445
tolower function,
   475-476
type conversions, 514
unary.c, 61
unions, 265-268
variables
   example, 48-49
   inaccessible, 275
   variable-argument
      functions, 497-498
void type pointers,
   211-212
while statement, 123-124
zombie processes,
   preventing
      waitpid function, 545
      wait function,
         543-544

lists, linked, 382-383
displaying data, 398
elements
   adding, 384-387, 392
   deleting, 388-389,
      400

empty, 383
head pointers, 383-385
implementing, 392,
   397-399
links, 397-400
modifying, 384
sample program,
   389-392
structure, 383-384
structure pointers, 257
visual representation,
   397
**literal character constants,
218**
literal constants, 45, 58
   declaring arrays, 163
   string constants, 220
      breaking lines, 57
      whitespace, 56
   versus symbolic
      constants, 46
literal text, 138
local scope, 282
**local variables, 90, 100,
276**
   automatic, 279, 282
   common uses, 286
   defining, 285-286
   of functions, 98-100
   initializing, 279
   listing, 99
   main() function, 284
   scope, 278
   static, 279
localtime function, 486
**locating GTK+ files,
593-595**
log function, 482
log10 function, 482
**logarithmic functions,
482-483**

logical operators, 76-77, 526-528, 531
AND, 76, 527
code examples, 77
OR, 527
precedence, 78-79
long keyword, 634
long type, 470
loops
busy-wait loops, 302
do...while, 128-132
for, 115, 117
infinite loops
code listing, 299-301
creating, 298
delay function, 301
menu function, 301
uses, 299
nested, 132-133, 313
terminating, 118
break statement, 292-294
continue statement, 294-295
while, 125

M

machine language, 14
Macintosh windows, 592
macros
character test functions, 471-475
errno.h header file, 493
expansion, 566
viewing, 566
function
(stringizing operator), 564-565
(concatenation operator), 565

#define preprocessor directive, 563-565
definitions, 563-564
functions comparison, 565-566
function parameters, 563
NDEBUG, 493
predefined, 571-572
substitution. *See* symbolic constants
main function, 29, 474
command-line arguments, 572, 587
main modules, 577-579
main modules, 577-579
main() function, 94, 100, 109
expenses.c, 162
local variables, 284
static variables, 284
make utility
compiling, 582
developing programs, 16
Makefiles, 581-585
code example, 582-584
comments, 583
dependencies, 581-584
targets, 583-584
Makefiles, 581-585
code example, 582-584
comments, 583
dependencies, 581-584
targets, 583-584
make_menu function, 612, 615
malloc function, 362, 368, 386, 516
allocating memory, 453
characters, 224
pointers, 223
strings, 222-227, 234

man pages, 477
managers (window), 596
managing disk files, 440-444
copying files, 442-444
deleting files, 440-441
renaming files, 441-442
manifest constants. *See* **symbolic constants**
manipulating memory blocks, 522-524, 531
mantissas, 42
math functions
abs, 483
ceil, 483
code example, 484-485
double type, 481, 507
exponential, 482-483
floor, 483
fmod, 484
hyperbolic, 483
logarithmic, 482-483
modf, 484
pow, 484
sqrt, 483
trigonometric, 482
validating data, 507
mathematical operators
binary, 62-64
precedence, 64
unary, 60-62
member operator. *See* **dot operator**
members
structures, 240
accessing, 241
arrays, 246-248
pointers, 255-257
unions, 265-266
memcyp function, 522-524, 531
memmove function, 522-524, 531

memory, 36. *See also* **type conversions**
addresses, 186-187, 214
allocation, 368
calloc function, 516-517
checking, 521
compilation allocation, 222
dynamic memory allocation, 222-227, 234, 515, 530
free function, 519, 521
free memory, 530
malloc function, 222-227, 234, 453, 516
memory availability, 515-516
overestimating, 517
overwriting issues, 227
realloc function, 518-519, 531
static memory allocation, 515
strcpy function, 453
strdup function, 456
strings, 221
arrays, 158
blocks
manipulating, 522-524
memcyp function, 522-524, 531
memove function, 522-524, 531
memset function, 522-524, 531
buffers, 522
file buffers, 430

freeing, 453
multidimensional arrays, 163
numeric variables, 39, 42
pointers, 189
arrays, 192-195
benefits, 214
cautions, 200
code example, 189-191
comparisons, 199
creating, 186-187
data types, 191-192
declaring, 187-188
decrementing, 196
dereferencing, 188, 211
differencing, 198
incrementing, 196
indirection (*) operator, 187-189, 214
initializing, 188
modifying individual variables, 215
naming, 186
operations, 199-200
passing arguments, 201-210, 215
pointer arithmetic, 196-198
pointer constants, 198
structure member pointers, 256
subscript notation comparison, 201
uninitialized, 200
void type, 210-213
reclaiming space, 389
variable lifetime, 274
memset function, 522, 524, 531

menu bars, 613, 615
menu callback functions, 94, 614
menu function, 301, 615
menu systems, 305-307
messages
displaying on screen, 138
signals, 549
X Protocol, 592
methods. *See* **functions**
military time, 487
mktime function, 487
modal windows, 606
modf function, 484
modular independence, 277
modular programming, 8, 576
benefits, 577
code examples, 577-578
external variables, 580-581
header files, 577-580
main modules, 577-579
object files, 578-579
secondary modules, 577-580
modules
main, 577-579
secondary, 577-580
source code, 577
modulus operator (%), 62
mulitiple indirection, 352
multi pointers, 357
multidimensional arrays, 162
cautions, 166
declaring, 354
dimensions, 358
initializing, 167
integers, 356
memory, 163

names, 355
   passing to funcitons, 358,
      360-361
   pointers, 353-356
   values, 357
**multiplication operator
   (*), 46, 62**
multiply.c, 27
   listing, 28-29
   running, 33
multitasking, 536

N

names
   arrays, 163-165,
      192-193, 354
   bit fields, 529
   C language, 9
   camel notation, 38
   filenames
      compiling multiple
         files, 587
      disk files, 416
      file functions, 447
      header files, 587
      #include preprocessor
         directive, 567
      paths, 416
      renaming, 441-442
   functions, 95
   pointers, 186
   tags (structures), 240,
      271
   variables, 37-38
NDEBUG macro, 493
nesting
   comments, 31
   for statements, 120-122,
      169

if statements, 73
loops, 132-133
   cautions, 133
   changing inner, 133
   indenting styles, 133
   switch statements
      comparison, 313
   parentheses, 65
   structures, 243-245
      initializing, 253
      limitations, 246
   while statements,
      126-128
networks
   fork functions, 543
   X, 592
new_rec pointer, 398
**not equal to operator (!=),
   67**
NOT operator (!), 76
null statements, 57
NULL value
   fopen function, 417-418
   pointers, 225
**numbering array
   elements, 158**
numbers
   floating-point, 42
   values
      displaying with printf
         function, 144
      reading with scanf
         function, 148-151
   variables, 39, 42, 352

O

object files, 578-579
**object-oriented
   programming, 8**

**objectives, planning
   programs, 10**
objects, 516-517
octal integers, 46
op keyword, 80
opening files, 416-420, 447
operands, 59
   modes, 60
   modulus operators, 62
   ternary operators, 81
   type promotion, 512
**operating system
   commands, executing,
   311-314**
operating systems
   memory allocation
      availability, 516
   operations
      pointers, 199-200
   processes, 542
   signals (software
      interrupts), 549
   system functions, 542
operators, 59
   address-of (&), 188, 214
   assignment
      compound, 80
      type promotion, 513
   assignment (=), 60
   binary, 62-64, 512
   bitwise
      complement, 528
      logical, 526-528, 531
      shift, 525-526, 531
   comma, 81
   compound assignment,
      80
   concatenation (##), 565
   conditional, 81
   defined, 569-570
   dot (.), 241, 252, 265
   increment (++), 260

indirection (*), 255
   passing arguments by
     reference, 208
   pointers, 187-189,
     214
logical, 76-77
mathematical, 60
precedence, 64-66, 78-79
   subexpressions, 66-67
   summary, 82-83
relational
   common mistakes, 74
   evaluating, 73-75
   list of, 67
   precedence, 75-76
sizeof, 171
stringizing (#), 564
code example, 565
unary (++, --), 60-62
OR conditions, 264
OR operator (||), 76, 527
OSs (operating systems)
   memory allocation
     availability, 516
   operations
   pointers, 199-200
   processes, 542
   signals (software
     interrupts), 549
   system functions, 542
out-of-range subscripts,
159
output. *See also* **input**
   devices, 318
   formatted output
     fprintf function,
      337-339
     printf function,
      337-343
   printf function, 138-139,
     142
   puts function, 146

redirecting
   | (pipe symbol), 346
   code example,
     344-345
   troubleshooting, 348
screen output, 334
   fputc function, 336
   fputs function, 336
   putc function, 336
   putchar function,
     335-336
   puts function,
     336-337
streams, 317
   equivalence, 320-321
   files, 319
   input/output
     functions, 320
   predefined streams,
     319
overestimating memory
allocations, 517
overwriting
   character arrays, 234
   gets function, 229
   scanf function, 232
   strings, 227, 257

P

parameter lists, 96
parameters
   argc, 572
   argv[], 573
   comparing to arguments,
     97
   function macros, 563
   receiving arguments, 97
   scope, 282
   sigaction function, 551

parent processes, 536
   fork function, 540-541
   sleep function, 541
   wait function, 543-544
   waitpid function, 546
   zombie process, 542
parentheses ( ), 65-66, 89,
104
passing
   arrays
     arrays of pointers,
      363
     multidimensional
      arrays, 358-361
   command-line
     arguments, 104
     argc parameter, 572
     argv[] parameter, 573
     getopt function,
      574-576
     main function,
      572-573, 587
     optional, 574
     pointers, 201-210,
      215, 375-376
     required, 574
     structures, 262-263
paths
   filenames, 416
   header files, 587
percent sign (%), 139
perror function, 494-496
PIDs (process identifiers),
536
pipes (|), 346
planning programs, 9-10,
93-94
pointer constants, 198
pointers, 189, 352
   arrays, 361
     array element storage,
      193-195
     array names, 192-193

declaring, 362-363,
365
multidimensional,
353-356
passing to functions,
201-206
strings, 361
subscript notation
comparison, 201
benefits, 214
calling different
functions, 374-379
cautions, 200
char, 362-363
code example, 189-191
comparison functions,
382
comparisons, 199
creating, 186-187
data types, 191-192,
210-213
declaring, 187-188, 352,
386
pointing to
multidimensional array
elements, 358
dereferencing, 188, 211
formatted file output,
421
head (linked lists),
383-385
incrementing, 357
indirect membership
operator
declaring, 257-258
linked lists, 257
passing as function
arguments, 263
indirection (*) operator,
187-189, 208, 214
initializing, 188, 371-373
malloc function, 223

memory address,
186-187, 214
modifying individual
variables, 215
multi, 357
naming, 186
NULL value, 225
operations, 200
passing arguments,
206-210, 215, 363,
375-376
pointer arithmetic
code example,
197-198
decrementing, 196
differencing, 198
incrementing, 196
operations, 199
pointer constants, 198
returned by functions,
380-382
storing, 352
strings, 221
structures, 257-259
members, 255-257
structure arrays,
259-262
target sizes, 357
typecasting, 514-515
uninitialized, 200
portability, 8
position indicators
files, 431-432
rewind function, 432
postfix mode, 60
pow function, 484
precedence, 64-66, 82-83
logical operators, 78-79
parentheses, 65
relational operators,
75-76
subexpressions, 66-67

**precision modifiers,
327-329**
precision specifiers, 339
**predefined macros,
571-572**
predefined streams, 319
prefix mode, 60
preprocessor, 561-562
**preprocessor directives,
570**
#define
function macros,
563-565
symbolic constants,
562
#elif, 568
#else, 568
#endif
conditional
compilation,
568-569
conditional
debugging, 569-570
#if
conditional
compilation,
568-569
conditional
debugging, 569-570
#include, 567
#undef, 571
**preventing zombie
processes, 543**
prev_rec pointer, 398
printarray_1 function, 360
printarray_2 function, 360
**printf function, 30, 100,
228-229, 337**
arguments, 145, 338
calls to, 145
code examples, 341-343

conversion characters, 142, 338-339

conversion commands, 338

displaying variables, 143

escape sequences, 139, 142, 340-341

expenses.c, 162

field-width specifier, 340

flags, 339-340

format strings, 138, 338-340

fprintf comparison, 349

precision specifier, 339

print_report function, 141-142

print_strings functions, 364

processes

child, 536

creating, 540

displaying, 536

getpid function, 537

parent, 536

PIDs, 536-537

replacing, 547-549

signals, 550

starting, 539

terminating, 542, 549

zombie, 542

preventing, 545

troubleshoting, 554-557

processor registers, 282

processors, 356

program control statements, 68-72

Program Development Cycle, 10, 12

program listings. *See* **listings**

programming

development tools, 12

GUIs

asynchronous events, 594-595

callback functions, 595

debugging programs, 595

widgets, 593-594

Hello World program

compiling, 19-21

debugging, 22-23

entering hello.c, 18-19

running hello.c, 19

IDEs (Integrated Development Environments), 12

make utility, 16

modular, 576

benefits, 577

code examples, 577-578

external variables, 580-581

header files, 577-580

main modules, 577-579

object files, 578-579

secondary modules, 577-580

object-oriented, 8

planning programs, 9-10

Program Development Cycle, 10, 12

shared libraries, 585-586

source code

ASCII format, 12

compiling, 15

debugging, 15-16, 21-22

text editors, 12-13, 23

structured, 92-94

writing source code, 12

programming languages. *See* **languages**

programs

comments, 31

development tools, 12

executing

controlling, 115

do...while loops, 128, 130-132

for statements, 114-122

while statements, 122-128

expenses.c, 161

functions, 28, 31

grades.c, 164-165

GTK+ example, 595-599

buttons, 599-602

dialog boxes, 602-608

text editors, 608-619

Hello World program

compiling, 19-21

debugging, 22-23

entering hello.c, 18-19

running hello.c, 19

IDEs (Integrated Development Environments), 12

list_it.c, 35

make utility, 16

multiply.c, 33

multitasking, 536

operating system commands, 311-314

planning, 9-10

Program Development Cycle, 10, 12

running in background, 538-539

sharing, 23
signals, 549, 553
source code, 277
    ASCII format, 12
    compiling, 15
    debugging, 15-16,
        21-22
    text editors, 12-13, 23
    writing, 12
structured
    advantages, 92-93
    functions, 103
    hierarchical structure,
        94
    menus, 94
    planning, 93
    tasks/subtasks, 93
    top-down approach,
        94-95
terminating, 310-311
typographical errors, 33
variables, 37
protocols, X Protocol, 592
prototypes, 89-92
    ellipses (…), 421
    semicolons, 103
    writing, 103-104
ps command, 537
ps_aux command, 536
ps_u command, 536
putc function, 336, 426
putchar function, 335-336
**puts function, 102,
    146-147, 227-228,
    336-337**

Q-R

qsort function, 500, 507
    strings example, 504-506
    values example, 501-504

quicksort algorithm, 500
quotation marks, 138

radians, 482
**RAM (Random Access
    Memory).** *See* **memory**
rand function, 169
random file access
    fseek function, 434-437
    ftell function, 432-434
    rewind function, 432-434
random.c, 167-169
reading
    disk files, 420
        character I/O,
            424-426
        direct file I/O,
            426-429
        EOF, 447
        formatted file input,
            423-424
        formatted file output,
            421-423
    strings
        fgets function,
            229-231, 234
        gets function,
            229-231, 234
        scanf function,
            231-233
**realloc function, 518-519,
    531**
**reaping zombie processes,
    543, 554**
**reclaiming memory space,
    389**
recursion, 106-108
redirecting input/output
    < symbol (redirection
        output), 344
    << symbol (redirection
        output), 344

    > symbol (redirecting
        input), 345-346
    | (pipes), 346
    code example, 344-345
    troubleshooting, 348
**register keyword, 282-283,
    634**
registers, 283
relational operators
    common mistakes, 74
    evaluating, 73
    list of, 67
    precedence, 75-76
remove function, 440-441
rename function, 441-442
renaming files, 441-442
replacing processes, 548
reserved words. *See*
    keywords
**return statements, 30,
    90-81, 101, 634**
return types, 95
reverse function, 379
rewind function, 432-434
Ritchie, Dennis, 9
root users, 17
running
    ddd debugger, 22
    gcc compiler, 14-15
    hello.c, 19

S

samples. *See* **listings**
save_filet function, 616
saving source code files, 24
**scanf function, 30, 147,
    150-151, 231-233**
    arguments, 151, 326-329
    code examples, 332-334

conversion
  specifications, 327-329
field width
  precision modifiers,
    327-329
  type specifiers, 328
conversion specifiers,
  148
format strings, 327
fscanf comparison, 349
handling extra
  characters, 329-332
scientific notation, 45
scope
  local, 282
  variables, 274-276
    data isolation, 276
    external, 276
    listing, 274
    local, 278
screen output, 334
  character output
    functions
      fputc function, 336
      putc function, 336
      putchar function,
        335-336
  formatted output
    functions
      fprintf function,
        337-339
      printf function,
        337-343
  string output functions
    fputs function, 336
    puts function,
      336-337
searching
  functions
    binary search
      algorithm, 500
    bsearch, 499-507

strings, 463-469
  code example,
    464-465
  strchr function,
    464-465
  strcspn function,
    465-466
  strpbrk function, 467
  strrchr function, 465
  strspn function,
    466-467
  strstr function,
    468-469
secondary modules,
  577-580
seconds.c, 62-63
selecting variable storage
  classes, 284
semicolon (;), 96, 103, 122
sequential file access,
  431-432, 447
servers
  fork functions, 542
  X, 592
Setup, ddd debugger, 21
shared libraries, 585-586
sharing programs, 23
shift operators, 525-526,
  531
short keyword, 634
sigaction function, 550-553
SIGALRM signal, 550
SIGCHLD signal, 550,
  554, 556-557
SIGCONT signal, 550
sigempty function, 552
SIGFPE signal, 550
SIGHUP signal, 550
SIGInt signal, 550, 554
SIGKILL signal, 550
signals, 549
  asynchronous, 549
  changing behavior, 551

GTK+, 619
handlers, 550-553
list of common, 550
SIG_DFL constant, 551
SIG_IGN constant, 551
synchronous, 549
trapping, 550
signed decimal integers,
  142
signed keyword, 634
SIGQUIT signal, 550
SIGSEGV signal, 550
SIGTERM signal, 550
SIGTSTP signal, 550
SIGUSR1 signal, 550
SIGUSR2 signal, 550
SIGWINCH signal, 550
SIG_DFL constant, 551
sig_handler function, 553
SIG_IGN constant, 551
sin function, 482
single-dimensional arrays,
  158-162
single-linked lists, 382. *See*
  also **linked lists**
sinh function, 483
SITSTOP signal, 550
size
  arrays, 170-172
  integers, 357
  unions, 271
sizeof operator, 40, 171,
  356, 635
sizeof.c, 39-41
sleep function, 302, 541
software interrupts. *See*
  signals
sort function, 369, 379
sorting
  changing order, 379
  elements in arrays,
    365-369

functions, 500-507
strings, 369
source code. *See also*
listings
array declarations, 159
ASCII format, 12
compiling, 15
files, saving, 24
formatting, 56
macro expansion, 566
modular programming,
576
benefits, 577
code examples,
577-578
external variables,
580-581
header files, 577-580
main modules,
577-579
object files, 578-579
secondary modules,
577-580
storing, 277
text editors, 12-13, 23
white space, 56
writing, 12
spaghetti code, 297, 313
sqrt function, 483
square brackets [], 159
square function, 104
standard input/output
files, 319
standards
C, 314
compilers, 313
statements, 30, 55. *See also*
keywords; preprocessor
directives
{} (braces), 33
blocks, 57
break, 292-294, 303-308

case, 309-310
compound, 57
continue, 294-295
do…while, 129-132
for, 115-120
arrays, 114
nesting, 120-122
structure, 115
functions, writing,
100-101
goto, 296-298
cautions, 297, 313
code listing, 296-297
debugger problems,
313
label statements, 298
target labels, 296
if, 68-70, 105
else clause, 71-72
listing, 69
nested, 73
semicolons, 69
in functions, 90
indenting, 71
iteration, 109
mathematical
executing, 61
null, 57
program control, 68
return, 30, 90-91, 101
switch, 302
basic code listing, 303
break statements,
including/omitting,
303-308
case statements,
309-310
menu systems,
305-307
nested loops
comparison, 313

while, 122-126
nested, 126-127
nesting, 128
structure, 122
whitespace, 56
static keyword, 635
static memory allocation,
222, 515
static variables
compared to automatic
variables, 281
external, 282
local, 279
main() function, 284
stdarg.h header file,
496-497
stderr stream, 319, 347
stdin stream, 319
stdio.h header, 141, 146,
426
stdlib.h header, 169
stdout stream, 319
storage classses
(variables), 284
storing. *See also* **memory,**
allocation
array elements, 158
data, 36
linked lists, 382, 400
registers, 283
integers, 356
pointers, 352
source code, 277
variables, 283
strcasecmp function, 463
strcat function, 457-458,
477
strchr function, 464-465
strcmp function, 460-462
strcpy function, 368
allocating memory, 453
code example, 454
structure array, 250

strcspn function, 465-466

strdup function

  allocating memory, 456

  code example, 456-457

streams, 317-319

  device independence,
   319

  direct file I/O, 430

  disk files, 415

    character I/O,
     424-426

    closing, 430, 447

    copying, 442-444

    deleting, 440-441

    direct file I/O,
     426-429

    EOF, 437-439

    file management,
     440-444

    file types, 416

    filenames, 416

    flushing, 431

    formatted file input,
     423-424

    formatted file output,
     421-423

    opening, 416-420,
     447

    random file access,
     432-437

    reading beyond EOF,
     447

    reading/writing, 420

    renaming, 441-442

    sequential file access,
     431-432, 447

    stream buffers,
     430-431

  equivalence, 320-321

  files, 319

  input/output functions,
   320

predefined streams, 319

stderr, 319, 347

stdin, 319

stdout, 319

**strftime function, 487-488,
491**

**string literal operator (#),
564-565**

**string output functions,
336-337**

strings, 220, 363. *See also*
characters

  allocating, 368

  character arrays,
   220-221, 234

  comparing

    case-sensitivity, 463

    entire strings,
     460-462

    partial strings,
     462-463

    return values, 462

  concatenating, 457-460

  copying, 453-457

  determining length,
   451-453

  displaying

    printf function,
     228-229

    puts function,
     227-228

  displaying onscreen, 370

  format

    scanf function, 231

    strftime function,
     487-488

  functions

    atof, 470-471

    atoi, 469-470

    atol, 470

    strcasecmp, 463

    strcat, 457-458, 477

strchr, 464-465

strcmp, 460-462

strcpy, 453-454

strcspn, 465-466

strdup, 456-457

strlen, 451-453

strncmp, 462-463

strncpy, 455-456

strpbrk, 467

strrchr, 465

strspn, 466-467

strstr, 468-469

initializing, 361

length of, finding, 368

literal, 220

memory allocation, 221

  compilation
   allocation, 222

  dynamic, 222-227,
   234

  malloc function,
   222-227, 234

  overwriting issues,
   227

numeric variable
  conversions, 469-471,
  477

overwriting issues, 234

pointers, 221, 361

printing, 364

reading

  fgets function,
   229-231, 234

  gets function,
   229-231, 234

  scanf function,
   231-233

realloc function, 531

searching, 463-469

sorting, 369

whitespace, 56

strlen function, 451-453
strlen library function, 368
strncat function, 458, 460
strncmp function, 462-463
strncpy function, 455-456
strpbrk function, 467
strrchr function, 465
strspn function, 466-467
strstr function, 468-469
struct keyword, 240-243, 635
structured programming
  advantages, 92-93
  functions, 103
  hierarchical structure, 94
  menus, 94
  planning, 93-94
  tasks and subtasks, 93
  top-down approach, 94-95
structures, 239. *See also* **unions**
  arrays, 248-252
    copying content, 250
    declaring, 249
    initializing, 253-254
  arrays pointers, 259-262
    code listing, 260-261
    increment operators (++), 260
  assigning, 271
  bit fields, 528-531
  data types, 240
  declaring, 240-241, 270
  defining, 240-241
  do...while loops, 128
  FILE, 417
  for statements, 115
  GtkItemFactoryEntry, 613-615
  initializing, 252

instances, 241, 270
linked lists, 383
members, 240
  accessing, 241
  arrays, 246-248
  pointers, 255-257
nesting, 243-245
initializing, 246, 253
passing as function argument, 262-263
pointers
  accessing, 258-259
  declaring, 257-258
  indirect membership operator, 258
  linked lists, 257
struct keyword, 242
synonyms, 269-270
tags, 240, 271
while statements, 122
subexpressions, 66-67
subscript notation, 201
subscripts, 114
  multidimensional arrays, 162
  out-of-range, 159
  single-dimensional arrays, 158
substitution macros. *See* **symbolic constants**
subtraction operator (-), 62
switch statements, 302, 635
  basic code listing, 303
  break statements
    including, 303-305
    omitting, 307-308
  case statements, 309-310
  menu systems, 305-307
  nested loops comparison, 313

symbolic constants, 46, 218
  #define directive, 47, 562
  defining, 47-49
  EOF, 426
  errno.h header file, 493-494
  versus literal constants, 46
synchronous signals, 549
synonyms, 269-270
system functions, 311-314, 439, 536
  exec family, 547
  fork, 542

T

tab escape character (\t), 142
tags, 240, 271
tan function, 482
tanh function, 483
target labels (goto statement), 296
targets, 583-584
tasks (structured programming), 93
templates, 266
temporary files, 445-446
temporary variables, 369
terminal windows, 17-18
terminating
  processes
    child processes, 554-556
    signals, 549
  programs, 310-311
ternary operators, 81
testing characters, 471-475

text, literal, 138
text editors
    compatibility, 23
    GTK+ program, 608-619
    Linux, 12-13
    source code, 12-13
text expressions, 118
text files, 447
third function, 104
three-dimensional arrays.
    See multidimensional
    arrays
time function, 486, 490
time functions, 487, 491
    calculating time
        differences, 488
    calculating time
        durations, 489
    clock, 489, 491
    code example, 489-491
    converting representation
        styles, 486-487
    ctime, 487
    difftime, 488, 491
    displaying time, 487
    formatting time, 487-488
    localtime, 486
    mktime, 487
    obtaining current time,
        486
    strftime, 487-491
        conversion specifiers,
            488
        format string, 487
    time function, 486, 490
    time representation
        styles, 485-486
    __TIME__ predefined
    macro, 571
tmpnam function, 445-446
tmp_rec pointer, 398

tolower function, 475-476
toolkits. *See* GTK+
top-down approach
    (structured
    programming), 94-95
toupper function, 475-476
trigonometric functions,
    482
troubleshooting
    error messages, 347
    input/output redirection,
        348
    zombie processes,
        543-546, 554-557
true values, 77
two-dimensional arrays.
    See multi-dimensional
    arrays
type conversions, 511
    automatic, 512-513
    typecasts
        arithmetic
            expressions,
            513-514
        pointers, 514-515
        void type pointers,
            210-211
type promotion, 512-513
type specifiers, 328
typecasting, 368
    arithmetic expressions,
        513-514
    pointers, 514-515
    void type pointers,
        210-211
typedef keyword, 635
    structure/union
        synonyms, 269-270
    tags comparison, 271
    variables, 43
typographical errors, 33

U-V

unary operators, 60-62
unary.c, 61
unbuffered character
    input functions, 321
unconditional jump state-
    ments
    goto, 296-298
        cautions, 297, 313
        code listing, 296-297
        label statements, 298
        target labels, 296
ungetc function, 324, 474
uninitialized pointers, 200
union keyword, 264, 635
unions. *See also* structures
    declaring, 264-269
    defining, 264-269
    initializig, 264
    members, accessing,
        265-266
    OR conditions, 264
    size, 271
    synonyms, 269-270
    union keyword, 266-269
unsigned decimal integers,
    142
unsigned keyword, 635
user-defined functions, 28,
    31, 87-89
users, root, 17
utilities, make
    compiling, 582
    developing programs, 16
    Makefiles, 581-585

validating data, 507
values
    of functions, 101-103
    garbage, 279
    initialization, 167

multidimensional arrays,
357
NULL, 225
true/false, 77
variable-argument
functions
argument data types, 496
code example, 497-499
declaring, 496
process, 497
setting number of
arguments, 496
stdarg.h header file,
496-497
variables, 36-37
arrays, 158, 162
automatic, 279-281
characters
declaring, 218-220
initializing, 218-220
counter, decrementing/
incrementing, 118
data types, 217-218
declaring, 42, 63, 277
defining, 29, 286
direct access, 189
displaying
printf function, 143
size in bytes, 39
values, 138
errno
code example,
494-495
errno.h header file,
493-494
explicit initialization,
281
external, 276
extern keyword, 580
modular
programming,
580-581

static, 282
when to use, 277
floating-point, 42
in functions, 89
global, 100
indirect access, 189
initializing, 43-44
lifetimes, 274
local, 90, 98-100, 276
automatic, 279
common uses, 286
defining within a
program block,
285-286
main() function, 284
static, 279
memory address, 186,
214
naming, 37-38
numeric, 39, 42
atof function, 470-471
atoi function, 469-470
atol function, 470
converting
strings to variables,
469-471
variables to strings,
477
pointers, 352
arrays, 192-195
benefits, 214
cautions, 200
code example,
189-191
comparisons, 199
creating, 186-187
data types, 191-192
declaring, 187-188
decrementing, 196
dereferencing, 188,
211

differencing, 198
incrementing, 196
indirection (*)
operator, 187-189,
214
initializing, 188
modifying individual
variables, 215
naming, 186
operations, 199-200
passing arguments,
201-210, 215
pointer arithmetic,
196-198
pointers constants,
198
subscript notation
comparison, 201
uninitialized, 200
void type, 210-213
scope, 274-276
data isolation, 276
external, 276
local, 278
static, 279
storage classes, 284
storing, 283
structures
accessing members,
241
declaring, 240-243
defining, 240-241
temporary, 369
typedef keyword, 43
visible, 274
View Data Window
command, 397
Viewing macro expansion,
566
void keyword, 635

void type
    pointers, 210-213, 514
        code example,
            211-212
        declaring function
            parameters, 210
        typecasts, 210-211
    return type, 106
volatile keyword, 635

W

waidpid function, 545
wait function, 543-544
waitpid function, 546
warning messages, 15, 24
**WEXITSTATUS macro,
    544**
while keyword
**while statements, 122-126,
    635.** *See also* **loops**
    condition, 123
    continue statement, 294
    listing, 123-124
    nesting, 126-128
    structure, 122
    versus for statements,
        124
whitespace, 56, 148
widget toolkits, 592. *See
    also* **GTK+**
widgets, 593-595
WIFEXITED macro, 544
windows
    managers, 596
    modal, 606
    terminal, 17-18
    X, 592

writing
    disk files, 420
        character I/O,
            424-426
        direct file I/O,
            426-429
        formatted file input,
            423-424
        formatted file output,
            421-423
    function macros
        # (stringizing
            operator), 564-565
        ## (concatenation
            operator), 565
        definitions, 563-564
        parameters, 563
    functions
        arguments, 96-98
        body, 98-103
        headers, 95-98
        local variables,
            98-100
        names, 95
        parameters, 96-98
        prototypes, 103-104
        return types, 95
        returning values,
            101-103, 380
        statements, 100-101

X-Y-Z

X (X Window System), 591
    GTK+. *See* GTK+
    history, 592
    Macintosh/Microsoft
        windows comparison,
        592

    widget toolkits, 592
    window managers, 596
    X clients, 592
    X Protocol, 592
    X servers, 592
    Xlib library, 592

Y2K bug, 487
**yesno_func function,
    606-607**
**yes_no_dialog function,
    606-608**

zombie processes, 542
    reaping, 543
    troubeshooting, 543-544
    troubleshooting,
        543-546, 554-557

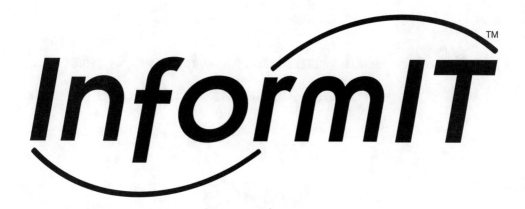

Get **FREE** books and more...when you register this book online for our Personal Bookshelf Program

http://register.samspublishing.com/

SAMS

 Register online and you can sign up for our *FREE Personal Bookshelf Program*...unlimited access to the electronic version of more than 200 complete computer books—immediately! That means you'll have 100,000 pages of valuable information onscreen, at your fingertips!

 Plus, you can access product support, including complimentary downloads, technical support files, book-focused links, companion Web sites, author sites, and more!

 And you'll be automatically registered to receive a *FREE subscription to a weekly email newsletter* to help you stay current with news, announcements, sample book chapters, and special events, including sweepstakes, contests, and various product giveaways!

 We value your comments! Best of all, the entire registration process takes only a few minutes to complete, so go online and get the greatest value going—absolutely FREE!

Don't Miss Out On This Great Opportunity!

Sams is a brand of Macmillan USA.

For more information, please visit *www.mcp.com*

What's on the Discs

The companion CD-ROM contains all the source code from the book, GNU gcc/gpp, GNU make, and ddd.

Installation

1. Insert the CD-ROM in your CD-ROM drive.

2. Mount the CD-ROM on your file system. Typically, this is done by typing

   ```
   mount -tiso9660 /dev/cdrom /cdrom
   ```

> **Note**
>
> The mount point must exist before you mount the CD-ROM. If you have trouble mounting the CD-ROM, please consult the man page for the mount command or contact your system administrator.

3. Please view the file README.1ST in the root directory of the CD-ROM for detailed installation instructions.

By opening this package, you are agreeing to be bound by the following agreement: